A COMPANION TO THE
ROYAL HERITAGE OF BRITAIN

A COMPANION TO THE
ROYAL HERITAGE OF BRITAIN

MARC ALEXANDER

Illustrative work by PAUL ABRAHAMS

SUTTON PUBLISHING

First published in 2005 by
Sutton Publishing Limited • Phoenix Mill
Thrupp • Stroud • Gloucestershire • GL5 2BU

British Library Cataloguing in Publication Data
A catalogue record for this book is available from the British Library.

ISBN 0 7509 3268 6

Half-title picture: William the Conqueror, statue in Falaise.
Frontispiece: The moment of crowning – Elizabeth II at her coronation on 2 June 1953. (*Getty Images*)

For Patrick Druce Andrew

Typeset in 9/10pt Times
Typesetting and origination by
Sutton Publishing Limited.
Printed and bound in England by
J.H. Haynes & Co. Ltd, Sparkford.

CONTENTS

Photographs by the author unless otherwise stated.

'The King is but a man, royalty is the gift of God.'
Alexandre Dumas

ACKNOWLEDGEMENTS

For encouragement and practical help in the preparation of this *Companion* I wish to thank Jennifer Hassell and Olivia Davies in particular for their support beyond the call of duty, also Richard Aldrich, Paul Alexander, Fraser Anderson, John Berry, Harold Elvin, Noel Hilliard, Caroline Jardine, David Leader, Patrick Macaskill, Reginald Massey, Alison Miles, Margaret Sandall and Peter Shephard.

Invaluable assistance has been provided by the Buckingham Palace Press Office, the Dean and Chapter of Canterbury Cathedral, the Dean and Chapter of Westminster Abbey, the Dean and Chapter of Winchester Cathedral, the custodians of Fontevrault Abbey, the British Library, the Colindale Newspaper Library and the National Trust.

Finally I wish to record my gratitude to my father Ronald Alexander, who infected me at an early age with his love of history.

INTRODUCTION

Although Egbert became overlord of the other kings who ruled parts of England after AD 825, effective monarchy began with King Athelstan, who was crowned in AD 924. When his kingdom stretched from the south coast to Hadrian's Wall, Athelstan realised that if a king was to be regarded as something more than a local ruler his role needed to be reinforced by ceremonial and pageantry. As a result he has been described as 'the first king to bring the concept of majesty to the country'. Soon religion bestowed kingship with a mystical quality which, while it did not approach the divinity of Japanese emperors, nurtured the 'divine right of kings'.

It is perhaps not extraordinary that royal ceremonial has survived in Britain and is still a part of national life in an age of technology. It would seem that ritual is necessary to the human condition. This appears to be borne out in some countries where monarchy has been replaced yet where the new rulers provide pageantry, which endorses their power and gives their subjects – sorry, people – a feeling of unity. However, to some the sight of a gilded coach escorted by cavalry in uniforms dating back to Waterloo is preferable to orchestrated rallies or processions of marching battalions.

A thousand years have passed since King Athelstan was crowned on King's Stone at Kingston upon Thames, during which England has had fifty-four sovereigns – splendid kings and queens, weak kings and queens, ruthless kings and queens, and even a few who have been described as saintlike. Whatever else, they have provided us with stories that are as entertaining today as they were in Shakespeare's time, as this *Companion* illustrates. And until a Scottish king inherited the throne of England, Scotland had its own monarchy every bit as varied and intriguing.

Throughout history there have been several royal houses, yet despite the dynastic changes the royal bloodline stretches back to pre-Athelstan days. Tracing it, one learns the fascination of genealogical charts which when studied reveal so much more than who succeeded

Statue of Richard I outside the Palace of Westminster. *(Photograph by Simon Alexander)*

whom. For example, the complex inter-relationship of the royal houses of England and those of Scotland and the Continent become suddenly apparent when the royal lines of kinship are traced. While England's royal houses have originated from abroad, equally foreign royalty has had its share of royal English genes. A prime example becomes clear with a glance at the genealogy of Queen Victoria.

As this book is a 'Companion', its object is to give the widest view of its subject; therefore, weighty matters such as the conflict between Crown and Church or the introduction of constitutional monarchy are balanced by such topics as royal pets or royal needlework. And as there would be no royal heritage without the sovereigns who have reigned in England and Britain since Athelstan, the endeavour has been to present them, as far as possible, as human beings rather than as royal figureheads. If this has involved a certain amount of trivia, so be it.

It is the plea of the author that in order to get the fairest picture of a past monarch the reader should try to judge him by the moeurs of his time. We, who pride ourselves in living in a democratic and caring society, understandably find such things as medieval execution or the burning of heretics shocking. Yet if medieval people could have time-travelled into the twentieth century, they would have been aghast at the use of weapons of mass destruction or genocide on a scale that would have been beyond medieval imagination.

Today, the challenge to the monarchy is to remain royal under the warts-and-all scrutiny of television and a media obsessed by 'celebrity' stories and exposés. But, as

OLIVER CROMWELL

1599
1658

this book shows, the royal road has ever been a rocky one and yet the institution has survived and is likely to continue into the future because it fulfils a requirement in society, of which society is only vaguely aware. Outside the Houses of Parliament stand two statues; one is of Oliver Cromwell, who briefly banished the monarchy, and the other is of Richard Coeur de Lion, the epitome of kingship. To the author the combination of these two historical characters in such a setting symbolises much of the British outlook.

The entries in this *Companion* are arranged in alphabetical order with cross references denoted by words printed in capital letters.

Marc Alexander
Gilsland, Cumbria

Statue of Oliver Cromwell in front of the Palace of Westminster – the antithesis of Richard Coeur de Lion.

A

ABDICATION In over eleven centuries of monarchy in Britain, one of the rarest events is abdication, a sovereign ending his or her reign by surrendering the Crown. In AD 962 King Ingulf of Scotland abdicated in order to join a holy order, but within a year his new vocation had ended when he was killed by marauding Vikings. Three centuries were to pass before the next abdication when John Balliol ('Toom Tabard') resigned from the throne of Scotland in 1296. He had been placed upon it by the influence of EDWARD I after the death of Margaret ('The Maid of Norway'), which had left the country without a direct successor to the Crown. A council of twelve disaffected nobles took control of the government and concluded an alliance with England's traditional enemy France. In reply King Edward invaded Scotland and, laying the blame on John, forced him to abdicate, after which he was imprisoned in the TOWER OF LONDON before he was finally allowed to retire to his estates in Normandy.

On 20 June 1327 EDWARD II was deposed by a parliament controlled by his wife Queen Isabella ('The She-wolf of France') and her paramour ROGER MORTIMER, Earl of March. On the 25th of the month the king 'dressed in black, fainting and sobbing' formally abdicated in favour of his son EDWARD III, and the Steward of the Royal Household broke his staff, signalling that his reign was ended. Nine months later the ex-king was murdered at Berkeley Castle.

The next English king to abdicate was RICHARD II, who, in August 1399, was captured by Henry Bolingbroke, who became HENRY IV. Richard formally abdicated the following month and, imprisoned in Pontefract Castle, he died mysteriously the following year.

MARY, QUEEN OF SCOTS, when a prisoner at Lochleven, was approached by Lord Lindsey, Lord Ruthven and Sir Robert Melville on behalf of the rebel lords who had taken control, and induced to abdicate on 24 July 1567 in favour of her infant son James VI of Scotland, who subsequently became JAMES I of England. Later she escaped from her island prison and found herself at the head of an army of her supporters. She was defeated by her half-brother James Stewart, Earl of Moray at the Battle of Langside on 13 May 1568, after which she unwisely fled to England to put herself at the mercy of ELIZABETH I. She was held a prisoner until her execution in 1587.

JAMES II was 'deemed by Parliament' to have abdicated on 11 December 1688 by fleeing to France at the onset of the GLORIOUS REVOLUTION. In his court of exile at St Germain he was still regarded as the rightful King of England by his supporters, who came to be known as Jacobites, and funded by the French he endeavoured to regain the Crown with an invasion of Ireland, but was defeated by WILLIAM III at the Battle of Boyne in 1690.

The next relinquishing of the British Crown came 248 years later in what came to be known as the Abdication Crisis. Then, EDWARD VIII abdicated on 11 December 1936 in favour of his brother

Mary Queen of Scots being forced to abdicate in favour of her infant son.

GEORGE VI in order that he might marry Wallis Simpson. The government and the Church of England had bitterly opposed the idea of the marriage to Mrs Simpson, as it was considered that it would be inappropriate for the king as head of the Church to marry a divorcee. The king had supporters sympathetic to his dilemma – the Crown or the woman he loved – and there was talk of a King's Party being formed, but Edward decided the only solution was his abdication, which he announced to the nation in a historic wireless broadcast.

AGINCOURT, BATTLE OF The most famous victory won by a king in the field, the battle was fought on St Crispin's Day, 25 October 1415. HENRY V, having taken Harfleur, led his army across Normandy towards his object of Calais. Close to the village of Azincourt they were met by a much larger force. As a frontal attack was launched against the English position, Henry's archers cut down the flower of French chivalry and gave Henry

Cut-out figures of Henry V's archers on the battlefield of Agincourt – a generous tribute to the English victors.

mastery of Normandy, making him a national hero, a role immortalised in Shakespeare's play *Henry V*.

AID The name given to the system whereby the tenants of medieval kings were called upon to provide 'aid', i.e. money, for exceptional circumstances. These could range from the cost of the marriage of an eldest princess to raising the ransom of a captured king. From a historical point of view this practice was important, as councils meeting to consider whether or not aid should be granted to the sovereign were the forerunners of Parliament.

ALBERT MEMORIAL *See* KENSINGTON GARDENS

ALBERT, PRINCE The second son of Ernest, Duke of Saxe-Coburg-Gotha, Albert married his cousin QUEEN VICTORIA in 1840, and two years later was made Consort. He was to labour with such dedication for the advancement of his adopted country that he often appeared haggard. As chairman of the Fine Arts Royal Commission, it was his aspiration to make London's South Kensington a centre for the arts and education. His interests ranged from the improvement of housing for the working classes to industrial development and the

furtherance of science. The Great Exhibition of 1851 in Hyde Park was his inspiration. When it opened in May it was a personal triumph for the Prince, who had seen it through against all manner of opposition. Its success was to underline Britain as the 'workshop of the world'.

Over the years, the prince wore down the mistrust felt towards him as a foreigner by both the public and ministers. When he became the Queen's husband he was practically unknown in England, and lacking position and wealth he was regarded by many as a 'Coburg adventurer on the make'. Indeed, it was not until 1857 that he was officially designated Prince Consort. Too intelligent to interfere openly in politics, his far-sighted advice was passed on to the Cabinet through the Queen. In one instance he is credited with averting a war between Great Britain and the United States of America.

The life of the royal couple was not wholly devoted to politics and advancement. Albert, raised in the romantic countryside of his father's little kingdom, sought to get away from London whenever possible to enjoy domestic life with Victoria and their family at BALMORAL in Scotland and OSBORNE HOUSE on the Isle of Wight.

It has been said that the Prince's most significant contribution to the British way of life was the example he and the Queen set of a decorous and devout family life after the scandals associated with previous Hanoverian reigns. Yet the behaviour of his eldest son Edward, the future EDWARD VII, caused him great anxiety. When Albert and Victoria became concerned about his matrimonial prospects, they were unaware of the talk in London clubs about Edward's liaison with Nellie Clifden, discretion not being one of the actress's virtues. When the story finally reached Windsor it dropped like a bombshell on the royal family. Prince Albert wrote to Edward 'with a heavy heart upon a subject which has caused me the greatest pain I have yet felt in this life'.

Albert travelled in a special train to Cambridge, where Edward was at Trinity, for a man-to-man talk which ended in a reconciliation between father and son. When Albert returned to London, he was in a low state of health, and his symptoms developed into typhoid fever from which he died on 14 December 1861. Believing that her beloved husband's illness had been caused by Edward's immoral behaviour, the Queen refused to send for him and it was only the result of a telegram, dispatched in secret by his sister Princess Alice, that

Edward travelled to Windsor early on the day that his father died.

Desperate in her grief, Victoria continued to hold Edward responsible, and she wrote to her daughter Vicky that 'I never can or shall look at him [Edward] without a shudder . . .'

ALFRED THE ATHELING Born *c.* 1008, the son of ETHELRED II ('The Unready') and his second wife EMMA, Alfred was known as 'The Atheling', the name denoting a prince of the blood royal or an heir apparent. A year after the death of Ethelred, Queen Emma married KING CANUTE, by whom she had a son and two daughters. This meant that Alfred and his brother, the future EDWARD THE CONFESSOR, were barred from the succession. They were taken to Normandy to be brought up, and on the death of Canute in 1035 Alfred made a rash visit to England. At Ely in Cambridgeshire he was taken prisoner by EARL GODWINE, then blinded and brutally murdered. His remains were interred in Ely Cathedral.

ALFRED THE GREAT As the legendary KING ARTHUR was to the Celts, so Alfred was to the Anglo-Saxons – a warrior king who held the line against foreign invaders. But Alfred is seen as more than a folk-tale hero, thanks to his biography by Bishop Asser, written in AD 893, which gives the first detailed account of an English king.

Alfred was born at Wattage in AD 849, the fifth son of Ethelwulf who was crowned King of Wessex five years later at Kingston upon Thames. He was said to be more interested in the kingdom of heaven

A coin from the reign of King Alfred.

King Alfred's statue in Winchester, the town where he held court after bringing peace to England.

In the year of Ethelred's accession a huge force of Danes, known as the Great Army, landed in East Anglia and prepared to attack systematically the various English kingdoms. It was led by the sons of the Viking Ragnar Lothbrok ('Hairy Breeches') who, after being captured by the Northumbrians, had been put to death in a snake pit. By AD 870 the Great Army had subdued Northumbria and East Anglia, where King Edmund became a living target for Danish archers when he refused to renounce Christianity.

The Great Army then advanced on Wessex, where on 8 January AD 871 it was checked at the Battle of Ashdown on the Berkshire Downs, the victory mainly due to the courage of Alfred. Soon afterwards King Ethelred died of wounds received at the Battle of Merton, fought on 23 April, and Alfred, the last of Ethelwulf's sons, was chosen as king by the WITAN. The Danes' incursions into Wessex continued and after Ashdown eight other battles were fought against them that year, with the result that the West Saxons earned some respite. Then, early in AD 878, Guthrum, King of the East Anglian Danes, made an attack for which Alfred was unprepared. As the Danes had never campaigned in winter before, the assault came as such a surprise that Alfred, with his wife Ethelswitha and their children, had to flee his palace at Chippenham, after which he became a lonely fugitive.

During the spring of AD 878 he was forced to hide on the marsh-surrounded Isle of Athelney and here the legendary tales surrounding him began. The best known tells how the disguised king took shelter in a cowherd's cottage. While he was sitting in front of the fire making arrows, the cowherd's wife asked him to watch some rye cakes baking on the hearth. Doubtless pondering on the plight of his occupied kingdom, Alfred did not notice that the cakes were being scorched until too late and he was berated in no uncertain terms. Alfred merely laughed over the episode and when he regained his kingdom the cowherd and his wife were rewarded.

By Easter AD 878 he had established a base on Athelney, on which his scattered followers began to converge. They were encouraged when the Earl of Devon's Saxons defeated a Danish army, slaying nearly a thousand Danes, though the real psychological blow to the invaders was the loss of their Raven Banner. This they regarded with superstitious awe, believing that the ill-omened bird, embroidered by the daughters of Ragnar Lothbrok, por-

than in his own kingdom of Wessex, and when Alfred was 6 years old he took him on a pilgrimage to Rome, seemingly not troubled by the fact that for the first time Vikings wintered on the Isle of Sheppey, which implied their designs upon England. The ruins of Rome and all they represented had a profound effect on the boy prince and left him with a lifelong ambition to restore learning to Wessex.

In AD 858 Ethelwulf died and was succeeded by his son Ethelbald. He died two years later and was followed by his brother Ethelbert. On his death in AD 865 the throne passed to Ethelred, who like his brothers was destined to have a short reign, spent in opposing the Danes, as the *Anglo-Saxon Chronicle* called the Scandinavian invaders.

tended victory or defeat by raising or lowering its wings.

It was at this point another incident occurred that was to become part of folklore. When Alfred was planning to meet Guthrum in battle he was anxious to know the disposition of his forces, so disguising himself as a minstrel he entered the enemy camp, where for several days he entertained the Danes. After his successful spying the order was secretly circulated for all men willing to fight the Danes to muster at Egbert's Stone in a lonely spot to the east of Selwood Forest. Soon afterwards one of the most significant battles in British history was fought when the English met the Danes at Edington in Wiltshire; after the Danes had fled the field, Alfred blockaded their base at Chippenham, where they were 'terrified by hunger, cold and fear'.

Finally Guthrum surrendered, offering hostages as an insurance for a peaceful withdrawal. Alfred was wisely magnanimous in victory and sent in food, and soon Saxon and Dane were feasting together, a remarkable peace celebration after so much blood-letting. Alfred's wish that he should be baptised was realised when the king 'stood god-father to him and raised him from the holy font'. Guthrum honoured his oath to leave Wessex in peace and settled with his followers in East Anglia, where he remained Alfred's staunch ally.

While Guthrum was no longer a threat, Alfred had to defend his kingdom against other invaders until in AD 879 they withdrew and the kingdom was finally at peace. By building ships with twice as many oars as those of the Danes, the king was able to defend the realm by heading off raiders before they could make landfall. His improved vessels, powered by sixty sweeps, shifted the balance of seapower so that Alfred earned the title of 'Father of the English Navy'.

King Alfred founded twenty-five towns, some of which were built on old Roman sites and some of which, like Shaftesbury and Oxford, were new. Although Alfred could now have claimed the title of King of the English, he preferred to remain officially the King of Wessex as he had no wish to weaken the country by regional jealousies. At his court the Witan was composed of Englishmen rather than just men of Wessex, as had been the rule. Part of the work of this broadly based Witan was to assist the king in drawing up a treaty with Guthrum which not only defined his territory, known as the Danelaw, but had more far-reaching objectives. It

An engraving of King Alfred being chided over the burnt cakes which became a piece of royal folklore.

stated that Englishmen living within the Danelaw should be treated as equals with the Danes, and Danes outside the Danelaw should have the same rights as Englishmen. The effect of this upon the country was so profound that it has been likened to MAGNA CARTA in importance.

Once the wars with the Danes were over, it is estimated that Alfred spent half the kingdom's revenue on bringing enlightenment to what had long been an illiterate land. Monasteries that had been destroyed were rebuilt, schools set up, and foreign craftsmen, artists and scholars were encouraged to come to teach in England. The king decreed that 'all the sons of freemen who have the means to undertake it should be set to learning English letters'. So eager was the king that he had himself taught Latin so he could translate Latin books into the language of his people. As a result he was not only regarded as the Father of the English Navy but the Father of English Prose. Among the works he translated was

Orosius' *History of the World*, which he brought up to date by writing extra chapters.

Alfred's days were so crowded that, at a time when hour-glasses and clocks were unknown in England, he devised a candle clock so he could divide up his time as profitably as possible. This was simply a candle marked with coloured rings, each of which represented an hour. When he was absorbed in writing, a servant watched the candle burn down until a new ring was reached, and it was his duty to announce that another hour had passed. To prevent draughts from making the candle clock unreliable the king invented a special draught-proof lantern to hold it.

Exhausted by his endeavours as a military commander, administrator and scholar, King Alfred – 'England's darling' – died in 899 at the age of 50 and was succeeded by his son EDWARD, who became known as 'The Elder'. Alfred was buried in Newminster Abbey, Winchester, and later his remains were translated to Hyde Abbey, where they stayed until the abbey was demolished following the Dissolution of the Monasteries. There is a possibility that one of Winchester Cathedral's mortuary chests may hold the king's bones.

ANGEVIN EMPIRE A name given to the dominions under the control of the counts of Anjou, known as the Angevins (also the Plantagenets), during their rule of England. Apart from England, it encompassed Anjou, Aquitaine, Maine, Normandy and Touraine. The 'empire' began with HENRY II when his marriage to ELEANOR, Duchess of Aquitaine and Countess of Poitou, in 1152 added Aquitaine to his existing territories, which then included England after he had succeeded his second cousin STEPHEN in 1154.

ANGLO-SAXON CHRONICLE At the end of the ninth century KING ALFRED inaugurated the *Anglo-Saxon Chronicle*, a year-by-year record of events written in Old English by clerks in various monastic centres. Existing copies provide rich accounts of the reigns of Alfred, Ethelred the Unready, Edward the Confessor and the Norman kings in particular.

ANNE The reign of Queen Anne, the last of the Stuarts to occupy the throne, was of great significance for the English monarchy. She was the last sovereign to preside at Cabinet meetings, the last to refuse assent to a parliamentary bill and the last to touch for the King's Evil. Born at ST JAMES'S PALACE on 6 February 1665 – the year of the Great Plague – Anne was the second daughter of JAMES, Duke of York, and Anne Hyde. She and her older sister Mary were the only children to survive out of the eight born to the duke and duchess, and from birth she was afflicted with ailments which were to cause distress all her life.

In 1667 Anne's mother died and two years later her father married Mary of Modena, a Roman Catholic like himself. As a future king of a Protestant country it was James's devotion to his faith that was his biggest drawback, and CHARLES II made sure that his little nieces, who were in the line of succession, were brought up as Protestants by Colonel Edward Villiers and his wife Lady Frances at Richmond. It was a claustrophobic world the sisters entered, for the Villiers had six daughters, and the only males they came in contact with were members of the clergy. This resulted in both Anne and Mary forming over-intense relationships with their childhood companions, especially with Frances Apsley, who subsequently became Lady Bathurst. Later Anne became infatuated with a friend named Sarah Jennings and when Sarah married John Churchill their relationship remained strong.

On 28 July 1683 Anne was married to Prince George of Denmark, the brother of King Christian V. The prince was 30 and unremarkable except for his faithfulness to his wife. With her married status Anne was given a regular establishment and her first act was to appoint her beloved Sarah Churchill as her Lady of the Bedchamber.

In her self-vindicating conduct of the Duchess of Marlborough Sarah explained that Anne 'grew uneasy to be treated by me with the ceremony due to her rank' and she proposed 'we might in all our letters write ourselves by feigned names such as would import nothing of distinction of rank between us'. Thus the queen became 'Mrs Morley' and Sarah 'Mrs Freeman'. The equality between the two did not last long, as timid 'Mrs Morley' allowed herself to be dominated by frank and forceful 'Mrs Freeman'.

When Charles II died in February 1685 Anne's father JAMES II succeeded him without difficulty despite his Roman Catholicism, and during her father's reign Anne lived in retirement, preoccupied with a series of unsuccessful pregnancies. In June

1688 she heard a son had been born to her father and his second wife, Mary of Modena. The arrival of a Catholic heir to the throne brought about the GLORIOUS REVOLUTION. Leading members of both the Whig and Tory parties secretly invited Protestant WILLIAM OF ORANGE and his wife MARY (Anne's sister), the daughter of James II, to take the English Crown. In November, William arrived at Tor Bay and when King James heard that his chief commander, John Churchill, had deserted him he realised his cause was lost. On 11 December 1688 he fled to France and into exile.

The powerful influence Sarah and her husband had on Anne became apparent in the following debates on the ACT OF SETTLEMENT, persuading her to acquiesce to William and Mary as joint sovereigns, and after their coronation in April 1689 John Churchill was created Earl of Marlborough.

Three months later Anne was successfully delivered of the heir presumptive who was christened William, Duke of Gloucester. Alas for Anne – five days after his 11th birthday on 30 July 1700, the little Duke of Gloucester died from hydrocephalus. The death of the heir presumptive caused Parliament to fear a Jacobite succession and at King

Queen Anne's statue in front of St Paul's. The fact that her back was to the cathedral was a subject for lampoonists.

William's suggestion the Crown was entailed so that if Anne failed to have more children, it would go to the Electress Sophia of Hanover, a granddaughter of JAMES I.

The following year the exiled James II died and Louis XIV recognised his son James (the Old Pretender) as the rightful King of England. As a consequence war with France came closer. Six months later King William died following a fall from his horse and Anne became queen. Due to gout and her many pregnancies, Anne was so obese that she had to be carried in a chair from Westminster Hall to the abbey for her coronation on 23 April 1702, but when she addressed Parliament her manner made a very good impression.

Now 37, with an ineffectual husband and unlikely to have another child, a lonely and difficult reign stretched before her. It seemed natural that she should turn more and more to the Marlboroughs for companionship. Marlborough was given the Order of the Garter, made Captain-General of England's forces and Master-General of the Ordinance and Ranger of Windsor Park, while his wife became Groom of the Stole, Keeper of the Privy Purse and Mistress of the Robes.

In the reign that followed affinities between political figures mingled, shifted and disintegrated like the colours of an oil slick. It was never a straightforward question of government by Whigs or Tories. Individual aspirations, religious schisms and the question of a Stuart or Hanoverian succession clouded the political scene. The key to everything was the queen's favour, as she could choose and dismiss ministers. To pluck the strings of the royal marionette was the object of 'Mrs Freeman'.

When Anne came to the throne she had been dominated by Sarah Churchill for years, and through this infatuation the Duke of Marlborough expected to become the real ruler of England. At this time the queen was pro-Tory but when it suited the Marlboroughs to align themselves with the Whigs, Anne dutifully changed her views. By now the queen, starting to tire of her favourite's domineering manner, turned to a young woman named Abigail Hill, who had been introduced into the court by Sarah to be her Mistress of the Bedchamber. Little is known about Abigail, though Sir Winston Churchill wrote that she was 'probably the smallest person who ever consciously attempted to decide, and in fact did decide, the history of Europe'. Abigail became as politically motivated as

A shilling coin from the reign of Queen Anne.

Sarah, especially after her marriage in 1707 to the queen's page, Samuel Masham.

Marlborough's four great victories in the Low Countries gave England more military glory than ever before, which encouraged Sarah to become ever more dictatorial.

In 1707 Lord Godolphin completed union with Scotland but now followed political strife between the ruling anti-Stuart Whig party and the Tories. The Whigs won the first general election covering all Britain in May 1708, and they demonstrated their new power by insisting that Prince George should give up his position as Lord High Admiral. Soon afterwards the prince suffered a serious attack of dropsy and it was obvious that he was dying. At the same time news came of Marlborough's victory at Oudenarde and on 19 August the queen was obliged to take part in a procession to St Paul's Cathedral to thank the Almighty for favouring the British side. As the procession entered the cathedral Sarah quarrelled bitterly with the queen, who retorted so loudly the duchess was alarmed in case the congregation should overhear and even join in. When they had taken their seats the queen continued to answer the criticism at the top of her voice, whereupon Sarah cried, 'Hold your tongue.'

The matter did not end there. The duchess, having received a letter from her husband criticising the queen, sent it to Anne with a note that read: 'I cannot help sending your majesty this letter, to show how exactly Lord Marlborough agrees with me in opinion that he has now no interest with you.' Soon afterwards, when the queen was at the bedside of her dying husband, a letter from Sarah was put in her hand which began: 'Though the last time I had the honour to wait upon your majesty, your usage of me was such as was scarce possible for me to imagine, or anyone to believe. . . .' Anne had only read this far when Sarah herself entered the chamber. Anne received her coldly and according to an eyewitness 'the deportment of the Duchess of Marlborough, while the Prince was actually dying, was of such a nature, that the Queen, then in the height of her grief, was unable to bear it'. 'Withdraw!' she cried, and for once 'Mrs Freeman' obeyed 'Mrs Morley'.

On the evening of 6 April 1710, 'Mrs Morley' met 'Mrs Freeman' for the last time. The extraordinary interview lasted an hour, during which all Anne would answer to Sarah's arguments was 'Whatever you have to say, you may write it.' When the Duke of Marlborough returned from his Flemish campaigns, he asked for a private audience with the queen when he tried to get his wife reinstated, but Anne's only reply was that she wished to receive back her gold keys as Mistress of the Robes. Obediently he asked Sarah for the keys, and in fury she flung them at his head. Anxious not to follow his wife into retirement, he took them meekly to Anne who received them 'with far greater pleasure than if he had brought her the spoils of an enemy'.

'Mrs Morley' had finally defeated 'Mrs Freeman' and the triumph was celebrated by Abigail being given Sarah's old post as Mistress of the Robes.

Apart from the rise to power of the Tories, the most significant development of the 'great change' was that following Marlborough's dismissal from his post of Captain-General, negotiations for peace with France went forward and the Treaty of Utrecht was signed in March 1713.

On 1 August 1714 the queen had an apoplectic fit. Two days later she died, and on the night of 24 August purple-draped horses drew her coffin, described as almost square because of her bulk, to WESTMINSTER ABBEY where it was interred in Henry VII's chapel beside Prince George.

ANNE OF BOHEMIA The sister of Bohemia's King Wenceslas, Anne was married to RICHARD II and crowned at Westminster Abbey in 1382; in the same year she was made a Lady of the Garter. She died of plague in 1394 and was interred in WESTMINSTER ABBEY.
See also RICHARD II

ANNE OF DENMARK The daughter of Frederick II of Denmark, Anne was married in 1589 to JAMES VI of Scotland by proxy as the match was opposed by ELIZABETH I. James then travelled to Norway to bring her to Scotland. She was noted for the extravagance of the royal court and her encouragement of art after her husband became JAMES I of England.

ANOINTING OIL The Old Testament alludes to the anointing and crowning of kings, and in medieval times the act of anointing with holy oil became an integral part of the coronation ceremony, investing the new king with a spiritual aspect which was later exemplified in the DIVINE RIGHT OF KINGS. Originally it was the head of the king that was anointed but later on other parts of the body; the breast, shoulders, arms and hands were included in the ritual. The oil used in coronations was known as 'the oil of the catechumens' (the name derives from Christian converts under instruction before baptism) and was second only to 'chrism', a consecration ungent prepared from olive oil and balsam and used only in the most sacred Church rites.

When Clovis, the King of the Franks, was crowned a very special anointing oil was used. It was said that the Holy Spirit in the form of a dove brought it down from heaven in a vessel that became known as the Sainte Ampoule and was placed in the altar for the coronation. In following French coronations a drop of this miraculous oil mixed with chrism was used for the anointing of kings. Later, chrism oil became part of the English ritual, probably being used for the first time at the crowning of EDWARD II in 1307. Meanwhile, a story of celestial oil became current in England in which the Virgin Mary appeared to THOMAS A BECKET and gave him oil to be used, at some future time, in crowning ceremonies of English kings. In 1318 Pope John XXII wrote to King Edward giving an account of this divine gift and the later discovery of the vessel that held it.

It was the use of chrism in the coronation ceremony that gave rise to the belief that the sovereign was able to cure scrofula by his or her laying on of hands which became known as KING'S EVIL. Although the use of chrism did not survive the Reformation, the royal touch as a scrofula cure persisted into the reign of Queen Anne.

AQUITAINE An independent duchy within the French kingdom, Aquitaine was originally a Roman province in the south-west of France. When HENRY II, who had married ELEANOR OF AQUITAINE, inherited the throne of England in 1154 Aquitaine became an English dominion. It remained so until 1453 when the French defeated the English at the Battle of Castillon, the last battle to be fought in the Hundred Years' War.

ARBROATH, DECLARATION OF Described as Scotland's 'Declaration of Independence', it was a letter written at Arbroath in 1320 by Scottish nobles to Pope John XXII. It sought recognition of Scottish independence and castigated England for its attempts to subjugate Scotland. In effect the letter was an answer to the pope's threat to excommunicate ROBERT I ('The Bruce') for failing to obey the papal injunction to observe a truce with England. As a result of the declaration Robert won papal recognition as Scotland's king.

ARMADA, SPANISH After attacking Cadiz early in 1587, Sir Francis Drake returned to England with the news that PHILIP II of Spain, the widower of QUEEN MARY, had prepared a fleet to invade England. His Armada consisted of 129 ships, carrying twenty thousand soldiers, and was intended to escort the Duke of Parma's Spanish army from Dunkirk. ELIZABETH I was averse to spending money in preparing warships to counter the Spanish fleet. Of the force which finally set out to meet the Spaniards, only a third were financed by the royal purse, the rest were fitted out by patriotic merchants and the smaller seaports. The sighting of the great enemy fleet off the Lizard in the third week of July caused Lord High Admiral Howard to beg 'for the love of God' to have powder and shot supplied to him.

The Spaniards were disconcerted by the superior speed of the English ships and their raking broadsides, which had been the inspiration of HENRY VIII. Despite this, their numbers were almost intact when they anchored off Calais. Then, as the Armada moved on to join the Duke of Parma, it was struck by strong winds and swept past the rendezvous point. The weather worsened, and while only ten galleons had been sunk by English ships, more than fifty were lost in the storms.

Although the Armada was dispersed, the remote possibility of invasion continued to perturb the public. On 8 August the Queen visited the army at

Tilbury and encouraged the troops with her famous speech: 'I know I have but the body of a weak and feeble woman, but I have the heart of a King, and a King of England too; and think foul scorn that Parma or Spain, or any other prince of Europe . . ., should dare to invade the borders of my realm . . . I myself will be your general – the judge and rewarder of every one of your virtues in the field. I already know by your forwardness that you have deserved rewards and crowns . . .'

As for the 'rewards and crowns', they had no relevance as far as the treatment of the wounded English sailors was concerned. Lord Howard declared, 'It is a pitiful sight to see men die in the streets of Margate.' In contrast, the defeated Spaniards had hospitals waiting for them on their return.

The defeat of King Philip's Armada resulted in England becoming the most commanding state in Europe and guaranteed the kingdom's security for the rest of Elizabeth's reign.

ARTHUR Although there is no historical evidence that Arthur existed, his story – or legend – is better known generally than the histories of many well-authenticated kings. No character from the past has been as widely commemorated in British place names; as the writer Dickenson has pointed out 'only the devil is more often mentioned in local association than Arthur'. Modern opinion concerning Arthur is that it is most likely he was a Romanised British war leader who opposed and temporarily halted the invading Saxons at some time after the Roman withdrawal from Britain in AD 410, when the so-called Dark Ages began. From then on records ceased to be kept and for a period equal to that between the reigns of Elizabeth I and Elizabeth II there are only three sources of 'historical' material available.

The first known reference to Arthur is to be found in the seventh-century Welsh poem 'Gododin'. Next, the Welsh author Nennius in his *Historica Brittonum*, written around the end of the eighth century, listed Arthur's twelve victories over the Saxons. Other Welsh reference to Arthur is in the twelfth-century manuscript *The Black Book of Carmarthen* and in the romance of Kilhwch and Olwen, the first Arthurian story which included such characters as Kay, Bedevere and Gawain.

According to the Cambrian Annals, compiled *c.* 954, Arthur defeated a Saxon army at the

King Arthur's statue standing in the Royal Chapel (Hofkirche) at Innsbruck. *(Courtesy of the Innsbruck Tourist Office)*

unidentifiable Mount Badon where he carried 'the cross of Lord Jesus on his shoulders'. Halfway through the sixth century the monk Gildas briefly referred to the Battle of Mount Badon in his *De Excidio Brittanniae* but made no mention of Arthur nor any other British leaders. The entry for the year AD 537 in the Cambrian Annals recorded the Battle of Camlann 'in which Arthur and Medraut [Mordred] fell'.

From such scant allusions and oral tradition the epic of King Arthur was to develop into the world's first best-seller and has continued as such. Between the years 1125 and 1130 William of Malmesbury, the librarian of the monastery of that name, visited Glastonbury Abbey to carry out research and was told by the Benedictine monks there of a Christian warrior king who had temporarily halted the Saxon invasion. Impressed by their accounts William wrote that Arthur was 'a man clearly to be pro-claimed in true histories', and included two passages about him in his *Gesta Regum Anglorum* which chronicled the kings of England from AD 449 to his own time.

His example was followed a few years later by Geoffrey of Monmouth who treated Arthur as a historical person in his *Historia Regum Britanniae*. He drew upon the folklore of his day and a myst-erious 'British book' which, if ever it existed, has certainly been long lost. Considering that printing had yet to be invented, the success of Geoffrey's book was phenomenal. Scribes toiled to produce hundreds of copies in Norman French – there are still over fifty extant – and the shadowy Celtic warrior was transformed into a historical hero.

On the Continent the story continued to evolve, and under the elegant genius of Chrétien de Troyes new elements were introduced, such as Sir Launcelot and his ill-starred love for Arthur's queen Guinevere, and the adventures of the individual knights of the ROUND TABLE. Above all he was responsible for the concept of 'courtly love' which so fired the imaginations of the members of QUEEN ELEANOR's court at Poitiers.

Following the WARS OF THE ROSES, the story of King Arthur and the Fellowship of the Round Table as we know it today burst into its full glory through William Caxton's printing of *Le Morte D'Arthur*, the 383,000-word masterpiece by Sir Thomas Malory. The story has magical elements and chivalrous adventures that would have had nothing in common with the life of the Arthur as a leader of Celtic warriors. Beginning with Arthur's magical conception at Tintagel Castle, Malory's epic continues with him proving his right to kingship by removing the sword from the stone, his receiving Excalibur from the Lady of the Lake, the formation of the Round Table Fellowship and the classic triangle of the king, Guinevere and Launcelot. A spiritual element enters the story with the vision of the Holy Grail and the knightly quests for it which lead to the break up of the Fellowship. Finally, Arthur slays Mordred, his secret son who has tried to usurp the Crown, at the Battle of Camlann and, grievously wounded, is borne away in a barge by three black-draped queens.

Malory did mention Arthur being taken to AVALON although earlier on a priest named Layamon had written in his work *The Brut*, the first long poem in Middle English, that 'The Britons believe yet that he is alive, and dwelleth in Avalon . . . and ever yet the Britons look for Arthur's coming.'

The importance of Arthur in the story of British monarchy is that regardless of whether he ever existed, his legend set a standard for kingship that was wise, just and heroic and, no matter how far sovereigns fell short of the ideal, this concept of what a king should be persisted down the ages in the minds of common folk.

ASHDOWN, BATTLE OF In January AD 871 the Danish 'Great Army', which had been ravaging the countryside from its base at Reading, suffered its first defeat at the Battle of Ashdown. The invaders were opposed by Ethelred, King of Wessex, and his brother ALFRED (the Great), at Ashdown on the Berkshire Downs. Both of the opposing armies were divided into two wings. The battle opened with Alfred leading his wing in a charge against the Danes, while his brother the King was still at his prayers. During the furious hand-to-hand fighting that followed Alfred was reinforced by the King's wing, but it was not until some time later that Ethelred, his devotions completed, arrived on the scene with his personal guards and tipped the battle in favour of the Saxons. By nightfall the Danes were defeated. Soon afterwards, Ethelred died of wounds he received at the Battle of Merton, and Alfred was elected as king by the WITAN. A white horse portrayed on a chalk hillside overlooking the battle site – the Ashdown Horse – has been traditionally regarded as a monument to the Wessex victory.
See also ALFRED THE GREAT

ASHINGDON, THE BATTLE OF When ETHELRED II died in 1016 he was succeeded by his son EDMUND IRONSIDE. However, CAN-UTE, the son of SWEYN FORKBEARD, who for a few weeks had been King of England, laid claim to the throne. The final battle between the two con-tenders took place at Ashingdon, close to the River Crouch in Essex, on 18 October 1016. Edmund had camped on Ashingdon Hill – then known as Assandun – while Canute occupied a defensive position on a low hill at Canewdon, just over a mile away. While Canute's followers were the more seasoned warriors, Edmund had superiority of numbers and this emboldened him to open the battle. He led his men in a charge down Ashingdon

Hill towards the Danes and the armies met halfway between the two hills.

Edmund lost his advantage of numerical superiority when Eadric, the Earldorman of Mercia, defected and led his followers from the field. In the battle that ensued, 'all the flower of the English nation' was slain and victory went to Canute. Soon afterwards the two leaders met at Deerhurst in Gloucester, where they agreed to share the kingdom until either one died, whereupon the other would become King of England. Edmund died on 30 November of that year and on 6 January 1017 Canute was crowned at Old St Paul's Cathedral. Later, to commemorate his victory, he built a church on Ashingdon Hill, which remains to this day.

ATHELSTAN The son of EDWARD THE ELDER and the grandson of ALFRED THE GREAT, Athelstan was born *c.* 895 and crowned at Kingston upon Thames in 924. The only flaw in the new reign was the new king's illegitimacy, his mother Egwina having been his father's mistress. Yet in this there was a hint of the marvellous. According

to legend, Egwina was the daughter of a shepherd and one day while she was guarding her father's flock she fell asleep and dreamed that a great globe of light 'resembling the moon' shone out of her body, miraculously sending its rays throughout the country. Later, she recounted her dream to the woman who had nursed EDWARD THE ELDER when he was a child, and seeing it as a divine omen, the royal nurse had Egwina groomed and educated, and introduced into court life where she was purposely put in the company of the king. The result was that he fell in love with her and she bore him two more children after Athelstan.

In the twelfth century William of Malmesbury described Athelstan thus: '. . . not beyond what is becoming in stature, and slender in body; his hair, as we ourselves have seen from his relics, flaxen, mingled with gold threads'.

Apart from being an inspired war leader, as one would expect from his pedigree, Athelstan became famous for his piety and enthusiasm for collecting holy relics. When Hugh, Duke of the Franks, was eager to arrange a match with the English king's sister, he had his envoys present Athelstan with the lance that was said to have pierced the side of Christ as he hung on the Cross, a fragment of the True Cross and the Crown of Thorns set in crystal. Apart from his veneration for such mementoes, Athelstan supported the Church by a vigorous programme of monastery building.

With such a pious reputation it is curious that he became the first King of England to be described as a murderer thanks to a reference to the year 933 made by the chronicler Simeon of Durham which read: 'King Athelstan ordered his brother Edwin to be drowned at sea.' The tradition behind this cryptic sentence is that when he became king, Athelstan faced hostility from those who objected to his illegitimacy and preferred his half-brother Edwin who had been born in wedlock. However, his first task was to secure his kingdom against the Danes and the Scots.

The Danes of York had elected as their king Olaf Sihtricsson, who was supported in his designs against the Anglo-Saxons by his uncle Guthfrith, King of the Danes in Ireland, and who brought an army across the Irish Sea to reinforce his nephew.

An imaginative representation of Athelstan's coat of arms in stained glass in the Great Hall of Winchester Castle.

In reply Athelstan marched resolutely upon York, causing Olaf to flee to Ireland while Guthfrith sought the protection of King Constantine of Scotland. Athelstan followed this success by marching into Strathclyde where he ordered that the northern rulers should formally submit to his authority. This ceremony took place at Eamont in Cumbria – believed to have been at a site where Dacre Castle stands today – in July 927 when Hywel of Strathclyde, Constantine of Scotland and Owain of Gwent accepted Athelstan as their overlord. This underlined the supremacy of the English king and England was united as never before, though it left resentment smouldering in the hearts of Athelstan's thwarted foes.

Having proved that he could be as formidable as his father, Athelstan turned to a more domestic threat to his Crown in 933. His cupbearer, hoping to profit from tale-bearing, warned him that Edwin was plotting against him and Athelstan had his half-brother arrested. Edwin denied any conspiracy but the king continued to believe in his guilt. Mindful how the execution of the young prince would affect his subjects, and not wishing to stain his hands with family blood, Athelstan ordered that Edwin should be placed in a small boat without provisions, oars, sail or rudder, and cast adrift out at sea so that he would perish through natural causes. Faced with a lingering death through thirst, Edwin preferred to throw himself over the side and drown.

When the news reached Athelstan the full impact of his act struck him and to assuage his guilt he founded the abbey of Middleton in Dorset where Masses were said regularly for the repose of Edwin's soul. One day the cupbearer who had

An early engraving of a ring worn by King Athelstan.

accused Edwin lost his balance as his foot slipped while serving at the high table. Using his other foot to save himself he made the fatal remark, 'See how one brother helps another.' The king read more into his words than the cupbearer had intended, and had him summarily executed.

In 937 Constantine formed an alliance with the Irish Danes under King Anlaf who sailed up the Humber in a fleet of over six hundred longships. The Scots and Danes joined forces with Owen, King of Cumbria and soon the North of England was at their mercy. It was not until the latter part of the year that Athelstan and his brother EDMUND were able to raise an army large enough to challenge the invaders. The two great armies – some estimates of the Danish–Scottish forces have been as high as sixty thousand – faced each other at a place known as Brunanburh. Historians have suggested three possible sites for the battle: Axminster; a spot between Rotherham and Derby; and Bromborough on the Mersey. Wherever it was, it became the setting for an extraordinary English victory after Athelstan began his dawn attack. The English army was divided into Saxon and Mercian contingents, the Saxons hurling themselves against the Scots while the Mercians attacked the Norsemen.

Following savage hand-to-hand fighting the invaders' line broke and, according to the *Anglo-Saxon Chronicle*, 'the whole day long the West Saxons with mounted companies kept in pursuit of the hostile peoples, grievously they cut down the

A coin dating from the reign of Athelstan.

fugitives from behind with their whetted swords'. During the fighting, five kings, the son of a Scottish king and seven earls were slain.

After the victory, the greatest so far achieved by the West Saxons, the Scots, Welsh and the Northumbrian Danes did homage to Athelstan, establishing him as the overlord of Britain and the most powerful monarch in west Europe.

In AD 940 Athelstan died and was interred in Malmesbury Abbey. He was succeeded by his half-brother Edmund.

ATTAINDER, ACT OF An Act used to condemn persons – usually adversaries of the Crown or a party in power – of treason without them being put on trial. Those accused under the Act were 'attainted', which meant their rights and property were forfeited, and their descendants were disinherited. One of the most celebrated cases was that of Thomas Wentworth, 1st Earl of STRAFFORD, who as a supporter of CHARLES I was attainted by Parliament, after which the King was pressured into signing his death warrant. During the WARS OF THE ROSES it was estimated that around four hundred persons were attainted. The last case of attainder was in 1798 and the Act was cancelled in 1870.

AURELIANUS, AMBROSIUS Described as 'the last of the Romans', Ambrosius Aurelianus was a legendary leader of Britons. Like KING ARTHUR, he was said to have fought the Saxons who invaded Britain following the Roman withdrawal, and was credited with a great victory at the Battle of Mount Badon in AD 516 – a victory also attributed to King Arthur. Legend tells that Ambrosius Aurelianus employed Merlin to transport a number of standing stones – then known as the Giants' Dance and today as Stonehenge – to Wiltshire as memorials to his warriors who had died fighting the Saxons.

AVALON Glastonbury has always been associated with the mysterious Isle of Avalon, pre-Norman Glastonbury being an 'isle' in that it was largely surrounded by swamps. GEOFFREY OF MONMOUTH wrote: '. . . the

Stonehenge, claimed in ancient legend to be a memorial to Ambrosius' warriors slain fighting invading Saxons.

renowned KING ARTHUR himself was wounded deadly and was borne thence unto the island of Avalon for the healing of his wounds, where he gave up the crown unto his kinsman, Constantine, son of Cador in AD 542.'

Glastonbury Tor, said to be the fabled Isle of Avalon to which King Arthur was borne wounded after his final battle.

B

BABINGTON PLOT In 1586 a Roman Catholic priest named John Ballard invited Anthony Babington to join a conspiracy to set MARY, QUEEN OF SCOTS upon the English throne with the assistance of Spain. Babington, who had been a page to the imprisoned queen and was one of her most enthusiastic supporters, fell in with the plan which would have involved the assassination of ELIZABETH I. The plot was discovered by Sir FRANCIS WALSINGHAM who used it to seal Mary's fate. Babington, arrested with five others, tried to put the blame on Ballard but still received the death sentence for treason.

BALMORAL QUEEN VICTORIA and her consort Prince ALBERT had been married for eight years when in 1848 they leased the Balmoral estate in Aberdeenshire with the enthusiasm that reflected their love of Scotland. Here Balmoral Castle, which had begun as a hunting lodge for ROBERT II of Scotland, would not only provide them with the opportunity to enjoy family life away from the capital, but presented Albert with the possibility of exercising his talent for architecture and design. This was not feasible while the property was leased, so in 1852 they bought the estate of over 17,000 acres in a private transaction with money that had come to Victoria in a bequest, which meant that, unlike Britain's royal palaces, Balmoral was not owned by the Crown.

Although the Queen wrote that the original house was 'a pretty little castle in the old Scotch style', it was decided to build a new residence. A site was chosen close to the existing building. Albert and his architect William Smith planned a 'Scotch baronial' castle whose numerous candle-snuffer turrets, castellated portico and high square tower evoked Scotland's 'chateau' castles that had been inspired by the 'auld alliance'. Its setting was particularly romantic with a backdrop of woods and hills surmounted by Lochnagar, scenery that reminded Albert of his youth in Thuringa. Gardens were laid

out and in the autumn of 1855 the original building had disappeared and the new granite castle with its 180 windows was ready for occupation.

While the new Balmoral was planned for Victoria and Albert to enjoy as a homely retreat with their children, the Queen could not escape the fact that she was sovereign of Great Britain and its empire, so a state drawing-room and a suite for visiting ministers were included, and remain for this purpose. Thus the advance of the railway into this previously remote area and the newly invented electric telegraph meant that the Queen could spend many weeks at Balmoral without neglecting her duties. The largest room in the castle is the ballroom, where the royal couple hosted an annual Gillies' Ball.

Victoria's pride in Albert's power shows in an entry in her journal: 'My heart becomes more fixed in this dear Paradise and so much more so now that all has become my dearest Albert's own creation, own work, own building, own laying-out, as at Osborne: and his great taste and the impress of his dear hand, have been stamped everywhere.'

Albert's creative interest did not end with the completion of the new Balmoral; his interior work included designing furniture of pine and maple whose silver hinges he had made incorporating his initials with those of the Queen. He also designed a special Balmoral tartan for the carpets and hangings. Indeed, his enthusiasm for tartans and things Scottish, such as bagpipe music, Highland reels and local dress, inspired jokes in the royal circle. He also enjoyed the outdoor life that the Highlands offered, including hunting. After his death in 1861 his grieving widow had a monument erected to his memory at the place where he had shot his last stag. During her long widowhood Victoria continued to visit Balmoral and obtain solace from its memories.

Today, Balmoral remains the summer holiday residence for members of the royal family where they attend the church in the nearby village of Crathie. In 1979 a part of the estate's forest was enclosed by the Duke of Edinburgh to create a regeneration project which, because of its progress, was enlarged by another 750 acres in 1995.

BALMORAL, COMTESSE DE In 1897, when Queen Victoria visited the south of France by train, she travelled under the pseudonym of the Comtesse de Balmoral.

BANNOCKBURN, BATTLE OF In the early part of 1314, ROBERT I ('The Bruce') of Scotland, laid siege to Stirling Castle. As the garrison's food supply dwindled Sir Philip de Mowbray, the governor, came to an agreement with the besiegers that if he was not relieved by 24 June he would open the gates to them. His tactic was to force EDWARD II to come to his aid and it also had the effect of forcing Robert Bruce into a pitched battle with an English army led by the English King, which was something he had always tried to avoid. On 23 June the two armies cautiously approached each other at the place where the Bannock burn flowed two miles south of Stirling. At the head of the main English column rode Sir Henry de Bohun. When de Bohun saw Bruce ahead of his troops and without an escort, the opportunity for gaining a victory before the battle had begun was too tempting to miss. Lowering his lance, the English knight spurred towards Bruce who, at the last moment pulled his horse to one side and, as Sir Henry went past, buried the blade of his battle-axe in his skull.

This opening engagement was a portent of the Scots' success. Though they fought well during the day, as darkness gathered Bruce considered retreating before the numerically superior enemy. It was an English deserter who convinced him that the morale of the troops had ebbed and that he should make a determined advance on the following day. This Bruce did and though Edward was said to have 'fought like a lion', according to the *Chronicle of Edward II*, 'he had to fly, and when the royal banner was seen retreating the whole army broke up.' The effect of the Scots' victory was to reaffirm Scotland's independence.

BANQUETING HOUSE Remembered in history as the place from where CHARLES I stepped out to his execution, the Banqueting House in Whitehall is all that remains of Whitehall Palace, which was destroyed by fire in 1691. Seventy-two years before, its original Banqueting House had been

The Banqueting Hall, from which Charles I stepped on to the scaffold, is all that remains of the royal Palace of Whitehall.

burned down, and its magnificent replacement, designed by Inigo Jones, was opened in 1622 and was celebrated by a performance of *The Masque of Angers* by Ben Jonson. Under the painted ceiling representing the blessings of Enlightened Rule, which Rubens completed in 1635, important state functions were performed such as the welcoming of foreign ambassadors, the traditional St George's Day banquet for the Knights of the Garter and the monarch's 'touching for the KING'S EVIL'.

It was on 30 January 1649 that King Charles calmly walked out through one of the windows to the scaffold, and it was there that CHARLES II celebrated his restoration eleven years later.

JAMES II had a weather vane set up on the building to warn of a wind that would bring his daughter and son-in-law to take his throne in the approaching GLORIOUS REVOLUTION. When WILLIAM AND MARY did arrive in England, it was in the Banqueting House that representatives of the Lords and Commons offered them the Crown.

Royal occasions ceased at the Banqueting House after the Whitehall Palace fire and Sir Christopher Wren converted it into the Chapel Royal as a successor to the one that had been burned. In 1890 it became a military museum, but in 1963 its interior was restored to its original appearance and opened to the public.

BARON The title baron was originally applicable to all vassals of kings, lords and bishops, but later was restricted to the greater barons who in England alone had the right to receive a writ of summons to Parliament. Today, the title is the lowest of the five ranks in the British peerage, being below that of VISCOUNT.

BARONS' WAR The name given to the conflict between HENRY III and the barons supporting Simon de Montfort in the four years following 1264.
See also HENRY III

BASILIKON DORON JAMES I wrote the *Basilikon Doron* for Prince Henry, his eldest son, in which he expressed his philosophy of government and kingship. It was published anonymously in 1599 and was less controversial than his *Trew Law of Free Monarchies*, issued the previous year, in which he expounded his belief in the DIVINE RIGHT OF KINGS.

BATH For centuries Britain's most famous healing waters flowed from the mineral springs of Bath. They were first recognised by Bladud, the father of King Lear, whose story was the inspiration of Shakespeare's play. Bladud was the leper son of the legendary British king Lud Hudibras and because of the horror his disease inspired he was exiled from his father's court. As an outcast he could only survive as a swineherd, wandering in the wilderness away from his fellow men. So contagious was his malady that the pigs in his care became infected, and in order to find relief one day they ran into a malodorous bog. When Bladud retrieved them he was amazed to see that their leprous sores had vanished. He then plunged into the mud and he too was wondrously cured and able to return to his father's court; he proved his identity by means of a ring his mother had given him. When he became king, he had well shafts dug in the vicinity of the bog where he had been restored to health and a settlement was established there.

With the arrival of the Romans, lavish baths were constructed close to a temple which, with typical Roman pragmatism, was dedicated to Sulis Minerva – Minerva being the Roman goddess of healing while Sul was a Celtic deity. Following the Roman withdrawal from Britain in the fifth century the baths were neglected and largely forgotten. Thanks to ANNE OF DENMARK, wife of JAMES I, 'taking the waters' of Bath for dropsy, the spa came into its own again. In the eighteenth century Beau Nash, as Master of Ceremonies, transformed it into a centre of fashion which was patronised by the Prince Regent.

BATH, ORDER OF THE Originally, initiation into the Order of the Bath was preceded by immersion in a bath symbolising the purity required of its members by the laws of chivalry. The Order goes back to the reign of HENRY IV and is composed of three classes: the first, Knights Grand Cross; the second, Knights Commanders; and third, Companions. Until 1847 it was a military order but since then civil servants have been eligible. Honorary membership may be bestowed on foreign nationals but the title of 'Sir' is withheld.

The Knights Grand Cross is composed of up to 150 knights and dames; Knights Commanders, 295; and Companions, 1455. The Order's chapel is Henry VII's Chapel at WESTMINSTER ABBEY where the arms of senior knights of the Grand Cross are displayed on their stalls above which their banners are suspended. Every four years members attend a service of remembrance in the chapel in the presence of the Grand Master, currently Prince Charles, and every eight years the service is attended by the sovereign.

The motto of the Order is *Tria juncta in uno* – 'Three united in one'.

BATTLE ABBEY After the Battle of Hastings, WILLIAM, Duke of Normandy knelt and promised God that he would build a magnificent Benedictine abbey on the battlefield in gratitude for his victory. Known as the Field of Senlac, it was so littered with

The ruins of Battle Abbey built by William the Conqueror on the spot where King Harold was slain at the Battle of Hastings.

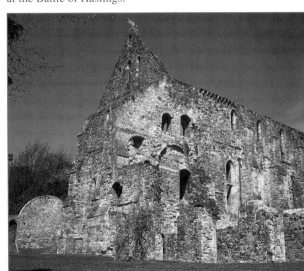

corpses after the fighting that in his poem *Harold* Lord Alfred Tennyson described it as

Sonlac! Sanguelac,
The lake of Blood.

Here amid the dead and dying William and his knights sat at trestle tables for a celebratory banquet.

After he became King of England, William kept his vow and the abbey, dedicated to St Martin, rose on the spot where King HAROLD and his loyal housecarls had made their last stand. The high altar marks the exact spot where Harold was killed. Time has eroded the building and today all that marks the location of Harold's death is a commemorative tablet.

BAYEUX TAPESTRY According to tradition it was Queen Matilda and her ladies who created the remarkable piece of embroidery, known as the Bayeux Tapestry, in which is depicted the conquest of England by her husband WILLIAM I. The events leading up to the Conquest and scenes of the Battle of Hastings are portrayed on a 20in wide band of linen 231ft in length. Worked in worsted threads of eight colours, the unique pictorial history begins just prior to Harold's visit to Bosham on his journey to Normandy, his entertainment at William's court, his swearing of fealty to William and other events which led up to the construction of the Norman fleet and the invasion of England. Of great interest to historians down the ages is the detail with which such subjects as shipbuilding, the serving of food and the construction of the Normans' earthworks at Hastings are depicted.

A scene from the Bayeux Tapestry depicting weapons and armour being transported for William the Conqueror's invasion of England.

The tapestry was first referred to in the fifteenth century when once a year it was brought out and displayed along the nave of Bayeux Cathedral. During the French Revolution it narrowly escaped destruction on two occasions but soon afterwards it was put on view in Paris at Napoleon's command. Later it was returned to Bayeux where it may be seen today.

BAYNARD'S CASTLE One of the oldest of Britain's vanished palaces – and the most rebuilt – was Baynard's Castle, which WILLIAM I built along with Montfichet's Castle and the White Tower in order to control the dangerous population of London. Built on the Thames bank at Blackfriars, it took its name from its first custodian, Ralph Baynard, who had come to England with the Norman Conquest. In 1111 it passed into the hands of the Fitzwalter family, lords of Dunmow in Essex, whose most celebrated member was Robert, who is remembered in history for leading the barons who forced KING JOHN to agree to MAGNA CARTA in 1215.

Three years previously the King had demolished the castle on account of Robert's growing opposition to him, but there is a more fanciful legend to explain the demolition. It was said that John developed an indelicate passion for Robert's beautiful daughter Matilda, but the girl, supported by her father, resolutely refused to become his mistress. To thwart the royal desires of a king such as John was to invite disaster. Matilda was imprisoned in the Tower of London, where, according to this piece of royal folklore, she was murdered by a poisonous powder sprinkled on a poached egg. Robert, meanwhile, had sought sanctuary in France and the king expressed his displeasure by destroying his home.

Sometime after John had died Robert Fitzwalter was able to return and rebuild the castle east of Blackfriars and overlooking the Thames as before. Later it became a royal property which HENRY VI bestowed on his uncle the Duke of Gloucester, the younger brother of HENRY V and known as the 'good Duke Humphrey', who had to rebuild it again after it was destroyed by fire in 1428.

After his victory over the House of Lancaster, Edward, Earl of March, was staying at Baynard's when the council, which included WARWICK THE

KINGMAKER and the Archbishop of Canterbury, arrived to offer him the Crown which he accepted to become EDWARD IV. It was also in the castle that RICHARD, DUKE OF GLOUCESTER, received a similar deputation led by the Duke of Buckingham and agreed to become Richard III.

After Henry VII came to the throne he decided to rebuild Baynard's, making it more of a palace and less of a castle. Its square fabric, which rose regally above the neighbouring buildings, enclosed a courtyard, and there was a walled garden and stairs running down to the river for embarking on royal barges. Its appointments gave a foretaste of the luxury that was to be the hallmark of Tudor courts.

In 1505 the ill-fated Prince Arthur and his betrothed CATHERINE OF ARAGON stayed there and later the place became the jointure of Catherine until it passed to Anne Boleyn, and after she fell from royal favour King Henry granted it to his illegitimate son the Duke of Richmond in 1536. He died soon afterwards and by 1540 Anne of Cleves was in residence.

After Henry's death LADY JANE GREY was proclaimed queen within its walls, and shortly afterward the procedure was repeated for MARY TUDOR. Before long a new wing replaced several former buildings and this was to be the last of the demolition and reconstruction that had been such a characteristic of the palace. The last sovereign to dine there was CHARLES II in 1666. A few days later it was destroyed in the Great Fire of London and was not rebuilt. Today a public house, suitably named 'The Baynard Castle', stands on the old palace site at the corner of Queen Victoria Street and St Andrew's Hill.

BECKET, THOMAS À When HENRY II proposed that his boon companion Thomas à Becket should become Archbishop of Canterbury – the king wishing to have an ally in the Church – Becket replied, 'You will take your favour from me and our love will become hatred.' Nevertheless he accepted the role and in a Damascene conversion changed from being a wealthy, pleasure-loving courtier, to a champion of the Church, defending it against the king's demands to a point where a feud developed between the erstwhile friends. On one famous occasion, provoked beyond endurance by Becket's behaviour, Henry fell into a rage that appeared to endorse the legend that the Plantagenets had satanic blood in their veins, and uttered the fateful words, 'What a parcel of fools and dastards have I nourished in my house! Not one of them will avenge me of this one upstart clerk.' Taking his

Right: Reliquary containing a revered relic of Thomas à Becket at East Finchley's All Saints Church. *(Photograph by Paul Abrahams)*

Far right: A life-like effigy of the martyred Thomas à Becket in his archbishop's robes in Canterbury Cathedral.

words literally, four knights – Reginald FirzUrse, William Trach, Hugh de Morville and Richard Brito – hurried from the king's Normandy court and reached Canterbury on 29 December 1170. At the cathedral Becket calmly greeted them but almost immediately was killed by a sword blow.

Thomas à Becket's murder sent a ripple of horror across Christendom. When the pope threatened to excommunicate Henry unless he unconditionally accepted the demands of the Church, the king hurried to Ireland. He landed at Waterford with an army of four thousand on 18 October 1171, having left an order that no one should follow unless summoned. This ensured that no letters of excommunication would reach him. Cut off from the outside world, Henry put into action his plan to get himself back in favour with the Vatican by subjugating Ireland which was then faithful to the Celtic Church. When the Irish clergy submitted to him formally at Cashel, the king was able to bargain with the pope – a Roman Catholic Ireland in return for lifting the threat of excommunication. In Normandy he was absolved from the crime after doing penance before papal legates.

In the death of Thomas à Becket the Church gained a hold over the English king, a new saint, and Ireland, while England gained the most remarkable shrine in its history, ranking only with St Peter's of Rome and the shrine of St James of Compostela. In 1173 Pope Alexander III canonised Becket and this added impetus to the expansion of his cult. Shiploads of Continental pilgrims were ferried over from France to swell the streams of hopeful humanity heading for Canterbury. Fifty years after St Thomas's death his remains were translated to the new chapel behind the high altar. In those days the altar was in a lower position than today, level with the present altar rails, allowing the shrine to become the glittering focal point of the cathedral. Covered with gold and gems, it has been described as being one of the greatest concentrations of portable wealth in England. Although Becket's shrine was demolished by order of HENRY VIII, its site in Canterbury Cathedral remains a place of pilgrimage today.

BLACK PRINCE A prince who should have been a king, Edward of Woodstock found a place in England's pantheon of semi-legendary heroes. According to Froissart he became known as the Black Prince because he was 'styled black by terror

of his arms'. On 15 June 1330 he was born at WOODSTOCK PALACE, the eldest son of EDWARD III who claimed that, following the death of Charles IV of France, he should have inherited the French throne through his mother Queen ISABELLA. In 1346 Edward took an army of fifteen thousand men to Normandy and with him went the 16-year-old Edward to win his spurs on the field of Crécy. A truce was finally agreed between King Edward and King Philip and the first act of the Hundred Years' War was over.

The second act came in 1356 when on 19 September the Black Prince won a victory at Poitiers in which he captured many nobles and John, the new King of France. These distinguished prisoners were taken to England where Edward entertained them with a series of pageants and tournaments. The ransom set for the French king was so high that his subjects resumed the war with England while he continued to live in England in great comfort.

Once more King Edward with his sons, the Black Prince and JOHN OF GAUNT, crossed the Channel with an army and on 28 October 1359 they reached the walls of Paris. According to a contemporary writer, it was a 'foul dark day of mist and hail, and

The beautifully wrought gilt effigy of the Black Prince, the victor of Poitiers, above his tomb in Canterbury Cathedral.

so bitter cold that sitting on horseback men died. Wherefore, unto this day it is called Black Monday, and will be for a long time hereafter.' Paris was blockaded for nearly two months, but its walls were too strong for the besiegers and in 1360 a treaty was signed in which Edward renounced his claim to the French crown and in return the French agreed to pay 3 million gold crowns for their king – a debt which was never honoured.

In 1361 Prince Edward married Joan, the daughter of Edmund, Earl of Kent, and granddaughter of EDWARD I. They had two sons, the first Edward, born in 1365, who lived for six years, and Richard, born in 1367 who later became RICHARD II.

Following the campaign in France King Edward took a less active interest in the affairs of state, handing over many of his responsibilities to John of Gaunt and the Black Prince who in 1362 was made Prince of Aquitaine. His administration was censured as harsh by Charles V of France, who had succeeded King John, and he was summoned to Paris to answer charges of misrule. In reply he attacked Limoges. The town's walls were too massive for the usual assault so a tunnel was dug which caused a section to collapse. At dawn on 19 September 1370 English troops streamed through the gap, and because he was then suffering from dropsy the Black Prince was borne on a litter in the tradition of RICHARD COEUR DE LION and EDWARD I. But while he had been a beau ideal of knightly virtue for so long, he was carried into a massacre. With his bearers slipping on bloody cobbles, the prince shouted encouragement to his men until the streets were piled with the corpses of innocent citizens.

In 1375 ill-health forced him to give up the governorship of Aquitaine and he died on 8 June the following year at the PALACE OF WEST-MINSTER and was interred in Canterbury Cathedral.

BLENHEIM PALACE As a reward for his devastating victory over the French and Bavarian armies at the Battle of Blenheim in 1704, John Churchill, 1st Duke of Marlborough was given the royal manor of Woodstock in Oxfordshire by QUEEN ANNE. It was here that the building of the magnificent Blenheim Palace was begun in the same year by Sir John Vanbrugh. The palace continued to belong to the Churchill family, Sir Winston Churchill being born there in 1874.

Following his death in 1965 he was interred in Bladon churchyard which is situated next to Blenheim Park.

BLOOD, COLONEL THOMAS Known in history as the man who nearly stole the CROWN JEWELS, the Irish adventurer Colonel Thomas Blood was on the Parliamentary side during the English Civil War with the result that he lost his estate at the Restoration. On the morning of 15 March 1671, dressed as a clergyman, he entered the TOWER OF LONDON with three friends. On reaching the chamber where the royal regalia was kept, Blood felled the Keeper of the Jewels with a mallet he had secreted under his clerical robe. The quartet then made off with the crown and orb.

The alarm was soon raised and the thieves pursued and apprehended. While the penalty for such a crime would have been the gallows or worse, CHARLES II, perhaps amused at Blood's audacity, visited the rogue in prison, gave him a pardon and a position at court, and returned his estate to him. Such royal benevolence led to the rumour that the king, who was always in need of money, had colluded with the reckless colonel in a plan to turn the regalia gems into hard cash for their mutual advantage.

BOLEYN, ANNE Born in 1504, Anne Boleyn was the daughter of Sir Thomas Boleyn and Elizabeth Howard, daughter of the Duke of Norfolk. In 1519 Anne went to the French court. When she returned to England in 1521 she became a maid of honour to QUEEN CATHERINE. At this time HENRY VIII had become dissatisfied with his marriage as the queen had failed to provide a male heir to the throne. Within a year he became infatuated with Anne, who realised from ELIZABETH WOOD-VILLE's association with EDWARD IV that virtue could be sometimes more profitable than vice. Marriage was the price of her bed. An elusive love was a new experience for the King and he delighted in wooing the reluctant maid of honour. Although he usually found writing tedious, he penned many lengthy letters to her and composed a poem, a verse of which read:

> Now unto my lady,
>> Promise to her I make
> For all other only
>> To her I me betake.

The object of this royal poetry was not generally considered – as the Venetian ambassador put it – 'one of the handsomest women in the world'. He added, 'She is of middling stature, swarthy complexion, long neck, wide mouth, bosom not much raised, and in fact has nothing but the English King's great appetite and her eyes which are black and beautiful.'

In 1527 Henry began his campaign to get his marriage to Catherine declared invalid, and Anne rewarded him with her favours. As the proceedings dragged on they became openly amorous. In one letter to Anne the king wrote: 'Mine own sweetheart, this shall be to advertise you of the great elengeness (loneliness) that I find since your departing. I think of your kindness and my fervencies of love; for otherwise I would not have thought it possible that for so little a while it should have grieved me . . . Wishing myself – especially of an evening – in my sweetheart's arms, whose pretty dukkys [breasts] I trust shortly to kiss.'

Anne was created Marchioness of Pembroke. She travelled with the royal retinue and had her own apartments, though at court she was referred to as 'The Concubine'. Determined not to remain 'The Concubine' Anne sensed that CARDINAL WOLSEY was opposed to a royal divorce and at supper one night she told Henry that Wolsey deserved to lose his head. It was the beginning of the cardinal's downfall. Early in 1531 Thomas Cromwell became one of the king's chief ministers and he engineered Henry's break with Rome, because of the Pope's refusal to grant an annulment.

In January 1533, with the Reformation under way, the King secretly married the now pregnant Anne. In May ARCHBISHOP CRANMER duly declared the marriage to be legal and in September Anne gave birth to the future ELIZABETH I. In January 1536 the discarded Queen Catherine died and on the day of her funeral Anne had a stillborn child, said to have been brought about by the shock of finding Henry with JANE SEYMOUR sitting on his lap. Once more the king despaired of having a son to inherit his crown.

On the following May Day, Henry and Anne attended a tournament at Greenwich, which the king suddenly quit to the bewilderment of the spectators. The next day Anne realised the significance of her husband's abrupt departure when she was charged with committing adultery with three gentlemen of the privy chamber and a musician, and with having committed incest with her brother Lord Rochford.

On 12 May her four alleged paramours were condemned for high treason, which meant that her case was in effect judged before she was brought to trial. One of the peers who pronounced them guilty was Anne's father, thereby implying the guilt of his daughter. Three days later she and her brother appeared before twenty-six peers and each gave a verdict of guilty. Anne's own uncle, Thomas Howard, 3rd Duke of Norfolk, presided over her judges and pronounced her death sentence.

On 19 May 1536, two days after her brother had been executed, Anne was led to Tower Green in the TOWER OF LONDON where she declared to the assembled nobility and London aldermen that she accused no one of her death, and, while not acknowledging the charges that had been brought against her, expressed submission to the law. The manner of her death was a novelty for the spectators, because an executioner had been brought from Calais to strike off her head with a sword, a French custom which until then was unknown in England. Her body was interred in the Tower's chapel of ST PETER AD VINCULA.

On the day of Anne's execution, Henry visited Jane Seymour, and Archbishop Cranmer issued a dispensation allowing their wedding to take place without the usual banns. The marriage was performed privately on 30 May. Cranmer also declared the King's union with Anne had never been legal because she was the sister of one of Henry's ex-mistresses, thus bastardising Anne's daughter Elizabeth – Queen Catherine's daughter Mary had already been declared illegitimate – which left the succession clear for any children Jane Seymour would bear.

BOSWORTH, BATTLE OF In the summer of 1485 RICHARD III was in Nottingham when word reached him that HENRY TUDOR, head of the House of Lancaster, had landed at Milford Haven on 7 August with two thousand mercenaries. As Welshmen flocked to Henry's banner the king marched his army in the direction of Leicester and set up camp near Market Bosworth. Here, on the night of 21 August, a couplet was pinned to the canvas of the Duke of Norfolk's tent with the warning:

Jack of Norfolk be not bolde
For Dickon thy master is bought and solde.

Norfolk ignored the warning and was to die valiantly in defence of the Yorkist Crown.

Next morning King Richard told his commanders, 'Everyone give but one sure stroke and the day is ours. What prevaileth a handful of men to a whole realm? As for me, I assure you this day I will triumph by glorious victory or suffer death for immortal fame.' The author of the Croyland Chronicle described how the king paraded his troops before Mass could be said or breakfast eaten, and was ready for battle by eight o'clock. He wore grey armour and sat astride a grey destrier, and over his helmet he placed his crown. Beneath it his face was pale and drawn but determined.

Richard arranged his forces on Ambion Hill overlooking the enemy camp with Norfolk's archers and cavalry forming the vanguard on the hill's crest. The king's own cavalry was stationed behind and the Earl of Northumberland's men were situated further back as the rearguard. On rising ground to the left Lord Thomas Stanley, the Steward of the Royal Household, waited with four thousand men. He had little enthusiasm for the campaign while his brother, Sir William Stanley, had been negotiating secretly with the Lancastrians and it has been suggested that the Stanleys positioned their men so that they would be able to join up with whichever side appeared to gain the advantage.

The royal army has been variously estimated to have numbered between eight and twelve thousand men, the rebels between five and eight thousand. This gave no advantage to Richard because when he advanced the Stanleys remained aloof, their troops idly watching the leading Yorkist ranks under Norfolk break against the tightly packed Lancastrians and then roll back to regroup. As the two vanguards clashed again, Richard ordered reinforcements from the rear but the Duke of Northumberland made no move to comply – 'Dickon' had indeed been bought and sold.

According to sixteenth-century writers Richard's lieutenants urged him to flee at this treachery but he refused with the words, 'I will die King of England. I shall not budge a foot.' Then shouting 'Treason! Treason!' he charged into the enemy ranks at the head of a hundred of his faithful supporters. He was said to have fought his way towards Henry Tudor who until then he had never seen before, knowing that his only chance of retaining the throne lay in killing his foe. Henry managed to avoid him but Richard got close enough to kill his standard-bearer

Richard III's white boar banner flying above the battlefield where Plantagenet rule ended with his death.

and the master of his cavalry before he was toppled from his saddle by a mace blow and stabbed to death on the ground.

The king's body was stripped and mutilated and then, with his long hair hanging down, slung across a packhorse and carried to Leicester. There the royal corpse was thrown in a ditch where for two days it was an object of ridicule, after which it was interred by charitable monks in Greyfriars Church. Thus perished the last of the Plantagenet kings whose forebears had ruled over England for more than three centuries.

BOUDICCA After the Roman conquest of Britain there was resentment over tax gathering, the annexation of land for the settlement of Roman veterans and the statues of the alien gods in new stone-built temples. Yet for many the changing way of life was agreeable. Chieftains left their draughty halls for centrally heated villas, learned Latin and enjoyed the benefits of Roman citizenship. Among these was Prasutagus, the King of the Iceni of East Anglia. A pro-Roman ruler, he borrowed heavily from Roman moneylenders, including Nero's wealthy tutor Seneca, in order to enjoy the benefits of the new civilisation imported from Rome. Before his death in AD 59 he arranged for the Emperor Nero to co-heir his kingdom with his daughters in order to safeguard their rights and those of the Iceni.

In the event this was no protection against the cupidity of Catus Decianus the procurator of

Britain. The preceding emperor, Claudius, who had died in AD 54, granted large sums of money to British chieftains to encourage their Romanisation, but Catus Decianus decided to reclaim these grants on the pretext that they were loans due for repay-

Bronze group of Boudicca and her daughters on the Thames Embankment. Prince Albert loaned his horses as models for those drawing the scene.

A woodcut illustration from Holinshed's *Chronicles* depicting the Roman army leaving London to the wrath of Boudicca's followers.

ment, and the Iceni were his first target. Meanwhile, in Rome Seneca demanded that Queen Boudicca, the widow of Prasutagus, should honour the debt incurred by her late husband.

Accompanied by a detachment of guards, Decianus's tax collectors entered the queen's palace at Norwich and ordered her to pay a huge sum of money. When she declared this would be impossible their response was brutal. 'Kingdom and household were plundered like prizes of war, the one by Roman officers, the other by Roman slaves', wrote Tacitus, the Roman historian whose father-in-law Agricola became the Governor of Britain in AD 77. 'As a beginning his [Prasutagus's] widow Boudicca was flogged and her daughters raped. The Icenian chiefs were deprived of their hereditary estates as if the Romans had been given the whole country.'

The Iceni watched impotently while their lands were confiscated but in secret forest enclaves Boudicca urged her people to revolt. She told them, 'Do not fear the Romans. . . . They provide themselves with walls and palisades and trenches. Why do they adopt such methods of fighting? Because they are afraid. We prefer a rough-and-ready action. . . . Our shields protect us better than their suits of armour. They cannot stand hunger, thirst, cold or heat as we can. . . . Let us show them that they are the hares and foxes trying to rule over dogs and wolves!'

A shamed queen eager to fight for the liberty of her people, Boudicca was an impressive figure and as such has remained a heroic symbol personified by her statue on the Embankment in the centre of London, the city she once razed. The Greek historian Dio Cassius wrote: 'She was very tall, in appearance terrifying, in the glance of her eye most fierce, and her voice was harsh. A great mass of the tawniest hair fell to her hips. Around her neck she wore a large golden necklace, and she wore a tunic of divers colours over which a thick mantle was fastened by a brooch.'

Boudicca's opportunity to revolt came in June AD 61 when Suetonius Paulinus, the Governor of Britain, took two-thirds of his army garrisoned in North Wales to crush the Druids who had retired to their holy isle of Mona. The destruction of their sanctuary was an extra incentive for the Iceni to revolt when most of the Roman legionaries were far away. The ashes of the Druids' groves were still smouldering when a message reached the victorious Suetonius that Camulodunum (now Colchester) had been razed by a rebel army led by Queen Boudicca whose Celtic name appropriately meant Victory. Almost immediately a second message reached the governor with the almost unbelievable news that an imperial legion had been annihilated.

When word of Camulodunum's destruction and the slaughter of twenty thousand Romans and pro-Roman Britons had reached the Roman garrison at Lincoln, its commander Petilius Cerealis set out with five thousand troops of the IXth Legion. They were marching through treacherous fen country when a host of Britons rose like phantoms from the reeds. Their attack was so unexpected in such marshland that only the cavalry managed to fight its way back to Lincoln. This meant that there was now no Roman force in the south or east of the province capable of halting the rebels, and the cities of Londinium (London) and Verulamium (St Albans) would be vulnerable. The flight of Catus Decianus, the procurator responsible for the rebellion, to the Continent further weakened morale.

Knowing that his foot soldiers would not be able to march the 250 miles to Londinium in time to defend it, Suetonius rode ahead with his cavalry, with the infantry following as best it could. He dispatched a courier to Gloucester, the base of the IInd Augusta Legion, ordering its *praefactus castrorum*, Poenius Postrumus, to rendezvous with him on his intended route. With his cavalry and the four thousand men of the IInd Augusta he believed he might be able to defend London until the main body of the army arrived. After two days' hard riding Suetonius reached the meeting place, but of Poenius Postrumus there was no sign. Tacitus wrote: 'Contrary to his military oath he disobeyed the commands of his general.' At this point Suetonius might have been tempted to wait for his army but the 60-year-old general was made of stern stuff and ordered his cavalry to continue. At the same time Queen Boudicca mounted her chariot, which according to legend had scythe blades fitted to its wheels, and led her people towards London. Moving down the Roman roads they resembled a human river, ever widening, as men constantly joined it, often with their families riding in ox carts. On the way Roman settlements were put to the torch and their inhabitants to the sword.

'They would have nothing but killing, whether by sword, cross, gibbet or fire, as though hungry to avenge themselves beforehand for the retribution which was to follow', wrote Tacitus. He appears to have had an inkling of Boudicca's motive for such slaughter as it committed her followers irredeemably to her cause, as Rome would show no mercy after such atrocities and the only outcome would be victory or death.

With an estimated following of a hundred and twenty thousand people her progress was naturally slow, and early in July Suetonius reached Londinium ahead of her but only to tell its citizens that he could not defend the city but would escort refugees to a safer area across the Thames. About ten thousand early Londoners left with the Roman cavalry while those who remained prepared to defend their city which had only been established seventeen years previously. Their efforts were in vain. When the queen's army arrived the city was destroyed in circumstances of particular horror, and historians believe that around twenty thousand people perished. Two millennia later there is still evidence of the holocaust in the form of a stratum of ash lying between 10ft to 20ft below the present-day surface of London. Similar layers of ash are to be found under St Albans which also fell to Boudicca. By now, according to Tacitus, seventy thousand Romans and Romanised Britons had been killed by the rebels.

Boudicca knew that although she had humbled the Romans she could not claim complete victory until Suetonius was vanquished and by August he was

According to local tradition this obelisk, situated 2 miles north-east of Waltham Abbey, marks the site of Boudicca's last battle. (*Photograph by Paul Abrahams*)

joined by his infantry and ready for the inevitable battle. The queen made the error of allowing him to take up position at the mouth of a defile with dense forest behind him and open sloping land in front. Perhaps it was thought that the site was unimportant as Suetonius was outnumbered by ten to one and, not having enough men to face the Britons' battle line, he was forced to split his army into three separate groups.

The supporters of the rebel queen were so confident of victory they brought their families in wagons to watch the spectacle of the Romans' defeat, ranging the vehicles in a tightly packed semicircle behind their vast army. Then wave after wave of Britons advanced up the slope to hurl themselves against the Romans' locked shields, but each time they were rolled back until the next wave surged forward. This was the pattern of the battle until the Britons were exhausted and the Roman divisions began an inexorable advance in wedge-shaped formations. The disciplined advance of a Roman army could strike an awesome fear into an enemy and it did so on this occasion. The Britons panicked, but as they attempted to flee they found themselves hemmed in by their own wagons. Suetonius showed no mercy. Not only the demoral-ised men but the women and children who a few hours before had been cheering spectators were put to the short Roman swords. Even horses and oxen were butchered between the shafts of the wagons which were then set alight. Roman historians calcu-lated that as many as eighty thousand rebels were killed by nightfall for the loss of four hundred Roman legionaries.

After his victory Suetonius waged a campaign of ruthless retribution in which the Iceni especially suffered, but once order was re-established through-out the province Emperor Nero uncharacteristically ordered a policy of reconciliation. Agricola replaced Suetonius, pardoned rebels and introduced reforms, and the practices which had ignited the rebellion were discontinued.

According to legend Queen Boudicca and her daughters managed to escape only to commit sui-cide by poison. Tacitus gave no clue as to the location of the battle but according to local tradition an obelisk standing in a field 2km north-east of Ambresbury Banks in Epping Forest marks the site.

BOYNE, BATTLE OF In March 1690 the deposed JAMES II sailed to Ireland from France with an army of six thousand French troops in an endeavour to regain his kingdom. The expedition was financed by Louis XIV. As the leading Roman Catholic king in Europe, Louis was the sworn enemy of Protestant WILLIAM OF ORANGE who had been invited by the English Parliament to assume the throne in what became known as the GLORIOUS REVOLUTION.

In Ulster, William's army consisted not only of Englishmen, but Dutchmen already hardened from fighting the French, Scots, Danes and French. On 30 June this multinational force reached the River Boyne on the south side of which James was encamped. With the addition of Irish Catholics, James's original army had grown to twenty-five thousand. While reconnoitring the river bank, William and his officers unwisely had an al fresco breakfast in full view of the enemy. Several cannon shots were fired at them and William was struck on the shoulder. Nevertheless, the next day he put himself at the head of his cavalry and, sword in hand, led them into the battle, which Ulster Protestants celebrate to this day.

After the Irish cavalry was broken James's regiments began to scatter and the battle became a rout. Observing this from a hill, James became the first to flee in the direction of Dublin. In the city he railed against the Irish for running away from the Protestant enemy until Lady Tyrconnel, angered by this criticism of her kinsmen, said sweetly, 'But Your Majesty won the race.'

BRAEMAR GATHERING Each September the Braemar Gathering for Highland sports and dancing takes place in the Aberdeenshire village of that name. The Gathering has been patronised by royalty ever since QUEEN VICTORIA attended it in 1848. She was attracted by the area and the games so much that she bought the Braemar estate five years later. It is said that some of the tougher sports, such as tossing the caber, go back to the reign of King Malcolm Canmore in the eleventh century.

BRETWALDA Meaning 'ruler of Britain', the word was first recorded in the *Anglo-Saxon Chronicle* entry for 829 which described EGBERT OF WESSEX as the eighth king to have that title.

BRIDEWELL PALACE In 1512 a fire destroyed the royal apartments in the Tower of London and another fire burned most of the Palace of

Bridewall Palace, built by Henry VIII, which later became a 'House of Correction' in use until 1855.

Westminster, with only the Painted Chamber and the Great Hall surviving. This double disaster meant that HENRY VIII's only London residence was BAYNARD'S CASTLE which could not be compared with Westminster or the Tower. The king therefore set about planning a new palace which would be suitably magnificent for a Tudor monarch and he chose a site on the bank of the River Fleet where it joined the Thames. The Fleet has long been bricked over but Bride Lane, which runs off New Bridge Street, marks where the northern wall of the palace once stood.

At the beginning of the sixteenth century CARDINAL WOLSEY acquired the land and when the king decided it would be a suitable location for his new residence the cardinal presented it to him. Construction work commenced in March 1513 under the supervision of Thomas Larke, Surveyor of the King's Work, and was completed in 1522. Although no architectural plan of the palace has survived, it is known that it was rectangular in shape with great courtyards which were hidden from the outside world by the high palace buildings that enclosed them like a great wall. The principal palace gateway, situated on Bride Lane, opened into the imposing quadrangle known as Chapel Court which boasted the Great Staircase, the first in England to have been conceived expressly to lend

majesty to state functions. A gateway led from Chapel Court into the Great Court, one side of which comprised the Great Hall, said to be 80ft in length, which covered the area known today as Bridewell Place.

It was here in November 1528 that Henry opened the proceedings for a royal divorce from Queen Catherine by addressing an assembly of nobles, prominent lawyers, dignitaries of the City and leading merchants. He explained that he feared that the marriage to the queen had been wrongful as she had been previously married to his brother Arthur and that his conscience required the ruling of a papal court in the matter. He added that if the Vatican ruled that Catherine was his rightful wife nothing would be 'more pleasant or more acceptable' to him. His words were wholly hypocritical as by now Henry, infatuated by Anne Boleyn, was desperate for the pope to grant him a divorce.

In the early months of 1529, during which legal argument was put forward that was to alter British history, Queen Catherine continued to live in the palace and became known as the 'Martyr of Bridewell'. In the same year Cardinal Wolsey fell from the king's favour, was impeached by the House of Lords and had his property confiscated by the Crown. This gave Henry the opportunity to take over York Palace, Wolsey's magnificent Thames-side palace at Westminster which the king renamed

Edward VI's head adorning an arch which is the sole relic of Bridwell Palace in London's New Bridge Street.

Whitehall Palace. He much preferred this splendid residence to Bridewell which he soon abandoned.

During the short reign of his son EDWARD VI part of the empty palace was converted into the Royal Bridewell Hospital, a 'house of correction' for vagrants, and later the remaining unused area became a school. The erstwhile dignity of the royal residence was further eroded in 1666 when its southern buildings were burned down in the Great Fire of London. In 1855 the Bridewell House of Correction was closed and today all that remains of the palace is a gateway, its arch surmounted by the sculpted head of Edward VI, at 14 New Bridge Street.

BRIGHTON PAVILION The most fantastical royal residence in Britain stands in the heart of Brighton, an amalgam of domes, minarets and lacy stonework that would not look out of place in an ancient oriental city. The creation of GEORGE IV when he was Prince Regent, the pavilion remains a reminder of how the influence of the Prince helped to turn a Sussex fishing village into England's most fashionable resort. In 1783, the year he attained his majority, George stayed with his Uncle Henry, Duke of Cumberland at Brightelmstone, later Brighton, which was attracting visitors because of the new fad for sea bathing.

The prince enjoyed his stay so much that when he secretly married MRS FITZHERBERT two years later he took a lease on a farmhouse at Brighton where he and his illegal wife could spend time together. But, with his taste for elegance, a farmhouse soon lost its charm and in 1787 the Prince commissioned the architect Henry Holland to turn it into a villa, its 'classical' design elaborated by chinoiserie within and domes reminiscent of Russian churches without. As it turned out, Mrs Fitzherbert never actually lived in the pavilion but discreetly took a house close by, and after 1811 when the prince ended their association she never set foot inside its exotic interior.

After George became Prince Regent he felt free to spend more on the Marine Pavilion, as it was then called, and while initially favouring a Chinese-style exterior for the remodelled house, his preference later veered to the Indian. Thus, in 1815 John Nash began transforming it into a palace that could have come straight from the *Arabian Nights*. The work was completed seven years later and resulted in a unique residence with an interior

theme that was the epitome of fantastic oriental decoration.

When WILLIAM IV ascended the throne he enjoyed stays at what was now the Royal Pavilion, and when at Brighton he made a point of remaining on friendly terms with Mrs Fitzherbert. QUEEN VICTORIA liked what she called 'this strange building' but now that Brighton had become so fashionable because of its royal connection she had little privacy and the seclusion of Osborne was much more to her taste. Royal interest in the pavilion waned and many of its furnishings were removed to Buckingham Palace, leaving its future in doubt until 1849 when it was purchased by Brighton Council and opened to the public. Over the years much of its former glory has been restored, with Buckingham Palace returning many of its original contents.

BRITANNIA This was a name used to denote Britain by the Romans and later reintroduced by the scholar and antiquary William Camden who titled his famous survey of the British Isles, *Britannia*, published in 1586. As a symbol of the nation, Britannia is represented as a seated woman with a shield, trident and Greek-style helmet. Modelled on CHARLES II's favourite, Frances Stewart, Britannia first appeared on the King's 'Peace of Breda' medal of 1667 and later on copper coins, the last being on the pre-decimal penny.

BRITISH EMPIRE, ORDER OF THE With the motto 'For God and Empire', the Order of the British Empire was instituted in 1917 and is awarded in recognition of exceptional work in the fields of art, science and charity work. Every four years the Order holds a celebratory service in its chapel which is St Paul's Cathedral. There is no limit to the number of the Order's members, of whom there are over a hundred thousand.

BRUCE, EDWARD The brother of ROBERT I ('The Bruce') of Scotland, Edward, Lord of Galloway and Earl of Garrick, proved himself to be an outstanding and ruthless soldier in the fight for Scottish independence. In 1308 he laid waste to Galloway, leaving the English caged in a small number of castles, followed by several campaigns on behalf of his brother the king. And at the decisive BATTLE OF BANNOCKBURN, fought in 1314, Edward commanded the foremost division.

The next year the nobles of Ulster proposed that he should have the crown of Ireland. With an army of six thousand he crossed from Ayr to Ulster and won a series of victories over the English which made him master of the province. He was crowned the King of Ireland on 2 May 1316 but on 14 October 1318 he was slain when his army was defeated by an Anglo-Irish force at the Battle of Dandled.

BUCKINGHAM PALACE Not only the official residence of QUEEN ELIZABETH II and her consort PRINCE PHILIP, Buckingham Palace is the chief venue for traditional royal ceremonies, the entertainment of state visitors and the holding of

Buckingham Palace. The Queen's official residence was built by the Duke of Buckingham in 1703, and did not become a royal residence until 1762.

investitutres. Yet when GEORGE II acquired it for the Crown at a cost of £28,000 in 1762 he wanted it merely to be a family residence so he could move from nearby ST JAMES'S PALACE, which he disliked, but where court ceremonial would continue.

The first house on the site had been built in 1633 by Lord Goring. It was destroyed by fire forty-two years later, rebuilt as Arlington House and passed into the ownership of the Duke of Buckingham in 1703, when it was rebuilt again and named Buckingham House.

King George, who had been crowned and married to Charlotte of Mecklenburg-Strelitz in September 1761, moved into Buckingham House the following May. The young couple were delighted with it, though the queen returned to St James's Palace for the birth of her first child, the future GEORGE IV.

However, their other fourteen children were born at what George renamed the Queen's House. During his reign the book-loving king added his famous library to the house, the completion of which was marked by a celebration that included the grounds being lit by four thousand coloured lanterns. When fire destroyed part of St James's Palace in 1809 it was found necessary to move a large number of official and social functions to the Queen's House.

After George IV came to the throne in 1820 he decided to transform the house into a truly royal palace where he could hold court and attend to affairs of state, and to this end he commissioned John Nash to draw up the plans. One of the problems faced by Nash was a lack of money, as Parliament was wary of the king's architectural ambitions after the vast amounts of money he had previously lavished on Carlton House, the Brighton Pavilion and Windsor Castle. Nevertheless, work went ahead, with the area of the main block of the Queen's House being doubled, and its wings lengthened to form a courtyard whose open end, facing The Mall, was railed off. For a ceremonial entry into the courtyard Nash designed a massive triumphal arch commemorating the victories of Admiral Nelson.

Nash used Bath stone to face the exterior of what was now being called 'The King's House at Pimlico'. The interior gained new state rooms including a throne room, music room, picture gallery, state dining-room and three drawing-rooms: the White Drawing Room, the Green and the Blue.

The Queen Victoria Memorial standing opposite Buckingham Palace, the work of Thomas Brock who was knighted on the spot by George V at its unveiling in 1911. The monument is 82ft in height and the group of figures is sculpted from a single block of marble.

The palace was not finished when WILLIAM IV came to the throne and entrusted the remainder of the work to the architect Edward Blore, who was more down to earth than his predecessor. William never took up residence in the palace; indeed, after the fire at the PALACE OF WESTMINSTER he suggested it might serve as the Houses of Parliament.

After QUEEN VICTORIA took up residence at the palace in 1837, marrying PRINCE ALBERT three years later, she found that it was not big enough for state functions, there being no room large enough to hold a state ball, or for her growing family. The answer was to build a new wing across the open end of the central courtyard, which meant that in 1851 Nash's triumphal arch was moved to Hyde Park at the end of Oxford Street where it became known as Marble Arch. Sir James Penthorne, a nephew of Nash, now took over the work on the palace, and at the queen's wish he added the south wing to accommodate the State Supper Room and the adjoining ballroom. At that time the latter, with its dimensions of 111ft by 59ft, was the largest room in London. Apart from its function as a ballroom, it became the setting for orchestral concerts performed by the queen's private orchestra.

Following the death of Prince Albert in 1861 the widowed queen lost interest in Buckingham Palace, though in 1868 she held the first royal garden party in the palace grounds. It later became a yearly occasion but during the four decades that followed Albert's death the palace was virtually closed up for most of each passing year. However, in 1873 the Shah of Persia and his entourage were installed in the palace during a state visit, an event that generated a number of dubious anecdotes such as when being escorted round a prison he expressed a wish to see the gallows operated and when informed that there was no condemned criminal available he is alleged to have said, 'Take one of my servants.'

When EDWARD VII came to the throne he found it necessary to have the interior redecorated, much of it being painted white with plenty of gilding. After the austere years of Victoria's reign her son transformed the palace into a scene of glittering social occasions, banquets and balls with the sure hand of a seasoned bon viveur.

GEORGE V had been on the throne for one year when, in 1911, the marble memorial from which Sir Thomas Brock's statue of Queen Victoria gazes down The Mall was erected in front of the palace. During an air raid on London on 13 September 1940 a number of bombs struck the palace and destroyed its chapel. The palace's state rooms were opened to the public in 1993.

BYE PLOT When James VI of Scotland became JAMES I of England in 1603, a plot to kidnap him was contrived by a Roman Catholic priest named William Watson. The plan, which became known as the Bye Plot, was to seize the king's person when visiting Greenwich Palace and induce him to avow toleration of Roman Catholics. The intrigue came to nothing but Sir Walter Raleigh was alleged to have been involved and was imprisoned in the TOWER OF LONDON. The investigation that the Bye Plot instigated uncovered the 'Main Plot', a scheme – said to have been encouraged by Spain – to remove the king and place his cousin Arabella Stuart on the throne.

Arabella, a third cousin to ELIZABETH I, managed to disassociate herself from the Main Plot, although previously she had been suspected of having been in love with William Seymour, later the Earl of Hertford, who had Tudor blood in his veins. This was overlooked until 1610 when she married Seymour secretly and their combination of royal blood was regarded as dangerous to the succession. They were imprisoned in the Tower of London from which both managed to escape. Seymour fled to Ostend but Arabella was recaptured and returned to the Tower where she died, insane, five years later.

C

CADE, JACK Little is known of Jack Cade's early life except that he came from Ireland, practised as a physician in Kent and married the daughter of a squire. From the manner in which he marshalled thousands of disaffected men and endeavoured to discipline them it is thought that he may have had a military background. In May 1450, over forty thousand men of Kent, dissatisfied with the rule of HENRY VI, and eager for Richard, Duke of York to be returned to favour, marched on London under the leadership of Cade who, having assumed the name of Mortimer, now called himself the Captain of Kent.

The rebels camped at Blackheath where for two days Cade managed to maintain strict order. During

Cadbury Castle, an Iron Age hill-fort and a centre of resistance against invading Saxons, making it a contender for the site of Camelot.

that time the Lord Mayor was forced to pass judgement on the king's hated favourite, Lord Sayle, who was summarily beheaded at Cheapside. On the third day a relatively small number of unruly rebels plundered some houses and this provoked the citizens to fortify London Bridge against the insurgents. Coupled with this setback, the promise of a royal pardon sowed dissension among Cade's followers as their enthusiasm for their cause evaporated. Cade attempted to make his way secretly to the coast but on 12 July he was cornered in a garden near Heathfield, Sussex, and killed by Sheriff Iden of Kent. Unlike the Peasants' Revolt of 1381, no reprisals were taken against the men of Kent following their leader's death.

CAMELOT Just as there is no tangible proof that KING ARTHUR ever existed, there is no evidence of Camelot having been built. Yet such is the

prominence of the Arthurian epic in British folklore it is argued that there must have once been actual people and sites upon which the legends were based. Sir Thomas Malory, the fifteenth-century author of *Le Morte d'Arthur*, declared that Winchester was the site of Camelot but archaeological discoveries point to the prehistoric hillfort known as Cadbury Castle, south-west of Wincanton. Covering an area of 18 acres and defended by four lines of ditches and banks, its connection with Arthur was first recorded in 1542 by John Leland, the chaplain to HENRY VIII who made him 'king's antiquary'. He wrote: 'At South Cadbyri standith Camallate, sumtyme a famose toun or castelle. The people can tell me nothing but that they hard say that Arture mych resortid to Camalat.'

The possibility that Cadbury Castle was the site of Camelot was investigated by the Camelot Research Committee under the chairmanship of the archaeologist Dr Ralegh Radford who had previously excavated Tintagel which was also associated with the Arthurian legend. In 1966 work commenced on the site and it was soon evident that, like an English Troy, it had various settlements, from Neolithic times onward, superimposed upon one another. It seems that the 'castle' fell out of use after the arrival of the Romans. However, shards of pottery similar to those found at Tintagel were found, indicating that the fort had been reoccupied after the Roman withdrawal and that new defensive drystone walls had been built which were definitely the work of Celts. Cadbury Castle is the only British Iron Age fortress to have been renewed on this scale, which leads to the conclusion that it was a unique centre of resistance against Anglo-Saxon invaders, providing a base for a Romanised British war leader such as the original Arthur would have been.

CAMLANN, BATTLE OF ARTHUR's last battle was fought at Camlann, the site of which has never been identified. Contenders for the battlefield include a spot by the River Cam in Cambridgeshire, the area around Slaughter Bridge on the River Camel in Cornwall and Camboglanna in Cumbria. The latter is an extensive Roman fort on Hadrian's Wall, known now as Birdoswald, situated between Lanercost Priory and Gilsland.

CANUTE Born *c.* 994 the son of Sweyn, King of Denmark, and his Polish queen Gunhilda, Canute

lived to become king of the English and the Norwegians. He was with his father when, angered over the murder of his sister Gunhilda in the St Bride's Day Massacre, he ravaged areas of England. After the defection of ETHELRED THE UNREADY Sweyn had been proclaimed King of England but then died unexpectedly at the beginning of 1014. The Danes who had come to England in Sweyn's war fleet elected Canute to succeed his father while his elder brother Harold became King of Denmark. However, at the request of the Witan Ethelred returned, raised an army and defeated Canute at Lindsey forcing him to sail back to Denmark for reinforcements after cutting off the hands, ears and noses of his English hostages.

In 1015 he returned with a mighty fleet and, after landing in Dorsetshire, devastated the surrounding countryside and by Christmas was master of Wessex. Early in the following year he led his army to York and received the submission of Northumbria.

The Danish poet Ottar the Black wrote in praise of Canute:

A copy of a manuscript illustration of King Canute and his wife Emma of Normandy, the widow of his late enemy King Ethelred.

The Danes

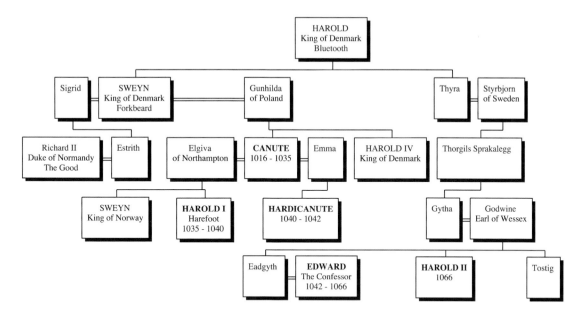

HAROLD
King of Denmark
Bluetooth

Sigrid — SWEYN King of Denmark Forkbeard — Gunhilda of Poland — Thyra — Styrbjorn of Sweden

Richard II Duke of Normandy The Good — Estrith — Elgiva of Northampton — **CANUTE** 1016 - 1035 — Emma — HAROLD IV King of Denmark — Thorgils Sprakalegg

SWEYN King of Norway — **HAROLD I** Harefoot 1035 - 1040 — **HARDICANUTE** 1040 - 1042 — Gytha — Godwine Earl of Wessex

Eadgyth — **EDWARD** The Confessor 1042 - 1066 — **HAROLD II** 1066 — Tostig

---

You made was in green Lindsey, Prince.
The Vikings wrought the violence they would.
In your rage, withstander of the Swedes,
You brought sorrow upon the English,
In Helmingborg to the west of the Ouse.
Young leader, you made the English fall close
  to the Tees.
The deep dyke flowed over the bodies of
  Northumbrians.
You broke the Raven's sleep, Waker of battle.

Apart from London, England was now Canute's but following the death of ETHELRED II in April 1016 he found the late king's son, EDMUND IRONSIDE, who had been elected king by Londoners, a powerful foe who reconquered Wessex. After several battles, Edmund and his Anglo-Saxons were defeated at Assandun (now Ashingdon) in Essex. Finally both sides faced each other across the River Severn and it was here that Edmund is said to have challenged Canute to single combat with the throne of England going to the victor. In reply Canute suggested that they should divide the country between them and live in peace. The two warrior kings met on the isle of Olney in the Severn where it was settled that Edmund should have Wessex and Canute the rest of England, and whoever lived the longest should rule all England. Within two months of this pact Edmund died mysteriously, which meant that Canute had control of the entire kingdom.

He was a king in the Viking tradition and one of his favourite sayings was 'He who brings me the head of one of my enemies shall be dearer to me than a brother.' His first act, in keeping with the

Canute's mortuary chest at Winchester Cathedral.

Ashingdon in Essex reminds the visitor of its historic connection with the Battle of Assandun with this sign.

by the fact that their new king had sent most of his army back to Denmark. In the same year, 1018, his brother Harold died so that he became King of Denmark as well as England, which meant the end of Danish raids which had been the bane of the English.

Canute summoned a national council at Oxford at which it was agreed to observe the laws and equal rights of KING EDGAR's time and he gradually replaced the Danish earls with native Englishmen, a Saxon noble named Godwine becoming the powerful Earl of Wessex in 1019, an appointment that was to have historical significance after the king's reign. He was also famous for his liberality to churches and monasteries, and to strengthen his position as King of England he married Ethelred's widow, Emma. Canute gained the sovereignty of Norway when King Olaf, later the patron saint of Norway, died in 1030. Thus what had been a divided England became part of a Scandinavian empire.

A tradition as popular down the ages as the story of King Alfred burning the cakes tells how Canute, weary of the flattery of his courtiers, ordered a chair to be set up on the seashore. Sitting in it he commanded the waves not to wet his feet, but as the tide rose and the water washed over the hem of his robe, it demonstrated his tenet that he was just another human being in the eyes of God.

When Canute died at Shaftesbury in 1035 he was mourned for his high ideals of a sovereign's duty. Today his remains, and those of Queen Emma, are housed in a mortuary chest in Winchester Cathedral.

then ruthless streak in his nature, was to hunt down the late king's relations and some of the most powerful English nobles, and to exile Edmund's two little sons.

In 1018 he levied a heavy tax – the hated Danegeld that had been introduced by Ethelred the Unready – which raised 82,500 pounds of silver which he used to pay off the Danish warriors who had come in his great fleet, retaining the crews of only forty ships. This demonstrated how secure he felt in his new kingdom which he divided into four earldoms of Mercia, Northumberland, Wessex and East Anglia.

It was at this time that he underwent a shift of character, changing from a violent Viking conqueror to a wise and temperate ruler who endeavoured to govern the country according to English ideas. One of the most important aspects of his reign was that he regarded England as his personal kingdom rather than a Danish colony. Under his reign the common folk were to enjoy the first peace and security that they had known for a long time and were reassured

CARACTACUS A son of the British king CUNOBELINUS, Caractacus divided his father's realm with his brother Togidumnus on their father's death in AD 40. The brothers fought against the Roman invasion and Tacitus wrote: 'The natural ferocity of the inhabitants was intensified by their belief in the prowess of Caractacus, whose many undefeated battles – and even many victories – made him pre-eminent among British chieftains.' In AD 43 he disappeared after being defeated in battle, after which Togidumnus had died. Five years later he reappeared as the leader of the Silures of southeast Wales until he lost his final battle to Ostorius near Ludlow. He fled north to the Brigantia tribe which he believed would aid him but instead he was handed over to his enemies by CARTIMANDUA, Queen of the Brigantes, who was anxious to please Rome.

In AD 51 he and his family were taken to Rome to be exhibited in the Emperor Claudius's triumph. According to Tacitus the British king held himself more like a conqueror than a captive and addressed the emperor with these words: 'Had my lineage and rank been accompanied by only moderated success, I should have come to this city as friend rather than prisoner and you would not have disdained to ally yourself peacefully with one so nobly born. . . . As it is, humiliation is my lot, glory yours. I had horses, men, arms, wealth. Are you surprised that I am sorry to lose them? If you want to rule the world does it follow that everyone else welcomes enslavement?'

Claudius responded well to the speech, perhaps the bearing of the captive fitted with the Roman concept of nobility, and pardoned Caractacus for having challenged the imperial might of Rome. He was given a villa in which he could live out his life with his family, and his last recorded words, spoken as he gazed at the magnificent buildings of the city, were, 'Why do you, who have got so many and so fine possessions, covet our poor tents?'

CARLTON HOUSE When GEORGE, PRINCE OF WALES reached the age of 21 his father GEORGE III allowed him to set up his own household at Carlton House, provided he agreed to be responsible for its taxes, repairs and the maintenance of the garden. Finding it in a sorry state of repair the prince commissioned his favourite architect, Henry Holland, to remodel it. Holland, who had been a pupil of 'Capability' Brown, commenced the work in 1783 and this continued on and off at astronomical cost for the next three decades.

The house, which stood in Pall Mall, had been built at the beginning of the eighteenth century by Henry, Lord Carlton. Its royal connection began in 1732 when it was bought by Frederick, Prince of Wales. After his death in 1751 his widow Augusta of Saxe-Gotha, the mother of George III, continued to reside there until her demise in 1772. Until it passed to the Prince of Wales it was undistinguished as a royal residence, its garden which had been laid out by William Kent and which extended as far as Marlborough House, being its only saving grace.

The prince was determined to turn it into a palace and in this he was successful. In 1785 Horace Walpole wrote: 'We went to see the Prince's new palace in Pall Mall and were charmed. It will be the most perfect in Europe . . . but whence the money is come I conceive not, all the tin mines in Cornwall could not pay a quarter.'

In order to achieve this perfection neighbouring houses were bought and demolished to provide space for new wings. Its most impressive exterior feature was a portico in the Corinthian style whose graceful columns gave it the dignity of an ancient Greek temple. Beyond this entrance was a magnificent hall leading to an octagon and an elegant double staircase to the state apartments and the prince's luxurious suite. One of the outstanding rooms was dedicated to Chinese decor and furnishings for which the prince had sent agents to the Far East to seek out and purchase such items. The silk hangings alone cost nearly £7,000, a very considerable sum in the eighteenth century.

In the garden the design of the Gothic conservatory appeared to have been inspired by Henry VII's Chapel in Westminster Abbey. The Gothic theme was continued in the library and the dining-room, the work of John Nash. Other rooms of splendour were the throne room, the golden drawing-room, the circular drawing-room and the rose satin drawing-room.

The prince's debts, most of which had resulted from the building of Carlton House, became so enormous that the king had to ask Parliament to clear them. A committee of inquiry was set up and finally it was agreed that the prince's liabilities would be cleared on condition that he married. This resulted in George's ill-fated marriage with PRINCESS CAROLINE OF BRUNSWICK-WOLFENBÜTTEL in 1795. Their unfortunate bridal night was spent at Carlton House and it was there that their daughter Princess Charlotte was born a year later. In 1816 she was married to Prince Leopold of Saxe-Coburg in the grand crimson drawing-room.

Often, Carlton House was the setting for many brilliant balls and receptions which the prince loved. One of the most notable was on 19 June 1811 when George became Prince Regent and the great dignitaries of the realm assembled for the swearing in and the kissing of the new regent's hand.

Despite the fact that it had been the prince's great project, when he became George IV in 1820 he decided that Carlton House was not splendid enough for his new status. One of the things that he disliked about it was that it was 'standing in a street'. He was determined to have a new, larger and grander palace and to this end he planned to build one on the site of BUCKINGHAM PALACE where his mother and father had resided. In order to raise money towards the project the king had Carlton House demolished in 1827. Its fittings and stone were sold and two terraces of houses designed by Nash were built on the site. Much of its furniture and fittings were sold by auction while a number of doors, fireplaces, stained-glass windows and even the ballroom floor were moved to Windsor. The Corinthian columns which had once been such a feature of the portico were incorporated in the new National Gallery, but of the house that was once hailed as a 'national ornament' nothing else remains.

CAROLINE OF BRUNSWICK-WOLFEN-BÜTTEL In 1794 George, Prince of Wales agreed to make a 'suitable' marriage in return for his father clearing his debts of £600,000 (approximately £38,250,000 today). Lord Malmesbury was dispatched to obtain consent for Princess Caroline, the daughter of Charles II, Duke of Brunswick-Wolfenbüttel and Augusta, a sister of GEORGE III of England, to marry the prince. When the match

Queen Caroline, whom the Prince Regent married in return for his vast debts being cleared by his father George III.

was agreed George remarked that 'one damned German Frau was as good as another'.

On the evening of 8 April 1795 the wedding took place in the Chapel Royal at ST JAMES'S PALACE. Just before the ceremony the prince said to his brother the Duke of Clarence, 'Tell MRS FITZHERBERT she is the only woman I shall ever love.' And no doubt it was the thought of the woman he had illegally married that made tears come to his eyes during the ceremony. Then, according to Princess Caroline, he spent the bridal night drunk in the fireplace.

When the prince fulfilled his obligation to the Crown by getting the princess with child, Caroline had a miserable pregnancy, painfully aware of the antipathy of her husband who was now infatuated with Lady Jersey. He forced Caroline to return the pearl bracelets he had given her as a wedding present in order to give them to his latest favourite who wore them openly in front of her. The only person to show her any consideration was King George.

Caroline gave birth to her daughter Charlotte on 7 January 1796 and soon afterwards the prince wrote: 'Nature has not made us suitable to each other, but to be tranquil and comfortable is, however, in our power; let our intercourse, therefore, be restricted to that.' And so they separated.

With relief Caroline set up her own household at Mongtague House, Blackheath. There she took into her personal care William Austin, the baby son of a destitute labourer, allowing his mother Sophia to visit him whenever she wished. This act of kindness led to the so-called Delicate Investigation. This began when an ill-natured rumour circulated that little William had been born to Caroline secretly in 1802 and a Royal Commission of Inquiry was appointed. In July 1806 it reported to King George that there was no doubt that William Austin had been born to Sophia Austin.

The Regency Bill was passed in 1810 and with the final collapse of the old king's health, Caroline lost her only royal sympathiser and the prince took the opportunity to stop her visits to their daughter Charlotte at Windsor. Anxious to escape the hostile atmosphere that surrounded her, Caroline decided to travel abroad and on 9 August 1814 she began her indecorous adventures by crossing the Channel in the navy frigate *Jason* accompanied by a number of English ladies and gentlemen.

It was in Milan that Bartolomeo Bergami entered the story. A handsome, bewhiskered figure, he became courier in the princess's travelling household where he soon became her chamberlain, and intimate companion. This gave rise to unseemly gossip and when Caroline was informed that her indiscretions were being reported to Carlton House, she is credited with remarking, 'I know it and therefore do I speak and act as you hear and see. . . . The Regent will hear it, as you say. I hope he will, I love to mortify him.'

It was at a ball in Genoa in May 1815 that Lady Bessborough encountered Caroline and wrote: 'I cannot tell you how sorry and asham'd I felt as an Englishwoman. The first thing I saw in the room was a short, very fat elderly woman, with an extremely red face (owing, I suppose, to the heat) in a Girl's white dress, but with shoulder, back and neck quite low (disgustingly so) down to the middle of her stomach. . . .'

The next year, after bestowing the title of Baron de la Francine on Bergami, the princess set out for the Holy Land. Here she showed an enthusiastic interest in visiting Biblical sites but this did not lessen what some described as outrageous behaviour. Commissioners were secretly dispatched to investigate her conduct and as their reports accumulated, the prince kept them in the notorious green bag which was later to be a godsend to cartoonists.

When George III died in January 1820 Caroline announced she would return to take part in the coronation now that her husband was George IV and she was Queen of England. Her arrival at Dover that June was greeted by cheering crowds and her journey to London was a triumphal procession. By acclaiming her, the people expressed their dislike of the king, and as he favoured the Tories, the Whigs gave the queen their backing. Prince George now placed the contents of the green bag before his Cabinet ministers and the Prime Minister suggested a Bill of Pains and Penalties, an obscure process which would result in an Act of Parliament dissolving the marriage if the allegations against Caroline were proved to be true. The coronation was postponed for the hearing in the House of Lords and Caroline appointed Lord Henry Brougham as her attorney-general while the prosecution was led by the king's attorney-general Sir Robert Gifford. Although the queen could not take part personally in the proceedings she was provided with a comfortable chair in the centre of the House in order to observe them.

Bartolomeo Bergami, whom Caroline, wife of the Prince Regent, elevated to chamberlain of her travelling court and caused a royal scandal.

On 17 August the 'trial' opened with the reading of the Bill of Pains and Penalties in which the grounds for the dissolution of the royal marriage were given as a 'most unbecoming and degrading' intimacy between the queen (then Princess of Wales) and one Bartolomeo Bergami 'a foreigner of low station'. If the first inquiry into Caroline's affairs was the Delicate Investigation, this was the Indelicate Investigation as detailed evidence was given by servants about stained sheets, 'white spots' on carriage cushions and the contents of chamber pots. Other evidence bordered on the absurd, an example being the prosecution witness who stated that Caroline had once blown her nose on one of Bergami's handkerchiefs – a handkerchief that he had already used!

Every day thousands converged on Westminster eager to hear and pass on the latest scandalous revelations. Broadsheet publishers became rich as the day's evidence was rushed off their presses and *The Times* broke with tradition by moving advertisements from the front page to make room for reports from the House of Lords.

In the opening address Lord Brougham said, with a sly dig at the king and the Duke of York, that he agreed that 'criminal intercourse was fatal to the honour of the royal family', but this was countered by the king's solicitor-general declaring that 'adultery in a man is in no way punishable'. There were ironical cheers for a piece of rhetoric by Thomas Denman, the queen's solicitor-general, when he declared in his first speech that Caroline was 'as pure as unsunned snow'.

The hearing lasted until 9 September and in his closing speech Denman thundered against 'those who had collected together a set of Her Majesty's discarded servants, who had ransacked filthy clothes-bags, who had raked into every sewer, pried into every water-closet, who had attempted to destroy all secrecies of private life. . .'. After speaking for 10 hours he concluded with a gaffe, declaiming in the direction of the queen, 'If no accuser can come forward to condemn thee, neither do I condemn thee – go, and sin no more.' Considering that he had spent so much time protesting that the queen had not sinned, the quote was gleefully seized upon by the king's supporters and a squib was circulated:

> Most gracious Queen, we thee implore
> To go away and sin no more;
> Or if that effort be too great,
> To go away at any rate.

On the third and final reading of the Bill of Pains and Penalties its majority had fallen so much that the Prime Minister changed the motion 'that the bill do now pass' to 'that the bill do pass this day six months' which meant in effect that it was dropped. It was carried against the most extraordinary scenes of jubilation Westminster had ever witnessed, while across the country bonfires were lit. Parliament voted the queen an annual £50,000 (approximately £2,400,000 today), the same sum that the king had offered her to renounce her claims.

The coronation was now held on 19 July 1821. On that morning Caroline went to Westminster Abbey but was turned away at the door on the pretext she did not have a peer's ticket. Eleven days later she was taken ill at the Drury Lane Theatre and died on 7 October. As the queen had expressed the wish to be buried beside her father in Brunswick, a funeral cortège bore her coffin to Harwich where according to Lord Brougham, 'multitudes had assembled from all parts of the country'. On 5 August 1821 the late queen had added a codicil to her will that the inscription upon her coffin should read: 'Here lies Caroline of Brunswick, the injured Queen of England.' As the coffin was placed aboard a vessel it was seen that the inscribed gilt plate had been torn off.

CARTIMANDUA Queen of the Brigantes, Cartimandua was a British queen in her own right. She entered into a treaty with the Romans which secured her realm and ensured that a native kingdom in the north was well disposed towards them. This resulted in the queen betraying CARACTACUS to her allies in AD 51, but antagonism between her and her ambitious consort, Venutius, led to civil war. In AD 69 Venutius seized the kingdom, and though Cartimandua was rescued by the Romans she never recovered her throne.

CASKET LETTERS After the followers of MARY, QUEEN OF SCOTS deserted her without engaging the army of the confederate lords at Carberry Hill on 15 June 1567, she was imprisoned at Lochleven while her husband, the Earl of Bothwell fled to Norway. One of his servants, George Dalgleish, was captured after his master's flight and under torture revealed the hiding place of the celebrated Casket Letters. These papers were contained in a gilt jewel case Mary had given Bothwell, and down the centuries scholars and historians have argued over their authenticity. They comprised eight letters which, if they were not forgeries, proved Mary's guilt in the planning of the murder of DARNLEY. The casket was also said to contain some sonnets in French written by the queen. The following example appeared in 1824 in Hugh Campbell's *Love Sonnets of Mary, Queen of Scots to James, Earl of Bothwell*:

> Friends may withdraw – afflictions dire may come
> But these are nothing to my ardent mind –
> With him, in hope, through enemies I'll roam,
> And hazard all, to fame and honour blind.
>
> For his sweet sake I will renounce the world;
> To make him great, even death itself were dear;
> Reft of a crown, or into exile hurled,
> Were naught to me, so Bothwell, lov'd be near.

Placed in his power, my son, my honour, life,
My country, subjects, soul, all, all subdued
by him, the conqueror of my will, in strife
If sweet emotions, that my love pursued.

Whatever the truth of the Casket Letters, Mary must have feared the effect they would have. At Lochleven she was given the choice of standing trial, at which the letters would be made public, divorcing Bothwell or abdicating in favour of her son. She chose the latter course and the infant James was crowned at Stirling five days later.

CATHERINE OF ARAGON A descendant of JOHN OF GAUNT and the fourth daughter of Ferdinand V, King of Aragon, and Isabella of Castile, Catherine was married to Prince Arthur, the Tudor heir of England, at the age of sixteen. The marriage took place in November 1501 and on 2 April of the following year the Prince, who suffered from ill health, died at Ludlow. In order to preserve the alliance between England and Spain, Catherine was affianced to her late husband's brother the future HENRY VIII, then eleven years old. In 1504 the Pope's dispensation allowing such a match of near relatives was obtained, and when Henry ascended the throne in April 1509 he honoured the agreement by marrying his brother's devout and witty widow. She was crowned Queen Consort in Westminster Abbey on 24 June.

Queen Catherine bore a son on New Year's Day 1511 and the King held a great tournament to mark the event but the continuing celebrations were curtailed when the child died a few days later. In all Catherine gave birth to five children but the only one to survive was the future QUEEN MARY. The lack of a male heir to the throne made Henry dissatisfied with the marriage and he feared it was Divine retribution as it was stated in the Book of Leviticus: 'If a man shall take his brother's wife, it is an unclean thing . . . they shall be childless'.

The King's decision to obtain a divorce from the Queen was strengthened when a sister of one of his ex-mistresses returned from the French court to become a maid of honour. She was ANNE BOLEYN and Henry became passionately interested in her. In 1527 he began the campaign to get his marriage nullified for which Anne rewarded him with her favours. Despite the difficulties that this entailed, ARCHBISHOP CRANMER pronounced the marriage invalid on 23 May 1533. The King, meanwhile, had secretly married Anne Boleyn on 25 January of that year.

Catherine retired to live a pious private life until her death at Kimbolton Castle on 7 January 1536 and was interred in Peterborough Cathedral. The site of her grave is still to be seen though her tomb was demolished at the beginning of the Civil War.

CERDIC, HOUSE OF The *Anglo-Saxon Chronicle* regarded Cerdic as the ancestor of ALFRED THE GREAT and the kings of the West Saxons. For the year AD 495 mention is made of the arrival of Cerdic with his son Cynric, but discrepancies in the entries made the details ambiguous.

CHAMPION OF ENGLAND The duty of the Champion of England was to challenge anyone who questioned the right of a newly crowned sovereign to his or her title. At a coronation banquet in Westminster Hall he would appear on his horse wearing full armour, throw down a gauntlet and issue his challenge. The custom went back to the dukes of Normandy when the Marmion family provided the champions. After the reign of EDWARD I the honour passed to the Dymoke family, the last Dymoke champion carrying out his traditional role at the coronation of George IV in 1821. The next king, thrifty WILLIAM IV, decided the banquet was too expensive and with it was abolished the role of the champion. As far as is known no one ever dared to accept the challenge of the royal protector.

CHANGING THE GUARD The ceremony of Changing the Guard takes place at BUCKINGHAM PALACE whenever the flying of the royal standard indicates that the sovereign is in residence. While security is the responsibility of the police, visitors to the capital find the ceremonial guarding of the sovereign by members of the elite Brigade of Guards one of the most popular sights. The soldiers who take part are from the regiments of the Coldstream Guards, the Grenadiers and the Scots, Irish and Welsh Guards.

At 11 a.m. the Guards' Band leads the New Guard from the Wellington or Chelsea Barracks to Buckingham Palace where the ceremonial routine takes place on the forecourt. The Old Guard waits in two ranks at the southern end where their colour is paraded. The New Guard, with its officers carrying drawn swords, marches through the north gate while the band plays a slow march.

The change-over drill is performed with exquisite precision with officers marching up and down in pairs as the new sentries take up their positions. The Old Guard then marches out of the main gate as the tempo of the band changes to a quick regimental march. A junior officer carries the colour of the regiment currently responsible for guard duty, and on the anniversaries of battles in which the regiment distinguished itself it is customary for it to be garlanded with a laurel wreath.

Ceremonial guard-changing also takes place at nearby St James's Palace, and at Horse Guards Building which is on the site of the old guard house of Whitehall Palace. Here the custom is carried out on horseback by troopers of the Life Guards, sometimes known as 'The Tins' or the Royal Horse Guards known as 'The Blues'. The former can be recognised by their red tunics, white horsehair plumes and white saddle sheepskins, while the latter have blue tunics, red plumes and black sheepskins. All wear buckskin breeches, black boots and steel cuirasses consisting of a breastplate and a back plate. It is said that some of these sets of cavalry armour were worn at the Battle of Waterloo and still have dents from that time. Changing the Guard is also carried out at WINDSOR CASTLE when the sovereign is in residence.

CHAPEL ROYAL, ST JAMES'S PALACE

Along with the gatehouse, the Chapel Royal remains part of the original ST JAMES'S PALACE and since it was built by HENRY VIII it has been famous for its nurturing of English church music. Its organists have included Thomas Tallis, William Byrd and Henry Purcell. QUEEN ANNE brought the choral foundation to it from the Banqueting House. It was there that CHARLES I took Holy Communion before crossing St James's Park to his execution at Whitehall. Two important royal marriages took place in the chapel: in 1840 QUEEN VICTORIA was married to PRINCE ALBERT, and fifty-three years later the future GEORGE V was married to Princess Mary of Teck.

CHAPELS ROYAL

The term is used for the chapels which were established in royal palaces after medieval courts became less migratory. The priests, who usually travelled with the court from place to place, were then able to perform their religious duties like their colleagues who served in conventional churches. The best known Chapels Royal are at Hampton Court Palace, St James's Palace and the Tower of London. There is also the Savoy Chapel in the Strand and a Chapel Royal in Buckingham Palace.

CHARLES I

The second son of JAMES VI of Scotland and ANNE OF DENMARK, Charles was born at Dunfermline Castle on 19 November 1600. As a child he was weak and suffered a speech impediment but he overcame his disabilities, though throughout his life – except at his most dramatic moment – a slight stutter remained.

The young prince studied architecture, music and painting, and his interest in the arts was fostered by his father's favourite, George Villiers, Duke of Buckingham.

The death of Charles's elder brother Henry in 1616 made him the heir apparent and four years later the French, anxious to woo England away from an alliance with Spain, suggested that HENRIETTA MARIA, the daughter of Henry IV, would make an ideal wife for the prince. In December 1625 the marriage treaty was agreed and on 1 May of the following year Charles was married to Henrietta by proxy at Notre Dame Cathedral, a month after the death of James I. The King met her at Dover Castle on 13 June, and the young couple arrived in London by river as the city was plague-

Charles I greeted by his loyal followers at Oxford following the inconclusive Battle of Edgehill.

stricken and this was thought to prevent contagion. The enthusiasm shown at the new queen's arrival soon evaporated, largely because she brought with her a Roman Catholic bishop and twenty-nine priests. The Protestant English were suspicious of foreigners and Catholic ones in particular. Henrietta's refusal to be crowned with Charles because it was a Church of England ceremony caused great disquiet, driving a wedge between the throne and Parliament.

Charles bitterly resented the influence of the French priests and courtiers of Henrietta's household and, unhappy in his marriage, came to rely more and more on Buckingham. His military adventures had ended in failure with the result in February 1626 that the Commons impeached him. In retaliation, Charles sent the leaders of the anti-Buckingham campaign to the Tower of London and the Commons refused to do any business until they were released. Charles dissolved Parliament and the situation escalated until it was dramatically resolved on 23 August 1628 when Buckingham was murdered by a dissatisfied army officer named Felton.

The King found an unexpected ally in Sir Thomas Wentworth, later the 1st EARL OF STRAFFORD, who stood by the King because, as he explained, 'the authority of the King is the keystone which closeth up the arch of order and government, which containeth each part in due relation to the whole'.

The next eleven years were the happiest in Charles's life as, bolstered by Strafford, he was able to rule without Parliament, and also because he had fallen in love with Henrietta after reconciliation between the royal couple followed the murder of Buckingham. On 29 May 1630 the birth of a son who was christened Charles after his father and an heir to the throne helped the king's position. Other children followed until there were three princes and three princesses.

In 1638 Scottish Covenanters signed a pledge to defend Presbyterianism against both the Church of England and Roman Catholics, and the Scottish Parliament abolished the office of bishops and prepared to defend the decision by military means. In the autumn of the following year Strafford returned from Ireland, where he had been Lord Deputy; and with his policy of 'Thorough' – the quelling of opposition by force – Charles now realised the necessity of working with Parliament again. When the so-called Short Parliament failed to endorse the 'Thorough' policy the Scots were encouraged to march south across the border and defeat a royal army at Newark, causing Charles to dissolve Parliament.

Soon afterwards he called the Long Parliament which immediately impeached Strafford as the 'principal author and promoter of all those counsels' which had led to 'so much ruin'. Strafford defended himself so brilliantly it appeared that he might escape conviction. His enemies, however, pressed for a Bill of ATTAINDER by which, provided it was passed by Parliament and the king assented, the Earl could be executed if it was necessary for the security of the state. For two days the King held out but on 9 May he gave in to the entreaties of the queen, and signed. He told the Privy Council, 'If mine own person only were in danger I would gladly venture to save Lord Strafford's life but, seeing my wife, children and all my Kingdom are concerned in it, I am forced to give way.'

Following Strafford's execution on Tower Hill – which was to haunt Charles for the rest of his life – the monarchy regained some popularity, to the alarm of Parliament which countered with the Grand Remonstrance listing unconstitutional acts of the king. During the summer debates the Commons split between the Puritans and those siding with the king. The prospect of civil war became inevitable.

Charles, encouraged by Henrietta, took halberdiers into Parliament to arrest five Members of Parliament, led by John Pym. The five had been warned to leave the PALACE OF WESTMINSTER in time to get away before the King's arrival.

The Great Seal of England introduced in 1651 by the Parliamentarian Government, two yars after King Charles had been executed.

CHARLES I

King Charles enters Parliament with a body of halberdiers to arrest Pym and his supporters, an act that branded him a tyrant.

Londoners now saw the king as a tyrant trying to deprive them of their traditional freedoms and on 10 January John Pym and his four supporters returned to Westminster in triumph. The humiliation and possible danger forced the royal family to flee Whitehall Palace and take refuge at HAMPTON COURT.

During the next few months the opposing sides prepared for the inevitable conflict, recruiting men, raising money and securing fortresses. Geographically the north and west of England remained loyal to the King while the south and east backed Parliament. When the royal standard was raised at Nottingham on 22 August 1642, signifying the start of the English Civil War, the Parliamentarians were believed to be in control of three-quarters of the country's wealth and two-thirds of its population.

On 23 October the first battle of the Civil War was fought at Edgehill, which ended with both sides claiming victory. The King, deeply shocked at his first experience of battle carnage, fell back to Oxford, which became his headquarters. The Earl of Essex, captain-general of the Parliamentarian army, led his men back to London, giving the Royalists a chance to regroup and re-equip for the war that was to drag on spasmodically over the next four years.

But there was discord again. Henrietta detested the King's nephew Prince Rupert of the Rhine, the charismatic and brilliant military leader of the Royalists, and old quarrels were revived between

Protestants and Roman Catholics. It was now that the name of OLIVER CROMWELL became known and feared. A Puritan squire and Member of Parliament before the war, he showed great military ability and quickly rose to the rank of lieutenant-general. Realising that the weakness of both sides was that their troops were badly trained, he created his famed New Model Army. It was his 'Ironsides' who defeated Prince Rupert at Marston Moor on 2 July 1644, said to be the first decisive battle of the Civil War. It was also the first time the Scots assisted the Parliamentary forces. When Cromwell won the Battle of Naseby on 14 June the next year it in effect ended the war.

After Naseby the King roamed the countryside as a fugitive until he gave himself up to the Scots who delivered him to the Parliamentarians for £400,000. Charles was held captive in his own palace of Hampton Court where he remained in comfortable captivity until, fearing for his own safety, he escaped to the Isle of Wight, where he was loosely guarded.

Enthusiasm for the Royalist cause began to revive. A Scottish army of thirty thousand invaded England as the result of an 'Engagement' the King signed in which he agreed to restore Presbyterianism if the Scots would restore him. This was known as the Second Civil War. Cromwell, willing to maintain the monarchy but mistrustful of the King, tried unsuccessfully to compromise with Charles, who remained adamant on all points which 'touched his clear conscience'. By the time the Second Civil War was over Cromwell and his supporters were ready to use sterner measures than debate.

In January 1649 Charles was escorted into Westminster to be tried for treason by levying war 'against Parliament and the kingdom of England'. Never had he appeared so calm and dignified when, dressed in black with the Order of the Garter on his left sleeve, he seated himself in a red upholstered chair opposite the table where the president of the court sat. To the supporters of the King he was acting out his finest hour and he lost his stutter when he declared, 'It is not my case alone, it is the freedom and liberty of the people of England; and . . . I stand more for their liberties.'

On 27 January the King was condemned to death and on the morning of 30 January 1649 he awoke at ST JAMES'S PALACE soon after five o'clock, putting on a second shirt as he did not wish to shiver and give the impression he was afraid.

At Whitehall Palace Charles had to wait for nearly four hours before the order was given for him to go through the Banqueting House whose ceiling he had commissioned Rubens to paint. Here he stepped through a window that had been specially enlarged onto a scaffold draped with black. He said a few words to the group on the platform, declaring his innocence and forgiving his enemies, saying it was God's punishment for his treatment of Strafford.

Charles's hair was tucked under his nightcap and, looking up into the sky, he prayed briefly. Then he took his position at the block, saying to the executioner, 'Stay for the sign.' Soon he gave the signal and was decapitated with a single blow. His coffin, snow on its black pall, was interred in ST GEORGE'S CHAPEL at WINDSOR CASTLE.

King Charles steps on to the scaffold built against the wall of the Banqueting House in Whitehall for his execution.

A youth who witnessed the execution wrote, 'there was such a groan by the thousands then present, as I never heard before and desire I may never hear again'.

It was the end of the DIVINE RIGHT OF KINGS.

CHARLES I, COMMEMORATION OF THE MARTYRDOM OF On the morning of 30 January 1649 Charles I was taken from ST JAMES'S PALACE to Whitehall Palace where he had to wait in the Banqueting Hall for four hours until an executioner willing to behead a king was found.

A lead bust of Charles I set in the wall of the Banqueting House, Whitehall, close to the spot where he was beheaded.

Today the anniversary of the event is still commemorated by a memorial service at WINDSOR CASTLE. In London choristers march from St Martin-in-the-Fields to Trafalgar Square where the statue of King Charles is specially decorated for the occasion, while wreaths are laid at the Banqueting House – once part of the old Whitehall Palace – in Whitehall.

CHARLES II Born on 29 May 1630 the son of CHARLES I and QUEEN HENRIETTA MARIA at ST JAMES'S PALACE, Charles's blood was more mixed than any previous British king, his grandparents being French, Danish, Italian and Scottish. His formal education ended with the outbreak of the English Civil War, and with his younger brother JAMES he was present at the Battle of Edgehill in 1642 where at one point he was in danger of capture. Later he was sent to Bristol as a figurehead of the Royalists under the direction of Sir Edward Hyde's council.

Following Royalist setbacks Charles went first to the Scilly Isles, thence to Jersey, and later to join his mother in Paris which he found exceedingly dull so the high-spirited prince turned to the company of the rakish Duke of Buckingham, the son of JAMES I's favourite, who introduced him to the pleasures of debauchery. At this time Charles was described as 'well made with a swarthy complexion agreeing with his fine black eyes, a large ugly mouth, a graceful and dignified bearing and a fine figure'.

In 1648 Charles tried to help his father by setting out with a fleet of nineteen vessels, but the expedition failed and after he returned to England victory went to the Parliamentarians so he was forced to withdraw to The Hague and the court of Prince WILLIAM II OF ORANGE. While in The Hague the prince met the first of his famous mistresses, Lucy Walter, the mother of his son James, DUKE OF MONMOUTH, born in April 1649. In January 1649 Charles learned of his father's trial and desperately tried to save him. His efforts failed and, when the King was executed on 30 January, he found himself the impoverished leader of the exiled Royalists.

Proclaimed as king in Scotland, Charles crossed to Edinburgh in 1650 and was crowned at Scone on 1 January 1651. In August 1651 he led a Scots' army south to Worcester where on 3 September he met a Parliamentarian force and although the young king fought desperately the outnumbered Royalists were defeated. Charles escaped to become a hunted fugitive.

While Cromwell's troopers hunted for him – and the £1,000 (approximately £77,000 today) reward offered for 'Charles Stuart a tall black man, six foot two inches high' – he was assisted by sympathisers whose loyalty was never forgotten. With the help of the Penderel family of Boscobel his cavalier locks were shorn and he was dressed in old clothes. In this disguise he and Richard Penderel travelled through remote countryside.

Soon afterwards came the adventure commemorated by hundreds of English inns with 'Royal Oaks' painted on their signboards. Penderel took Charles to Boscobel House and afraid that the house would be searched, Charles, in company with a Captain Carless, returned to the wood at the edge of which stood a massive oak. The two fugitives hid in its branches from where they viewed a detachment of Roundheads hunting for them. At sunset the troops

Prince Charles escaping in disguise from Cromwell's soldiers eager for the £1,000 reward offered for his capture.

retired and Charles and the colonel went back to Boscobel House.

After more adventures the King sailed secretly from Brighton to join Queen Henrietta Maria at their poverty-stricken and quarrelsome court at St Germain. An agreement between Cromwell and Cardinal Mazarin forced the exile to leave France. He went to Brussels where he waited for the call that would one day invite him back to England.

On 25 May 1660, after nine years of impoverished exile, Charles landed at Dover to be welcomed by General Monk amid scenes of near hysterical enthusiasm. In the euphoria that followed the Restoration, Charles became aware of the magnitude of the problems facing him. After expenditure incurred during the Commonwealth, England was almost bankrupt; the standing army, costing £55,000 a month, was dangerously in arrears of pay, and there was an inherited naval war with Spain. Equally pressing problems included religious discord, the ownership of land which had been confiscated by the Parliamentarians and Royalist thirst for revenge – and those who had suffered in the king's cause now thronged Whitehall in the hope of compensation.

The King did all he could to restore confiscated properties though he lost some popularity among his old supporters. When the ACT OF INDEM-NITY AND OBLIVION was passed cynical Royalists declared it was indemnity for their old enemies and oblivion for them. It was from this disillusioned faction that the Whig party was formed.

Charles now took Barbara Palmer as his mistress. Her maiden name was Villiers and she was related to the Duke of Buckingham. Her husband, Roger Palmer, was created Earl of Castlemaine in the autumn of 1661 in recompense for being cuckolded. In February 1662 she bore the King a daughter named Anne, who became the Countess of Sussex, and then three sons in succession.

On 21 May 1662 Charles married Catherine of Braganza, Princess of Portugal, as he needed a legitimate heir and she had the added attraction of a splendid dowry including Bombay, gateway for the Indian trade, Tangier, which gave England a base in the Mediterranean, and, most welcome of all, a huge cash sum. In return the Portuguese wanted English support against Spain. The couple spent their honeymoon in HAMPTON COURT which, after a strict convent upbringing, must have appeared a dazzling new world to the young queen.

Catherine of Braganza, who brought Charles II a magnificent dowry including Bombay but who failed to provide a royal heir.

By the end of the year Queen Catherine was delighted by signs of pregnancy but this was to be the first of a series of false hopes, for although Charles was to have a total of twelve children by his mistresses he had no legitimate heir to the throne.

While the king continued to take supper with Lady Castlemaine an added complication was the arrival at court of fair-haired, 15-year-old Frances Stewart. He was greatly attracted to her but the girl managed to retain both her virtue and Charles's affection. Charles gave Frances immortality by choosing her as the model for Britannia on the national copper coinage.

In October of the following year Queen Catherine became dangerously ill while taking the waters at Bath. Charles remained by her bed and as the fever increased he knelt and with tears in his eyes implored her not to die. Although she began to improve she was delirious for some days and under the delusion that she had given birth to a son.

In 1664 war threatened between England and her sea rival Holland, and Charles wrote to his sister Henrietta Anne – his dear 'Minette' – and wife of the Duke of Orléans: 'You will have heard of our taking of New Amsterdam which lies just by New England. It is a place of great importance to trade. It did belong to England heretofore, but the Dutch by degrees drove our people out and built a very good town, but we have got the better of it, and it is now called New York.'

The situation reached a climax on 4 June 1665 when the English fleet sank eighteen Dutch warships off Lowestoft. There were victory bonfires in London, but it was the last celebration to be held for a long time as the Great Plague was soon to spread across the city. Then on 2 September 1666 Samuel Pepys, civil servant and diarist, informed the King at Whitehall that fire had broken out during the night in Pudding Lane and now, fanned by an east wind, was engulfing the city.

The King took control of the fire-fighting, and fire lanes were cut through the vast maze of wooden buildings. With a bag of gold coins he provided encouragement while directing operations and at times jumping down to heft water buckets. Almost before the ashes cooled he consulted Sir Christopher Wren on plans for the new London.

In June 1667 a Dutch fleet under Admiral de Ruyter sailed up the Thames and destroyed several warships including the famous flagship *Royal Charles*. It was the worst naval defeat England had

The Great Seal of Charles II, struck after his return to England in 1660.

suffered but soon a peace was concluded with Holland.

Charles had now met his most famous mistress NELL GWYNNE who had begun her theatrical career as an orange girl at the Theatre Royal in Drury Lane, London. She had a son by him named Charles Beauclerk, created Duke of St Albans, but a politically more important mistress was Louise de Keroualle, created Duchess of Portsmouth. An agent of the French court, she was first noticed by the King when she accompanied his sister Henrietta to London in 1670 to arrange the signing of the secret and later notorious Treaty of Dover in which Louis XIV of France agreed to pay Charles an annual subsidy for an alliance against Holland and a declaration that he was a Roman Catholic.

In 1672 war was resumed with Holland and Charles issued a Declaration of Indulgence to end penal laws against Catholics and Nonconformists, but delayed his conversion to Catholicism. The Declaration was highly unpopular with the King's subjects and the following year Parliament forced him to withdraw it. When peace was finally agreed with Holland it was cemented by the marriage of Charles's niece MARY to the Prince of Orange, later WILLIAM III.

In 1678 the so-called Popish Plot created a wave of anti-Catholic feeling when Titus Oates claimed to have discovered a plot in which the Pope and the King of France conspired to have Charles assassinated and his Roman Catholic brother James put on the throne.

In March 1683 Charles was returning from Newmarket where he had been watching horse races. Being ahead of schedule he missed assassination by snipers' bullets on the road at Rye House near Ware. Had the plan worked messengers were to have spurred to London to proclaim Charles's illegitimate son James, Duke of Monmouth as king. One of the conspirators revealed that some leaders of the Whig party were behind the Rye House Plot as well as Monmouth himself. Charles was deeply saddened to learn his favourite natural son with Lucy Walters was implicated in a plot to kill him yet he was reluctant to have him punished and allowed him enough time to flee to Holland.

Two years later, on 2 February 1685, Charles suffered an apoplectic fit and his physicians subjected him to severe bleeding. For the next three days the doctors continued to torture the dying monarch with their savage treatments. A Catholic priest was smuggled into the royal bedchamber to hear the king's confession and administer Extreme Unction.

On one occasion Queen Catherine was so overcome emotionally that she fainted by his bed and had to be carried away. On recovering she sent Charles a message begging his forgiveness to which he answered, 'Poor woman! She ask my pardon? I beg hers with all my heart. Take back that answer.'

In the early hours of 6 February there was a flash of the King's old humour when he apologised to those about him for taking an 'unconscionable' time to die. He then asked his brother James to look after the Duchess of Portsmouth and 'not let Nelly starve'. A little later he said that a clock in his horological collection should be wound up that day or it would stop. He said nothing more and just after noon it was announced that he had died. He was interred in WESTMINSTER ABBEY.

CHARLES, PRINCE The son of the then PRINCESS ELIZABETH and PRINCE PHILIP, Charles was born at BUCKINGHAM PALACE on 14 November 1948. Christened Charles Philip Arthur George, he became the Duke of Cornwall and Rothesay, Earl of Carrick, Lord of the Isles and Baron Renfrew. When his mother ascended the throne he became the heir presumptive and in 1958 he was created Prince of Wales. He read archaeology, anthropology and history at Cambridge University and in 1969 was invested as Prince of Wales at Caernarvon Castle. The next year he took

his seat in the House of Lords. In 1971 he learned to fly a jet aircraft in the RAF, after which he served in the Royal Navy until 1976. He also qualified as a helicopter pilot during his military training and holds the ranks of Rear Admiral in the Royal Navy, Major-General in the Army and Air Vice-Marshal in the Royal Air Force. In 1976 he established the Prince's Trust which helps disadvantaged youngsters to set themselves up in business. His concern with the environment became evident when he made a television programme *The Earth in Balance*.

In 1981 he married Lady Diana Spencer in St Paul's Cathedral. Their first son Prince William was born in 1982 and the second Prince Henry in 1984. The couple's marriage was dissolved in 1996.

On 9 April 2005 Prince Charles married Camilla Parker Bowles, the ceremony being a day later than planned due to the Prince travelling to Rome to represent the Queen at the funeral of Pope John Paul II. When the wedding was announced it caused a certain amount of controversy from legal and

The Queen placing the coronet of The Prince of Wales on Charles, Prince of Wales' head during his investiture ceremony, while an official holds the Seal of Letters Patent. (Getty Images)

doctrinal points of view. The problem for the Church of England was that Prince Charles, a future head of the Church, was a divorcé, as was Camilla Parker Bowles, and therefore the couple could not be allowed a church ceremony.

This situation was solved by them having a register office wedding at Windsor Guildhall, after which a service was held in St George's Chapel in Windsor Castle at which Rowan Williams, the Archbishop of Canterbury gave the couple a blessing.

Another question was whether it would be legally possible for the Prince to marry Camilla Parker Bowles, clauses of various Marriage Acts being cited, but it was finally settled by a statement in Parliament that there was no legal obstacle to the marriage.

One issue that became prominent in the press was the status of Camilla Parker Bowles once she was married. The possibility of a morganatic marriage was raised, but as Prime Minister Stanley Baldwin told Parliament in the 1936 CONSTITUTIONAL CRISIS, 'There is no such thing as what is called a morganatic marriage known to our law.'

Camilla's position became clear when it was officially stated that when Prince Charles succeeded to the throne she, as the wife of the King, would automatically become Queen, just as when she

The postage stamps issued by Royal Mail to commemorate the marriage of Prince Charles and Camilla Parker Bowles. (© *Royal Mail*)

married Charles she automatically became the Princess of Wales and the Duchess of Cornwall. She made it clear that she wanted to be known by the latter title and that when her husband ascended the throne she would be referred to as the Princess Consort rather than the Queen.

With these questions behind them the couple were married in what was a semi-private celebration but which still had the atmosphere of a royal occasion.
See also HIGHGROVE

CHURCHILL, ARABELLA It was said that the excitement of returning to Britain at the Restoration damaged the morals of JAMES, Duke of York which up to then had compared favourably to those of his elder brother CHARLES II. As soon as he was established at court he began a string of brief affairs, which did not cease when his secret marriage to Anne Hyde was announced publicly in September 1660.

Arabella Churchill, then aged 17, came to court as a maid of honour to Anne Hyde in 1665. The

daughter of Sir Winston Churchill – her younger brother was to become the 1st Duke of Marlborough – she came to the notice of James one day on the hunting field when her horse bolted and she was thrown to the ground. The prince galloped up and was so captivated by her that he made her his first regular mistress. She was to bear him four children, two girls and two boys who were made the Duke of Berwick and the Duke of Albermarle respectively.

She was still his mistress when Anne Hyde died in 1671. After his marriage to Catholic Mary of Modena two years later, Arabella Churchill was pensioned off to Ireland.

CITY OF LONDON, ENTRY INTO Said to date back to 1588 when ELIZABETH I attended a service of thanksgiving at old St Paul's for the defeat of the Spanish Armada, this custom has reflected the independence of the City of London. It is still practised on state occasions when the sovereign is required to enter the City. At the site of Temple Bar, marking the boundary between the City and the rest of London, the royal party is met by the Lord Mayor. As a symbol of peaceful intent the royal sword and mace are reversed, after which the Lord Mayor holds out the City's Pearl Sword with the blade pointing down. The sovereign briefly touches the hilt and returns it, thus symbolising royal predominance. The Lord Mayor then carries it before the sovereign who is now permitted to enter the City precincts.

CLARENCE HOUSE Standing in Stable Yard Road, ST JAMES'S PALACE, Clarence House was reconstructed by John Nash for William, Duke of Clarence and was completed in 1828. When the duke became WILLIAM IV he continued to live there as work on BUCKINGHAM PALACE was unfinished. The King and Queen Adelaide did try residing in St James's Palace, but found they were hampered by lack of space, having their books and personal belongings moved from state rooms whenever receptions were held there. The answer was to join St James's to Clarence House by means of a passage.

When the King died in 1837 the house was occupied by his niece, Princess Augusta, until her death three years later. It then became the home of the Duchess of Kent, the mother of QUEEN VICTORIA, for the next twenty-one years. After this the house became the official residence of

Victoria's second son Prince Alfred, Duke of Edinburgh in 1866 and he remained there until his death at the end of the century, after which the queen's third son Prince Arthur, Duke of Connaught resided there until he died in 1942. Following this the house became the headquarters of the Red Cross, and after 1947 the home of PRINCESS ELIZABETH. It was there that her daughter Princess Anne was born in 1950.

After Elizabeth ascended the throne in 1953, Clarence House became the home of Queen Elizabeth, the Queen Mother, until her death in 2003. It is now the Prince of Wales's official London residence.

CLIFFORD, ROSAMOND The mistress of HENRY II, Rosamond Clifford, known as 'Fair Rosamond', was the cause of the redoubtable QUEEN ELEANOR, turning against the king to such an extent that she supported their sons when they rebelled against him. Rosamond's legend was told by Higden, a monk at Chester, who wrote: 'She was the fayre daughter of Walter, Lord Clifford, concubine of Henry II and was poisoned by Queen Eleanor AD 1177. Henry made for her a house of wonderful working, so that no man or woman might come to her. This house was named Labyrinthus and was wrought like unto a knot in a garden called a maze. But the queen came to her by a clue of thredde and so dealt with her that she lived not long after.'

In reality Queen Eleanor was her husband's prisoner at Winchester when Rosamond Clifford died in 1176 and was buried at Godstow Nunnery near Oxford.

COMMONWEALTH, HEAD OF Her Majesty Queen ELIZABETH II is the Head of the Commonwealth made up of 53 independent countries, most of whom were previously under British rule. The Queen also remains the sovereign of Australia, Canada and New Zealand.

CONSTITUTIONAL CRISIS In 1934 Edward, Prince of Wales and the future EDWARD VIII, invited Ernest Simpson and his wife WALLIS SIMPSON to join his party at Biarritz in France. Ernest's business interests took him to the United States at that time, so Wallis went to Biarritz with her aunt Bessie Merryman as chaperon. From Biarritz the party took a cruise on the yacht *Rosaura* during which the Prince and Wallis (to quote her own

words) 'crossed the line that marks the indefinable boundary between friendship and love'.

This event was to set in motion the most remarkable drama involving a British – or any other – monarch for no other king has willingly renounced his throne for the sake of love. It is thought that at the end of the following year the prince intended to tell his father GEORGE V of his deep feelings towards Wallis, but refrained out of consideration for his failing health. Soon afterwards, on 20 January 1936, King George died at Sandringham.

In June, Edward, now Edward VIII, and Wallis, who was still married to Ernest Simpson, embarked on the steam yacht *Nahin* for a cruise along the Dalmation coast. This made headlines throughout Europe and America, but not in Britain. Thanks largely to the efforts of Lord Beaverbrook, the owner of the *Daily Express*, the British Press maintained a conspiracy of silence on what was developing into a national crisis.

After the cruise, Wallis joined Edward at BALMORAL and filed a divorce action against her husband. This was heard at the Ipswich Assizes on 27 October and reported in the British Press without comment, but it was becoming clear that the newspapers would not keep silent much longer. Edward summoned Stanley Baldwin, the Prime Minister, to BUCKINGHAM PALACE on the evening of 16 November.

Baldwin told the King that a marriage with a divorced woman, whose two husbands were still living, would not 'receive the approbation of the country'. Edward replied, 'I want you to be the first to know that I have made up my mind and nothing will alter it. I mean to abdicate to marry Mrs Simpson.'

'Sir, this is a very grave decision and I am deeply grieved,' said Baldwin and left. The King then dined with his mother Queen Mary and the Princess Royal and announced his decision, which was received with shock.

On 3 December the British Press told its readers what the rest of the world had known for weeks, and the country was thrown into a constitutional crisis.

The next day, in the House of Commons, the Prime Minister told Parliament: 'Suggestions have appeared in certain organs of the press yesterday and again today, that, if the King decided to marry, his wife need not become queen. These ideas are without foundation. There is no such thing as what is called morganatic marriage known to our law. The lady whom he marries, by the fact of her marriage to the King, necessarily becomes queen. The only way in which this result could be avoided would be by legislation dealing with a particular case. His Majesty's Government is not prepared to introduce such legislation.'

On 19 December the Dukes of York, Gloucester and Kent assembled at FORT BELVEDERE, Edward's home when he was Prince of Wales, to witness their brother sign the Instrument of Abdication. The next evening Edward had a farewell dinner with his family, including his brother who was now GEORGE VI, and then he made his famous broadcast to the nation, which his supporter Winston Churchill is said to have helped to compose.

'You all know the reasons which have impelled me to renounce the throne,' he said. 'But I want you to understand that in making up my mind I did not forget the country or the Empire which as Prince of Wales, and lately as King, I have for twenty-five years tried to serve. But you must believe me when I tell you that I have found it impossible to carry the heavy burden of responsibility and to discharge my duties as king as I would wish to do without the help and support of the woman I love.'

On 3 June 1937 Edward, now the Duke of Windsor, married Wallis at Maine-et-Loire in France.

CORONATION CEREMONY
A magnificent feast was the most likely event marking an early English king's assumption of royal power but as the concept of royal succession became established his inheritance of the throne was marked by a religious ceremony. It was ST DUNSTAN, as Archbishop of Canterbury, who introduced the concept of a coronation rite as it is known today when in May AD 973 he crowned EDGAR THE PEACEFUL at Bath Abbey. With some refinements, the present coronation service goes back to that time. The rite was advantageous to both king and Church. By going through a religious ceremony and being anointed with holy oil the king was no longer an ordinary man but a king ordained by God, a concept that led to the DIVINE RIGHT OF KINGS, while the Church increased its power as the spiritual authority necessary for the consecration of kings and queens and thus the continuation of the monarchy.

In order that the crowning of a sovereign should impress his or her subjects with its almost mystical

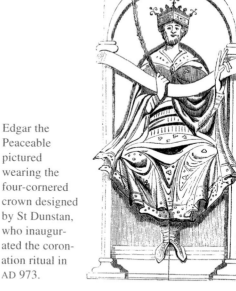

Edgar the Peaceable pictured wearing the four-cornered crown designed by St Dunstan, who inaugurated the coronation ritual in AD 973.

significance, the service became a majestic ceremony of religious ritual with rich vestments and seemingly priceless regalia, and accompanied by inspiring music. Having seen the crowning of CHARLES II at WESTMINSTER ABBEY on 23 April 1661, Samuel Pepys wrote in his diary: 'Now after all this, I can say that besides the pleasure of these glorious things, I may now shut my eyes against any other objects . . . being sure never to see the like again in this world.'

After the execution of CHARLES I the coronation regalia was disposed of during the Interregnum with only the three swords of state, representing temporal justice, spiritual justice and mercy, and the anointing spoon remaining. Following the Restoration, Charles II spent £12,000 (approximately £1,200,000 today) on regalia fashioned by the royal goldsmith Robert Vyner. Today this regalia forms part of the Crown jewels to be seen in the Jewel House in the TOWER OF LONDON.

CORONATION CHAIR
At early coronation ceremonies part of the ritual was for the new king to be seated on a stone that was recognised as having a mystical or sacred quality. In Scotland kings were crowned on the STONE OF DESTINY; in England it was the KING'S STONE which was last used for the coronation of ETHELRED II ('The

The Coronation Chair in Westminster Abbey when the Stone of Destiny rested beneath the seat. Now the Stone has been returned to Scotland.

Unready') in AD 979. After this coronations were conducted mainly at cathedrals until WILLIAM I ('The Conqueror') became the first king to be crowned at Westminster Abbey, which has been the venue for such observances ever since. When EDWARD I ascended the throne in 1272 he installed the wooden coronation chair which has been the focal point of the coronation ritual ever since. It was originally placed on a gilded step but in the sixteenth century this was replaced by four carved lions. A confusion of names of Edward I and EDWARD THE CONFESSOR resulted in the chair being known as St Edward's Chair, although the latter Edward was crowned at Winchester Cathedral.

Edward I seized the Stone of Scone in 1296 and had it placed beneath the seat of the coronation chair where it remained for seven centuries. In 1997 it was returned to Scotland where it is held at HOLYROODHOUSE PALACE though it is likely to be used at coronation ceremonies in the future.

CORONATION CLOTH So-called 'coronation cloth' was introduced to the public at the time of EDWARD VII's coronation. Produced in England in wool and worsted, it had single-thread stripes of tinsel or gold yarn running lengthwise and set an inch apart. Later yarns of red, white and blue were used in the material which then became known as

'inauguration cloth'. At the same time as coronation cloth came on to the market a related cloth known as 'queen's mourning' was produced in black with a white hairline which ladies wore as a mark of respect for the late QUEEN VICTORIA.

CORONATION MISHAPS For every sovereign the most important day in his or her reign must be the day on which they are anointed and crowned so that by the end of the great ceremony in WESTMINSTER ABBEY they emerge as a historical figure. Down the centuries the ritual has been solemn, full of symbolism and performed with fitting dignity but there have been occasions when protocol suffered from the unexpected.

William, Duke of Normandy was crowned WILLIAM I on Christmas Day 1066 in Westminster Abbey. At a certain point in the ceremony a bishop had to demand if those assembled would accept Duke William as their king. The Normans affirmed in Norman French but when the English shouted their consent in Anglo-Saxon the Norman guards outside the abbey mistook their response for cries of revolt. Their immediate reaction was to set nearby

William the Conqueror in Westminster Abbey for his coronation which became a fiasco when a riot caused the congregation to flee.

houses on fire in retaliation, and in the smoky confusion the congregation bolted. The Conqueror and the clergy were left alone to conclude the enthronement in the deserted abbey.

On 3 September 1189 RICHARD I ('Coeur de Lion'), walking beneath a silken canopy supported on the lances of the four greatest barons of the kingdom and escorted by the bishops of Bath and Durham, entered Westminster Abbey for his coronation. It was a magnificent occasion but, just as William the Conqueror's ceremony had been marred by bloodshed, so was Richard's. He had issued a proclamation banning women and Jews during the ceremony and the following banquet, it being thought by some historians that he feared an act of witchcraft and at that time Jews were believed to have the power of sorcery. Many prominent Jews had assembled in London from all over the country with gifts for the new sovereign, no doubt hopeful that the protection they had enjoyed under HENRY II would be continued. Despite the prohibition some tried to enter Westminster Abbey. Servants drove them from the building and the mob outside, inflamed by a false rumour that Richard had ordered a massacre, began a terrible slaughter. News of this reached the king at his coronation banquet in Westminster Hall and he tried to halt the massacre by sending the justiciar, Ranulph de Glanville, and other officials to restore order but they were forced back to the hall in fear of their lives.

GEORGE IV planned to have the most magnificent coronation in British history – his robes alone cost £24,000 – but when his estranged wife QUEEN CAROLINE tried to gain entrance to Westminster Abbey she was turned away by his order. It would appear that this unseemly incident did not distress the new monarch. Mrs Arbuthnot, the wife of a Member of Parliament, was present and later wrote in her journal: 'The king behaved very indecently; he was continually nodding and winking at Lady Conyngham and sighing and making eyes at her. At one time he took a diamond brooch from his breast, and looking at her, kissed it, on which she took off her glove and kissed a ring she had on!'

On 28 June 1838 VICTORIA was enthroned in Westminster Abbey where two incidents occurred which were illustrative of her character. When Lord Rolle fell as he tried to ascend the steps to the throne she stepped down to help him. Then during the ceremony the Bishop of Bath and Wells, fumbling with his prayer book, turned over two pages in error. When the sub-dean informed the young queen that as a result the service had ended too soon she demanded that it should be restarted from the point where the bishop had made his mistake. After being crowned the queen retired briefly to St Edward's Chapel and afterwards wrote in her journal: 'The Archbishop came in and ought to have delivered the Orb to me, but I had already got it and he (as usual) was so confused and puzzled and knew nothing, and – walked away. . .' The procession then re-formed and Victoria continued that it 'proceeded through the Abbey, which resounded with cheers, to the robing-room. The Archbishop had (most awkwardly) put the ring on the wrong finger, and the consequence was that I had the greatest difficulty to take it off again, which I did at last with great pain.'

GEORGE VI wrote an account of his own coronation: 'I knew I was to spend a most trying day and to go through the most important ceremony in my life. The hours of waiting before leaving for Westminster were the most nerve-racking . . . On our arrival our pages and train-bearers met us to carry our Robes to our retiring rooms. Elizabeth's procession started first but a halt was soon called, as it was discovered that one of the Presbyterian chaplains had fainted . . . I was kept waiting, it seemed for hours due to this accident, but at last all was ready for my progress into the Abbey. This went well . . . I bowed to Mama and the Family in the gallery and took my seat.' Having described the ritual to the point where he moved to the coronation chair, the king continued: 'Here various vestments were placed upon me, the white colobium sindonia, the surplice which the Dean of Westminster insisted he put on inside out had not my Groom of Robes come to the rescue . . . I had two Bishops, Durham and Bath and Wells, on either side to support me and to hold the form of Service for me to follow. When this great moment (the taking of the Coronation Oath) came neither Bishop could find the words so the Archbishop held his book down for me to read, but horror of horrors his thumb covered the words of the Oath.

'My Lord Great Chamberlain was supposed to dress me but I found his hands fumbled and shook so I had to fix the belt and sword myself. As it was he nearly put the hilt of the sword under my chin trying to attach it. The supreme moment came when the Archbishop placed St Edward's Crown on my head. I had taken every precaution as I thought to see that the Crown was put on the right way round, but the Dean and Archbishop had been juggling with it so much that I never did know whether it was right or not. The St Edward's Crown, the Crown of England, weighs 7lbs and it had to fit. Then I rose to my feet and walked to the throne in the centre of the amphitheatre. As I was turning after leaving the Coronation Chair I was brought up all standing, owing to one of the Bishops treading on my robe. I had to tell him to get off it pretty sharply as I nearly fell down.'

CORONATION OATH At the coronation of QUEEN ELIZABETH II the Archbishop of Canterbury administered the coronation oath by asking the Queen if she was willing to take the oath and upon the affirmative asked the following question:

Archbishop Will you solemnly promise and swear to govern the Peoples of the United Kingdom of Great Britain and Northern Ireland, Canada, Australia, New Zealand, the Union of South Africa, Pakistan and Ceylon, and of your Possessions and other Territories to any of them belonging or pertaining, according to their respective laws and customs?
Reply I solemnly promise so to do.
Archbishop Will you to your power cause Law and Justice, in Mercy, to be executed in all your judgements?
Reply I will.
Archbishop Will you to the utmost of your power maintain the Laws of God and the true profession of the Gospel? Will you to the utmost of your power maintain in the United Kingdom the Protestant Reformed Religion established by law? Will you maintain and preserve inviolably the Settlement of the Church of England, and the doctrine, worship, discipline, and government thereof, as by law established in England? And will you preserve unto the Bishops and Clergy of England, and to the Churches there committed to their charge, all such rights and privileges, as by law do or shall appertain to them or any of them?
Reply All this I promise to do.

The Queen then rose from her chair and, with the sword of state carried before her, went to the altar and made her solemn oath in the sight of all the people. The archbishop brought the great Bible from the altar for her to lay her right hand upon as she knelt upon the steps and declared, 'These things which I have here before promised, I will perform, and keep. So help me God.' She then kissed the Bible and signed the oath.

CORONATION OF ELIZABETH II The order of the coronation of ELIZABETH II on 2 June 1953 began with the Preparation. Having made certain that the ampulla was filled with oil for the anointing and placed with the spoon on the altar in WESTMINSTER ABBEY, the archbishops and clergy went in procession to the west door of the church to await the Queen after her royal progress from BUCKINGHAM PALACE. On her arrival an anthem was sung as she walked through the choir and, passing her throne, made her 'humble adora-

Queen Elizabeth II wearing the State Crown and carrying the State Orb in a royal carriage after her coronation ceremony, 2 June 1953. *(Getty Images)*

tion' and knelt at the faldstool in front of her chair of estate on the south side of the altar and then, after private prayers, seated herself in King Edward's Chair, also known as the CORONATION CHAIR. The Lords who carried the regalia in procession then came from their places and it was deposited upon the altar.

The Recognition followed in which the Queen stood by King Edward's Chair showing herself to the congregation while the Archbishop of Canterbury declared, 'Sirs, I here present unto you Queen Elizabeth, your undoubted Queen: Wherefore all you who are come this day to do your homage and service, are you willing to do the same?' This was signified by a universal cry of 'Save Queen Elizabeth', followed by the CORONATION OATH, after which the moderator of the General Assembly of the Church of Scotland presented a Bible to the queen with the words, 'Here is Wisdom; This is the royal Law; These are the lively Oracles of God.'

The Queen returned the Bible and the ceremony continued with the beginning of the Communion service in which the creed was said followed by the Anointing. With a rich pall held over her by four Knights of the Garter, the Dean of Westminster poured holy oil into the spoon taken from the altar and the archbishop anointed her on both hands, the breast and the head. After this followed the Presenting of the Spurs and Sword and the Oblation of the said Sword, the investing of the Armills, the Stole Royal and the Robe Royal, and the Delivery of the Orb. After the Dean of Westminster took the orb from the Queen and placed it on the altar, the Keeper of the Jewel House delivered the Queen's Ring – a sapphire with a ruby cross – to the archbishop who placed it upon the fourth finger of the queen's right hand. Then the archbishop placed the St Edward's Crown upon the head of the Queen, whereupon the princes and princesses, peers and peeresses put on their coronets and caps while the moment was marked by a salute from the TOWER OF LONDON's guns.

This was followed by the Benediction and then the Enthroning, which, in the official 'form and order' of the coronation, is described thus: 'Then shall the Queen go to her Throne, and be lifted up into it by the Archbishops and Bishops, and other Peers of the Kingdom; and being enthroned, or placed therein, all the Great Officers, those that bear the Swords and the Sceptres, and the Nobles who carried the other Regalia, shall stand round about the steps of the Throne; and the Archbishop standing before the Queen, shall say: Stand firm, and hold fast from henceforth the seat and state of royal and imperial dignity, which is this day delivered unto you, in the Name and by the Authority of Almighty God, and by the hands of us the Bishops and servants of God, though unworthy. And the Lord God Almighty, whose ministers we are, and the stewards of his mysteries, establish your Throne in righteousness, that it may stand fast for evermore. Amen.'

After the Enthroning came the Homage in which the archbishop put his hands between the Queen's and swore to be 'faithful and true'. He kissed her right hand and then the Duke of Edinburgh knelt before the Queen and said, 'I Philip, Duke of Edinburgh do become your liege man of life and limb, and of earthly worship; and faith and truth I will bear unto you, to live and die, against all manner of folks. So help me God.'

The Communion service was then continued and finally came the Recess when the Queen descended from her throne and was escorted into St Edward's Chapel where the Groom of the Robes removed the robe royal, which was replaced by a robe of purple velvet. Then, wearing her imperial crown, the Queen left the chapel and proceeded in state to the west door of the abbey from where she returned to Buckingham Palace in the state coach.

COUNCIL OF STATE During the absence or illness of the sovereign counsellors of state are appointed to act on behalf of him or her. The last Council of State was appointed in December 1929 when six counsellors were nominated because of the grave illness of GEORGE V. This council consisted of the Queen, the Prince of Wales, the Duke of York, the Archbishop of Canterbury, the Prime Minister and the Lord Chancellor.

CRANMER, THOMAS One of the principal architects of the Church of England, Archbishop Cranmer was born in 1489 in Aslocton in Nottinghamshire and when he was 14 his widowed mother sent him to Jesus College, Cambridge. In 1510 he gained a fellowship but his marriage to 'black Joan' of the Dolphin Tavern resulted in it being rescinded. After Joan died the fellowship was restored and Cranmer took holy orders in 1523 and became a divinity tutor. It was his suggestion that the universities of Christendom should be appealed to on the question of the legality of HENRY VIII's marriage to CATHERINE OF ARAGON that won him the favour of the King who appointed him as an advocate in the divorce proceedings and as a royal chaplain.

His rise continued and on 30 March 1533 he was consecrated Archbishop of Canterbury, taking the oath of allegiance to the pope which he later dismissed as having done it merely as a matter of form. In May he pronounced that the marriage between the king and Queen Catherine was null and void, and soon afterwards that Henry's marriage to Anne Boleyn was valid. In September of that year he was invited to become godfather to Queen Anne's daughter ELIZABETH.

He continued to be Henry's obedient servant in matters of his matrimony, annulling his marriage to Anne in 1536. Four years later he presided over Henry's divorce from Anne of Cleves and in 1541 was responsible for informing him of Queen Catherine Howard's alleged prenuptial liaison with a kinsman – the same charge that had brought about the death of Anne Boleyn – and endeavoured to obtain her confession of guilt.

He owed so much to Henry, but he did not always see eye to eye with him. Although he had arranged the king's divorce from Anne Boleyn, he spoke up on her behalf, as he did later on behalf of Thomas Cromwell who had encouraged the king to declare himself supreme head of the Church, but later fell from favour and was beheaded on Tower Hill in 1540. The previous year Cranmer had spoken out against the Statute of the Six Articles, known as the 'Whip with Six Strings'. Although Henry had broken with Rome, he wished to maintain the doctrines of the Roman Catholic Church and his statute endorsed transubstantiation, Communion, celibacy of the clergy, vows of chastity, private Masses and spoken confession.

Cranmer did have a personal reason for opposing the articles, as in 1532 he had married the niece of the Lutheran reformer Osiander in Nuremberg and brought her secretly to England where, under the Articles, death was the penalty for a priest who married. However, his opposition to them had no effect and he sent his wife back to Germany, recalling her after the king's death in 1547.

When Henry's sickly son, EDWARD VI, was dying in 1553, Cranmer reluctantly acquiesced to his last wishes and signed the document that switched the succession from MARY to LADY JANE GREY. As a result, on 14 September 1553 –

a few weeks after Mary had taken the throne – he was arrested and imprisoned in the TOWER OF LONDON, and on 13 November was charged with treason, to which he pleaded guilty. With the queen reintroducing Roman Catholicism, Cranmer was taken to Oxford in March 1554; he was put on trial before the papal commissioner but steadfastly refused to acknowledge his authority. Meanwhile, all statutes passed during Edward VI's reign had been annulled, the new prayer book was banned and the Mass restored. The Protestant bishops Hugh Latimer and Nicholas Ridley, at one time Cranmer's chaplain, were found guilty of heresy and on 16 October 1555 were burned at the stake in front of Balliol College. Cranmer witnessed the fiery execution from his prison.

Early in the next year Cranmer signed – under the promise that his life would be spared – several recantations of his Protestant faith, each more abject than the last. On 21 March he was taken to St Mary's Church where he realised that he was about to be executed after all. Instead of reading his last admission of guilt aloud as ordered, he retracted all he had written and when he was taken to the stake and the fire started he thrust his right hand – the hand that had written his recantations – into the flames with the words, 'This hath offended! Oh, this unworthy hand!'

Thomas Cranmer had not only supported Henry in his separation from Rome but had been ahead of the king in the advancement of Protestantism. He promoted the translation of the Bible, and as Archbishop of Canterbury oversaw the religious changes that divided the Church of England from Rome.

CROMWELL, OLIVER In the reign of CHARLES I the DIVINE RIGHT OF KINGS was still acknowledged in Britain and Europe and was the keystone of state structure. The idea that an anointed king could be judged as other men was unthinkable; he was on the throne by God's will and for good or ill he was the master of his kingdom. The man who swept this time-honoured system away in Britain was Oliver Cromwell, and though he rose to ultimate power by deposing a king, his reign as Lord Protector ended with the trappings of royalty apart from the actual wearing of a crown. Nevertheless it could be argued that the upheaval he generated began a long process that led to the emancipation of the common man.

Part of an autographed letter written by Oliver Cromwell following his victory at the Battle of Naseby on 14 June 1645.

I wish this action may begett thankfullness, and humilityo in all that are concerned in itt, Her that ventures his life for the libertyo of his cuntrie, I wish Her trust God for the libertyo of his conscience, and you for the libertyo Her fights for, In this Her rests whose is

Juno. 14.th/1645. Haurubrowe.

your most humble servant

Oliver Cromwell

The son of a country gentleman, Oliver Cromwell was born at Huntingdon in 1599. He was educated at a local grammar school and in London where he studied law. His father died in 1617, leaving him a modest estate, and three years later he married Elizabeth Bourchier, the daughter of a London merchant. Soon afterwards he enthusiastically embraced Puritanism, the extreme form of Protestantism which held that HENRY VIII had not gone far enough in removing the Roman Catholic Church from England. In those days Parliament did have a say in the country's finances, and in 1626 its members refused to sanction the money the king required for a war with Spain. In retaliation Charles used his right to dissolve Parliament, but being short of funds he was compelled to call a new one within two years and Cromwell attended as the member for Huntingdon.

Oliver Cromwell, Lord Protector of England who gradually assumed aspects of the monarchy that he had deposed.

In his opening address Charles made it clear that the royal will would be done, declaring, 'If you should not do your duties in contributing what this state needs, I must in discharge of my conscience use those other means which God has put in my hands.' No agreement was reached between Parliament and king and finally Charles sent a message to the Speaker of the House of Commons commanding him to adjourn the session. Cromwell returned to farming until 1640 when he represented Cambridge in what came to be known as the Short Parliament, so called because when it would not agree to the king's policies it was dissolved. In November of that year Charles called the fateful Long Parliament in which Cromwell campaigned for Parliament to be held annually rather than when it suited His Majesty.

It was during this session that Parliament issued the Grand Remonstrance, demanding that it should appoint ministers of state and not the king. At this point Charles decided to act against the five main members of Puritanical opposition. On 4 January 1642 Charles entered Parliament with two hundred halberdiers at his back. Secretly warned in advance, the five members he came to arrest had fled, but that armed soldiers should enter the House of Commons shocked England and Londoners made preparations for the triumphal return of the outlawed Members of Parliament.

Inevitably the English became polarised. The Royalists, or Cavaliers as they came to be called, were mostly made up of nobility, country squires and citizens of cathedral towns. Due to the style of their Puritan haircuts the Parliamentarians were nicknamed Roundheads, and their followers came from the merchant classes, freeholders and artisans.

Both sides knew that the time for negotiation was over and during the next few months the opposing sides prepared for the inevitable conflict. Cromwell raised a troop of cavalry for the Parliamentarians which he led at the Battle of Edgehill, the first action in the English Civil War.

From then on Cromwell's military genius developed. To him the Civil War was a holy war and therefore should be fought by 'honest and godly men' dedicated to the Puritan cause. He recognised that both sides lacked military discipline and he formed a body of fighting men who combined psalm-chanting with total obedience, and who became known as 'Cromwell's Ironsides'. Thanks to their victories, Cromwell rose to become commander of the Parliamentarians' New Model Army which completely defeated the king's forces at the Battle of Naseby on 14 June 1645, thus ending the Civil War.

King Charles surrendered to the Scots at Newark who sold him to the Parliamentarians for £400,000. By now there was a split between Parliament and the leaders of the New Model Army, and for some months Charles was kept in comfortable captivity while the victors failed to agree on what should happen next. It appeared that the king's fortunes might revive for many army officers had sympathy for him; after all he was still an anointed king who had worn his Crown by Divine Right. And while a prisoner he was allowed to lay his hands on scrofula sufferers to cure what was known as the 'King's Evil', as it was believed that the touch of a king would cure it. Thus, despite the fact that Charles had been defeated, an almost superstitious belief in the monarchy persisted.

With his usual inability to understand or make the best of a situation, Charles entered into a secret engagement with the Scots in which he promised to restore Presbyterianism to Scotland if they would restore him. A Scottish army of thirty thousand invaded England and were routed by Cromwell who by now had gained control of Parliament. He tried vainly to come to a compromise with Charles but he refused to surrender his royal rights and Cromwell decided to use sterner measures than debate to get his way. On 1 January 1649 Parliament declared that Charles had committed treason by levying war 'against Parliament and the kingdom of England'. Nineteen days later he was escorted into Westminster Hall to be tried before a mere fifty-three members – most had deserted Cromwell as they had no wish to sit in judgement upon a lawful king. On 27 January the trial was brought to an abrupt close with the king being condemned to death and executed three days later.

Soon a Council of State was formed, with Cromwell as its dominant member, and the period known as the Commonwealth began, the only time Britain's head of state has not been of royal blood. In March 1649 Cromwell took over command of

Moment at Marston Moor where royalists commanded by Prince Rupert were defeated so soundly he had to hide in a bean-field.

Ireland where he waged war upon rebel Roman Catholics with such a traumatic effect upon Ireland's psyche that the 'Curse of Cromwell' is still spoken of. His exultation in the bloodshed is apparent from a report he sent to Parliament after the storming of Drogheda in September 1649. Part of the document reads:

> that night they [Cromwell's troops] put to the sword about 200 men; divers of the Officers and soldiers being fled over the Bridge into the other part of Town, where about 100 of them possessed St. Peter's Church steeple, some the west Gate, and others a strong Round tower next to the gate called St. Sunday's. These being summoned to yield to mercy, refused. Whereupon I ordered the steeple of St. Peter's Church to be fired and one of them was heard to say in the midst of the flames: God damn me, God confound me: I burn, I burn. The next day, the other two towers were summoned in one of which were about six or seven score. . . . When they submitted, their officers were knocked on the head; and every tenth man of the soldiers killed; and the rest shipped to the Barbados [as slaves]. I am persuaded that this is a righteous judgement of God upon these barbarous wretches.

Afterwards, death sentences were passed on all who had assisted in the rebellion; those who had resisted Parliament forfeited two-thirds of their land and those who had not shown 'constant good affection' one-third.

With Scotland and Ireland subdued Cromwell wished to achieve a constitutional settlement but could make no progress with Parliament. In an act similar to that which had fired his antagonism to the late king, he marched to the House of Commons with a detachment of musketeers. In the chamber he told the members that their time had come. When one member had the courage to remind Cromwell that he was a servant of Parliament, he cried, 'Come, come, I will put an end to your prating. Call them in.' At these words the soldiers appeared and Cromwell dismissed the shocked members. The dramatic scene closed with his famous remark as pointing to the Speaker's mace – the symbol of Parliament's authority – he said, 'Take away that bauble.'

A reformed House of Parliament was inaugurated but this fared no better and ended by presenting Cromwell with a 'humble petition and advice' requesting that he should become king. Aware that republican elements in the army would regard acceptance of this as blasphemy, Cromwell refused the royal title, but in a ceremony similar to a coronation was installed as Lord Protector with the power to name his successor.

Many of the Lord Protector's subjects resented the Puritanical laws imposed upon them. Observance of the Sabbath became so strict that even travel was declared illegal, adultery was punishable by death and maypole dancing banned. What was resented most was Cromwell holding power through the army, and it was from this time that the British traditional aversion to the use of the military in civil matters began.

Before he died on 3 September 1658 Cromwell named his son Richard as his successor but Richard had scarcely taken over as Lord Protector when the republic collapsed and he abdicated. Charles II, the son of the late king, was invited back to England, but the absolute power of the monarchy was diminished for ever.

Richard Cromwell inherited his father's title and position but abdicated when Charles II was invited back to England.

CROWN JEWELS Apart from the regalia used in the coronation ceremony, there are a number of crowns which are kept at the Jewel House in the TOWER OF LONDON. Foremost of these is St Edward's Crown. The original crown worn by EDWARD THE CONFESSOR, who was later canonised, and possibly by ALFRED THE GREAT was destroyed in 1649 by order of the Parliamentary commissioners. At the Restoration CHARLES II's goldsmith Sir Robert Vyner made a new St Edward's Crown. Apart from three occasions this crown has been the one placed upon the sovereign's head in coronation ceremonies since then. When GEORGE IV was crowned in 1821 he had a crown made for the occasion. This was subsequently used in the coronations of WILLIAM IV and EDWARD VII. The traditional use of St Edward's Crown was revived by GEORGE V. St Edward's Crown, which is made of solid gold, weighs over 6lb and is decorated with over four hundred precious and semi-precious stones.

The Imperial State Crown was made for QUEEN VICTORIA in 1838 and is famous for the magnificence of its jewels. The most outstanding of these is the great balas-ruby which is set in the middle of the cross patée – a square of gold with a diagonal cross cut in it – on the front of the crown. This jewel is known as the BLACK PRINCE's ruby, which according to tradition was presented to him by the King of Castile, Pedro the Cruel, after he had won the Battle of Najera in 1367. At the BATTLE OF AGINCOURT in 1415 HENRY V wore a coronet over his helmet in which the ruby was set. During the Interregnum it was sold for £15 (approximately £1,400 today) but came back into royal possession at the Restoration and was set in Charles II's State Crown. Later it was to be seen in the crown worn by MARY II at the joint coronation with her husband WILLIAM OF ORANGE who wore the State Crown that had been made for King Charles. This crown was later used at the coronation of GEORGE II by which time the Black Prince's ruby had been reset in it. After the coronation of GEORGE III the crown was dismantled and the ruby was set in the present Imperial State Crown. Set below it is a square diamond of 317.4 carats, known as the Second Star of Africa, having been cut from the famed Cullinan diamond. Apart from these historic gems, the crown incorporates 4 rubies, 11 emeralds, 17 sapphires, 277 pearls and over 3,000 diamonds.

Other crowns numbered among the crown jewels include a small diamond crown which Queen Victoria wore in place of the Imperial State Crown, which she found uncomfortably heavy. Another small crown is known as Mary of Modena's Crown, Mary being the consort of JAMES II and thus it is also known as the Queen Consort's Crown and was used by several queens up to the reign of WILLIAM IV but has not been used since then.

Also on display in the Jewel House is the crown made for Queen Mary when, as George V's consort, she was crowned in 1911. In 1937 Queen Elizabeth, known later as the Queen Mother, had a crown made for her crowning as GEORGE VI's queen consort in which is set the fabled Koh-i-noor diamond. The story of this diamond, whose name means 'Mountain of Light', goes back to Sultan Baber who founded the Mogul empire in India, and for a long time it was in the possession of his descendants, one of whom was Shah Jehan who built the Taj Mahal. Finally it came into the ownership of the Sikh ruler Ranjit Singh and when his empire foundered after his death the Punjab was taken over by the British and the diamond was removed from the treasury to become a gift to Queen Victoria.

Another crown with an Indian connotation is the Imperial Crown of India which George V wore when he became Emperor of India in 1911 at the Delhi Durbar. As there is no longer an empire, the crown, with its six thousand Indian diamonds, is of historical value only. The Jewel House also displays two Prince of Wales's crowns. The oldest was made for Frederick, the son of George II, when he was proclaimed Prince of Wales in 1729, and the other was made for Prince George, later George V, to wear at the coronation of his father Edward VII. A third Prince of Wales's crown, specially made for Prince Charles, is kept at Caernarvon where his Investiture was held in 1969.
See also CORONATION CEREMONY

CULLODEN, BATTLE OF The last battle to take place in Great Britain was fought at Drummossie Moor, known as Culloden today, on 16 April 1746. On that day the Jacobite dream of re-establishing the House of Stuart ended in disaster for the rebel army led by Prince Charles Edward ('Bonnie Prince Charlie'). The rebellion against the new House of Hanover began promisingly with Edinburgh surrendering to the Jacobites in September 1745, followed by the defeat of a royal army. Plans were made for GEORGE II and his court to retire to Hanover as the rebels advanced south to Derby. Here, under the threat of a royal army, the prince was persuaded by his bickering commanders to withdraw to Scotland where at Inverness he waited to confront the advancing force under command of

WILLIAM AUGUSTUS, 1st DUKE OF CUMBER-LAND, the second surviving son of the king.

John O'Sullivan, the prince's quartermaster, who was more successful as a flatterer than a strategist, chose the site for the battle which, tragically for the Jacobites, was well suited for Cumberland's disciplined troops supported by cannon. The battle began with the royal gunners sending shot through the lines of Highlanders who fell like skittles while the prince sat upon his horse unable to decide on what order to give. Finally the desperate Jacobites could wait no longer and broke ranks to make a wild Highland charge through volleys of musket fire and grape shot. Despite this a number of rebels managed to reach the royal line where they fought with such fury that over three hundred of Cumberland's troops were cut down. But this was at a terrible cost, as when the fighting ended almost two thousand Jacobites lay dead upon the moor. When he saw the day was lost the prince was the first to gallop from the field. Dragoons hunted the remnants of the rebel army but it was what happened after the victory that the name of the battle became synonymous with anguish, which has lingered down the generations.

The chevalier Johnstone wrote in his memoirs of the revolution: 'The Duke of Cumberland had the cruelty to allow our wounded to remain amongst the dead on the field of battle, stript of their clothes, from Wednesday, the day of our unfortunate engagement, till three o'clock on Friday, when he sent detachments to kill all those who were still in life; and a great many, who had resisted the effects of the continual rains which fell all that time, were then dispatched.'

CUMBERLAND, WILLIAM AUGUSTUS, 1st DUKE OF Born on 15 April 1721, William Augustus was the second son of GEORGE II and Queen Caroline. Created the Duke of Cumberland in 1726 and a Knight of the Garter four years later, he chose a military career and at the start of the War of the Austrian Succession in 1743 was wounded at the Battle of Dettingen. Two years later he was defeated without loss of honour by Marshal Saxe at Fontenoy after which he was recalled to England to suppress the second Jacobite rebellion. This he did at Culloden in April 1746. The cruelties inflicted upon the wounded followers of Bonnie Prince Charlie earned him the epithet of 'The Butcher'.

For his service to the Crown in crushing the rebellion he was granted an annual income of £25,000. In 1747 he was again defeated by Marshal Saxe at Laffeld and after the outbreak of the Seven Years' War he capitulated at Kloster-Zeven. He left the army, but remained a powerful political influence into the early part of GEORGE III's reign.

CUNOBELINUS In AD 1 the Catuvellauni tribe, situated in the area now known as Hertfordshire, conquered and absorbed the Trinovantes of Kent and Essex. Nine years later Cunobelinus, the King of Catuvellauni on whom Shakespeare based Cymbeline, built his capital where Colchester stands today. He named it Camulodunum, meaning the 'stronghold of Camulos' the Celtic god of war. From here he ruled his kingdom which took in Essex, part of Kent, the lower Thames region and the Chilterns. He encouraged Roman merchants to settle in his kingdom and in return for wine, glass, jewellery and other Mediterranean products, he traded slaves, minerals, cattle and hunting dogs which were in great demand with the Romans because of their exceptional intelligence. Roman-style coins – several of which are extant – were minted with his profile on one side. Suetonius, the Roman historian, gave him the title of Rex Brittonum, King of the Britons. He died *c.* AD 43.

Jacobite monument at Culloden where the Duke of Cumberland, son of George II, defeated Bonnie Prince Charlie.

D

D'ALENÇON, DUC England and the Protestant world was stunned by the massacre of many thousands of Huguenots in France on the morning of St Bartholomew's Day, 24 August 1572. ELIZABETH I was reluctant to grant the French ambassador an audience and when he was finally admitted to the royal presence he found the entire court in mourning. The nobles turned from him in silence, but this did not prevent him passing a letter to the Queen from Francis, Duc d'Alençon, son of Catherine de' Medici, who had organised the massacre, nor did it prevent Elizabeth reading it on the spot.

The reason was that Elizabeth had embarked upon a bizarre love affair. The unlikely object of her affections was the Duc d'Alençon, who was twenty-three years younger than the Queen and has been described as a 'hideous dwarf', smallpox having left his face scarred and his body stunted. His blotched skin coupled with his misshapen body gave him a frog-like appearance and Elizabeth nicknamed him her '*petit grenouille*'. He accepted the appellation cheerfully as his saving grace was a rough heartiness to which Elizabeth responded.

When it seemed the two were about to contract a marriage there was universal panic in England. A certain John Stubbs published a pamphlet entitled *Discovery of a Gaping Gulf wherein England is likely to be swallowed by another French Marriage*. Elizabeth was so enraged that she ordered that Stubbs should have his hand cut off. Yet he had no quarrel with the Queen, and when the executioner severed the offending right hand Stubbs removed his hat with his left, waved it above his head and shouted, 'God save the Queen!' before collapsing unconscious.

In November 1582, d'Alençon and Elizabeth exchanged rings in front of the Spanish ambassador, Elizabeth telling him, 'You may write this to the king, the Duc d'Alençon shall be my husband.' That night Elizabeth was persuaded by her ladies-in-waiting (who had been coached by Leicester and Hatton) not to run the risk of suffering as her sister MARY had done at the hands of a foreign consort. In the morning she told the duke about her conflict between love and duty, and that she was 'determined to sacrifice her own happiness for the welfare of her people'. In his chamber, d'Alençon hurled his ring to the floor, declaring 'the women of England are as changeable and capricious as their own climate'.

DARNLEY, LORD HENRY STEWART The son of the Earl of Lennox by his marriage with a granddaughter of HENRY VII of England, Henry Stewart Lord Darnley was among the closest heirs to the throne of England. It has been said that MARY, QUEEN OF SCOTS' infatuation with him began at first sight. He was handsome and his courtly grace, something that Mary had missed since leaving France, temporarily won her heart. Ignoring opposition from the Scottish Protestant nobles, Mary married Darnley on the morning of 29 July 1565 and he was proclaimed King. Mary, however, was reluctant to grant him the crown matrimonial, whereby if she died without issue the throne of Scotland would be inherited by his heirs.

His attitude towards her changed dramatically and he no longer bothered to conceal his true nature behind his mask of charm. He was frequently drunk, spoke lewdly of his royal wife to his tavern friends and was grossly unfaithful. Having achieved the bed of the highest lady in the land, some quirk in his character made him seek the lowest whores in Edinburgh. It was his involvement in the murder of DAVID RIZZIO, Mary's secretary, in front of her that ended any lingering affection Mary felt for him.

At the beginning of 1567 Darnley was taken ill with either smallpox or syphilis, and his once handsome face became so ravaged he had to wear a gauze mask. On 31 January it was arranged that he would stay in Edinburgh at a house standing in a square known as Kirk o' Field, within walking distance of HOLYROODHOUSE PALACE. On the night of 9 February Mary had a meal with him before going back to the palace to attend a masque.

That night Darnley's lodging was destroyed by a gunpowder blast and his body and that of his valet were found in the garden. Suspicion fell on the Earl of Bothwell. When the Queen married him three months later she was accused of complicity in Darnley's murder and her downfall began.

DAVID II OF SCOTLAND When ROBERT I died in 1329 his only son and heir David was 5 years old. He had been born at Dunfermline Palace on 5 March 1324, his mother Elizabeth de Burgh being his father's second wife. In 1325 he was created Earl of Carrick, after which it became the custom for the eldest sons of Scotland's sovereigns to be given that title. Following the death of his father a parliament held at Cambuskenneth endorsed the right of the little boy to become King David II, and agreed that in the event of his death the succession would go to Robert Stewart, the son of ROBERT THE BRUCE's daughter Marjorie.

Before the crown was put on the boy's head he was married to Joan, the 7-year-old daughter of the ill-fated EDWARD II of England and Queen Isabella. David was enthroned on 24 November 1331 at Scone Abbey, and at the same ceremony Joan was crowned Queen Consort, being the first Scottish queen to receive this honour. As the new king was still a child Thomas Randolph, Earl of Moray, was appointed Regent of Scotland.

Moray was not destined to enjoy this position for long. In 1332 EDWARD III encouraged a number of dissatisfied Scottish nobles to revolt. The reason for their discontent was that, having unsuccessfully backed the English against David's father, their estates had been confiscated. Now their aim was to replace the child king with Edward Balliol, the son of John Balliol, and to this end they landed at Kinghorn in Fife. Earl Randolph led a force against them but died before reaching the enemy and the Earl of Mar took his place as regent only to be slain soon afterwards at the Battle of Dupplin Moor on 11 August near Perth.

The rebels followed their victory by crowning Edward Balliol on 24 September at Scone. Realising the need to be on good terms with England, the newly crowned king immediately offered Berwick to Edward III as a gesture of friendship, but by the end of the year he was forced to flee south across the border 'in his shirt and one

The carved figure of Lord Henry Darnley, the ill-fated husband of Mary, Queen of Scots, beside the tomb of his mother the Countess of Lennox.

boot' by angry Scots led by Archibald Douglas and Andrew Moray. This provoked King Edward to intervene and in the spring of 1333 he personally laid siege to Berwick. Archibald Douglas went to the rescue of the town with a large army which found itself facing the English at Halidon Hill on 19 July. As the Scots advanced up the hill the arrows of Edward's archers took a terrible toll which included Douglas.

After this victory a large number of Scots and nobles changed sides with the result that the Scottish Lowlands came under English control. At this dangerous time young King David and Queen Joan were removed to the safety of France, and King Robert Bruce's grandson Robert Stewart became regent. There followed a period of sporadic warfare in which Robert campaigned against the English. In 1339 he took Perth with the help of a French force and by the following year English garrisons north of the Forth had been eliminated. This meant that David was able to return to Scotland as king.

Following the devastating defeat of the French at Crécy in 1346 David agreed to the King of France's plea for a diversion to reduce English military pressure on him and invaded England. He reached Durham and on 17 October 1346 he faced a local army under the command of the Archbishop of York at Neville's Cross. The battle was a disaster for the Scots. David was captured and taken to London. For the next eleven years he remained a contented prisoner, preferring life at King Edward's court to the stress of ruling a disorderly kingdom where Robert Stewart was once more the regent.

In 1355 the French sought another diversion by the Scots and this time it was more successful, Berwick being recaptured and an English army defeated at Nesbit Muir. In retaliation Edward III invaded the Lowlands, but the campaign was a failure and he made a truce with Scotland. King David, rather reluctantly, was returned to his uneasy throne for a ransom of 100,000 marks.

In 1362 Queen Joan died, having been unable to provide an heir, and the next year the King proposed to the Scottish Parliament that the succession should go to Edward III's son Lionel, a suggestion that outraged the Scots. In the same year David married a widow, Margaret Logie, the daughter of Sir Malcolm Drummond, but his wish for an heir was unfulfilled and he divorced her in 1370. Still in hope of an heir, David was about to take a third wife, Anne Dunbar, when he died on 22 February 1371 at Edinburgh Castle and was interred in Holyrood Abbey. The throne went to his nephew Robert Steward who, as ROBERT II, was the first of the Stewart kings of Scotland.

DEE, DR JOHN *See* ELIZABETH'S MERLIN

DEFENDER OF THE FAITH The year 1521 saw the publication of the then Roman Catholic HENRY VIII's treatise attacking Martin Luther's reforming doctrines entitled *Assertio Septem Sacramentorum*. It had been written with CARDINAL WOLSEY's encouragement and found such favour with Pope Leo X that he bestowed the title of 'Defender of the Faith' on the English king. The title was withdrawn after Henry's break with Rome, but was reaffirmed by Parliament in 1544 as part of the official designation of the British crown. 'Fid.Def.' or 'F.D.' (standing for *Fidei Defensor*) still appears on British coins.

DELICATE INVESTIGATION, THE *See* CAROLINE OF BRUNSWICK-WOLFENBÜTTEL

DETTINGEN, BATTLE OF The last British king to take part in a battle was GEORGE II who distinguished himself at Dettingen on 27 June 1743. The battle, fought between the French and the British armies, was part of the War of the Austrian Succession, Britain having entered into the conflict in support of Maria Theresa. In endeavouring to separate a superior French army from their Bavarian allies, the British forces became trapped near the village of Dettingen on the Main. The situation became desperate, then King George, sword in hand, led a counter-attack, which not only saved his army but defeated the French army. The French retreated to Alsace and peace negotiations were begun. In honour of the King's victory, HANDEL composed the Dettingen *Te Deum*.

DEVEREUX, ROBERT, EARL OF ESSEX In 1588, when ELIZABETH I was 55 years old, her final favourite appeared on the scene. Thirty-three years her junior, he was Robert Devereux, the second Earl of Essex and the stepson of ROBERT DUDLEY, Earl of Leicester, who had been the Queen's earliest paramour. As with Elizabeth's previous favourites, the rise of Robert Devereux was fast. In 1593 he became a Privy Councillor, and Foreign Secretary the following year. In 1596 Essex was put in charge of an expedition to capture Cadiz and on 20 June the city was taken by surprise. It was the last great naval success of Elizabeth's reign and it established Essex as the most powerful man at court, where he often spent the evening with Elizabeth 'playing at cards or other games until the birds were singing the morning'.

On 4 August 1598 Cecil, the architect of Elizabeth's greatness, died and his son Robert became the new Secretary of State. Essex had hoped for the post himself, but had fallen out with the Queen. The quarrel began over who was to become Lord Deputy of Ireland, and at its height the Queen struck his ear, bidding him 'Go and be hanged!' Before he could control himself Essex laid his hand on his sword hilt. It was the most fatal moment of his life, and soon it was he who was on his way to tackle the Irish problem.

In September 1599, Essex made a truce with Tyrone, the rebels' leader, to the indignation of Elizabeth who had warned him against concluding any agreement with the Irish. In desperation he left Dublin against orders and on 28 September he burst into the royal bedchamber at NONSUCH PALACE to find the Queen in her nightclothes. At first she was pleased to see her impetuous favourite, but by the afternoon of the next day she had a change of heart, some saying it was because he had seen her without her wig.

The Privy Council charged him with disobeying the Queen and deserting his command. He answered these accusations with such logic that many were in favour of releasing him, but the angry Queen ordered that he should remain a prisoner in his house. Her temper was not improved when news came that Tyrone had broken the truce.

Essex now believed that Robert Cecil and his faction were in league to arrange the English succession for the Spanish Infanta and, declaring he must save the country from its recent enemy, he plotted to take possession of the court and force the Queen to renounce Cecil. He recruited more than one hundred followers – some of them wild young men from the Mermaid Tavern – and arranged that Shakespeare's *Richard II* (whose theme was the deposing of a monarch) should be staged at the Globe Theatre.

When news of this reached the Queen, Essex was summoned by the Council, but instead he galloped through Cheapside at the head of his men-at-arms crying, 'For the Queen! The crown of England is sold to a Spaniard! A plot is laid for my life!'

The citizens were bewildered rather than inspired by this performance and all Essex could do was surrender. When found guilty of treason he said, 'I would not that any man should give the Queen to understand that I condemn her mercy, which notwithstanding I believe I shall not fawningly beg.'

There was no mercy. On 25 February 1601 the fallen favourite was beheaded.

DIAMOND JUBILEE In 1897 the length of QUEEN VICTORIA's reign, stretching from 1837 to 1901, exceeded that of GEORGE III which had hitherto been the longest of any British sovereign. Her record reign was marked by the Diamond Jubilee but due to the infirmities of age Victoria

remained in an open carriage outside St Paul's Cathedral while the service of thanksgiving, the highlight of the jubilee, was celebrated inside.

DIVINE RIGHT OF KINGS The divine right of kings was most aptly expounded by Louis XIV of France with the words 'l'état, c'est moi'. Such absolutism was reinforced by the fact that kings were crowned and anointed by the Church. In Britain the belief that kings derived their authority from God and as such should be exalted was set out by JAMES I (James VI of Scotland) in his *Trew Law of Free Monarchies* (1598) and *Basilikon doron* (1599). They were written as an answer to the Calvinistic theory of government advocated by George Buchanan in his *De Jure Regni*. When Buchanan had been a tutor to James his insistence that kings should be elected and as servants of their subjects should be responsible to them only reinforced the young king's opposition to such a concept. After he ascended the throne of England in 1603 his new subjects were alarmed by his assertion that kings, being gods in their own right, were above the law. CHARLES I followed his father's credo but the doctrine of divine right was discredited with his execution, although it was re-introduced in the later Stuart period. The concept of royal absolutism finally ended in Britain with the GLORIOUS REVOLUTION of 1688–9 and the advent of WILLIAM OF ORANGE.

DOMESDAY BOOK In 1085 WILLIAM I commissioned the great survey of his kingdom, which he named 'The Description of England'. It became known as the Domesday Book, from 'doomsday' when there is no appeal against one's earthly record. It was essentially a register of those who had held land and manors during the reign of EDWARD THE CONFESSOR. The information was gathered by a number of panels of commissions, each covering a separate group of counties. Their findings were then compiled into the book by the King's clerks. As a historical source the Domesday Book has been invaluable. Computer-based study on the register continues to produce new data on the medieval age.

A typical monument erected to mark Queen Victoria's Diamond Jubilee which, after her semi-seclusion, generated universal rejoicing.

DUDLEY, ROBERT, EARL OF LEICESTER
After attaining the throne ELIZABETH I made no
attempt to conceal her affection for her handsome
MASTER OF HORSE, Robert Dudley, Earl of
Leicester, the son of the Duke of Northumberland
who had been executed for his support of LADY
JANE GREY in the previous reign. He was rarely
absent from the Queen's side despite the fact that he
was married. In September 1560 Dudley's wife
Amy Robsart died alone and under mysterious
circumstances at her home, Cumnor Place, after
sending all her servants to Abingdon Fair. An
extraordinary aspect of the mystery was that prior to
September ambassadors reported to their royal
masters that the Queen and Dudley would marry,
yet all knew it was impossible while Amy lived.
Even the normally circumspect Secretary of State,
Cecil, remarked that Dudley was 'infamed' by his
wife's death, while on the Continent there was little
doubt about his – and even the Queen's – guilt in
the matter, especially when rumours spread that the
marriage would take place.

From pulpits throughout England sermons against
the marriage were daringly delivered, and English
ambassadors abroad informed the Council it must
not take place, because the world regarded Dudley
as his wife's murderer. Elizabeth's dilemma was
that if she married Dudley it would be construed as
condoning his guilt; if she did not it would be said
she doubted his innocence. Her solution was not to
marry him but to continue to treat him as her
honoured favourite.

Although Elizabeth decided that for political
expediency he should become the husband of
MARY, QUEEN OF SCOTS, he refused, and
parried the Queen's anger by flattering her with the
explanation that he found her more attractive than
Mary and could not leave her side. Elizabeth was
appeased, and created him Earl of Leicester in
1564.

In 1573 Dudley married the Dowager Lady
Sheffield, a union that was kept secret from the
Queen. Five years later he bigamously married the
widow of Walter Devereux, Earl of Essex, without
royal permission, which greatly angered Elizabeth,
though as before her displeasure soon abated. In
1588 he was appointed as commander of the forces
assembled at Tilbury when England was threatened
by the Spanish ARMADA. In September of that
year he died unexpectedly. Rumours spread that he
was the victim of poison that had been intended for

his wife, but there was no evidence – such rumours
not infrequently followed the demise of prominent
members of the court.

DUDLEY WARD, FREDA Edward, Prince of
Wales and the future EDWARD VIII, met Freda
Dudley Ward towards the end of the First World
War. They were both sheltering in the cellar of a
Mayfair house during an air raid and after the 'all
clear' they went dancing until the small hours.
When Edward returned to civilian life she became
his mistress.

Freda was the wife of William Dudley Ward, the
Vice-Chamberlain of the Royal Household. She was
to be Edward's great support during the next sixteen
years. There was a curious coincidence regarding
the meeting of the couple. Mrs Kerr-Smiley, at
whose house they met, was the sister of Ernest
Simpson, who was destined to marry an attractive
American divorcee named Wallis Spencer.

When Edward told his father, GEORGE V, that
Freda was the only woman he really loved, it only
added fuel to the King's growing disapproval of his
heir. He associated the fashions and attitudes of his
own youth with what was correct, while he viewed
the post-war world and its dress styles with distrust.
Thus he detested his son's casual way of dressing as
much as his circle of friends and their 'modern'
ways.

On one occasion the King was reported to have
shouted at the prince, 'You dress like a cad. You act
like a cad. You are a cad!' It was Freda who helped
Edward through his fits of depression, caused by his
father's attitude towards him.

In 1930 the prince acquired FORT BELVEDERE
near Virginia Water, and Freda enthusiastically
helped him with its redecoration and the restoration
of its grounds. It was to 'The Fort' that the prince
invited Ernest Simpson and his wife Wallis to be his
guests on the weekend of 30 January 1932. This
event was the prelude to what become known as the
CONSTITUTIONAL CRISIS.

The mutual attraction that developed between
Wallis and the prince was reflected by the dismissal
of Freda in 1934. In May of that year her eldest
daughter had to undergo a major operation. For
several weeks she was seriously ill, during which
time Freda stayed by her side night and day in the
nursing home. When the girl began to recover Freda
realised that for the first time in fifteen years the
prince had not been in touch with her when they

were apart. Puzzled, she telephoned York House only to be told by an embarrassed switchboard operator that she had orders not to put her through to the prince. She was never in contact with him again.

DUKE The highest title in the British peerage, the word 'duke' owes its origin to the Latin *dux*. It was bestowed only on men of royal blood, usually the sons of kings, until 1448 when HENRY IV rewarded William de la Pole for his military achievements in France by pronouncing him Duke of Suffolk. Principal Whig supporters of the GLORIOUS REVOLUTION received dukedoms but after GEORGE II ascended the throne in 1727 he reintroduced the rule that only allowed members of the royal family to be granted the title.

DUNFERMLINE, THE ABBEY OF In the eleventh century QUEEN MARGARET, later St Margaret, endowed a Benedictine abbey at Dunfermline which was to become Scotland's pantheon after the nave of the present church was built on its foundations by her son David I, known as 'The Saint'. Since then twenty-two members of Scotland's royalty have been interred within its precincts yet the only one whose resting place is marked today by a memorial is ROBERT I ('The Bruce'). St Margaret, the daughter of Edward the Atheling of England and the wife of Malcolm III, was buried in the abbey in 1093, though later her

remains were translated to the Escorial in Madrid. However, her shrine remains outside the eastern wall of the church and since medieval times it has been an object of pilgrimage.

Dunfermline's days as an abbey ended with the Reformation, but part of the building continued as a parish church which is known today as the 'Old Church' and leads into the latter day church whose carved pulpit is one of the finest in Scotland.

In 1329 Robert I was interred in the abbey but over the centuries his grave site was forgotten and it was not until 1818 that it was rediscovered. Then, when preparing the ground for the new abbey church, workmen happened upon a vault containing an oaken coffin sheathed in lead in which lay a skeleton in a cloth-of-gold shroud. On examination it was found that the breast bone had been cut in order to allow the heart to be removed, and it was remembered that King Robert had ordered that this should be done so that the embalmed relic could be carried to the Holy Land. The following year, when there was a great revival of Scottish nationalism, the royal remains were placed in a grave beneath the pulpit and covered by a brass memorial plate engraved with a representation of Scotland's greatest king.

Apart from royal offspring and consorts, Scottish sovereigns who have been interred in the abbey include Duncan II, King Edgar, Malcolm III, Alexander I, David I, Malcolm IV, Alexander III, and the aforementioned Robert I.

Dunfermline Abbey, Scotland's Pantheon, in which many members of Scottish royalty were interred, including Robert the Bruce. *(Photograph by Mark Ronson)*

E

EARL Originally the title of earl was the Old English word for a Danish sub-king, but after the Norman Conquest it became the equivalent of the Continental count. In the peerage today it ranks between a viscount and a marquess, the latter being second only to a duke. The premier earl is Arundel, now united with the dukedom of Norfolk. An earl's wife is a countess.

EARLY ENGLISH KINGDOMS

BERNICIA By the seventh century the Kingdom of Bernicia stretched between Tees and the Forth, having originally been several Anglo-Saxon settlements situated on the Tyne and Wear rivers. The first known king of Bernicia was Ida, who reigned *c.* 547–59. In the seventh century Bernicia merged with Deira to form Northumbria, but when Northumbria was conquered by the Vikings' Great Army in the ninth century, part of the old Bernicia became a province ruled by what were known as the ealdormen of Bamburgh.

DEIRA Between the Tees and the Humber the Anglo-Saxon kingdom of Deira became fully established in the sixth century and lasted until Ethelfrith merged it with Bernicia to form the kingdom of Northumbria.

DUMNONIA Following the withdrawl of the Romans from Britain, the area we know as Cornwall became part of the kingdom of Dumonia. Its geographical position made it relatively easy to defend and it lasted until AD 814 when it was conquered by KING EGBERT of Wessex.

EAST ANGLIA Settled by Anglo-Saxons towards the end of the fifth century, the kingdom covered the counties named Suffolk and Norfolk today. Its best-known king was Redwald who died *c.* 627 and who is thought to have been given a ship-burial at Sutton Hoo. In the ninth century Danish incursions overpowered the kingdom. The last East Anglian king EDMUND was martyred in AD 870, after which the territory was ruled by Scandinavian kings until EDWARD THE ELDER and ATHELSTAN reclaimed it to become part of the kingdom of England.

ESSEX The kingdom of the East Saxons, Essex was formed by the arrival of Anglo-Saxon settlers in the seventh century. Although it had its own kings until the ninth century, Essex remained a minor kingdom, its influence being reduced by the rise of the West Saxons following their successes against the Mercians in the early part of the ninth century. When KING ALFRED set the boundary of the Danelaw, Essex was included within it until the next century when it became part of the English kingdom.

KENT According to legend, the Jute Hengist was the first King of Kent towards the end of the fifth century. The *Anglo-Saxon Chronicle* relates that the Romano-British ruler Vortigern employed Hengist and his brother Horsa to act as mercenaries against the invading Picts. They were so successful that they were granted the Isle of Thanet, but eager for more land they revolted against Vortigern. Though they were defeated at Aylesford, where Horsa was slain, Hengist seized Kent and became king. Kent's most powerful period was during the reign of King Ethelbert, who took over London and established his rule over the East Saxons. After he was converted to Christianity he founded the see of Canterbury, but subsequent kings were unable to prevent the kingdom being dominated by Mercia and then Wessex.

MERCIA Based on Anglo-Saxon settlements in the north Midlands, Mercia became equal to Northumbria and Wessex when the formidable pagan PENDA became King in AD 633. In that year, and in alliance with Cadwallon of Wales, he defeated Edwin – later St Edwin – of Northumbria. Nine years later he defeated Northumbria again and killed King Oswald, but in AD 655 the Northumbrians had their revenge when he was slain at the Battle of Winwaed. Mercia became the dominant power in the 8th and early 9th centuries and demanded tribute from other Anglo-Saxon kingdoms. Apart from military success, Mercia produced the first coinage of silver pennies, undertook ambitious public works, including OFFA's DYKE, and achieved a status that allowed King Offa to deal with Charlemagne as an equal. In AD 825 Mercia was defeated by King Egbert of Wessex at the battle of Ellendun, which signalled the start of the kingdom's decline. This was further continued by Viking incursions.

NORTHUMBRIA Prior to the Viking invasion of England, Northumbria ranked with Mercia and Wessex as a major kingdom. It originated in the seventh century when Ethelfrith merged the kingdoms of Bernicia and Deira. At the height of its power, Northumbrian territory was bounded by the Clyde and the Firth of the Forth to the north and the Humber and Mersey to the south. In AD 685 the Picts defeated the Northumbrians at the Battle of Nechtanesmere, after which the kingdom waned while its rival Mercia rose to a paramount position. From then on Northumbria suffered from savage rivalry between family factions aspiring to the throne. In the latter part of the ninth century the kingdom was overwhelmed by the Great Army of the invading Danes. The invaders remained in control at York until AD 954 when KING EDRED drove out ERIC BLOODAXE and Northumbria became part of the unified English kingdom.

WESSEX Although the origins of the West Saxons' kingdom of Wessex are obscure, it is thought that it began in the Thames valley region under the rule of CERDIC at the end of the fifth century. By subduing neighbouring Britons the kingdom expanded west. In the seventh century Cadwalla, calling himself King of the Saxons, conquered the Jute-held Isle of Wight and gained control over Surrey and Sussex. King Ine further extended the kingdom across southern England. Nevertheless, paramount power remained with Mercia until EGBERT secured Kent and the Southwest, so that Wessex dominated all of England south of the Thames. Prior to ALFRED THE

GREAT's success against the Vikings in the ninth century, the Danes' Great Army had eliminated Wessex's rival kingdoms. This meant that the only remaining line of effective Anglo-Saxon royalty was that of Wessex, which evolved into the monarchy of England.

EDGAR Born *c.* 944 the younger son of EDMUND THE MAGNIFICENT and his wife St Elgiva, Edgar came to the throne on the death of his brother the unhappy EDWY THE FAIR in 959, though it was not until 973 that the crown was actually placed upon his head. During his reign, which was largely shaped by DUNSTAN, Archbishop of Canterbury, Edgar was fortunate that for the time being the Norsemen had lost interest in England, with the result that the kingdom enjoyed unusual prosperity and Edgar was able to turn his attention to revising the laws of England which he decreed were 'to be common to all the nation, whether English, Danes or Britons, in every province in my dominion'. Such popular rule earned the king the sobriquet of 'the Peaceable'.

One aspect of Edgar's reign that was to have a lasting effect on the monarchy was his coronation. This did not take place until fourteen years after his brother's death because Dunstan would not agree until he amended his moral life. When the time for the coronation came Dunstan introduced an impressive new ceremony which switched the emphasis from the actual crowning to the anointing. This stressed the spiritual nature of the rite and with it the role of the Church. Kings had been known to place crowns on their own heads, but self-anointing would be impossible so would remain the Church's prerogative, endorsing its power in the kingdom. Dunstan's ceremony has remained the basis of coronation services up to the present time.

Edgar's crowning was held on Whit Sunday 973 at Bath and was followed by the best remembered event of his reign. The newly anointed king was rowed voluntarily down the River Dee by eight tributary kings as an act of homage, and with Edgar at the helm it seemed to symbolise that Anglo-Saxon England had reached nationhood.

Although Edgar was hailed as 'the Peaceable', he could be ruthless in his private life. After the death of his wife Ethelfleda the Fair whom he had married *c.* 961, the king wished to marry for a second time. He was impressed by reports of the beauty of a lady named Elfrida, daughter of the Earldorman of

After being crowned in AD 973 King Edgar was rowed down the River Dee by eight tributary kings as an act of homage.

Devon, Earl Ordgar, and to assure himself that she was as beautiful and accomplished as hearsay claimed, he sent his friend and favourite courtier Athelwold to her father's hall. He was to find that descriptions of Elfrida had not been exaggerated, and he fell in love with her himself. Not having told the earl or his daughter the real reason for his visit he declared that he sought her for himself. To his royal master he sent word that the lady had not lived up to her description and would be an un-suitable queen as she was simple-minded.

Earl Ordgar agreed to the marriage and after the ceremony Athelwold took his bride to his estate at Wherwell in Hampshire. Here he was so devoted to her that when he would have to leave home for the court at Winchester Elfrida must have wondered why he did not take her with him – and so must King Edgar. Before long a courier arrived to say that as the King was hunting in the area he intended to spend the night at his old friend's hall. The news forced Athelwold to confess to Elfrida the deception he had practised because of his love for her, and

then ordered her to appear before the king in decrepit clothing and act stupidly to bear out his false description. While Athelwold waited to greet his royal master Elfrida retired to her chamber to prepare for the visit.

According to Grafton's Chronicle: 'She trimmed and decked herself in the most costly and shewing apparell. And over that, if dame Nature had anything forgotten or misprinted in her, she left not what be done by woman's help to have it amended and reformed, and at the King's comming receyved him with all joye and gladnesse. By which means the amorous King was soone caught in the Devil's snare, so that he set reason apart and followed his awne sensulaite . . . to bring his purpose the better about, he kept forth a countenance as he had been well contented with all thing.'

Edgar asked Athelwold to go hunting with him in the wood of Welverley and there slew his erstwhile friend with his spear. He married Elfrida *c.* 964 and she bore him two sons, one of whom was to become ETHELRED II. King Edgar died in 975 and was interred in Glastonbury Abbey.

EDITH SWAN-NECK One of the first royal mistresses to be mentioned in history dates from the

Norman Conquest. When Duke WILLIAM was victorious at the Battle of Hastings in 1066 he wanted to honour his defeated adversary HAROLD by building a great cairn over his corpse. But Harold had been so mutilated in the fighting that his body could not be found among the dead who littered the Field of Senlac. His mistress, Edith Swan-neck, was brought to the battlefield to look for him. She finally recognised the corpse of her royal lover by 'a familiar mark known only to her'.

EDMUND IRONSIDE Surnamed 'Ironside' either on account of the armour he wore or his powerful stature, Edmund II was acclaimed as king by Londoners on the death of his father ETHELRED THE UNREADY in April 1016. Meanwhile, in Southampton CANUTE, King of Denmark, claimed the English throne and was elected by the Witan. The Danish army was already menacing London but Edmund and his followers broke out before the city was completely surrounded and succeeded in reconquering Wessex. This was followed by Edmund raising the siege of London and then with a fresh army he was victorious over the Danes at Otford, but this was to be his final victory. When he met the Danes again at Assandun (now Ashingdon) in Essex he was defeated and saw the flower of the Saxon nobility slain.

Finally, the opposing armies faced each other across the River Severn and here, according to legend, Edmund challenged Canute to single combat

The meeting of Edmund Ironside and Canute on Olney Island in the River Severn to divide England between them.

with the kingdom as the prize for the victor. Canute, who was smaller than Edmund, suggested that instead they should divide England between them and live in peace. The two redoubtable leaders met on an island in the river and it was agreed that Edmund should have Wessex and Canute the rest of England, and whoever outlived the other would rule the whole of England. Within two months of this agreement King Edmund died at Oxford and was buried at Glastonbury. His death was said to have been arranged by one of his thanes named Edric Streona who was eager to gain Canute's favour. According to legend Edmund retired to an outside privy one night after his evening meal. The privy was in reality little more than a deep pit in which Edric's son hid himself and waited for his victim. When Edmund sat down, the assassin plunged his knife into his entrails. Another version, written by the chronicler Geoffrey Gaimer, tells that a more ingenious method was devised in which the act of sitting on the privy seat activated a crossbow fixed in the cavity below. It should be remembered, however, that crossbows did not come into use until much later.

However Edmund was slain, Edric lost no time in going to Canute and declaring, 'Hail, you who are the sole King of England!' 'I will exalt you higher than all the nobles of the land,' Canute told him when he heard the details of Edmund's murder. He then ordered the traitor to be executed and his head mounted on a tall pole.

EDMUND THE MAGNIFICENT When KING ATHELSTAN died at Gloucester in AD 939 he was succeeded by his 18-year-old brother Edmund who had proved himself at the Battle of Brunanburh two years earlier. He soon earned the sobriquet of 'The Magnificent' because of the pleasure he took in fine things, though during his short reign he had little time to enjoy them as he was constantly defending his realm against incursions by England's traditional enemies, the Danes. He had hardly been crowned on the KING'S STONE at Kingston upon Thames when a Norse army left Ireland to invade England where they were welcomed by their fellow Norsemen who had settled in the Danelaw. The tide of conquest and reconquest was to ebb and flow across northern England for the next six years, and when Edmund was murdered in his hall at Pucklechurch in Gloucestershire, he had managed to regain control of the kingdom he had inherited from his brother.

We will never be sure whether Edmund's killing was as straightforward as the chroniclers recorded or whether it was as the result of a conspiracy. From today's viewpoint no one would have gained by his death yet it seems strange that an outlaw should have been allowed to enter the royal residence so openly. We shall probably never know more than the following account of what happened on 26 May 946 that appeared in Holinshed's *Chronicles* published in the sixteenth century:

> On the day of Saint Augustine the English apostle as he [the king] was set at table, he espied where a common robber was placed neere unto him, whomme sometime he had banished the land, and now returned without licence, he presumed to come into the kings presence, wherewith the king was so moved with high disdaine, that he suddenlie arose from the table, and flew upon the theefe, and catching him by the heare of the head threw him under his feet, wherewith the theefe, having fast hold on the king, brought him downe upon him also, and with his knife stoke him into the bellie, in such wise that the kings bowels fell out of his chest, and there presentlie died. The theefe was hewn in peeces by the kings servants, yet he slue and hurt divers before they could dispatch him. This chance was lamentable, namelie to the English people, which by the overtimelie death of their king, in whome appeared manie evident tokens of great excelencie, lost the hope which they had conceived of great wealth to increase by his prudent and most princlie government. His bodie was buried at Glastenburie where Dunstane was then abbot.

EDRED When EDMUND THE MAGNIFICENT was slain by an outlaw in AD 946 the English Crown passed to Edred who was born the youngest son of EDWARD THE ELDER *c.* 923. Despite a certain physical weakness the new king proved that the blood of ALFRED

A coin from the reign of King Edmund.

The murder of King Edmund by an outlaw who 'presumed to come into the king's presence' at Pucklechurch in Gloucestershire.

was in his veins when he put down a revolt by Northumbria and forced the rebels to take oaths of loyalty to him. When those vows were broken he promptly defeated them for a second time. He also won several victories over the ever troublesome Danes who were now led by the famous Viking, ERIC BLOODAXE, who, for a brief period, was the last independent King of York. In the latter part of his nine-year reign he chose DUNSTAN, the Abbot of Glastonbury, to be his High Treasurer. Dunstan's hold over the king became so powerful that he allowed himself to be scourged by the abbot as a penance for his sins. Edred died in 955 and was interred in Winchester Cathedral. He was followed by his nephew EDWY ('The Fair').

EDWARD THE CONFESSOR The last Anglo-Saxon king of the old line, Edward the Confessor earned his pious nickname for his monk-like qualities, generosity to the poor and his uncon-summated marriage to Queen Edith. The son of ETHELRED II and Emma of Normandy, he was born *c.* 1003 and became King of England in 1042 on the death of his half-brother HARDICANUTE. Thus the Danish dynasty ended and the Crown was once more worn by a descendant of CERDIC.

The new king was supported by GODWINE, EARL OF WESSEX, the most influential noble in the kingdom. Although Godwine was regarded as responsible for the death of Edward's half-brother

Drawing from a manuscript illustration of Edward the Confessor emphasising the pious nature of the King.

ALFRED THE ATHELING in 1035, Edward married the earl's daughter Edith and for much of his reign he was dominated by the Godwine family. The marriage was not consummated, to the disgust of the queen's family, and the kingdom was left without an heir because Edward had taken a vow of chastity some time before coming to the throne. The King was nicknamed 'The Confessor' as a result of his excessive piety and his neglect of his wife for his devotions.

Having been brought up in Normandy with his half-brother Alfred during the reign of CANUTE, Edward's sympathies were entirely Norman and

The seal of Edward the Confessor.

once he was king he invited Norman clerics to occupy English sees. At court his favourites were Normans, Norman French was spoken and he followed the Norman practice of authenticating documents by means of a great seal instead of drawing a sign of the cross as his predecessors had done. This favouring of Normans was deeply resented by the English 'party' led by Godwines, and this came to a head in 1051 when Earl Godwine refused a royal order to punish the citizens of Dover who had been involved in a fracas with the King's brother-in-law Eustace, Earl of Boulogne. As a result the Godwine family was banished to Flanders, and it was during this time that WILLIAM, the 18-year-old Duke of Normandy, visited the English court where it was said that Edward promised to make him his heir to the throne of England. In 1053 Earl Godwine was restored to favour by the Witan but he only lived seven months after his return and his son HAROLD became Earl of Wessex, taking over his father's role as England's principal noble.

During his reign Edward had the laws of England revised and translated into Latin. He saw holy visions and had the power of curing by his touch, and because of his 'saintliness' his name was used as the English battle-cry before it changed to St George during the Crusades. His great achievement was the building of WESTMINSTER ABBEY to which he devoted a tenth of his wealth. It was consecrated on 28 December 1065 but Edward was too ill to attend the ceremony. Several days later he rallied and managed to whisper to Harold Godwineson and Queen Edith, who was warming his feet against her breasts. Anxious over the succession, his last words were that Harold should have the Crown.

After Edward's death there were reports that healing miracles were occurring at his tomb before the high altar in Westminster Abbey. This led to his canonisation by Pope Alexander III in 1161, making him the only English king to become an official saint.

EDWARD MEDAL Instituted by EDWARD VII in 1907, the Edward Medal, bearing the figure of its founder, was awarded for courageous acts in civil life and was mainly conferred upon miners and quarrymen. Its ribbon was dark blue with a narrow yellow edge to which bars could be added for additional acts of valour.

EDWARD THE ELDER When KING ALFRED died in AD 899 he had not named his successor, which meant that there were two royal contenders for the Wessex throne, one being his son Edward ('The Elder') who had been born *c*. AD 870. The other was Ethelwald, son of Alfred's elder brother ETHELRED I. In those days primogeniture – the

A coin from the reign of Edward the Elder.

right of succession belonging automatically to the first-born – did not apply, and a new king was often elected by the late king's councillors. In this case the Witan voted for Edward because he had already earned a formidable military reputation campaigning against Danish invaders during the latter part of his father's reign.

Ethelwald refused to accept the Witan's decision and defied his cousin by seizing the royal residence at Wimborne, declaring that if he could not live there he was ready to die there. These bold words were forgotten when Edward arrived with his army. Deserting his followers, Ethelwald travelled to Northumbria to win the support of the Danes. Since Alfred's pact with the Danish leader Guthrum, the Danes had honoured their agreement to remain in that part of England known as the Danelaw whose frontier roughly followed the line of Watling Street between London and Chester. But in AD 902 the treaty was forgotten when, under Ethelwald's urging, a Danish force entered Edward's kingdom.

King Edward's response was unexpected and spectacular. Instead of trying to engage the invaders, he led his army straight into the Danelaw where he struck terror into Danish settlements as far as the fen country. Then, leaving the Danes in no

doubt as to the retribution that would follow any further incursions into his territory, he led his men home. On the march they met the Danes returning from Wessex and in the ensuing Battle of the Holm Ethelwald was slain along with the Danish king who had succeeded Guthrum.

Several years later, in the belief that the Danes were still a threat to Wessex, Edward decided that the time was ripe for the reconquest of Britain. An entry in the *Anglo-Saxon Chronicle* in the year 909 stated: 'King Edward sent an army both from the West Saxons and from the Mercians, and it ravaged very severely the territory of the northern army, both men and all kinds of cattle, and they killed many men of those Danes.' From then on, year by year, Edward remorselessly rolled back the frontier of the Danelaw. The historian Richard Humble wrote: 'It is typical of the English that the humiliating Norman Conquest of 1066 remains the best remembered event in their history while the glorious English Reconquest of Edward, 150 years earlier, remains sunk in almost total oblivion. The Reconquest was a series of military operations without parallel in early medieval warfare, ranking Edward with the greatest of England's warrior kings.'

Edward the Elder died in 924 and was interred in Winchester Cathedral. He had assumed the title of 'King of the English', having extended his realm over Mercia, East Anglia and Northumbria, and was succeeded by his son ATHELSTAN.

EDWARD THE MARTYR In 978 King Edward, later to be known as 'The Martyr', was assassinated outside Corfe Castle in Dorset. Born the son of

A coin from the reign of Edward the Martyr.

EDWARD THE MARTYR

The Martyr's Gate at Corfe Castle where King Edward was assassinated at the behest of his stepmother Queen Elfrida.

EDGAR THE PEACEABLE *c.* 962, he had the misfortune to have the ambitious QUEEN ELFRIDA as his stepmother. When her husband King Edgar died in 975 she endeavoured to have her son Ethelred proclaimed king but the clergy favoured Edgar's older son by his first wife Ethelfleda and Edward was crowned at the KING'S STONE at Kingston upon Thames.

On a March day in 978 the young king was on a hunt in Devon when he decided to ride alone to Corfe Castle to see his step-brother ETHELRED for whom he had deep affection, and who lived in the castle with his mother Queen Elfrida. It was twilight when he rode up to the castle's gate, today signposted as 'The Martyr's Gate', and as the queen's cupbearer held up a wine horn in the traditional welcome, one of her retainers stabbed him fatally. The dying king spurred away but soon fell from the saddle. His foot being caught in the stirrup he was dragged down the hill to where his horse halted by a brook. Men from the castle came and threw the mutilated body down a well, and

following the unexplained disappearance of the king young Ethelred was duly crowned to become known in history as 'the Redeless' or 'the Unready'. Local people soon noticed that a mysterious ray of light shone from the mouth of a well and word spread that it was a holy sign. When Edward's followers searched the well their master's corpse was brought to the surface and on 18 February 979 it was interred at the church of St Mary of Wareham where the now empty stone coffin is still to be seen.

The murder shocked England, the *Anglo-Saxon Chronicle* commenting: 'No worse deed than this for the English people was committed since first they came to Britain . . . men murdered him but God honoured him. In life he was an earthly king, he is now after death a heavenly saint.' The suggestion that he had become a 'heavenly saint' was inspired by the miracles that followed his death. It was found that the well in which the body had been hidden had gained healing properties and was named St Edward's Fountain. Then an old woman came forward with an amazing story. Before the assassins took the body to the well they hid it under a covering in her hut, confident that she could never testify against them because she was blind. At midnight the room was filled with unearthly light and the old woman found that her sight was restored. As such stories of miracles increased it was decided that St Mary's Church was not grand enough for such a spiritual treasure and in 980 Edward's body was translated to Shaftesbury Abbey with magnificent ceremony. Healing miracles began to occur at the new tomb and soon the Abbey found itself the possessor of a famous shrine while in 1001 the murdered king was officially styled a martyr.

EDWARD I To his English subjects Edward I was a heroic warrior king, a reincarnation of RICHARD COEUR DE LION, but to the Welsh and Scots he is remembered as the cruellest oppressor. Either way legends gathered about him, and the leaders of those who opposed him became folk heroes.

The eldest son of HENRY III and ELEANOR OF PROVENCE, Edward was born at Westminster in 1239. When he was 15 his father arranged for him to be married to 10-year-old Eleanor of Castile, the daughter of Ferdinand III, and he was created Earl of Chester. As such he became responsible for the Welsh Marches which were frequently harried by insurgents. Though Edward is best remembered as one of England's most warlike kings he was far from successful at the start of his military career. Matthew Paris wrote that he 'was much ashamed to be unable to repress the Welsh rebels'.

Later, Edward spent much of his time in France where he enjoyed taking part in tournaments. He was now a fine figure of a man whose height earned him the nickname of Longshanks and it seemed that in him the earlier Plantagenet spirit had returned. But in 1263 Simon de Montfort's civil war broke out and Edward returned to aid his father with a force of mercenaries, though again he was to be disappointed. He found difficulty in paying the foreign troops who made up for this by looting which alienated the citizens of London.

King Henry was captured by Simon de Montfort and soon afterwards Edward too was taken and imprisoned in Dover Castle. In May 1265 he was at Hereford where he was allowed to exercise his horses and on a certain day he waited until the escorts were tired, then leapt onto a fresh horse and galloped to freedom. He assembled an army and after capturing Gloucester and Worcester, caught up with Simon de Montfort's army at Evesham, where at last he had a resounding victory.

The gilt figure of Queen Eleanor above her tomb in Westminster Abbey, said to be one of the most beautiful medieval effigies in existence.

When Edward was returning to England from the Seventh Crusade the news reached him of the deaths of his small son and King Henry. It was the death of the latter that affected him most, saying, 'I may get more children but never another father.'

In August 1274 Edward was crowned with Eleanor at Westminster Abbey and then, more than any English sovereign since the Norman Conquest, he devoted himself to serious ruling.

After three years Edward began the first of his campaigns, leading an army against Llewellyn ap Gruffydd, the Lord of Snowdonia who also bore the title of Prince of Wales and became known in history as Llewellyn the Last. The king still resented his early failures on the Welsh Marches, nor was he likely to forget that Llewellyn and his men had fought for de Montfort at the Battle of Evesham. Now he used Llewellyn's refusal to do him homage as his feudal overlord to attack him, and he was aided by the fact that many chieftains supported the English including Llewellyn's brother David.

Wales was transferred to Edward's dominion by the Statute of Wales in 1284. To this end he built the castles of Conway and Caernarvon and a circle of fortresses surrounding Snowdonia. In the same year at Caernarvon Queen Eleanor gave birth to a son EDWARD II. The event inspired a piece of royal folklore which became as popular as Alfred burning the cakes or Canute ordering back the tide. In order to placate his new subjects Edward was said to have promised to find them a prince that was 'born in Wales who knows not a word of English' and then presented his baby son to them from the tower of Caernarvon Castle. It certainly made a good story in Tudor times, from when it originates, but the castle tower had not been built at the time and Edward's son did not receive the principality of Wales until his seventeenth year in 1301. Since then there have been twenty-one English Princes of Wales, all of them heirs apparent to the throne though, unlike the dukedom of Cornwall, the title does not come automatically but is bestowed at the sovereign's discretion.

In 1286 Alexander III of Scotland died, leaving the throne to his 6-year-old granddaughter Margaret who was known as the Maid of Norway. With such a young heiress to their throne the Scots feared violence over the succession and they agreed to the king's suggestion that his son Edward should marry the little princess. This plan collapsed when the little girl died on the voyage from Norway. Meanwhile, in the autumn of 1290 Edward was stricken with grief when his beloved Eleanor died at Grantham.

There were thirteen claimants to the Scottish throne and the Scots asked Edward to nominate one as their next king. The man he chose was John Balliol who was a fair choice though what was not taken into account was the way the English king exploited Balliol to establish himself as suzerain of Scotland. Then encouraged by Anglo-French conflict, the Welsh took to arms in the winter of 1295 capturing many castles and towns. The king sent an army to Gascony to oppose the French there and then set out to quell the Welsh. It was no easy task and on one occasion after his convoys had been captured 'he had to drink honey and water and eat salt meat'.

In 1295 Madoc, the Welsh leader, surrendered and he and other chieftains were incarcerated in dungeons for the rest of their lives. John Balliol renounced his loyalty to the English Crown. On 28 April the Scottish nobility were defeated by the Earl of Surrey at Dunbar. Balliol surrendered to the king in a churchyard at Angus and was sent to London where he was imprisoned in the TOWER OF LONDON for the next three years. The earl was made Governor of Scotland and Edward returned to England with the great seal of Scotland and the STONE OF SCONE.

Edward next took an army of a thousand troops to France and after a six-month campaign a truce was agreed with the French. Meanwhile, WILLIAM WALLACE, destined to become one of his country's greatest heroes, led a new rebellion. On 11 September 1297 he and his army of Scots defeated the Earl of Surrey at Stirling after which Wallace was proclaimed the guardian of Scotland. In July the following year Edward had his revenge when his army encountered Wallace's army near Falkirk. Wallace escaped but was later betrayed to his enemies. In London he was executed as a traitor even though he had never acknowledged Edward as his sovereign.

In 1299 Edward took as his second wife Margaret, daughter of Philip III of France, who bore him a son Thomas. Within a year Edward was at Winchester when news reached him that made him prepare for his final campaign against the Scots. Following the English victory at Falkirk two men had been elected as guardians of Scotland: John Comyn and ROBERT BRUCE. The latter had been raised as a Scot though his family traditionally supported the Plantagenets, so that Bruce suffered from conflicting loyalties. These were resolved

Lanercost Priory in Cumbria where Edward I wintered before attempting his final campaign against the Scots.

The monument at Burgh-on-Sands, Cumbria, where King Edward died after trying to lead his army to Scotland despite his illness.

dramatically when he killed his rival John Comyn in the cloisters of the Minorites in Dumfries and had himself crowned King of Scotland at Scone on 25 March.

Though he was now ailing, Edward gave a banquet at which he knighted his eldest son Edward and vowed publicly 'by the God of Heaven I will again go to Scotland and living or dead avenge Comyn'. Now 67 years old and weak enough that he had to be carried on a litter when his army marched north that autumn, on reaching Cumbria he was forced to winter at Lanercost Priory. With the arrival of summer he declared he would lead his troops in person against his old foes, offered up his litter in Carlisle Cathedral and mounted his war-horse. The effort proved too much for him and on 7 July he died at Burgh-on-Sands, a few miles from Carlisle, after making his son swear to carry his body at the head of the English army until the last Scot surrendered, a vow that the new king did not keep.

Edward I was interred in Westminster Abbey beside Queen Eleanor in a plain tomb on which was inscribed the words: *Edward Primus Malleus Scotorun* – Edward I the Hammer of the Scots.

EDWARD II The fourth but only surviving son of EDWARD I and Queen Eleanor of Castile, Edward II was born at Caernarvon on 25 April 1284. As he grew older contemporary authors complained that he preferred the company of common folk to that of his peers and in this he was joined by Piers Gaveston, the son of a Gascon knight, who in 1298 became the prince's official companion.

In 1300 King Edward decided it was time for his son to be blooded on the battlefield so the prince, accompanied by Gaveston, joined the siege of Caerlaverock Castle in Dumfriesshire, winning his father's approval. This changed when the ailing king was incensed when Edward wanted to bestow his late mother's territory of Ponthieu upon Gaveston, and Gaveston was banished to France.

When Edward I died on 6 July 1307 his son inherited daunting problems, not least the financial cost of his father's glory. One of his first acts was to recall Gaveston from exile. The nobility, jealous of the royal favours showered upon the favourite, were infuriated when in January 1308, Edward made him regent of England when he crossed the Channel to attend his own wedding.

On 27 January, in the church of Notre Dame in Boulogne, Edward II married Isabella the Fair, daughter of Philip IV of France. It appeared to be an ideal match; the bride was said to be the most beautiful princess in Europe while Edward, tall, fair-haired and exceptionally strong, was regarded as the most handsome prince.

In April, the barons, under the leadership of Thomas of Lancaster, demanded the banishment of Gaveston. The king, supported only by Sir Hugh Despenser, gave way to avert conflict between the barons and the Crown. He deprived Gaveston of his titles, decreed that he should leave England and then got his own back by sending him to Ireland as the King's Lieutenant. Within twelve months Gaveston was back.

At the beginning of 1310 a new threat beset Edward and Gaveston in the form of the Lords Ordainers, a committee of twenty-one members made up of bishops, earls and barons, whose purpose was to reform the governing of the kingdom. Edward had no choice but to sign letters patent

The Great Seal of Edward II.

Ordainers. For the following six years England suffered from chaotic government and during this troubled period Edward became more and more intimate with the son of his old supporter Sir Hugh Despenser, also named Hugh. Like Gaveston the new favourite was mistrusted by the Lords Ordainers and in 1321 Parliament forced Edward to banish him with his father.

A few months later Queen Isabella was on a pilgrimage to Canterbury when, on the evening of 13 October 1321, she requested a night's lodging at Leeds Castle near Maidstone. The castle's governor, Lord Badlesmere, was absent and his wife refused to admit the queen. Furious at the insult Isabella ordered her guards to force their way into the castle and six men were killed in the ensuing fracas. The queen turned to her husband who was as incensed as his wife over the slight. By hiring mercenaries and raising local levies he was able to lead a formidable force into Kent to besiege the castle, which soon surrendered.

With a successful army under his command, Edward knew his moment was at hand. The Despensers were recalled and a royal campaign began. The first targets were the Mortimers and other marcher lords of the Welsh borders who had mustered forces in support of Lord Badlesmere and therefore were technically traitors. The Mortimers – Roger Mortimer of Chirk and his nephew ROGER MORTIMER of Wigmore – surrendered at Shrewsbury and were sent to the Tower of London. Edward took castle after castle of those who opposed him and then turned his attention to Lancaster in the North.

It had been Edward's devotion to an unpopular favourite that had led to his tribulations, and now that his authority was restored he began to repeat his folly, heaping riches upon Hugh Despenser as he had upon Piers Gaveston. After Gaveston's death his relationship with the queen had greatly improved, as is shown by the fact that she bore him four children between 1312 and 1321. In 1324 it seemed that hostilities would break out between France and England and Edward was persuaded to sequester Isabella's estates because she was a Frenchwoman, but the next year she was permitted to visit Paris to arrange a settlement with her brother Philip V. At the French court she met and fell in love with Roger Mortimer of Wigmore who had escaped from the Tower of London and sought sanctuary across the Channel. Together they

transferring power to them. Though the Ordainers may have grasped the sceptre, their hatred for Gaveston remained and among the forty-one articles they presented to the king the following year was one stating that Piers Gaveston had 'misled and ill-advised our lord the King, and enticed him to do evil in various deceitful ways'.

For the third time Gaveston was exiled and although the banishment was to be perpetual, Edward yet again brought him back with all his titles and property restored. As a result of this defiance Gaveston was excommunicated, the barons took up arms and the king fled to York. At Scarborough Gaveston was besieged in his castle by the earls of Pembroke and Surrey and Henry Percy, and after three weeks was forced to negotiate. It was agreed he would be escorted south to present his case to Parliament while his followers retained the castle. On the journey he fell into the hands of the Earl of Warwick at the village of Deddington and on 19 June 1312 he was beheaded on Blacklow Hill.

Although Edward was distraught at the death of his friend, politically Gaveston's death improved the king's position by removing the nobles' main cause of discontent, and then to universal rejoicing the queen gave birth to the future EDWARD III in November.

On 24 June 1314 the English army was defeated by the Scots at the Battle of Bannockburn which weakened Edward's position at home and when the next Parliament met at York, Lancaster and his allies did not hesitate to exploit the situation and control of the kingdom passed back to the Lords planned to bring down the Despensers. Edward remained unaware of this so that when Isabella wrote suggesting that their 13-year-old son, Edward, Prince of Wales, should join her to make the traditional homage to the French king, he raised no objection. After the ceremony he ordered her to return but, having now got her son, she declared that 'marriage was a bond between husband and wife, and until the middleman who divided them was gone she would live single or in a convent'.

At her refusal to return the Despensers persuaded the king to outlaw both her and Prince Edward but while in France she corresponded with the anti-Despenser faction in England. Then on 24 September 1326 she landed near Harwich with Roger Mortimer in command of a small force of English exiles, barons and mercenaries: her campaign had begun. On learning that Isabella's ever growing army was advancing on London, Edward and the Despensers left for Gloucester to raise troops. The king fell back to Bristol where on 26 October the queen's forces were welcomed by the citizens and the elder Despenser was captured and hanged.

According to Froissart's Chronicle the king and Sir Hugh the younger, who were in Bristol Castle when the execution took place, tried to escape by boat but were overtaken and captured. Sir Hugh was hanged while the king was removed to Kenilworth where on 16 January 1327 a parliamentary deputation declared he should be deposed and his place taken by Prince Edward. If he refused to abdicate voluntarily, his son would be denied the Crown and another sovereign found, presumably Roger Mortimer. In order to safeguard his dynasty, Edward finally agreed.

The next month Edward III was crowned and Queen Isabella and Roger Mortimer acted as regents for the young king, and in effect had full control of the realm. At first Edward was treated reasonably at Kenilworth Castle but on 5 April 1327 the humiliated ex-monarch was incarcerated in Berkeley Castle

Berkeley Castle, the final prison for the deposed Edward II, where he was assassinated in the 'Italian manner' in 1327.

and little was known of him until the official announcement of his death on 21 September. During that time he was an increasing embarrassment to Isabella, as she was still his wife and his continued existence made her relationship with Mortimer adulterous.

After Edward III was crowned royal power remained with his mother and her paramour who had taken the title of Earl of March. The couple retained two-thirds of England's tax revenue for their own purposes and the nobility began to see they had exchanged a foolish king for an avaricious tyrant. Isabella and Mortimer realised that the deposed king could become a focus for revolt and it was no longer a question of if Edward should be murdered but how. It was then the custom for the body of a dead king to be exposed to public view before burial to prove he was not a victim of foul play. Isabella and Mortimer could not afford to be accused of the murder of the new king's father, therefore it was decided that Edward should meet his death in what was known as the 'Italian Manner'.

According to Grafton's Chronicle: 'Sir Roger sent a letter unto them [Edward's captors, Thomas de Gourney and John de Maltravers] signifying how and in what wise he [Edward] should be put to death. . . . And being in his sound sleep, these traitors and false forsworn persons against their homage and fealty, came privily into his chamber and their company with them. . . . Then the murderers took a horn and thrust it up into his

fundament as far as they might, and then took a hot burning spit and put it through the horn into his body and in the end killed and vilely murdered him, but yet in such wise that after his death it could not be perceived how he came by his death.'

The ex-king was embalmed and his heart given to the publicly mourning Isabella as a memento mori in a silver casket. In December he was given a spectacular funeral at Gloucester Cathedral where his tomb became an object of pilgrimage.

EDWARD III The eldest son of EDWARD II and Queen Isabella, Edward III was born at Windsor on 13 November 1312, six months after his father's favourite, Piers Gaveston, was beheaded. When he was 13 years old he was created Duke of Aquitaine and as such joined his mother in Paris to perform customary homage to the King of France. At the French court Isabella formed a liaison with ROGER MORTIMER and together they laid plans for the downfall of King Edward. In September 1326 the young prince was back in England where his mother and Mortimer succeeded in imprisoning the king. Although young Edward was offered his father's throne he refused to accept it until his father officially abdicated.

After the death of the ex-king Edward II was announced, the prince was crowned King Edward III in January 1327, but he was the king in name only as the real power remained with Isabella and Mortimer. A year later he married Phillipa, the daughter of William V of Hainault and, like Edward, a great-grandchild of Philip II of France. Although it was an arranged marriage the young couple fell deeply in love.

Aged eighteen, Edward resolved to avenge his father. Now the father of Edward of Woodstock, later the BLACK PRINCE, this new responsibility encouraged him to end his role as a crowned puppet. Isabella and Mortimer resided in Nottingham Castle, guarded by Mortimer's Welsh troops. At midnight on 19 October 1330 twenty-four of the king's companions crept up a tunnel and burst into the queen's chamber. Ignoring Isabella's plea in Norman French of 'Bel fitz, bel fitz, eiez pitie de gentil Mortimer!' Edward seized Mortimer. He was tried for usurping the king's authority and having killed his father, though no mention was made of his liaison with Queen Isabella. On 29 November he was drawn on a hide from the TOWER OF LONDON and hanged at Tyburn. Queen Isabella

was imprisoned for the remaining twenty-eight years of her life at Castle Rising in Norfolk where Edward paid her a formal visit once a year. The young king was now free to govern his kingdom, and not for many years had an English monarch been held in such high regard.

When ROBERT BRUCE died in 1329 he was succeeded by his only son DAVID II who was enthroned with his wife Joanna, Edward's sister, at Scone. In 1332 Edward Balliol, who had briefly worn the Scottish crown in the days of EDWARD I, landed at Kinghorn in Fife with over three thousand followers in an attempt to win back the kingdom; and on 24 September he was crowned King of Scotland at Scone. It was a brief triumph as by the end of the year he took refuge in England. Edward supported Balliol, using the activities of Scottish reivers as an excuse to break the Treaty of Northampton.

On 19 July 1333 a Scottish army led by Sir Archibald Douglas arrived 3 miles north-east of Berwick where Edward's army was positioned on Halidon Hill overlooking a protective stretch of swampy ground. Although Edward venerated the concept of chivalry, he was ready to try any tactic likely to bring him victory and at Halidon Hill he broke tradition by ordering his knights to fight on foot. The Scots struggled across the marsh only to be crushed by ranks of fighting men in massive armour. It has been estimated that through Edward's tactics over nine thousand Scots were slain while the English casualties were less than a hundred. Following this triumph Balliol was reinstated and in return for Edward's assistance he transferred most Scottish territory south of the Forth to England, which inspired generations of Scottish patriots to fight for its return.

Edward's success at Halidon Hill fired his military aspirations. In France English possessions had been reduced, and as a pretext for a campaign to recover the lands lost by his forebears he boldly claimed he was the rightful King of France. His argument was that his mother was the sister of the late Charles IV, disregarding the fact that the French recognised Salic Law which debarred women from the throne. In order to emphasise his claim Edward quartered the lilies of France with the English leopards on his coat of arms and bestowed upon himself the title of King of France, which was retained by the English monarchy until 1801.

But if some of his earlier campaigns were disappointing he retained his enthusiasm for

The Battle of Crécy is commemorated by this representation of an English archer close to the site of the battle.

determined to make the most of their surrender. It was decreed that six principal burghers should walk barefoot from the town, hangman's nooses round their necks, to hand over the keys of Calais before being executed. Reaching the royal dais the captives fell to their knees, handed the keys to the king and implored mercy. Their pleas were rejected until Queen Phillipa knelt beside the condemned and begged her haughty spouse to show compassion. The king was satisfied, and the story spread across Europe. Following the fall of Calais a truce was made between Edward and Philip VI, and the first act of the HUNDRED YEARS' WAR was over.

In 1348 the Black Death swept into Europe from the East reducing England's population by over a third. With the workforce drastically reduced surviving labourers realised their own value and the practice of service for land tenure was changed to that of rent, and the yeoman class was born.

During the plague there was no official war between France and England but after the plague passed, war with France resumed and on 19 September 1356 the Black Prince won a great victory at Poitiers. John II, the new King of France, was taken prisoner and brought to England. The ransom for him was set so high that his subjects preferred to continue the war while he remained in great comfort in England. Edward and his sons crossed the Channel and on 28 October 1359 the English army reached the walls of Paris. But the walls of the city were too strong for the besiegers and on 7 May 1360 a treaty was signed in which Edward renounced his claim to France and in return retained Calais, Poitou, Guienne and Gascony. The French also agreed to pay 3 million gold crowns for their king – a debt that was never honoured. From then on Edward took a less active interest in the

chivalry, establishing the MOST NOBLE ORDER OF THE GARTER for twenty-four knights who were to be 'co-partners both in peace and war'. According to tradition it was inspired during a dance when the Countess of Salisbury's garter fell to the floor. There was knowing laughter from the bystanders when the king picked it up, whereupon he uttered the famous phrase '*Honi soit qui mal y pense*'.

In 1346 Edward returned to France with an army of fifteen thousand and won everlasting fame through his victory at Crécy. Next he laid siege to Calais but it was to be eleven months before the town surrendered, during which time the inhabitants resorted to eating their cats and dogs. Peeved by the length of time he had been defied, Edward was

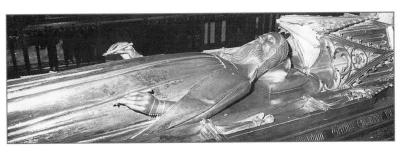

Effigy of Edward III in Westminster Abbey.

affairs of state, handing much of his responsibility to his sons JOHN OF GAUNT and the Black Prince. In 1369 Queen Phillipa died of the plague, having borne Edward eleven children.

During the latter years the king had enjoyed affairs with various women and made Alice Perrers, one of the queen's ladies-in-waiting, his mistress. He was so enamoured of her it was said that she was able to influence the government of the country. While the old Edward thought of little else but Alice Perrers, the glory the young Edward had given England faded. The death of the Black Prince so grieved the king it probably hastened his death, which came on 21 June 1377. He was yet another English king to be deserted in his last hour. Courtiers fled from his chamber to safeguard their own interests and Alice Perrers is said to have tarried just long enough to pull the rings from the dying king's fingers. Only a priest remained to hear his last words: 'Miserere Jesu.' His body was interred in a magnificent tomb in WESTMINSTER ABBEY.

EDWARD IV When Edward was born at Rouen on 28 April 1442 his father Richard, Duke of York was acting as HENRY VI's regent in France. The duke was descended from the fourth surviving son to EDWARD III and he believed this made him the successor to the childless king. Edward's mother was Cecily Neville, a granddaughter of JOHN OF GAUNT and known as the 'Rose of Raby'. With such a background it was inevitable that Edward would be drawn into the looming power struggle that became known as the WARS OF THE ROSES.

Soon after King Henry VI became insane in 1453, his wife Queen Margaret gave birth to a baby who was christened Edward and created Prince of Wales. The arrival of the royal heir nullified Duke Richard's chance of inheriting the throne but this did not deter his ambition to win it. After the Wars of the Roses broke out the duke was attainted and forced to flee to Ireland in 1459. His son Edward escaped across the Channel in a fishing boat steered by his formidable cousin, the Yorkist Earl of Warwick, soon to be known as 'The Kingmaker'. He remained in Calais for eight months under the influence of the powerful earl, learning the three things that were to shape his career: diplomacy, military tactics and intrigue.

Edward was now a handsome youth, over 6ft tall, highly gifted and with his gallantry and graceful manners he was the antithesis of his pious cousin King Henry.

In the following year Edward and Warwick returned to England and, after being warmly welcomed by Londoners, defeated the Lancastrian army at Northampton. King Henry was made a prisoner and after the battle it was agreed by Parliament that Henry would remain king until he died, then the Crown would pass to the Duke of York. Unwilling to see her son Prince Edward disinherited, Queen Margaret raised an army which in December 1460 defeated the Yorkists at Wakefield. The duke was killed and his son Edmund was murdered after the battle. Then came the news that the Lancastrian earls of Pembroke and Wiltshire had landed on the Welsh coast. Edward waited for the invading force at Mortimer's Cross; proving his ability as a military leader, the Yorkists won a notable victory. Victory then went to the Lancastrians at St Albans which reunited King Henry with his queen, but this did not prevent Warwick having Edward proclaimed Edward IV in London.

The labyrinthine politics and bloody battles of the Wars of the Roses kept Edward and the Kingmaker occupied until 1465 when the fugitive King Henry was captured and Queen Margaret fled to Flanders. It seemed that peace had finally come to England

Elizabeth Grey, daughter of Sir Richard Woodville, whom Edward married secretly in 1464 and who became the mother of Edward V.

and after the troubled reign of Henry VI Edward must have appeared as an attractive king, good-natured, golden-haired and impressive. Appropriately he chose a radiant sun as his emblem.

Believing it was time for the young king to marry, Warwick was ambitious to see an alliance between England and France and negotiated the king's marriage with the French queen's sister. Edward shattered his hopes by announcing that five months earlier, on 1 May 1464, he had been secretly married to Elizabeth Grey. The daughter of Sir Richard Woodville and the widow of a Lancastrian knight slain at the second Battle of St Albans, Elizabeth already had two sons and was five years older than the king when they met. While Edward certainly loved her, he recognised the value of a Lancastrian connection, seeing the Woodville family as a counterbalance to the domineering Neville clan of whom Warwick was the leading member.

Warwick's next move was to secretly arrange a marriage between the king's ambitious brother George, Duke of Clarence to his elder daughter Isabella without royal approval. The wedding took place on 11 July 1469 and the next day Warwick, Clarence and Archbishop Neville signed a paper calling upon all 'true subjects' to assemble at Canterbury to assist them in calling the king's attention to the 'deceivable covetous rule and guiding of seditious persons'. In the rebellion that followed, Edward was captured and taken to Middleham Castle where Warwick was savouring his greatest triumph: he now held King Edward captive while in London King Henry was languishing in the Tower. It seemed that he was in a position to bestow the Crown upon his eager son-in-law but first he executed a number of Edward's allies, which lost Warwick the support of the people. They had been ready to side with him when he promised to reform the realm but his ruthless arrogance contrasted with Edward's good-humoured character and King Henry's Christian piety. In London the citizens rioted and the Duke of Burgundy offered to come to their aid if they would support King Edward. Warwick realised he had overplayed his hand and freed Edward.

By the end of the year Warwick and Clarence were back at court. With the kingdom still restless the king and the earl needed each other. Warwick had finally learned that his power still depended on royal authority while Edward still required the support of the most powerful noble in England.

Early in 1470 a rebellion broke out in Lincolnshire and when Edward suppressed it documents were discovered revealing that Warwick and Clarence had planned it with the intention of Clarence being put on the throne. The two conspirators fled to France where Warwick visited his old enemy Queen Margaret, telling her he would now support the Lancastrian cause and restore Henry to the throne, suggesting this new alliance would be sealed by his daughter Anne Neville marrying Margaret's son Prince Edward. The queen agreed and a force of Lancastrian supporters, backed by Louis XI of France, landed unopposed at Portsmouth and Dartmouth. So many men flocked to the Lancastrian standard that Warwick is said to have had an army of sixty thousand when he approached London. It was now Edward's turn to flee across the Channel.

In the TOWER OF LONDON Henry VI suddenly found his old enemy kneeling before him and then he heard cheering as he was escorted to the PALACE OF WESTMINSTER and felt the weight of the crown on his head. With Henry back on the throne and Warwick returned to power, those concerned in the coup were satisfied, except the Duke of Clarence.

As Louis of France had supported Warwick and Clarence, so the Duke of Burgundy assisted the fugitive Edward. On 11 March 1471 he set sail from Flushing with fifteen hundred troops in what seemed like a forlorn hope, but Edward knew he had one clandestine ally. His mother had arranged a secret reconciliation between him and his brother Clarence. The brothers met on 3 April 1471 and Clarence fell on his knees before his brother who raised him to a fanfare of trumpets. Thanks to Clarence's betrayal of Warwick, Edward was now confident to march on London and entered the city to an enthusiastic welcome on 14 April.

When news came that Warwick had joined with Lancastrian forces in the south, Edward led an army of ten thousand to Barnet to intercept him. There on a foggy Easter Sunday the armies of the red rose and the white rose met in battle, which ended in the defeat of the Lancastrians and the death of Warwick. On 4 May Queen Margaret's army was defeated at the Battle of Tewkesbury in which Clarence fought on behalf of Edward and was said to have assisted in the murder of Queen Margaret's son Prince Edward.

On 20 May 1471 Edward made a triumphant entry into London; the next night King Henry died mysteriously in the Tower. At last Edward was the

Drawing from a manuscript illustration of the Battle of Barnet where Warwick the Kingmaker died fighting against Edward IV.

undisputed sovereign of England. Three years later he undertook an expedition to Calais presenting a challenge to the King of France, but instead of fighting it was agreed that the dauphin should be betrothed to Edward's daughter Elizabeth and peace should be maintained between the two countries for ten years; in return the English king would receive an annuity of 20,000 crowns from France.

Edward IV receiving a religious book while his ill-fated son, who was briefly Edward V, stands beside him.

On his return to England Edward settled down to enjoy his reign. A great patron of the arts, ST GEORGE'S CHAPEL at Windsor Castle is a tribute to his knowledge of architecture. His interest in books led him to becoming a patron of William Caxton when he set up England's first printing press in Westminster in 1476.

In a bizarre attempt to discredit the queen and the Woodville faction, in fury Clarence burst into a Council meeting, shouting that Edward was a bastard and a sorcerer. He was arrested, charged with treason and sentenced to death. He was not tried or executed publicly but died mysteriously in the Tower of London, reputedly drowned in a butt of Malmsey, his favourite wine. With his troublesome brother out of the way Edward was free to continue a life of self-indulgence while his remaining brother, RICHARD OF GLOUCESTER, guarded his frontiers. Then in 1482 the Burgundians offered an alliance to Louis of France who promptly accepted it. Not only did this mean that Edward's daughter would not marry the dauphin as agreed but it jeopardised his pension. The following January he planned to invade France but during the preparations he was taken ill with fever and died on 9 April 1483. Edward IV is buried in St George's Chapel, Windsor.

EDWARD V Twelve years old when he succeeded his father in April 1483, Edward was destined to reign for no more than two months, and his fate – and that of his younger brother Richard – remains England's longest running historical controversy. He was born on 2 November 1470 while his mother Elizabeth Woodville was in sanctuary at Westminster, his father EDWARD IV having fled to Flanders when, in the volatile climate of the Wars of the Roses, WARWICK THE KINGMAKER had briefly restored the Crown to the bemused HENRY VI.

Six months later his father returned to wrest back the throne, and following the Battle of Tewkesbury Edward was created Prince of Wales. When his younger brother Richard, Duke of York was aged 4 he was married to Anne, the 6-year-old heiress of the wealthy Mowbray family. When the princes' uncle, Richard of Gloucester, attended the ceremony and spoke kindly to the children, none dreamed that he would be remembered down the centuries as the most wicked of all wicked uncles.

Following the triumph of the House of York, Richard, the king's younger brother, had been made

Great Chamberlain of England and before his death on 9 April 1483 Edward IV named him Lord Protector until the royal heir should be of an age to rule in his own right.

Dressed in blue velvet, Edward was presented to the people as their new sovereign before being taken to the house of the Bishop of London. The Council, after ratifying Richard's position as Lord Protector, fixed Edward's coronation for 22 June. Then following the usual procedure, on 19 May he took up residence in the TOWER OF LONDON, then a royal palace as well as being a fortress and prison, and his brother Richard joined him three days later. It was then announced that the coronation would be postponed until November.

On 22 June a certain Friar Ralph Shaa, preaching at St Paul's on the text 'Bastard slips shall not take root', revealed that when Edward IV secretly

Queen Elizabeth, widow of Edward IV, bidding farewell to her sons in Westminster Abbey before their uncle Richard escorts them to the tower.

married Elizabeth Woodville he already had a pre-contract with Lady Eleanor Butler, the daughter of the Earl of Shrewsbury, and consummation had taken place. As the law stood this made the children of the king and Elizabeth Woodville technically illegitimate. Robert Stillington, the Bishop of Bath and Wells, then declared to the Council that knowing of the contract between the late king and Lady Eleanor his conscience would not permit him to see a bastard ascend the throne. His words convinced the Council and were later written into an Act of Parliament. Detractors of Richard of Gloucester suggest that Bishop Stillington was playing a key role in a plot to get the Lord Protector onto the throne but an intriguing point emerges in the writings of THOMAS MORE, who certainly had no love for Richard. He described a letter written by Edward IV's mother, the Duchess of York, imploring him not to commit bigamy at the time of his infatuation with Elizabeth Woodville.

Meanwhile, the uncrowned Edward and his brother remained in the Tower, and later

HOLINSHED published the accepted Tudor version of their imprisonment, his account inspiring compassion for the 'Princes in the Tower' to this day. He wrote: 'When he had shewed it unto him [Edward V] that he should not reigne but his uncle should have the crowne he was sore abashed and began to sigh and said "Alas I would that my uncle would let me have my life yet though I would lose my kingdom." Both the young princes were now shut up and all others removed from them, onlie one called Blacke Will set to serve them and see them sure.' After that they were never seen again. According to the Croyland Chronicle a rumour spread that they had been murdered in the Tower that autumn so that the ambitious Richard could gain the Crown. In April 1484 the assassination of Edward V and his brother was mentioned by the French chancellor. Apart from this nothing more was known about the boys' fate for twenty years.

The Wars of the Roses finally ended with King Richard being killed at the Battle of Bosworth in 1485 and HENRY TUDOR becoming king. The strongest argument against the conventional view of Richard is the fact that Henry, who had every reason to discredit the king he had usurped, had an act of attainder passed on the dead Plantagenet in which he was accused of all manner of crimes – except the assassination of his nephews. Nineteen years were to pass before Henry gave a verbal explanation of Edward V's disappearance. In May 1502 a certain Sir James Tyrrell, who had been a trusted friend of both Edward IV and RICHARD III, was executed in the Tower for 'matters of treason'. Afterwards Henry announced that Tyrrell had confessed to playing a part in the murder, stating that when Richard III was on his royal progress following his coronation in August 1483 he sent him to arrange the assassination. This was carried out by three men, one of whom was Tyrrell's groom John Dighton, by smothering them with pillows, after which their bodies were buried at the foot of the stairs in the White Tower. When this account was made public only John Dighton was still alive but instead of being punished for regicide he was provided with a pension on condition he resided in Calais.

In 1674, when excavations were carried out at the Tower, workmen found two small skeletons beneath the foundations of the White Tower thought to be those of the two princes. CHARLES II commissioned Sir Christopher Wren to design a tomb for them in WESTMINSTER ABBEY.

In 1984 London Weekend Television staged *The Trial of Richard III* in which two leading QCs took part as advocates, with Lord Elwyn-Jones of Lanelli and Newham, who had been a prosecutor at the Nuremburg war crimes trial and attorney general, acting as judge. Witnesses were historians, authors of books on Richard and specialist experts, while the jury of six men and six women were painstakingly selected by the company's research department as being a cross-section of the public as they would be in a regular court hearing. The transcript of the 'trial', conducted exactly as if it was in a Crown court, provides all the arguments of the prosecution and defence as to whether the king was responsible for the deaths of his nephews. After the closing speeches and the summing up the jury retired and then returned a verdict of 'not guilty'.

EDWARD VI England braced itself for a power struggle when the boy king Edward VI succeeded to the throne in January 1547. His father HENRY VIII had defied the Pope and created the Church of England with himself at its head, but many of his

The boy king Edward VI, who died at the age of sixteen after catching a chill, the last male Tudor sovereign.

subjects had remained devoted to the old faith and were eager for its return. Certain noble families who had been held in check during the reigns of the first two Tudor monarchs now had the opportunity to reassert themselves. As it turned out there was conflict, but this was confined to the court and hardly affected ordinary folk.

Edward was born, to his father's joy, on 12 October 1537 and the sponsors at his christening personified the forces at work in the kingdom. They were the Protestant Archbishop CRANMER, the pro-Catholic plotter Norfolk and Edward's half-sister Mary, who defied her father in her allegiance to the pope to the point where her life was endangered.

Edward's mother Queen Jane Seymour had died within a few days of his birth and therefore a household was set up for the little prince at HAMPTON COURT where he was cared for by his wet-nurse Mother Jak. As an infant he attempted to walk before his first birthday and we are told that when minstrels played he 'danced and played so wantonly that he could not stand still'. This is the only record of any gaiety on his part as he was soon studying for his role of future king with a scholastic enthusiasm remarkable in one so young. Like his father he developed an intense interest in the subtleties of theology and there is a strong suggestion that over devotion to study weakened his already delicate constitution. He had only one childhood friend, a boy named Barnaby Fitzpatrick, the son of an Irish aristocrat. When Barnaby was sent to the French court to finish his education the two boys corresponded and in one letter Edward wrote: 'Shortly we will prove how ye have profited in the French tongue, for within a while we will write to you in French. . . . For women, as far forth as ye may, avoid their company. Yet if the French King demand you, you may sometimes dance, else apply yourself to riding, shooting or tennis . . . not forgetting sometime, when you have leisure, your learning, chiefly reading of the Scriptures.' Barnaby replied: 'Ye make me think the care ye take for me is more fatherly than friendly.'

Edward was nine and staying at Hatfield with his half-sister Elizabeth – whom he called in sombre playfulness 'my sister Temperance' – when news came that Henry VIII had died. Immediately the boy was taken to the TOWER OF LONDON by the Earl of Hereford who had been one of his father's chief advisers. A Council of Regency was formed, Somerset was created a duke and given the title of

Lord Protector while his brother Thomas Seymour, who was to marry Queen Catharine Parr, the widow of the dead king, took the post of Lord High Admiral.

When Edward was enthroned on 20 February 1547 it signalled a new round of court intrigue. One of the conditions of Henry VIII's 1543 peace settlement with Scotland was that in due course his heir should marry MARY STEWART, later Mary, Queen of Scots. Following Henry's death the Scots revoked the agreement and Somerset hurried north to force them to reinstate it. With memories of Somerset's destruction of Leith, the Scots had no trust in him and a war broke out which, on 4 September, culminated at the Battle of Pinkie Cleugh where Scotland suffered an even worse defeat than at Flodden. On returning to London Somerset found that many of the Council members had turned against him and he suspected that it was the work of his brother Thomas Seymour. Somerset removed this threat early in 1549, shortly after Seymour's wife Catherine, widow of Henry VIII, died in childbirth and he expressed the wish to marry the Princess Elizabeth. Somerset had him charged with treason and executed.

As Lord Protector, Somerset had a dual character. Personally he was ambitious for wealth and glorification, using material from despoiled churches to build the magnificent Somerset House, for which he even tried to have WESTMINSTER ABBEY demolished. On the other hand he had a feeling for the common man which made him popular with the people. It was the execution of his brother that earned him the enmity of his peers and it was not long before the king sided with Somerset's enemies, led by John Dudley, Earl of Warwick, and agreed to him being imprisoned in the Tower of London.

For some months Dudley took over the role of Lord Protector but this ended when Somerset made his submission, was released, and returned to power. In order to maintain peace in the Council, Somerset married his daughter to Dudley's eldest son but this was to no avail. Dudley had enjoyed his taste of power too much not to hanker after it again and he schemed against Somerset by increasing his influence over the boy king who was impressed by his Protestant zeal. Dudley was created Duke of Northumberland and in 1551 he was able to have Somerset sent to the Tower of London for the second time on a doubtful charge of plotting against the lives of his fellow councillors.

In his diary Edward recorded that Somerset had declared 'if he were overthrown he would run through London and cry "Liberty! Liberty!" to raise the apprentices and rabble'. Although Somerset denied this, it might have saved him if he had. When a false report circulated that he had been acquitted, the mob at Westminster 'made such a shriek and casting up of caps it was heard into Long Acre beyond Charing Cross'. Bells pealed and bonfires blazed as far away as Bath. Alarmed by this demonstration of popular support for Somerset, his enemies had him executed. Edward noted in his diary: 'The Duke of Somerset had his head cut off upon Tower Hill between eight and nine a clock in the morning.'

Dudley now had full control of the kingdom but discontent found expression in revolts, the most serious being in June 1549 when sixteen thousand peasants followed a tanner named Robert Kett in an effort to end enclosures, reduce rents and abolish bondage 'since Christ had died to make men free'. Twice they entered Norwich, on the second occasion holding the town until Dudley arrived with an army of Welsh artillerymen and German mercenaries. In the ensuing battle three thousand of Kett's followers were slain and afterwards three hundred were hanged, including Kett himself. Dudley realised that the reign of King Edward was likely to be a short one and planned to secure the succession to his own family. To this end he arranged a marriage between LADY JANE GREY, the king's first cousin, and his son Lord Guildford Dudley.

In January 1553 Edward caught a chill as the result of taking a cold drink while overheated from a game of tennis. This led to consumption and as he lay ill in GREENWICH PALACE Dudley suggested that he should nominate the 'heirs males' of Lady Jane Grey as the successors to the throne. Edward approved of Lady Jane because she shared his religious beliefs and signed a document to this effect. Edward died on 6 July, his last words being 'I am faint. Lord have mercy on me and take my spirit.' He was interred in Henry VIII's Chapel in Westminster Abbey.

EDWARD VII The eldest son of Victoria and Albert was born at BUCKINGHAM PALACE on 9 November 1841, and was christened Albert Edward. He was soon known by the royal family as Bertie.

Within a month after his birth he was officially created Prince of Wales, and QUEEN VICTORIA wrote to her Uncle Leopold, King of the Belgians, saying how she prayed that her son would grow up to be like 'his dearest papa'.

The queen and Albert planned a formidable course of education for the little prince, who, denied the company of children of his own age except his brothers and sisters, was made to study six days out of seven with a team of tutors and under such pressure that he sometimes dissolved into tears of exhaustion. At 18, he went to Christ Church College, Oxford, where after his first term he declared it had been the happiest time of his life.

In 1860, studies were temporarily interrupted to visit Canada and the United States. A member of the British royal family making an official visit to a country which had rejected monarchy could have been difficult, but the prince won over the Americans with the natural charm and tact that was his hallmark in later life.

In 1861 the prince broke his studies at Cambridge, where he had gone from Oxford, to train at the Curragh outside Dublin and where he was attached to the 2nd Battalion, Grenadier Guards. For the first time in his life he enjoyed the personal freedom that other young men took for granted. Several brother officers introduced him to 'dissipations which were new to him' by smuggling a young actress named Nellie Clifden into his quarters.

Meanwhile, plans were going ahead for a match between the prince and Princess Alexandra of Denmark, the most suitable of the European princesses. A private meeting was contrived for the young people at Speir Cathedral in September 1861. Although he found Alexandra beautiful and to his liking he hesitated.

The prince's future matrimony occupied his parents, who were unaware of the talk in London clubs about his liaison with Nellie Clifden, discretion not being one of the actress's virtues. When the story finally reached Windsor it had a devastating effect. Prince Albert wrote to Edward 'with a heavy heart upon a subject which has caused me the greatest pain I have yet felt in this life'. He asked if the affair was the cause of his delay in coming to a decision about marriage.

Edward was contrite. In pardoning his son for the 'terrible pain' he had inflicted upon his mother and father, the prince consort urged him to make an early marriage. On 25 November Prince Albert

Above: The beautiful art nouveau memorial to Queen Alexandra set in the wall of Marlborough House.

Right: The wedding photograph of Edward and Alexandra in which Queen Victoria steadfastly gazes at a bust of the late Prince Albert.

visited Cambridge and there was a reconciliation between father and son.

When he returned to Windsor, Albert was in a low state of health and his symptoms developed into typhoid fever, from which he died on 14 December 1861. Believing that her beloved husband's illness had been caused by Edward's immoral behaviour, the Queen refused to send for him and it was only because of a secret telegram, sent by his sister, Princess Alice, that Edward travelled to Windsor early on the day that his father died. Queen Victoria, in her grief, held Edward responsible.

On 9 September 1862 Edward and Princess Alexandra were betrothed in Belgium. 'The all-important event has taken place today,' he wrote to his mother. 'I proposed to the Princess at Laeken and she accepted me; and I cannot tell you *how* grateful I am for it.' When Princess Alexandra arrived in England on 7 March 1863 she was greeted enthusiastically by the public, and the Poet Laureate Tennyson wrote:

Sea King's daughter from over the sea, Alexandra!
Saxon and Norman and Dane are we,
But all of us Danes in our welcome of thee,
Alexandra!

The marriage ceremony, which included three dozen members of European royalty, took place in ST GEORGE'S CHAPEL on 10 March 1863, followed by a honeymoon at OSBORNE HOUSE on the Isle of Wight. The couple then moved into Marlborough House in London where they led a glittering social season. While the queen continued to grieve at Windsor, Edward and his beautiful bride established a brilliant alternative court.

On 8 January 1864 Princess Alexandra gave birth two months prematurely to a prince. At the insistence of Victoria he was christened Albert Victor, the queen declaring that it was her wish that all future heirs to the throne should have Victoria or Albert with one other name. She expected her own son to be known as Albert Edward when he came to the throne.

A second son, the future GEORGE V, was born to Princess Alexandra in June 1865 at Marlborough House, followed by three daughters at yearly intervals. As a result of her confinements, the princess suffered a painful form of rheumatism which left her with a slight limp and increasing deafness.

By now Princess Alexandra was not only worried about her health but she had to come to terms with her husband's notorious tangle of infidelities. However, the prince did not allow these distractions to shadow the great affection he felt for his wife and children, while, for her part, she accepted the situation, finding great enjoyment in her family, to whom she was always 'Motherdear'.

With the advent of the popular press, scandals in high places, once kept discreetly hidden in aristocratic circles, became known to the public at large. Edward's problem as Prince of Wales was that while he performed such royal functions as laying foundation stones and opening institutions, Queen Victoria would not allow him any definite responsibility in the affairs of the country. As a result he had

Marlborough House, originally built for Sarah, Duchess of Marlborough in 1711, became the home of Edward and Alexandra.

plenty of time to indulge in a life which was partly that of a man-about-town enjoying London club life and being lavishly entertained and partly the Squire of Sandringham. As a sportsman in winter he enjoyed shooting, and throughout the year he regularly went racing, having founded a most successful stud at SANDRINGHAM, where he bred three outstanding Derby winners. Edward was very much a prince of pleasure. The feelings of the man in the street towards the Prince of Wales were of great affection. He might be a rake but above all he was such a likeable gentleman.

In 1877 Edward met Lillie Langtry, the daughter of the Dean of Jersey and the wife of Edward Langtry. When she burst upon the London social scene, her vivacity and beauty were the talk of the town, and almost immediately she became the prince's first official mistress. But it was when on a visit to Cannes that Edward began his longest affair, which was to last ten years. The object of his

Edward VII, King of Great Britain and Emperor of India (1841–1910) wearing state robes for his coronation, 1902. *(Getty Images)*

affections was 'Darling Daisy', Lady Brooke, who later became the Countess of Warwick.

Edward was 59 when in January 1901 he sent a telegram to the Lord Mayor of London, who traditionally announced the death of a sovereign. The telegram read: 'My beloved Mother the Queen has just passed away surrounded by her children and grandchildren.' After a reign of sixty-three years, seven months and two days, Queen Victoria had died, and when the king addressed the Privy Council the following day, he declared that as long as there was breath in his body he would work for the good of the people. He also announced 'I have resolved to be known by the name Edward, which has been borne by six of my ancestors'. For Prince Albert Edward the long wait for the throne was over.

At last Edward could exercise his diplomatic talents that had been blocked during his mother's reign, and probably his greatest achievement was the part he played in 1904 in establishing the Entente Cordiale with France.

To help Anglo-French relations Edward was invited to meet President Loubet privately at the Elysée but on his insistence this became a state visit. And again, as so often throughout his life, as a result of his great natural charm and diplomacy, the British Ambassador was able to report the visit 'a success more complete than the most sanguine optimist could have foreseen'.

Edward felt that conflict was soon to engulf Europe. In 1908 he had his secretary write to the Prime Minister, Mr Asquith: 'His Majesty wishes me to ask you whether in framing the Budget, the cabinet took into consideration the possible (but the King hopes improbable) event of a European war.'

By early 1909 the king was suffering from bronchitis, and despite a heavy cold he and Queen Alexandra made a state visit to Berlin in February, for the benefit of Anglo-German relations. On his return Edward wrote to his friend and confidant Sir Ernest Cassel, 'My bronchial catarrh was not improved by my visit to Berlin though the visit was in every respect a great success'. By 1910 the king's health began to seriously deteriorate and despite heart troubles and bronchitis he went slowly about his daily duties and appointments granting audiences and signing official documents at Buckingham Palace. On 6 May he managed to dress in his usual fastidious style and smoke one of his big cigars but in the afternoon he suffered a heart attack and collapsed while playing with his two pet canaries. Even then he refused to be put to bed, remaining in an armchair while old friends came to see him. Among these was his last and most important mistress, Mrs Alice Keppel, who was admitted to his room by order of Queen Alexandra. Soon after 5pm he was informed that one of his horses had come in first in Kempton Park's Spring Two-Year-Old Plate. 'I'm very glad,' he murmured before he fell into a coma. He was finally laid on his bed and 15 minutes before midnight he died peacefully.

Edward VII's reign had brought prestige and power to the Crown of England and the empire, and on the last stage of his final journey from Windsor station up the hill to St George's Chapel nine sovereigns followed the gun carriage. Further down the procession a footman led the late king's imperious little terrier Caesar, who faithfully followed his master to St George's Chapel, where Edward had been christened and married and where he is buried.

See also SANDRINGHAM

EDWARD VIII In one respect the birth of Prince Edward – or David as he was always known to his family – on 23 June 1894 was unique. QUEEN VICTORIA, in a letter to her daughter Vicky, wrote: 'It seems that it has never happened in this Country that there shd. [*sic*] be three direct Heirs as well as the Sovereign alive.'

The little boy, who had been born to the Duke of York, the future GEORGE V, and Mary of Teck at White Lodge in Richmond Park, did not have a happy childhood; later in life he described it as 'wretched'. It seems that the traditional Hanoverian rift between father and eldest son was to become manifest again between Edward and his father. In the rather cramped York Cottage at SANDRING-HAM the elder children were put under the care of a neurotic nurse who, while her neglect of little Prince Albert led to a stomach ailment, adored Edward to such a degree that she could not bear to be parted from him for even a few minutes. Consequently, when he was taken to the drawing-room to be inspected by his parents, she would secretly pinch him so that his screams resulted in him being immediately returned to her care. Edward escaped her pinches when she finally had a nervous breakdown.

The child learned early on that he was destined to be a king, announcing in his fourth year that when

he was crowned he would pass a law against 'cutting puppy dogs' tails'.

In 1907 the duke enrolled his son at the Royal Naval College in the grounds of OSBORNE HOUSE. It was a month prior to his 13th birthday when Edward, upset at the prospect of leaving home, was taken on the journey to the Isle of Wight by his father. When he bid his young son farewell, he said, 'Now that you are leaving home David and are going out into the world, always remember that I am your best friend.' However, the generation gap defeated this well-intended wish. Edward's waywardness was to be a deep disappointment to the duke and already there was a hint of sadness about him that his father could not understand or perhaps did not recognise.

If Edward had not been particularly happy at York Cottage, his introduction to life as a naval cadet was no improvement. With thirty other boys he lived in a bleak dormitory where he was expected to begin a long discipline-filled day at six o'clock in the morning. Every action the boys had to undertake, whether cleaning their teeth or saying their prayers, was regulated by the note of a gong. Part of the preparation for the day was a plunge into cold water. Edward wrote in his autobiography: 'Today I have only to close my eyes to see again that pathetic crowd of naked, shivering boys, myself among them, being herded reluctantly towards that green-tiled pool in the first light.'

Edward's royal status did not save him from any of the rigours of the college or bullying by his fellows. On one occasion they reminded him of the fate of his ancestor CHARLES I by being 'guillotined'; a dormitory window sash was dropped down on his neck, which held him prisoner until his cries finally brought help.

The prince commenced his final period of naval training at the Royal Naval College at Dartmouth in May 1909 and a year later Edward VII died. After the funeral Edward returned to Dartmouth, but his father, now GEORGE V, decided he should receive the title of Prince of Wales and that as the heir apparent he needed to widen his education and experience. Edward duly went to Magdalen College where, unlike his grandfather, he was allowed to live as an ordinary undergraduate. At last he began to enjoy life, particularly sports which included fox-hunting, shooting, tennis, golf and playing association football for the Magdalen 2nd XI. And like many young men of his day, he succumbed to banjo-playing.

King Edward VIII, Duke of Windsor (1894–1972) salutes as he leaves the War Office wearing his Major-General uniform, 1939. *(Getty Images)*

His natural charm soon made him popular with fellow students and professors alike but from an academic point of view his progress was not outstanding. The president of Magdalen declared, 'Bookish he will never be', a phrase that amused the prince so much that it became one of his favourite quotations for the rest of his life.

To sit on a horse well was a requirement of a sovereign and in order to improve his horsemanship Edward was briefly attached to the 1st Life Guards when his time at Oxford ended in June 1914. When war broke out with Germany in August of that year he was as keen as any of the hundreds of thousands of young men to 'do their bit' for the country in what was expected to be a quick war. When he was not permitted to rejoin the navy his request for a commission in the Grenadier Guards was granted. But when his battalion was to go to France he was transferred to another which was remaining in England. Disappointed at being left behind, Edward obtained a meeting with Lord Kitchener, Secretary of State for War, and declared, 'What does it matter if I am shot? I have four brothers.' To this the old hero of Omdurman replied, 'If I was certain you

would be shot, I do not know if I should be right to restrain you. What I cannot permit is the chance, which exists until we have a settled line, of the enemy securing you as a prisoner.'

Undeterred, Edward continued to press to be allowed to cross the Channel and finally in 1915 he joined the staff of the Guards Division under the command of Major-General Lord Cavan. On 29 September he accompanied Cavan to the Guards HQ in the Loos front-line area. As they walked through a shattered landscape towards the head-quarters in a ruined farmhouse, an enemy artillery barrage began and as shells fell about them they had to shelter in trenches strewn with corpses. After reaching the farmhouse they crawled forward to an observation post which gave the prince an even more graphic picture of the horror that was taking place round him.

On hearing of the danger in which the prince had been placed, Sir John French, Commander-in-Chief of the British Expeditionary Force, ordered that the prince should be transferred to a safer zone. The king, sympathetic to his son's wish to do something more positive, informed Lord Cavan that neither he nor any of his officers would be blamed if Edward became a casualty. Yet a gulf remained between father and son. Edward had seen men die horribly in the mud of the trenches and he could not reconcile this to the parade ground pageantry of war. This surfaced when the King demanded he should wear his decorations, including those presented to him by Tsar Nicholas II. The prince answered that he could not countenance the wearing of medals given to him merely because of his position while there were thousands of brave soldiers who deserved to be decorated.

In 1916 Edward was sent to Alexandria where he met troops from Australia and New Zealand who had recently been mauled in the fiasco of Gallipoli. The easy manners which came so naturally to him were appreciated by the democratic Anzacs, and when he bathed with them in the Suez Canal near Ismailia the incident became something of a legend in the Commonwealth. When the Armistice came the prince was attached to the Australian Corps in Belgium.

Edward returned to civilian life and the young woman who had become his mistress in February 1919. Mrs Freda DUDLEY WARD, the wife of William Dudley Ward, the Vice-Chamberlain of the Royal Household, met the prince when they were both sheltering in a cellar of a Mayfair house during an air raid. After the 'All Clear' they went dancing until the small hours and so began a love affair which was to last sixteen years, during which Freda was Edward's great support.

There was a curious coincidence regarding the meeting of the couple. Mrs Kerr-Smiley, at whose house they met, was the sister of Ernest Simpson, who was destined to marry an attractive American divorcee named Wallis Spencer.

When Edward told his father that Freda was the only woman he really loved it only added fuel to the king's growing disapproval of his heir. George V still associated the fashions and attitudes of his own youth with what was correct, while he viewed the 'modern' world and the fashions that followed it with distrust. Thus he detested his son's casual way of dressing as much as his circle of friends and their modern ways. On one occasion the King was reported to have shouted at the prince, 'You dress like a cad. You act like a cad. You are a cad. Get out!' There is no doubt that Freda Dudley Ward helped Edward through his fits of depression caused by his father's humiliation of him.

But if Edward frequently felt frustrated in private life, in public he was a great success. Soon after the war was concluded he became Britain's ambassador extraordinary, not only paying visits to different parts of the empire but also to the United States where – if one can go by newspaper reports – people fell in love with him and he fell in love with all things American.

Thus the years passed with the prince attending to his official duties, doing all he could for ex-servicemen through Toc H and the British Legion, taking a sympathetic interest in the plight of the unemployed and enjoying himself in his own circle whenever possible.

His greatest pleasure came in 1930 with the acquisition of Fort Belvedere close to Virginia Water. Freda Dudley Ward was with Edward when he first saw the castellated residence of mellow stone which had been built in the eighteenth century and which the prince first described as a 'pseudo-gothic hodgepodge' though he fell in love with it, no doubt because it represented his first real taste of independence. It had been neglected for many years and the garden had run wild. But Freda helped him with its redecoration and he became an enthusiastic gardener as he laid out borders and laboured to restore the grounds. Indeed, his love of gardening

overtook his enthusiasm for hunting and even to some extent his passion for golf.

It was here that the prince invited Wallis Simpson and her husband to be his guests on the weekend of 30 January 1932. This event set in motion the most remarkable drama involving a British – or any other – monarch, for no other king has willingly re-nounced his throne for the sake of love.

Bessie Wallis was born in 1896 in Pennsylvania, the only child of Alice and Teackle Wallis Warfield. The Warfield family was one of America's oldest and most successful, having arrived in the New World in 1662. Alice was a member of the equally ancient Montague family, so from an American point of view Wallis's antecedents were impeccable which gave a lie to the pre-Abdication rumours that she was devoid of 'breeding' or a social background.

In 1916 she married a US Navy pilot, Earl Winfield Spence, whom she described in an ecstatic letter home as 'the world's most fascinating aviator'. They divorced in 1927 to the outrage of the Warfields and Montagues for whom divorce was the ultimate disgrace. The following year Wallis married former Grenadier officer Ernest Simpson and they set up house close to Hyde Park. Ernest's sister, Mrs Kerr-Smiley, introduced them into London society, which finally led them to meeting the Prince of Wales in 1930, though it was not until 1932 that he invited them to his house which was then known as The Fort.

The mutual attraction which developed between Wallis and the prince was reflected in 1934 by the dismissal of Freda. In May of that year her eldest daughter had to undergo an operation. For several weeks she was seriously ill, during which time Freda stayed by her side night and day in the nursing home. When the girl began to recover Freda realised that for the first time in sixteen years the prince had not been in touch with her when they were apart. Puzzled, she telephoned York House only to be told by an agitated switchboard operator that she had been ordered not to put her through to the prince. She was never in contact with him again.

In the summer of 1934 the prince asked Wallis and Ernest Simpson to join his party at Biarritz. Ernest's business interests took him to the United States at that time so Wallis went with her aunt Bessie Merryman as chaperone. From Biarritz the party took a cruise on the yacht *Rosaura* during which the prince and Wallis (to quote her own words) 'crossed the line that marks the indefinable boundary between friendship and love'. It has been thought that the prince intended to tell his father of his love for Wallis Simpson but he refrained out of consideration for his failing health. Then, on 20 January 1936, King George died at Sandringham.

In June Edward, now Edward VIII, and Wallis Simpson embarked on the steam yacht *Nahin* for a cruise along the Dalmatian coast, which made headlines throughout Europe but not in Britain. Thanks largely to the efforts of Lord Beaverbrook, the British press maintained a conspiracy of silence on what was becoming a national crisis. In September Wallis was panicked by the situation and the effect her relationship with the King could have

The postage stamp of an uncrowned king. Although a crown appears on the stamp, Edward VIII did not have a coronation before his abdication.

upon him. She wrote that while they had had 'lovely beautiful times together' he must now attend to his job. The King's reply – 'I do love you so entirely and in every way' – touched her so deeply she abandoned any idea of parting. She joined him at BALMORAL and filed a divorce action against her husband Ernest. This was heard at the Ipswich Assizes on 27 October and reported in the British press without comment. But it was now clear that the newspapers would not keep silent much longer and the King summoned Stanley Baldwin, the Prime Minister, to BUCKINGHAM PALACE on the evening of 16 November.

Baldwin told the King that a marriage with a divorced woman whose two husbands were still living would not 'receive the approbation of the country'. Edward replied, 'I want you to be the first to know that I have made up my mind and nothing will alter it. I mean to abdicate to marry Mrs Simpson.' 'Sir, this is a very grave decision and I am deeply grieved,' said Baldwin and left. The King

then dined with his mother Queen Mary and the Princess Royal and announced his decision, which was received with shock.

On 3 December the British press told its readers what the rest of the world had known for weeks and the country was thrown into the thick of a constitutional crisis. The next day in the House of Commons the Prime Minister told Parliament: 'Suggestions have appeared in certain organs of the Press yesterday and again today, that, if the King decided to marry, his wife need not become queen. These ideas are without foundation. There is no such thing as what is called morganatic marriage known to our law. The lady whom he marries, by the fact of her marriage to the King, necessarily becomes queen. The only way in which this result could be avoided would be by legislation dealing with a particular case. His Majesty's Government are not prepared to introduce such legislation.'

At Fort Belvedere on 19 December 1936 the dukes of York, Gloucester and Kent arrived to witness their brother sign the Instrument of Abdication. The next evening Edward had a farewell dinner with his family, including his brother who was now GEORGE VI, and then he made his famous broadcast to the nation which his supporter Winston Churchill is said to have helped him to compose.

'You all know the reasons which have impelled me to renounce the throne,' he said. 'But I want you to understand that in making up my mind I did not forget the country or the Empire which as Prince of Wales, and lately as King, I have for twenty-five years tried to serve. But you must believe me when I tell you that I have found it impossible to carry the heavy burden of responsibility and to discharge my duties as King as I would wish to do without the help and support of the woman I love.'

At midnight Edward said goodbye to his brothers, bowing to the new sovereign, and left for Portsmouth where HMS *Fury* waited to carry him across the Channel into exile.

When Edward reached Vienna, where he planned to stay until Wallis's divorce was finalised, he was met by the British ambassador to Austria. 'What is my name?' Edward asked anxiously as he descended from the train. 'Sir, you are His Royal Highness the Duke of Windsor,' the ambassador replied.

As the Duke of Windsor, Edward married Wallis Simpson in the Chateau de Candé near Tours in France on the morning of 3 June 1937. To the ex-king's anger his wife was not allowed the honorific

The Duke and Duchess of Windsor in New York with their pet pug terrier called Disraeli, *c.* 1951.
(Getty Images)

title of 'Highness'. This was compounded by the fact that it was made clear that he was not to return to England. The couple lived in France until 1939. During the Second World War the Duke served as Governor of the Bahamas, after which he returned to France from where he was allowed to make occasional visits to England and meet his relatives.

Edward, the uncrowned ex-king, died in 1972 and was interred in the royal burial ground at Frogmore. His duchess died fourteen years later and was buried beside him.

EDWY THE FAIR The son of KING EDMUND, Edwy ('The Fair') was born *c.* 941 and ascended the English throne on the death of KING EDRED, who had died without an heir, in 955. Like several kings before him, he was crowned on the KING'S STONE at Kingston upon Thames. At the coronation feast, the Archbishop of Canterbury was infuriated when he noticed that the new king was missing from the high table, and he sent DUNSTAN, the Abbot of Glastonbury, to find him. Monkish chroniclers biased in favour of Dunstan made much of the incident that followed. The abbot entered the King's chamber to find Edwy seated on a couch with his cousin Elgiva, with whom he was in love, and her mother Ethelgiva. His crown lay discarded on the floor and Dunstan, who had been allowed to scourge the previous king for the good of

his soul, had no compunction in dragging Edwy ignominiously back to the banquet. The King was never to forgive the abbot for this humiliation.

Ignoring the opposition of the Archbishop and Dunstan, Edwy announce that he was going marry Elgiva. The clergy professed themselves shocked because it would be a marriage of cousins, but the King refused to be cowed by the clerical party and struck back by calling upon Dunstan to account for the huge sums of money with which the previous king had entrusted him. He refused, arguing that the money was given to him for religious purposes and he was answerable only to God. Thereupon Edwy banished him and Dunstan went to a monastery in Flanders, from where he mounted a whispering campaign against the King. Soon afterwards a revolt flared up in Northumbria and Mercia in favour of the King's brother, Edgar. When the Mercian nobles were considering their choice of a leader a mighty voice, as though from heaven, echoed through the hall, commanding them to choose Edgar, who also happened to be Dunstan's choice. Another miracle occurred when a statue of Christ became vocal and endorsed Dunstan's policies.

Legend tells that Queen Elgiva was kidnapped from a royal residence, branded on the forehead and shipped to Ireland as a slave. When she was recognised she was released, healed of her wound and

Above: St Dunstan dragging the newly crowned Edwy back to his coronation feast after finding the youth with his cousin Elgiva.

Below: The mortuary chest in Winchester Cathedral which contains the remains of King Egbert who died in AD 839.

returned to England in September 959. Travelling to rejoin her husband she was in the vicinity of Gloucester when her cavalcade was set upon by armed men who attacked her with their swords and left her to die. When the news reached Edwy he was so distraught that he died at Gloucester on 1 October 959; it was said, of a broken heart. He was interred in Winchester Cathedral.

Even out of this tragedy Dunstan was able to make a holy capital, revealing that he had a vision in which he saw Edwy's soul being borne away by demons but, as a result of his prayers, the demons fled and the late king was saved from the torments of hell.

EGBERT The son of Ealhmund, King of Kent, Egbert was born sometime in the decade following AD 769. For attempting to claim the West Saxon kingship, following the death of Cynegils in AD 786, he was forced to flee to the court of Charlemagne. However, in AD 802 he succeeded Beorhtrica as King of Wessex. In a war with the Mercians his great victory of Ellandune, probably fought near Winchester, gave him the overlordship of Mercia. In AD 829 he was accepted by the Northumbrians as their suzerain which made him the first real King of England, although that title was not used. He died in AD 839.

ELEANOR CROSSES On 28 November 1290 QUEEN ELEANOR died of a fever at Harby Manor in Nottinghamshire while travelling to Scotland with her husband EDWARD I. For thirty-six years she had been the king's companion on his journeys and campaigns, and had borne him sixteen children including the future EDWARD II. In his anguish at her death the king wrote: 'My harp is tuned to mourning, in life I loved her dearly, nor can I cease to love her in death.'

At the twelve places where her cortège halted for the night on its way to London Edward had a memorial cross erected and no other English king left such enduring tokens of the love he bore his

The Northampton Eleanor Cross, one of the three original crosses to have survived of the twelve set up by the grief-stricken Edward I.

wife. The most splendid of these crosses was the Charing Cross where the procession halted before Eleanor was interred in WESTMINSTER ABBEY. Built of Caen stone at a cost of £650 it included eight figures of the queen and survived until 1647 when it was demolished by order of Parliament. In 1863 the present replica was erected by the London, Clapham & Dover Railway Company. Three of the original crosses are still to be seen, at Geddington, Northampton and Waltham. In Westminster Abbey Queen Eleanor's gilt bronze effigy above her altar tomb is perhaps the most beautiful of such figures to have survived from medieval times.

ELEANOR OF AQUITAINE When William X, Duke of Aquitaine died on a pilgrimage to the Shrine of St James of Compostela, his dying wish was that his daughter Eleanor, the 15-year-old heiress to his vast dominions, should marry Louis, the son of King Louis the Fat of France. The king approved the match as it meant that the south-west of France, from the borders of Brittany and Anjou to the Pyrenees, would be added to his kingdom. The magnificent marriage ceremony took place at Bordeaux in April 1137, the bridegroom being escorted by five hundred knights.

As a child, Eleanor's new husband had been educated at the abbey of St Denis. It was his dearest wish to take holy orders, but when his elder brother was killed he became heir to the throne and was told that he must concentrate on the kingdom of France rather than on the kingdom of heaven. In contrast Eleanor was worldly and highly talented; her skill in writing poetry and music was admired by the troubadours of Provence and she was famous for her Courts of Love, an aristocratic game in which its noble company debated the philosophy of courtly love.

Within a month of the wedding, King Louis the Fat died and Eleanor became Queen of France when her husband was crowned Louis VII.

On 31 March 1146 Bernard, Abbot of Clairvaux, later known as St Bernard, preached to a huge crowd. He began by repeating the news from Outremer, the Christian enclave in the Holy Land, that Edessa had fallen to the heathen Turks who had massacred its Christian inhabitants, and he announced that Pope Eugenius III had approved a crusade. When his oration came to its emotional climax with an appeal to men to go forth and defend the true faith, King Louis stood up and 'took the

Cross'. Never before had a sovereign left his kingdom to do battle with the infidel, but the cheers which greeted Louis's declaration reached a level of hysteria when Eleanor rose and vowed to go on the crusade with him and so the Second Crusade began its ten-month journey to Antioch.

The royal couple were welcomed by Eleanor's uncle, Raymond of Poitou, Prince of Antioch who, only seven years older than the Queen, was 'more handsome than any man of his time', according to a contemporary description. The King, suffering from the effects of the great march, brooded while his wife and Raymond joked and conversed in the *langue d'oc*, the language of Provence, and listened to the prince's troubadours. For Eleanor it was not only a case of flirting with a handsome relative but it was a return to the way of life she had enjoyed in Aquitaine.

The situation became tense when Raymond urged that the Christian army should recapture Edessa, the purpose of the crusade, but King Louis announced he would visit Jerusalem before engaging on anything else. Raymond pointed out the vulnerability of his kingdom unless the Turks were defeated, asking the King to attack Edessa first. Eleanor supported him and soon she and Louis were shouting at each other. When he threatened to force her to go with him to Jerusalem she replied – according to the Chronicle of Guillaume de Nangis – 'that she would not live as the wife of a man whom she had discovered was her cousin, too near by the ordinance of the Church'.

Nevertheless, Eleanor was compelled to go with the French army to Jerusalem while Louis joined the Emperor of Germany in a futile siege of Damascus. At Easter 1149 Eleanor and Louis left the Holy Land in separate ships; the crusade failed because of the king's refusal to retake Edessa.

There was a temporary reconciliation between the King and Queen until Geoffrey the Fair, Count of Anjou, arrived at court. He was married to Matilda, Lady of England, the daughter of HENRY I of England, and as his only heir she had claims to both Normandy and England where STEPHEN, a descendant of WILLIAM I, had seized power. Eleanor was charmed by this new arrival, but when he died of fever she transferred her attentions to his 18-year-old son who was soon to become HENRY II of England. The intimacy that burgeoned between the two became such a scandal that the King forced Henry to return to Anjou and the Queen applied for a divorce on the grounds that Louis was a fourth cousin. Doubtless aware that Eleanor was pregnant by Henry, King Louis agreed and on 18 March 1152 the royal marriage was annulled on the grounds of consanguinity. Six weeks later Eleanor and Henry were married and four months later their son was born.

From his new wife Henry obtained the men and ships he needed to claim his English inheritance. He crossed the Channel in January 1153 and with an army so powerful that King Stephen agreed to him becoming Justiciar of England, with a guarantee that he would succeed to the throne. Stephen died in October 1154 and with the crowning of Henry and Eleanor on 19 December of that year at Westminster the PLANTAGENET dynasty began – and the beginning of strife between England and France that was to remain through the following centuries. King Louis had hoped the two daughters Eleanor bore him would ultimately inherit her duchy of Aquitaine, but when Eleanor married Henry and he became King of England it meant Aquitaine became an English possession which together with Normandy and Anjou was an additional danger to France.

Geoffrey the Fair, Count of Anjou who married Henry I's daughter Matilda and became the father of Henry II.

In England the new reign brought prosperity to the kingdom and happiness to the queen. Although her first son William died in 1156, she was to bear Henry three daughters and four sons, and of the latter RICHARD and JOHN were to wear the Crown.

Following the birth of John her love for Henry began to give way to enmity. She discovered that he had a mistress famously known as FAIR ROSAMOND and in 1173 the rift between the royal couple became so final that Eleanor actively encouraged her sons Henry and Richard to revolt against their father. When this failed, Henry and Richard fled to the French court and Eleanor was captured in male attire attempting to flee to Normandy. For the rest of Henry's life she was kept in 'honourable confinement'.

During an insurrection in 1183 Prince Henry died from fever, filled with remorse that he had taken up arms against his father. The shock of his death temporarily reconciled Henry and Eleanor, who was seen at court for several months before returning to comfortable captivity, but two years later their son Geoffrey was killed at a tournament.

Henry died of fever on 6 July 1189 at Chinon and was succeeded by Richard I who was with him. He immediately sent orders to England for the release of his mother. After being a prisoner for sixteen years she found herself Regent of England. Soon afterwards the new king departed for the Third Crusade while Eleanor arranged a marriage for him with Berengaria of Navarre. She then escorted the girl to Cyprus where the wedding took place before Richard continued to the Holy Land and military glory.

Eleanor was to help Richard again when he was captured on his journey back in 1192 and held for ransom by the German emperor. Thinking that the Pope was not doing enough for her son after he had taken a leading part in the crusade, she sent him several incensed letters which she signed 'Eleanor, by the wrath of God, Queen of England.' The ransom was finally set at the then colossal sum of £100,000, raised from the King's reluctant subjects in England, Normandy, Anjou and Aquitaine. Then, although she was now over 70, Eleanor travelled with the convoy carrying the ransom to Cologne for fear that the King's brother John might waylay it. She had no illusions about her youngest son and his conspiracy against Richard while he was out of the kingdom, but later she reconciled the brothers and John remained the royal heir. In February 1194 Richard was liberated when the ransom was paid.

Five years later King Richard was mortally wounded by an arrow he received while besieging the castle of Chaluz. Eleanor was summoned from the abbey of Fontevrault and arrived at his deathbed in time to hold him before he died. When John succeeded to the throne Eleanor remained a potent political figure, crushing an Angevin rising against John in favour of her grandson Prince Arthur. On 1 April 1204 Queen Eleanor died and was interred in Fontrevault Abbey beside her husband Henry II and her son Richard, and for centuries their effigies have gazed serenely at the high vaulted ceiling without a hint of the turbulent passions they once shared.

ELEANOR OF PROVENCE Surnamed 'La Belle', Eleanor of Provence and wife of HENRY III, was probably England's most unpopular queen consort. She was not cruel, did not tyrannise her subjects or encourage war and was loyal to her husband. Yet her extravagance affected the kingdom, and for this she became hated. The second of the five beautiful daughters of Count Berenger of Provence, Eleanor had a talent for poetry. When as a girl she wrote a romantic epic on the Cornish folk hero Blandin and sent a copy to Richard, Earl of Cornwall, he thought so highly of the verses and their charming author that he suggested to his brother Henry that she would make him a suitable wife. The King had already been rejected in turn by princesses of Scotland, Bretagne, Austria and Bohemia, but these disappointments had been political rather than personal for Henry who was renowned for his unusual celibacy.

The effigy of Eleanor of Aquitaine above her tomb in Fontevrault Abbey near Chinon, France. (*Photograph by Paul Abrahams*)

In 1235 the Earl of Ponthieu had accepted Henry as a prospective son-in-law and ambassadors set out to seek papal approval, but before they reached Rome they were overtaken by a courier who told them to return to England. The King had changed his mind about the earl's daughter, so influenced was he by Richard's eulogies on Eleanor that he was determined that she should be his queen. As Louis IX of France had married one of Eleanor's sisters, the King's advisers were enthusiastic for the match because of its obvious political advantages. The couple were married on 4 January 1236 and magnificent preparations were made for the coronation of the new queen.

A column of 360 leading citizens in robes 'embroidered with gold and silk of divers colours' conducted Henry and Eleanor to WESTMINSTER ABBEY from the TOWER OF LONDON, each man holding high a silver or gold goblet as a wedding gift. The King's famous piety did not hamper his passion for finery and display, not only for himself, but for members of his court and his bride. It has been estimated that for her coronation he gave Eleanor jewels then worth £30,000, a sum difficult to translate into today's money but its magnitude may be deduced from the weekly wages of between 6d and 1s paid to manual workers.

Despite the troubles that had been associated with the reign of Henry's father JOHN, England was now enjoying a period of prosperity and the King's subjects doubtless regarded the display of royal opulence as a reflection of their own improved circumstances. But it was not long before enthusiasm for the new queen was replaced by complaint.

After Eleanor had given birth to the future EDWARD I, her mother Beatrice brought Eleanor's sister Sanchia to England to be affianced to the King's recently widowed brother, the Earl Richard. Eleanor prevailed upon Henry to entertain her kinsfolk so lavishly that the King soon found that he could not afford to continue such hospitality. He therefore devised a scheme – which he was to use over and over again – in which he demanded from every sheriff in the kingdom the names of the six richest Jews in each large town and the two richest in smaller ones. Those named were ordered to assemble before him in order to 'treat with him for their mututal benefit' in what was to become tagged as the 'Jews' Parliament'. It was soon obvious that the only ones to benefit from the meeting were Eleanor's relations, the Jews being told that they must raise a sum of 20,000 marks.

In 1242 Henry set out on an ill-fated expedition against the King of France on behalf of his mother, Isabella of Angoulême, now married to Hugh de Lusignan of Gascony, who demanded aid against French oppression. Eleanor travelled with the army despite the fact she was pregnant and the campaign's timetable became geared to her confinement.

When the French army advanced on Henry his Gascon allies deserted and the English were mauled on their retreat to the safety of Bordeaux. During the campaign the King's military chest and portable chapel with its costly plate were lost, but this loss, coupled with the cost of the campaign, did not inhibit the royal couple. After Eleanor gave birth to a daughter she and Henry ordered tournaments and pageants as though celebrating a victory rather than a debacle, to the extent that the last of the campaign funds were spent. Most of the disillusioned nobles went back to England, but it was a year before Henry and Eleanor could follow as he 'had sunk into such poverty that despite the heavy taxes he had levied he was tied to Gascony by his debts'.

Queen Eleanor at the banquet held for her after her coronation, which was one of the most extravagant in British history.

In October 1243 the King and Queen returned to the kingdom where they arranged extravagant festivities to celebrate Sanchia's marriage to Earl Richard. The cost was borne by the Jews, one of them being the famous Aaron of York who was forced to contribute 400 gold marks and 4,000 silver. Matthew Paris wrote: 'The King thought he could not do enough to testify his love for the Queen . . .' When the royal debts reached 1 million marks the king turned to his Council for help. This was given in return for certain concessions, such as a say in the appointment of ministers. Meanwhile, Eleanor had her own method of raising money. Part of the revenue provided for queen consorts was raised from customs dues levied at their own wharf, known as Queenhithe, and to the resentment of London merchant ships with valuable cargoes were forced to unload at Eleanor's quay.

The reign continued to be one of royal profligacy and insolvency. On one occasion Henry, having already pawned the CROWN JEWELS and unable to pay the officers of the Chapel Royal at Windsor, pawned 'the most valuable image of the Virgin Mary for the sum required'.

Unrest against the monarchy spread through England as Henry failed to keep his promise to the Council and his subjects, and at Easter in 1262 anti-Semitic rioting ended with an attack on Eleanor. The contemporary chronicler Thomas Wikes wrote: 'Besides plundering and killing five hundred of this devoted race, the mob turned the rest out of their beds, undressed as they were. The next morning they commenced the work of plunder with such outrageous yells that the Queen, who was then at the Tower, seized with mortal terror, got into her barge with many of her great ladies, the wives and daughters of the noblest, intending to escape by water to Windsor Castle.'

As the royal barge approached London Bridge a hail of 'everything vile' was flung down on it by a mob chanting, 'Drown the witch!' This referred to a slander spread by the Queen's enemies that she had obtained help from a woman proficient in black magic to kill a beautiful girl who had caught the attention of the king. The tale was very similar to the libel spread about ELEANOR OF AQUITAINE, its perpetrators not having the imagination to change the victim's name from Rosamond. When the missiles hurled at the queen became stones and balks of timber, the rowers did not wait for an order to race back to the Tower.

Civil war followed between the king and the barons, led by Simon de Montfort, and when Henry was captured, Eleanor crossed the Channel to sell her jewels in order to pay for an invasion of the rebellious kingdom. This sacrifice, however, was not needed after royalist forces won the Battle of Evesham, where Simon de Montfort was killed. Back on his throne Henry, remembering the insult to his queen by the London mob, levied a collective fine of 20,000 marks on the city, all of which was paid to the Queen.

Henry died on 16 November 1272 and some years later Eleanor, with the kingdom under the firm hand of her son EDWARD I, became a nun at Amesbury Abbey after obtaining permission from the pope to retain her dower. She died in 1291 and was buried in the abbey.

ELIZABETH I The daughter of HENRY VIII and Anne Boleyn, Elizabeth was born at Greenwich Palace on 7 September 1533. When only 14 she received her first marriage proposal from Thomas, Lord Seymour, who saw the advantages of marrying into the royal family as the reigns of Elizabeth's sickly half-brother EDWARD VI and his half-sister MARY were likely to be short. But in a letter Elizabeth thwarted his ambitions, writing: 'My Lord

A Victorian engraving from an early portrait of Elizabeth with her coronation regalia.

Admiral . . . I confess that your letter very much surprised me, for besides that neither my age nor my inclination allow me to think of marriage, I never could have believed that anyone could have spoken to me of nuptials at a time when I ought to think of nothing but sorrow for the death of my father.'

Roman Catholic Queen Mary knew that the Protestants regarded her half-sister Elizabeth as their champion and sent her to the TOWER OF LONDON. She arrived in the rain at Traitor's Gate on 17 March 1554. But in May the same year Elizabeth was sent into custody at Woodstock Palace, where she was so scrupulous in her practice of the Roman Catholic religion that by Christmas she was back in court.

When Queen Mary died in November 1558 ROBERT DUDLEY hurried to Hatfield to offer homage to the new queen and, as her MASTER OF HORSE, escorted her regal entry into London on 28 November. When she was crowned on 15 January 1559 at WESTMINSTER ABBEY she was given an enthusiastic reception by her subjects, who approved her boast that she was 'the most English woman in the kingdom'.

Protestants and Roman Catholics wondered whether Elizabeth favoured the faith of her father or her sister. Catholics were delighted when she allowed Queen Mary to be interred with Catholic rites and permitted Mass to be heard in private, but when at her coronation the oath of allegiance styled her the Supreme Governor of the Church of England, it became apparent she favoured neither party.

After ascending the throne Elizabeth made no attempt to conceal her affection for her handsome Master of the Horse and, although married, Robert Dudley was never absent from her side. Then in September 1560 Dudley's wife Amy Robsart died alone and under mysterious circumstances at her home after sending all her servants to a country fair. The extraordinary thing was that prior to September ambassadors reported that the Queen and Dudley would marry, yet all knew it was impossible while Amy lived. Elizabeth's dilemma was that if she married Dudley it would be seen as condoning his guilt; if she did not it would be said she doubted his innocence. Although they did not marry, Dudley remained her favourite courtier and in 1564 was created Earl of Leicester. In 1563 the future marriage of MARY, QUEEN OF SCOTS, arose and with great political acumen Elizabeth suggested Dudley as a possible husband for her Scottish rival. Mary, however, chose her cousin Henry Stuart, Lord Darnley.

Mary, Queen of Scots, posed a tremendous problem for Elizabeth. She knew that Mary would be a focus for Catholic plots. In November 1569 rebellion broke out in the North. Characteristically the Queen was more upset by the cost of the campaign against the rebels than the threat they posed to her throne and Elizabeth's nobles crushed the revolt.

To the displeasure of Leicester and the court Elizabeth found a new favourite. He was a young lawyer named Christopher Hatton who owed his good fortune to the queen being impressed by his graceful dancing at a masque. She appointed him Captain of the Guard after which his rise was meteoric, culminating in his appointment as Lord Chancellor in 1587. Elizabeth treated him with extravagant affection. Missives flowed between them and to the delight of the queen he was as skilful at penning compliments as he was at dancing.

On the morning of 24 August 1572 – St Bartholomew's Day – Protestants were stunned by the massacre of many thousands of Huguenots in France. Elizabeth was reluctant to grant the French ambassador an audience and when he was finally admitted to the royal presence the entire court was in mourning. Nobles turned him away, but this did not prevent him passing a letter to the Queen from Francis, the DUC D'ALENÇON, the son of Catherine de' Medici who had ordered the massacre, nor did it prevent Elizabeth reading it on the spot.

The Queen had started a bizarre relationship with the Duc d'Alençon who was twenty-three years younger than her and has been described as a 'hideous dwarf', smallpox having left his face

The signature of Elizabeth I. A practical purpose of the scrolled line was to prevent a postscript being added by another hand.

scarred and his body stunted. His blotched skin coupled with his misshapen body gave him a frog-like appearance and Elizabeth nicknamed him her 'petit grenouille'.

In November 1582 d'Alençon and Elizabeth exchanged rings in front of the Spanish ambassador, Elizabeth telling him, 'You may write this to the king, the Duc d'Alençon shall be my husband.' However, the Queen was persuaded not to run the risk of suffering as Queen Mary had done at the hands of a foreign consort. In the morning she told the duke that she was 'determined to sacrifice her own happiness for the welfare of her people' – d'Alençon hurled his ring to the floor, declaring 'the women of England are as changeable and capricious as their own climate'.

In middle age Elizabeth suffered from ill-health and melancholia, yet her tremendous vitality always overcame physical disabilities and she never lost her vanity.

Plots centring round Mary Stuart continued, culminating in the BABINGTON PLOT of 1586. On 15 October at Fotheringhay Castle Mary was charged with conspiring to bring about the death of the queen and the invasion of England. The results of the hearing were laid before both Houses of Parliament and on 12 November they presented a petition to the queen that Mary Stuart should be executed without delay.

Elizabeth demurred, knowing that if the execution was carried out the political consequences would be enormous. Then, in January 1587, false rumours spread that Mary Stuart had escaped and Spaniards had landed at Milford. Against a background of public turmoil Elizabeth signed Mary's death warrant on 1 February, but still she hesitated to implement it. Two days later William Cecil persuaded the Privy Council to risk the queen's displeasure and dispatch the warrant.

While the final drama of Mary, Queen of Scots, was played out Sir Francis Drake was away on his piratical activities, in which Elizabeth took a financial interest. After attacking Cadiz he returned with the news that Philip II of Spain, the widower of Queen Mary, had prepared a fleet to invade England. His Armada consisted of 129 ships carrying 20,000 soldiers intended as an escort for the Duke of Parma's Spanish army which was to cross from Dunkirk in barges.

Elizabeth loathed the thought of spending money in preparing warships to counter the Spanish fleet.

Of the force that finally met the Spaniards only a third were financed by the royal purse, the rest being fitted out by patriotic merchants and the smaller seaports.

The Spaniards were disconcerted by the superior speed of the English ships and their raking broadsides which had been the inspiration of HENRY VIII. Despite this their numbers were almost intact when they anchored off Calais. Then, as the Armada moved on to join the Duke of Parma, it was struck by such strong gales it was swept past the rendezvous point. Although only ten galleons had been sunk by English ships, over fifty were lost in the storms.

On 8 August Elizabeth visited the army at Tilbury and encouraged the troops with her famous speech: 'I know I have but the body of a weak and feeble woman, but I have the heart of a King, and a King of England too; and think foul scorn that Parma or Spain, or any other prince of Europe . . . , should dare to invade the borders of my realm. . . . I myself will be your general – the judge and rewarder of every one of your virtues in the field.' The defeat of King Philip's Armada resulted in England becoming the most commanding state in Europe and guaranteed the kingdom's security for the rest of Elizabeth's reign.

Elizabeth was 55 when a final favourite appeared on the scene. Thirty-three years her junior, he was Robert Devereux, the second Earl of Essex and the stepson of Leicester who had recently died. As with the Queen's previous favourites his rise was fast and in 1593 he became a Privy Councillor, Master of Horse and a member of the Order of the Garter. In 1596 he was put in charge of an expedition to capture Cadiz and on 20 June he took the city by surprise. It was the last great naval success of Elizabeth's reign and it established Essex as the most powerful man at court where he often spent evenings with Elizabeth 'playing at cards or other games until the birds were singing the morning'.

The French ambassador wrote a description of the ageing Queen: 'As for her face, it appears very aged. It is long and thin, and her teeth are yellow and unequal. Many of them are missing, so that one cannot understand her easily when she speaks quickly.'

On 4 August 1598 William Cecil, the architect of Elizabeth's greatness, died, and his son Robert became the new Secretary of State. Essex had hoped for the post himself but he had quarrelled with the Queen over who was to become Lord Deputy of

William Cecil, Elizabeth I's chief minister for forty years and one of England's greatest statesmen.

Ireland. At its height the Queen struck his ear, bidding him 'Go and be hanged!' Before he could control himself Essex laid his hand on his sword hilt. It was a fatal moment, and soon he was sent to tackle the Irish problem.

In September 1599, he made a truce with Tyrone, the rebels' leader, to the fury of Elizabeth, who had warned him against concluding any agreement with the Irish. In panic he left Dublin against orders for

The Great Seal of Elizabeth I.

an audience with the queen at NONSUCH PALACE. At first she was pleased to see her impetuous favourite, but by the afternoon of the next day she had had a change of heart. The Council charged him with disobeying the queen and deserting his command. He answered these accusations with such logic that many were in favour of releasing him but the angry queen ordered that he should remain a prisoner in his house. Then came news that Tyrone had broken the truce.

Essex now believed that Robert Cecil and others were in league to arrange the English succession for the Spanish Infanta and, declaring he must save the country from its recent enemy, he plotted to take possession of the court and force the Queen to renounce Cecil. When news of this reached Elizabeth, Essex was again summoned by the Council and when found guilty of treason he said, 'I would not that any man should give the Queen to understand that I condemn her mercy, which notwithstanding I believe I shall not fawningly beg.' There was no mercy. On 25 February 1601 the fallen favourite was beheaded.

Early in February 1603 Elizabeth caught a cold and went to Richmond where she became very ill. Not wishing to become bedridden she 'stood upon her feet for fifteen hours'. When Robert Cecil told her that she must go to bed she retorted, 'The word must is not to be used to princes. Little man, little man, you know I must die, and that makes you so presumptuous.'

Elizabeth's nobles begged her to name her heir and as she could no longer speak, they asked her to make a sign when they spoke the name of the person she favoured when a list of candidates was read. At the name of one the Queen was so indignant that she forced herself to say, 'I will have no rascal's son in my seat. It is the throne of kings.'

These words were her last. She died early on 24 March and was interred in Westminster Abbey on 28 April 1603.

ELIZABETH II The first child of Albert, Duke of York and Elizabeth Bowes-Lyon, Princess Elizabeth Alexandra Mary was born at her parents' home at 17 Bruton Street, London, on 21 April 1926. Destined to become Elizabeth II of England, her royal blood line can be traced back to the Saxon KING ALFRED and to ROBERT RAGNDVALSSON, 1st Duke of Normandy. When she was 9 years old she made her first public appearance during the Silver Jubilee of her grandfather GEORGE V. Following his

ELIZABETH II

Princess Elizabeth and Princess Margaret Rose on their ponies in Windsor Great Park. *(Getty Images)*

death in 1936 Elizabeth's uncle, Edward, became king but abdicated in December of that year in order to marry Wallis Simpson. Changing his name to George, Elizabeth's father ascended the throne on 11 December 1936, thus making his daughter heiress presumptive.

In 1940, following the outbreak of the Second World War, Elizabeth made her first wireless broadcast to the children of the Empire who were in danger or separated from their parents. When she was 18 an Act of Parliament made her eligible to become one of the counsellors of state to act for the King when he travelled abroad visiting the British Empire.

After the end of the war the princess accompanied her parents on a South African tour and soon afterwards came the announcement of her engagement to her cousin PHILIP MOUNTBATTEN who, like her, is a great-great-grandchild of QUEEN VICTORIA. They were married in WESTMINSTER ABBEY on 20 November 1947 and Prince Philip was created Duke of Edinburgh. On 14 November of the following year CHARLES, the first of their three sons, was born at BUCKINGHAM PALACE. On 15 August 1950 a daughter was

born to Elizabeth and Prince Philip at CLARENCE HOUSE and was named Anne Elizabeth Alice Louise. In 1987 she was designated Princess Royal.

When King George VI died on 6 February 1952 Elizabeth and her husband were on a Commonwealth tour. They flew urgently from Kenya to London where she held her first Privy Council and began her royal duties which she has performed tirelessly throughout her reign. As queen her official title is: Her Most Excellent Majesty Elizabeth the Second (Elizabeth Alexandra Mary of Windsor) by the Grace of God, of the United Kingdom of Great Britain and Northern Ireland and of Her other Realms and Territories; Defender of the Faith; Head of the Commonwealth; Sovereign of the British Orders of Knighthood and Sovereign Head of the Order of St John; and Lord High Admiral of the United Kingdom. Among her numerous royal duties the Queen is Colonel-in-Chief to twenty-nine military corps, ranging from the Life Guards to the Malawi Rifles; she is Captain-General of ten others, mainly overseas. She is also Head of the Civil Defence Corps and Master of the Merchant Navy and Fishing Fleets.

The Queen was to have two more sons. On 19 February 1960 Andrew Albert Christian Edward was born at Buckingham Palace. In 1986 he was created Duke of York, Earl of Inverness and Baron Killalee. His younger brother Edward Antony Richard Louis was born on 10 March 1964 and in 1999 was created Earl of Wessex.

No sovereign before Elizabeth has had a reign in which there has been so much social change and in which, since Lord Altrincham's famous attack on the monarchy, there has been so much critical intrusion by the media. Apart from national tensions relating to economic problems, the troubles in Ulster and minor wars, the Queen has had her domestic problems. In the spotlight of publicity she has had to face the failure of marriages within her family which made her refer to an unhappy year as the 'annus horribilis'. Yet despite the changing attitudes and values of her subjects she has managed, with the encouragement of Prince Philip, to retain the dignity required by her role as figurehead and ambassador of the kingdom. Her success as a tradi-

Opposite: Queen Elizabeth II (left) with Queen Mary (centre) and Queen Elizabeth the Queen Mother at King George VI's funeral, 15 February 1952. *(Getty Images)*

Elizabeth & Philip

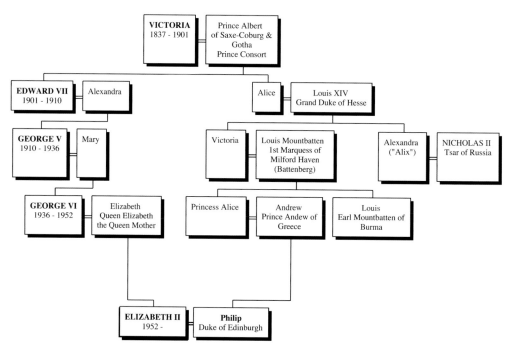

tional monarch in a changing world was endorsed by the vast public enthusiasm for her Golden Jubilee celebrations in 2002.

ELIZABETH'S MERLIN Dr John Dee, born in 1527, was regarded – and feared – as a wizard after he studied at St John's College, Cambridge, and became one of the original Fellows of Trinity. His interests were alchemy, astrology, astronomy and mathematics, subjects regarded as arcane in Tudor times. During the reign of MARY I he was charged with using witchcraft to harm the queen but he was freed through lack of evidence. On Mary's death ELIZABETH I asked him to predict an auspicious date for her coronation, and subsequently he was frequently at court where he advised the queen on her health and other matters, earning the sobriquet of 'Elizabeth's Merlin'. He travelled abroad to further his alchemic studies, and was thought to have acted as a secret agent for the queen. His magical practices were said to have included scrying with a magical mirror and summoning spirits by means of a crystal globe.

In the last decade of the sixteenth century Dee was made Warden of Manchester College. When he died in 1608 and was buried in Mortlake Church he left behind seventy-nine works on subjects ranging from the calendar to an account of a conversation with an angel.

ELTHAM PALACE For several centuries Eltham Palace in Kent was a favourite retreat for England's sovereigns as it had the pleasant advantages of a country manor and yet royal parties had only to travel a few miles south from London to reach it. When the DOMESDAY BOOK was compiled between 1084 and 1086 it was owned by BISHOP ODO, the half-brother of WILLIAM I. In 1295 it was largely rebuilt and made 'fit for a king' by Antony Bek, the Bishop of Durham, before being presented to the future EDWARD II. During his ill-starred reign the king had further building work carried out for Queen Isabella who spent much of her time there, doubtless reflecting on the short-comings of her husband.

Their son EDWARD III also found the palace greatly to his liking and it was there that he entertained his royal prisoner, King John II of France. At this time the French chronicler Jean Froissart wrote that Eltham was 'a very magnificent palace which the king possessed seven miles from London'. After RICHARD II came to the throne he employed Geoffrey Chaucer to oversee further building work which was later continued by HENRY IV. In 1444 HENRY VI married Margaret of Anjou by proxy and extensions to the palace were undertaken urgently in order that it would be suitably splendid for the arrival of the new queen.

It was during the reign of EDWARD IV which followed that the palace's magnificent Great Hall, still to be seen, was constructed and remains a gem of late medieval architecture. It is noted in particular for its great hammer beam, the third largest in England after those of WESTMINSTER and HAMPTON COURT.

Soon after HENRY VIII came to the throne he added to the palace by building a chapel there, and it was from the palace that he issued the Statutes of Eltham. These were regulations for the running of the royal household produced for the king by THOMAS WOLSEY, then Lord Chancellor. Highly detailed, they included such directives as ordering the king's barber to avoid 'vile persons' while attendants serving food were forbidden to wipe their hands on the royal tapestries.

The palace had been allowed to deteriorate in the first half of the seventeenth century. Its connection with royalty virtually ended with the execution of CHARLES I and it was taken over by Parliament. It was purchased by Colonel Nathaniel Rich who began to demolish it and, after visiting Eltham in 1656, John Evelyn wrote, 'Both the palace and chapel in miserable ruins, the noble wood and park destroyed by Rich, the Rebel.'

With the Restoration what remained of the palace was returned to the Crown but its days of glory were over. In 1663 the manor was leased to Sir John Shaw who left the ruins as they were but rebuilt the manor lodge which, as Eltham Lodge, today is the clubhouse of the Royal Blackheath Golf Club. The Great Hall remained standing and was used as a barn and its now humble interior was the subject of a painting by Turner in 1790. Thirty-eight years later the building was repaired enough to preserve it but it was not until 1931 that Stephen Courtauld gained the lease of the property and began the proper restoration of the Great Hall, which was completed six years later. Towards the end of the Second World War Eltham Palace was acquired by the War Department, and today its lease is held by the Institute of Education which allows public admittance to the Great Hall.

EMMA The daughter of Richard I, Duke of Normandy, Emma was the mother of two kings of England. In 1002 she became the second wife of ETHELRED II ('The Unready') and their son was the future EDWARD THE CONFESSOR. After Ethelred's death in 1016 she married KING CANUTE and bore him KING HARDICANUTE. Her importance in history is that through her, England and Norway established a dynastic connection. It was to Normandy that she sent her son Edward for safety during Danish rule of England, which was one of the factors that led to the Norman Conquest.

ERIC BLOODAXE If ever a king was rightly named it was Eric Bloodaxe, the son of Harold Fairhair of Norway. For a short period he followed his father as King of Norway, during which time he slew his brother and achieved a reputation for ruthlessness and ferocity, which led to him being driven out of his kingdom in AD 946. The following year he became King of York. Eight years later the Northumbrians banished Eric when KING EDRED led his army north. Eric made for the Norse kingdom of Dublin, but was slain at the Battle of Stainmore, which marked the end of Scandinavian control of York. Typically, the symbol on his coinage was a sword.

ETHELBERT It is generally reckoned that Ethelbert, King of Kent, achieved the hegemony over England south of the Humber about the year AD 590. Some time before this he had married Bertha, the Christian daughter of Charibert, the Frankish King of Paris. When she came to England Bertha brought Bishop Liudhard with her and her pagan husband allowed them to practise their religion. When St Augustine arrived in Kent in AD 579, on his mission to convert the English, the King showed the same tolerance by allowing him to preach on a site in Canterbury which later became the cathedral church. Encouraged by his queen, Ethelbert became a convert and was followed by many of his subjects which, because of the size of his kingdom, had a profound effect on the re-establishment of Christianity in England. Ethelbert was also responsible for the first written English laws.

A coin from the reign of Ethelred.

ETHELRED II Born in AD 968, Ethelred was the son of KING EDGAR and his second wife Elfrida. During his life he became known as 'The Redeless' or 'The Unraed' – both sobriquets meaning 'without counsel' – which evolved into 'The Unready'. He was only 10 years old when he came to the throne following the assassination of his half-brother EDWARD THE MARTYR. And with his reign came what could be termed the twilight of Saxon England. When he stood by his mother and saw his beloved half-brother Edward murdered at her command he cried so bitterly that she beat him violently with a long candle, so that for the whole of his reign he refused to have candles carried in procession before him. On his coronation day

The Saxon Kings

Archbishop Dunstan was said to have forecast that his reign would be an evil one because he had become king as a result of murder.

For a while the boy king was greatly under the influence of his fiercely ambitious mother but as he grew up this declined and finally she retired to a nunnery which she established at Wherewell to spend her remaining days in prayerful repentance. The other dominating influence in the king's life was Dunstan, the Archbishop of Canterbury, and only when he died in AD 988 was Ethelred at last able to rule as he thought fit. His first significant act of kingship came in AD 991 when there was a Norwegian invasion led by Olaf Tryggvason who later became king of Norway. Ethelred decided to buy peace and agreed to pay 22,000 pounds of silver and gold to the invaders in return for them leaving his kingdom and promising not to attack English shipping. The Norsemen – known in old chronicles as Danes regardless of what area of Scandinavia they came from – were ready to agree to anything for such a vast amount of treasure, but soon their longships were sailing back to England to demand an even greater tribute. Ethelred agreed to pay and a special tax, known as 'Danegeld', was levied on all English subjects to buy peace. When the next demand came, which once more the king agreed to pay, many Englishmen felt they would rather face warfare with the Vikings than pay this humiliating tax.

In 1002 a Danish fleet was once more prowling off the shore of England and once more it was decreed that Danegeld should be collected. This time Ethelred secretly prepared to pay his enemies with cold iron rather than bright silver, and messages were dispatched to every town in the realm ordering that on St Brice's Day, 13 November, all the Danes who had settled in England since King Alfred's agreement to the establishment of the Danelaw should be put to the sword. As there was a state of peace with the immigrants at

English subjects paying Danegeld, a tax introduced by Ethelred to buy off Danish invaders rather than fight them.

the time, England's Danish population was taken completely by surprise on the day of the mass execution. Among the thousands who perished in the massacre was a Danish lady named Gunhilda who was the wife of an English noble. Unfortunately for England she was also the sister of Sweyn FORKBEARD, the King of Denmark.

Ethelred, in a charter dated 1004, referred to the massacre as a most 'just slaughter', but it had the opposite effect to what he wanted. For one thing the Danes who perished were peaceful settlers who probably wanted nothing better than to be on good terms with their Saxon neighbours, not the mail-coated 'sea wolves' who only stayed long enough to collect their tribute. Worse, the murder of Gunhilda inspired in Sweyn a remorseless blood feud against the English king which no amount of Danegeld would ever assuage.

Earlier in the same fateful year as the St Brice's Day massacre Ethelred had married his second wife Emma, the daughter of the Duke of Normandy. By his first wife, Elgiva, who had died in 1003, the king had three sons, and Emma was to bear him two more. These were brought up in their mother's

113

homeland thus creating the relationship between the two countries that was destined to bring about the end of Anglo-Saxon independence.

The next year, as soon as the weather was favourable, Sweyn led his war fleet across the North Sea to mount an attack on the west of England in which Wilton and Salisbury were razed. Following this the Danish ships sailed to the coast of East Anglia, and Norwich and Thetford were reduced to ruins. In 1005 there was another massive raid and the harvest spoiled in the fields while the English took up arms to defend themselves but to little avail. The Danes plundered at will, then set up their base on the Isle of Wight from where they continued their work of revenge during the winter.

Yet again Ethelred bought temporary peace with Danegeld but in a series of raids in the following decade Sweyn realised there was more to be gained than silver in England – there was a crown to be won. In 1013 he brought an army from Denmark to occupy the north of England, after which Mercia was pillaged and then the invaders appeared before London. Ethelred prepared to stand siege in the city which managed to hold out until he boarded a ship in the Thames and sailed away to find refuge in Normandy. At his defection the Londoners laid down their weapons and such was their disillusion with Ethelred the Redeless that they were ready to regard Sweyn as a deliverer. He was proclaimed King of England but on 3 February 1014 he died unexpectedly at Gainsborough. The Danes chose Sweyn's son CANUTE as king but the English Witan sent a message to Ethelred inviting him back if only he would 'rule them rightlier than he had before'. In reply Ethelred sent his son EDWARD – later to be known as 'The Confessor' – to the Witan to announce that his father would be a good lord to them and 'abide by their will in all things'.

Following this promise Ethelred returned to England to be declared king again, after which he gathered a large army which defeated Canute at Lindsey. Canute returned to Denmark to raise fresh forces while Ethelred wrought terrible retribution on the local people who had sympathised with his enemy. Canute returned in 1015 when Ethelred was lying sick at Corsham in Wiltshire. His son EDMUND raised an army to meet the Danes and confused fighting followed in various parts of the kingdom. The next year, on 23 April, the king died in London and was interred in old St Paul's Cathedral as Canute was preparing to besiege the city.

F

FAIR ROSAMOND *See* CLIFFORD, ROSA-MOND

FALKLAND PALACE Though administered by the National Trust, Falkland Palace belongs to QUEEN ELIZABETH II, as does the PALACE OF HOLYROODHOUSE and Edinburgh Castle. The earliest castle buildings on the site date back to the twelfth century and vestiges of their foundations are still to be seen in the palace grounds. It was in 1402 that DAVID, DUKE OF ROTHESAY and the eldest son of ROBERT II, King of Scots, was imprisoned at Falkland by his uncle the Duke of Albany. On 26 March 1402 he died; it was claimed of dysentery, though it was widely believed that he was starved to death. Sir Walter Scott was convinced by the starvation theory and incorporated it into his novel *The Fair Maid of Perth*.

It was in the first half of the sixteenth century that the royal palace was built on the site of the old castle by JAMES IV of Scotland and, after his death on FLODDEN Field, by his son JAMES V. It was during the reign of the latter that a royal tennis court was built at the palace and today it remains the oldest in Britain. The architecture of the palace was a mixture of Scottish and French Renaissance styles, the south wall with its buttresses and battlements being Scottish Gothic while French masons created the walls in the central courtyard that were ahead of their time in 'auld alliance' design. The only interior part of the palace to survive from that period was the Chapel Royal which was finished shortly before James IV's death.

After the House of Stewart was established by ROBERT II in 1371, Falkland Palace was used as a superior hunting lodge by subsequent Scottish kings and queens when they followed the chase in the forest of Fife. After an exploding cannon killed JAMES II in 1460 his 9-year-old son became JAMES III while his mother Mary of Gueldres became Regent of Scotland. She was particularly fond of Falkland where she gave sanctuary to HENRY VI's queen Margaret of Anjou when she fled England as a result of the Wars of the Roses. MARY, QUEEN OF SCOTS made Falkland her preferred palace, a place where she could relax and enjoy something of the court life she had known in France without the criticism she received in Edinburgh.

When Mary's son JAMES VI married ANNE OF DENMARK in 1589 he gave her the palace, but after he became the first Stuart King of England fourteen years later the importance of Falkland faded. During the Civil War the east wing of the palace was destroyed by fire when Parliamentary soldiers were quartered there. The last monarch to visit the semi-ruined palace after a period of three centuries was ELIZABETH II who went there in 1958 for the 500th anniversary of Falkland receiving the charter that created it a royal borough.

FEUDAL SYSTEM A remarkable aspect of the reign of WILLIAM I was the speed with which the feudal system was established within nineteen years of the Conquest. Under the pyramidal social structure, with the king at its apex, the whole of the kingdom was divided into over sixty thousand *fiefs*, all of which belonged to the Crown. Varying numbers of these *fiefs* were allotted to the nobles as tenants, mainly men who had supported William in his crusade to claim the English throne, which gave many Norman barons vast manors. In return for these domains the nobles, known as *tenants-in-capite*, accepted that they were the vassals of the king and were bound to provide military service at their own cost for forty days in the year, and to pay certain charges. These élite *tenants-in-capite* then underlet land on similar conditions to subordinate tenants, known as *mesne-tenants*, who in turn could sublet to lesser vassals.

Under this system the king, if in need of military support, could call upon his vassal *tenants-in-capite*, who in turn would call upon their vassals and so on down the feudal chain, with the result that

115

it was possible for an army of around sixty thousand armed men to be raised. One of the advantages of the king being able to command such an army was that after the Conquest there were no more Norse invasions.

In order to keep control over his barons William made it law for all those who held land from the *mesne-tenants* down to take an oath of allegiance to the king as well as their own particular lord. At a great *gemot*, or assembly, held at Salisbury both English and Norman landholding nobles gathered to pay HOMAGE to the king in respect of their domains. This public confirmation of loyalty to the king increased the authority of the Crown in curbing refractory barons and began the process of unifying English and Normans into a single nation. William took care that the barons' great domains were spread widely across the kingdom, in order to prevent them amalgamating to form independent enclaves, and he also abolished the great pre-Conquest earldoms apart from those of Kent and Chester, and the bishopric of Durham.

Feudalism in England broke down in the fourteenth century, though remnants of the system continued until the reign of CHARLES II.

FIELD OF CLOTH OF GOLD In June 1520 HENRY VIII met Francis I of France at the Val d'Or near Guines with the idea of fostering a much needed friendship between their kingdoms. Both monarchs sought to eclipse the other by such extravagant displays of wealth that the area became known as the Field of the Cloth of Gold. For more than a fortnight the two kings enjoyed splendid tournaments and entertainments, wrestled together, jousted and concluded the great assembly with a Mass and banquet. The meeting remains famed for its magnificence, its site is still marked, but as a diplomatic exercise it was a failure.

FITZHERBERT, MARIA In 1756 Maria Anne Smythe – better remembered in history as Mrs Fitzherbert – was born into a Roman Catholic family which, while not aristocratic, moved in aristocratic circles, and as a girl Maria visited the French court. At the age of 19 she was married and widowed within a year. In 1778 she married again but in less than three years she was widowed for a second time. She now lived at Richmond and, thanks to her wit and pleasant manner, her home became the centre of a very fashionable set. When

she was introduced to George, Prince of Wales, later GEORGE IV, he fell in love with her. The fact that Maria was a widow six years his senior added to his infatuation. He was seeking a mature mistress, having had unfortunate experiences with younger women. One of these was the actress Mary Robinson who threatened to publish the prince's impassioned letters which his father GEORGE III bought back for £5,000 (approximately £450,000 today), plus an annual pension of £500.

The prince rightly recognised that such a lady as Mrs Fitzherbert would never take advantage of him, but to his chagrin Maria – described as being graceful with fine dark eyes and a splendid bosom – had no intention of becoming a royal concubine. This display of virtue fired the prince's desire to the point where he was determined to have her even if it meant flouting two Acts of Parliament – the ROYAL MARRIAGES ACT which stated that no son of the sovereign could marry under the age of 25 without his father's consent, and the ACT OF SETTLEMENT which stated that no heir to the throne could marry a Roman Catholic.

When Maria heard the prince declare his intention of marrying her regardless of the consequences she decided her best course was to make a prolonged visit to the Continent. When George learned of her plan its effect was melodramatic. In November 1784 four members of his household raced to Richmond to entreat Maria to return with them to CARLTON HOUSE where George had just stabbed himself, explaining that, according to his doctor, only her presence was likely to save the heir to the British throne. She agreed with the proviso that the Duchess of Devonshire should accompany her as a chaperone.

George's chest was still covered with blood when she entered a room in Carlton House and she was so distressed by the gory spectacle that she almost fainted. George explained that the thought of her departure had caused him to turn his sword upon himself, adding that 'nothing would induce him to live unless she would promise to become his wife'. In her shocked state Maria agreed. When this highly charged meeting was over the enormity of the situation struck Maria and she made the duchess sign a statement that 'promises obtain'd in such a manner are entirely void'. Next day she fled across the Channel and began a long Continental tour. The intriguing question was whether the prince had really tried to kill himself. Stories of the incident abounded, one suggesting he had not stabbed himself, having been bled by his doctor to relieve tension, he had rubbed blood over his chest.

Whatever the truth of the matter, the prince recovered rapidly and bombarded 'dearest and only beloved Maria' with letters of up to forty pages in length. Due to this persistence Maria was finally persuaded to return to England on condition that she and the prince should go through a formal marriage ceremony. This was performed secretly one evening at Maria's house in Park Street by the Reverend Robert Burt. It was claimed he was paid £500 (approximately £45,000 today) to clear his debts but there is no existing proof of this. George wrote on a sheet of plain paper: 'We, the undersigned, do witness that George Augustus Frederick, Prince of Wales, was married unto Maria Fitzherbert, this 15th of December 1785.' It was signed by the prince, his bride and the two witnesses. It was then given to Maria as her 'marriage lines'.

The couple now lived openly together in London though their marriage was denied in Parliament, to the distress of Maria who knew that while it might be valid under canon law it was invalid under civil law. At first George was happy with his 'wife' but when he was approaching 30, and had lost his boyish figure, he became enamoured with Frances, Lady Jersey who was determined to replace Maria. By now the prince was so deeply in debt he decided to fall in with his father's wish for him to make a legal and dynastic marriage in return for financial deliverance.

A marriage was arranged with Princess CAROLINE OF BRUNSWICK-WOLFENBÜTTEL but George parted from her after the birth of their daughter Charlotte. As the prince's ardour for Lady Jersey waned he tried to win Maria back but now he was officially married she remained aloof until she received a ruling from the Vatican stating that she could return to him without sin as she had been married to him by a priest first. With this papal endorsement the next eight years were happy ones for Maria but George began to find the relationship becoming too platonic and he turned to the statuesque Isabella, Marchioness of Hertford.

The final break came in 1803 when George planned an extravagant reception at Carlton House. Unable to end the relationship with dignity, he invited Maria to the function, but not to sit at his table; she was to be seated 'in order of her rank' which was very low down as she did not have a title. 'I can never submit to appear in your house in any place or situation but that where you yourself first placed me,' she told George, and she retired from court to Brighton with an annuity of £6,000.

FLODDEN, BATTLE OF In 1513, when HENRY VIII was involved in military activity across the Channel, France invoked the 'auld alliance' to persuade JAMES IV of Scotland to declare war on England. The Scots army crossed the River Tweed at Coldstream and seized the castles of Norham, Etal, Wark and Ford. An English army under the command of the Earl of Surrey left Newcastle and on 9 September confronted the invaders at Branxton Hill, close to Flodden. During the four-hour battle King James was slain and the Scots suffered the worst defeat in their history. The cream of Scotland's nobility died on the field of battle and Flodden has remained an almost legendary catastrophe in Scotland's annals. It is still commemorated in the lament *Flowers of the Forest*, the 'flowers' being the young Scots who died in the battle.

FOREST LAWS Hunting is traditionally associated with British royal families and no king took greater pleasure in it than WILLIAM THE CONQUEROR,

Hunting was so popular with the Norman kings that the detested Forest Laws were introduced to prevent the poaching of deer.

who created the New Forest as a vast game reserve by confiscating common land and demolishing hamlets. In order that common folk would not poach the royal deer – a key element in the Robin Hood legend – the Forest Laws were introduced which earned the king and his successors the enmity of their rural subjects. Under these laws no dogs were to be kept within miles of the royal hunting domains except mastiffs, which were used to guard households, provided they were crippled by the amputation of three claws of the forefeet so they could not chase deer. A Court of Regard was held every three years to ensure that no one owned a dog fit for hunting.

No Saxon Englishman dared enter hunting reserves unless he was some dispossessed wretch whose hunger drove him to poach and who knew that if he was caught he would be hanged with his own bowstring. The evidence required for such summary execution was impressed into the minds of the peasants by the couplet:

> Dog draw – stable stand,
> Back berand – bloody hand!

'Dog draw' meant holding a dog by a leash; 'stable stand', standing concealed with a drawn bow; 'back berand', bearing away a dead deer, and 'bloody hand', hands stained with deer blood.

See also WILLIAM II

FORT BELVEDERE Situated on the boundary of Windsor Great Park, this mock-castle house became famous briefly during what was known as the 'abdication crisis' as it was the home of the Prince of Wales before he became EDWARD VIII. William Augustus, Duke of Cumberland and fourth son of GEORGE II, had the original structure built as a gazebo overlooking the lake he had created known as Virginia Water. It was enlarged during the reign of GEORGE IV, a tower being added which gave it the appearance of a small castle or fort. In 1930 Prince Edward was greatly attracted by the house despite the chaotic state of its grounds and obtained permission from his father GEORGE V to take it over. He set about restoring it and took great delight in working to create a new garden, a task that was enthusiastically shared by his mistress FREDA DUDLEY WARD. Famed among the smart set for its weekend parties, Fort Belvedere remained a happy retreat for the prince until he abdicated on 11 December 1936. The house is no longer in royal ownership.

The frontispiece to the foundation charter of New Minster, Winchester, dated 966, although it may have been produced a little later. King Edgar, standing between the Virgin Mary and St Peter, is shown offering his charter to Christ. *(British Library, MS Cotton Vespasian A. viii, fol. 2v)*

Above: The ancient church of Ashington, built by Canute in thanksgiving after his victory at the battle of Assandun in 1016.

Right: The *Liber Regalis*, or 'Royal Book', fourteenth century. It contains the Order of Service for coronations, and was probably used by kings and queens at their coronations from the time of Henry IV in 1399 to Elizabeth I in 1559. *(Copyright: Dean and Chapter Westminster)*

Below: Stained glass roundel depicting Edward the Martyr by Rupert Moore in the Shrine of St Edward at the ruins of Shaftesbury Abbey.

St Stephen's Abbey, Caen, built by William I to fulfil his promise to the Pope for having his invasion of England declared a holy crusade.

The effigy of Henry V, the hero of Agincourt, above his tomb in Westminster Abbey.

The Traitor's Gate in the Tower of London, through which passed such doomed prisoners as Lady Jane Grey, Anne Boleyn, Catherine Howard, Sir Walter Raleigh and the Duke of Monmouth.

The descent of Henry VI as King of England and France from St Louis of France (top centre), through the French kings (left) and the English kings (right). *(British Library, MS Roy 15.E. vi)*

Banners, helms and crests of the senior Knights Grand Cross of the Most Honourable Order of the Bath above their stalls in Henry VII's Chapel, Westminster Abbey. *(Derek Forss)*

Stall plates at St George's Chapel, Windsor, of knights of the Most Noble Order of the Garter: Walter, Lord Hungerford, d. 1449 (left); Henry Bourchier, Earl of Essex, d. 1483 (centre); Sir John Grey of Ruthin, d. 1439 (right).

Left: Statue of a Queen's Beast at Windsor Castle.

Below: St George's Chapel, Windsor.

Above: Extract from the *Rous Roll* (*c.* 1483) showing the figures, arms and other devices of Queen Anne Neville, Richard III and their only son, Edward Middleham. *(British Library, MS Add 48976, fol. 17)*

Right: Henry VIII, the first King of England to be addressed as 'Majesty'. *(Belvoir Castle, Leics/Bridgeman Art Library)*

Above: Hampton Court Palace.

Left: Mary I by Giacomo Antonio Moro.
(Prado, Madrid/Bridgeman Art Library)

G

GARTER, CEREMONY OF THE Each year in June Her Majesty Queen Elizabeth attends a service for the Most Noble Order of the Garter, Britain's highest order of chivalry, in St George's Chapel at Windsor Castle. A procession of twenty-five Knights of the Garter, in traditional robes, is led by the queen and the Duke of Edinburgh from the castle to the chapel. The Household Cavalry line the route while Yeomen of the Guard provide an escort. *See also* MOST NOBLE ORDER OF THE GARTER

GAVESTON, PIERS In 1298 the lonely 14-year-old Edward, Prince of Wales (the future EDWARD II), was given an official companion of his own age, Piers Gaveston, the son of a Gascon knight. The boys spent most of their time at Langley Manor in Hertfordshire, where the Prince and 'Perrot', as he called his friend, were free to indulge in uncourtly pastimes, such as training dogs, thatching cottages and digging ditches. To the censure of chroniclers they also enjoyed the company of minstrels and drinking with 'vylans an vyle persons'.

It was not surprising that a strong bond developed between them. In February 1307 Edward was with his father, EDWARD I, at Lanercost Priory in Cumbria, when he demanded that his late mother's territory of Ponthieu should be bestowed upon his friend. This caused the formidable old King to retort,'Do you want to give lands away now, you who have never gained any? As the Lord lives, if it were not for fear of breaking up the kingdom you should never enjoy your inheritance!' As a result, Gaveston was banished to France and Edward was forced to swear upon the Host that he would never recall him without Parliament's consent

Six months later Edward succeeded his father. He brought back Gaveston – whom he created Earl of Cornwall, a title traditionally reserved for members of the blood royal – and arranged for him to be married to his niece, Margaret de Clare. In January 1308, the new King married Isabella the Fair, daughter of Philip IV of France at Boulogne, leaving Gaveston as Regent of England. A chronicler wrote: 'It was thought remarkable that one who had recently been in exile from the land should now be its keeper.' Although Isabella must have heard rumours of her bridegroom's affection for his boyhood companion, she was not prepared for the scene that awaited her arrival at Dover. Edward leapt ashore before the mooring ropes were tied and embraced the waiting Gaveston, almost overwhelming him with caresses. And if Isabella's French courtiers looked aghast at the scene it was merely a prelude to a greater outrage when it became known that the King had bestowed upon his favourite gifts that his father-in-law had given him, together with the best pieces of Isabella's jewellery.

At Edward's coronation on 25 February 1308 the barons were enraged that Gaveston – 'so decked out that he more resembled the god Mars than an ordinary mortal' – was given the high honour of carrying the crown, while the new Queen's uncles were furious at the wedding feast when the King preferred to share a couch with Gaveston rather than the Queen.

In April the barons, under the leadership of Thomas of Lancaster, demanded the banishment of Gaveston. The King, supported only by Sir Hugh Despenser, gave way to avert conflict between the baronage and the crown. He then set to work to get Gaveston reinstated in England, bribing his opponents 'one after another to his will with gifts, promises and blandishments'. Within twelve months Gaveston was back. Believing that the King had established his royal authority, Gaveston did not feel constrained to be tactful to the barons who had opposed him and subjected them to ridicule. At court he nicknamed the Earl of Lancaster 'the Old Hog', the stout Earl of Lincoln 'Burst Belly', while the Earl of Gloucester became 'The Cuckold's Bird' in a reference to his mother's morality. The appellation Gaveston was to regret most was that of 'The

Black Dog of Arden', which he bestowed on the Earl of Warwick.

These nicknames did as much as any other factor to seal Gaveston's fate. The earls' deep resentment of his pinpricks is confirmed by the prominence given to them in medieval chronicles.

At the beginning of 1310 a new threat beset Edward and Gaveston in the form of the Lords Ordainers, a committee of twenty-one members made up of bishops, earls and barons, whose purpose was to reform the governing of the kingdom. One of their acts was to declare that Piers Gaveston had 'misled and ill-advised our lord the King, and enticed him to do evil in various deceitful ways'.

For the third time Gaveston was exiled. Although the banishment was decreed to be perpetual, Edward yet again brought Gaveston back, with all his titles and property restored. As a result of this defiance, Gaveston was excommunicated, the barons took up arms and the King fled to York. At Scarborough, Gaveston was besieged in his castle by the Earls of Pembroke and Surrey and Henry Percy, and after three weeks was forced to negotiate. It was agreed he would be escorted south to present his case to Parliament, while his followers retained the castle. To guarantee his safekeeping, the earls swore oaths to the agreement on the Host. Yet when the cavalcade spent the night at the village of Deddington, Gaveston was awakened by the words 'Get up traitor, you are taken'. As he opened his eyes he saw armed men and a figure in full armour who said, 'I think you know me. I am the Black Dog of Arden.'

Gaveston was taken to Warwick Castle where the Earls of Lancaster, Hereford and Arundel now joined the Earl of Warwick and decided that the royal favourite should be put to death. On 19 June 1312 Gaveston was beheaded on Blacklow Hill. Edward's anguish at the death of his friend inspired his contemporary biographer to write: 'I am certain the King grieved for Piers as a father grieves for his son, for the greater the love the greater the sorrow.' *See also* EDWARD II

GEOFFREY OF MONMOUTH A Benedictine monk from Monmouth, Geoffrey worked at Oxford and wrote *Historia Regum Britanniae* in *c.* 1136 in which he claimed to give the histories of British kings over a period of nearly two thousand years up to Cadwaller in AD 689. His work was important in literature as he wrote about ARTHUR as an actual king, maintaining that his source was a 'most ancient book in the British tongue', which is taken to mean in Welsh, and this stimulated the popularity of the Arthurian myths which remains to this day. He was created Bishop of St Asaph in 1152 and he died three years later.

GEORGE I The arrival of George Louis, Duke and Elector of Hanover in 1714 to become George I of Britain changed the role of British monarchy for all time. No longer would the decision of a sovereign sway the destiny of the nation – future kings and queens would be constitutional figureheads and the kingdom would be controlled by Parliament. The man who ushered in this new era had no ambition to influence his new subjects or earn their respect. He did not learn to speak English, and the only reason he found himself on the throne was that he was a great-grandson of JAMES I on his mother's line, and he was a Protestant.

The Guelph family of Brunswick-Lüneberg into which George Louis was born was noted for eccentric traits. His father Ernest Augustus, Elector

Engraving of George I, whose arrival in England from Hanover in 1714 established the House of Hanover.

of Hanover, was famous throughout Europe for his excessive drinking and the pursuit of amorous pleasure. His more esoteric interests included astrology and alchemy. No doubt the idea of turning base metal into gold was attractive to him when faced with the heavy financial demands of his sumptuous court. One of his most profitable methods of raising money was to hire out his well-drilled troops. He once supplied over six thousand to the Seignory of Venice out of which only fourteen hundred returned to Hanover.

George's mother was Sophia, youngest daughter of Frederick of Wittelsbach, Elector Palatine and titular King of Bohemia, and Elizabeth, the eldest daughter of JAMES I of England. After being in labour for three days, Sophia gave birth to George Louis on 28 March 1660 at Osnabrück. The boy received an education suitable for a young German prince of his time – though his main interest was stag hunting – until the age of 15, when he went on his first military campaign 'bearing himself bravely at the battle of Conz on the Imperial side'. On his return he showed that he had inherited his father's sensual appetite by getting a governess pregnant. History does not record what happened to her and the child.

In 1680 George travelled to England where he met PRINCESS ANNE whom it was thought he might marry, but he was recalled by his father who had other plans for him. In a move toward consolidating the Hanoverian fortunes, the elector arranged for his eldest son to marry SOPHIA DOROTHEA, the only child of George's uncle, the Duke of Brunswick-Lüneberg-Celle. It was said the bridegroom was 'purchased in hard cash' by the duke who saw many political advantages in the match. An agreement was reached whereby he would pay Ernest Augustus a large cash sum plus an annual payment of £10,000 (approximately £1,150,000 today) for the next ten years. George, reluctant to follow his father's plan, only agreed on condition that he could keep Sophia Dorothea's handsome dowry, which was separate from the payment to the Elector, for himself.

The wedding took place quietly in her apartment on 21 November 1682. The only person to be completely satisfied with the marriage was the Elector. With the injection of cash from Celle in his exchequer, he ordered his architects to design a new hunting lodge and magnificent new stables. Meanwhile, George Louis did not disguise the fact that he

preferred the military camp to the company of his high-spirited wife. He was at the siege of Vienna when she bore him his only son, the future GEORGE II of England. He then went on a series of campaigns, being at Buda when it was captured from the Turks, then soldiering in Greece, Germany and Flanders.

Left alone, Sophia fell in love with Count Philip Christopher von Königsmarck and most likely would have eloped with him had he not disappeared mysteriously on the night of 1 July 1694 when it was thought he set out to visit her. The Elector instituted proceedings on behalf of his son George before an ecclesiastical court which, on 28 December 1694, granted a divorce and gave the 'innocent party' permission to marry again if he wished. This was granted on the grounds of desertion by Sophia, and throughout the case there was no mention of Königsmarck or adultery. She was confined in the castle of Ahlden until her death in 1726.

In 1704 the Duke of Marlborough, not only one of England's greatest military commanders but a veteran in intrigue, visited George Louis in Hanover where their common tastes and political convictions led to a friendship that was to have significance later. In England, when Princess Anne lost her only surviving child, the ACT OF SETTLEMENT was introduced whereby the inheritance of the English Crown would go to George's mother, the Electress of Hanover, provided an heir was not subsequently produced. The Whigs supported the idea of a Hanoverian succession as they wanted a Protestant on the throne, while the Tories were in favour of the exiled House of Stuart.

In June 1714 the Electress died and George became heir presumptive to the English Crown. On 1 August QUEEN ANNE died and immediately George Louis was proclaimed King of Great Britain, the Whigs taking advantage of the fact that the Tories and Jacobites (supporters of the Stewart heir) were not prepared for the event.

On 16 September George Louis embarked on the yacht *Peregrine* at Oranie Polder and, accompanied by twenty British men-of-war, arrived at Greenwich two days later. There have been few less sympathetic monarchs ever to claim a kingdom; hardly a drop of the new King's blood was English, he never tried to learn the language of his new kingdom and despite the fact that he was the country's first constitutional monarch he had no enthusiasm for constitutional monarchy, though he was wise enough to appreciate that he owed his position to accepting it. And this policy he followed, immediately appointing a Whig ministry which was to control the country for the next half-century.

George I was crowned with great pomp on 20 October 1714 at WESTMINSTER ABBEY. Although London remained quiet, anti-Hanoverian feeling was demonstrated by riots in other parts of the country. Five months later the King attended his first Parliament where his speech was read for him by the Lord Chancellor, after which business continued without royal interference. But it did not take long for the foreign sovereign to earn the dislike of his subjects 'partly from his own want of graces, but still more from the cupidity attributed to his German mistresses and dependants'.

These two ladies were Mademoiselle Schulenerg, and Madam de Kilmandsegge, later the Countess of Darlington. Neither lady was popular with the public and were jeered by the mob when their coaches were driven through the streets of London. On one occasion one of them put her head out of the carriage window and said in imperfect English, 'You mistake, my friends. We come here for your goods.' The remark was received with delight as the royal mistresses were blamed in part for royal extravagance, as indeed were the rest of the foreign courtiers. But if the English disliked the King, the King equally disliked them and often regretted leaving Hanover and the pleasures of his rural palace at Herrenhausen.

During the thirteen years of his reign, he returned to his electorate seven times, sometimes remaining there for six months. His only regret about these absences was that he had to leave his son George representing him in England, as between George I and the future GEORGE II there was deep and mutual dislike. The prince was antagonistic to his father because of the way his mother had been treated.

In 1715 the Jacobite Rebellion broke out in favour of Prince James Edward, the son of James II, known in history as the Old Pretender. In August the Scottish Earl of Mar raised the prince's standard and proclaimed him James III of England and James VIII of Scotland. The ill-fated rising greatly damaged the Tory party on account of its previous Jacobite sympathies, and the triumphant Whigs elected Robert Walpole as their leader. Because of his lack of English, the king did not sit at Cabinet meetings and was content to follow Walpole's advice. In effect the patronage of the Crown was surrendered to the Whig leaders and once the Jacobite Rebellion was concluded George hurried back to his beloved Hanover where his subjects welcomed him with enthusiasm and he revelled in stag hunts, operas and galas.

Meanwhile, apart from the South Sea Bubble, the kingdom flourished. Walpole's policy was for peace and for twenty years there were fewer wars than the British could remember. The religious and political struggles of the previous century were forgotten and industry burgeoned. And while George did not win the affection of the English his reign gave them an unusual sense of security.

In 1726, his ex-wife Sophia Dorothea died in her castle of exile, and George celebrated by setting fire to her will. A curious story was told by Horace Walpole who claimed that the King had received a deathbed letter from Sophia warning that he would follow her within a year, a prediction which greatly disturbed him. Some months later, on a journey to Osnabrück, the King suffered a stroke which was blamed on eating melons after a rough Channel crossing. When he had recovered consciousness, he intimated by signs that the journey should be resumed. When he arrived at his destination he was paralysed and two days later, on 12 June, he died and was buried in the Chapel of the Leine Schloss in Hanover.

GEORGE II Born in Hanover at the country palace of Herrenhausen on 10 November 1683, George Augustus spent his early days with his mother SOPHIA DOROTHEA OF CELLE until she was disgraced and imprisoned in 1694 as a result of her clandestine relationship with Count Philip von Königsmarck who met a fate still shrouded in mystery. After his father, later the Elector of Hanover and GEORGE I of Great Britain, divorced Sophia her situation had a profound effect on him. As a youth, he attempted to rescue her from the castle of Ahlden where she was a captive but this was foiled by the elector's guards.

George learned to speak English, though with a heavy accent, from his grandmother the Electress Sophia. She was a granddaughter of England's JAMES I and, proud of her Stuart blood, she made sure that her grandson was well aware of his. In 1700, when Queen Anne's last remaining child died, the Electress became heir to the English

The last British king to lead troops into Battle, George II fought sword in hand at the Battle of Dettingen in 1743.

throne and in 1705 an Act was passed in London naturalising her and her children, and George was created Duke of Cambridge and a Knight of the Garter. The same year he was married to Caroline, the daughter of the Margrave of Brandenbury-Anspach, an attractive and intelligent girl who was destined to have a considerable influence on her husband and the political life of Britain.

At this stage of his life George Augustus was described as a short, stiff, dapper man, fair-haired and red-faced, with large blue eyes and a strutting though dignified gait. The military tradition of his family was strong in him and his army career began in 1708 when he saw service under the Duke of Marlborough at Oudenarde. There he led his Hanoverian dragoons in a desperate charge during which his mount was shot from beneath him. It was probably the most glorious day in his life and on special occasions afterwards he would wear his old army coat and hat.

In 1714 George made his first visit to London for his father's coronation and on 17 March he enthusiastically entered the House of Lords, having declared with great patriotism and greater inaccuracy, 'I have not a drop of blood in my veins which is not English.' In September of that year, at George I's first council, he was declared Prince of Wales, but the rift already existing between him and his father widened when it became apparent that he was more popular with the English than the King who could not speak their language.

Londoners found him easy-going compared with his father, and they approved of his calm bravery when he left ST JAMES'S PALACE early one morning to help fight a fire at Spring Gardens. A few days later his coolness in the face of danger was demonstrated again at the Drury Lane Theatre when a would-be assassin tried to enter his box and was arrested after having shot a bodyguard. In return for his popularity, the prince declared that the English were the 'handsomest, best-shaped, the best-natured and lovingest people in the world'.

The prince's antagonism to his father brought him into favour with the Tories whose past pro-Stuart sympathies had led them into the political wilderness. But it also created him enemies among influential men in the ruling Whig party who privately warned the King that they considered the prince too ambitious. The antipathy of the Whigs towards the prince increased when George I made his first return visit to Hanover and left his son as guardian of the kingdom. George made the most of the situation and Lady Cowper wrote in her diary: 'The King was no sooner gone than the Prince took a Turn of being civil and kind to Everyone – he went to Hampton Court where he resided with great splendour.' When the King returned he repaid what he regarded as his son's arrogance by dismissing several of his friends from court and the next time he visited his beloved Hanover the kingdom was in the care of a council of regency.

Meanwhile, George Augustus became so keen on his adopted country that, unlike his father, he decided to have an English mistress. For this honour he chose one of his wife's maids of honour named Henrietta Howard who had no objection to becoming the prince's recognised mistress. When George succeeded to the throne she was given apartments in ST JAMES'S PALACE while her husband was bought off with an annual pension.

The ill-feeling between the King and the prince reached a climax in 1717 when Princess Caroline bore a son they named Frederick Louis. George I declared that the Lord Chamberlain, the Duke of Newcastle, who was the prince's bête noire, should be one of the baby's godfathers. When the christening ceremony ended the prince went up to the Lord

GEORGE II

Chamberlain and shouted, 'you are a rascal but I shall find you out'. This so infuriated the King that he had his son placed under arrest and then forced him to leave the palace. George and Caroline took up residence in Leicester House where an alternative court was formed, attended by ambitious young politicians and pretty society women. The King retaliated. The prince lost the custody of his children and his income was limited. There was even a plan for him to be kidnapped and taken to the American colonies as a last resort, a draft of the plan being found among the king's papers after his death.

The royal feud became such a scandal that the ruling Whigs were adamant that a reconciliation must take place. Walpole gained a powerful ally in Princess Caroline, and as a result of their efforts the tensions between father and son lessened. For the rest of the reign the prince lived quietly, paying more attention to his wife's maids of honour than to politics.

On 14 June 1727 George I died. George expressed no emotion, but held a council meeting at Leicester House where the Archbishop of Canterbury presented him with his father's will, expecting that he would read it out. The new King merely pocketed it and there the matter ended. On 11 October 1727 George was crowned with grandeur while Queen Caroline glittered with hired gems. But many whose hopes had run high at the splendid coronation were soon to be disappointed. Ambitious young Tories who had formed George's alternative court in the days of his disfavour were dismayed when George suddenly adopted his father's policy of favouring the Whigs. He also quarrelled with Frederick, his son and heir, just as his father had quarrelled with him. In turn Frederick, the new Prince of Wales, did what George had done in the same circumstances – he established his own court to which dissatisfied Tories flocked, and he parodied his father's amorous adventures in a skit he wrote entitled *Les Adventures du Prince Titi*.

There was no shortage of material for such burlesques. Until now George's principal mistress had been Mrs Howard but on a visit to Hanover, of which he was now elector, he met Madame de Walmoden who earned herself the title of Countess of Yarmouth in the traditional manner, after which he gave his affections to his daughter's governess, Lady Deloraine. As in the reign of George I royal

mistresses had apartments in St James's Palace close to those of the Queen but, whatever her feelings, Caroline was too wise to interfere. She bore George eight children, three of whom were to survive him, and always gave the appearance of being submissive though in reality she became the power behind the throne. Using Walpole's advice, she devoted herself to the guidance of the king, doing it so skilfully that it is doubtful if George ever suspected he was being manipulated.

Though now formal in public, George nevertheless came to be a popular king. His common sense prevented him from making mistakes which would have alienated his subjects; he accepted parliamentary government and while he was on the throne the country was fortunate both in peace and war. When Queen Caroline died in 1737 George was stricken with grief. Despite his moods and affairs, he loved her, as letters he sent her of over thirty pages long demonstrated. On her deathbed she told him to marry again and his voice choked with sobs as he exclaimed, 'No, no! I shall have mistresses.'

At a loss without Caroline's guidance, George took advice direct from Walpole, his Prime Minister, and remained loyal to the Whig party. In 1742 Walpole resigned after his position was weakened on account of his unpopular foreign policy. His defeat coincided with England's involvement in the War of the Spanish Succession, owing to the supposed threat to the king's Hanoverian territories.

Three years later the Jacobite Rebellion ended when the king's son William Augustus, Duke of Cumberland ended the Stuart hopes with his defeat of Prince Charles Edward ('Bonnie Prince Charlie') at CULLODEN.

After the Forty-five, as the rebellion became known, George had to accept ministers against his will, now that Walpole had gone. When William Pitt the Elder, who had been a friend of Frederick, Prince of Wales, was given office he was said to have shed tears of rage. In 1751 the friction between father and son ended with the death of Prince Frederick. He died of pleurisy brought on, it was believed, by getting wet while gardening at Kew. It was he and his wife Augusta who established Kew as a centre for the study of plants when they leased a house there.

Although the King hated Pitt, his last years were marked by a series of brilliant victories which brought him colonies all over the world as a result of Pitt's policy. Despite his age George kept good health apart from failing eyesight and, while he continued to be absorbed by foreign affairs, he did not seek to influence his ministers. He enjoyed card-playing and the company of his mistresses. In July 1760 he playfully enquired of the Duchess of Hamilton what she would most like to see. 'A coronation,' she replied. 'Well, you will not have long to wait,' he said. On 25 October he died from the bursting of a blood vessel, having reigned for thirty-three years. The funeral service was performed in WESTMINSTER ABBEY on the night of 11 November. Showing an unusually romantic streak for a Hanoverian, George had ordered that his remains should mingle with those of Queen Caroline and so, as his coffin was laid beside hers, the adjacent sides of the caskets were removed. Both were then enclosed in a stone sarcophagus in the royal vault in Henry VII's chapel, this being the last royal internment in the abbey.

GEORGE III When George William Frederick was born at Norfolk House on 4 June 1738, the eldest son of Frederick, Prince of Wales, and his wife Princess Augusta, he was two months premature and not expected to live. To everyone's surprise he survived and grew to be a tall young man with the ruddy complexion of the Hanoverians. As a boy he was taught elocution so that his accent would not be ridiculed like that of his grandfather, GEORGE II.

When he reached manhood a rumour circulated that he had secretly married a Quaker girl named HANNAH LIGHTFOOT who bore his children. There is no evidence that the story was true but later it was to be a source of irritation to George's queen, Charlotte, implying that her children were illegitimate.

Following the death of George II in 1760 a marriage was arranged for the new king with Charlotte Sophia, the younger daughter of the Duke of Mecklenburg-Strelitz. Small and plain, the 18-year-old girl had grown up in the simple atmosphere of a petty German court yet she took her transition to Queen of England in her stride and for the next six decades made George an excellent wife. They were married in the Chapel Royal, ST JAMES'S PALACE on 8 September 1761, followed two weeks later by their coronation in WESTMINSTER ABBEY.

Once he was crowned, George determined to retrieve the lost power of the monarchy. In 1770 the power of the Whigs was finally broken when Frederick, Lord North became Prime Minister. In him George found a pliable minister after his own heart who was to remain at the head of the government for the next twelve years. Too ready to give in to the King, he was largely responsible for the measures which led to Britain's loss of her American colonies. The opinion in London was that the answer to the colonists' independent attitude was to deal with them firmly. The King cannot be blamed entirely for this disastrous approach as his ministers had a substantial Commons majority in favour of the stern policy. Things came to a head on 8 April 1775 when actual fighting broke out between the colonists and British troops under General Gage. In the following year the American Continental Congress issued the Declaration of Independence and by 1781 Britain realised it would

The dominating statue of George III overlooking Windsor Great Park, known colloquially as 'the Copper Horse'.

be impossible to deny the American demand for independence and the formation of the United States.

In the spring of 1788 George was taken ill with what were believed to be bilious attacks and on 21 June he went to Cheltenham 'to take the waters' for his complaint. While at the spa he appeared to improve, but on returning to WINDSOR he was taken ill again and began to show signs of derangement. A story, first recounted by a page who had been dismissed from the royal household, quickly spread that while driving in Windsor Great Park the King stopped his carriage and spoke to an oak tree in the belief that it was the King of Prussia.

Rumours of the King's 'madness' could no longer be denied. The Whigs clamoured for his son George, Prince of Wales to be appointed regent and medical bulletins on the King's condition provided rich propaganda for the pro-regency party. Doctors decided that the King's head should be blistered in order to draw malignant 'humours' from his brain which inspired a Whig versifier to write:

> If blisters to the head applied
> Some little sense bestow
> What a pity 'tis they were not tried
> Some twenty years ago.

George's condition deteriorated, no doubt due in part to the savage medical treatment of his time. Today there is medical opinion that the King was never insane in the usual sense, but suffered from a rare disease known as porphyria which only came to be understood in the middle of the twentieth century. It is a malfunction of the porphyrin metabolic process which manufactures red pigmentation and a blood disorder. If too much red pigmentation is produced it attacks the brain and nervous system. Whatever the cause of the King's malady, he was regarded as mad and against his will transferred to Kew.

On 19 February 1789 the announcement that the King was convalescing was greeted by widespread rejoicing as his illness had won him much popular sympathy. A service of thanksgiving for his recovery was held at St Paul's on 15 March and London was illuminated to celebrate the withdrawal of the proposed Regency Bill. In May the King was well enough to travel to Weymouth where he led a simple life, sailing, bathing and riding, and everywhere he went he was greeted with acclaim.

A coin from the reign of George III.

There were several attempts on his life. The most dramatic of these occurred when he stood in the royal box in the Drury Lane Theatre and a would-be assassin fired two shots at him from the pit. The pistol balls missed him by inches, but the King calmly ordered that the entertainment should continue and actually fell asleep during the interval.

As the King grew older his frugal life became a subject of many cartoons, particularly those by Gillray. When he stayed at Weymouth he had his household goods sent from Windsor in order to avoid the high prices of the watering-place. Yet such homely traits renewed his popularity, particularly with the middle classes, and he developed the habit of visiting his subjects' houses at random, rather like a latter-day Haroun al Raschid, to see how they were faring. His keen interest in agriculture – he wrote articles on the subject – earned him the affectionate nickname of 'Farmer George'.

In 1801 he gave up the traditional title of King of France, and the same year union with Ireland was achieved. This was followed by another attack of illness which lasted for four months. Again he convalesced in Weymouth where it was observed that his illness had greatly aged him. Yet he still managed to carry out his duties and in 1803, when there was fear of a French invasion, he reviewed 27,000 volunteers in Hyde Park, promising that if Napoleon's forces landed he would meet the attack at the head of his troops.

Yet it was an unhappy time for the king. He was saddened by what he saw as the scandalous conduct of the Prince of Wales, while the Queen, fearful of another outbreak of insanity, lived apart from him.

He resided quietly at Windsor, appearing only to go to chapel or listen to music in the evening. To pass the time he liked to work with his hands, making buttons and adjusting the mechanisms of watches.

In the autumn of 1810, greatly upset by the illness of his favourite daughter Amelia, he showed signs of derangement once more and in January of the following year the Regency Bill was passed in favour of the Prince of Wales. For the remainder of his life George's mind was clouded. He was kept in his own apartments at Windsor where he spent much time playing hymns upon his harp. He died on 29 January 1820 and was buried in St George's Chapel at Windsor. On his accession, GEORGE IV gave his father's magnificent collection of books to the British Museum. Known as the KING'S LIBRARY it is now housed in the British Library.

GEORGE IV Known as 'The First Gentleman of Europe', George was born at ST JAMES'S PALACE on 12 August 1762. He was the eldest child of GEORGE III and Queen Charlotte and within the first few weeks he was created Prince of Wales and given the new preventive medical treatment of vaccination. As a child his education was remarkably thorough, including modern languages, drawing, elocution, the classics and agriculture, subjects that reflected the interests of his father. At the age of 18 he asked to join the army. King George refused but allowed him to set up his own household in a private suite at Buckingham House, now BUCKINGHAM PALACE. The prince then began his career as a flamboyant man about town – welcomed in London as a contrast to his frugal and retiring father.

Friendly with the Whig leader Charles James Fox, he was thronged by dissatisfied Whigs. At this time he was described as a stout young man with a florid complexion, a charming manner, and a fine sense of fashion, spending £10,000 a year on dress.

In 1780 the prince met his first mistress, the actress Mary Robinson. The affair lasted for two years, then the prince became interested in another young woman. Mary threatened to publish certain intimate letters and King George paid her £5,000 (approximately £450,000 today), plus an annual pension of £500, for their return.

The prince's answer to his father's warning was political opposition to the king's policies, so that when a Whig government came to power in 1782 the Prince of Wales was voted a civil list of over £60,000 a year and a further £30,000 to cover his debts. Coming of age in August 1783, he took his seat in the House of Lords and established himself at CARLTON HOUSE. At the same time he began building the oriental pavilion at Brighton which to this day remains his most extravagant creation.

The prince's expenses soared. He spent over £30,000 a year on his stables and stud alone, and before long his debts amounted to £160,000 (approximately £11,460,000 today). Finally he was forced to appeal to his father for help, even offering to live incognito in Europe so the debt could be cleared out of his income but the king refused both money and permission to go abroad. The prince shut Carlton House, his horses and carriages were auctioned and he lived in friends' houses on borrowed money until it was decided an appeal should be made to Parliament early in 1787.

Further embarrassment was caused by an allegation that the prince had flouted the ROYAL MARRIAGES ACT of 1772 which King George had passed forbidding any member of the royal family under the age of 25 to marry without the

The bronze equestrian statue of George IV overlooking Trafalgar Square, originally intended to stand in front of Buckingham Palace.

consent of the reigning sovereign. The sensational rumours were correct. The prince had secretly married a widow, MARIA FITZHERBERT, without the necessary consent and his bride was a Roman Catholic which contravened the Act of Settlement.

Rumours of this clandestine marriage were an obstacle to the prince getting parliamentary assistance in 1787 and the leading Whigs would not help for fear of repercussions on the party. In Parliament the member for Devonshire raised the question of the supposed marriage, and on 30 April Fox, following the prince's instructions, denied publicly that any form of marriage had taken place and that he had the Prince of Wales's direct authority for saying so.

Fox was stunned into the realisation of the predicament he was in through supporting the prince when a certain Orlando Bridgeman, a friend of the prince who had guarded the door during the ceremony, said to him, 'Mr Fox, I hear that you have denied in the House the Prince's marriage to Mrs Fitzherbert. You have been misinformed. I was at the marriage.' Fox knew that if he was to reveal the truth he would brand the prince a liar and this would be the end of his aspirations, as he believed that without the prince's support the Whig party would never return to power. He decided to remain silent and for the next twelve months he avoided the prince's company.

Finally there was a truce between the King and the prince, whose income was increased; over £160,000 was voted to clear his debts and another

£20,000 (approximately a total of £1,750,000 today) was allowed for the renovation of Carlton House. The prince's extravagances were blamed for the King's mental breakdown in 1788, and relations with his mother became very strained.

George III's restoration to health was greeted with popular rejoicing and ended the question of a regency and by 1789 the prince was again deeply in debt. He had spent more than double the allocation made by Parliament for the improvements to Carlton House and his creditors again became desperate. The prince continued to be short of money and once, to get the bailiffs out of Mrs Fitzherbert's house, he had to pawn his diamonds, but he did not allow this state of affairs to interfere with his love of racing. In 1788 the Derby was won by his horse Sir Thomas, and in the following four years he won 185 prizes. When his debts reached £½ million he was obliged to sell off nearly five hundred of his horses and Carlton House was again closed. His financial position was so disastrous that by August 1794 he decided to escape it by falling in with his father's wishes to make a suitable marriage.

PRINCESS CAROLINE, the daughter of the Duke of Brunswick-Wolfenbüttel was chosen as his bride and in 1795 She came to England. When the couple met for the first time George turned to his friend Lord Malmesbury and cried, 'I am not well. Get me a glass of brandy'. The wedding took place at the Chapel Royal, St James's Palace on the evening of 8 April 1795 and the prince only got through the ceremony by the prompting of the King after which, according to Princess Caroline, he spent the night in the fireplace dead drunk.

The relationship between George and Caroline was unhappy from the start, but as a result of his obedience to his father's wishes £600,000 worth of his debts were liquidated. On 7 January 1796 Caroline had a daughter who was named Charlotte. After separation from Caroline, George lived with Mrs Fitzherbert at Brighton or Carlton House, while the princess resided at Blackheath.

In the summer of 1803 the prince tried to get a military post, writing to his father that he wanted 'to shed the last drop of my blood in support of Your Majesty's person, crown and dignity'. The King replied that 'should the implacable enemy so far succeed as to land, you will have an opportunity of showing your zeal at the head of your regiment'. So the prince continued his dissolute way of life

A coin from the reign of George IV.

and amused himself by establishing restaurants and gaming clubs and designing military uniforms.

In 1810, when King George was stricken with his final onset of insanity, the Regency Bill was passed, and on 5 February 1811 George took the oath as regent and, in effect, began his reign. Soon afterwards his relationship with Mrs Fitzherbert was finally over.

In 1815 Princess Caroline left England and the next year Princess Charlotte was married to Prince Leopold of Saxe-Coburg. Her happiness was short-lived; eighteen months later she died in childbirth, leaving the country without a direct heir.

When George III died on 29 January 1820, Caroline announced that she was returning to England. The new George IV offered her an annual £50,000 to renounce her title, but now as Queen of England Caroline was determined to claim her rights. George then tried to divorce her on the grounds of improper conduct and, being the Queen, she was 'tried' by the House of Lords.

There was much salacious evidence, that even related to the contents of chamber pots. The public loved it, the cartoonists loved it, and *The Times* actually moved advertisements from its front page to feature the latest reports from the House of Lords. The case against the Queen was dropped amid the most extraordinary scenes of jubilation seen in Westminster, and Parliament voted her £50,000 per annum.

Caroline declared that she was going to take part in the coronation, but George was equally determined to be crowned alone, at a ceremony of incredible magnificence, his robes alone costing £24,000 (approximately £1,150,000 today). On coronation day the Queen arrived at Westminster Abbey only to be turned away from the doors. A few weeks later she died on 7 August 1821 and George's relations with his subjects reached their lowest ebb. Dozens of caricatures and cartoons lampooning him were circulated and when he drove to the opening of Parliament, stones and insults were hurled at his coach, after which he avoided public appearances. One reason for his unpopularity was the debts which accumulated while so many were impoverished after the long, expensive Napoleonic wars.

In 1823, acutely aware of his unpopularity, George hid himself at Windsor or Brighton and elaborate precautions were taken to prevent people seeing him even when he drove in Windsor Park, and it was obvious that his mind was clouded when he delighted in describing his imagined exploits on the field of Waterloo. With Wellington, whom he used to kiss and call his 'dear Arthur', he would reminisce over their equally non-existent adventures together in Spain or Flanders. By the beginning of 1830, the King had become partially blind and would stay in bed for days in his over-heated chamber at Windsor, drinking large quantities of cherry brandy and laudanum. He died on the night of 25 June 1830 and was buried in ST GEORGE'S CHAPEL, Windsor.

See also CARLTON HOUSE, CAROLINE OF BRUNSWICK-WOLFENBÜTTEL and FITZHERBERT, MARIA

GEORGE V Born on 3 June 1865 George was the second son of ALBERT EDWARD, Prince of Wales, and Princess Alexandra. As his elder brother Edward, Duke of Clarence, would be groomed for the throne, George's career would lie with the Royal Navy. At the age of 12 he joined HMS *Britannia* at Dartmouth where he and his brother were among two hundred cadets. Recalling his Dartmouth days later in life he said, 'It never did me any good to be a prince, I can tell you, and many a time I wish I hadn't been . . . the other boys made a point of taking it out on us on the grounds that they'd never be able to do it later on.'

Two years later he passed out of Dartmouth and was posted for the next three years to HMS *Bacchante*. His feelings about naval life were summed up in a letter: 'The sights of England's oaken and iron walls combined, a tearing through black water, fills one with a strength and joy such as nothing else can give.'

In December 1891 the engagement was announced of George's brother Prince Edward and Princess Mary of Teck, known as Princess May, the daughter of Francis, Duke of Teck. The great-granddaughter of GEORGE III on her mother's side, Princess Mary grew up at White Lodge in Richmond Park. Although she was very regal later in life, as a girl she was something of a tomboy and one of her greatest pleasures was riding her pony in the park. Her studies included German, the court language of Europe, water-colour sketching and singing under Paolo Tosti.

Less than two months after the engagement was announced Edward died from typhoid at SANDRINGHAM, thus putting George in line for the throne after his father.

Seafaring days were now over. He was created Duke of York, his official duties started, and he began to attend the House of Commons in order to acquire political understanding. Meanwhile, QUEEN VICTORIA was determined that he should marry his late brother's fiancée. George acquiesced, dutifully proposed to Princess Mary and on 2 May 1893 they were betrothed. The wedding took place in the CHAPEL ROYAL two months later and their marriage turned out to be one of the most successful in the history of the British monarchy. The couple had five sons and one daughter, and despite their great affection for the children, relations between them were never relaxed. George once remarked, 'My father was frightened of his mother; I was frightened of my father, and I'm damned well going to see that my children are frightened of me.'

After the wedding the couple lived quietly, staying frequently at SANDRINGHAM HOUSE, his best loved home among the royal residences. Part of George's time was spent studying constitu-

King George V of Great Britain with his cousin Tsar Nicholas II of Russia, *c.* 1915. *(Getty Images)*

tional history, and in an exercise book he presented his personal view of kingship, writing that an English type of monarch offered 'a splendid career for an able monarch; he is independent of political parties and therefore impartial, his position ensures that his advice would be received with respect, and he is the only statesman in the country whose political experience is continuous', a philosophy George endeavoured to practise all his life.

In 1901, when his father came to the throne, George and Princess Mary embarked on the longest royal tour ever made. Over a period of eight months they travelled over 45,000 miles visiting the empire; it was estimated the royal couple shook hands with 25,000 people.

George was 45 when on 6 May 1910 he recorded in his diary: '. . . beloved Papa passed peacefully away and I have lost my best friend and the best of fathers'. The prospect of the new reign must have seemed formidable to George.

In November 1911 King George and Queen Mary travelled on the P & O liner *Medina* to India where the famous Coronation Durbar was held in Delhi on 12 December. For the first time an important royal event was recorded by newsreel cameras. A platform was built to enable fifty thousand people to watch while their emperor and empress, wearing their specially designed Durbar crowns, sat enthroned in an arena and reviewed a 5-mile procession of Indian princes and their retinues.

In 1913 the King and Queen were guests of the Kaiser in Berlin at his daughter's wedding to the only son of George's uncle, the Duke of Cumberland, who would have been King of Hanover if his family had not lost the kingdom following the Austro-Prussian war of 1866. Tsar Nicholas II of Russia was also in Berlin and as the three royal heads of state enjoyed the celebrations they could not have guessed that within eighteen months their countries would be locked in the most terrible war in history, sparked by the murder of Archduke Franz Ferdinand, heir to the Austro-Hungarian Empire, at Sarajevo on 28 June 1914. Europe was used to the bloody rough-and-tumble of Balkan politics but few guessed the consequences of the archduke's murder.

At the time war was declared on 4 August 1914, the king and queen were somewhat remote from the people. The King, with his sincere but earnest manner, did not have the popular appeal of his flamboyant father. It was not until 1915 that any public feeling for George was shown, when he became a war casualty. In October while in France visiting the Royal Flying Corps the horse lent by General Haig reared and fell backwards, rolling on the King and causing a cracked pelvis and other internal injuries. It was two months before he recovered and thus he was identified with the countless wounded troops. He devoted himself to the war effort, visiting troops in France and inspecting hospitals and factories to boost morale. He also played a lesser known role in trying to heal the breaches between Britain's military and political leaders.

In 1917 George made a patriotic and much appreciated gesture of changing the name of his House, from Saxe-Coburg-Gotha to Windsor.

Although by the end of war in November 1918 the King's prestige was enhanced, elsewhere the world had changed for monarchy. All over Europe thrones had toppled; the British monarchy, once part of the much greater European royal family, was now almost alone. In Britain there were those who shared the Continental disillusionment with royalty, feeling that the time was ripe for the country to be rid of 'the ancient trappings of throne and sceptre'.

The greatest upheaval was in Russia. King George and Tsar Nicholas were first cousins and when Nicholas abdicated under pressure in 1917 and a provisional socialist government was established under Alexander Kerensky, it was suggested that the imperial family might find refuge in England. In Moscow the Soviet of Workers' Deputies had demanded the Tsar's execution, but the moderate Kerensky hoped Britain would send a cruiser to carry the imperial family to safety. Concerned about the well-being of his relatives, King George sent a telegram to Nicholas saying, 'Events of the last week have distressed me. My thoughts are constantly with you and I shall always remain your true and devoted friend.'

In London the offer of asylum had been received coldly by the Prime Minister, David Lloyd George, who regarded the Tsar as a tyrant, and as opposition grew the Foreign Office announced that 'His Majesty's Government does not insist on its former offer of hospitality to the Imperial family.' The King, too, was persuaded to change his loyalties. By the end of March 1918 his private secretary sent

a letter to the British Foreign Secretary doubting whether it was advisable that the imperial family should take up their residence in Britain.

When Lenin arrived in Russia and Kerensky's provisional government was overthrown by the Bolsheviks, the imperial family ended up as prisoners at Ekaterinburg in the Urals. At midnight on 16 July 1918 Nicholas, his wife Alexandra (a granddaughter of Queen Victoria) and their five children were shot by Red Guards.

During the war the Irish problem continued to cause anxiety to the king. In 1916 the Easter Rising in Dublin was followed by the setting up of an independent parliament two years later which culminated in the Government of Ireland Act of 1920 dividing Eire from Ulster. In 1921 the Northern Ireland Parliament was opened at Stormont by the King and Queen.

On 3 May 1926 the General Strike began and lasted nine days, bringing the country almost to a standstill. Churchill announced that the military would receive support for any action they might take for ensuring the continuation of essential services. The King ordered his private secretary to write to the War Office: 'His Majesty cannot help thinking that this is an unfortunate announcement.' The King had a surprisingly good insight into labour problems through his strong friendship with J.H. Thomas, MP, the railwaymen's leader, who warned the government against a plan to stop banks paying out money to striking unions.

In his private life George took comfort from the troubles of the day in his collections. He was a most

King George V preparing to give a radio broadcast from a room at Sandringham, 1932. (Getty Images)

knowledgeable philatelist; posters, clocks and mechanical toys, and old ship models formed part of his collections. His 'Silver Squadron' of nautical miniatures was the most valuable in the world. Queen Mary had the same enthusiasm for her collections of lace, fans, tortoiseshell and Wedgwood china.

In 1929 the King's health, much weakened by his accident in 1915 and wartime stress, declined alarmingly. His doctor had to guide his hand when he put his signature to a document appointing a COUNCIL OF STATE, and throughout the country churches remained open night and day so that prayers could be said for his recovery. The interest with which the bulletins on his health were followed left no doubt as to his popularity. Then, after three months, a service of thanksgiving for his recovery was celebrated. On 6 May 1935 King George and Queen Mary's Silver Jubilee was celebrated and vast crowds cheered when they toured the East End. Everywhere, the King was met with such acclaim that he declared simply: 'I'd no idea they felt like that about me. I'm beginning to think they really like me for myself.' At the end of the day he said on BBC radio, 'How can I express what is in my heart? I dedicate myself to your service for all the years that I may still be given time.'

But there was little time left. That autumn the King's health deteriorated. He was particularly depressed by the death of his beloved sister, Princess Victoria, with whom he had always enjoyed a deeply affectionate and humorous relationship. In January 1936 a Council of State was again appointed and again the King's hand had to be guided as he put his name to the document. He was now unable to write in the diary that he had kept for half a century. The last entry was made by Queen Mary who wrote: 'My dearest husband, King George V, was much distressed at the bad writing above and begged me to write his diary for him the next day. He died on January 20th five minutes before midnight.'

GEORGE VI Prince Albert Frederick Arthur George, the second son of George, Duke of York and Mary of Teck, was born at York Cottage in the grounds of SANDRINGHAM HOUSE on 14 December 1895. The date was also the anniversary of the death of QUEEN VICTORIA's beloved Albert thirty-four years earlier so the baby was christened Albert, though always known as Bertie.

The early part of the prince's life left its mark on him just as it had on his elder brother EDWARD.

Apart from his father's strict code of discipline, little Albert suffered neglect by his neurotic nurse and the irregularity of his meals, which led to severe stomach trouble, a precursor of what he was to suffer in later life. When his father discovered that he was left-handed, he forced the young prince to write with his right hand, probably causing his stammer, and lifelong acute embarrassment.

In 1907 the Duke of York decided that Albert should be enrolled in the Royal Naval College at Osborne on the Isle of Wight where his brother Edward was in his final term. As with Edward, the duke gave orders that the young prince should be treated like any other boy. But Albert was insecure and at a disadvantage, never having mixed with boys of his own age from different backgrounds. So it was with relief he joined his brother in the naval college at Dartmouth in January 1911. Here his self-confidence was bolstered by one of his officers, Lieutenant Henry Spencer-Cooper, who fostered his love of riding and encouraged him to go in for long-distance running at which he began to excel.

In January 1913 Albert joined the cruiser HMS *Cumberland* and was then posted as a midshipman to HMS *Collingwood* in the home fleet. After the outbreak of the First World War the prince was a sub-lieutenant and saw action at the Battle of Jutland on 30 May 1916. Soon afterwards he had to undergo an operation for a duodenal ulcer, after which his father, now GEORGE V, decided he should not return to sea but join the Royal Naval Air Service which was soon to be incorporated into the Royal Air Force.

Although the prince disliked flying he felt he should become a pilot and with his usual determination to overcome obstacles he became the first member of the British royal family to become a qualified pilot. A year at Trinity College, Cambridge, followed, studying history, economics, civics and the development of the constitution. He was now performing an increasing number of public engagements which he found a real ordeal because of his speech defect, yet he did not shirk these appearances and struggled with his speeches. In June 1920 the King showed his appreciation of Albert's efforts by conferring on him the titles of Duke of York, Earl of Inverness and Baron Killarney.

In the summer of 1920 the prince paid a visit to GLAMIS CASTLE in Forfarshire – once the residence of Macbeth – where he met 20-year-old

Lady Elizabeth Bowes-Lyon, the ninth of the Earl of Strathmore's ten children. He was greatly attracted by the vivacious young woman and when he visited Glamis again he proposed marriage, only to be rejected. It seemed Lady Elizabeth was reluctant to give up the freedom she enjoyed, but the prince continued to see her and in January 1923 they became engaged. The marriage took place in WESTMINSTER ABBEY on 6 April 1923. Princess ELIZABETH was born on 21 April 1926 and the following year they were scheduled to visit Australia and New Zealand. Before the tour the prince, greatly encouraged by his wife, determined to have one more attempt at improving his speech. He heard about the remarkable results achieved by an Australian named Lionel Logue, whose outstanding gift was his ability to convince his patients that it was possible for them to be cured. After the prince left for Australia he wrote to Logue: 'I have ever so much more confidence in myself, and don't brood over a speech as in the old days. I know what to do now, the knowledge has helped me over and over again.'

King George VI and Queen Elizabeth talking to a workman in a bomb-damaged area of London, 18 October 1940. *(Getty Images)*

On 20 January 1936 EDWARD VIII succeeded George V, making Prince Albert a direct heir to the throne. He soon became worried by his brother's infatuation with WALLIS SIMPSON and the ABDICATION crisis. When Edward decided to give up the throne for the woman he loved, Prince Albert was proclaimed King, with George VI as his official name. Now came the biggest challenge. Britain and the empire had lost two kings within a year and, because of his father's attitude, the new King had never even seen a state paper. However, he wrote to the Prime Minister: 'I am new at the job but I hope that time will be allowed to me to make amends for what has happened.'

The coronation took place at WESTMINSTER ABBEY on 12 May 1937. The service was broadcast throughout the world by the BBC, which the king supported despite considerable opposition. There were several changes to the service: the sermon was omitted while the old method of anointing was revived.

Soon after the coronation Neville Chamberlain became Prime Minister. Although he was more austere than his predecessor Stanley Baldwin, his relations with the new King were always of a warm nature. George agreed with him that every effort

should be made to avoid another European war, but despite all efforts, on 15 March 1939 German troops entered Prague and Hitler declared, 'Czechoslovakia has ceased to exist'. So had the Munich agreement.

In May 1939 the King and Queen made an arduous state visit to Canada. The King presided over the Canadian Parliament in Ottawa and on 9 June they crossed the border into the United States at Niagara Falls. The visit was an immense success, with newspapers printing such headlines as 'The British retake Washington'.

The triumph of the tour, however, was soon overshadowed by the situation in Europe. On 23 August, Chamberlain wrote to the King of the pact between Germany and Russia. Britain and France let it be known that they would stand by their pact with Poland. On 1 September German forces crossed into Poland and on 3 September Britain and France declared war on Germany.

In the global conflict that followed, King George and Queen Elizabeth established a relationship with their subjects unique in the history of the British monarchy. Despite air raids and the fact that BUCKINGHAM PALACE was bombed nine times, they remained in London, only sleeping at Windsor at the height of the blitz.

In 1940 the king was saddened by the resignation of Chamberlain. He sent for Winston Churchill, who formed a coalition War Cabinet, and a somewhat wary relationship soon became a deep friendship.

Together the King and Queen began their famous series of visits to war centres, touring shipyards, armament factories and industrial centres. Using the train which had been built for Queen Victoria, they visited troops and factories all over the country.

In 1940 the King created the George Medal for civilian bravery and despite air raids he refused to postpone honouring men and women at Buckingham Palace. It has been estimated that between 1940 and 1945 over thirty-two thousand people received medals from his hands. The King felt the tragedy of war even more deeply in August 1943 when his younger brother the Duke of Kent was killed in a flying accident while on active service.

In June of the following year he went to North Africa where he covered 7,000 miles visiting the troops. Before D-Day on 6 June 1944 he visited the combined forces who would be involved in the D-Day landings. Ten days later he was at General Montgomery's headquarters in Normandy.

When the war in Europe ended on 8 May 1945 Buckingham Palace became the focal point of jubilant Londoners, as it had at the end of the First World War. That evening the King made a broadcast, thanking the nation and making a plea for a better world in the future. On 15 August 1945, when Japan surrendered, the war was finally over. Following the victory of the Labour party in the general election, the King wrote: 'I saw Winston at 7 p.m. and again it was a very sad meeting. I told him the people were very ungrateful after the way they had been led in the War. He was very calm . . . I asked him if he should send for Mr Attlee to form a government and he agreed. We said goodbye and I thanked him for all his help to me during the five War Years.'

In 1948 plans for a royal visit to Australia and New Zealand were postponed as the King had symptoms of arteriosclerosis. He underwent surgery on 12 March 1949 in an operating theatre set up in Buckingham Palace. A few days later he had sufficiently recovered to hold a Privy Council meeting and in June drove in an open carriage to watch the ceremony of TROOPING THE COLOUR. The King's health remained a matter of concern both to his family and the public. His untiring efforts during the war had taken their toll and in 1950 there was still much cause for anxiety. The economic outlook for Britain was gloomy, relations with the Eastern Bloc were increasingly bleak and in June the Korean War began.

By September cancer of the lung was diagnosed, a condition blamed on his heavy smoking. The exact nature of the disease was never made public and the king never knew he had cancer, but on 23 September 1941 his left lung was removed. That year the King spent Christmas with his family at Sandringham and this time he did not have the stress of making his traditional radio broadcast live. The operation had left him hoarse so his speech was recorded sentence by sentence. On 31 January 1952 he went to London airport to bid farewell to Princess Elizabeth and her husband, who were departing on a Commonwealth tour. Afterwards he felt well enough to enjoy a day out shooting with friends at Sandringham. Before retiring the King planned the next day's sport but when his valet entered his room early the following morning he found the King had died during the night.

On 15 February the King was buried at Windsor to the genuine grief of the nation he had served so unexpectedly and well. Among the floral tributes was one from Winston Churchill in the shape of a George Cross with the legend 'For Gallantry'.

GLAMIS CASTLE Apart from being known as the most haunted castle in Britain, Glamis Castle in Angus owes much of its fame to Shakespeare's *Macbeth* in which it provided the setting for the murder of Duncan. In reality the murder did not take place there, though the King was either murdered by Macbeth elsewhere or died fighting him in 1040 at the Battle of Bothganowan. However, the castle does have one genuine royal murder in its history when in 1034 Malcolm II died there at the hands of his kinsmen.

In 1376 ROBERT II, the first Stewart King of Scotland, presented his Chamberlain and son-in-law, Sir John Lyon, with the royal estate of Glamis and it has remained in the possession of the Bowes-Lyon family, apart from one tragic break, until the present day. In 1537 Lady Janet Douglas, widow of the 6th Lord of Glamis, was arrested for practising witchcraft, William Lyon falsely accusing her, her son Patrick and her second husband Archibald Campbell of using magic in an attempt to bring about the death of JAMES V. Archibald Campbell fell to his death while attempting to escape from Edinburgh Castle.

Lady Janet's fate was more terrible. She was burned as a witch on Edinburgh's Castle Hill where,

Glamis Castle, famous for its association with Macbeth and as the home of Elizabeth Bowes-Lyon, later the wife of George VI.

in the words of an old chronicle, she met her death 'with great commiseration of the people, being in prime years, of a singular beauty, and suffering all, though a woman, with a manlike courage'. Her son's death sentence was suspended until he should reach his 21st birthday. Meanwhile, Glamis returned to royal ownership and the king and his queen, Mary of Guise, often stayed at the castle.

Young Lord Glamis was later released from prison and had his estates restored to him when William Lyon made a deathbed confession that there had been no truth in the evidence he had given against Lady Janet. In 1562 his son, the 8th Lord Glamis welcomed MARY, QUEEN OF SCOTS to the castle with her retinue, which included her treacherous half-brother James Stuart, Earl of Moray and her ladies known famously as her 'Four Maries'.

In the following century Glamis Castle was rebuilt, the work being completed after Parliamentary troops billeted there had ransacked the interior. When the first Jacobite Rebellion broke out in 1715, PRINCE JAMES EDWARD, the Old Pretender, stayed at Glamis where he demonstrated his heritage by touching for the KING'S EVIL with satisfactory results.

The latest royal connection with Glamis began in 1923 when the Duke of York, the future GEORGE VI, and his bride Elizabeth Bowes-Lyon went to Glamis which had been Elizabeth's girlhood home, which they frequently revisited, having been provided with a suite of rooms in an old part of the castle. Their second daughter Princess Margaret Rose was born at the castle in 1930, the first royal birth in Scotland since 1602 when JAMES I's son Robert was born, and died in the same year, at Dunfermline Palace.

GLASTONBURY THORN Each Christmas Day flowers from a legendary thorn tree decorate the sovereign's dining table at BUCKINGHAM PALACE. The background to this custom is the famous Glastonbury Thorn (*Crataegus monogyna praecox*), which was first referred to in a poem written in 1502. It blossomed at Christmas which, being so early, was regarded as a holy sign. A thorn tree, said to be a descendant of the original bush, still grows in the grounds of the ruined abbey and it became a tradition – that still continues – that some of its unseasonable flowers be sent to the sovereign.

In 1714 the antiquary Eyston wrote in his *A little Monument to the once famous Abbey and Borough*

The Glastonbury Thorn, which legend tells is a descendant of St Joseph of Arimathea's hawthorn staff, and which is said to bloom at Christmas.

of Glastonbury: 'St Joseph of Arimathea landed not far from the town, at a place where there was an oak planted in memory of his landing, called "the Oak of Avalon"; that he and his companions marched thence to a Hill, near a mile to the south side of the town, and there being weary rested themselves, which gave the Hill the name of Wearyall Hill, that St Joseph stuck on the Hill his staff, being a dry hawthorn stick, which grew, and constantly budded and bloomed upon Christmas Day.'

The belief that Britain was the first country to receive the Gospel as a result of St Joseph's mission 'immediately after the Passion of Christ' was to provide some political advantage. At the great Church Councils of Pisa (1409), Constance (1417), Siena (1424), and Basle (1434), precedence was given to English bishops, and English ambassadors demanded similar treatment. ELIZABETH I declared that her father HENRY VIII claimed the same right of precedence.

GLORIOUS REVOLUTION The general unpopularity of JAMES II on account of his Roman Catholicism, coupled with the Whigs' aim of deposing him in order to limit the power of the monarchy,

led to what is known in history as the 'Glorious Revolution'. In June 1688 WILLIAM OF ORANGE, the husband of MARY, the eldest Protestant daughter of James by Anne Hyde, was invited to come to England by several Whigs and Bishop Compton, who feared the king would weaken the Church of England, a view held by the Tories. It was the birth of James's son that month which escalated the situation as the little prince became heir to the throne in place of the king's daughter Mary.

After William landed at Torbay on 5 November many of the officers in the royal army defected and James realized that he could not look to the army to defend his position. Defeated, James fled to France and in 1689 the Bill of Rights declared that in doing so he had abdicated and confirmed William and Mary as joint sovereigns.

See also JAMES II, WILLIAM OF ORANGE, JACOBITES

GODWINE, EARL OF WESSEX The most influential noble during the reigns of four kings of England, Godwine was born *c*. 987, the son of Wulfnoth of Sussex. He became a favourite of CANUTE early in his reign and was made an earl in 1018. The next year he married Thyra, daughter of King Sweyn, and following her untimely death married Sweyn's sister Gytha. In 1920 he became Earl of Wessex and Kent. After Canute died in 1035 he continued to hold his position of power under HARDICANUTE and his successor HAROLD I. It was during the latter's reign that he was held responsible for the death of ALFRED THE ALTHELING, the half-brother of the future EDWARD THE CONFESSOR, who had a claim to the English throne.

In 1042 he was influential in raising Edward to the throne and arranged for him to marry his daughter Edith. Because the pious Edward had taken a vow of chastity in his youth the marriage was unconsummated, to the disgust of the earl and his family, as history had shown that the need for a royal heir was of paramount importance. The earl was now virtually the uncrowned King of England but his opposition to the burgeoning Norman influence at the king's court led to the normally compliant Edward banishing him and his family and confiscating his estates in 1051. The following year he and his formidable sons returned and were welcomed so enthusiastically by all sections of society that Edward had no option but to reinstate them.

After Godwine died of apoplexy at Winchester Castle in 1035 his son HAROLD became the principal noble in the kingdom and succeeded The Confessor for one of England's briefest reigns in 1066.

See also EDWARD THE CONFESSOR

GOLD STATE COACH *See* ROYAL MEWS

GOLD STICK IN WAITING It was during the hysteria of the Popish Plot that concern for the sovereign's safety manifested itself in the appointment of a special bodyguard known as Gold Stick in Waiting. In 1678 the anti-Catholic fabrications of Titus Oates and Israel Tonge, warning of a Jesuit conspiracy to assassinate CHARLES II, so concerned the King's illegitimate son JAMES, DUKE OF MONMOUTH, that he persuaded his father of the necessity of being guarded 'from his rising to his going to bed'.

At the time the duke was colonel of the 1st Troop of Life Guards, and Charles agreed that the special protectors should be drawn from the Household Cavalry. The insignia of office was to be an ebony staff with a gold top engraved with a crown and the royal coat of arms which gave the bearer the title of Gold Stick in Waiting. If military duty impeded a colonel from attending the king, the responsibility was temporarily transferred to one of his lieutenants with the junior title of Silver Stick in Waiting.

After the Battle of Waterloo, the cavalry regiment known as the Blues was raised to the status of Household Cavalry for the part it had played in the victory, and since then the role of Gold Stick has been shared between its colonels and those of the Life Guards. Today the office has become largely ceremonial, though when the sovereign travels by carriage or coach Gold Stick is in attendance.

GREENWICH PALACE From the reign of HENRY V to that of GEORGE II, the palace at Greenwich was one of the most popular royal houses with the monarchy. Its great advantage was that, while it was in countryside ideal for hunting and rural pursuits, it was but a short journey down the Thames from London by royal barge. The site goes back to the time of ALFRED THE GREAT when his niece Ethelruda presented what was known as the Greenwich Manor to the abbey of St Peter at Ghent. When foreign priories in England were suppressed by HENRY V, the estate passed to his younger brother Humphrey, Duke of Gloucester – the 'Good Duke Humphrey' – who in 1437 rebuilt the manor as Bella Court, and five years later was allowed to enclose 200 acres which became GREENWICH PARK. The duke was not only a distinguished soldier but a patron of the arts and an avid book collector, his library at Greenwich being England's first great privately owned library, which he bequeathed to Oxford University and which became the basis of the Bodleian Library.

In 1445 the duke lent the palace to HENRY VI following his marriage to Margaret of Anjou, and early in 1447 the king claimed it when the duke died mysteriously after he had been arrested for treason. Renamed 'Placentia', the palace was further improved by Henry; the work included the fitting of glass panes in the windows. Following the WARS OF THE ROSES HENRY VII, the first Tudor king, occupied Placentia and on 28 June 1491 his wife Elizabeth of York gave birth to the future HENRY VIII there.

Ten years later the palace was the scene of the wedding of Prince Arthur, the king's eldest son, to CATHERINE OF ARAGON. Six months after the

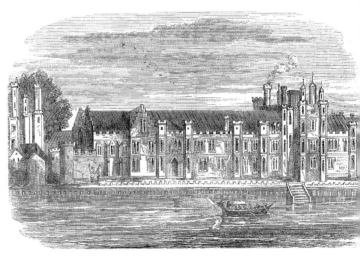

Greenwich Palace, with royal connections reaching back to Henry VI, became the National Maritime Museum in 1937.

wedding Arthur died and after the death of Henry VII in 1509 his son Prince Henry married Arthur's widow at Greenwich Palace a fortnight before his coronation.

Greenwich Palace, as it was now called, became the new king's favourite residence. He was in easy distance of his capital and also his naval dockyards at Woolwich and Deptford, while the great park provided the hunting which he enjoyed with an ardour shared by so many of England's sovereigns. And like his predecessors he improved the palace, adding a banqueting hall, an armoury and tiltyard where knightly tournaments were held. On 18 February 1516 Queen Catherine gave birth to the future queen MARY at the palace which, the following Christmas, became the setting for the first masquerade to be staged in the kingdom. A less happier time for the queen was in 1529 when she was effectually held prisoner there for denying that her marriage to the King was invalid.

At the beginning of 1533 Henry secretly married ANNE BOLEYN and it was at Greenwich Palace that the future ELIZABETH I was born to the royal couple in September that year. The palace was the scene of a distressing time for Queen Anne when she was delivered of a stillborn son in January 1536 and disappointed the King's wish for a male heir. On the following May Day the Queen was watching a tournament at the palace tiltyard when she dropped her handkerchief, which was construed to be a signal to a lover. The next day she was arrested, conveyed to the TOWER OF LONDON and, after being convicted of high treason, was executed. The King married Jane Seymour eleven days later.

It was at Greenwich that Henry reluctantly married his fourth wife Anne of Cleves in January 1540, but the non-consummated marriage was annulled in July. The next event of significance was when Henry's successor, the ailing EDWARD VI, took up residence at the palace where it was hoped its wholesome surroundings would improve his failing health, but to no avail as he died there in July 1553.

After Mary was crowned queen her only interest in Greenwich was to invite Franciscan friars to take it over but after Elizabeth was enthroned the palace regained its royal status when she banished the friars and made it her summer residence. It was at Greenwich that Sir Walter Raleigh's act of throwing his cloak over a puddle in the queen's path became

part of royal folklore and the MAUNDY ceremony was revived when Elizabeth washed the feet of thirty-nine poor women and gave them Maundy money. Here, too, Elizabeth signed MARY, QUEEN OF SCOTS' death warrant.

England's first Stuart king, JAMES VI of Scotland and JAMES I of England shared the Tudor appreciation of Greenwich Palace, which he settled on his wife ANNE OF DENMARK. He employed Inigo Jones to design a Palladian-style house in the grounds, subsequently known as the Queen's House, but it was not completed when Anne died in 1619. The king gave the incomplete house to his son CHARLES and after his marriage to Catherine of Braganza the house was completed. It was formed of two buildings, one providing views of the Thames and the other of Greenwich Park, situated on either side of the road and joined by a bridge. The queen was so pleased with it that it was named the 'House of Delights', and little wonder as the panels of her drawing-room and bed chamber were decorated by Rubens and Jacob Jordaens. Paintings from Charles I's famous collection, which included works by Raphael, Rubens and Van Dyck, were displayed there, but were later sold off during the Commonwealth.

Stripped of its furnishings, Greenwich Palace was used to house Dutch prisoners of war, and such was its state when CHARLES II was restored in 1660 that he planned to replace it with a new palace to be named the King's House, but when he died in 1685 only the west wing of the proposed three blocks was finished. After the GLORIOUS REVOLUTION of 1688, which brought MARY II and her husband WILLIAM OF ORANGE to the throne, the queen decided that, following the naval Battle of La Hogue, what had been completed of the King's House should become the Royal Hospital for Seamen, which in 1869 was transformed into the Royal Naval College.

After the House of Hanover was established, royal interest in Greenwich Palace waned and the last member of royalty to be associated with it was CAROLINE OF BRUNSWICK-WOLFEN-BÜTTEL, who was welcomed there by Lady Jersey, the mistress of her intended husband, in 1795. Ten years later the Queen's House was made over to the princess, but soon afterwards it was sold to provide a school for the orphans of seamen. In 1933 the school moved, leaving the once-gracious house in a sad state of repair. Thanks to the Office of Works the house was restored and in 1937 it became the National Maritime Museum.

GREENWICH PARK When he built a fine house on the banks of the Thames in 1427, HENRY V's brother Humphrey, Duke of Gloucester, enclosed a large area of land between Greenwich Hill and the river. Six years later HENRY VI granted him the right to enclose 200 acres of pasture and woodland which remains the royal park of today. When the duke died in 1447 his house and park passed into the ownership of Henry VI to become one of England's premier palaces. It reached its peak as a royal residence when HENRY VIII came to the throne and, in order to have adequate game for royal hunting parties, stocked it with deer. Henry took great pleasure in 'a-maying' in the park, and in holding tournaments on the level green at the base of the hill.

It was at such a tournament, held on May Day 1536, that ANNE BOLEYN was said to have signalled to a lover with her handkerchief. Henry abruptly left the tournament and the queen's fate was sealed. Her brother Lord Rochford and four commoners were imprisoned in the TOWER OF LONDON that night, to be accused of having adulterous relations with the queen. Anne was arrested the next day. Her daughter ELIZABETH I's delight in the park began when her accession in 1558 was celebrated there by a sumptuous pageant mounted by the City of London.

Fourteen years later the City provided a more serious spectacle in the park when it paraded 1,400 armed men before the queen following the discovery of the conspiracy of Thomas, 4th Duke of Norfolk who had been in treasonable communication with MARY, QUEEN OF SCOTS. After the royal review the militia proved its enthusiasm by staging a mock engagement which, it was said, 'had all the appearances of a regular battle except for the spilling of blood'.

In 1619 JAMES I had the entire park encircled with a wall of brick at the then cost of £2,000. Following the Restoration Le Nôtre, the landscape gardener to Louis XIV of France, was brought over by CHARLES II to enhance the park. He did this by making the Queen's House, which had been designed by Inigo Jones in 1615, the central feature from which radiated leafy avenues lined with Spanish chestnuts. The next addition to the park was the Royal Observatory built by Christopher Wren on Greenwich Hill in 1675. In 1690 Charles Sackville, Earl of Dorset and Middlesex took up residence in the Queen's House as the park's first ranger. A royal ranger was Princess Caroline, the wife of the Prince Regent, who sold her right to the office in 1806.

The park has been open to the public since the eighteenth century.

GREY, LADY JANE The most tragic of English queens is Lady Jane Grey, remembered in the classroom mnemonic as 'queen for a day' though in fact her reign lasted nine days. Born in 1537 Jane was the daughter of Henry Grey, Duke of Suffolk, and Lady Frances Brandon who in turn was the daughter of Charles Brandon, Duke of Suffolk, and Mary the youngest sister of HENRY VIII. Thus Jane was EDWARD VI's first cousin.

As a young girl Jane proved to be a remarkable scholar. Under her tutor John Aylmer, who later became Bishop of London, she mastered Latin, Italian, French and Hebrew. Despite her accomplishments her parents treated her with sternness 'more than needed to so sweet a temper'. Roger Ascham wrote in 1550 how she confided in him that they punished any fault in her embroidery or deportment with 'pinches, nips and bobs'. When Jane's father became Duke of Suffolk she lived at court where she was often in the company of Princess Mary, the daughter of Henry VIII and CATHERINE OF ARAGON, and the young Edward VI who greatly approved of her intellectual abilities.

John Dudley, Duke of Northumberland and the real master of the kingdom, was aware that the reign of the sickly boy king was likely to be a short one. He planned to secure the succession to his own family and to this end he proposed a marriage between Jane and his son Lord Guildford Dudley. A Venetian visitor to England at that time reported that the girl hated the idea of such a match and it was only when her ambitious father – aware of how much he stood to gain from the union – became violent that she gave in and became Guildford Dudley's wife.

In January 1553, when Edward lay ill at GREENWICH PALACE, Northumberland suggested that he should nominate the 'heirs male' of his daughter-in-law Jane as successors to the throne. Such a proposal was contrary to Henry VIII's statutes, but Edward approved of his cousin because she shared his Protestant beliefs and he was afraid of his half-sister, the bastardised Princess Mary, inheriting the throne because of her ardent Roman Catholicism. He therefore signed a document putting Northumberland's wishes into effect.

As Edward's condition worsened the duke realised that he would die before his daughter-in-law could produce any 'heirs male' and so the wording of the document the king had signed was secretly altered to read 'Lady Jane and her heirs male'. In June he forced the Council, along with the judges and bishops including ARCHBISHOP CRANMER, to accept this forgery. On 6 July 1553 the 15-year-old king died and two days later Northumberland took Jane before the Council where the shock of being told that she was to be queen caused her to faint. On 10 July she was taken in state by barge to the TOWER OF LONDON where she was led through the great hall with elaborate ceremonial to the royal apartments, and on the same day she put her signature to a proclamation announcing her succession in accordance with the late king's will. Her husband Guildford Dudley now put pressure on her to proclaim him king but

The tragic Lady Jane Grey – 'Queen for a day' – who was beheaded on Tower Green at the age of seventeen.

she resisted, saying that such a decision must come from Parliament.

Meanwhile, Princess Mary claimed that she was her half-brother's legitimate heir and her supporters rallied to her at Framlingham Castle in Suffolk. On 13 July they proclaimed her queen in Norwich and six days later the princess arrived in London with thirteen thousand supporters. In one of the most shameful acts of betrayal in English history, Jane's father, Thomas Grey, pronounced MARY queen at the gates of the Tower and informed his daughter that she was now a prisoner. His volte-face earned him a pardon on 3 August when Mary made a triumphant entry into the city and was welcomed by the Lord Mayor at Aldgate.

On 14 November Lady Jane Grey, in company with her husband, her two brothers and Archbishop Cranmer, were charged with treason at the Guildhall. A chronicler described her calmly entering the chamber in a 'black gown of cloth, a French hood, all black, a black velvet book hanging before her, and another book in her hand, open'. She pleaded guilty and although arguments for her immediate execution were put forward, Queen Mary was reluctant to order the death of the girl whom she knew in the past as a pleasant companion and who had merely been a reluctant pawn in the political chess game. It was expected that she would be allowed to withdraw into private life and this would probably have been the outcome had not her father switched his allegiance yet again and become involved in a conspiracy against the new queen. On learning of the plot Mary saw Jane as a potential threat as long as she was alive, and so on 12 February 1554 Lady Jane Grey and Lord Guildford Dudley her husband were executed. Jane did not take the opportunity for a final meeting with her husband lest it should upset 'the holy tranquillity with which they prepared themselves for death'.

Dudley was beheaded first on Tower Hill and Jane had to pass his headless body as it was brought back when she was led to her own execution on Tower Green, where at least she did not have to endure the jeers of the mob. Before kneeling at the block she stated that it had never been her desire to be queen and that she would die 'a true Christian woman'. A handkerchief was bound round her head and being thus blindfolded she was unable to locate the block. 'What shall I do?' she cried as she groped for it. 'Where is it?'

After the execution she and her husband were interred in the Tower church of ST PETER AD VINCULA. Meanwhile, her father fled to Astley Castle in Warwickshire where he hid until his park-keeper betrayed him and he suffered the same fate as his daughter.

GROOM OF THE STOLE The popular idea of the Groom of the Stole was that this functionary was in charge of the royal wardrobe, but the *Oxford English Dictionary* explains: 'In accounts of coronation ceremonies the king is said to have worn an ornament resembling a stole until modern times. This view that the Groom of the Stole derived his designation from this ornament is quite improbable.' In fact, the groom had a far more intimate role in the monarch's daily life. The word 'stole' was an old spelling of 'stool', and in this case the stool was a commode. The king's 'stool chamber', a room containing the royal 'close stool' – a utensil enclosed in a stool or box – was served by the Groom of the Stole. When the king travelled the groom at all times carried a soft linen napkin and a light three-legged stool with a circular hole, which in effect was a symbol of his office and which he kept ready in case His Majesty should experience what might be termed a sudden call of nature.

The Groom of the Stole at the Tudor court was a highly prized position, second only to that of vice-chamberlain, because it gave the holder the privilege of being alone with the king at his most private moments. Therefore he had to be a person whose loyalty was considered beyond reproach. However, in 1536, during the reign of HENRY VIII, Sir Henry Norris, the King's Groom of the Stole, was executed after being found guilty of adultery with ANNE BOLEYN.

In 1647 Henry Hyde, 1st Earl of Clarendon, referred to a Groom of the Stole in his *History of the Rebellion and Civil Wars in England* thus: 'A seuth (whome I woalde gesse by his writing to bee Groome of the Stoale to some Prince of the bloude of Fraunce) writes a beastly teatise onely to examine what is the fittest thing to wipe withal, aledging that white paper is too smooth.'

In the household of a queen or a princess the office and title were held by a lady, but since QUEEN VICTORIA ascended the throne no Groom of the Stole has been appointed.

GUNPOWDER PLOT When the Roman Catholics of England failed to obtain religious toleration from JAMES I, Robert Catesby and other conspirators hatched a plot to kill the king, destroy Parliament and proclaim for Princess Elizabeth, James's eldest daughter, in order that the true faith be re-established. In furtherance of this they invited Guy – or Guido – Fawkes to return from the Netherlands where he had been fighting with the Spanish army. The son of Protestant parents, he had embraced Roman Catholicism with the zeal of a convert and he responded enthusiastically to Catesby's invitation. His mission was to hire a cellar beneath the House of Lords – it was not unusual for such cellars to be used for the storage of merchandise – place thirty-six barrels of gunpowder in it, and at the opening of Parliament on 5 November 1605 light a slow fuse. It has been

Below left: The signature of Guy (Guido) Fawkes before and after torture. *Below:* The Gunpowder Plot conspirators.

estimated that such an amount of gunpowder would have laid waste the area within a half-mile radius of the Palace of Westminster.

Shortly before the fateful date Lord Monteagle received a letter from his brother-in-law Francis Tresham, one of the conspirators, warning him not to attend Parliament. When this letter was shown to the king on 4 November he ordered a search to be made of the Palace of Westminster. Fawkes was discovered in the cellar with the explosive and taken to the TOWER OF LONDON where he was put to torture. It was only when he learned that his fellow conspirators had either been killed or captured that he made a confession. He was sent to the scaffold at Westminster on 31 January 1606.

As a result of the plot more repressive laws were passed against Roman Catholics, but curiously it was not until the discovery of the 'Popish Plot' seventy-three years later that the traditional search of the vaults of the Palace of Westminster was inaugurated.

See also JAMES I.

GWYNNE, NELL After CHARLES II discarded BARBARA VILLIERS with a pension and the title Duchess of Cleveland, his next paramour was to become the most celebrated of Britain's royal mistresses. Born at Hereford *c.* 1650, Eleanor ('Nell') Gwynne was forced to become a barmaid in a brothel after her ne'er-do-well father died in the debtor's prison. From there she became an orange girl and then one of the first English actresses, as until then it had been the custom for boys to play female roles. She was famous at Drury Lane, London, for her dark ringlets and shapely legs which made her performances in 'breeches parts' popular. Her best role was in Dryden's *Secret Love* in which she played the part of Florimel.

Her first protector was Lord Buckhurst but when she became the king's mistress she gave him all her affection. As for Charles, he delighted in the contrast between his aristocratic paramours and 'pretty, witty Nelly' who called him Charles III because she had known two lovers of that name before him. Even when he took another mistress,

the French noblewoman Louise de Keroualle whom he made Duchess of Portsmouth, he remained as fond as ever of Nell. Because Louise was French and a Roman Catholic she was suspected by English Protestants of being a spy for King Louis. Her unpopularity was demonstrated one day when Nell Gwynne was driven out in the fine carriage Charles had provided for her and was hooted by a mob who mistook her for the Duchess of Portsmouth. Opening the window she cried out, 'Pray, good people, be civil! I am the Protestant whore!' The jeers turned to laughter and Charles was highly amused when the story reached him. What pleased both him and his subjects about Nell was the fact she had no wish to play politics. A popular doggerel at the time summed it up:

> Hard by Pall Mall lives a wench call'd Nell
> King Charles the Second he kept her.
> She hath got a trick to handle his prick
> But never lays hands on his sceptre.

When the king had his famous stag parties Nell presided over them with all the skill of a comedienne – on one occasion hoisting her skirts to show the French ambassador her legs which she boasted were better than those of the Duchess of Portsmouth. Yet Nell showed another side to her character when she urged Charles to found Chelsea Hospital.

In 1684 she bore the king a son named Charles Beauclerk, and it became a piece of royal folklore that in a fit of pique Nell held the baby over a pond and threatened to drown him because he had not been enobled like Charles's other bastards. 'God preserve the Duke of St Albans!' was the instant reply of the urbane king.

When he was on his deathbed in 1685 Charles told his brother JAMES to take care of the Duchess of Portsmouth, and added, 'Let not poor Nelly starve.' Nell Gwynne was to live for only another two years, during which time she remained faithful to the memory of her royal lover, rejecting one would-be suitor with the words, 'Shall the dog lie where the deer once crouched.'

H

HAMPDEN, JOHN It was the attempted arrest of John Hampden and four other members of Parliament by CHARLES I in 1642 that precipitated the English Civil War. Born in 1594, Hampden was educated at Magdalen College, Oxford, and subsequently entered Parliament where he became a leading member of those opposed to the king's policies. In 1636 he refused to pay his share of Ship Money, an occasional tax on property in port towns in return for naval protection, which in previous years the king had extended across the country without the consent of Parliament. Hampden was prosecuted before the Court of the Exchequer, which had the effect of making him a popular hero. Later he was involved in the parliamentary proceedings that led to the execution of STRAFFORD. When the Civil War broke out he took a colonel's commission and raised a regiment for the Parliamentary army. After seeing action at Edgehill and Reading, John Hampden died on 24 June 1643 at Thame, after being wounded at the Battle of Chalgrove Field where PRINCE RUPERT suddenly turned on Hampden's pursuing force and defeated it.

HAMPTON COURT Sometimes described as the 'Versailles of England', Hampton Court Palace was the grandest residence ever used by the British monarchy, though it began as a private house – if a building containing a thousand rooms can be described merely as a house. In 1514 THOMAS WOLSEY had just been appointed Archbishop of York, a mark of HENRY VIII's favour for services rendered to the Crown. The same year he acquired an area of Thames-side land, 12 miles upstream from London, from the Knights Hospitallers of St John of Jerusalem. Attracted to the spot by its 'extraordinary salubrity', Wolsey chose it as a site for a country residence that, in the full thrust of his meteoric rise to power and wealth, would reflect his position as a king's most powerful minister since the days of THOMAS A BECKET, a position endorsed by the fact that he was made both Lord Chancellor and a cardinal the following year.

He built Hampton Court round two large courtyards known as the Clock and Base Courts, and at the same time enclosed, 1800 acres of land which now form Hampton Court Park and Bushy Park. When the building was completed he delighted in lavish entertaining – he is said to have had luxurious accommodation for 280 guests – but the splendour of his residence was to earn him the envy of his peers rather than their admiration, and the opinion flourished that he was living more like a king than

A monument to John Hampden close to the site of his unexpected defeat at the Battle of Chalgrove Field.

143

A Victorian painting of the Great Hall at Hampton Court.

the king himself. The Venetian ambassador reported that to reach his audience chamber one had to go through eight chambers, each hung with a tapestry which was changed on a weekly basis.

Wolsey's fall was even more dramatic than his rise. His prevarication over Henry's divorce not only lost him Henry's favour but earned him the hostility of the Boleyn faction. In 1529 he had to surrender the Great Seal when he was prosecuted under THE STATUTES OF PRAEMUNIRE, and in a vain endeavour to save himself he presented Hampton Court to the king, who also became the possessor of Wolsey's London residence which became WHITEHALL PALACE.

Under the royal owner Hampton Court did indeed become a palace; Henry enthusiastically transformed Wolsey's chapel into the amazing Chapel Royal, added a third court bounded by royal apartments, and created the Great Hall which remains an outstanding example of medieval design at its height. In the grounds the king installed archery butts, a tiltyard and a tennis court.

Five of Henry's six wives lived at Hampton Court, Anne Boleyn having apartments there before his divorce from CATHERINE OF ARAGON. It was there that Jane Seymour gave birth to the sickly EDWARD and where Catherine Howard was arrested after being questioned by ARCHBISHOP CRANMER on her alleged adultery with the musician Mannock. The king spent the last period of his life there with his sixth wife Catherine Parr.

His daughter MARY chose Hampton Court for her honeymoon with Philip, son of Charles V, King of Spain, and later resided there when she willed herself into believing that she was to have his child. ELIZABETH I, who had been under house arrest in Hampton Court's Water Gallery, did not feel the same aversion to it as she did to her other prison, the TOWER OF LONDON, but enjoyed going there where she took great interest in the palace's gardens, which remain one of its great features. The Chamberlains' Company – which included Shakespeare among its actors – put on productions for the queen in the Great Hall and continued to do so for her successor JAMES I. At the end of the Civil War CHARLES I was held at Hampton Court before his short-lived escape to the Isle of Wight, and later OLIVER CROMWELL, the Lord Protector, having sold off many of the palace's works of art, made it his home.

When WILLIAM AND MARY came to the throne they found the palace much to their liking and asked Sir Christopher Wren to remodel it on the lines of Versailles, which was being copied with varying success across the kingdoms of Europe, but before the work could be completed the money set aside for the project was spent, though

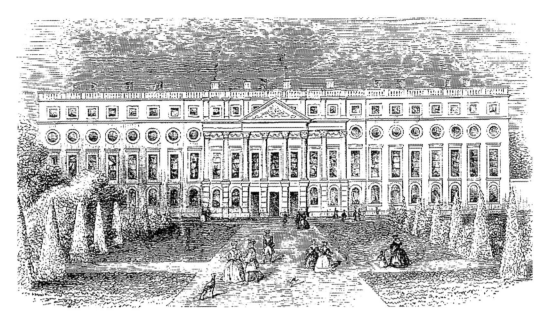

Wren left his mark with the state apartments, one set for the king and another for the queen as they were joint sovereigns, built round the Fountain Court.

After GEORGE I was presented with the throne he often stayed at Hampton Court with his two mistresses, whom his irreverent subjects nicknamed 'the Elephant and the Bean Pole', and for their entertainment Colley Cibber provided them with London plays. His son, GEORGE II, was the last king to live in the palace. GEORGE III did not like it because, so it was said, when he was a boy he had his ears severely boxed there by his grandfather George II. From then on the palace was used for grace and favour residences which today take up around a thousand rooms.

When QUEEN VICTORIA came to the throne, one of her early acts was to give the public access to Hampton Court and its gardens including the famous maze that goes back to the beginning of the eighteenth century.

HANDEL, GEORGE FREDERICK Born in Halle in 1685, Handel remains the best known composer of 'royal' music. At the age of 17 he became the Halle Cathedral organist while also studying law. Gaining a great reputation as a keyboard player he spent four years as a successful operatic composer. In 1710 he was appointed Court Musical Director to the Elector of Hanover.

An early engraving of Hampton Court, which was given public access by Queen Victoria.

However, his habit of taking time off to make frequent visits to England, where his opera *Rinaldo* was first performed, put a severe strain on relations with his royal patron. In 1713 QUEEN ANNE granted him a royal pen-sion and the following year the elector became GEORGE I.

As a peace offering Handel wrote his *Water Music* to be played for the king who was travelling by barge from Whitehall to Chelsea. King George doubled his pension and it was later raised again by QUEEN CAROLINE and lasted for the rest of his life. He was appointed composer to the CHAPEL ROYAL in 1723 and four years later became a naturalised citizen of Britain. The same year he composed the anthem *Zadok the Priest* for the coronation of GEORGE III, which has been performed at every coronation since. *Messiah* was composed in 1741 and in 1746 he produced the oratorio *Judas Maccabaeus* with the chorus 'See, the conquering hero comes' as a compliment to the DUKE OF CUMBERLAND returning from his victory at CULLODEN. *Music for the Royal Fireworks* was written in 1749 in celebration of the Treaty of Aix-la-Chapelle.

Handel died in 1759 and is interred in WEST-MINSTER ABBEY. In London his house is open to the public.

HANOVER, THE HOUSE OF Following the death of QUEEN ANNE in 1714 the House of Hanover was established in Britain through the ACT OF SETTLEMENT of 1701. The Act ensured that a Protestant would come to the throne if WILLIAM III or Queen Anne should die without issue, by naming a granddaughter of JAMES I, Sophia, Electress of Hanover or her heir, as the royal successor. The Act had a number of stipulations such as the sovereign should be a member of the Church of England and that the consent of Parliament had to be obtained before engaging in war to defend overseas territory that did not belong to Britain.

Thus the Crown went to Prince George Ludwig of Hanover, which set aside the Roman Catholic Stuarts' hereditary claim. When GEORGE I was crowned the Stuart claimant was the son of JAMES II, Prince James Francis Edward ('the Old Pretender'), who was excluded from the succession because of his Roman Catholicism. In 1715 his followers – the Jacobites – mounted a rebellion to restore the House of Stuart which, despite the public antipathy to the new German-speaking king, failed, as did the second Jacobite uprising of 1745.

Up to the reign of QUEEN VICTORIA the Hanoverian kings were better known for their private lives than acts of kingship, though to be fair they reigned but no longer ruled while the government and contending Whigs and Tories made the serious news of the day. One aspect of the Hanoverians was the almost traditional animosity between father and eldest son, with sides being taken by political parties. And of all royal houses the Hanoverians were the most scandal ridden. Morganatic and illegal marriages, royal mistresses being given public status, and adultery, were commonplace and reported to the public by a

The Hanoverians

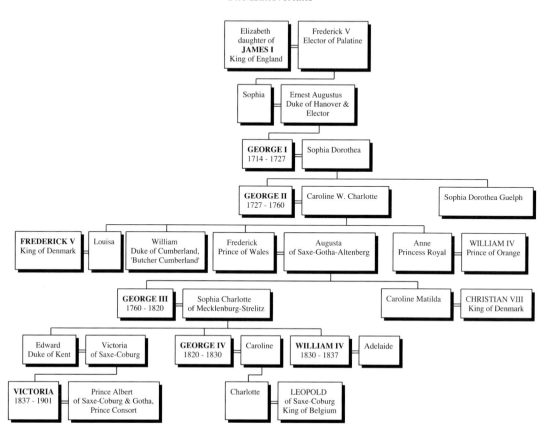

The coat of arms of George, the first Hanoverian king of England.

burgeoning press. The exception was GEORGE III but the popularity he enjoyed with the people was eroded by his extravagant and bigamous son. Indeed, it could be argued that Victoria with her family values restored respect and affection for the monarchy which continued with her successors.

The House of Hanover ended with Victoria's death in 1901 and was replaced by the House of Saxe-Coburg-Gotha. The change of name did not reflect a change in the royal line but came about because EDWARD VII was the son of Prince Albert of Saxe-Coburg-Gotha. During the First World War there was such detestation of things German that in 1917 GEORGE V eliminated all traditional German titles from his House and renamed it the House of Windsor.

The Hanoverian dynasty was also known as the House of Brunswick, as Britain's Hanoverian kings were also dukes of Brunswick-Wolfenbüttel, and until Victoria came to the throne they were electors of Hanover as well. As the Hanoverians were descended from the old Guelph family they were also known as Guelphs.

HARDICANUTE The son of CANUTE and his second wife EMMA, the widow of ETHELRED THE UNREADY, Hardicanute became the King of

Denmark on the death of his father in 1035. His elder half-brother HAROLD HAREFOOT became King of England in the same year despite the fact that some Anglo-Saxon nobles, led by EARL GODWINE of Wessex, favoured Hardicanute. In 1040, encouraged by Queen Emma, Hardicanute was preparing to sail to Britain to seize the Crown when news reached him that Harold had died. Thus he inherited the kingdom peacefully, but soon demonstrated his harsh nature by having the body of his brother disinterred at St Clement Danes in London, decapitated and thrown into the Thames. He revived the unpopular Danegeld tax for his own benefit, and this alienated him throughout the kingdom. There were several insurrections and in Worcester rebellious citizens killed his tax collectors. In revenge he razed the city.

However, his subjects did not have to endure his tyranny for long. In 1042, at the age of 24, he was a guest at the wedding feast of his Danish standard-bearer, Towed the Proud, when, according to the *Anglo-Saxon Chronicle*, 'he was standing at his drink and he suddenly fell to the ground with fearful convulsions, and those who were near him caught him and he spoke no words afterwards. He died on 8 June . . .' He was interred in Winchester Cathedral and was succeeded by his half-brother EDWARD THE CONFESSOR.

HARDRADA, HAROLD Known as 'The Ruthless', Harold Hardrada became the King of Norway in 1047 after a Viking career that earned him his nickname. In 1066 he invaded England with the aid

A monument to the Battle of Stamford Bridge where King Harold defeated Harold Hardrada. *(Photograph by Mark Ronson)*

147

of HAROLD II's brother Tostig on the pretext that KING HARDICANUTE had promised the kingdom to his predecessor King Magnus. On 25 September of that year he fought King Harold at Stamford Bridge where he was defeated and killed. Although it was a great victory for Harold, it had drawn him away from the south of England where WILLIAM THE CONQUEROR was able to land his army unopposed and therefore Hardrada's incursion may have altered history.

HAROLD II Although Harold Godwineson, the last Saxon King of England, was without royal blood he was elected to the throne, an event which led to the greatest change in English history. The son of EARL GODWINE and his wife Gytha, CANUTE's sister-in-law, he was born *c*. 1022. On the death of his father in 1053 he succeeded to the earldom of Wessex and rose to be the power behind EDWARD THE CONFESSOR's throne, in effect ruling the kingdom with great energy so that he was to become known as the 'Duke of the English'. His brother Tostig became Earl of the Northumbrians.

Around 1058 – the exact date is not certain – Harold made a pilgrimage to Rome where he had an audience with Pope Benedict X and acquired a collection of holy relics. Returning to England he was attacked by bandits, but managed to escape with his saintly fragments. His veneration for these was such that on his return he built a church at Waltham to house them, which was dedicated by the Bishop of York in the spring of 1060. The church also contained a famous rood, or Cross of Christ, which was believed to have miraculous powers, and before which Harold was to pray in his time of despair.

In 1063 Gruffydd ap Llywelyn (*see* WALES, KINGS OF), King of Wales, was making forays into England which caused Harold and Tostig to mount a campaign against him. Harold ordered his troops to lay aside their heavy armour and weapons and, instead of fighting in the usual close formation they were ordered to spread out when they met the enemy. They lived off the land and moved as quickly as the Welsh guerrillas, and these tactics met with spectacular success. Wales was ravaged and at every point where Gruffydd was defeated a stone monument was set up on which was carved the words 'Here Harold was victorious'. In August 1063 the Welsh sued for peace and as a token of submission a deputation brought Harold a bundle of bloodied cloth in which was wrapped Gruffydd's head.

The following year Harold and his sister had embarked on a pleasure voyage from Selsey Bill when a storm drove their vessel on to the French coast at Ponthieu. The bedraggled crew was captured by a local count and Harold was handed over to WILLIAM, Duke of Normandy, at Rouen. Although he was treated as an honoured guest it became clear that he would not be allowed to return to England until he had agreed to the duke's

A scene from the Bayeux Tapestry depicting Harold taking his vow to assist William the Conqueror.

conditions. One of these was a promise that he would marry one of William's daughters when she was old enough. The duke, who had been promised the English Crown by Edward the Confessor when he visited the English court, considered that this would gain him a useful alliance. But the main condition was that Harold should vow that he would do everything within his power to ensure that Duke William would be crowned as King Edward's successor when the English throne became vacant.

Harold swore to this with his hand on a small leather box known as a phylactery. Most likely he did so under the conviction that a vow made under duress could not be held to be valid, but after taking the oath he was shown that the phylactery contained relics of saints which gave it religious significance. Yet, after his return to England, Harold broke part of the vow by marrying Edith, the widow of Gruffydd the Welsh leader he had defeated.

In 1065 there was a rebellion in Northumbria against the misgovernment of Harold's brother, Earl Tostig. The rebels marched on York, declared Tostig to be an outlaw and elected Harold's brother-in-law Morcar in his place. King Edward ordered Harold to put down the insurrection by force, but fearing that to do so could spark off civil war Harold parleyed with the rebels and, although Tostig was his brother, he agreed to Morcar becoming the new Earl of Northumbria.

When King Edward was dying in the first days of January 1066 he is said to have told Harold that he should be his successor. The Witan confirmed this by endorsing Harold's claim to the throne, and he was crowned on 6 January 1066, most likely at old St Paul's in London. Duke William sent messengers to the new king reminding him of the 'holy' oath he had taken. Although Harold argued that an oath made under duress was invalid, he knew that soon more than messengers would arrive from Normandy, and he began preparations to meet an invasion by raising the fyrd – freemen required to perform military service when called upon – and fortifying strategic positions on the south coast.

On the ninth day after Easter 1066 a strange light appeared in the sky. To Harold and his subjects it was a portent of ill-omen and was later incorporated into the BAYEUX TAPESTRY. In fact it was a comet which, after reappearing in 1759, was named Halley's Comet.

Months passed during which Harold kept his fleet in readiness to meet a Norman invasion but when preparations for such an invasion were completed Duke William was held back by contrary winds. In September Harold learned that another claimant to the throne, HAROLD HARDRADA, King of Norway, was invading England ahead of the Normans. In this he was supported by Earl Tostig who could not forgive his brother for allowing his earldom of Northumbria to pass to Earl Morcar.

Harold Hardrada arrived at the mouth of the Tyne with a fleet of three hundred ships and sailed up the Ouse to Riccall, south of York. Harold's brothers-in-law, Morcar, Earl of Northumbria, and Edwin, Earl of Mercia, prepared to resist the invaders. Battle was joined on 20 September 1066 at Gate Fulford, 2 miles south of York. Although it is one of England's forgotten battles it was one of the most significant. Had the English won, it would have meant that Harold could have remained in the south of England with his army and the Norman Conquest might never have succeeded. As it was, Harold Hardrada was victorious and he camped outside York while negotiations were arranged for the surrender of the city.

When news of the Fulford defeat reached Harold, he was ill with an agonising pain in his leg. Distressed at being unable to lead his men, he spent the night in prayer before the holy rood in Waltham church. Meanwhile, the Abbot of Ramsey had a vision in which Edward the Confessor commanded him to tell Harold that he would triumph. On hearing this Harold found that his pain had vanished and he was able to march north to quell one invasion, but leaving the south vulnerable to another. The troops marched by night as well as by day

A coin from the reign of Harold II.

under the baleful glare of the sinister comet. On 25 September the two armies faced each other at Stamford Bridge on the River Derwent, 9 miles north-east of York. On the first day of October Harold celebrated England's greatest victory over the Norsemen with a feast at York. In the middle of the festivities a messenger arrived with the news that Duke William had landed his army at Pevensey. Harold's army, exhausted after the forced march from London to do battle at Stamford Bridge, were now faced with a return march. Harold summoned all thegns and shire militia to follow and hurried south with his housecarls – his élite bodyguard of men of rank – raising new levies on the way. Meanwhile, the Normans moved several miles inland from their landing place, set up a prefabricated castle, sent out raiding parties, and had ample time to prepare for the inevitable battle.

On 13 October Harold had marched south from London with seven thousand men, a number equal to that of Duke William's army. Although his force was less than half of England's trained warriors, Harold chose not to wait to build up his army and defences but hurried to meet his enemies instead of forcing them to march against him through hostile country. One explanation for this apparent military misjudgement was that Harold was anxious to protect his own people and lands in Sussex from being harried by the invaders.

The next day the battle that was to alter the whole course of English history was fought 10 miles north-west of Hastings. Harold positioned his army, weary from a forced march from London, on a ridge where BATTLE ABBEY stands today. At half-past nine Duke William ordered the first advance against English 'shield wall' lines, but it was driven back, as were subsequent attacks. During the morning and early afternoon the fighting continued inconclusively but by mid-afternoon the Normans began to gain ascendancy. The King's two brothers, Gyrth and Leofwine, were killed, and then Harold was brought down by a chance arrow. The housecarls fought on, but after dusk the English survivors left the field leaving William to give thanks to God for his victory.

The following day Harold's mother, Gytha, sent a message to the victors offering the weight of her son's body in gold if she could have it for proper burial. William refused, declaring that it should be laid under a great cairn on the shore of the kingdom Harold had defended so valiantly. Because of the

A stone memorial marking the spot where King Harold is believed to have been buried at Waltham Abbey. *(Photograph by Paul Abrahams)*

wounds that disfigured the king, he could not be identified among the dead until his mistress Edith Swan-neck, by whom he had several children, was brought to the battlefield where she finally recognised his body by a familiar mark. Harold was buried in the area, but later his remains were translated to Waltham Abbey where today his grave is marked by a stone.

HAROLD HAREFOOT Following the death of CANUTE in 1035 two of his sons were candidates for the throne of England. One was Harold, born *c.* 1016, whose mother, Elgiva of Northampton, had

A coin from the reign of Harold Harefoot.

been Canute's first wife. The other contender was
HARDICANUTE who was already King of Denmark. His mother was EMMA the widowed wife of
ETHELRED before she became Canute's second
wife. Although Canute had hoped that Harold
would inherit his English kingdom, many Saxons,
led by Earl Godwine of Wessex, favoured Hardicanute. With the danger of civil war hanging over
the land, the succession was debated at a meeting of
the Witan at Oxford with the result that Harold was
named king. His reign only lasted five years during
which he spent much of his time hunting and
because of his unusual ability in running, earned the
nickname 'Harefoot'. When he died in 1040 his
half-brother was planning an invasion of England
with the support of his mother Queen Emma.

HARPIST TO THE PRINCE OF WALES In the
reign of JAMES I the office began when Robert ap
Huw became the first of a long line of court
harpists. Up until the reign of VICTORIA the
holders of the office invariably came from Wales,
but this changed when the queen took Thomas
Chatterton, an English harpist, into her private band.
On his death the post went back to a Welshman,
John Thomas, to whom EDWARD VII gave the new
title of Honorary Harpist to the King after the death
of his mother. When John Thomas died in 1913 it
seemed that the chain of royal harpists had ended.

When the investiture of PRINCE CHARLES as
Prince of Wales was planned in 1969 the possibility
of reinstating the post of royal harpist was considered and then rejected as being too archaic. But
in the millennium year of 2000 this view changed,
with the appointment of a harpist whose duty it is to
play for the prince, especially when visiting Wales.

HASTINGS, BATTLE OF Early on Saturday 14
October 1066 DUKE WILLIAM OF NORMANDY,
having arrived at Pevensey with his invasion force
several days previously, led his men on to the Field
of Senlac. Facing them was KING HAROLD's
army of between seven and eight thousand men
weary after a forced march from London. The
English had taken up position on the ridge where
the ruins of BATTLE ABBEY stand today, and here
Harold waited beneath his banner embroidered with
the figure of a warrior. William's army, which
numbered roughly the same as the English, was
arranged in three divisions with the Normans in the
centre, flanked by French and Flemings on the right

Norman cavalry charging up the slope at Senlac to
attack Harold's foot soldiers, as portrayed on the
Bayeux Tapestry.

and the Bretons who had joined his expedition on
the left. At half-past nine William ordered the first
attack. With flights of arrows providing covering
fire the Normans rushed upon the defenders' shield
wall, but shouting their battle cry of 'Holy Cross!
Holy Cross!' the English drove them back.

This was followed by a heavier assault in which
the duke's infantry was supported by mail-clad
cavalry, but again the English held the line.
Harold's famed housecarls – two thousand élite
warriors who had brought him victory at the Battle
of Stamford Bridge – gave the Bretons such a
bloody reception with their axes that they turned
and fled. In their confusion the cry went up that

A monument marking the spot where Harold,
England's last Saxon king, was slain at the Battle of
Hastings.

William had been slain. On hearing this the duke removed his helmet and rode among his men to calm the panic. At one point Harold's brother Gyrth hurled a spear that killed William's horse. The duke leaped clear, ran straight at Gyrth and slew him. In the course of the day three of his horses were killed under him but he remained unscathed.

For several hours the fighting continued without either side gaining the advantage. As well as directing the defence, Harold fought wherever the mêlée was thickest and his valour was afterwards praised by Norman writers who declared that no one escaped who came within range of his terrible war axe.

At mid-afternoon Duke William executed his famous ruse, ordering his men to advance and then pretend to flee in panic. Scenting victory, many of the English troops disobeyed the commands of their captains, broke their shield walls and charged down the slope only to be cut down by an onrush of Norman cavalry. With the tide of battle now running in his favour, William ordered his archers to shoot upwards so that their arrows would fall like deadly rain on the English who were so tightly packed there was hardly room for the slain to fall to the ground.

One of these arrows struck Harold in the eye. As he fell, twenty Norman knights, who had vowed to carry off his standard, made a fanatical charge into the English ranks. Four managed to break through and hacked the last Anglo-Saxon King of England to death with their swords. The faithful housecarls surrounded their master's body and defended it until the last man was cut down. Then Duke William – now truly the Conqueror – ordered his standard to be unfurled where Harold's had stood, and gave thanks to God for his victory. Then, according to an old chronicle, 'he sat down to eat and drink among the dead'.

HATFIELD PALACE Only briefly in royal ownership, Hatfield Palace is chiefly associated with ELIZABETH I as it was where she spent most of her life before she became the Virgin Queen. It had its beginnings in the twelfth century when it was a manor belonging to the bishops of Ely, which gave it the name of Bishop's Hatfield. During the reign of HENRY VII John Morton, Lord Chancellor and Archbishop of Canterbury, was responsible for transforming Hatfield into such a grand residence that before long it caught the covetous eye of HENRY VIII. He acquired it after the death of Thomas Goodrich,

Bishop of Ely, by reaching an understanding with his successor who surrendered Hatfield in return for several far less impressive manors. Thus in 1533 it became a royal palace, though its association with royalty was to last for only seventy-four years.

Although Henry had been eager to take possession of Hatfield he rarely visited it and it became a home for his two daughters, MARY, the daughter of divorced CATHERINE OF ARAGON, and Elizabeth. The latter arrived there when she was only 3 months old and her mother Anne Boleyn was still hoping to produce a male heir. Later PRINCE EDWARD, Henry's only son, who was born to Jane Seymour, went to live at Hatfield where he and Elizabeth were given lessons together. The sickly little prince must have felt genuine affection for his half-sister as he granted the palace to her after he became Edward VI.

It was a happy time for Elizabeth. She was free to enjoy Hatfield's great park – she was always keen on alfresco occasions – and under her tutor Roger Ascham she studied to become probably the most learned monarch in the Europe of her day.

Elizabeth's pleasant life in the palace ended abruptly when her half-sister MARY ascended the throne. She was imprisoned in the Tower of London on the suspicion, or so it was alleged, of having been linked in some way with Thomas Wyatt, who, in the company of the father of LADY JANE GREY, led a rebellion of Kentish men and paid for his folly with

An early engraving of Hatfield House as it was when Elizabeth I lived there under virtual house arrest.

his life. Later she was moved to WOODSTOCK PALACE, where she was under house arrest, and then finally she was allowed to return to Hatfield where a careful watch was kept on her.

It was said that she was sitting under a tree in the palace grounds reading a Greek testament when a delegation arrived to announce that Mary I was dead and that she was now Queen of England. Her first act was to make William Cecil her Principal Secretary of State, a post he filled with remarkable skill for the next forty years. Then, escorted by her new MASTER OF HORSE, ROBERT DUDLEY, Earl of Leicester, the new queen left the palace for London.

Elizabeth only returned to Hatfield on rare occasions for the hunting, and it was not long after her death that the palace passed out of royal hands. In 1607 Robert Cecil, the son of William Cecil, acquired it from JAMES I. Four years later his splendid new Hatfield House replaced the old palace which had largely been demolished to provide building material, though the Great Hall was spared and is all that remains of the once royal residence today.

HATTON, CHRISTOPHER In 1564 ELIZA-BETH I found a new favourite to the chagrin of LEICESTER and the court. He was a young lawyer named Christopher Hatton and he owed his good fortune to the Queen being impressed by his graceful dancing at a masque. She appointed him Captain of the Guard, after which his rise was meteoric, culminating in his appointment as Lord Chancellor in 1587.

Elizabeth treated him with extravagant affection, calling him 'her mutton' and 'her sweet lids', a reference to his eyelids. Missives flowed between them to the delight of the Queen, who was never averse to flattery. Hatton was as skilful at penning compliments as he was at dancing.

'My spirit and soul, I feel, agreeth with my body and life, that to serve you is heaven; but lack you, is more than hell's torment unto them,' he wrote in one letter to her.

Taking up residence in Ely Place, the London palace of the Bishops of Ely, Hatton spent large sums of money on improving it – money which he borrowed from the Queen. It was said that when she demanded repayment of the loans he died of a broken heart. Today, the area that adjoined Ely Palace is known as Hatton Garden.

HENRIETTA MARIA Born at the Louvre Palace on 26 November 1609, Henrietta Maria was the daughter of Henry IV of France and Marie de' Medici. Six months later she was taken to the abbey church of St Denis for the funeral of her father.

A curious story is connected with his death. Henry, who was crowned before his marriage, heard a prophecy that on the day after his future wife's coronation he would die. Consequently, when he married Marie de' Medici, he postponed her enthronement year after year. After the birth of Henrietta, the queen begged to be formally enthroned, arguing that if he was killed on a forthcoming campaign against Hapsburg forces, her children's position would be more secure if she had been formally crowned. He agreed reluctantly and the ceremony took place at St Denis on 10 May 1610. The next day the royal party returned to Paris and in the busy rue de la Ferronerie a bystander leaned through the window of the coach and stabbed the king in the heart.

The assassin, Francois Ravaillac, was under the delusion that Henry was about to make war on the Pope. He paid the penalty for the regicide by having ropes tied to his arms and legs, the other ends being

Queen Henrietta Maria, a power behind the throne of Charles I and the self-styled 'she-majesty generalissima over all'.

attached to four teams of horses. Then, watched by the mourning court, he was slowly pulled apart.

Queen Marie was appointed regent when her 9-year-old son was crowned Louis XIII at Rheims Cathedral, and Henrietta with her brothers and sisters was brought up at a royal hunting lodge at Saint-Germain-en-Laye away from the epidemics which regularly infected Paris.

In 1620 it was thought politically advantageous that Henrietta should marry JAMES I's son, the future CHARLES I. When the English ambassador expressed the view that the princess's Roman Catholicism would raise difficulties, the 10-year old Henrietta declared that 'a wife ought to have no will but that of her husband', words that were to have an ironical ring in later years. The plan did not develop until the death of James I in 1625, when Charles married Henrietta by proxy on 1 May 1625 at the cathedral of Notre Dame in Paris. On her arrival in London the new queen was welcomed enthusiastically by its citizens.

For the next two years the royal couple lived apart, meeting when state occasions required. Meanwhile, the queen's popularity evaporated,

The Palace of St Germain, Paris, where exiled English royalty held court and plotted. (Photograph by Mark Ronson)

largely because of her Roman Catholic entourage which included a bishop, twenty-nine priests and over four hundred attendants. The English, remembering the Marian persecutions, were suspicious of Roman Catholic foreigners. Matters were not helped when Henrietta refused to be crowned with Charles in a Church of England coronation ceremony.

The King's resentment of the Queen's clergy was matched by her aversion to his influential favourite George Villiers, 1st Duke of Buckingham. This ended on 23 August 1628 when the duke was assassinated by John Felton, a discontented army subaltern. Henrietta comforted her distraught husband with such understanding that at last love began to grow between them. When she gave birth to a premature baby who died after its christening, she was so moved by Charles's consideration that later she wrote: 'I was the happiest and most fortunate of queens; for not only had I every pleasure the heart can desire; I had a husband who adored me.'

In October the Queen was pregnant again and this time the birth was normal, Henrietta being delivered on 29 May 1630 of a healthy son who was christened CHARLES after his father. An heir to his throne greatly strengthened the King's position and increased the love he felt for his wife. Other

children followed in quick succession and though political problems were looming, the tenor of daily life continued pleasantly. Charles arranged extravagant court masques for Henrietta's entertainment and on one occasion a dwarf in a tiny suit of armour jumped out of a pie placed before her.

Inevitably the civil unrest grew. The King's greatest supporter, Thomas Wentworth, Lord STRAFFORD, was tried in Westminster Hall and condemned to death, which required the King to sign the death warrant. He refused, having promised his friend he would not let him 'suffer in life, honour or fortune'. Outside Whitehall Palace a mob shouted for Strafford's death but for two days Charles still held out. Finally the Queen, who feared for her children, both beseeched and bullied him, until on 9 May 1641 he signed the fateful document, an act which was to haunt him.

Charles now regained some popularity with his subjects to the concern of Parliament which countered with the Grand Remonstrance, accusing him of unconstitutional acts. In reply he decided to take action against the five leading members of the opposition, a plan that some historians claim was the result of Henrietta's 'taunts and reproaches'. Whatever the truth of this, on 4 January 1642 Charles set out from Whitehall for Westminster with 200 halberdiers to make the arrests, having told Henrietta, 'If you find one hour elapses without hearing ill news from me, you will see me return the master of my kingdom.'

After an hour the Queen told her disloyal friend Lady Carlisle, 'Pym [the king's principal opponent] and his confederates are arrested!' Lady Carlisle immediately sent a warning to the five so that when Charles, delayed by a crowd of petitioners, reached the Commons his intended victims had fled. Realising the result of her words, Henrietta threw herself into Charles's arms, blaming herself, and later said to her friend Madame de Motteville, 'Never did he treat me with less kindness than before it happened, though I had ruined him.'

On 10 January Pym and his four companions returned triumphantly to London while the royal family took refuge at HAMPTON COURT. Soon there was an emotional farewell at Dover when Henrietta and her daughter Mary Henrietta boarded the *Lion*. The Queen carried some of the Crown jewels and her personal jewellery to sell for the royal cause while the princess was on her way to her husband WILLIAM II OF ORANGE, event-

ually becoming the mother of WILLIAM III, who was to ascend the English throne. As the *Lion* sailed away Charles rode along the cliffs, waving until it was lost to view. On 23 October the English Civil War started in earnest, with the Battle of Edgehill.

Although William of Orange welcomed his mother-in-law, the Protestant Dutch feared her presence would lead to trouble with the English Parliament. They expressed their feelings towards her by not removing their hats in her presence, but the queen had more on her mind than the rudeness of burghers. In Breda dealers were wary of the

The site of the Battle of Edgehill today. Here the Civil War started in earnest although the outcome of the battle was inconclusive.

Crown jewels but the Queen's personal jewellery found a ready sale. 'You may judge how, when they know we want money, they keep their foot on our throat,' she said in a letter to Charles. 'You cannot imagine how pretty your pearls were when they were taken out of the gold settings and made into a chain.'

On 2 February 1643 the Queen sailed from Scheveningen in the English ship *Princess-Royal*, accompanied by eleven transports filled with munitions. A storm forced the fleet to turn back with the loss of two ships, but her second attempt was successful and on 22 February her ships anchored off Bridlington, when she and her party moved into the village to wait for the Royalists to collect the vital stores. Early the next morning a naval squadron opened fire on the port, the captain of one ship having landed secretly to ascertain in which house the queen was staying so guns could be trained upon it.

Henrietta wrote to Charles: 'The balls whistled so loud about me, that my company pressed me earnestly to go out of that house, the cannon having totally beaten down the neighbours' houses. . . .' She pulled on a dress and ran barefoot into the street, then remembered that she had left her little dog Mitte in the bedroom. She raced back and then with Mitte in her arms followed her fleeing household. 'I went on foot to some little distance from the town,' she wrote, 'and got into the shelter of a ditch . . . the cannon bullets fell thick about us and a servant was killed within seventy paces of me. The firing lasted till the ebbing of the tide.'

York was the Royalist headquarters of the North and from here the Earl of Newcastle dispatched two thousand men to escort the Queen and a baggage train of over 200 wagons loaded with arms, ammunition and six cannons. It was then that she decided that the war in the North was going to be her war in which she would lead an army. Writing about herself in the third person she said, 'She rode on horseback throughout all the march as a general; she ate her meals in sight of the enemy, without seeking shelter from sun or rain; she spoke frankly to her soldiers, who seemed infinitely delighted with her; she took a town . . . very useful to the royal cause.'

She then wrote to Charles that she was bringing him an army of three thousand, thirty companies of horse and dragoons and six cannon, describing herself as 'she-majesty generalissima over all'. On 13 July PRINCE RUPERT escorted her to Keinton where, waiting to take her to Oxford, was Charles and their two eldest sons. It was a joyful reunion after sixteen months. Before long Henrietta was pregnant and her campaigning days were over.

On 17 April 1644 at Abingdon the King and Queen had their final parting, she going to the safety of Bedford House in Exeter where on 16 June she became the mother of her ninth child. When Exeter was threatened by Parliamentary forces the Queen, who had been suffering from puerperal fever, left her sickbed and, accompanied by one of her ladies, a priest and her doctor, set off for Falmouth. Some 3 miles from Exeter Gate she was forced to hide in a hut for two days, without food and lying beneath a pile of rubbish. From Truro she wrote to Charles of her intention to go to France, concluding: 'Adieu, my dear heart. If I die, believe

that you will lose a person who has never been other than entirely yours, and who by her affection has deserved that you should not forget her.'

Setting out from Falmouth on 2 July the Queen's ship was fired upon by a Parliamentary vessel. Rather than fall into enemy hands and used to pressure the King in negotiations, she declared that the powder magazine must be fired if her capture was likely. To everyone's relief the ship outsailed its pursuers.

In France Henrietta sold her remaining jewellery and sent the money to Charles while experiencing her second civil war as the troubles with the Fronde tore France apart. On hearing of her husband's capture she showed her courage by applying for a passport to travel to London in order to plead for his life. But on 30 January when the news of the king's execution reached Henrietta at St Germain, where she had sought refuge from the disturbances in Paris, she went into a trance-like state for over an hour. Her active political career was now ended, but she maintained a court for exiled Royalists and after the Restoration she visited England twice. She died in 1669 as a result of being prescribed an overdose of opium, inspiring an epigram which also referred to the deaths of her father and her husband:

Tous tois morts par assassin,
Ravaillac, Cromwell and medecin.

HENRY I When WILLIAM I ('The Conqueror') lay dying in Rouen in 1087 his youngest son Henry listened while he divided his dominions between Henry's two elder brothers, Robert ('Curthose') and William ('Rufus'). When Henry asked what he would receive, the king said, 'Five thousand pounds in silver from the treasury.' Henry then asked what good was silver if he had nowhere to live, and his father replied prophetically, 'Let your brothers peacefully precede you . . . you in your own time will have all the honour which I have obtained and you will excel your brothers both in riches and power.'

Henry was born to King William and Queen Matilda in 1068 at Selby, Yorkshire, and was their only son to be born in England. This made him more acceptable to the Anglo-Saxons than his 'foreign' brothers, and his father, aware of this advantage, had him educated entirely in England where he learned to speak English as well as Norman French.

A manuscript portrait of Henry I, known as the 'Lion of Justice' on account of his reforms.

After the death of their father there was discord between William and Robert with Henry sometimes siding with one and then with the other. In 1090 William bribed the citizens of Rouen to revolt against his brother Robert and on this occasion Henry supported his eldest brother. When the insurrection was suppressed, Conan, the rebel leader, was brought before Henry who took him to the top of the castle tower and told him to gaze over the land he had failed to win. Realising his hours were numbered, Conan asked for a priest to shrive him but Henry's answer was to hurl him to the ground far below.

Duke Robert, the most easy-going and romantic of the three brothers, joined the First Crusade. In order to finance his army he mortgaged his duchy for 10,000 marks to his brother William so that for a while England and Normandy united again. In 1099 Jerusalem was captured by the crusaders and news reached England that Duke Robert would soon be returning to reclaim Normandy. Henry knew that once this happened he would have little chance of claiming the Crown on William's death. Then, on 2 August 1100, while hunting in the New Forest, the king was killed by an arrow and Henry, realising he must act swiftly, immediately galloped to Winchester, demanding the keys of the royal treasury; it was vital for a claimant to the throne that he had control of the kingdom's financial assets. The next day the semblance of a WITAN dutifully proclaimed Henry the new sovereign and on 5 August he was crowned at WESTMINSTER ABBEY.

At the time of his coronation Henry was physically a powerful man of middle height with black hair lying thick on his forehead and mild, bright eyes which gave little indication of his harsh character. Wisely he promised peace for his subjects, healed the rift with the Church created by his late brother and reinstated the laws of King Edward. This made him popular with his subjects. He also restored Saxon blood to the royal line by marrying Matilda, the daughter of Malcolm III of Scotland (*see* SCOTLAND, EARLY KINGS OF) and a great-granddaughter of ETHELRED II.

Meanwhile, Duke Robert returned a hero from the Crusades. When he reached Normandy, Ranulf Flambard, once his father's favourite minister, urged him to fight for the English Crown which was his rightful inheritance. Battle-hardened after Palestine, Robert took little urging and on 20 July 1101 his fleet arrived at Portsmouth, and soon afterwards at Alton in Hampshire. English and Norman armies confronted each other again, but the expected battle did not take place as at a parley Henry agreed to relinquish all rights to territory in Normandy and Robert renounced his claim to the English throne.

William the Conqueror's prophecy still had to be fulfilled and in 1106, on the pretext of saving the Norman people from his brother's misrule, Henry crossed the Channel with his army. On 2 September a battle was fought between the brothers' armies at Tinchebrai and the Normans were defeated. The victorious English saw it as a reversal of the Battle of Hastings fought forty years earlier.

Henry now had control of both England and Normandy and he began the reforms for which he became known as the 'Lion of Justice'. He reorganised the methods of taxation and the judicial system, and established the Curia Regis or King's Court. As well as being a court of law, its members were employed to bring remote districts into the tax system and make the population familiar with justice. The president of this new body was called the Justiciar, and whoever held the post became the most important minister in the kingdom. The first Justiciar was Roger, Bishop of Salisbury, who found royal favour by the speed with which he could say Mass.

Henry also reformed the coinage and saw to it that quick justice was meted out to forgers, and though his rule was harsh it did bring security to the kingdom. The *Anglo-Saxon Chronicle* stated: 'Good man he was, and great awe there was of him. No man durst misdo another in his time. Peace he made for man and beast.' The length of his arm was established as the universal unit of measurement.

Queen Matilda bore two children, a son named William and a daughter who was named Matilda after her mother. In May 1118 the queen died. Neglected by the king who had married her for political reasons, she had occupied herself with charitable works and her sole pleasure was listening to minstrels' romances. Henry's taste for numerous mistresses resulted in thirteen illegitimate offspring. Two years later at the Battle of Brémule fighting

A medieval artist's impression of the sinking of the *White Ship* in which the royal heir Prince William perished.

Louis of France he was wounded twice. A victorious Henry returned to England on 25 November 1120, Prince William deciding to follow in a vessel known as the *White Ship*.

What followed was recorded by William of Malmesbury: '. . . the young man who was just over seventeen and himself king in all but name, commanded that another vessel should be prepared for himself, and almost all of the young nobility, being his boon companions, gathered round him. The sailors, too, who had drunk over much cried out with true seamen's hilarity that they must overtake the ship that had already set out. . . . Wherefore these rash youths, who were flown with wine, launched this vessel from the shore although it was now dark . . . but the carelessness of her drunken crew drove her on to a rock which rose above the waves not far from the shore. . . . A boat was, however, at last launched and the young prince taken into it. He might easily have reached the shore in safety had not his bastard sister, the Countess of Perche, now struggling with death in the larger vessel implored his assistance. . . . He ordered his boat to return to the ship that he might rescue his sister, and it was thus that the unhappy youth met his death. The boat overcharged by the multitude that leapt into her capsized and sank and buried all indiscriminately in the deep. No ship ever brought such misery to England.' With William was drowned his brother Richard, Henry's only other legitimate son.

The Great Seal of Henry I.

With the sinking of the *White Ship* Henry lost the male heir to the throne and in an attempt to gain a new one he married Adela, the daughter of Geoffrey VII, Count of Louvain, but there were no children. Accepting that he was unlikely to father a male heir, he declared that his newly widowed daughter Matilda would assume the throne on his death, resulting in renewed unrest across the Channel. To counter this he arranged an alliance with Anjou by marrying Matilda to Geoffrey, the son of Count Fulk. The youth was surnamed PLANTAGENET, from two French words '*Plante Genet*' relating to his custom of wearing a sprig of yellow broom on his helmet instead of a feathered plume.

For the next few years Henry held court in Normandy, but the Normans, being the hereditary foes of Anjou, deeply opposed the idea of having Geoffrey as a future overlord and when Matilda gave birth to a son, the future HENRY II, it was with great difficulty that the king forced them to take an oath of allegiance to her and the child.

In November 1135 after a day's hunting, Henry ate a 'surfeit of lampreys' – small water creatures that attach themselves to stones. Though it was a dish of which he was fond, it poisoned him. After a week's illness King Henry died on 1 December. His body was embalmed and brought to England to be interred at Reading Abbey which he had founded.

HENRY II If ever England needed a strong ruler it was after the 'nineteen long winters' of STEPHEN's reign, and when Henry Plantagenet and his wife ELEANOR OF AQUITAINE were crowned at Westminster on 19 December 1154 the unhappy country found one. The young king brought order to his new kingdom with a vigour that made him one of the country's outstanding sovereigns.

His energy was reflected in his appearance. In a contemporary account, Peter of Blois wrote: 'His eyes were full, guileless and dove-like when he is at peace, gleaming like fire when his temper is aroused. He has a broad, square, lion-like face. . . . His hands show by their coarseness that he is careless and pays little attention to his person. Although his legs are bruised and livid from hard riding, he never sits down except on horseback or at meals. He always has weapons in his hands when not engaged in consultation or at his books.'

Henry was born on 5 March 1133 at Le Mans, the eldest son of Geoffrey, Count of Anjou, by Matilda, the only daughter of HENRY I of England. He lived with his mother in France until the death of her father. Then, in the belief that the kingdom was rightfully hers, Matilda set out to win it from the 'usurper' Stephen, Count of Blois. When Henry reached 16 Matilda conferred her Norman dominions and her claim to the English throne upon him, and three years later he inherited Anjou from his father. These possessions were extended again in 1152 when he married Eleanor of Aquitaine, previously married to Louis VI of France. This marriage was tactfully annulled on the grounds of consanguinity, Louis being her fourth cousin. Six weeks later she married Henry and four months later their son William was born.

Eleanor's wealth enabled Henry to obtain the men and ships he needed to claim his English inheritance, but instead of resuming the civil war which had been so damaging to the kingdom an agreement was reached whereby he became Justiciar with a guarantee that he would succeed to the throne. Stephen died in October 1154 and with the crowning of Henry the Plantagenet dynasty began.

Henry revived his grandfather's system of sending judges on circuit. In their work they were to be assisted by twelve local men sworn to tell the truth and thus trial by jury was firmly established. He also began the abolition of trial by combat and ordeal. In this work Henry was supported by his boon companion THOMAS A BECKET, the son of a Norman-born merchant and a Saracen princess. Henry made him his Chancellor and in 1162 suggested that he should become Archbishop of Canterbury, reasoning that with his friend in control, he could limit the vast power of the Church in England. Thomas, reluctant to give up his luxurious lifestyle, warned Henry, 'You will take your favour from me and our love will become hatred.' But Henry insisted, and in May 1162 Thomas was consecrated. The effect on him was dramatic. From a jovial soldier-statesman, he became an ascetic priest ready to defend the Church against his old companion. Soon there was disagreement over the legal rights of the Church and the claiming of estates from nobles which Thomas claimed were rightful Church property. Henry then accused his friend of the misappropriation of £20,000. The court found Thomas guilty of treason but the archbishop's reply was to deny the power of the court, after which he fled to Flanders and put himself under the pope's protection.

HENRY II

In 1170 Henry had his eldest son Henry crowned to remove any future problems over the succession, his first-born William having died at the age of 3. From his exile Thomas objected because as Archbishop of Canterbury he should perform the ceremony, but the coronation went ahead in his absence. In reply Thomas let it be known that the clerics involved in the ceremony would be excommunicated. Finally a meeting was arranged between Henry and Thomas at Amboise in France in an attempt to heal the rift between Church and state. The result was a letter from the king stating: 'I remit to the Archbishop of Canterbury all my anger and offence . . . and I restore him the Church of Canterbury.'

In December 1170 Thomas returned to Canterbury and on Christmas Day he preached in the cathedral, announcing the excommunication of the bishops of Salisbury and Lincoln for their part in Prince Henry's coronation. When news of this reached the king in Normandy he shouted in fury, 'What a parcel of fools and dastards I have

The Great Seal of Henry II.

nourished in my house! Not one of them will avenge me of one upstart clerk.' Taking his words literally, four knights hastened to Canterbury on 29 December and murdered the archbishop in the cathedral.

The martyrdom of Thomas à Becket sent a shockwave through the Christian world and a

The Chateau of Amboise where Henry II and Thomas à Becket became briefly reconciled. *(Photograph by Paul Abrahams)*

chronicler wrote that Henry . . . grieved more terribly, more than it is possible to say: for three days he would eat nothing nor speak to anyone, and for five weeks his doors were closed and he led a solitary life.'

Pope Alexander III threatened excommunication unless the king yielded unconditionally to the demands of the Church. Henry's response was to take an army to Waterford in October 1171. Isolated from the rest of the world, he conquered most of the country, which until then had been independent of the Church of Rome. When the Irish clergy made formal submission to him at Cashel, Henry was in a position to offer the Pope the loyalty of the Irish in return for the lifting of the threat of excommunication. He then went to Normandy where he did penance before the papal legate and was absolved. In the death of Thomas à Becket the Church gained not only a saint but power over the king who had brought Ireland into its fold.

The murder of the archbishop was not the only problem that beset Henry; he also had to face the hostility of his queen. Their first son William had died in 1156, but Eleanor bore him seven more children. It was following the birth of John in 1166 that Eleanor's love for Henry died when she discovered that he had a mistress known as FAIR ROSAMOND. As a result Eleanor actively sided with her son Prince Henry when he demanded a kingdom for himself. When the king refused the plotting began, and he learned of his danger at Toulouse when Count Raymond, kneeling before him in the usual act of homage, whispered, 'Beware your sons and your wife.' The warning came just as Prince Henry left for Paris, and in company with his brothers, Richard and Geoffrey, and Louis VII of France, William the Lion of Scotland and various barons, he declared war on his father. Only his youngest son John, who had no territorial prospects and was thus nicknamed 'Lackland', appeared to be uninvolved.

Henry's response was swift and energetic. He had Eleanor arrested as she was fleeing disguised in male clothing to join her rebellious sons. Then, recalling his troops from Ireland, he set about crushing his enemies one after the other. The King of France was defeated on the Normandy border, rebellion in Brittany was quelled and Aquitaine subdued.

On 7 July 1174 Henry returned to save his English kingdom. He went straight to Canterbury, entering the cathedral barefoot and in pilgrim's rags to do public penance before the tomb of Thomas à Becket. Here he was scourged by seventy monks and then he spent the night before the altar. Four days later news reached him that King William of Scotland, pinned beneath his horse, had surrendered to one of Henry's loyal knights while he was on his knees at Canterbury. On the same day the Count of Flanders called off the invasion as adverse winds had held back his fleet so long that he no longer had the money to pay his troops.

Henry Plantagenet had triumphed. In the following years his reforms prospered but in 1183 Prince Henry again rebelled and William of Newburgh related: 'Having made an alliance with his brother Geoffrey, Count of Brittany and some magnates from Aquitaine, he provoked his father by his warlike movements. . . . Shortly after, the younger Henry was stricken with fever . . . his physicians despairing of his life, he was smitten with remorse and sent to his father, humbly confessing his fault and begging as a last favour from his affectionate father that he would condescend to visit his dying son . . . but, being persuaded by his friends it would not be safe for the King to trust himself to those wicked conspirators who were about his son's person . . . the King did not go. Instead he dispatched to his son a familiar ring as a token of mercy and forgiveness and a pledge of his parental affection. On receiving the ring the son kissed it and immediately expired.'

Three years later Prince Geoffrey was killed while taking part in a tournament. Philip Augustus, the new King of France, claimed the custody of Geoffrey's son ARTHUR – a claim which Henry, as the boy's grandfather, emphatically rejected. Richard, fearing he might be dispossessed in favour of his younger brother John was by the end of 1188 at war with his father again and by the middle of 1189 Henry's town of Le Mans fell to Richard and Philip. Stricken by fever, he sought refuge in Chinon where news reached him that Tours, the city of his birth, was in the hands of his enemies and there was no other option but to agree to their demands.

One of the terms Richard and Philip insisted upon was that Henry should officially pardon all who had plotted against him and a list of their names was brought to his sick chamber. As he glanced at the scroll he uttered a groan and turned his face to the wall – the first name on the list was that of his best

Effigy of Henry II in Fontevrault Abbey, close to the tomb of his wife Eleanor of Aquitaine. (*Photograph by Paul Abrahams*).

loved son John who he believed had always been loyal. 'Let things take their course,' he said. 'I care no longer for myself or anything in this world.'

Henry II died on 6 July 1189 and was buried in the nearby abbey of Fontevrault where his tomb and effigy remain.

HENRY III Because the royal regalia was lost when KING JOHN's army was crossing the Wellstream estuary, Henry, his 9-year-old heir, was crowned with a golden collar belonging to his mother, Isabella of Angoulême. The ceremony took place at Gloucester on 28 October 1216, nine days after John met his unlamented death at Newark Castle where he entrusted William Marshal, Earl of Pembroke with the future of his divided kingdom. This powerful noble decided that the enthronement of the boy prince, with himself as regent, would be best for the kingdom as the grievances that had led to civil war were removed by the late king's death.

Henry III, born at Winchester on 1 October 1207, developed into one of the most complex characters to have worn the Crown up to that time. He was

enthusiastic about music, painting and architecture, and was famed for his religious devotion. Against this was his inability to keep his word, lack of decision, and reckless extravagance.

In 1220 Henry was enthroned for a second time at Westminster where he laid the foundation stone for the rebuilding of the new abbey that was to become his life's achievement. His education was in the hands of priests, who had such a profound effect

Portrait of Henry III in Westminster Abbey, where he was interred, having reigned for fifty-six years.

on his outlook that he found his greatest satisfaction in sacred ceremonies. His chastity – a virtue not generally associated with medieval English kings – was regarded as remarkable. On gaining his manhood the king was described as dark-complexioned, short in stature and ungainly in his movements, while his facial appearance was marred by a drooping eyelid.

In 1230 he took an army to Bordeaux and spent the summer besieging castles. The cost of the campaign was excessive and the king found it necessary to levy heavy taxes to pay for his military adventure, which caused the first wave of popular resentment.

At the age of 28 Henry recognised the need to marry and produce an heir. His choice was ELEANOR OF PROVENCE, surnamed La Belle, the second of the five beautiful daughters of Count Berenger of Provence. Henry's advisers were delighted with the political advantages of the match as Eleanor's elder sister was already married to Louis IX of France. On 4 January 1236 the 14-year-old Eleanor was married to Henry at Canterbury.

Stained glass portrait of Henry III in the Great Hall of Winchester Castle.

Henry had an excessive love of finery, not only for himself but for his courtiers. Costly materials such as satin, velvet, cloth of gold and ermine were the order of the day and at the ceremony the King was the first to wear the luxurious material 'baudekins' which was like a tissue of pure gold. According to Matthew Paris, Henry 'glittered very gloriously'.

Lavish preparations were made to welcome the new Queen. WESTMINSTER PALACE was redecorated and over three hundred leading citizens escorted the royal party from the TOWER OF LONDON to the palace. But before long there was resentment over the way royal favours were heaped on the queen's relations. William de Valence, one of Eleanor's uncles, gained undue influence over the king and within a year practically controlled the administration.

Another foreigner arrived in England who was destined to become Henry's greatest enemy. A Frenchman named Simon de Montfort came to claim the earldom of Leicester he had inherited from his English grandmother and in 1238 he married the king's sister, Princess Eleanor. In the following year Queen Eleanor bore a son later to become EDWARD I, and at her churching Henry gave another example of his unpredictable character. Having named his brother-in-law Simon de Montfort as the baby's godfather, he suddenly accused him of having seduced his sister, causing such a scandal that de Montfort fled to France with his wife.

In 1242 Eleanor accompanied Henry across the Channel on an ill-fated expedition against her brother-in-law the King of France. It was on behalf of Henry's mother Isabella of Angoulême, now married to Hugh de Lusignan of Gascony, who had long complained of French aggression. In May the English army, which included three hundred knights, sailed for Bordeaux. When nearly there Henry was overtaken by the French and in the ensuing battle Henry was so rash that he was only saved from capture by Simon de Montfort who

The Great Seal of Henry III.

muttered that he ought to be shut up at Windsor, for which remark he was never forgiven. Having lost his military chest, it was to be a year before Henry returned to England, 'deluded and defrauded he had sunk into such poverty and ignominy that despite the heavy taxes that he levied he was tied to Gascony by his debts.' The following year the royal debt became so immense that in desperation Henry sought help from the Council. Led by Richard of Cornwall, Simon de Montfort and the Bishop of Lincoln, its members declared that financial aid was dependent on the king agreeing to the setting up of a committee to supervise the government. He refused but was still allowed just enough money to subsist on.

The next year Simon de Montfort led the barons into what became known as the 'Mad Parliament' at Oxford. Their objective was to have the kingdom governed by a committee of twenty-four members, half of whom they would chose and the other half chosen by the king. Ministers would be selected by this committee and a parliament would meet three times a year. Henry had to agree to what became known as the Provisions of Oxford. This form of government soon suffered due to ill-will between Simon de Montfort and the powerful Earl of Gloucester, and the rift gave the king the chance he needed. In June 1261 he announced that he had received a dispensation from all his oaths by the pope and this enabled him to repudiate the Provisions of Oxford. This reunited the barons and they summoned a parliament without royal authority to which Henry replied by calling the knights of the shire to a meeting at Windsor. Gloucester now came over to the king's side and a disgusted Simon de Montfort went to France. The situation took another turn when Gloucester died and his successor declared himself for de Montfort who returned to England at the beginning of 1262.

Civil war – known as the Barons' War – broke out in 1264 after Henry refused to confirm the Provisions of Oxford and declared that he would accept the arbitration of Louis IX of France. This was first welcomed in England until the French king – Henry's brother-in-law – declared the Provisions invalid at Amiens in January 1264. Encouraged by this support Henry began a campaign against rebellious barons and on 12 May his army faced the enemy at Lewes and surrendered to Simon de Montfort after fighting until his horse had been killed beneath him. De Montfort took his royal captive to London where for the next fifteen months he was king in name only. Meanwhile, the barons arranged for Parliament to meet at Westminster in January 1265 which was not only attended by magnates, prelates and barons but also by burgesses and knights of the shire, and as a result Simon de Montfort became known as the 'founder of Parliament'.

Now that the king was ineffective, the barons grew jealous of de Montfort's power, his ambition and the introduction of the 'town element' into Parliament. A royalist faction formed to oppose him which was strengthened when the Pope excommunicated the king's enemies. Prince Edward now rallied royalist sympathisers who engaged Simon de Montfort's army at Evesham on 4 August 1265. During the battle many Welsh spearmen slipped away and the remaining troops were crushed by the weight of royalist cavalry. Simon de Montfort, his son Henry and nearly four thousand of their followers were killed. The result was that the Dictum of Kenilworth cancelled the Provisions of Oxford and restored the King's authority on condition he confirmed the MAGNA CARTA. The civil war had affected Henry deeply and from then on he dedicated himself to his religious interests. By 1270 the kingdom was so peaceful that Prince Edward felt it safe to join the Seventh Crusade.

Throughout his adult life Henry had added to his debts through his rebuilding of WESTMINSTER ABBEY and by 1269 he saw the work almost completed. He attended EDWARD THE CONFESSOR's translation where he carried the sainted relics to the splendid new tomb.

On 16 November 1272 Henry III died at the Palace of Westminster, having reigned for fifty-six years. He was buried in Westminster Abbey in the old coffin of Edward the Confessor whom he especially revered. Four years later Queen Eleanor took the veil and remained a nun for the rest of her life.

HENRY IV Born on 3 April 1367 at Bolingbroke Castle in Lincolnshire, Henry IV was the eldest surviving son of John of Gaunt, the fourth son of EDWARD III and Lady Blanche Plantagenet, the great-great-granddaughter of HENRY III.

On the death of his brother the BLACK PRINCE in 1376 Henry's father took over the government as his ailing father was no longer capable of ruling. King Edward died of a stroke on 21 June 1377 and young Henry was the ceremonial sword-bearer at the coronation of his cousin RICHARD II. At the age of 14 Henry married Lady Mary de Bohun, the co-heiress of the last Earl of Hereford. They had four sons – the eldest being the future HENRY V – and two daughters before Lady Mary died in her twenties.

In 1387, when his son Henry was born, he plunged into politics by joining the LORDS APPELLANT in their campaign against Richard II's favourites. After the royal favourite Robert de Vere fled into exile the five lords entered the TOWER OF LONDON 'with linked arms' to make terms with King Richard. During the proceedings Henry took his cousin onto the walls to see a huge crowd below which he explained had gathered there 'for the salvation of the King and kingdom'.

Richard heeded the message, and agreed to the demands of the Lords Appellant. John of Gaunt, who had a deep sense of loyalty to the Crown, cautioned his son on the importance of being on good terms with the king. Henry minded this advice and supported Richard even when he arrested three of the Lords Appellant – Arundel, Gloucester and Warwick. At Arundel's trial he assisted in the prosecution of his old comrade.

King Richard was at the height of his power, and Henry feared that, despite his recent proof of loyalty, the King might secretly plan revenge for the day he led him onto the walls of the Tower to see the mob. This fear was shared by Thomas Mowbray who like Henry had transferred his allegiance to the King. Mowbray made the mistake of warning Henry of a royal conspiracy to bring down a number of nobles including Henry and John of Gaunt.

Henry knew that the King was watching those who had once opposed him and he safeguarded himself by repeating Mowbray's conversation to the King. Henry was then offered a full pardon under the Great Seal for all past treasons and offences if he would repeat Mowbray's words about the King to the Council. Mowbray defended himself by declaring Henry's accusation as 'the lies of a false traitor'. The King had both men arrested and he banished them both – Henry for ten years and Mowbray for life. Henry's banishment was no hardship. Granted a pension by the King he left London for France in October. The King also granted Henry's request for letters patent, allowing him to appoint attorneys to take possession of any inheritances which might fall to him during the period of exile. Four months after leaving England news reached Henry in Paris that his father had died and he immediately applied to the king for his inheritance under the terms of the letters patent. Richard assembled a great council of his supporters who dutifully declared that the letters were illegal and void. Added to this Henry's term of exile was changed to banishment for life.

In claiming possession of the House of Lancaster for the Crown, Richard made a fatal error. The nobles resented this high-handed action against one of their peers, and the ordinary people, remembering the King's false promises to Wat Tyler's followers, saw it as yet another example of royal trickery. Such was the discontent at all levels of society that Henry, now Duke of Lancaster, realised that he had the excuse needed to fulfil his greatest ambition, especially as the royal heir Roger Mortimer, Earl of March had died recently.

Henry landed at Ravenspur in Yorkshire on 15 July 1399, publicly protesting that he had merely come to claim his duchy, but the thousands who flocked to his banner had little doubt about his real ambition. Within weeks Richard II abdicated and on 30 September Parliament met in the Great Hall of Westminster. Here, according to the chronicler Sir John Froissart, 'the Duke of Lancaster challenged the crown of England, and claimed it for his own, for three reasons – first, by conquest; second, from being heir to it, and third from the pure and free resignation which King Richard had made of it. The

Henry IV, the first Lancastrian king, holding court as depicted in an early manuscript.

Parliament then declared that it was their will he should be King'.

During the coronation ceremony on 13 October 1381 Henry was anointed with holy oil which was said to have been miraculously given to St Thomas à Becket by the Virgin Mary when he was praying one night in the church of St Colombe at Sens. The oil was sealed in a crystal bottle which fitted into an eagle shaped out of gold which was then enclosed in a vessel of lead together with a description of the miracle written by the saint himself. Later it was brought to England by John of Gaunt and stored in the Tower of London. The golden eagle flask is still used to hold the anointing oil at coronations. In contrast to the splendour of the ceremony, Adam of Usk, who was present, noted that lice were falling from Henry's hair.

Though Henry became the first Lancastrian king, he was aware his claim to the throne was precarious and that he was dependent on the goodwill of the barons who were determined to deny him the absolute power that Richard had wanted so badly. His first intimation of the price of a usurped crown came when Henry learned of a conspiracy in which a double of the deposed Richard would impersonate the royal captive in leading a revolt. The new King's enemies were 'hanged, drawn and quartered', the prelude 'to those scenes of blood and cruelty which followed in the long contest between the houses of York and Lancaster, occasioned by the fatal ambition of Henry IV'.

The Great Seal of Henry IV.

Having taken the throne from a legal and anointed king, Henry had no illusions about his own position. As long as the deposed Richard remained alive, even as a secret prisoner, he would be a focus for Henry's enemies and early in 1400 the deposed king died mysteriously in Pontefract Castle.

When Charles VI of France learned of his son-in-law's death he demanded the immediate return of Queen Isabella with her jewels and dowry intact. Henry had plans for marrying her to his son Henry, now Prince of Wales, and as he was short of money he had no intention of returning the dowry. France could use this as an excuse to invade England's Continental territories.

A serious situation in Wales forced Henry to face the threat posed by Owain Glyndwr (see WALES, KINGS OF) who, having declared himself the rightful Prince of Wales, urged his fellow Welshmen to free themselves from the English yoke. Henry marched against Glyndwr's followers but he was unable to engage the enemy. The Welsh used their time-honoured tactic of retiring to their mountains until the way was clear to resume guerrilla raids into England.

For the next two years Henry realised it was one thing to win a crown and quite another to hold it. He found that the support he had received in deposing Richard II had been a popular gesture against an unpopular king rather than an act of loyalty to himself. As time passed he was conscious of growing antipathy from his subjects and his insecurity was heightened when an assassination plot was discovered.

Henry's assets as a king were his energy and efficiency, and he set about winning the goodwill of the country's peers and prelates to stabilise his position. Related to many peers he flattered them, calling them cousins while courting the prelates by attacking the Lollards. The approval of the Church was won by introducing a statute forbidding criticism of the Catholic faith known as the *De heretico comburendo*, which authorised the burning of heretics in England.

To strengthen his position against the French, Henry married Joan, the daughter of Charles of Navarre, and widow of the Duke of Brittany. The wedding ceremony took place at the beginning of 1403 at the church of St Swithin in Winchester, but the celebrations did not last long.

The English army's involvement with Owain Glyndwr's rebellion gave the Scots ample opportunity to raid the north of England, especially lands belonging to the Earl of Northumberland, the head of the Percy family, and his son HENRY PERCY, known in history as 'Hotspur'. In the summer of 1402 a Scottish force of 10,000 reached Newcastle where there was so much looting they had to return to Scotland with it. On the march they reached Homildon (now Humbleton) Hill, to find an army under the Earl of Northumberland, the Earl of March and Hotspur waiting. The Scots took up position on the hill and English archers sent squalls of arrows against them until in desperation they charged down the slope only to find that the archers would flee ahead of them, then turn and continue to pour arrows into their ranks. The raiders were completely routed. Fifteen hundred men were killed as they attempted to escape across the Tweed. Seven leading Scottish nobles died and over eighty knights were captured as well as the Earl of Douglas.

When news of the victory reached Henry he sent congratulations to the Percys but forbade them the traditional right to ransom their prisoners. His reason was to keep Scotland quiet by holding her leaders captive, but this command coming at their moment of glory so deeply offended the independent Percys they formed an alliance with his old enemies the Scots and Owain Glyndwr.

In July 1403 Hotspur led an army into Cheshire on the way to join up with the Welsh. Here he handed out White Hart badges to the locals, telling them that King Richard still lived. The King hastened to Shrewsbury to occupy the town before the rebels arrived and on the morning of 21 July he confronted his enemies. At a spot known today as 'Battlefield' he arranged his army in two divisions, the rear formation under the command of his son Prince Henry. The following battle continued without respite for three hours. Finally, Hotspur and the Earl of Douglas found that the ranks through which they had charged had closed behind them and they were assailed from all sides. Hotspur, nearly suffocating in his armour, raised his visor for air and at that instant an arrow struck him in the face and he fell dead from the saddle. Seeing this, Henry spurred towards the enemy shouting, 'Henry Percy is dead! St George! Victory!'. The Percys' lines broke and their men fled the field. Hotspur's body was divided into four and spiked in Bristol, Chester, Newcastle and London as a warning to those who would challenge the king's authority.

After his victory at Shrewsbury, Henry was temporarily secure from revolt but in 1404 a parliament met at Coventry – the 'Unlearned Parliament' as there were no lawyers in it – to check the expenditure of the royal household and demand freedom of speech in return for subsidies. The government of the country became known as the 'Lancastrian Experiment' in which the king and Parliament became joint rulers of the realm.

Worn out by his campaigns and the intrigue that surrounded him, Henry's health deteriorated and it was said that he suffered from leprosy. He died on 20 March 1413 and curiously it was his wish to be buried in Canterbury Cathedral, close to the tomb of his uncle the Black Prince whose son he had deposed.

HENRY V Destined to become England's most popular medieval king, Henry V was born on 9 August 1387 in Monmouth Castle. The eldest son of Henry Bolingbroke – later HENRY IV – and his wife Lady Mary de Bohun, he was a sickly child and owed much to the devoted care of his nurse Joan Wiring on whom he settled a generous annual pension in later life. In 1394 his mother died and four years later his father was banished by RICHARD II. Henry, with his three brothers and two sisters, remained in England under the care of the king who treated them kindly despite his quarrel with their father. When the King made an expedi-

A manuscript illustration of Henry V granting an audience.

tion to Ireland in 1399 he took Henry, who acquitted himself so well in a dangerous skirmish that he was dubbed a knight on the field.

A year after his father became Henry IV in 1399, young Henry accompanied him on his expedition against the Welsh, at the end of which he was left in command of the frontier with his headquarters at Chester. His chief companion was HENRY PERCY ('Hotspur') whose powerful northern family were loyal supporters of the House of Lancaster. But the quarrel between these northern lords and the King flared into rebellion, and on 31 July 1403 young Henry found himself at the Battle of Shrewsbury where his erstwhile friend Hotspur was killed. After the defeat of the rebels Henry remained in control of the Welsh border until his 20th year when his father's illness forced him to take a more active part in government. By 1410 he was virtually ruler of the country until the King, suspicious of his son's increasing power, made him retire from court.

It has been written that it was his father's jealousy in keeping him out of state affairs that obliged him 'to amuse his active mind by those youthful dissipation and escapades which have gained him a merry immortality from the pen of Shakespeare'. Typical of the stories handed down about Prince Hal's wild exploits is the following from John Stow's annals, published in 1580: 'The Prince used to disguise himself and lie in wait for the receivers of crown lands, or of his father's patrimony, and in the disguise of a highwayman, set upon and rob them.' When he became Henry V and after his coronation during a snowstorm on Passion Sunday, 9 April 1413, the contemporary historian Thomas Walsingham wrote: 'As soon as he was made King he was changed into another man, zealous for honesty, modesty and gravity; there being no sort of virtue that he was not anxious to display.'

The new King felt strongly that the Crown had been usurped from its anointed owner by his father, and therefore his position was dependent upon the goodwill of the nobility and the Church. To keep the favour of the former he hoped for a profitable war; to the latter he promised to continue his father's policy of repressing the Lollards.

Having secured the allegiance of the Church by supporting it on the Lollard question, Henry sought the goodwill of the aristocracy. Before he died, Henry IV warned his son not to allow his nobles to remain inactive for a long period otherwise, with

Henry V's signature.

only hunting to occupy their minds, it was inevitable that dangerous factions would be formed. So, in order to 'bury restless minds in foreign quarrels', Henry decided to seek military glory in France and wage a successful war.

There could not have been a better time for such an adventure. During the frequent bouts of insanity suffered by Charles VI of France, his brother the Duke of Orleans and his cousin the Duke of Burgundy vied for supremacy. In 1407 a band of eighteen assassins murdered the Duke of Orleans on the rue Barbette in Paris, sparking off a civil war which had brought the country close to ruin. Taking advantage of the situation, Henry demanded from France the restoration of Normandy, Anjou, Maine and Touraine – and the hand of the French king's youngest daughter, Catherine of Valois. Soon he went further by announcing at Westminster his determination 'to recover his inheritance by arms', which meant reviving EDWARD III's claim to the throne of France.

The French reply came from the dauphin who sent Henry a barrel of tennis balls with the message that such a game would be more suitable for him than fighting. On 11 August 1415 an English army of about ten thousand men-at-arms and archers set out from Southampton and landed on the Normandy coast near Harfleur. The town surrendered after six weeks and Henry challenged the dauphin to meet him in single combat. When by 8 October he received no response he set out on a cross-country expedition to Calais. Soon his troops became aware they were being shadowed by numerically superior forces while ahead of them a large army under the Constable of France laid waste to the countryside to prevent the English living off the land. On

25 October, the two armies met at a battlefield which lay between the villages of Tramecourt, Maisoncelles and Agincourt – known as Azincourt today – and here, thanks to the skill of his archers, Henry scored the most renowned victory of any English monarch.

In London he received a hero's welcome and Parliament now allowed him all the money he required to take another army across the Channel to consolidate the Agincourt victory. On 1 August 1417 he entered Normandy and secured Caen, Bayeux and Alençon. In the summer of the following year the English army laid siege to Rouen, one of the richest and most powerful cities in France. It was too strong to be taken by assault and Henry declared that war had three handmaids – fire, blood and famine. And it was mainly through the latter handmaid that the city surrendered on 13 January 1419. Henry entered the silent city on a black charger and rode straight to the cathedral to give thanks to God for another victory. He then made arrangements to get food supplies for the hungry inhabitants.

Henry now met Princess Catherine – whose hand he had demanded earlier on – at Troyes where it had been agreed he would negotiate with her father Charles VI. As the French king was mentally ill at the time he was represented by the Duke of Burgundy and Queen Isabella. Henry was impressed by Catherine's beauty as well as her political desirability, and a treaty was agreed whereby he would marry her and become Regent of France until Charles VI died, whereupon he would ascend the throne. Henry and Catherine were married at Troyes Cathedral on 2 June 1420 and at the end of the year he brought Catherine to England where she was crowned in WESTMINSTER ABBEY on 23 February 1421.

In the spring Henry made a pilgrimage through the Midlands, visiting various shrines, but news soon reached him that the dauphin had taken up arms against the English and that his brother Clarence had been defeated and slain at Beaux. By June the King was back in France where he sent the dauphin's army to retreat across the Loire. Six months later the Queen bore him a son who was destined to become HENRY VI.

Campaigning and the strain of soldiering began to tell on the king and his strength was further weakened by dysentery. By August he was so weak that he handed over the command of the army to his

A coin from the reign of Henry VI.

brother Bedford before being conveyed by barge to Vincennes where it became obvious that his death was close. He sent for his brothers and charged them to protect his son and then asked his confessor to recite the seven penitential psalms.

Henry V died on 31 August 1422 and it was ironical that had he lived for another eight weeks the death of Charles VI would have enabled him to realise his ambition of becoming King of France. His body was conveyed to Calais on a carriage of crimson and gold, escorted by 500 knights in black armour, and on to London where it was interred in Westminster Abbey.

Queen Catherine later married a Welsh gentleman named Owen Tudor and so became an ancestress of England's most powerful royal house.

HENRY VI The only English king to have been crowned in Paris, Henry VI was born on 6 December 1421 at Windsor. Within a year of his birth his father HENRY V died and the baby became King of England on 1 September 1422; through the Treaty of Troyes he succeeded to the French throne, so his uncle John, Duke of Bedford was appointed Protector of England and Regent of France. The boy king was crowned at WEST-MINSTER ABBEY on 5 November 1429 and at Notre Dame Cathedral in Paris on 16 December 1431.

The King's coronation in November 1429 was the year that Joan of Arc's army forced the English to raise the siege of Orleans. The previous year Joan claimed that voices had commanded her to rescue the Paris region from English domination and have the dauphin crowned Charles VII in Rheims Cathedral. Wearing white armour, this extraordinary young woman so inspired the French soldiers that the English were driven back and finally the dauphin was crowned as she had predicted.

On his sixteenth birthday Henry became King, though he did very little ruling other than the giving of charters and pardons. Apart from his devotions and charitable works he endeavoured to act as a peacemaker between his uncle Humphrey, Duke of Gloucester, and Cardinal Beaufort in their contest to control the kingdom.

In 1443 William de la Pole, Earl of Suffolk – a prominent member of the Lancastrian 'peace' party – went to France to negotiate the marriage of Henry and Margaret, the daughter of the cultured but impecunious Duke René of Anjou, titular King of

Margaret of Anjou, an engraving from a tapestry that hung in St Mary's Hall, Coventry.

Henry VI and Queen Margaret being presented with a religious book.

Sicily. Inevitably Gloucester, who led the Yorkist party, opposed the match so it was only natural that when Margaret arrived in England she favoured the Lancastrians. The marriage took place at Titchfield Abbey on 23 April 1445 and on 30 May Margaret was crowned in Westminster Abbey. She soon became aware of the maelstrom of intrigue that surrounded her naive husband and she impressed on Henry that their new-found happiness was endangered by the machinations of his uncle. This galvanised the king into uncharacteristic action. In February 1447 he called for a parliament to be held at Bury St Edmunds whose citizens supported the Lancastrians. There Gloucester was requested to present himself before the king and accused of slandering the queen and plotting against the king.

The duke was arrested and five days later he mysteriously died. To the people he became a posthumous hero and Henry's problems increased when Cardinal Beaufort died two months after the duke. Suffolk now had full control of the Lancastrian party but there was still the Duke of York, who was heir to the Crown should the King die without issue.

In March 1449 Charles VII of France renewed his campaign against the English by invading Normandy which ended Suffolk's peace policy, and Duke René, father of the queen on whom the policy had been based, supported the French king. There were strong opinions that Suffolk's policies had lost the English territory which had been so hardily won by the king's glorious father Henry V. On 26 January, 1450, Parliament impeached him and he was only saved from execution by Henry enforcing his banishment. Suffolk left for Flanders, but in the Channel his ship was overtaken by a Yorkist boat. He was abducted and, after a mock trial, beheaded.

The King needed a champion to replace the murdered Suffolk, and chose Edmund, the 2nd Duke of Somerset, the ineffectual commander of the English forces in France. The country was stunned when this man, responsible for England's defeats, was made Constable of England. The Duke of York confronted the King, declaring, 'The great rumour is that in this your realm justice is not duly ministered.' Henry's reply was to promise him a larger share in the government. Somerset met the EARL OF WARWICK in the Temple Gardens by the Thames and as angry words were exchanged Somerset plucked a red rose whereupon Warwick picked a white one. Their companions followed their example so that the flowers became their symbols, the red rose for the House of Lancaster and the white for York.

In 1453 the HUNDRED YEARS' WAR ended when the French reclaimed Gascony. In August that year the queen gave birth to a prince named Edward, but the King, now suffering bouts of mental collapse, merely stared vacantly when he saw his son. The birth of Prince Edward may have ended York's chances of ever succeeding to the throne, but it increased his chances of gaining power in another direction. As the King's oldest adult relation he saw himself in control of the kingdom as regent during the King's illness and was given the title of Protector and Defender of the Realm.

At Christmas 1454 the King, now lucid, dissolved Parliament. The Duke of York retired to his castle at Sandal where the Duke of Norfolk, the Earl of Salisbury and his son the Earl of Warwick, soon to be known as the 'Kingmaker', agreed that the only hope for the Yorkist cause lay in open war. On 20 May 1455 they arrived at Royston with 3,000 troops. The next day Henry led a Lancastrian army of 2,000 to St Albans where the two armies met. It was the first battle of the WARS OF THE ROSES – or the Cousins' War – with victory going to the Yorkists. Somerset was slain and Henry was captured and taken to London where he had no option but to summon a Yorkist Parliament. The shock of his defeat, coupled with an arrow wound he had received in the fighting, caused the return of mental disturbance and in July 1455 the king was again shut away from public sight. The Duke of York was declared Constable of England but his triumph was lost when sanity returned to the king, who made a surprise visit to Westminster in February 1456 where he told Parliament 'that being now recovered by the blessing of God, he did not think his kingdom was in need of a protector'. A token peace was celebrated on 25 March when Henry led a procession of Lancastrians and Yorkists to St Paul's.

The peace did not last for long. Deep in the tangle of plot and counter-plot Queen Margaret was determined to destroy the Yorkist party and in spring of 1459 she had a warrant issued for Warwick's arrest and there was civil war again. There followed a series of battles. At Northampton the king again fell into Yorkist hands and was taken to London, where he remained a captive figurehead. In the North Queen Margaret raised an army, winning a victory over the Yorkists at Wakefield when the Duke of York was killed. The Queen's army marched south to save King Henry from the

The Great Seal of Henry VI.

Earl of Warwick. On 17 February 1461 Warwick was defeated in the second Battle of St Albans where Henry was found beneath an oak tree from where he had watched the battle, singing and 'smiling to see the discomfort of the army'.

For some obscure reason the Lancastrians turned north again, giving Warwick the chance he needed to earn his nickname of Kingmaker. With Henry in care of the triumphant queen he knew that he must give the country a new sovereign. On 4 March he had Edward, Earl of March, son of the slain Duke of York, proclaimed king at old St Paul's in London. Both Warwick and the new King EDWARD IV knew that this was merely a gesture. The Crown still had to be won by force of arms and this took place in the frozen fields between the villages of Towton and Saxton, 10 miles south of York, on Palm Sunday, 29 March 1462, and ended in defeat for the Lancastrians.

When news of the defeat reached Henry at York he fled to Harlech, while Queen Margaret journeyed to Brittany to solicit help from Louis XI. In October 1462 she landed her small army on the Northumbrian coast near Bamburgh Castle which she captured along with the castles of Alnwick and Dunstanburgh. But on 15 May 1463 her army was routed at the Battle of Hexham. She returned to France with her son and lived in Anjou for the next seven years.

Henry was finally captured at Cantlow and in June 1465 he was escorted to London astride a miserable hack, his legs bound to his stirrups and a mocking placard on his back. Warwick met the fallen King at Islington where he encouraged the mob to jeer him. Henry did not respond to the insults until he received a blow in the face whereupon he rebuked the man who had done it with 'Forsooth and forsooth, ye do foully to smite a king anointed so.' Then, for the next five years he remained a prisoner in the TOWER OF LONDON, 'dirty, sickly, ill-dressed and neglected'.

It was a bitter falling out with Edward IV that motivated Warwick to visit his old enemy Queen Margaret in France and convince her he would now espouse the Lancastrian cause. Their combined armies would invade England and in his role of Kingmaker he would restore Henry to the throne, and this alliance would be sealed by his daughter Anne Neville marrying Margaret's son Prince Edward. The thought of a return to power conquered the queen's aversion to Warwick and she agreed.

In September 1470 King Edward was involved in the suppression of a revolt when Warwick's army of thousands backed by Louis XI of France, landed unopposed in southern England. So many men flocked to the Lancastrian standard that Warwick is said to have had an army of sixty thousand when he approached London and it was Edward's turn to flee across the Channel. Two bishops sought Henry in the Tower, dressed him in a blue velvet gown and took him to Westminster where, as Warwick's puppet, he wore the Crown of England.

In March 1471 Edward IV returned to England, raising an army, and in London the fickle mob, having cheered King Henry a short while before, welcomed him back as their king.

Warwick was defeated and killed at Barnet on Easter Day and Henry was returned to the Tower. Some weeks later Queen Margaret landed with French troops at Dorset attempting to win back Prince Edward's birthright but a Yorkist army

The chamber in the Tower of London where it is believed the captive Henry VI was secretly done to death in 1471.

defeated her at Tewkesbury on 4 May and Prince Edward was killed. On 21 May 1471 King Henry died in the Tower, it was said, 'disconsolate and of pure melancholy on hearing of the death of his son'. But it is known for certain there was another cause. In 1911 Henry's bones were disinterred and the back of the skull was found to have been crushed by a blow. Henry was originally buried at Chertsey Abbey, but in 1485 his remains were translated to St George's Chapel, Windsor.

HENRY VII When Henry was born at Pembroke Castle on 28 January 1457, his father Edmund Tudor, Earl of Richmond had died two months previously and his mother Margaret Beaufort had still not celebrated her 14th birthday. Although Henry had important ancestors and was to become head of the House of Lancaster, he had little right to the throne of England.

Henry's early life was influenced by the struggle between the Lancastrian and Yorkist factions, and he later confided to a contemporary historian Phillip de Commines that 'from the time he was five years old he had been an exile or a prisoner'. When WARWICK the Kingmaker restored HENRY VI to the throne in 1470 young Henry was taken to London by his uncle, Jasper Tudor, to meet him. The king was so impressed by his intelligence that he remarked, 'One day this child will get all that we are fighting for.'

A few months later EDWARD IV returned in triumph, Henry VI was murdered in the TOWER OF LONDON, and his son killed after the Battle of Tewkesbury, making young Henry of Richmond head of the Lancastrians. His uncle took him out of the country for his own safety, and for the next twelve years he lived in Brittany. Here he grew up 'fair and slender, pale-faced but comely, active and well formed'.

When Edward IV died in 1483 Henry was 26 and ready to seize the opportunity this presented. The Yorkist party had divided itself into two factions – one supporting the Woodville family which had been shown favour by the late king who had married Elizabeth Woodville, and the other loyal to the late king's brother RICHARD OF GLOUCESTER.

A number of nobles, including Yorkists who were at odds with Richard III, as the Duke of Gloucester soon became, raised money for Henry to return to England and try to seize the Crown. On 12 October 1483 he set out from St Malo with a fleet of forty

Henry VII after his coronation following the Lancastrian victory over Richard III on Bosworth Field.

vessels but a storm forced Henry's return to Brittany. Despite this ill-fated expedition Henry did not lose heart and at Christmas he appeared in the cathedral of Rennes where Lancastrian exiles hailed him as their future king. Henry vowed that 'though his love was promised elsewhere' he would marry Elizabeth of York, the eldest daughter of the late Edward, thereby uniting the Houses of Lancaster and York.

On 1 August 1485 Henry sailed from Harfleur to Milford Haven, then on to Shrewsbury, his army marching under the red dragon of Wales. By 21 August he reached Atherston and on the next morning he won the Crown of England at the BATTLE OF BOSWORTH. One of Henry's first acts was to send Sir Robert Willoughby to Sheriff Hutton in Yorkshire to take Elizabeth of York and the young Earl of Warwick to London – the former to be his bride; the latter, who was the son of Edward IV's brother the Duke of Clarence, was imprisoned in the Tower.

Henry's coronation took place at WESTMINSTER ABBEY on 30 October. At this time he instituted the Yeomen of the Guard to be his special bodyguard, which suggests he did not altogether trust his new subjects. After his coronation Henry went before Parliament, claiming he had come to the throne by just title of inheritance and the sure judgement of God who had given him victory over his enemies in the field, adding that 'every man should continue to enjoy his rights and hereditaments, except such persons as in the present parliament should be punished for their offences against his royal majesty'.

Henry's claim was confirmed without question and he was requested to marry Elizabeth of York as he had promised. They married on 18 January 1486 after a papal bull gave the necessary dispensation for marriage between cousins, and detailed Henry's various rights to the English throne – by conquest, inheritance, election and Act of Parliament. As a graceful gesture at her wedding the princess carried a bouquet of red and white roses.

Nine months later she bore Henry his first son who was christened Arthur 'in honour of the British race', and who it was hoped would herald in an age as famous as the legendary days of Camelot. The birth of a royal heir strengthened those still opposed to Henry, and the first of the two imposters who were to plague him appeared upon the scene. Lambert Simnel, thought to have been born about 1475, was groomed to impersonate one of the 'Princes in the Tower', the two sons of EDWARD IV, by a priest named Richard Simon. This plan changed when a rumour spread that Edward of Warwick, the son of the Duke of Clarence with a strong claim to the throne, had escaped from prison. In Dublin Simon then presented Simnel as Edward of Warwick. Henry did his best to discredit Simnel by having the real Earl of Warwick taken from the TOWER OF LONDON and paraded through the streets but this had no effect on Simnel's supporters. On 24 May 1487 he was crowned in Dublin Cathedral as Edward VI of England. Next month he and his followers landed in England but on 16 June were defeated at the Battle of Stoke, the last battle in which an English king personally fought against a rival claimant. Richard Simon was imprisoned for life and the imposter pardoned and given a humiliating job as a scullion in the royal kitchens.

Henry returned to London to get on with his work of ruling the kingdom. He had his Queen Elizabeth crowned, a Council committee was set up in the Star Chamber to deal with those who were so powerful that they were beyond ordinary law, and preparations were made to go to the aid of Brittany under attack from the French.

The Great Seal of Henry VII.

Henry had always been hard pressed financially, and when he became King he was obsessed with acquiring money. He employed two tax-gatherers, Dudley and Empson, both Speakers of the House of Commons, who became famous for the way they 'fleeced the people to the bone'.

The King soon had to face another threat to his crown from a second imposter, a threat that was to haunt him for five years. The imposter claimed to be Richard of York, the younger son of Edward IV, who had been placed in the Tower of London with his elder brother by Richard III. Perkin Warbeck was a convincing claimant. Born in 1472 at Tournai, he was the son of a prominent citizen, coming into contact with adherents of the House of York. At the age of 17 he entered the service of a Breton knight named Pregent Meno with whom he sailed to Ireland where he was presented as Richard of York. As such he was invited to the French court and in Flanders Margaret, Duchess of Burgundy, hailed him as her nephew. In order to counteract this plot Henry stopped trade between England and Flanders, and immediately Londoners rioted at their loss of income. In 1497 Warbeck landed in Cornwall at the invitation of Cornish rebels, proclaiming himself Richard IV. His attempt to take Exeter failed and after surrendering at Beaulieu and confessing to the imposture he was imprisoned in the Tower.

Henry had no wish to make a martyr out of him and soon he was released and kept at court under surveillance. In the summer of 1498 he tried to escape but was captured at Syon monastery and returned to the Tower. Here he met the true Earl of Warwick, the only real threat to Henry's crown, and they hatched a plot to seize the Tower. When the authorities learned of the plan, Warbeck, Warwick and other prisoners were indicted at the Guildhall. The pretender was hanged at Tyburn and the unhappy Earl of Warwick beheaded.

These abortive attempts on his crown made Henry nervous and he sought to strengthen his position by dynastic alliances. He arranged for his eldest daughter Margaret to marry JAMES IV of Scotland while in 1501 he saw the success of his plan for Prince Arthur to marry CATHERINE OF ARAGON, the daughter of Ferdinand and Isabella of Spain. Six months after the marriage Prince Arthur died and the next year he was followed by his mother Queen Elizabeth. Anxious not to return Catherine's dowry to Spain, Henry suggested that as he was now a widower, he should marry his daughter-in-law. This idea horrified Queen Isabella so much that she wrote to the Spanish ambassador in London telling him to forget about the dowry and get her daughter back to Spain by any means possible. Finally it was agreed that Catherine should marry her late husband's younger brother – the future HENRY VIII – and that Ferdinand and Isabella would renounce all claims to her dowry.

Henry had other interests. He tried to persuade the Pope to canonise HENRY VI, who had been murdered in the Tower. He also built a magnificent chapel as a shrine to the late king, but when the court of Rome demanded a larger sum for the canonisation than Henry was prepared to pay, the idea was dropped and the body of Henry VI remained at Windsor.

Henry went ahead with building a chapel in Westminster Abbey, which was to be dedicated to the Virgin 'in whom', Henry stated in his will, 'hath ever been my most singular trust and confidence.' He planned it as a place of burial for himself and his family, a shrine that would glorify the dynasty that he had founded.

By the end of 1508 Henry's health began to fail. During the winter his condition worsened, and aware that his end was near, he discharged the debts of all prisoners in London committed for sums under 40*s* and expressed regret at the harsh methods employed by his tax-gatherers Dudley and Empson, though he could not bring himself to halt their work.

Effigy of Henry VII, who was interred beside his wife Elizabeth of York in Westminster Abbey.

He died at his palace in Richmond on 21 April 1509 and was buried beside Queen Elizabeth in his chapel in Westminster Abbey. Above his tomb was carved the red dragon of Wales which had been his device when he seized the throne.

HENRY VIII The second son of Henry VII and Elizabeth of York, Henry VIII was born at GREENWICH PALACE on 28 June 1491. As he grew up he was renowned for his physical appearance and grace and after his coronation in 1509, Pasqualio, the Venetian diplomat, wrote: 'His Majesty' – Henry was the first English king to be thus addressed – 'is the handsomest potentate I ever set eyes on: above the usual height, with an extremely fine calf to his leg; his complexion fair and bright, with auburn hair combed straight and short in the French fashion.'

Soon after becoming King in April 1509, Henry honoured his father's old agreement with Ferdinand and Isabella of Spain by marrying his brother Arthur's widow, the witty and devout CATHERINE OF ARAGON. Both were crowned at Westminster on 24 June after which Henry celebrated his accession with a long round of entertainments and pageants. There was plenty to celebrate: the Treasury was full, the realm at peace and the nobility suitably respectful.

Queen Catherine bore a son on New Year's Day 1511 and the King held a great tournament to mark the event, but the celebrations ended when the child died a few days later, the first of many such disappointments.

Henry preferred his own pleasures to affairs of state and more and more administrative responsibility fell upon THOMAS WOLSEY. The son of an Ipswich butcher, Wolsey rose to become a cardinal and then Lord Chancellor.

In 1520 both Francis I of France and the Emperor Charles V made overtures for Henry's alliance. First Charles stayed with him at Canterbury, then Henry visited Francis at Guisnes where the two monarchs tried to outdo each other in splendour on the famous FIELD OF THE CLOTH OF GOLD. Here Henry's grandeur was only exceeded by his insincerity – he had already come secretly to agreement with the emperor.

The following year saw the publication of a book attacking Martin Luther's reforming doctrines entitled *Assertio Septem Sacramentorum*. Written by Henry with Wolsey's encouragement, it found such favour with the Pope that he bestowed the title of 'Defender of the Faith' on the English king, a relic of this honour being the 'Fid. Def.' or 'F.D.' (standing for *Fidei Defensor*) which still appears on British coins.

For some time he had been dissatisfied with his marriage because although the queen had borne him a daughter, the future MARY I, she had not been able to provide a much-wanted son. Now he was

A Victorian engraving of Henry VIII, from a painting in what was known as the New Palace of Westminster.

The Field of the Cloth of Gold, where Henry VIII and Francis I competed in magnificent display.

troubled with the thought that God was punishing him for the sin of his marriage which was summed up thus in the Book of Leviticus: 'If a man shall take his brother's wife, it is an unclean thing . . . they shall be childless.' While the king was wrestling with this problem, a sister of one of his ex-mistresses returned from the French court to become a lady-in-waiting to the queen. She was ANNE BOLEYN, the daughter of Sir Thomas Boleyn, and Henry became passionately interested in her. In 1527 he began his campaign to get his marriage declared invalid, for which Anne rewarded him with her favours.

Although the King's divorce went against everything Cardinal Wolsey believed in, he knew how important it was for Henry. To this end he set in motion the whole machinery of the state, but Pope Clement II refused to cooperate and all Wolsey could achieve was to arrange a 'trial' before Cardinal Camoeggio. This proved very humiliating for Henry who was forced to appear as a supplicant before foreign envoys in his own capital.

Anne believed that Wolsey was purposely delaying the legal proceedings, telling Henry the cardinal deserved to lose his head. The impatient king heeded her. Aware of the danger of his position, Wolsey sought to win back favour by presenting Henry with HAMPTON COURT, the magnificent Thames-side palace he had built. Although Henry accepted the gift, in October 1529 Wolsey was fined, relieved of the Great Seal and forced to relinquish his property. The new Chancellor was Sir THOMAS MORE, a staunch Roman Catholic and boyhood friend of the King.

Early in 1531 Thomas Cromwell, a former agent of the late cardinal, became Henry's chief minister. He boldly planned to ignore the Pope's authority if an annulment would not be granted, and he solicited legal opinions from all over Europe in support of Henry's cause. He was so successful that Parliament agreed to the royal divorce 'after being shown above an hundred books drawn by doctors of strange regions'. Next Henry and Cromwell charged the English clergy with the treasonable offence of PRAEMUNIRE, which was a statute originally passed in 1388 with the object of diminishing the power of the Roman Catholic Church in Britain by making it a crime to owe obedience to the Pope. The Convocation of Bishops, panicked by the resurrection of this statute, agreed to pay Henry £100,000 and recognise him as 'protector and supreme head

of the church and clergy of England' in return for a universal pardon. This act was too much for Sir Thomas More who, seeing clearly where it would lead, asked to be relieved of the Great Seal.

On 25 January 1533, Henry secretly married the pregnant Anne Boleyn. Archbishop CRANMER confirmed the king's marriage with Anne, who in September gave birth to the future ELIZABETH I. Though Henry felt satisfaction over the progress of the Reformation there was still no male heir. In 1534 Anne added another to the unhappy list of royal miscarriages and Henry solaced himself by falling in love with Queen Anne's lady-in-waiting, Jane Seymour.

On May Day 1536, the King and Queen attended a tournament at Greenwich which Henry suddenly quit to the bewilderment of the spectators. The next day Anne realised the significance of her husband's abrupt departure when she was charged with committing adultery with three gentlemen of the privy chamber and a musician, and with having committed incest with her brother Lord Rochford. On 12 May her four alleged paramours were condemned for high treason which meant that the Queen's case was in effect judged before she was brought to trial. One of the peers who pronounced them guilty was Anne's father, thus endorsing the guilt of his daughter. Three days later she and her brother appeared before twenty-six peers, each of whom gave a verdict of guilty. Anne's own uncle, the Duke of Norfolk, passed the death sentence and an ecclesiastical court ruled that her marriage to the King was invalid.

On 19 May 1536, two days after her brother had been executed, Anne was led to Tower Green in the Tower of London. The manner of her death was a novelty because an executioner had been brought from Calais to strike off her head with a sword, a French custom.

A coin from the reign of Henry VIII.

On the same day Henry visited Jane Seymour, and Archbishop CRANMER issued a dispensation allowing their wedding to take place without the usual banns. This was privately performed on 30 May at York Place. Henry's delight when Queen Jane became pregnant was tempered by a revolt in the North sparked by Roman Catholic opposition to the closing down of religious establishments. As the revolt, known as the Pilgrimage of Grace, gathered dangerous momentum Henry followed the tactics of earlier English monarchs and parleyed with the rebels until he was in a position to crush them. In October 1537 Henry's dearest hopes were fulfilled when Queen Jane bore him a son, later to become EDWARD VI, but shortly afterwards she died. Henry was genuinely grief-stricken, and she was the only one of his deceased wives for whom he wore mourning.

Now that the succession appeared to be secure Henry did not remarry for two years, during which he had much to occupy him. The Pope excommunicated him which reinforced his zeal for the Reformation. Although the Roman Catholic style of worship remained in the churches, statues were obliterated and religious pilgrimages banned. Probably the most important effect on the country at this time was the publication of the Great Bible, which by law had to be placed in all churches. At last the English were free to read their sacred book in their own language.

Disregarding the doctrinal differences between Henry's English Church and the German Protestants, Thomas Cromwell decided an alliance between them against the Pope would be politically expedient, and a marriage was arranged in September 1539 between the King and Anne, the daughter of John, the Lutheran Duke of Cleves. Anne was escorted to Rochester where Henry, found her watching a bull-baiting through a casement. Enveloped in a cloak, Henry presented her with a token of himself which, while she received it politely, was not enough to draw her away from the window. The King left the gallery, shed his cloak and reappeared in a coat of royal purple which convinced the lady that here was her husband-to-be. This revelation came as a shock as Henry, now nearly fifty, was a sadly different figure from the golden prince who had once been the idol of his subjects.

After the wedding ceremony on the Twelfth Day of 1540, Thomas Cromwell was created Earl of Essex for arranging the marriage. This turned out to be a hollow honour because after two months Henry could no longer stand 'the mare of Flanders', as he termed the queen, and Cromwell was imprisoned in the Tower of London. An Act of Attainder was passed against him and he was forced to admit that His Majesty had never loved the Queen and that the union had not been consummated. Essex was executed on Tower Hill by a bungling headsman on 28 July. An Act of Parliament was passed nullifying the King's marriage. In this Henry was assisted by Anne herself who, in return for lands which would provide her with £3,000 (approximately £1,250,000 today) per annum, admitted a pre-contract and agreed cheerfully to the dissolution of the marriage, after which she led a life of peaceful retirement.

Parliament then petitioned the King to marry for a fifth time 'for the good of the people'. He complied by marrying a cheerful, ambitious, auburn-haired girl of 18 named CATHERINE HOWARD who, like Anne Boleyn, was a niece of the Duke of Norfolk. It seems that Catherine had her first love affair with a musician named Henry Mannock who taught her to play the virginals. Later she had an affair with Francis Dereham, a member of the Duke of Norfolk's household. Love tokens passed between the couple – Dereham giving Catherine a silk hearts-ease – and they considered themselves to be engaged. But this relationship ended when the girl was summoned to court where the Catholic party planned to use her to charm Henry away from the Protestant Queen by becoming his mistress. The scheme worked better than they could have hoped because instead of becoming Henry's mistress she became his wife.

But soon the marriage became another 'Great Matter' for the King. On the day after All Saints Day 1541 – when Henry had given thanks for the good life he enjoyed with Catherine 'after sundry troubles of mind which happened to him by marriage' – Archbishop Cranmer slipped a paper into his hand and begged him to read it when he was alone. The note claimed that prior to her marriage the Queen had been intimate with the musician Mannock and Francis Dereham. The latter was arrested on a euphemistic charge of piracy and admitted under questioning that he had enjoyed intercourse with Catherine when she was single. When Mannock's turn came to be interrogated he denied having had intercourse with Catherine.

Archbishop Cranmer and Catherine's uncle the Duke of Norfolk were sent to question the Queen

A waxwork tableau of Henry VIII and his wives made with painstaking attention to historic detail at Madame Tussaud's, London.

who made a confession of her 'immorality' which Cranmer copied down. She claimed, however, that since her marriage she had been faithful to Henry, and even torture could not force Dereham to contradict her. Despite the fact that under the harshest probing no confession of adultery could be obtained, Catherine was imprisoned in the Tower of London. On 12 February 1542 she was informed that she was to be executed the following morning.

Henry's final marriage was celebrated a year later, his new wife the scholarly Catherine Parr who was to outlive him. Widowed twice, she was 31 when she was first courted by the King and told him 'that it was better to be his mistress than his wife'. They were married on 12 July 1543 at Hampton Court.

In the year following his marriage to Catherine Henry had to mount military campaigns in France and Scotland where he had been deserted by his allies. The King sent his commander these instructions: 'Sack Leith and burn it and subvert it and all the rest, putting man, woman and child to fire and sword without exception . . . extend the like extremities and destruction in all towns and villages whereunto ye may reach conveniently.' Such ruthless tactics gave the king a strong foothold in Scotland and the French agreed a peace by which England was to remain in possession of Boulogne.

By 1546 Henry's physical state had deteriorated and he was unable to walk, while gout so crippled his hand he could not write his signature. It was clear to all except Henry that he did not have long to live but as it was considered high treason to speak of the sovereign's death, no one had the courage to tell the King that his end was near until his Groom of the Bedchamber delicately told him.

Archbishop Cranmer was brought to Henry's bed at midnight on 27 January 1547 to find him unable to speak. The archbishop asked him to give some token of his trust in Christ and in reply Henry held his hand. He died soon afterwards and in accordance with instructions in his will was interred beside Queen Jane in St George's Chapel at Windsor.

HEPTARCHY, THE Derived from the writings of Henry of Huntingdon in the twelfth century, the word Heptarchy was used to describe England when it consisted of seven separate kingdoms in the seventh century. These were East Anglia, Essex, Kent, Mercia, Northumbria, Sussex and Wessex.

HEREWARD THE WAKE The last Anglo-Saxon resistance to WILLIAM I ended in 1071 with the capture of 'the Camp of Refuge' in the fenland near Ely. The previous year the presence of a Danish fleet off the coast encouraged the locals, many of whom had some Norse blood, to challenge the newly imposed rule of the Normans. Supported by the Danes and led by Hereward, a shadowy figure known as 'The Wake', meaning 'the watchful one', Peterborough was sacked. Hereward's secret base, the Camp of Refuge, was established on an island amid the fens, from which resistance to the Normans continued. It was said that the monks of Ely, no doubt troubled by the destruction of Peterborough monastery, betrayed its location to the Normans. In order to reach it William gave instructions for the building of a 2-mile causeway through the marshes which allowed his soldiers to overwhelm the partisans. Hereward escaped the attack and after that nothing definite is known of him. In the fifteenth century Ingulf of Croyland wrote the *Gesta Herewardi* which purported to be an account of his wanderings, but this is thought to be a work of fiction on which later material was based.

HIGHGROVE Located within what was the old manor of Doughton in pleasant Gloucestershire countryside near Tetbury, the site of PRINCE CHARLES's home of Highgrove had its first royal connection in the reign of EDWARD III. The manor then passed into the hands of his son Edmund of Langley and later was given to Elizabeth of York as part of her dower when she married HENRY VII in 1486. In 1798 the present Highgrove was built by a local worthy, John Paul Paul, whose curious name came about through his father changing the family name from Tippetts to Paul in consequence of an inheritance. The three-storeyed house, built of brick dressed with Cotswold stone, contains thirty rooms, four of which are main reception rooms including a spacious library.

In 1980 the house was bought on behalf of the prince, by the Duchy of Cornwall. One of the reasons it was selected was its easy accessibility to the west of England, where much of the Duchy's property is situated; Wales, of which Charles is the prince, and London. One of the aspects of High-grove which attracted the prince, who has an abiding interest in ecological farming, was its estate of 347 acres.

HOLINSHED, RAPHAEL Early in the reign of ELIZABETH I Raphael Holinshed, a 'minister of God's word', was employed as a translator by the publisher Reginald Wolfe. During this time he prepared the chronicles – often referred to as Holinshed's Chronicles – which, written by several authors and illustrated by woodcuts, were published in 1577. It has been described as 'the first authoritative vernacular and continuous account of the whole of English history' from which Shakespeare took material for his plays relating to British kings. Holinshed's own literary work was the *Historie of England*.

HOLYROODHOUSE, PALACE OF Standing at the end of Canongate in Edinburgh's Old Town, the Palace of Holyroodhouse is the sovereign's official residence in Scotland. The name of the palace goes back to 1128 when DAVID I of Scotland established an abbey of Augustinian canons on the site and bestowed upon it a relic of the Holy Rood, the archaic word 'rood' meaning the cross of Christ. It wasn't until the reign of JAMES IV of Scotland that the abbey buildings were largely rebuilt as Scotland's royal palace by the king who wanted to establish Edinburgh as the capital of the kingdom. After James was killed at the BATTLE OF FLODDEN in 1513 his baby son JAMES V inherited the throne and later continued his father's work on making Holyrood Scotland's premier palace. The building, whose exterior was built in the French style, had a large square courtyard at its centre and today the surviving Great Tower remains as a monument to his work.

MARY, the daughter of JAMES V of Scotland, was a week old when she became Queen of Scots on her father's death in 1542. The regent Arran promised her in marriage to EDWARD, the son of HENRY VIII, but when the Scottish Parliament rejected the match, war with England followed, during which Holyroodhouse was badly damaged. Mary was then betrothed to the Dauphin of France and was brought up as a member of the brilliant French court, marrying the dauphin in 1558. Soon afterwards her husband became Francis II of France but following his death in 1560 Mary returned to Scotland and took up residence in Holyroodhouse.

The Palace of Holyroodhouse, Edinburgh, has been a royal palace since the reign of James IV of Scotland.

weeks and, full of optimism at that stage of the campaign, gave a magnificent ball.

It was not until 1822 that the palace came into its own again with GEORGE IV's visit to Edinburgh, supervised by Sir Walter Scott. Huge crowds waited outside the palace to cheer him when he made public appearances in a kilt – and tights.

QUEEN VICTORIA, with her love for Scotland, established the tradition – which lasts to this day – of the British sovereign staying at the palace for a short period every year when there is a garden party and appropriate state functions. During that period the Royal Company of Archers acts as the sovereign's traditional bodyguard. It was the result of Queen Victoria's wish that the royal apartments were first opened to the public in the middle of the nineteenth century. The next monarch to take a personal interest in the palace was her grandson GEORGE V who was responsible for restoration and redecoration while Queen Mary supervised much of the refurnishing.

HOMAGE Coming from the French word *homage*, the act of homage was a medieval rite in which a tenant declared that he held his holding as a fief from a local lord and that he was 'his man'. The custom went right up the social layers of the feudal pyramid with the nobility having to pay homage to the king at the apex. In the ceremony the tenant knelt and placed his hands between those of his lord, a symbolic act of loyalty that is still part of the coronation ceremony.
See also FEUDAL SYSTEM

HOMILDON, BATTLE OF When the army of HENRY IV was occupied with Owain Glyndwr's rebellion in Wales, the Scots had ample opportunity to raid the North of England, especially lands belonging to the Earl of Northumberland, the head of the Percy family, and his son HENRY PERCY known in history as 'Hotspur'.

In the summer of 1402 a Scottish force of ten thousand, under command of Lord Archibald Douglas, reached Newcastle, where they took so much loot it became necessary for them to return with it to Scotland. On the march they reached Homildon (now Humbleton) Hill to find an army under the Earl of Northumberland, the Earl of March and Hotspur, waiting for them.

The Scots took up position on the hill. English archers sent squalls of arrows against them until,

On 29 July 1565 she married her cousin Henry Stewart, LORD DARNLEY, in the palace chapel. Disappointed that he was not granted the crown matrimonial, Darnley became involved with a number of Protestant lords in a conspiracy against the queen's Roman Catholic secretary David Rizzio. On the night of 9 March 1566 Rizzio was murdered by the conspirators and the Outer Chamber where the murder took place remains a place of morbid interest to visitors.

The next dramatic event at the palace during Mary's reign was her rash wedding on 15 May 1567 to James Hepburn, 3rd Earl of Bothwell. The earl was suspected of involvement in the death of Darnley, who was found dead in the garden of his house after it had been blown up by gunpowder.

In July 1567 Mary abdicated in favour of her son JAMES VI of Scotland and when he reached the age of 12 he took up residence in Holyroodhouse and spent more time in the palace than any other Scottish king. However, when he became James I of England it fell into disuse and it was not until the Restoration that much of it was rebuilt and refurbished in the expectation of CHARLES II visiting Edinburgh. In the event the royal visit never materialised but the king's brother JAMES stayed at the palace during the Exclusion crisis which, beginning in 1679, was an attempt to exclude him as heir to the throne on account of his Roman Catholicism.

During the Jacobite rebellion of 1745 Bonnie Prince Charlie stayed in Holyroodhouse for five according to accounts of the time, those without armour bristled with shafts like hedgehogs. In desperation the Scots charged down the slope only to find that the archers would flee ahead of them, then turn and continue to pour arrows into their ranks. The raiders were completely routed. In addition to the carnage on the hill, fifteen hundred men were killed as they attempted to escape across the River Tweed. Seven leading Scottish nobles died and more than eighty knights were captured.

HONOURABLE CORPS OF GENTLEMEN-AT-ARMS Established by HENRY VIII, the ceremonial duties of this company of thirty-two members include being present at BUCKINGHAM PALACE garden parties and at the STATE OPENING OF PARLIAMENT. For their ceremonial duties the gentlemen wear helmets decorated with swans' feathers, scarlet jackets and blue trousers. The captain of the corps is traditionally the chief whip in the House of Lords.

HONOURS OF SCOTLAND *See* SCOTTISH CROWN JEWELS

HORSE GUARDS PARADE Originally the tilt-yard of Whitehall Palace, today the parade ground is the scene of TROOPING THE COLOUR which is held annually on the sovereign's official birthday. It first came into prominence in 1540 when HENRY VIII held a famous tournament there which attracted chivalrous contestants from all over the Continent. When ELIZABETH I came to the throne in 1558 it became the tradition for her birthday to be celebrated by military displays which continued during the following reigns and later included the ceremonial presentation of medals.

HOTSPUR *See* PERCY, HENRY

HOWARD, CATHERINE In 1540 Parliament petitioned HENRY VIII to marry for a fifth time 'for the good of the people'. He complied by marrying a cheerful, auburn-haired girl of 18 named Catherine Howard who, like ANNE BOLEYN, was a niece of Thomas Howard, Duke of Norfolk.

It seems that Catherine had her first love affair with a musician named Henry Mannock who taught her to play the virginals. Later she had an affair with a certain Francis DEREHAM who was a member of the Duke of Norfolk's household. Love

tokens passed between the couple – Dereham giving Catherine a silk hearts-ease – and they considered themselves to be engaged, which in those days was regarded as so binding that it could invalidate any later marriage either had with a third party.

This relationship ended when the girl was summoned to court where the Catholic party planned to use her to charm Henry away from his queen, the Protestant ANNE OF CLEVES, by becoming his mistress. The scheme worked better than they could have hoped for, because instead of becoming Henry's mistress she became his wife after his marriage to Anne was annulled.

Soon the marriage became another 'Great Matter' for the King. On the day after All Saints Day 1541 – when Henry had given thanks for the good life he enjoyed with Catherine 'after sundry troubles of mind which happened to him by marriage' – ARCHBISHOP CRANMER slipped a paper into his hand and begged him to read it when he was alone. The note claimed that prior to her marriage the Queen had been intimate with the musician Mannock and Frances Dereham. The latter was arrested on a euphemistic charge of piracy and admitted under questioning that he had enjoyed intercourse with Catherine when she was single. When it was Mannock's turn to be interrogated he denied having had intercourse with Catherine.

Cranmer and Catherine's uncle, the Duke of Norfolk, were sent to question the Queen who made a confession of her 'immorality', which Cranmer copied down. She claimed, however, that since her marriage she had been faithful to Henry, and even torture could not force Dereham to contradict her.

Despite the fact that under the harshest probing no confession of adultery could be obtained, Catherine was imprisoned in the TOWER OF LONDON. On 12 February 1542 she was informed that she was to be executed the following morning. Her response was to ask that the block be brought to her cell so that she could rehearse her part in the grim ceremony.

HUNDRED YEARS' WAR This was the name given to hostilities between England and France from 1337 to 1453, but in fact was a continuation of wars fought in the previous century over the sovereignty of Aquitaine. In 1152 the marriage of ELEANOR OF AQUITAINE to HENRY II meant that Aquitaine became part of the Angevin empire, the territory in France controlled by the counts of

Anjou, better known as the Plantagenets in England where they formed the royal house. One aspect of the acquisition of Aquitaine was that the English kings, as dukes of Aquitaine, owed homage to the French crown.

HYDE PARK Like some other royal parks, Hyde Park was appropriated by HENRY VIII after the Dissolution of the Monasteries in 1536. Originally the land, which had been bequeathed to the monks of Westminster, comprised three properties, one of which was named Hyde. The king sold off two properties but Hyde he kept as a hunting domain, deer being hunted there into the late eighteenth century. By that time it had already been open to the public since the beginning of the previous century and had become a place for fashionable folk to promenade and mingle. During the Commonwealth it was divided into three and sold, but following the Restoration CHARLES II saw to it that it was returned to royal ownership. A brick wall was built to encompass it and once more the park became a centre for the fashionable and aristocratic, the latter being driven round the enclosure known as the Ring in their magnificent carriages.

The way that led from St James's Palace through the park was known as the *route du roi*, the name evolving into 'Rotten Row', and after WILLIAM III and MARY came to the throne in 1689 it became the first road in England to be artificially illuminated. This was achieved with three hundred oil lamps that the king had suspended along the way in an effort to deter the robbers who prowled in the park after nightfall. It seems that the scheme was not all that successful, as in 1749 one of the illustrious victims of a couple of armed highwaymen was the author Horace Walpole who was relieved of cash and his watch. The park also gained a sinister reputation as a venue for duelling. The most famous duel there took place in 1712 between the Duke of Hamilton and Lord Mohun, which

concluded with Lord Mohun lying dead and the duke so badly wounded that he expired a few minutes later.

QUEEN CAROLINE possessed an enthusiastic eye for landscaping and in 1730 her ideas resulted in the Westbourne river, which flowed through the park, being damned to form the Serpentine, a sewer being built to carry away excess water. Two boats were kept on the Serpentine for the pleasure of the royal family. Ninety years on, GEORGE IV, who had planned to have one of the most magnificent coronations in the history of England, had the event celebrated in the park by balloon ascents and stupendous firework displays. Two years later Wellington's triumphs were commemorated by Sir Richard Westmacott's statue of Achilles, erected in the park by 'the women of England'. It was cast in bronze melted down from French cannons and had the novelty of being England's first nude public statue.

Royal connections with the park continued with the constructing of the Albert Gate in 1845 and the Prince of Wales's Gate 1847. In 1851 the Great Exhibition, the inspiration of PRINCE ALBERT, was held in the Crystal Palace which had been erected near the Prince of Wales's Gate.

Perhaps the best known aspect of Hyde Park around the world is Speakers' Corner, opposite Marble Arch, which goes back to 1827 when the right of assembly came into being. Here anyone can express his or her views freely as long as they are not obscene, offensive to religious convictions or likely to cause a breach of the peace.

In the Dell at the eastern end of the Serpentine is what appears to be a megalith. Weighing 7 tons, it is known as the Standing Stone and there is a tradition that it was taken from Stonehenge and placed in the park by command of CHARLES I. Alas for a romantic legend, the stone was part of an old fountain that once stood in the park.

I

INDEMNITY AND OBLIVION, ACT OF At the Restoration CHARLES II faced the problem of reuniting a kingdom that had been bitterly divided by civil war. Supporters who had suffered in the Royalist cause looked for compensation, while those who had supported Parliament feared reprisals. Before he returned to England Charles issued the Declaration of Breda, stating there would be a general amnesty, arrears of troops pay settled and that there would be consideration for 'tender consciences' in religion. The Act of Indemnity and Oblivion passed in 1660 was designed to put Charles's promise into effect and 'bury all seeds of future discords'. The way in which Charles did conciliate the country was a remarkable feat of kingship, but because changes in the ownership of property resulting from the civil war could not be redressed without civil dissension, the status quo remained and disappointed Royalists complained it was oblivion for them and indemnity for the king's erstwhile enemies.

INN SIGNS A number of inn signs were originally chosen to compliment personages in authority, a local aristocrat or the sovereign of the day. While some of the latter merely expressed respect to the monarchy, such as the King's Head or the Queen's Arms, others were more specific and expressed loyalty to a sovereign or a royal faction by the use of an appropriate symbol which could be easily recognised. Thus an inn named the White Rose represented the Yorkists in the WARS OF THE ROSES while the Red Rose referred to the Lancastrian badge, emblems bestowed with consideration to local allegiance. Specific sovereigns, referred to by signs usually based on their coat of arms, were:

Edward III – The White Swan
Richard II – The White Hart
Henry IV – The White Swan
Henry V – The Swan and Antelope

Edward IV – The White Lion (when Earl of March)
 and The Three Suns (when king)
Richard III – The Blue Boar
Henry VII – The Red Dragon
Henry VIII – The Bull's Head
Charles II – The Royal Oak
The House of Stuart – The Chequers.

IONA Lying just off the west coast of Mull in the Inner Hebrides, the Isle of Iona was once regarded as the most holy spot in the British Isles and therefore an appropriate burial place for kings. Although the island was originally known as Innis-nam Druidbneach ('The Isle of Druids'), it was after the arrival of St Columba and his small band of followers in AD 563 that Iona became a hallowed Christian sanctuary. After Columba had established his monastery – its stone foundations are still to be seen – he began his evangelical expeditions to the mainland and Iona became the gateway through which Christianity was introduced into Scotland.

In the eleventh century Malcolm Canmore, King of Scotland, crossed to Iona with his English wife Queen Margaret who, being an ardent Roman Catholic, induced some of the monks to change allegiance from the Celtic Church in return for which she rebuilt the monks' chapel dedicated to St Oran and which remains to this day.

Such was the veneration with which Iona was held by Scots and Scandinavians that it came to be regarded as a spot of unparalleled sanctity. A tradition grew up round it that when the second flood swamps the world only the holy island will be free from inundation. Another belief was that Iona was so hallowed that those buried there would be absolved from mortal sin and therefore would avoid purgatory but instead would go directly to heaven. This belief caused the Reilig Odhrain, the burial ground beside St Oran's Chapel, to become a royal necropolis. The royal dead arrived by ferry from Mull across the Sound of Iona or directly by ship to the island's landing place, and were then carried

along a cobbled track, known as the Road of the Dead, to their last resting place. It is said sixty kings and chieftains were interred there, including eight from Norway and four from Ireland. Duncan I was buried in the Reilig Odhrain in 1040, as was his cousin, successor – and possible murderer – King Macbeth who was laid there in 1057. Other Scottish kings to be interred in the sacred soil were Kenneth I

The Road of the Dead, Iona, along which dead kings of Scotland and Scandinavia were brought for burial in the island's holy soil.

(859), Constantine I (877), Donald II (900), Malcolm I (954), Kenneth II (995) and Lulach (1058).

J

JAMES I OF SCOTLAND Born the second son of King ROBERT III at Dunfermline in 139I, James I was the most remarkable of the Stewart kings of Scotland. After his elder son David had disappeared at Falkland, supposedly murdered by his uncle the Duke of Albany, the ailing king was apprehensive over his surviving son's safety and in 1406 sent him to France. On the voyage he was captured by the English on 22 March and held as a hostage by HENRY IV. Although he technically became the King of Scotland on the death of his father on 4 April, James was to remain in England for the next eighteen years. Albany, who as Regent of Scotland was ruling the kingdom as an uncrowned king, had no wish for James to return to claim his throne and connived to have him kept in England.

Although he was a hostage, he was well treated and Henry IV ensured that he was educated as befitted a prince. As for James, he grew up with a strong belief in the English form of government which was to influence him when he finally returned to his kingdom. During his years as a royal hostage James became accomplished in the field of sport and in music and literary work. In particular he is noted for his poem 'Kingis Quair' ('The King's Book') in which he wrote of his captivity, his love for, and his prospective marriage to, Joan Beaufort. A daughter of the Earl of Somerset, Joan was a niece of RICHARD II. She and James were married at Southwark on 12 February 1424 and were to have six daughters and twin boys.

The Duke of Albany died in 1420 and the regency of Scotland was inherited by his son Murdoch who lacked the authority – or ruthlessness – of his father. Unable to cope with the anarchy caused by the feuding of the nobles which was afflicting the kingdom yet again, HENRY VI finally arranged for James to return to Scotland.

The kingdom that James found he had inherited was in turmoil. Ordinary folk were suffering from poverty and lawlessness while the power of the unruly nobles had expanded to the detriment of the Crown which, as the chaotic administration demonstrated, had lost its authority. There was resentment against the newly arrived king because of his wife's connection with English royalty and the fact that in order to gain experience in military matters he had taken part on the English side against the French. Undeterred, with remarkable energy James immediately began to tackle the problems that beset his kingdom. After he had only been back in the country for a week Parliament was presented with a large number of statutes which he considered necessary to bring stability to the country, so that he became known as 'The Law-giver'. During his reign he was to bring back law and order, introduce new and necessary taxes and institute reforms that were not always welcomed. A minor example of this were laws against poaching and fishing for salmon out of season.

James's initial concern was to remove what he saw as threats to the stability of the Crown – and savour personal revenge. In 1425, eight months after he had returned to Scotland, his cousin Murdoch, the previous regent, two of his sons and his father-in-law the Earl of Lennox, were arrested and executed at Stirling and their estates forfeited to the Crown. In this stroke the power of the Albany Stewarts, which had dominated Scotland for so many years, was ended. For the rest of his reign James never hesitated in taking pre-emptive military action against those nobles whom he saw as menacing his rule.

In 1427, aware of opposition brewing in the Highlands he summoned the chiefs of that turbulent area to a parliament and promptly had forty seized and a number of the ringleaders put to death. Meanwhile, he worked to improve Scotland's economy by encouraging trade with the Low Countries and concluding a treaty with Denmark, Norway and Sweden. In 1428, after a failed attempt to come to terms with Henry VI of England he revived the Auld Alliance with France and sent troops to support Charles VII against the English. This action was highly popular with his subjects for as the future Pope Pius II remarked after a visit to Scotland, 'Nothing pleases the Scots more than abuse of the English.'

Having experienced the court life of Henry IV and HENRY V James had a firm concept of the status of royalty and became renowned for his fine raiment and his liberal use of the royal purse. Linlithgow Palace was transformed into a royal residence the magnificence of which had not been seen in Scotland before.

In restoring order to the kingdom and curbing power-seeking nobles, James earned the enmity of those who resented his rule, particularly that of three of his relations who led a plot dedicated to his removal. These conspirators were his uncle and chamberlain Walter Stewart, his cousin Sir Robert Stewart and Sir Robert Graham. In February 1437 the King was staying at the monastery of the Friars Preachers in Perth when on the night of the 20th assassins entered through a door from which the bolts had been previously removed. The King endeavoured to hide in a vault beneath the floor of his chamber but he was discovered and although he put up a desperate fight he was stabbed to death in front of his wife. The assassins were seized and Queen Joan avenged her husband, who had always been loyal to her, by having them horribly tortured before they finally died in a manner which was regarded as shocking even in those cruel days.

JAMES II OF SCOTLAND The younger of the twin boys born to JAMES I of Scotland and Queen Joan at Holyrood Palace on 16 October 1430, James became the Duke of Rothsay on the death of his brother Alexander a few months later. He is the first Scottish monarch of whom there is an idea of his appearance. In a portrait he was depicted with his hand on a dagger at his belt and a look of confidence on his face the left side of which was scarred by a livid birthmark.

James was six years old when he succeeded to the throne following the assassination of his father in 1437, and once more there was a regent in control of Scotland. Without a strong sovereign to uphold Parliament and curb the ambitions of the great nobles, the country suffered from the sort of power struggles that James I had to contend with when he began to rule his kingdom. The regent, who was also the heir to the throne, was Archibald, 5th Earl of Douglas, the head of the immensely

powerful 'Black' Douglas family which was to be James's bête noir. Earl Douglas died in 1439 and his son William became the 6th Earl. The role of regent went to Sir William Crichton who greatly feared the Douglases and the fact that until the king produced an heir, the throne would go to Earl William, then aged 17, in the event of his death.

One day in November 1440 Sir William invited the youthful earl and his younger brother David to Edinburgh Castle to have supper with the 10-year-old king. Both boys duly arrived and in the Great Hall, so it was said, saw a black bull's head placed before them, a traditional portent of death which was realised when they were immediately beheaded. The effect of the murders was to temporarily weaken the House of Douglas, while the earldom was granted to Sir William's great uncle James, known as 'the Gross' who, it was whispered, had connived at the murders. James the Gross died in 1443 and his son William became the 8th Earl of Douglas and was made lieutenant-general of the kingdom the following year.

It was not until 1449 that James assumed the duties of kingship. In the same year he married Mary, the daughter of the Duke of Gueldres, who was crowned Queen Consort on 3 July, the day of the wedding, at Holyrood Abbey. Like his father, James displayed great energy once he held the reins of power, continuing his father's policy of sustaining the position of the sovereign against the power-hungry nobles. James did attempt to effect a reconciliation with William Douglas but the earl rejected this and the feud between the Black Douglases and the Crown was to continue, with the earl entering into a confederacy with other disaffected lords against the king and becoming involved in a treasonable alliance with the Yorkists in England.

In February 1452 the king invited William Douglas to come to Stirling Castle for a meeting under a guarantee of safe conduct. Perhaps inspired by a scene he had witnessed as a child, James dined with Douglas and during the course of the meal stabbed his adversary to death. Following the demise of Douglas, his brother James, now the 9th Earl of Douglas, and his three brothers engaged in open warfare against the king. A month after the murder James was fortunate to escape with his life from Stirling when the Douglases arrived with their followers. At this point it appeared likely that with English help the Douglas faction might even defeat

James, but then the royalist Parliament passed judgement on the murder of William Douglas in James's favour, declaring, 'The Earl was guilty of his own death by resisting the King's gentle persuasion.' Then on St Andrew's Day Queen Mary gave birth to a male heir which reinforced James's popularity with his subjects who wanted stability in the royal succession. They were also aware that James had endeavoured to improve the welfare of the common people although his efforts in this direction had been frustrated by many of the nobles, the House of Douglas in particular.

In 1455 the King, confident of his subjects' loyalty, set out for the final conflict with the House of Douglas, laying siege to Abercorn and Threave. James Douglas fled to the Isles and thence to England where he was to spend many years. Meanwhile, his three brothers who remained to continue the struggle were slain at the Battle of Arkinholm. This signalled the finish of the House of Douglas, the earldom being ended by forfeiture.

In England the WARS OF THE ROSES had begun and James tended to side with the Lancastrians as the Yorkists had not only provided refuge for James Douglas but had renewed a claim to the overlordship of his kingdom. Thus in 1456 he campaigned in Northumberland and in the summer of 1460 besieged Roxburgh Castle, which the English had garrisoned since 1346 and which was now under Yorkist control. On 3 August 1460 he was watching a bombardment of the castle ramparts when a cannon close to him exploded and he was killed in the blast. He was buried in Holyrood Abbey.

JAMES III OF SCOTLAND Aged 8 years, James III of Scotland inherited the throne on 3 August 1460 when his father JAMES II was killed by an exploding cannon at the siege of Roxburgh. A week later he was crowned at Kelso Abbey and once more Scotland came under the control of a regent. In this case it was Bishop Kennedy of St Andrews while the Earl of Angus was appointed the country's lieutenant-general. Under these two prudent men the government of Scotland continued soundly until the earl died in 1462 and the bishop in 1466.

Following this Scotland was yet again bedevilled by the rivalries of ambitious nobles. Foremost among these was the High Justiciar, Lord Boyd of Kilmarnock, who followed Bishop Kennedy as regent. While he held this post he had his son

Thomas created 1st Earl of Arran and in 1467 Thomas was married to the young king's sister Mary. Two years later, as a consequence of James II's Treaty of Copenhagen, James III was married to Margaret, the daughter of Christian I of Denmark, Norway and Sweden. Unable to afford Margaret's dowry, King Christian pledged the earldom of Orkney and the lordship of Shetland, both of which were annexed by the Scottish Crown in 1472.

After his marriage to Margaret at Holyrood Abbey in August 1469 James became king in deed as well as in name. His first act was to free himself from the influence of the ex-regent Lord Boyd whose arrogance infuriated him to such an extent that Boyd and his son fled, the latter's marriage to Princess Mary being declared null and void in 1473.

With a cultivated mind and deep interests in intellectual pursuits, James was unlike the previous Stewart kings whose prime interest had been in holding a kingdom that required stern rule to save it from its propensity for conflict. He was fascinated by astrology and the arts, and preferred the company of musicians, artists and architects to the aristocratic members of the court. In turn the nobles resented the coterie of these low-born favourites, blaming their influence on the King for the poverty and lawlessness which was plaguing the kingdom. These discontents gravitated to the King's younger brothers, Alexander, Duke of Albany, and John, Earl of Mar, who in effect led an alternative court. The popularity of his brothers troubled James who feared that they could become a threat to his Crown, and in 1479 he had them arrested. While in prison, Mar died mysteriously while in his bath but Albany escaped from Edinburgh Castle by climbing down a rope after dispatching his guards. The suspicious death of one brother and the sensational escape of the other increased the King's unpopularity with his subjects, who already compared him unfavourably with his father and grandfather.

In 1482 Scotland was threatened by an English invasion and James set out with a small army to counter it at the border. He was followed and overtaken at Lauder and made captive by a number of noble malcontents led by Archibald Douglas, 5th Earl of Angus, who had declared, 'I shall bell the cat.' Before the King was taken back to Edinburgh he saw his favourites hanged from Lauder bridge.

Meanwhile, Albany had been summoned from exile in France by EDWARD IV of England and, in company with the Duke of Gloucester, marched north to capture Berwick. He then continued to Edinburgh where he liberated his royal brother with whom he had a brief reconciliation, becoming his lieutenant-general. This only lasted until March 1483 when James learned that Albany had made a treasonable agreement with Edward IV. Once more the duke had to flee the country and was later injured fatally when taking part in a tournament in France.

In 1488 a number of rebellious nobles proclaimed James's 15-year-old son James, Duke of Rothesay, as king in place of his father. James tried to come to an understanding with the rebels but when this attempt failed he went to Stirling with his troops only to find the gates of the city barred against him. On 11 June the royal and rebel armies faced each other at Sauchieburn within sight of Stirling Castle. At the start of the battle James carried the sword of Robert Bruce, but once it was obvious that the rebels were gaining the ascendancy he galloped from the field. Soon afterwards he was badly injured by a fall from his horse and took shelter in a cottage near Bannockburn. There the king called for a priest and an unknown man who claimed to be one, entered and stabbed him to death. James was buried in Cambuskenneth Abbey.

JAMES IV OF SCOTLAND Fifteen days after his father JAMES III was murdered on his flight from the Battle of Sauchieburn on 11 June 1488 the 15-year-old James IV was crowned at Scone Abbey. Having nominally been in command of the rebel army that brought disaster to his father, the youthful king was said to have suffered from remorse and to have worn a chain round his body as a penance for the rest of his life. But although he may have suffered remorse over the manner by which he came to the throne it did in fact serve him well. The nobles who rebelled against James III had chosen him to be his father's replacement and were therefore – for a while at least – unlikely to continue Scotland's tragic tradition of magnates versus the Crown. They were content with their victory not only because they had a king of their choice but they were able to take state offices, the royal treasury and even the jewels that had belonged to the dead king. Barons who had remained loyal to him during the rebellion were accused of treason and lost their estates.

From the start of his reign James IV showed the energy and understanding that was to make him one of the most popular and successful of Scotland's Stewart kings. Until it ended in sudden disaster, his reign was one of prosperity for the country, which he raised to the rank of other European kingdoms. He secured his subjects' affection by constantly travelling about the kingdom and showing himself to them, unlike his father who rarely moved from Edinburgh. He was the first Scottish king – albeit well guarded – to visit the Highlands and Islands, that wild region which for so long had been a law unto itself and a menace to his predecessors. The Spanish ambassador, Pedro de Ayala, reported to Ferdinand and Isabella, 'The king even speaks the language of the savages who live in some parts of Scotland and in the islands.'

James was, in fact, a natural-born king. Like EDWARD IV or ELIZABETH I, he had what might be termed today 'royal glamour' that not only impressed but often delighted his subjects. He not only looked the part but was admired for his warm nature, generosity and regal ostentation. His court has been described as 'glittering' and it was said that the tournaments he held were equal to those of England and France, countries famous for the splendour of such chivalric contests. He spent unstintingly on lavish building projects, such as Holyrood Palace and the Great Hall at Stirling Castle, which reflected his concept of how royalty should live. He was particularly fond of music, being a proficient performer on the lute, and he took the court musicians with him wherever he went.

In those pre-Calvinistic times his numerous love affairs, and the royal bastards that resulted, earned him the envious popularity such as his descendant CHARLES II was to enjoy. And like Charles the flamboyant side of his nature was balanced by a cool intelligence. The prosperity enjoyed under his rule, combined with the increasing influence of the Renaissance, generated an expansion of learning and the arts while literature flourished under royal patronage. Impressive churches were built, many castles that had hitherto been grim and uncomfortable fortresses assumed the style and comfort of grand houses, and in the cities wood began to give way to stone as a building material.

Up until James's reign Scottish military activity had been confined to land battles but the king was dedicated to the building of a Scottish navy, especially as England was developing as a sea power. In October 1511, when the king watched the launching of the *Great Michael*, it was then the largest ship of war in northern Europe.

James's reign proved to be free from internecine strife due in part to the fact that he regarded parliaments as providing opportunities for opposition to the Crown and thus he called only three in twenty-five years.

Despite an abortive plot by some Scottish nobles to seize James and deliver him to HENRY VII of England, there was a period of relative peace between the two countries during the early part of his reign. In 1491 Henry concluded a five-year truce with the Scots, but in 1495 PERKIN WARBECK, the pretender to the English throne, arrived in Scotland. He claimed to be Richard, Duke of York, the younger of the two sons of EDWARD IV who had vanished in the TOWER OF LONDON. James made him welcome at his court, gave him his kinswoman Catherine Gordon, the daughter of the Earl of Huntly, in marriage and proposed to go to war on his behalf. It is impossible to know how much of Warbeck's story James believed and how much his support for the pretender was politically motivated. As it turned out, what had been planned as an invasion of England was confined to border raiding, and two years later a seven years' truce was agreed between the two countries.

It held, and on 25 January 1502 James was married by proxy at Richmond Palace to Margaret Tudor, the daughter of Henry VII and Elizabeth of York. On 8 August of the following year the couple went through a marriage service in person at Holyrood Abbey, Margaret being crowned Queen Consort at the same time. This union linking the two royal houses led to the House of Stewart ascending the English throne a hundred years later.

The peace that Henry had sought between the two kingdoms did not last when his son HENRY VIII succeeded him and English hostility towards France increased. To support Scotland's old ally James signed a treaty of alliance with Louis XII in 1512. France was hard pressed by both the English and the Spanish and, urged on by King Louis, James prepared to honour the alliance by invading England despite doubts voiced by his advisers.

In August 1513 James's army of twenty thousand men crossed into England at Coldstream and captured the castles of Norham, Etal, Wark and Ford. Meanwhile, Thomas Howard, Earl of Surrey led the English north from Newcastle to Wooler and on 9 September battle was joined at Branxton Hill near Flodden. After four hours of hand-to-hand fighting King James, who had fought on foot, had been slain

along with the cream of Scotland's nobility. With the king perished his natural son Alexander Stewart, Archbishop of St Andrews, nine earls, fourteen lords and many Highland clan chiefs. As for the ordinary fighting men the English claimed that ten thousand were killed that day. The BATTLE OF FLODDEN is the most famous and the most disastrous in Scottish history and the tragedy is still echoed in 'The Flowers of the Forest', the most evocative lament to be played by Scottish pipes.

A curious legend grew that James survived the battle and went on a pilgrimage to the Holy Land where he remained. There was no evidence for this, yet when Queen Margaret petitioned for a divorce from her second husband in 1527 it was on the grounds that her first husband was still alive.

There is also a mystery concerning the fate of the King's body. After the battle it was transported to Henry VIII who refused his dead brother-in-law proper burial. One story relates that during Henry's reign it remained in a store room at Richmond Palace, another that he was interred in Sheen Abbey in Surrey and yet another that his head may lie in the Church of St Michael in the City of London.

JAMES V OF SCOTLAND James V was just 18 months old when he inherited the Crown from his father JAMES IV who had been killed at the calamitous BATTLE OF FLODDEN on 9 September 1513. The same month he was crowned King of Scotland at the Chapel Royal in Stirling Castle and his mother Queen Margaret became regent so that Scotland, already suffering from the loss of an able king and so many of its leading men, was once more condemned to a repetition of the uncertainty and power struggles that had blighted previous Stewart minorities. At that time the only thing in Scotland's favour was that the English did not invade the country following their success at Flodden.

The lines that were to divide Scotland were drawn up when Queen Margaret married Archibald Douglas, 6th Earl of Angus in August 1514 and the regency was passed to John Stewart, Duke of Albany. Angus led the party that sought good relations with England while Albany, who had been educated in France, headed the pro-French faction which favoured the Auld Alliance. Both camps sought to obtain the person of the King; at one stage Angus and Margaret planned to have him kidnapped and taken to HENRY VIII. The plot failed and the couple fled to England where they fell out, Margaret finally divorcing Angus in 1527.

Against this background of rivalry between the English and French supporters and feuds between the nobles who had survived Flodden, the country was reduced to a state of anarchy. Albany sought to impose his authority as regent but his efforts were fruitless and, disillusioned, he withdrew to France in 1524. With Albany out of the way, those who had been hostile towards him now turned their energies to quarrelling among themselves. In the same year the Scottish Parliament, coerced by Henry VIII, declared that the young king, who had been in the care of Sir David Lyndsay, was fit to govern with the advice of his mother and a council. However, in 1525 James fell into the hands of Angus and was held as a prisoner in Falkland by the Douglas family, of which the earl was chief.

In May 1528 the 16-year-old King put on the clothing of a groom and escaped to Stirling where he was met by loyal supporters. Considering the chaotic background to his life, the way in which James took control of his kingdom and brought order to it was remarkable. One of his first acts was to banish those who had held him captive and then he turned his attention to the border marauders and rebellious Highlanders. He created the College of Justice and earned the nickname of 'King of the Commons' through his sympathetic interest in his ordinary subjects and his protection of the peasantry against oppression by the barons. In order to understand the situation of the ordinary people he developed the habit of disguising himself and, in the tradition of Haroun al-Raschid, visiting them in their homes.

Like his father, James spent lavishly on maintaining his court and on architectural work at Falkland, Linlithgow and Stirling to create settings that asserted the majesty of the Crown.

In 1534 he signed a peace treaty with Henry VIII who wanted him to marry his daughter MARY, later to be known as Bloody Mary. Instead, to Henry's chagrin, he chose to marry Madelaine, the daughter of Francis I of France, on 1 January 1537 at the cathedral of Notre Dame in Paris. She died in July the same year and eleven months later the King married Mary, the daughter of the Duke of Guise-Lorraine.

While King Henry disapproved of his nephew's choice of French brides, he wanted his support for the Reformation, which could lead to Scotland becoming Protestant and therefore an enemy of Roman Catholic France. James, however, refused to abandon his ties with Rome, one of the reasons being that he needed the support of the Scottish clergy to balance the power of the nobles. Still hoping to gain his support, Henry invited James to a meeting at York in 1541, but he waited in vain six days for his guest to arrive – James, it was said, feared that he might be kidnapped by his uncle. From then on relations between England and Scotland deteriorated. In 1542 James was offered the Crown of Ireland by some disaffected Irish chiefs and this motivated Henry to send an army into Scottish territory.

James endeavoured to reply by invading the north of England but his nobles, who in their traditional fashion had become at odds with the King, halted at the border and refused to go further. A second army was levied and put under the command of the King's favourite, Oliver Sinclair. The plan was to march down the Esk Valley to Carlisle but when the army reached Solway Moss on 25 November it was surprised and overwhelmed by a smaller English force and a large number of prisoners were taken. Although he had not been present at the battle and therefore was not responsible for the outcome, James was filled with shame at the defeat. He retired to Falkland Palace where, already ill, he developed a fever and died on 14 December, a week after he had learned of the birth of his daughter, the future MARY, QUEEN OF SCOTS.

JAMES VI OF SCOTLAND, JAMES I OF ENGLAND It was ironical that when the Tudor era ended with the death of ELIZABETH I, England's next royal dynasty – the HOUSE OF STUART – should have begun with the son of her enemy MARY, QUEEN OF SCOTS whose death warrant she had signed. While Mary was in prison she was given the choice of standing trial for the murder of her husband Henry Stewart, LORD DARNLEY, or abdicating in favour of her infant son. She chose the latter and on 24 July 1567 the child was crowned James VI of Scotland at Stirling. He had been born on 19 June of the previous year, the son of Lord Darnley.

As a boy James was a pawn rather than a king in Scotland's turbulent politics, and at 16 he was kidnapped by enemies. Although treated with respect he remained a prisoner until a year later he escaped to St Andrews. When he approached the Duke of Guise in France with a plan to free his mother, Queen Elizabeth defused the project by offering him

James VI of Scotland and James I of England, known as 'the wisest fool in Christendom'.

an annual pension of £4,000. It was fear of losing this that caused him to make only a token protest when Mary, Queen of Scots was executed in 1587.

Although he had shown little interest in the opposite sex, in August 1589 James was married by proxy to Anne, daughter of Frederick II of Denmark. The next decade was hard for him when he was at odds with both the nobles and clergy. Although he was a Protestant he was not a Presbyterian, yet by the end of the century he had managed by playing one faction against another to invest the throne of Scotland with more security than had been known for a long time.

In March 1603, when Elizabeth was close to death Robert Cecil, her Secretary of State, was secretly in touch with James and as soon as the queen died James was proclaimed James I of England. The new King's slow progress into his unfamiliar kingdom was that of an impoverished country cousin coming to take over a rich inheritance. Passing through Newark he was so elated with the absolute power of being a king of England that he ordered an execution without trial.

In London ministers looked forward to a monarch who could make quick decisions. His gradual assumption of power in Scotland had given him a reputation for efficiency and many looked upon him – as he described himself – as 'an old experienced king, needing no lessons'. Politically the new reign opened well. James ended hostilities with Spain and kept Cecil as his counsellor, but soon his popularity began to wane and courtiers were taken aback by the uncouthness of their new king. Sir Anthony Weldon, the King's Clerk of the Green Cloth, wrote: 'He was of middle stature, more corpulent through his clothes than his body, the doublets quilted for stiletto proof, his breeches in great pleats and well stuffed. He was naturally of a timorous disposition, which was the reason for the quilted doublets. . . . His beard was very thin, his tongue too large for his mouth which made him speak full in the mouth, and made him drink uncomely, as if eating his drink. His skin was as soft as taffera sarset. He never washed his hands, only rubbed his finger ends slightly with the wet end of a napkin.'

With a huge extravagant style his amusements were lavish entertainments and entertaining; cockfighting, cards, golf and gardening, in which he was particularly interested, planting mulberry trees where Buckingham Palace now stands. But his main enjoyment was hunting and for much of the year he would progress from one hunting seat to another spending nearly all day in the saddle.

But while James enjoyed himself with revels and hunting, he did not neglect the serious side of his nature of which he was very proud. Described as 'the wisest fool in Christendom' he was one of the most literary of British sovereigns, writing and publishing poetry and writing books which included *A Counterblast to Tobacco* and *Daemonologie*, demonstrating the belief he had in the devil and

The coronation of King James in Westminster Abbey in 1603, uniting the crowns of Scotland and England.

witchcraft. He also ordered a new translation of the Bible and in 1611 the Authorised Version was published, which was not only a work of supreme importance from a religious viewpoint but a milestone in English literature.

Soon after coming to the throne James alienated the English Roman Catholics who had expected more toleration for their faith. Plots were hatched against him and in November 1605 the King's life was threatened by the GUNPOWDER PLOT.

In the following years the royal finances deteriorated until in 1610 Cecil introduced the Great Contract, an agreement between the Commons and the king whereby he would renounce his feudal revenues in return for a guaranteed income of £200,000 per annum. At first it was agreed, but when a heated dispute arose James dissolved the last of the great Tudor parliaments. Royal displeasure at the breakdown fell on Cecil who died in May 1612 and with him the final link with the Tudor era. James announced that from then on he would be his own Secretary of State though in practice the power went to his favourite Robert Carr whom he created Viscount Rochester.

There was now little goodwill left between the King and his subjects and with power falling into the hands of favoured courtiers the rift widened. The King had shown that he did not care much for the company of women or for Queen Anne, who lived apart from him in Denmark House, and his doting treatment of favourites such as Carr gave rise to rumours.

Then in 1616 Robert Carr fell from grace due to the OVERBURY SCANDAL and soon afterwards the penniless George Villiers filled the vacuum left by Robert Carr in the affections of the 50-year-old king. Within a few months Villiers was made an earl, a Knight of the Garter and Master of Horse. Ultimately he was created Duke of Buckingham and became the second richest noble in the kingdom. In 1619 the Queen died and soon afterwards James became ill and left most of the affairs of state to Buckingham. But the King wanted to make an alliance with Spain by marrying his son CHARLES to the daughter of Philip IV of Spain and it was because of this that James, the most peaceful and merciful king England had known for centuries, committed his only infamous act.

Sir Walter Raleigh, a victim of court intrigue, imprisoned in the TOWER OF LONDON for thirteen years, was released in 1616 to undertake an expedition to the Orinoco to find the legendary El Dorado. James only agreed to the adventure because it had been advocated by Buckingham and ordered Raleigh not to engage upon any piratical activity that would upset the Spaniards. Two years later Raleigh returned from Guiana. The quest had failed and worse, while Raleigh was lying fever-stricken aboard his ship the *Destiny*, his men had razed a Spanish settlement. The Spanish ambassador complained to James who, rather than jeopardise the possibility of his son marrying the infanta, had Raleigh sent to the block. However, when he made his plan for the Spanish marriage public, Parliament was whole-hearted in its disapproval and when the Commons declared it was proper for them to discuss all matters of state the king referred to them as 'three hundred kings' and dissolved both Houses.

James was now ailing so Buckingham began to safeguard his position by cultivating a warm friendship with Prince Charles who, after the death of his elder brother Henry in 1612, was heir to the throne. In February 1624 James was petitioned by Parliament to break off negotiations with King Philip and reluctantly agreed. It was his last act as a reigning monarch as from then on he allowed his royal authority to pass to Buckingham and his son. In September 1624 a treaty was concluded with France for Prince Charles to marry HENRIETTA MARIA, the daughter of Henry IV of France.

Buckingham and Charles had been urging the king to go to war with Spain after Spanish troops

A coin from the reign of James I of England.

194

invaded the Palatinate, which was ruled by his Protestant son-in-law, Elector Frederick Henry, who was married to his daughter Elizabeth. James had no wish for the forthcoming war and it was over this that he quarrelled with Buckingham. The now feeble James was pathetically in need of his favourite's affection, as can be seen by these lines he sent him before Christmas 1624: 'I cannot content myself without sending you this billet . . . that we make at this Christmas a new marriage, ever to be kept hereafter; for, God so loved me, as I desired only to live in this world for your sake, and that I had rather live banished in any part of the world with you, than live a sorrowful widow-life without you.'

At the beginning of March 1625 King James suffered an attack of tertian ague and went to Theobalds Park in Hertfordshire where he was nursed by Buckingham's mother. There he died on 27 March and was buried in WESTMINSTER ABBEY. Of the seven children he had fathered only two survived him, his son Charles I and his daughter Elizabeth, through whose line the HOUSE OF HANOVER was later to be established.

JAMES II The second surviving son of CHARLES I, James was born at ST JAMES'S PALACE on 15 October 1633 and known as Duke of York from birth. Like his brother CHARLES his education was cut short by the outbreak of the English Civil War in 1642. At the Battle of Edgehill he was nearly killed by a cannon ball and when Oxford surrendered to the Parliamentarians he was captured and held in St James's Palace. He escaped and joined his mother QUEEN HENRIETTA MARIA in Paris.

By the time he was 19, James was bored with the poverty-stricken court-in-exile at St Germain and became a professional soldier. While waiting to return to England after the death of OLIVER CROMWELL in 1658 he signed a contract of marriage with Anne Hyde, the daughter of Sir Edward Hyde who was to become the Lord Chancellor of England. After Charles II was invited to claim his throne a deputation brought James a gift of £10,000 (approximately £950,000 today) and appointment as Lord High Admiral, and in this role he commanded the flotilla that carried his brother to Dover.

The heady atmosphere of the Restoration affected the morals of the young duke and in the new court he followed the example of Charles in his amorous adventures, though he lacked his brother's tact and charm. His marriage to Anne Hyde in no way restricted his extramarital affairs.

When war broke out in Holland in 1665 James commanded the fleet that dramatically defeated Admiral Opdam off Lowestoft on 3 June, whereupon a grateful Parliament awarded him £12,000 for the victory. During the Great Fire of London the following year he was at his best, organising the firefighting with the king and taking his share of physical toil and danger.

When James's wife Anne, a professed Roman Catholic, died in March 1671 her last words were 'Duke, Duke, death is terrible! Death is very terrible!' This had such a profound effect on him that he publicly converted to the Catholic faith.

It was now unlikely that Charles and Catherine would produce an heir so plans were made for James to remarry. In September 1673 James married by proxy Mary, daughter of Alfonso III, Duke of Modena and Laura Martinozzi. As a Roman

A bronze statue of James II in Roman dress by Grinling Gibbons looking over Trafalgar Square from the front of the National Gallery.

Catholic her arrival in England angered the Protestant population and a scandalous libel spread that her real father was the Pope. But James found his bride charming and good-looking, but so unworldly that 'she had never heard of England nor the Duke of York'. She had no wish to be wedded, having set her heart on retiring to a convent. The Pope had to write commanding her to follow her Catholic mother's wishes over the marriage so that Protestant England might be led back to the true faith. The next spring Mary had the first of a series of miscarriages and whenever a baby was born alive it died an early death. To Mary it must have seemed she was following the tragic Queen Catherine by failing to provide an heir, while her husband fathered two sons and two daughters by his mistress Arabella Churchill. Meanwhile, in 1677 Mary, James's daughter by Anne Hyde, married William, Prince of Orange. The following year – the year of the Popish Plot – James became infatuated with CATHERINE SEDLEY and it seemed strange that he, a devout Catholic, should take a Protestant mistress. In March 1679 she bore him a daughter whose paternity he acknowledged.

When the accusations of Titus Oates released the full anti-Catholic fury of the Protestant English James found himself in a dangerous situation. Oates refrained from laying charges against him but letters discovered in the house of Edward Coleman, secretary to Mary of Modena, showed that he had corresponded with the French king's Jesuit confessor about the conversion of England as agreed in the secret 1670 Dover Treaty, which gave ammunition to Lord Shaftesbury when he demanded James's removal from public affairs in October 1678. To prevent him from being excluded from the succession the king had to dissolve two parliaments and order his brother out of the kingdom by a letter, written in affectionate terms, in February 1679. James went to Holland and what he later referred to as his 'years of vagabondage' began. It was the effect of the Rye House Plot, which was directed as much at James as the King, and the marriage of his second daughter Anne to the Protestant Prince George of Denmark, that soothed public opinion and in 1684 he was able to resume his seat in the Council and his place at the Admiralty.

The king died in February 1685 and James succeeded without difficulty or delay. The new reign began auspiciously when he made a temperate speech to the Council and appointed moderates as his main ministers, but this popular start was soon overshadowed by his zeal for Roman Catholicism. As the Catholic king of a Protestant country James would have been wise to keep his devotions private but he heard Mass in public and at his coronation on St George's Day the Church of England rites were curtailed. Protestants, and especially the Whigs, were alarmed, though public opinion was mollified when the new King banished his late brother's mistress, the Duchess of Portsmouth, back to France.

On 11 June 1685, within five months of his uncle's accession, James, DUKE OF MONMOUTH landed at Lyme Regis and having declared his right to the Crown raised an army who saw the duke as their defender against a Catholic king. But at Sedgemoor on 6 July his followers, many of them armed only with scythe blades lashed to poles, were disastrously defeated in battle. Monmouth was found hiding in a ditch and when interviewed by his uncle the King, he swore to become a Roman Catholic if his life was spared. James commented afterwards, 'The Duke did behave himself not so well as I expected, nor so as one ought to have expected from one who had taken it upon himself to be king.' On 15 July Monmouth was beheaded.

In April 1687 James issued a Declaration stating, 'We cannot but heartily wish all the people of our dominion were members of the Catholic Church.' The pope now made Queen Mary's brother a cardinal, naming him Protector of the English Nation at Rome. In April of the following year James's second Declaration of Indulgence was published.

The Great Seal of James II.

His first Declaration had failed because it was aimed at suspending penal laws against Catholics and nonconformists but anti-Catholic nonconformists defeated it by refusing to accept toleration. The second Declaration was basically the same and James commanded it should be read in all churches. The Archbishop of Canterbury and six bishops petitioned that it was illegal, insisting that the sovereign did not have the right to dispense with the penal code and they should not be compelled to break the law by publishing it. James had them imprisoned in the TOWER OF LONDON, thus firmly setting his course for disaster.

On 10 June Queen Mary gave birth to a son, JAMES EDWARD, later to be known as the 'Old Pretender'. The consternation of the Whigs grew, especially when the Pope was asked to be the child's godfather, and they retaliated with the story that the baby had been smuggled into the Queen's chamber in a warming pan, ignoring the fact that over sixty people were present at the birth.

The same month the Bishop of London and six leading members of both the Whig and Tory parties sent a secret document to WILLIAM OF ORANGE inviting him to come and free England from tyranny. Prince William, the Protestant champion of Europe, had a strong interest in England as he was the only son of James's eldest sister Mary and the husband of his eldest daughter who, prior to the arrival of Prince James Edward, had been heiress presumptive of England.

The signature of James II.

James became aware of the danger when William began military preparations in response to the clandestine invitation. He tried to mollify his subjects but it was too late. The English were now looking across the sea to William of Orange.

Early in November William's fleet slipped into Torbay and what became known as the GLORIOUS REVOLUTION began. On 19 November James took command of the army at Salisbury as William's forces moved through the West Country, attracting local support while the royal army was weakened by desertion. When James learned that his chief commander Lord Churchill, his nephew the Duke of Grafton and his son-in-law Prince George of Denmark had joined the deserters, he knew that it was impossible to expect support from the army. Returning to London on 26 November he found that his daughter Anne had also abandoned him. He sent envoys to Prince William at Hungerford who returned with the ultimatum he should renounce Roman Catholicism. Whatever James's mistakes, he never faltered in his loyalty to his chosen faith and the idea of abandoning it for political gain was unthinkable. Instead he resolved to leave his kingdom and on Christmas Day 1688 he arrived in France. In March 1690 he sailed to Ireland with an expedition financed by Louis XIV who, as the leading Catholic king in Europe, was the sworn enemy of William of Orange.

On 1 July 1690 James had an army of twenty-five thousand facing Prince William's army of English and Dutch Protestants on the banks of the River Boyne. Although William was wounded he continued to command and his regiments scattered James's forward ranks. Observing this from a hill James became the first to flee in the direction of Dublin and the battle became a rout.

James returned to France and in 1692 a second planned invasion foundered and a third attempt also failed. When the French realised James would never regain his crown, the Peace of Ryswick was concluded with Louis recognising William as the sovereign of England. Powerless without French support, it was the end of James's hopes and he turned his attention to spiritual matters, devoting himself to fasting and penances.

James II died on 6 September 1701 and was interred in the St Germain parish church of St Edmund. Soon it became known for miracle cures attributed to his remains and this resulted in parts of his body being distributed as holy relics.

JOHN The youngest son of HENRY II and QUEEN ELEANOR was born on 24 December 1167. As he grew up he was known as 'Lackland' because of the various Plantagenet possessions claimed by his three elder brothers. Just as Richard was his mother's darling, John became his father's favourite and Henry proposed he should be crowned King of Ireland but the coronation never took place.

In 1186 his prospects brightened when his older brother Geoffrey was killed. But Geoffrey's widow

Constance, a sister of Philip of France, bore a posthumous son christened Arthur. The arrival of this child meant that he was ahead of John in succession to the English throne.

When his brother Richard joined Philip of France against Henry, John became involved in their secret alliance, and after defeating the fever-stricken king, one of the terms they insisted on was a royal pardon for those who had plotted against him. As the King had to know who they were a list was brought to his sick chamber. The first name on the scroll was that of his best loved son John. Henry turned to the wall with the words, 'I care no longer for myself or anything in this world.' Soon afterwards he died.

John took a leading part in his brother Richard's coronation and four days before the ceremony he married Isabella of Gloucester who brought him the lordship of Gloucester as her dowry. Despite this new-found affluence John was soon to suffer a disappointment which led to his treachery against Richard.

In December 1189 Richard joined the Third Crusade, leaving William Longchamp the papal legate in control as Justiciar. Though Richard treated his brother generously, he had shrewd doubts about his loyalty, and to protect his interests he made it a condition that John should not enter England for three years and the new king acknowledged his 4-year-old nephew Arthur of Brittany as his heir. John may have consoled himself that the laws of succession were still fluid in Europe, and should Richard be killed fighting in the Holy Land, he still might be able to persuade the Council that he was the right prince to take the Crown. In 1190 he was allowed to return and, exploiting the unpopularity of William Longchamp, caused the Justiciar to flee the country.

When Eleanor arrived in England from her court in Aquitaine she found that John had control of the TOWER OF LONDON and was supported by a number of barons and bishops. She sent a message to Richard to return home. On the homeward journey Richard fell into the hands of the emperor Henry VI who alerted King Philip of France. Philip and Richard's friendship had not stood the stresses of the Holy Land and the French king passed the news to John suggesting that they should divide Richard's French dominions between them, to which John agreed, telling the Council that King Richard was dead. When John attempted to make himself king he found that public feeling was

King John paying homage to the Papal legate after the Pope placed his kingdom under interdict.

against him and sent for French mercenaries. This was thwarted by Queen Eleanor who rallied troops loyal to Richard and forced John to make a truce.

In March 1194 the King returned and summoned John to appear before the Council within forty days to stand trial as a rebel. Meanwhile, King Philip invaded Normandy and Richard crossed the Channel for the last time to defend his territory. He repulsed a French force at Lisieux where John threw himself at his brother's feet in submission and was pardoned. John proved his loyalty by capturing Evreux for Richard, a victory he signalled by beheading three hundred members of the defeated garrison and lining the town's walls with their heads.

After Richard died on 6 April 1199, from an arrow wound received while besieging the castle of Chaluz, John rode to Le Mans finding that the town was about to be taken over by a number of Prince Arthur's supporters and a French army. Arthur was not only a nephew of John but also of King Philip of France.

In England John was crowned at Westminster on 21 May and he then obtained a divorce from

Isabella. The following August he married the beautiful 13-year-old daughter of the Count of Angoulême, also called Isabella, who was already betrothed to Hugh de Lusignan, who burned to revenge himself on the man who had taken his fiancée. Supported by Philip of France and Constance of Brittany, de Lusignan attacked John's Poitou lands, and in May 1201 John was forced to take an army across the Channel to meet the threat. Meanwhile, King Philip had betrothed Prince Arthur to his daughter and had taken up his cause as the rightful heir to the English throne, ordering John to come to Paris to hand over his French fiefs to Arthur in compensation. John ignored the summons, and in July 1202, news reached John at Anjou that his mother, Queen Eleanor, was besieged at Mirabeau by Hugh de Lusignan. Mirabeau lay over a hundred miles away, but after forty-eight hours' hard riding John and his men entered the town so unexpectedly that the resistance was short-lived. In one stroke the king had Prince Arthur, his sister Eleanor and Hugh de Lusignan at his mercy. Arthur was imprisoned in Falaise Castle and later moved to Rouen where he vanished mysteriously. It was believed that John had arranged his murder or had even carried it out himself.

The disappearance of Prince Arthur was the watershed in John's career. After it nothing went well and the most shattering blow was in March 1204 when Chateau Gaillard, the great bastion against the French which had been built by Richard I, fell to its besiegers. Three months later Queen Eleanor died at Fontevrault and her death removed any parental influence she might have exercised over John; it also broke the last tie which held his empire together. By that summer King Philip had won control of all Normandy, and Anjou, Maine and Touraine fell one after another. Within two years all that remained of England's Continental territories was a portion of Aquitaine.

In 1205 John quarrelled with the Church over a disputed election of the Archbishop of Canterbury. When Pope Innocent III consecrated Stephen Langton against the wishes of the king, who refused to recognise Langton, Innocent placed an interdict upon England. This meant that church services were suspended throughout the kingdom and the only sacraments priests could perform were baptism and hearing the confessions of the dying. John retaliated against the clergy by confiscating their property. Finally Innocent launched a decree against him

The Great Seal of King John.

which, in the eyes of the Church, released the English from their allegiance to their sovereign and this made John see the necessity of making peace with Rome. In May 1213 he agreed to Innocent's demands that he acknowledge Archbishop Langton, recall the banished bishops and compensate the monasteries he had oppressed. More dramatically he did homage for his kingdom, first surrendering it to the Pope and then receiving it back as a fief of Rome with the condition he paid an annual tribute of 1,000 gold marks.

The King's quarrel with the Church was now replaced by one with his nobles. He had made himself hated by many through bad government and, it was said, improper advances to their wives and daughters. If he enjoyed such intrigues, he could not stand being cuckolded himself. After Queen Isabella tired of his behaviour and took lovers herself, John had two of them hanged above her bed and then led her to view the scene.

In 1214, while John was at war with France, his discontented barons decided upon the concessions they would force from him, 'to restore the liberty of the Church and the Kingdom, to abolish the evil customs which his father, brother and himself had introduced and to renew Henry I's charter'. Despite the King's delays they finally forced him to put his seal to the MAGNA CARTA in a field near Runnymede on 15 June 1215. This charter of privileges is regarded as the foundation stone of British liberty, and among the clauses was the vital one stating that there could be no punishment without trial according to the law of the land, and another that taxation could not be imposed without the consent of the Council. Although the document was a charter of human rights, it was the barons rather than the commoners who benefited from it as from then on their power was greatly increased.

John, though, had no intention of keeping to the terms of the charter and petitioned his enemy King Philip and the Pope for aid, which resulted in the papal legate excommunicating the barons. This polarised them into two factions, one still loyal to the Crown and those who invited Prince Louis, the Dauphin of France, to come to England as their leader. In October 1215 civil war began.

In September 1216 John went on the offensive, entering Lincolnshire with his army to create a barrier between his enemies to the south and those to the north. On 12 October he set out in the direction of Swineshead Abbey. To reach it the column had to cross the Wellstream estuary, now known as the Wash, 5 miles across with the tide out. Behind the lines of troops straggled the royal baggage train which included wains carrying the King's treasure. In the autumnal mists the vehicles missed the track and their wheels sank in quicksand. Roger of Wendover wrote: 'The ground opened in the midst of the waters and whirlpools sucked in everything, men and horses.'

John left the scene of the disaster, reaching Swineshead Abbey sick in heart and body. HOLINSHED wrote: '. . . after he lost his armie, he came to the abbie of Swineshead in Lincolnshire, a monke, being moved with zeale for the oppression of his countries, gave the king poison in a cup of ale wherreof he first tooke the assaie, to cause the king not to suspect the matter, and so they both died in manner at one time.'

Certainly death was close when the King left the abbey to continue on to Newark, carried on a makeshift litter. He reached the Bishop of Lincoln's castle at Newark on 16 October, and on the night of the 18th he expired halfway through making his will, naming his eldest son Henry heir. He died on 18 October 1216 and was interred before the high altar in Worcester Cathedral where his effigy is still to be seen. Queen Isabella returned to France where she married her former suitor Hugh de Lusignan.

The effigy of King John on his tomb in Worcester Cathedral.

JOHN OF GAUNT The fourth son of EDWARD III, John of Gaunt was born in 1340 at Ghent and rose to be one of the most powerful nobles in the history of England. He married his cousin, Blanche of Lancaster, in 1359 and three years later was created 1st Duke of Lancaster. His enormous wealth allowed him to have the largest company of knights in the kingdom, and during his father's declining years and the period before RICHARD II reached the age of majority he was effectively England's ruler. Following the death of Blanche in 1372 he married Constance, the daughter of Pedro the Cruel

An early manuscript illustration of the legend that a monk gave John a cup of poisoned ale.

John of Gaunt's Savoy Palace was destroyed in the Peasants' Revolt and only his restored chapel remains as the King's Chapel of the Savoy.

of Castile, and through this union claimed the title of King of Castile, though his attempt to seize the country failed.

Nonetheless he remained the most influential magnate in England and it was believed, and feared, that his ambition was the throne itself. His protection of the religious reformer John Wycliffe, which at one stage saved the reformer's life, coupled with his famous quarrel with the Bishop of London, gained him the opposition of the clergy and the disapproval of the people, which resulted in his Savoy Palace being sacked by a London mob in 1381.

Young King Richard feared his ambition and in 1386 encouraged him to leave the country in another attempt to win the crown of Castile. The enterprise ended with a treaty by which John's daughter Catherine would marry the future King of Castile. On his return to England John convinced the king he had nothing to fear from him, and indeed it was his backing that became Richard's most valuable asset and in return John was made

Duke of Aquitaine. After his second wife Constance died in 1394 John married his mistress, Catherine Swynford, by whom he already had three children. They were legitimated by the Pope in 1396 but debarred from the succession by a Charter of Richard II.

John of Gaunt died in February 1399 and was interred in old St Paul's Cathedral, London. In the following September his fourth son by Blanche of Lancaster became HENRY IV on the abdication of RICHARD II.

JORDAN, DOROTHEA Born in 1762 near Waterford, Ireland, Dorothea Bland was 14 when she made her stage debut as Phoebe in Shakespeare's *As You Like It*. Seduced by Richard Daly, the Dublin theatre manager, she crossed to England where her first child was born. Here she continued as an actress under the stage name of Mrs Dorothea Jordan, being especially popular in comedy and 'breeches' parts which showed off her shapely legs. William Hazlitt, the essayist, wrote: 'Her smile had the effect of sunshine, and her laugh did one good to hear.' The poet Lord Byron described her with one word: 'Superb.' In 1785 she appeared with enormous success in *The Country Girl* at Drury

Lane and for many years continued to take leading roles. In private life she became the mistress of Sir Richard Ford, by whom she was to have four children.

In 1790, when she was at the height of her career, she met William, Duke of Clarence and the future WILLIAM IV, and became his mistress. In this capacity she provided him with the happy home he had always wished for and was popular with his royal brothers whom she frequently entertained. Even GEORGE III succumbed to her charm and went to Drury Lane to watch her perform. There was no question of her giving up the stage as she could not afford to. Apart from the fact that the duke's household was always short of money, she provided for her previous children as well as a number of poor relations. Later in life she was to write: 'From my first start in life, at the early age of fourteen, I have always had a large family to support. My mother was a duty. But on brothers and sisters I have lavished more money than can be supposed.'

As a leading actress she received £30 a week while William allowed her £1,000 a year. When his father suggested that this sum should be halved Mrs Jordan sent the king the bottom half of a playbill on which were printed the words: 'No money returned after the raising of the curtain.' At first the couple resided at St James's, then in a house at Bushey Park where William was given the post of ranger. It was a jolly if somewhat chaotic household, and here Mrs Jordan was to bear the duke ten children over the next twenty years, five boys and five girls, all of whom were given the surname of FitzClarence.

The relationship between Mrs Jordan and the duke was a happy one, but finally William decided that the only way to solve his money problems was to follow the example of his elder brother GEORGE who became Prince Regent early in 1811, and make a dynastic marriage. It was at this time that Mrs Jordan, while acting at Cheltenham, received a letter from William asking her to meet him at Maidenhead for a final separation. She accepted the situation with equanimity, saying she understood that the parting was forced by lack of money and she remained friendly with William. She was provided with an income of £4,000 per annum with the proviso that she would not continue her acting career.

As for William, a convenient marriage was more difficult to arrange than he imagined – young princesses had little desire to wed the bluff, middle-aged duke with ten illegitimate children. Finally, Princess Adelaide of Saxe-Meiningen, then half his age, became his bride. She bore William two daughters who died in their infancy, so that when he came to the throne in 1830 the royal heir was his niece Victoria.

The new king continued to enjoy the company of his children by Mrs Jordan, to the outrage of the *Morning Post* which declared: 'Can anything be more indecent than the entry of a Sovereign with one bastard riding before him and another by the side of his carriage.' Meanwhile, in trying to help her son-in-law who was desperately in debt, Mrs Jordan got into such financial difficulties herself that she was forced to go back on the stage, thereby losing her allowance. Now 50, plump and ailing she was no longer the attraction she had been for so long, and she was unable to earn the money she needed so badly. In order to avoid the debtor's prison, she fled to Paris and settled in a rambling old house in the suburb of St Cloud. Here she spent her time 'sighing on the sofa' and waiting anxiously for some mysterious communication from England. It never came. On 13 July 1816 she died and was buried in the St Cloud cemetery. Not until years later was a stone memorial raised above her grave.

K

KENSINGTON GARDENS In the same year that WILLIAM and MARY came to the throne in 1689, the king bought Nottingham House, to be transformed into Kensington Palace, and the land belonging to it became Kensington Gardens adjoining HYDE PARK. Under the supervision of Queen Mary royal gardeners laid out the grounds, and as a reminder of the king's background yew hedges were planted in the formal patterns that were popular in Holland. These only lasted until the accession of QUEEN ANNE who disliked them so much that she had them removed. More to her liking was the bower that Sir Christopher Wren designed for her, and which was later moved to its present site close to Marlborough Gate in Hyde Park.

GEORGE II had the gardens opened on Saturays to people who were respectably dressed and the Broad Walk became a popular promenade with fashionable Londoners. During the king's reign the Round Pond – the delight of generations of model-boat captains – was established. It became the habit of George to take a solitary walk round the gardens each morning, and it was on one of these walks that he was robbed by an intruder. The man, who had climbed over a wall, was very respectful to the king and apologised for the fact that reduced circumstances compelled him to take drastic action. When he had taken money and a watch from his royal victim, he knelt to remove his shoe buckles and the king asked if he could have back a seal that was on his watch-chain which he particularly liked. He promised he would return the seal the following day when he had detached it from the chain, provided His Majesty kept silent about the incident. George agreed and the next day the robber returned to the garden at the agreed time and the seal was duly returned.

Soon after WILLIAM IV ascended the throne in 1830 he opened the gardens to the public all the year round. The most spectacular addition to Kensington Gardens was the Albert Memorial which was completed in 1872. A committee had

been established by QUEEN VICTORIA to advise her on the design of a national monument to PRINCE ALBERT, who had died in 1861, and finally Gilbert Scott, later knighted for his work, was selected to be the architect. His design was inspired by that of an ELEANOR CROSS, and the final cost of the work was £120,000, which was raised by public subscription and a government grant. The structure, which is the largest and most elaborate of any dedicated to a member of a British royal household, measures 180ft from its base to the top of the inlaid cross surmounting the spire, which is constructed of gilt and enamelled metal tabernacle work. The statue of the Prince Consort by John Foley is set beneath this Gothic canopy and was not unveiled until 1876 due to the death of the first sculptor whose work was not considered satisfactory. The 14ft bronze figure of Albert shows him seated and holding a catalogue of the Great Exhibition. There are four groups of statuary at the corners of the memorial representing Africa, America, Asia and Europe, while round the base is a frieze of marble against which are set 169 natural-sized figures representing the arts while bronze allegorical statues are portrayed against the memorial's pillars.

Completely lacking the size and grandeur of the ALBERT MEMORIAL, but certainly possessing more charm, is the statue of Victoria overlooking the Broad Walk which has the added interest of being the work of the queen's remarkable daughter, Princess Louise. The white marble figure represents the queen as she appeared after her coronation and was put up in 1893.

KENSINGTON PALACE When WILLIAM AND MARY became the joint sovereigns of Britain in the winter of 1689, their problem was to find a suitable residence in the capital. On arrival in London they lived in Whitehall Palace but the king found the damp air from the Thames, which had no embankment at that time and not infrequently flooded the royal cellars, affected his asthma to the extent that he would not stay there. They moved to HAMPTON COURT but as the new king and queen were required to spend much of their time in the capital the search began for a suitable London residence. The answer was Nottingham House, a Jacobean mansion in the then village of Kensington, which belonged to the Secretary of State, Daniel Finch, 2nd Earl of Nottingham, who accepted £20,000 for it.

The house was renamed Kensington House – the 'Palace' came later – and Sir Christopher Wren was directed to begin work on enlarging it for the royal couple and their court, with Nicholas Hawksmoor acting as Clerk of the Works. In order to save valuable time the original building was allowed to remain, with new three-storey blocks or 'pavilions' being erected at its four corners, royal apartments taking up two of these and the Council Chamber in another. A road was built through Hyde Park to the house and the work was completed in 1690, but Queen Mary did not have long to enjoy it, dying there of smallpox in December 1694. When QUEEN ANNE came to the throne in 1702 she moved into the palace where she left her mark with the delightful Orangery, which she commissioned Sir John Vanburgh to build in the year of her succession. Here she spent some of her most pleasant hours, often in the company of her bosom friend SARAH, DUCHESS OF MARLBOROUGH, who as Mistress of the Robes had her own apartments in the palace until the friends famously quarrelled in 1710 and never saw each afterwards.

When the queen's consort, Prince George of Denmark, died at Kensington Palace on 28 October 1708 it affected her so deeply that over a year and a half passed before she could bring herself to reside there again.

After GEORGE I was invited to take the throne in 1714, his accession on 1 August was heartily celebrated by courtiers and staff with a huge bonfire in the palace gardens, being repeated annually on that date. During the king's reign a large number of alterations and improvements were made to the palace, which included part of the original building being dismantled to make way for three state rooms, the ceilings of which were intricately decorated by William Kent. His work pleased the king and he was commissioned to paint the ceilings of the royal apartments and decorate the plain walls of Sir Christopher Wren's King's Grand Staircase. This magnificent staircase is of particular interest as

Kent painted a vast mural on the upper north and east walls, depicting a gallery with arches and balustrades behind which were animated likenesses of people associated with the court, some of whom can still be identified. These included Mahoment and Mustapha, the Grooms of the Chamber, who as boys had been captured during fighting in Turkey, and the king's dwarf, Jorry. Perhaps the most curious portrait was that of Peter the Wild Boy who had been found on all fours, leading an animal-like existence in the Bavarian forest in 1726, and who was brought by the king to England where he lived until 1785 on a royal allowance.

Although GEORGE II liked the palace and spent up to half of each year there, few alterations were made to it during his reign, though he and Queen Caroline were largely responsible for Kensington Gardens. After his death in 1760 his son GEORGE III abandoned the palace and it was never used again by a reigning sovereign. However, members of royalty continued to reside there, such as the king's fourth son Edward, Duke of Kent, and his wife Victoria of Saxe-Coburg-Saalfield. On 10 February 1819 their daughter VICTORIA was born at Kensington Palace, but the duke died in the following January. Victoria and her mother continued to live at the palace and it was early on the morning of 20 June 1837 that she was wakened to be told that she was now Queen of Great Britain, where upon she moved to BUCKINGHAM PALACE.

Among other 'royals' who resided at Kensington were CAROLINE OF BRUNSWICK, the alienated wife of the future GEORGE IV, and their daughter Princess Charlotte.

Another resident was Princess Louise, the sixth child of Queen Victoria, with her husband the Marquis of Lorne. She was a remarkable sculptress – as she was termed in her day – and at twenty had exhibited at the Royal Academy, and when she took up residence in the palace she set up her studio there. Her best known work is the marble statue of her mother as she appeared at the time of her coronation and which overlooks Kensington Gardens' Broad Walk.

On 26 May 1867 a daughter was born to the Duke and Duchess of Teck, the first of their four children, all of whom were born at the palace. She was christened Mary Augusta there by the Archbishop of Canterbury, and she was destined to become Queen Mary, the wife of GEORGE V. Throughout her life she retained her affection for Kensington Palace,

The statue in Kensington Gardens of Victoria as she appeared after her coronation, sculpted by her gifted daughter Princess Louise.

where she had spent a happy childhood, until the family left for Florence in 1883; the rooms she and her mother had occupied were preserved in their Victorian form.

Towards the latter end of the nineteenth century it became obvious that Kensington Palace was in need of expensive repair and restoration. Controversy as to its future included an argument for its demolition, but Queen Victoria would have none of this and in 1897 Parliament agreed to provide the refurbishment of the state apartments, conditional on them being opened to the public. On the queen's 80th birthday in 1899, the opening ceremony took place.

In 1911 the recently founded London Museum took over the state apartments and mounted a collection of royal effects, including court dress from the past, coronation robes and dresses that had belonged to the last three queens: Victoria, Alexandria and Mary. Such was the public interest in the exhibition that on the first day of its opening thirteen thousand visited it.

During the Second World War the state apartments were damaged by enemy bombs and it was not until 1949 that restoration work was completed

and the palace reopened. Today it remains one of Britain's important attractions, with its ceremonial dress collection, the various state apartments and more personal links with the royal past such as the Duchess of Kent's dressing-room, Queen Victoria's bedroom and Queen Mary's dining-room.

KEW PALACE The most unpalatial of British palaces is the brick Kew Palace, also known as the Dutch House, which remains Kew Gardens' only surviving royal building. Yet despite its lack of magnificence, it provided a happy ambience for royal domesticity. In 1631 Samuel Fortrey, a London merchant of Dutch extraction, built the house over the vaults of a Tudor house that had once stood on the site. Almost a hundred years later Queen Caroline took out a 99-year lease on the property for the annual rent of £100 and 'a fat doe'. The great advantage of the Dutch House was that it was only a mile away from RICHMOND LODGE, the favourite residence of GEORGE II, and so became a suitable place for the royal couple's daughters. The eldest of these, Princess Anne, was living there when she married WILLIAM IV, Prince of Orange, in 1734.

Close to the Dutch House was a two-storey mansion known as the White House which in 1731 became the home of Frederick, Prince of Wales, and it was here that his son GEORGE III spent much of his boyhood. When Frederick died in 1751 his widow Augusta continued to reside in the White House until her demise twenty years later. Following the death of her husband the dowager princess became interested in gardening and in 1759 designed a private botanic garden which, opened to the public in 1841, is known today as the Royal Botanic Gardens.

In 1771 George III and Queen Charlotte took over the White House following the death of Princess Augusta. When they found it was not large enough to accommodate their expanding family, the Dutch House came into its own as an annexe for some of their children including the future GEORGE IV. In 1802 the White House was pulled down on the order of the king who decided to live in the Dutch House until his Gothic style NEW PALACE, also known appropriately as the 'castellated palace', should be finished on the nearby Thames bank. Never completed, the New Palace was eventually demolished by George IV whose artistic taste was affronted by its design.

The king and Queen Charlotte left the Dutch House towards the end of 1805, and when Charlotte returned eight years later she was a woman saddened by the distressing illness of her husband. The last royal occasion at the Dutch House took place on 13 July 1818 when the Duke of Clarence, the future WILLIAM IV, married Adelaide, daughter of the Duke of Saxe-Meiningen, and on the same day his brother Edward, Duke of Kent and future father of QUEEN VICTORIA, married Victoria, daughter of the Duke of Saxe-Coburg-Saalfield. The Prince Regent wheeled his mother from her bedroom so that she could observe the ceremony, but four months later she died and for the next eight decades the Dutch House remained empty. It was Queen Victoria's DIAMOND JUBILEE in 1897 that brought the house to life again. As part of the great celebration it was refurbished and opened to the public.

KEYS, CEREMONY OF THE British royalty is associated with the world's oldest military ceremony which takes place every night at the TOWER OF LONDON. It is known as the Ceremony of the Keys and goes back seven centuries. Just before 10 p.m. the Chief Warder of the Yeomen Warders of the Tower of London – often referred to as Beefeaters – goes to the Bloody Tower where the Escort of the Keys, comprising four guardsmen, is waiting. In his traditional dress and carrying a lantern, the Chief Warder walks to the West Gate which he locks while the Escort presents arms. This is repeated at the Middle and Byward Towers. Back at the Bloody Tower the party is halted by a sentry who demands:

'Halt! Who goes there?'
'The Keys,' is the ritual reply.
'Whose Keys?'
'Queen Elizabeth's Keys.'
'Pass, Queen Elizabeth's Keys. All's well.'

The Escort then marches through the archway to the Main Guard of the Tower where the officer-in-charge gives the order to present arms in honour of the Keys. The Chief Warder removes his Tudor-style hat and shouts, 'God preserve Queen Elizabeth', to which the Escort and Guard respond with an amen to coincide with the clock striking ten, which demonstrates the precision with which the ceremony is performed. The Last Post is sounded by the Tower bugler after which the Chief Warder takes the Keys to the Queen's House where they are given to the Resident Governor for safekeeping.

The ceremony has been repeated every evening since it was inaugurated, and even the bombing of London during the Second World War did not interrupt it. On 16 April 1941 a German bomb injured members of the Escort, but despite this the ceremony was continued to its conclusion. It should be noted that the ceremony is not open to the general public, but application to see it can be made to the Governor of the Tower.

'KINGMAKER', THE *See* WARWICK, EARL OF

KING'S EVIL The custom of the sovereign touching a person suffering from the disease once known as the King's Evil, began during the reign of EDWARD THE CONFESSOR. The condition was actually scrofula, a disorder affecting the lymph glands which, it was believed, could be remedied by contact with a royal hand. This healing ability was regarded as proof of the DIVINE RIGHT OF KINGS. HENRY VII turned the practice into a formal ceremony in which each sufferer was given a gold coin.

According to Macaulay the tradition reached its peak during the reign of CHARLES II when it was estimated that the king laid his hand on nearly a hundred thousand people. In 1684, at the end of Charles's reign, John Evelyn wrote in his diary: 'There was so grette and eager a concourse of people to be touched of "the Evil" that six or seven crushed to death by pressing at the chirurgeon's door for tickets.'

The last sovereign to touch for the King's Evil was QUEEN ANNE, who touched Dr Johnson for his affliction without success. From the reign of CHARLES I to the early part of the eighteenth century an office for the practice was included in *The Book of Common Prayer*.

KING'S LIBRARY In the centre of the British Library, situated by London's St Pancras station, is a glass-walled edifice rising tower-like through the library. Known as the King's Library, it contains over sixty-five thousand volumes, many of almost priceless historical value, and has been described as 'probably both larger and finer than any like

Collection ever made by any one man, even under the advantageous conditions of royalty'. That 'one man' was GEORGE III. Today the King is remembered more for his so-called madness than for his intense interest in science, the arts and books from which the nation has profited.

In 1760, when George ascended the throne at the age of 22, there was no national library as such. His grandfather GEORGE II had presented a neglected accumulation of books to the British Museum in 1757 where it duly became known as the Old Royal Library to distinguish it from George III's vast collection. It became the King's ambition to build up a library that would not be a mere collection of valuable books, but a practical place of reference for the use of scholars and men of letters from abroad as well as Britain.

Within the first two years of his reign the king began his great undertaking which from first to last he financed out of his own purse so that no public contributions were involved. He was represented at all of London's book sales, while on the Continent his agents relentlessly sought out suitable books. In this they were helped by the fact that in 1773 Pope Clement XIV suppressed the Jesuits, with the result that books from the order's libraries became available.

George was not only interested in acquiring books for his library, but looking after them correctly after they had been purchased. To this end four great rooms were included by Sir William Chambers's remodelling of the Queen's House, now BUCKINGHAM PALACE, which not only housed the ever increasing number of books but also the royal collection of coins and maps. A bindery was established on the premises for volumes that required re-binding, some of which were decorated with the royal coat of arms. The King was particular about the appearance of his books and his collection included volumes of royal bindings that had been created for Britain's kings and queens from the time of ELIZABETH I.

Today it would be impossible to put a value on the books of the King's Library as so many can be truly described as priceless, with such treasures as a Gutenberg Bible, first editions of the *Canterbury Tales* and *Paradise Lost*, all four folios of Shakespeare and a number of Caxtons, to name but a few.

When the King died in 1820 the library was inherited by his son GEORGE IV who, not being a bibliophile like his father, decided that it took up too much space in the Queen's House, which he was adapting to his own taste. He therefore decided to present the library to the nation, and that the great collection should be housed at the British Museum in a specially constructed gallery which was completed in 1827. Thus it remained as a working library as George III would have wished, until the Second World War when in 1940 an enemy bomb struck the British Museum, destroying 124 priceless volumes while several hundred others were damaged. In 1998 the King's Library was transferred to the new British Library where it remains one of the most splendid monuments to a British monarch.

KING'S STONE Protected by iron railings in the centre of Kingston upon Thames, London, is a square block of stone that gave the town its name. Known as the King's Stone, Anglo-Saxon kings knelt upon it for their crowning ceremonies. Kings known to have been anointed on it are Ethelwulf (*c.* 839), Ethelbald (858), Ethelbert (860), Ethelred I (*c.* 865), possibly Alfred (871), Edward the Elder (900), Athelstan (*c.* 924), Edred (946), Edwy (955), Edward the Martyr (975) and Ethelred II (978).

KNIGHTHOOD Although once only awarded for military excellence, today knighthoods are conferred for exceptional service in all aspects of society. The honour is either conferred by the queen or by members of the royal family on her behalf. In the investiture ceremony the recipient kneels before the sovereign, or her deputy, and in the act known as 'dubbing', his right shoulder and then the left is touched by a sword blade. He then stands and is invested with the insignia of the Order of Knighthood to which he has been assigned. Foreign citizens may become honorary knights but without the title of 'Sir'.

L

LANCASTER HOUSE Standing in Stable Yard and adjoining ST JAMES'S PALACE, Lancaster House goes back to the seventeenth century when it was known as Godolphin House. It began its royal association in 1807 when Frederick, Duke of York and Albany (the 'Grand Old Duke of York') and the second son of GEORGE III, took up residence in the house, which was renamed York House. When Princess Charlotte died in childbirth in 1817 it meant that the duke became the heir to the throne and in order that his residence should reflect his new status, Sir Robert Smirke, the architect famous for his design of the British Museum, was engaged to remodel York House. His plans did not meet with the approval of GEORGE IV who was fastidious in his architectural tastes, and the project was passed to Benjamin Dean Wyatt. The work commenced in 1825 but was not completed when the impoverished duke died two years later. The government cleared the mortgages on the house and then sold the lease of the still uncompleted house to the Marquess of Stafford – later the 1st Duke of Sutherland – with the result that the name was changed to Stafford House.

The house was in the care of the 2nd Duke of Sutherland when it was finally completed with walls of Bath stone and an interior reflecting the extravagant style inspired by French designers in the reign of Louis XV. On the first floor were the magnificent state rooms and the Great Gallery, in which there was a collection of paintings by such artists as Raphael, Rubens, Van Dyck and Velasquez. The duke's wife Harriet was QUEEN VICTORIA's Mistress of the Robes and frequently visited Stafford House, as it was now called, remarking on one occasion, 'I have come from my house to your palace.' The house was the scene of splendid entertainments and a meeting place for leading liberals including Lord Shaftesbury, William Garrison, the American abolitionist, and Garibaldi. In 1848 the queen, accompanied by Prince Albert and the Duke of Wellington, visited the house to hear Chopin play.

Sir William Lever, the manufacturer of Sunlight Soap and later the 1st Viscount Leverhulme, acquired the house from the 4th Duke of Sutherland in 1912 and it was renamed yet again as Lancaster House after the county of Sir William's birth. The following year he presented it to the nation for the setting up of the London Museum – which remained there until 1946 and is now situated at the Barbican – and as a venue for special government functions. The most important of these was in 1953 when Lancaster House was the setting for ELIZABETH II's coronation banquet. Today the house continues to be used for receptions and conferences.

LIGHTFOOT, HANNAH The daughter of a Quaker shoemaker from Wapping, Hannah Lightfoot won the heart of young Prince George, the son of GEORGE II, and became the cause of an intriguing royal mystery. Unlike the other Hanoverian kings notorious for their lax morality, the future GEORGE III was not interested in mistresses and it was widely believed at the time that he legally married Hannah in April 1759 and they subsequently had three children. As the date of the reputed wedding was thirteen years before the passing of the ROYAL MARRIAGES ACT, it meant that such a marriage with the 21-year-old prince would be legal, unlike that of his future son's marriage to MRS FITZHERBERT.

Papers said to have been signed by George validating the marriage were put before the Attorney General in 1866 with the result that legal opinion tended to regard them as genuine. If it was true that George had thus been legally married to Hannah, it would have meant that his marriage to Queen Charlotte was bigamous. Thus his rightful heirs would have been Hannah's children, and technically the sovereigns descended from George III and Charlotte would not have been entitled to wear the Crown.

Such a possible technicality was used by a woman named Olivia Wilmot in her attempt to prove a royal connection. Born in 1772, she became a talented artist who not only exhibited at the Royal Academy, but obtained the position of landscape artist to the Prince of Wales, later GEORGE IV. It was at this time that she began a campaign to win recognition as the daughter of George III's brother, Henry Frederick, Duke of Cumberland. To this end she produced over seventy documents, one of which purported to prove that the duke had privately married her mother also named Olivia, a daughter of the Reverend James Wilmot, before he bigamously married Anne, daughter of the 1st Earl of Carhampton, while Olivia was still alive. Another document that Olivia believed would help her case cast doubt on the succession was an alleged marriage certificate affirming that George had indeed married Hannah Lightfoot. These papers failed to persuade the public of the authenticity of the claim, though the claimant became popularly known as 'Princess Olivia of Cumberland'. When she died in 1834 her daughter Lavinia continued to assert the royal connection and went to court in an endeavour to substantiate her right to the title of Duchess of Lancaster and a sizeable legacy. The case was thrown out by the Lord Chief Justice and *The Times* reported: 'All the declarations and protestations of the great personages, introduced into the story, are written on mere scraps, and the petitioner attempted to account for their size by alleging that they had been cut so small that they might be easier kept.'

LINLITHGOW PALACE During the reign of David I of Scotland (*see* SCOTLAND, EARLY KINGS OF) in the twelfth century it was first recorded that a royal residence named Linlithgow stood on the shores of Linlithgow Loch, 16 miles west of Edinburgh. Although the palace is now in a semi-ruinous condition, it retains an atmosphere of ancient grandeur that inspired Sir Walter Scott to write in his poem 'Marmion':

> Of all the palaces so fair,
> Built for the royal dwelling,
> In Scotland, far beyond compare
> Linlithgow is excelling.

EDWARD I wintered at Linlithgow in 1301 and used it as a base for attacking Stirling Castle, but twelve years later the English were driven out and after ROBERT I's victory at Bannockburn in 1314 the fortifications erected by the English were

dismantled. The palace was restored by DAVID II, the son of King Robert, but his work was destroyed by fire in 1423.

When JAMES I of Scotland returned to his country in 1424 from his eighteen-year stay in England as a royal hostage, he set about rebuilding Linlithgow which, with its high walls set round a quadrangle with a square tower at each corner, has hardly changed down the centuries.

In 1461 EDWARD IV was crowned King of England after his victory at Towton and the deposed HENRY VI and his queen, Margaret of Anjou, were given sanctuary in Linlithgow Palace by the boy king JAMES III who had inherited the throne of Scotland the previous year. When JAMES IV married Princess Margaret, the daughter of HENRY VII of England, by proxy in 1502, the palace was decorated and hung with cloth of gold and tapestries for her reception. Much of her time there was spent in what came to be known as 'Queen Margaret's Bower', an octagonal chamber at the top of the palace's north-western tower, which gave her a far distant view of the Grampians. It was from this vantage spot that she watched for the return of the king when he was away fighting her fellow countrymen. Scott described her vigil in 'Marmion' thus:

> His own Queen Margaret, who, in Lithgow's tower
> All lonely sat, and wept the weary hour.

Her watch was to no avail, King James had been slain at Flodden Field on 9 September 1513. His posthumous son Alexander was born eight months later.

Six days before JAMES V of Scotland died on 14 December 1542, his queen, Mary of Guise, gave birth at Linlithgow to their daughter MARY who, on the day her father died, became Queen of Scotland. Mary saw the palace for the last time twenty-five years later when after leaving it she was 'abducted' by Patrick Hepburn, 3rd Earl of Bothwell whom she married disastrously a short while later. Her son, JAMES VI of Scotland, spent a lot of his time at Linlithgow before he became JAMES I of England, and when he married ANNE OF DENMARK the palace was included in her marriage settlement. Their son CHARLES I was the last king to stay in the palace, after which it began to fall into disrepair.

In September 1745 BONNIE PRINCE CHARLIE paused at Linlithgow before being given the

The frowning ruin of Linlithgow Palace on the shore of Linlithgow, first recorded as a royal palace in the twelfth century.

welcome in Edinburgh that reinforced his hopes of reviving the House of Stuart. After those hopes had perished, the advancing Hanoverian army under the command of the DUKE OF CUMBERLAND reached Linlithgow, and on 31 January 1746 the palace was burned, as a result of soldiers leaving fires unattended in it when they continued their march. Linlithgow Palace has remained a shell since then but in July 1914 it was once again the scene of a royal event when GEORGE V and Queen Mary held court in the Great Hall which, open to the sky, was filled with summer sunshine.

LORD HIGH CHANCELLOR OF GREAT BRITAIN Like the great majority of their subjects, early kings had little knowledge of reading and writing and therefore required scribes, or secretaries, who they could trust to set down their declarations and write letters to other heads of state. So important was this work that EDWARD THE CONFESSOR created the post of Lord Chancellor, or chief secretary to the king, a position that was to evolve into the most powerful appointment outside that of the sovereign and the head of the Church. Several of the most dramatic episodes in the history of British royalty have

involved the relationship between kings and their chancellors.

As it was vital that documents of state were seen to be authentic, Saxon kings safeguarded their decrees by attaching their Great Seals to them, a method that was continued by royalty after the Norman Conquest. These Great Seals were placed in the keeping of the Lord Chancellor and, apart from the seal being his symbol of office, it meant that every state document had been passed by him when it had its seal affixed. Thus the Lord Chancellor gained the additional title of Keeper of the Great Seal. Only when a new Lord Chancellor was handed the Great Seal by the reigning monarch did his appointment become official.

As Speaker of the House of Lords, the Lord Chancellor sat on the Woolsack. The reason for this was that he was not necessarily a peer, and according to tradition the Woolsack was considered not to be part of the Lords' Chamber at the Palace of Westminster. When the Lord Chancellor was thus seated the Mace and Great Seal were placed on the Woolsack behind him to denote his authority. At the State Opening of Parliament it was his duty to present the sovereign with his or her speech.

It also fell to the Lord Chancellor to preside over the highest court of appeal and appoint the most senior judges, and therefore the majority of those chosen for the post over the centuries had legal backgrounds. Another of the Lord Chancellor's titles was 'Keeper of the Royal Conscience', which came about in the fourteenth century when he was expected to take over the sovereign's obligations to subjects in need of care, ranging from students in colleges founded by royalty to sufferers of mental disorders. From this developed the Court of Chancery.

British sovereigns appointed their own Lord Chancellors until the executive power of the Crown was transferred to the government, and in effect choice was made by the Prime Minister. At the time of writing the Lord Chancellor is referred to in over three hundred parliamentary Acts. In June 2003 the abolition of the office of Lord High Chancellor was announced by Prime Minister Tony Blair.

See also THOMAS A BECKET and THOMAS WOLSEY.

LORDS APPELLANT *See* RICHARD II

M

MAGNA CARTA In 1214, while KING JOHN was at war with France, his discontented barons decided upon the concessions they would force from him – 'to restore the liberty of the Church and the Kingdom, to abolish the evil customs which his father, brother and himself had introduced and to renew Henry I's charter'.

Despite the king's delays they finally forced him to put his seal to the MAGNA CARTA in a field near Runnymede on 15 June 1215. This charter of privileges is regarded as the foundation stone of British liberty, and among the clauses was the vital one stating that there could be no punishment without trial according to the law of the land, and another that taxation could not be imposed without the consent of the Council. Although in a sense the document was a charter of human rights, it was the barons rather than the common folk who benefited from it as from then on their power was greatly increased.

MARBLE ARCH Inspired by Rome's Arch of Constantine, John Nash designed Marble Arch which, constructed to face BUCKINGHAM PALACE, was completed in 1827. It was intended that the arch should be surmounted by an equestrian figure of GEORGE IV but the plan was changed and the statue was sited in Trafalgar Square. In 1851 it was decided to remove the arch to its present position at the junction of Park Lane and Bayswater Road. The only persons permitted to use it as a gateway are members of the royal family and the King's Troop, Royal Horse Artillery.

MARLBOROUGH HOUSE In 1709 Sarah, Duchess of Marlborough, laid the foundation stone of Marlborough House on land adjoining ST JAMES'S PALACE which she had secured on a fifty-year lease from her friend and long-time confidante QUEEN ANNE. The duchess engaged Christopher Wren to design the house but the plans were probably drawn by his son under his guidance.

However, Wren was dismissed before the work was finished, the duchess believing that he was being duped by the building contractors, and she personally directed the final stage. The red Dutch bricks used in the construction of the house had come to England as ballast in the ships that had provided her husband, John Churchill, 1st Duke of Marlborough, with men and munitions for his campaigns in the war of the Spanish Succession.

The house was completed in 1711 and for the next thirty-three years Sarah used it as her London residence. The duchess died at Marlborough House in 1744 but the Marlborough family continued to use it until it reverted to the Crown in 1817 and was refurbished to accommodate Princess Charlotte, daughter of GEORGE IV and the royal heir, and her husband Prince Leopold of Saxe-Coburg-Saalfield, but before the couple could take possession she died in childbirth, to the sorrow of the nation. The prince took up residence in the house until 1831 when he became the first King of the Belgians.

The next royal occupant was the Dowager Queen Adelaide who stayed there from 1837 until her death in 1849. Later the house became a centre for the smartest society, dubbed the 'Marlborough House Set', when EDWARD, Prince of Wales resided there. In 1865 his son the future GEORGE V was born in the house and he lived there after becoming the Prince of Wales until 1910 when it became the home of the Dowager Queen Alexandra until 1925.

Following the death of George V in 1936 his widow Queen Mary took up residence until her death in 1953. Six years later the house was presented to the government to be used as the Commonwealth Centre.

MARMION The family name of the men who were the heredity champions at English coronations, an office that was introduced by WILLIAM I but which ended with the reign of EDWARD I.

MARQUESS The title of marquess, or marquis, ranks below that of a duke and above an earl. It was the last title to be introduced into the peerage when RICHARD II created the first marquis in 1385, making his boyhood friend Robert de Vere, 9th Earl of Oxford, Marquis of Dublin. The wife of a marquess is a marchioness.

MARRIAGES ACT Until 1753 an exchange of vows between a man and woman was regarded as a legitimate marriage. This practice explains how such a contract could cause a later church marriage made with a different party to be held unlawful. The children of such a union were considered to be illegitimate, as was the case with EDWARD V, who was declared illegitimate by Act of Parliament and deposed. After the Marriages Act of 1753 only marriages held in churches according to the English *Book of Common Prayer*, after banns had been called, were legal.

MARY I Born at GREENWICH PALACE on 18 February 1516 Mary – later to earn the epithet of 'Bloody' – was the only surviving child of HENRY VIII and CATHERINE OF ARAGON. When Henry broke with the Church of Rome in order to divorce the queen and marry ANNE BOLEYN, the girl was parted from her mother and declared illegitimate, thereby losing her rights as the royal heir. Following the birth of Anne Boleyn's daughter ELIZABETH in 1533 her household was disbanded and she was ordered by the Privy Council to cease

Drawing from a painted portrait of Mary I, the only surviving child of Henry VIII and Catherine of Aragon.

using the title of princess. She replied with a letter which was not only courageous but showed maturity for a 17-year-old girl who had seen her world fall about her. 'My lords', she wrote. 'As touching upon my removal from Hatfield, I will obey his grace . . . but . . . my conscience will in no wise suffer me to take any other than myself for princess, or for the king's daughter born in lawful matrimony, and that I will never wittingly or willingly say or do ought whereby any person might take occasion to think that I agree to the contrary.'

Thomas Cromwell, who had urged Henry to declare himself supreme head of the Church in England, was now Chancellor and, aware there was much sympathy throughout the kingdom for Mary, he had her papers searched, forbade her pen and paper and had several people sent to the TOWER OF LONDON for styling her 'princess' in letters she received. When her half-brother EDWARD VI came to the throne in 1547 her life got easier, despite her detestation of his Protestantism, and his occasional disapproval of her not only on account of her Roman Catholicism, but for dancing too much. Two years later her troubles began again when the Council tried to stop Mass being said for her privately and she began to suffer from a disorder of the womb which was later to give her the illusion of being pregnant.

The Great Seal of Queen Mary.

When King Edward died on 6 July 1553 John Dudley, Duke of Northumberland, eager for his daughter-in-law LADY JANE GREY to assume the throne, kept the king's death secret for two days in order to get Mary, the rightful heir, into his power. She, however, avoided his trap and was crowned. She was now 37 and suffered greatly from toothache, headaches and pain from her womb, yet she was determined to fulfil her role as a responsible sovereign. Giacomo Soranzo, the Venetian ambassador, wrote admiringly: 'She rises at daybreak when, after saying her prayers and hearing Mass in private, she transacts business incessantly until after midnight . . . she chooses to give audience, not only to all members of her Privy Council, and to hear from them every detail of public business, but also to all other persons who ask it of her.'

It is likely Mary would have reprieved the Protestant Lady Jane Grey – who had been sentenced to death for her role in Northumberland's plot to usurp the queen – and allowed her to live in retirement had not her father Thomas Grey, Duke of Suffolk joined a conspiracy against the new queen, despite the fact he had been pardoned. It was then feared that as long as the tragic Lady Jane Grey lived she would provide a focal point for rebellion and she was therefore executed on 12 February 1554 on Tower Green in the Tower of London.

The conspiracy Suffolk supported was led by Thomas Wyatt who was violently opposed to the queen's intended marriage to Philip, the son of Charles V, Holy Roman Emperor and King of Spain. In January 1554 Wyatt led fifteen thousand anti-Philip rebels from Kent to Southwark. Mary's response was to go to the Guildhall where she made a speech which has been likened to the famous 'Armada' speech made by her half-sister Elizabeth I. 'I am come in mine own person to tell you what you already see and know,' she declared. 'I mean the traitorous and seditious assembling of the Kentish rebels against us and you. They pretend to object to the marriage with the Prince of Spain.'

On 7 February when Wyatt entered London the queen refused to flee to the safety of Windsor but watched the marching rebels from the gatehouse of ST JAMES'S PALACE. The unrest over the proposed marriage had the effect of hardening Mary's determination to wed Philip and restore Roman Catholicism to her kingdom. The Mass was reintroduced, altars were set in churches again, and

clergy who had married were given the ultimatum of either losing their wives or their benefices.

Mary and Philip had only one private meeting before the wedding ceremony was held at Winchester Cathedral on 25 July 1554. Although he was attentive to Mary in public, before long rumours of his extramarital adventures were rife, especially with females of 'low condition'. Mary continued to hold opulent court to entertain her husband and it

A coin depicting Mary I and her husband Philip of Spain.

was announced that she was 'quicke of childe'. At the same time Parliament was busy following the Queen's wishes by passing Acts to confirm papal authority and revive old laws against heresy.

The effect of the latter was demonstrated on 4 February 1555 when the first Protestant martyr, John Rogers, a married prebend of St Paul's, was burned at the stake. Apologists for Mary claim that she was encouraged to persecute 'heretics' by her Spanish husband, but he actually argued moderation because he knew these spectacular executions were less acceptable in England than in Continental countries. Nevertheless, in April all justices of the peace were ordered to search out heretics and the dismal procession to the stake continued. As yet the majority of the queen's subjects did not anticipate the approaching reign of terror, and when on 30 April news spread that Mary had given birth to a prince at Hampton Court, bells pealed and bonfires of joy rather than punishment blazed in the streets of London. Next day it was officially announced that the rumour was false. Mary had mistaken her condition due to the disease of her womb.

Philip, disenchanted with a wife unable to conceive and conscious of his growing unpopularity, visited his other realms and at the end of August Mary bade him an anguished farewell at Greenwich.

By the end of the year the toll of victims reached ninety, including Hugh Latimer, Bishop of Worcester, who with THOMAS CRANMER, Archbishop of Canterbury, had taken part in establishing the Protestant Church in England, and Nicholas Ridley, Bishop of London who had supported Lady Jane Grey. The executions took place opposite Balliol College at Oxford. As the two prisoners were chained back-to-back Latimer cried out, 'Play

Archbishop Cranmer meeting his death at the stake in Oxford, one of the three hundred martyrs of Queen Mary's reign.

the man, Master Ridley. We shall this day light such a candle in England as, by the grace of God, shall never be put out.' It was estimated that in total nearly three hundred persons were burned at the stake besides those who suffered imprisonment and confiscation of property.

To Mary's joy Philip returned to England in March 1557 but for political motives rather than regard for her. His father, the Emperor Charles, had abdicated to devote himself to religious exercises and clock-making, thus giving his son the crowns of Spain and the Netherlands. The old conflict between Spain and France was renewed and the purpose of Philip's visit was to involve England in the quarrel. Although an English army won the Battle of St Quentin in August, in January 1558 Calais, which had been part of the English kingdom for over two centuries, fell to the French.

In April 1558 the queen announced she was pregnant. Hope that this would cause Philip to return died when he refused and she realised that for a second time she had been deluded by her medical condition. Added to this she was now suffering from heart trouble and dropsy, and it became apparent that her reign was nearing its end. According to HOLINSHED, when a lady-in-waiting suggested to her that Philip's absence was the sole sorrow in her illness the queen replied, 'Not only that but when I am dead and opened you will find Calais lying upon my heart.'

Queen Mary died on 17 November 1558 and was interred in Henry VIII's chapel in Westminster Abbey. Her husband Philip II of Spain outlived her by forty years.

MARY, QUEEN OF SCOTS No royal figure in British history has been regarded as more romantic than Mary, Queen of Scots. The fascination with her life is reflected in the fact that there are over three hundred biographies devoted to her in the British Library. The daughter of JAMES V of Scotland and his second wife Mary of Guise, Mary was born on 7 or 8 December 1542 at Linlithgow. Her father died almost immediately after her birth which meant that she became a queen when she was just a week old. Six years later the child was taken to Paris to be affianced to Francis, the eldest son of King Henry II of France and Catherine de' Medici. Her next ten years were spent at the French court where she was carefully educated and in 1558 she was married to the sickly dauphin who was a year younger than herself. At this point she was persuaded to sign a secret agreement that in the event of her dying without issue, Scotland and her claim to the English throne would pass to France. This claim to the English succession was due to the fact that she was the great-granddaughter of HENRY VII, and in consequence styled herself Queen of England, an affectation that was never forgiven by ELIZABETH I.

In 1559 Mary's father-in-law died and when her husband the dauphin was crowned Francis II she became Queen of France. A few months later the new king died and then came news that her mother, Mary of Guise, had died and she was needed urgently in Scotland. On 19 August 1561 she arrived at Leith and on the way to Edinburgh her first act as Queen of Scotland was to give a royal pardon to James Kellone, who had been sentenced to death for playing games on the Sabbath. This incident brought home to Mary that she was a Roman Catholic queen of a country in the throes of the Lutheran reformation, personified by John Knox. Mary was happy for men to worship as they pleased, but she expected the same tolerance to be extended to her. It was a forlorn hope as when the Mass was celebrated for her in the chapel at

Engraving of Mary, Queen of Scots as a young girl.

Holyrood, John Knox did not hesitate to castigate her publicly as 'the whore of Babylon'.

Mary now chose her illegitimate half-brother James to be her chief minister, bestowing upon him the title of Earl of Moray, which reassured her subjects as he was a Protestant. The question of the Queen's marriage now became a vital matter in Scotland and many suitable husbands, including several kings, were suggested but Mary made her own choice. She surprised everyone by choosing her Catholic cousin Henry Stewart, LORD DARNLEY, the son of the Earl of Lennox by his marriage with a granddaughter of Henry VII of England. This meant that Darnley was among the closest heirs to the throne of England, a point that did not escape Queen Elizabeth. It has been said that Mary's infatuation with Darnley began at first sight. He was handsome and his courtly grace, something that Mary had missed since leaving France, temporarily won her heart. Ignoring opposition from the Scottish Protestant nobles Mary married Darnley on the morning of 29 July 1565 in Holyrood Chapel and he was proclaimed king.

The Queen was to fall out of love with her consort as dramatically as she had been attracted to him. Once the wedding was over he no longer bothered to conceal his true nature behind his mask of charm. He was frequently drunk, spoke lewdly of his royal wife to his tavern friends and was grossly unfaithful. Having achieved the bed of the highest lady in the land, some quirk in his character made him seek the lowest whores in Edinburgh. What made this worse for Mary was that soon after the wedding she found that she was pregnant.

In her distress she was supported by her Italian secretary DAVID RIZZIO who, because of his Catholicism, had earned the enmity of the Protestant lords. Under the leadership of Lord Ruthven they devised a way to get rid of him and at the same time discredit the equally hated Darnley. A document was prepared which, while it did not name Rizzio, stated that anyone who injured Darnley's honour should be dispatched. Darnley was induced to sign this and then, on the night of 9 March 1566, Darnley with Lord Ruthven, Moray and a number of other Protestant conspirators entered HOLYROODHOUSE PALACE and went to the cabinet of the Queen who was with several friends, her doctor and her doomed secretary. Realising their errand, Rizzio clung to the Queen's skirt and begged her to save him. The author of *The*

Narrative of Lord Ruthven wrote: '. . . Lord Ruthven took the Queen in his arms and put her into the King's arms, beseeching her majesty not to be afraid. And David [Rizzio] was thrown downstairs from the place where he was slain. The King's dagger was found sticking in his side.'

Rizzio's body had fifty stab wounds and during the bloody assassination Mary fainted. When she recovered consciousness James Hepburn, Earl of Bothwell, burst in and demanded an explanation. In reply Ruthven took the document with Darnley's signature from his pocket and said, 'What has been done was done in the King's name.' Despite her distress Mary was reassured to see Bothwell, the turbulent border lord who was already playing a significant role in her life. She had first met him at the French court six years earlier, and now disillusioned by her husband her interest in him had ripened. Fearful of remaining in the hands of Rizzio's assassins, the heavily pregnant queen soon left Holyrood House for the safety of Dunbar Castle.

When Mary returned to Edinburgh there were eight thousand men marching behind her under Bothwell's command. The conspirators fled and her son JAMES, later to be James I of England, was born at Edinburgh Castle. Amid the rejoicing at the safe arrival of the royal heir there was speculation as to who had fathered him. Only three months earlier the queen's husband had been involved in the murder of Rizzio – could Rizzio have been the father? This doubt over his parentage was to dog James all his life and when he became known as the 'British Solomon', wits said it was because he was the son of David.

There can be no doubt of the intensity of Mary's feelings for Bothwell after the birth of her baby. Four months later he was wounded by an outlaw and when he lay ill at Hermitage Castle in the desolate heart of the Roxburghshire Moors, Mary rode from Jedburgh to Hermitage and back in one day – a total distance of 50 miles – to assure herself that he was still alive. The strain of the journey made her ill and the target of gossip but this was nothing compared to what was to come.

At the beginning of January 1567 Darnley was taken ill with either smallpox or syphilis, and his once handsome face became so ravaged he had to wear a gauze mask. On 31 January it was arranged that he would stay in Edinburgh at a house standing in a square known as Kirk o' Field within walking distance of Holyroodhouse Palace. On the night of 9 February Mary had a meal with him before going back to the palace to attend a masque. After the entertainment ended an explosion echoed across the city and crowds gathered at Kirk o' Field to gaze at the ruins of the house that had been shattered by a gunpowder blast – the bodies of Darnley and his valet were found in the garden. Soon afterwards Bothwell arrived at Holyroodhouse Palace crying 'Treason!' and it was commented upon that his face was blackened.

On 12 April, after what has been described as a mock trial, he was acquitted of any involvement in the assassination. Although Mary was aware of the problems that had beset Elizabeth in England over the scandal surrounding the mysterious death of Robert Dudley's wife, Amy Robsart, on 15 May she nonetheless married the man who was believed by many to have murdered her husband, three days after his previous marriage had been annulled. Scotland and the whole of Europe was stunned and the nobles could not forgive Mary for making Bothwell the most powerful man in the kingdom and they began taking up arms against the royal couple.

The queen and her new husband left Edinburgh for Borthwick Castle where Bothwell hoped to rally his borderers to the royal standard. Instead the castle was surrounded by their enemies who sent a message declaring that if Mary left Bothwell and returned to Edinburgh she would receive the respect due to a sovereign. She refused contemptuously and, disguised as a boy, escaped from the castle and she and Bothwell spent their last time together at Carberry House.

The armies of the queen and the rebel lords faced each other at Carberry Hill on 15 June, but as the day wore on the royal forces melted away and she had to surrender without a shot being fired, parting from Bothwell. In Edinburgh she was met with shouts of 'Burn the murderess!' When the procession was diverted into Kirk o' Field, so Mary had to pass the ruins of the house in which Darnley was killed, she was in danger of being lynched. Soon afterwards she was taken to her island prison in Lochleven. She said that she was seven months pregnant which, if true, meant that she had conceived before the death of Darnley. What happened next remains a mystery. One tradition suggests that she had stillborn twins, another that she gave birth to a daughter who was smuggled to France. Meanwhile, Bothwell escaped to Norway and was finally

Carberry House today. Here Mary, Queen of Scots and her husband Bothwell spent their last night together.

imprisoned by the King of Denmark at Dragsholm in Zealand, dying in 1578.

Under the threat of indiscreet letters to Bothwell attributed to her – the controversial CASKET LETTERS – being made public Mary agreed to abdicate in favour of her infant son and on 24 July 1567 the child was crowned JAMES VI of Scotland at Stirling.

The following year Mary escaped from Lochleven and for a few weeks found herself with an army of her old supporters. On 13 May 1586 they were defeated at Langside by her half-brother, the Earl of Moray, who was now Regent of Scotland. With a small party Mary fled to Dundrennan Abbey.

Here her counsellors advised her to take a ship to France where her powerful Guise relations would look after her; instead she chose to throw herself upon the uncertain mercy of Elizabeth of England. On 16 May she crossed the Solway to become a prisoner for the rest of her life.

At first Mary was lodged in Carlisle Castle. She had been unable to bring any spare clothes with her and Elizabeth sent a parcel to her by Sir Francis Knollys. When opened it was found to contain a couple of torn petticoats, some pieces of black velvet and two pairs of worn shoes. Sir Francis, embarrassed by this display of spite, muttered that 'Her Highness's maid had mistaken and sent such things necessary for such a maidservant as she was herself.'

From Scotland Moray sent Queen Elizabeth copies of the Casket Letters, which gave her the excuse to imprison her royal cousin for nineteen years, first at Carlisle and then at a number of places, until she was taken to a manor at Chartley in Staffordshire at the order of SIR FRANCIS WALSINGHAM, who was determined to end the machinations of Mary's pro-Catholic supporters. It was here that she became fatally involved in the BABINGTON PLOT, named after Anthony Babington who had once been a page in her household.

Gilbert Gifford, an ex-Catholic who secretly allied himself to Walsingham, persuaded the royal captive that he had devised a safe method of smuggling letters out from Chartley to her friends. He explained that messages for her would be placed in a waterproof case and hidden in a cask of ale which would be brought in by a sympathetic brewer. Letters to her supporters would go back in the empty cask. What Mary did not know was that Walsingham's secretary intercepted these letters and copied them before replacing them in the cask.

On 6 July 1586 a letter was recovered in which Babington addressed Mary as 'My dread Sovereign Lady and Queen unto whom I owe only fidelity and obedience' and then set out the plans of his conspiracy. These included the elimination of the 'usurper', meaning Elizabeth, Mary's liberation and the arrival of an invasion army from overseas. He asked for Mary's approval and an assurance that the 'six noble Gentlemen' who were to carry out the 'tragical execution', would be well rewarded if they escaped or that their heirs would be

Effigy of Mary, Queen of Scots above her tomb in Westminster Abbey, erected by her son James I.

reimbursed if they failed. This letter was passed on via the brewer on 9 July and on 17 July Walsingham read Mary's reply which gave full approval of Babington's plan and enquired how the 'six Gentlemen deliberate to proceed'. The deadly document was then passed on to the unsuspecting Babington with a forged postscript asking for the names of the six Gentlemen. Early the next month Walsingham was able to arrest Babington and his associates, who had been so full of confidence that they had posed for a group portrait. At Chartley Mary's papers were seized and in the TOWER OF LONDON Babington and the would-be assassins admitted their guilt. On 20 September they were drawn on hurdles to St Giles Fields where they were executed with such barbarity that, despite the callousness of the age, there was a wave of public revulsion.

Mary was brought to trial and was sentenced to death on 25 October 1586 though it was not until 1 February of the following year that Elizabeth nerved herself to sign the warrant. The execution of Mary, Queen of Scots, took place on 8 February at Fotheringay Castle and her body was first buried at Peterborough, then in 1612 moved to WESTMINSTER ABBEY where it lies in a regal tomb erected by her son James.

MARY, QUEEN OF SCOTS, EXECUTION OF

Robert Wyngfield, in a detailed description sent to Lord Cecil of the execution of MARY, QUEEN OF SCOTS at Fotheringhay Castle in 1587, wrote:

The said eighth day of February being come, and time and place for the execution, the Queen being of stature tall, of body corpulent, round shouldered, her face fat, and broad double-chinned and hazel eyed . . . her gown was of black satin printed, with a train and long sleeves to the ground, with "Acorn Buttons of Tett", trimmed with pearl, and short sleeves of satin black cut, with a pair of sleeves of purple velvet whole under them, her kirtle whole of figured black satin, and her petticoat skirts of crimson velvet...Thus apparelled she departed her chamber.'

'All the world is but vanity,' she told the assembled commissioners and knights, 'and subject still to more sorrow than a whole ocean of tears can bewail. Carry this message for me, that I die a true woman of my religion, and like a true queen of Scotland and France, but God forgive them that have long devised my end.'

Without any terror of the place, the persons, or the preparations she came out of the entry into the hall, stepped up to the scaffold, being two foot high and 12 foot broad, with rails around about with black, with a low stool, a long cushion and a block also covered in black.

Then she, lying very still upon the block, one of the executioners holding her slightly with one of his hands, she endured two strokes of the other executioner with an axe, she making very small noise or none at all, and not stirring any part of her from the place where she lay: and so the executioner cut off her head, saving a little gristle, which being cut asunder, he lifted up her head to the view of all the assembly and bade God Save the Queen . . .

Her lips stirred up and down a quarter of an hour after her head was cut off. Then one of the executioners, pulling off her garters, espied her little dog which had crept up near her clothes, he could not be gotten forth but by force, but came laid between her head and her shoulders, and being imbrued with her blood was carried away and washed.

MARYLEBONE MANOR HOUSE In 1544 the Lord of the Manor of Marylebone, Thomas Hobson, came to an agreement with HENRY VIII to exchange his manor house for some land that had been confiscated from the Church by the king's commissioners. Wishing to hunt close to his capital, Henry had the manor converted into a hunting lodge and here the royal children, Mary, Elizabeth and Edward, enjoyed the pleasures of the chase. It was eventually sold by JAMES I and in the eighteenth century it was in the ownership of John Holles, Duke of Newcastle. When the area around it was developed it lost its appeal as a manor house, became a boarding school and then in 1791 was demolished. The site of the Tudor hunting lodge is now covered by Devonshire and Beaumont streets.

MASTER OF HORSE Although the role of the queen's Master of Horse is now only a ceremonial one, the post was once so important that five of those who held it ended their careers at the hands of the royal executioner, which in Tudor times especially might be regarded as something of a commendation. It has been said that 'the Normans ruled England from horseback' and thus it was the responsibility of the early Masters of Horse to ensure that the court and the army was never short of suitable mounts. It was an exacting task, especially when England was at war. For example, it was reckoned that destriers, the massive horses that carried armour-clad knights, were only good for one battle.

Across the kingdom the breeding of horses was a vital industry and it fell to the Master of Horse to organise it, his importance peaking when the House of Tudor came to power. HENRY VII insisted that his Master of Horse, Thomas Brandon, should obtain horses that would emphasise the majesty of the new dynasty on state occasions. The FIELD OF THE CLOTH OF GOLD, where HENRY VIII and Francis I of France sought to outshine each other in regal splendour, underlined this objective. Apart from being in charge of the horse transport that this entailed, the duty of Henry's Master of Horse, Sir Henry Guildford, was to ride directly behind him, leading his second mount as tradition required.

It was from this period that the power of the Master of Horse increased beyond the sphere of the procurement and training of horses. When ELIZABETH I was called from her exile at Hatfield Palace in 1558 to take the throne of England she immediately appointed ROBERT DUDLEY to be her Master of Horse and as such he escorted her into a jubilant London. It was a post he held for fourteen years and which led to him becoming one of the most influential courtiers in the kingdom, being made a Knight of the Garter, a privy councillor and Earl of Leicester.

The post evolved from organising the royal need of horses into a political office. The Master of Horse chosen by the sovereign automatically received a peerage and membership of the Privy Council, but in the latter part of the eighteenth century it became a government appointment and today the role is a ceremonial one. The Master of Horse, on a white mount, accompanies the sovereign on state occasions that involve horses. A symbolic link with the past is the pair of golden cords worn as part of his uniform, representing the fact that in bygone days he had to be on hand to secure the royal mount whenever the king dismounted.

MAUNDY MONEY The celebration of Royal Maundy was already an established custom in the reign of ELIZABETH I. It is celebrated on Maundy Thursday, the day before Good Friday, and was inspired by the episode at the Last Supper in which Christ washed his disciples' feet. The word 'maundy' is derived from the Latin *mandate* which refers to the words Jesus said, 'A new commandment I give you, that ye love one another.' The symbolic act of feet-washing was observed in monasteries before it became a royal tradition, and it is known that EDWARD II washed the feet of the poor as a gesture of humility. His son EDWARD III established the royal custom of annually giving maunds or gifts of food to the same number of poor people as the years of his age.

During the reign of Elizabeth I Royal Maundy became an elaborate observance which, according to contemporary accounts, differed from the original act as the feet that the queen touched had been thoroughly scrubbed before the ceremony. In the modern version of Royal Maundy the sovereign and attending clergy still hold posies which were originally carried as defence against contagion and distasteful smells.

JAMES II was the last king to physically wash the feet of the poor, his successor WILLIAM OF ORANGE ordered his almoner to take over the ritual. Later, money replaced the food gifts and in 1946, when silver ceased to be used in the production of coins, it was decided that silver would continue to be used for the minting of special

Maundy money. Until 1952 the ceremony was held each year in WESTMINSTER ABBEY but since then it alternates between the abbey and different churches.

Following tradition, today's Maundy ceremony is attended by the Yeomen of the Guard, and after a special service the sovereign leads a procession of clergy between two lines of recipients whose number equals her age. A Yeoman carries small drawstring purses of either red or white leather, the red ones containing ordinary 'dole' money while the white ones hold Maundy money in the form of small silver coins. They are still legal tender but are worth very much more than their official value to numismatists.

MERIT, ORDER OF Created in 1902, the Order of Merit is awarded to men and women who have contributed considerably to the arts, education and science. The Order is restricted to twenty-four members and its motto is 'For Merit'.

MEY, CASTLE OF Overlooking the sea and situated 6 miles west of John o' Groats, the Castle of Mey, previously known as Barrogil, was saved from becoming a ruin by Queen Elizabeth, the Queen Mother after she bought it privately in 1952. When she first visited the sixteenth-century house she found that the roof had suffered from storm damage and the ceilings were in a dangerous condition due to damp which also affected the walls. It took three years for the castle to be restored and when it was completed in 1955 QUEEN ELIZABETH II and PRINCE PHILIP travelled to the house-warming celebration aboard the royal yacht *Britannia*.

Many of the contents of the castle were sought out enthusiastically in local antique shops by the Queen Mother, who made the castle into her favourite retreat. As patron of the Aberdeen Angus Cattle Society, she enlarged Mey's 25 acres by purchasing an adjoining farm to accommodate her own herd of pedigree cattle.

Originally the castle was a house belonging to the Bishop of Caithness but *c.* 1560 it was purchased from him and transformed into a castle by George Sinclair, 4th Earl of Caithness, whose family members were remote ancestors of the Queen Mother.

MILITARY KNIGHTS OF WINDSOR As it was impossible for Knights of the Garter to attend daily service in the Order's chapel of St George at Windsor Castle they were – and are – represented by the Military Knights of Windsor. Selected on account of distinguished army service, the Military Knights are provided with modest incomes and residences close to the chapel. Their distinctive scarlet uniforms, worn in the chapel and on ceremonial occasions, were chosen by WILLIAM IV in 1833, the same year that their original title of 'Poor Knights of Windsor' was dropped in favour of the present title.

See also MOST NOBLE ORDER OF THE GARTER

MONARCHIES EXTANT Following political upheavals, particularly in the twentieth century, many countries did away with monarchy and became republics. Outside Britain the remaining monarchies are Belgium, Bhutan, Denmark, Japan, Jordan, Nepal, Morocco, Norway, the Netherlands, Saudi Arabia, Spain, Sweden, Thailand and Tonga.

MONMOUTH, JAMES, DUKE OF Although Lucy Walter claimed that her son James, born at Rotterdam in 1649, was fathered by the exiled CHARLES II there was a suspicion that his real father was Colonel Robert Sidney. Whatever the truth of the allegation, Charles regarded him as his son and put the child in the care of Lord Crofts. Two years after the Restoration in 1660 the dowager queen HENRIETTA MARIA brought 'James Crofts' to England and the next year he was created Duke of Monmouth and married Anne, Countess of Buccleuch who was possessed of a large fortune. Later Lord Shaftesbury – the 'wickedest dog in England' according to Charles – who had no wish to see the king's Roman Catholic brother JAMES succeed to the throne, promoted Monmouth, the 'Protestant Duke', as the alternative heir. He involved him in the Rye House Plot, on the discovery of which Monmouth fled to Holland.

Following the death of King Charles on 6 February 1685, Monmouth landed at Lyme Regis on 11 June to claim the kingdom and was proclaimed King James II at Taunton by his followers. He raised an army of over three thousand men, mostly Cornish peasants and miners, but suffered a devastating defeat at the Battle of Sedgemoor on 6 July. He fled the field, was captured two days later and taken before the real King James who, ignoring his nephew's tears and offer to embrace

James, Duke of Monmouth, who was beheaded after his bungled attempt to seize the throne of his uncle James II.

the Roman Catholic faith, had him beheaded on Tower Hill. Monmouth had asserted that he was legitimate because Charles and his mother had been married, and that he had a marriage certificate to that effect, but this was never produced.

MONTROSE, JAMES GRAHAM, MARQUIS OF

One of the most brilliant commanders ever to fight in Britain's internal wars, Montrose returned to Scotland from extensive travels on the Continent in 1637 and became one of the four nobles who drew up the Presbyterians' National Covenant against the use of the English Liturgy which CHARLES I was endeavouring to enforce. As time passed he began to have doubts about the Covenant and expressed these at the Scottish General Assembly of 1639.

In the next year he took a leading part in what was known as the Second Bishops' War – so-called, because it was fought on behalf of the bishops advocating Church of England ritual – which ended in the defeat of the English at Newburn. However,

the Scottish Parliament imprisoned him for five months in Edinburgh Castle on a charge of being in communication with King Charles.

Following the outbreak of the English Civil War, the General Assembly of Scotland and the English Parliamentarians entered into the Solemn League and Covenant from which came the designation 'Covenanters', whose rallying cry of 'Jesus, and no quarter!' showed the strength of their anti-Royalist feeling. Although this dealt a blow to Charles's cause, he did not entirely give up hope of raising an army in Scotland to fight for him in England, as many Scots were against the Covenant.

In 1644 Montrose, now the king's lieutenant-general and a marquis, travelled in disguise to Perthshire, where the Highland clans were rallying to the Royalist cause. Here he took command of twelve hundred Irish and Scottish auxiliaries and in a few months welded his diverse followers into a small but formidable army that was to vanquish all the forces that were sent against it. On 1 September,

James Graham, Marquis of Montrose, who fought a brilliant campaign in Scotland on behalf of Charles I.

223

although greatly outnumbered, he won his first battle against the Covenanters on the moors of Tippermuir, 3 miles west of Perth, and twelve days later he took Aberdeen.

Montrose was forced to retreat under the threat of a superior force under Archibald, 8th Earl of Argyll and a leading Covenanter, but by his genius for bewildering his enemies, he suddenly appeared in Angus where he ravaged the estates belonging to pro-Covenant nobles. His success earned him reinforcements from the clans and soon he forced Argyll to flee from his castle of Inverary. He then pressed on towards Inverness.

The Covenanters endeavoured to trap him by placing a new army in front of him while Argyll with three thousand Campbells should smash his rear. It was now the depth of winter but Montrose, aware of his enemies' strategy, led his men over remote snowbound moors to Inverlochy where on 2 February 1645 Argyll's army was taken by complete surprise and destroyed. Montrose then marched 'with fire and sword' through Moray and Aberdeenshire, sacked Dundee and on 9 May, with odds of about six-to-one, gained the victory at Auldern after which he defeated another Covenanting army at Alford.

Montrose's greatest triumph came on 15 August at Kilsyth where his army of five thousand inflicted such a defeat on a force of six thousand that only a few hundred escaped with their lives. At this point it appeared that Montrose had won Scotland and, in bringing Scottish aid to the Royalists in England, would turn the course of the war. What he did not take into account was the fickleness of the clansmen, who deserted by the thousand in order to carry their loot back to their Highland homes. At Philliphaugh on 13 September Montrose's force, which had dwindled to five hundred loyal Irish and a hundred Scottish troopers, was ambushed and crushed by an army of six thousand. Montrose escaped to Athole and after a year of trying to rally the Highlands, travelled to Norway and thence to Holland. When news reached him that Charles had been executed on 30 January 1649 he swore to avenge the king and prepared to invade Scotland with a small army, most of which he lost through shipwreck on the voyage from Orkney to Caithness. With his depleted force he marched to the border of Ross-shire but it was a forlorn hope and he was defeated at Carbisdale on 27 April 1650. For a brief while he was a fugitive in remote parts of Sunderland, but was betrayed and taken to Edinburgh where he was hanged in the High Street on 21 May. Some years later the dismembered parts of his body were brought together and buried in St Giles where a monument was later erected to him.

MORDAUNT CASE Although scandals have not been unknown involving members of reigning families, Prince Edward – later EDWARD VII – was the first to attend a court as witness where it was alleged he had been involved in what became known as the 'Mordaunt Case'. The affair came to public notice when Sir Charles Mordaunt sought to divorce his wife Harriet on the grounds of her adultery with Viscount Cole, Sir Frederick Johnstone and 'other persons'. It then became common knowledge that the other persons included the Prince of Wales, but rather than remain out of sight when the case came to court he bravely attended every sitting for ten days.

Sir Charles said in evidence that three days after the birth of her baby, Harriet (perhaps in the grip of post-natal depression) declared, 'Charlie, I have deceived you. You are not the father of that child . . . I have done wrong.'

'Who with?' her husband demanded.

'Lord Cole, Sir Frederick Johnstone, the Prince of Wales, and others, often, and in open day.'

When the prince was called as a witness on 16 February 1870 he was asked, 'Has there ever been improper familiarity or criminal act between yourself and Lady Mordaunt?' There was applause in the courtroom when he answered firmly, 'No.'

The case was thrown out when it was decided that Lady Mordaunt was unfit to plead because she was held to be insane before the hearing. Although the prince was exonerated, the press made the most of the situation and his image was tarnished. For a time Alexandra was cheered and Edward was booed when they visited the theatre.

See also THE TRANBY CROFT AFFAIR

MORE, SIR THOMAS Canonised four hundred years after he was beheaded, Sir Thomas More was one of the greatest intellectuals of Tudor times. He was born in 1478 the son of a judge and followed his father into law and towards the end of HENRY VII's reign he became the under-sheriff of London. CARDINAL WOLSEY brought him to the attention of HENRY VIII who immediately recognised his talents and he was made Treasurer of the Exchequer

The gold-faced statue of Sir Thomas More on London's Chelsea Embankment which was erected in 1969.

and then Chancellor of the Duchy of Lancaster. He became Speaker of the House of Commons and went on diplomatic missions, and when Wolsey fell from favour the king appointed him Lord Chancellor.

Meanwhile, he had written his *Utopia* in which an imaginary island provided a vehicle for a political work on social, economic and moral problems in England, and his made-up name for the island became part of the language. Among More's other works were *The History of Richard III* and *A Dialogue Concerning Heresies* which he directed against the religious reformer William Tyndale. With his loyalty to Roman Catholicism, More was dismayed by the king breaking with Rome over his wish to divorce CATHERINE OF ARAGON and in 1532 he resigned as Lord Chancellor as a matter of principle and wrote *An Apology of Sir Thomas More* in which he justified his action.

Two years later a bill was passed in Parliament requiring all subjects to acknowledge by oath the supremacy of Henry over the Pope as head of the new Church of England. More refused to acknowledge this and the King, his erstwhile esteem of the ex-Lord Chancellor replaced by animosity, had him arrested and tried for high treason. He was imprisoned in the TOWER OF LONDON for a year and, when he still refused to acknowledge the authority of the King, was beheaded on 7 July 1535.

MORTIMER, ROGER, 1st EARL OF MARCH
A landowner in Ireland as well as the Welsh Marches, Roger Mortimer was appointed Lieutenant of Ireland by EDWARD II and countered EDWARD BRUCE's invasion there in 1316. When Hugh Despenser gained influence over the king, Mortimer joined an ill-fated revolt against the king and his favourites, and as a result was sentenced to life imprisonment in the TOWER OF LONDON. In 1323 he escaped by climbing up a chimney and found sanctuary in Paris where he and Queen Isabella became lovers and planned the downfall of Edward. Their campaign was successful, the king was forced to abdicate in favour of his son EDWARD III who was still in his minority, and the country was in effect ruled by Isabella and Mortimer. There is little doubt that Mortimer arranged the murder of Edward and became the de facto king. He took over the Dispenser estates, made himself Earl of March and had the ex-king's half-brother Edmund, Earl of Kent executed. Inevitably popular feeling swung against him and Isabella. On 19 October 1330 the 17-year-old Edward III entered Nottingham Castle by a secret passage and arrested him. For having 'murdered and killed the king's father' Mortimer was taken to London and hanged at Tyburn where his body was left on the gallows for two days.
See also EDWARD II.

MOST NOBLE ORDER OF THE GARTER
Inspired by his love of chivalry EDWARD III established an élite order of knights, rather as the legendary King Arthur created the Fellowship of the Round Table. Thus on St George's Day 1348 was inaugurated the Most Noble Order of the Garter with twenty-six founder knights, which remains Britain's oldest chivalric order. The story of how its name came about is one of history's choice anecdotes ranking with Canute defying the tide or

Alfred letting the cakes burn. During a dance at a celebration of the king's capture of Calais a garter worn by Joan, the beautiful Countess of Salisbury, slipped to the floor whereupon Edward, ignoring the sniggers of the assembly, retrieved it and bound it on his own leg with the words which became the motto of the Order, 'Honi soit qui mal y pense' – 'Evil be to him that evil thinks'.

King Edward built ST GEORGE'S CHAPEL within the precincts of Windsor Castle to be the spiritual centre of his new Order and established the College of St George, consisting of a number of priests who would serve the chapel and conduct a daily service for the Garter knights, which included the prayer 'God save our Gracious Sovereign and all Companions, living and departed, to the most Honourable and Noble Order of the Garter'. Apart from the period of the Commonwealth the service has been conducted daily for six centuries. As it was impossible for every member of the Order to attend these services stand-ins were introduced originally known as the Poor Knights of Windsor and the MILITARY KNIGHTS OF WINDSOR today.

Each Garter knight had his stall beneath his banner in the choir to which was attached a heraldic plate showing his coat-of-arms. In the beginning the membership of the Order was reserved for the sovereign's subjects but later it was an honour occasionally bestowed on members of foreign royalty who were termed 'Strangers Elect'. Later recipients did not necessarily need to have military backgrounds, and statesmen ranging from Benjamin Disraeli to Sir Winston Churchill became Garter knights.

Today the membership of the Order remains at twenty-six – the sovereign and twenty-five men and women who have held public office – plus foreign recipients. The emblem of the Order, worn on the left shoulder, is a blue 'garter' with a silver badge, in the centre of which is the red cross of St George encircled by the famous motto.

'MRS MORLEY AND MRS FREEMAN' In her youth, the future QUEEN ANNE developed a particularly deep friendship with Sarah Jennings who had entered the service of Anne's father, the Duke of York, later JAMES II. In 1677 Sarah married John Churchill who was destined to become the 1st Duke of Marlborough, but this did not affect the bond between the two young women,

which was to last for most of Anne's life and was to have political repercussions after she ascended the throne in 1702.

In her self-vindicating *Conduct of the Duchess of Marlborough*, Sarah explained that Anne 'grew uneasy to be treated by me with the ceremony due to her rank . . . It was in this turn of mind which made her one day propose to me that whenever I should happen to be away from her we might in all our letters write ourselves by feigned names such as would import nothing of distinction of rank between us.' Thus the queen became 'Mrs Morley' and Sarah 'Mrs Freeman'. The equality between the two did not last long, timid 'Mrs Morley' allowing herself to be dominated by frank 'Mrs Freeman'. Sarah later used the Freeman–Morley correspondence in her support of the Whig Party, with such remarks as, 'I beg that Mr and Mrs Morley may see their errors and reflect that the greatest of your family has been occasioned by ill advice and obstinacy.'

During Anne's reign affinities between political figures mingled, shifted and disintegrated like the colours of an oil slick. It was never a straightforward question of government by Whigs or Tories. Individual aspirations, religious schisms and the question of a Stuart or Hanoverian succession clouded the political spectrum. The key to everything was the Queen's favour, as she could choose and dismiss ministers. Thus to pluck the strings of the royal marionette was the object of 'Mrs Freeman'. Initially the queen was pro-Tory, but when it suited the Marlboroughs to align themselves with the Whigs, Anne dutifully changed her views. But when Sarah became too confident in her influence over her friend, Anne began to tire of her favourite's hectoring manner and turned to her young bed-chamber woman, Abigail Hill.

Abigail became as politically motivated as Sarah, intriguing on behalf of her ambitious cousin Robert Harley, later 1st Earl of Oxford. Sir Winston Churchill wrote that she was 'probably the smallest person who ever consciously attempted to decide, and in fact did decide, the history of Europe.'

The year 1708 saw the first general election covering all of Britain. It was won by the Whig party, championed by Sarah, now the Duchess of Marlborough. The Whigs demonstrated their new power by insisting that Prince George, Queen Anne's Danish husband, should resign his position as Lord High Admiral. Soon afterwards the prince suffered a serious attack of dropsy and it soon became obvious he was dying.

Before he died, Anne was obliged to take part in the obligatory procession to St Paul's Cathedral to give thanks to the Almighty for Marlborough's victory at Oudenarde. Sarah, smiling in the reflected glory of her warrior husband, was halfway up Ludgate Hill when she noticed that the Queen was without her jewels. This made her furious because, as Mistress of the Robes, she had arranged the royal gems in a certain fashion for Anne to wear – for her to ignore this was tantamount to rebellion. As the procession entered the cathedral, Sarah quarrelled bitterly with Anne who retorted so loudly that Sarah was alarmed in case the congregation should overhear and even join in. When they had taken their seats Anne continued to answer the criticism at the top of her voice, whereupon Sarah cried, 'Hold your tongue.'

The matter did not end there. When Anne was at the bedside of her dying husband a letter from Sarah was put in her hand which began: 'Though the last time I had the honour to wait upon your majesty, your usage of me was such as was scarce possible for me to imagine, or anyone to believe . . .'

Anne had only read this far when Sarah herself entered the chamber. Anne received her coldly and according to an eyewitness 'the deportment of the Duchess of Marlborough, while the prince was actually dying, was of such a nature, that the Queen, then in the height of her grief, was unable to bear it.'

'Withdraw!' she cried, and for once 'Mrs Freeman' obeyed 'Mrs Morley'.

The final act of the tragicomedy began when Sarah upbraided Anne for not having consulted her when she ordered her laundress a daily bottle of wine. While she raged, Anne started to leave, whereupon the Duchess 'clapped her back against the door and told her that she should hear her out'. In the usual acrimonious letter that followed such scenes, Sarah drew attention to *New Atlantis*, Mrs Manley's scandalous work which contained material 'not fit to be mentioned of passion between women.'

Sarah, encouraged by the Whigs who were in despair over the increasing ascendancy of the pro-Tory Abigail Masham (née Hill), demanded an interview with the Queen to try and explain away her conduct. Thus, on the evening of 6 April 1710, 'Mrs Morley' met 'Mrs Freeman' for the last time. The extraordinary interview lasted an hour during which all Anne would answer to Sarah's arguments was, 'Whatever you have to say, you may write it.'

Thanks to the influence of Abigail Masham, the Tory government was firmly in power when the Duke of Marlborough returned from his Flemish campaigns. He asked for a private audience with the Queen at which he tried to get his wife reinstated, but Anne's only reply was that 'she wished to receive back her gold keys of GROOM OF THE STOLE and Mistress of the Robes'. Finally, Marlborough went on his knees and begged for ten days' grace to prepare Sarah for the shock. Reluctantly Anne granted three. Obediently he went to Sarah and asked for the keys, and in a fury she flung them at his head. Anxious not to follow his wife into retirement, he took them meekly to Anne who received them 'with far greater pleasure than if he had brought her the spoils of an enemy'.

'Mrs Morley' had finally defeated 'Mrs Freeman' and the triumph was celebrated by Abigail Masham being given Sarah's old post as Keeper of the Privy Purse.

N

NATIONAL ANTHEM The authorship of the national anthem has long been a matter of controversy. It has been ascribed to John Bull (*c.* 1563–1628), an organist to JAMES I, and also to Henry Carey (*c.* 1690–1743), a poet and musician whose best known poem is 'Sally in our Alley'. Great use was made of the song during the Jacobite Rebellion and its popularity dates from that time. The lines 'Confound their politics, Frustrate their knavish tricks' are thought to refer originally to the Jacobites. Some of the words were first used as watchwords in the navy as early as 1545 – 'God save the King' with the countersign 'Long to reign over us'.

GEORGE V showed great interest in the anthem's proper interpretation and in 1933 an Army Order laid down regulations for tempo, dynamics and orchestration. The official score was then published by Boosey & Hawkes.

The National Anthem in full:

> God save our gracious Queen!
> Long live our noble Queen!
> God save the Queen!
> Send her victorious,
> Happy and glorious,
> Long to reign over us,
> God save the Queen.
>
> Thy choicest gifts in store,
> On her be pleased to pour,
> Long may she reign!
> May she defend our laws,
> And ever to give us cause,
> To sing with heart and voice,
> God save the Queen!
>
> O Lord God arise,
> Scatter our enemies,
> And make them fall!
> Confound their knavish tricks,
> Confuse their politics,

> On you our hopes we fix,
> God save the Queen!
>
> Not in this land alone,
> But be God's mercies known,
> From shore to shore!
> Lord make the nations see,
> That men should brothers be,
> And form one family,
> The wide world o'er.
>
> From every latent foe,
> From the assassin's blow,
> God save the Queen!
> O'er her thine arm extend,
> For Britain's sake defend,
> Our mother, prince, and friend,
>
> God save the Queen!

NEVILLE, ANNE A daughter of Richard, Earl of Warwick ('The Kingmaker'), Anne was married to Richard of Gloucester in 1472. She was crowned Queen Consort in 1483 when her husband became RICHARD III but died two years later and was interred in WESTMINSTER ABBEY.
See also RICHARD III

NEW PALACE The New Palace, built on the bank of the Thames at Kew, was Britain's only royal palace that was never used by a sovereign. It was the inspiration of GEORGE III who in 1800 was determined to build a Gothic masterpiece on the site of the old White House palace which had to be demolished for the purpose two years later. The projected cost for the new building was then £40,000, and the work was entrusted to the Surveyor General of Works, James Wyatt, who had been responsible for redesigning the state apartments at WINDSOR CASTLE.

Today all that remains of the New Palace are the plans, which are preserved in the library at Windsor

Castle. They show that the building was rectangular in shape with round towers at the four corners. In front was a large quadrangle whose outer walls resembled those of a medieval castle, while the whole complex was dominated by a large square tower on which was mounted a remarkable weather vane; this had the same dominating effect as a central flagpole. In total the palace had thirty-six crenellated towers and turrets. As the king's project began to take shape criticism was levelled at it from those who did not approve of its romantic appearance. Sir Nathaniel Wraxall wrote in his memoirs that it formed a 'structure such as those in which Ariosto or Spencer depicted princesses detained by giants or enchanters'.

Inevitably the cost of the building exceeded its original estimate so that four years after the White House had been demolished £100,000 had been spent on its successor and the king, troubled by increasing illness, began to lose interest in it. Although the structure was complete by 1806, further work was halted in April of that year. GEORGE IV, who had an abiding interest in architecture, found his aesthetic sensibilities affronted by his father's palace and in 1872 ordered its demolition by explosives. Before the order was carried out the doomed palace's staircase and floors were taken to be installed in BUCKINGHAM PALACE.

NONSUCH PALACE In 1538 HENRY VIII planned his projected palace of Nonsuch to be 'the pearl of the realm' after finding a suitable site for it near Ewell in Surrey. First, he persuaded the owner of Cuddington Manor to exchange it for a manor in Suffolk, then the folk of the nearby village were forced to leave and their homes were demolished to complete the setting for the residence. The parkland around it covered 1,200 acres and was walled about when it was stocked with deer. A nearby priory, a victim of the Dissolution, was demolished and its stones transported to the site where a workforce of over five hundred labourers, carpenters and masons was accommodated under canvas in order to put in as many daylight hours as possible each day.

Nonsuch Palace, Henry VIII's 'pearl of the realm'.

The palace's entrance, a three-storeyed gatehouse, led into the Outer Court whose buildings, though only two storeys high, were described as 'strong and graceful'. The ground floor housed domestic offices and servants' quarters while the floor above provided accommodation for members of the court. Archways led to the stables and the kitchen court, and a tall gatehouse was surmounted by the palace clock. This opened on to the Inner Court which contained the magnificent royal apartments, whose white and gold decoration inspired Antony Wagon, a vicar whose parish was close by, to write:

When you have greeted its threshold and seen with dazzled eyes, the shining lustre of the stone glittering with purest gold it is not surprising that it should hold you senseless . . . The King's way is guarded night and day by Scorpio, clothed in bronze garments. Setting foot, with Scorpio's permission, into the royal quarters you will first see the spacious chamber of the royal guard. From there the way goes up by generous winding steps, leading to the most glorious precincts of the royal presence. The precincts look out one way on the riches of the courtyard, the other way on the perplexing twists of the maze and the scented beauty of the garden, From there, leaving the closets on the right, extends the dignified approach to the king's privy chamber.

A door leads into the garden. From there if you turn your gaze to the lofty towers, the turreted walls, the projecting windows, the plaster-work, the exquisite statues, you will wonder whether you are walking in a court-yard or garden, for the face of each has the same splendour and majesty.

A marble fountain in which water gushed from the jaws of a griffin was the centrepiece of the Inner Court while at the two corners of the opposite end of the gatehouse rose two towers ornately decorated with heraldic beasts, flagstaffs and wind vanes, and which were regarded as the palace's outstanding feature.

Although Queen Catherine Parr visited Nonsuch in 1544 when building work was still ongoing, the King did not make a royal progress to the new residence until June 1545 after he had expressed himself forcibly over what he considered the time being taken on the plasterwork. When he died two years later there was still some work to be done.

As has been the case with some other vanished palaces, once the sovereign who inspired the project is gone, subsequent monarchs lose interest in it. After his father's death young EDWARD VI hardly ever set foot in Nonsuch and when his half-sister MARY ascended the throne she even considered demolishing it. In the end she sold it to the Earl of Arundel, her Lord Steward of the Household, who then put the final touches to the palace.

In the summer of 1559, the year following her accession to the throne, ELIZABETH I visited Nonsuch where Arundel provided the extravagant entertainment that was to become the feature of the Queen's visits to the establishments of her courtiers. In 1592 Nonsuch became a royal residence once more when the queen repurchased it and it was here in 1599 that ROBERT DEVEREUX, Earl of Essex – after leaving Ireland, where he was Lord Lieutenant – burst into Elizabeth's bedchamber against her wishes. This foolhardy action of the erstwhile favourite ended with his execution at the TOWER OF LONDON and the birth of a royal legend.

William the Conqueror's troops sailing for England in 1066, as depicted in the Bayeux Tapestry.

When JAMES I came to the throne he spent over £5,000 on the palace then gave it to his wife ANNE OF DENMARK. His son CHARLES I likewise gave it to HENRIETTA MARIA who lost it during the English Civil War but regained it with the Restoration. CHARLES II inherited the palace in 1669 and shortly afterwards he gave it to his mistress BARBARA VILLIERS whom he created Duchess of Cleveland and Baroness Nonsuch. It was said that the King, becoming weary of her hectoring ways, used Nonsuch as a parting gift. As the result of a bitter dispute with the park keeper, the 1st Earl of Berkeley, she demolished the greater part of the palace, and later its parkland was sold off and the part known as the Great Park became Worcester Park.

NORMAN KINGS The Norman line of succession went back to ROBERT RAGNDVALSSON, 1st Duke of Normandy, who is better remembered in history as Rollo. In AD 912 he secured a large area of land from Charles the Simple which expanded into the Duchy of Normandy. WILLIAM I ('The Conqueror') was the 5th Duke of Normandy after Robert and with him began the reign of the Norman kings of England. This lasted for eighty-eight years from the Norman Conquest of 1066 to the death of STEPHEN in 1154.

William I took the English throne on the grounds that it had been promised to him by EDWARD THE CONFESSOR. It had also been promised to HAROLD GODWINESON although the young

EDGAR THE ATHELING, the grandson of ETHELRED II ('The Unready'), was the legitimate heir. Harold became the last Saxon king in January 1066 and although his claim was endorsed by the Witan he was without royal blood, whereas William could claim distant links to Ethelred II and CANUTE through his great aunt EMMA who had been married to both kings. William's wife Matilda had closer ties with the English monarchy as she was a descendant of KING ALFRED.

At the Battle of Hastings fought on 14 October 1066, Harold was slain and the Norman regime began. William was followed by his son WILLIAM II ('Rufus') who left no heir when he was killed in the New Forest. His brother HENRY I joined the Norman line to that of Britain by marrying Edith, the daughter of Malcolm III (*see* SCOTLAND, EARLY KINGS OF) of Scotland. Edith, who found it politic to change her Saxon name to the Norman one of Matilda, was the great-granddaughter of Ethelred II and this was welcomed by the English.

The sinking of the *White Ship* robbed England of Henry I's male heirs so that when he died in 1135 his daughter the Empress Matilda was his successor.

The Normans

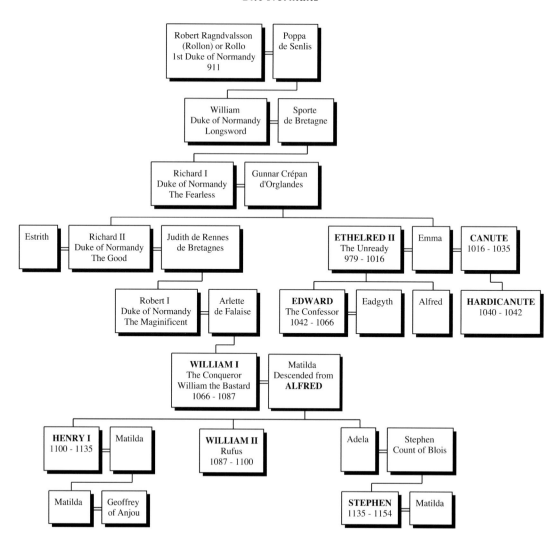

However, the throne was seized by her cousin STEPHEN of Blois which led to civil war. His death in 1154 signalled the beginning of the Plantagenet dynasty.

NURSERY RHYMES It has been a common opinion that certain nursery rhymes were satirical comments on royalty before becoming verses for the amusement of young children. It is not possible to prove definitely the origin of individual nursery rhymes as they developed orally before being finally collected and published. Thus some authorities find differing explanations for rhymes thought to have been inspired by regal figures. For example, the following rhyme, first published in Tom Thumb's *Pretty Song Book, c.* 1744, which is generally thought to refer to MARY, QUEEN OF SCOTS is also claimed to apply to the Roman Catholic Church.

> Mary, Mary, quite contrary,
> How does your garden grow?
> With silver bells and cockle shells,
> And pretty maids all in a row.

The unfortunate Catholic queen, arriving in Scotland from the glittering French court, was considered 'contrary' in the eyes of her dourly Protestant critics. Indeed, John Knox publicly named her 'the whore of Babylon'. The 'cockle shells' were said to have been the motif decorating a gown she wore that had been given to her by her late husband Francis II of France, while 'pretty maids all in a row' were her ladies-in-waiting. Known as the 'Four Marys', these famed companions of the queen were Mary Beaton, Mary Livingston, Mary Fleming and Mary Seaton. Although not one of the quartet, a Mary Carmichael was introduced in the still popular ballad 'The Queen's Maries', the first verse of which stated:

> Yeste'en the Queen had four Maries,
>   This nicht she'll hae but three;
> There was Marie Seaton and Marie Beaton,
>   And Marie Carmichael and me.

There can be no doubt about the historical events that inspired the following rhyme:
> William and Mary, George and Anne,
> Four such children had never a man.
> They put their father to flight and shame,
> And called their brother a shocking bad name.

The first line names the daughters and sons-in-law of JAMES II who was deposed in the GLORIOUS REVOLUTION of 1688 that brought WILLIAM and MARY to the throne of England. They were succeeded by ANNE and her husband Prince George of Denmark. That they 'had never a man' alluded to the fact that neither couple produced a successful royal heir, Queen Anne's son William dying at the age of 12. 'Their brother' was Prince James Francis Stewart, the only son of James II and known as the 'Old Pretender', who inspired the Jacobite rebellion of 1715.

> What is the rhyme for poringer?
> What is the rhyme for poringer?
> The king he had a daughter fair
> And gave the Prince of Orange her.

This rhyme comes from a Jacobite song mocking William of Orange who had taken the throne of his father-in-law.

> Hush-a-bye baby, on the tree top,
> When the wind blows the cradle will rock;
> When the bough breaks the cradle will fall,
> Down will come baby, cradle and all.

First published in *Mother Goose's Melody* in 1765 the rhyme was said to be a 'lampoon on the British royal line' in the reign of James II.

> Little Jack Horner
> Sat in a corner,
> Eating a Christmas pie;
> He put in his thumb,
> And pulled out a plum,
> And said, What a good boy am I!

Historically, Richard Whiting, the last abbot of the Benedictine abbey of St Mary at Glastonbury, had a steward named Jack Horner. In 1534 the abbot and his monks signed the Act of Supremacy which separated the Church of England from the Roman Catholic Church, but when the Dissolution of the Monasteries began two years later he is said to have endeavoured to preserve Glastonbury Abbey by sending Jack Horner to London with a gift for HENRY VIII. This took the form of a Christmas pie, inside the crust of which were hidden the title deeds of twelve manors for His Majesty. According to tradition Jack Horner

The ruins of Glastonbury Abbey. From here Jack Horner set out with a gift for Henry VIII.

managed to extract the deed to the Manor of Mells during the journey, and it is recorded that after the Dissolution he took up residence at Mells. Despite the pie, Richard Whiting was arrested when he refused to surrender the abbey and was hanged on Glastonbury Tor with two of his monks in 1539.

'Sing a Song of Sixpence' is also said to have been inspired by Henry VIII.

> Sing a song of sixpence,
>   A pocket full of rye,
> Four and twenty blackbirds,
>   Baked in a pie;
> When the pie was opened,
>   The birds began to sing;

> Was not that a dainty dish
>   To set before the king?

> The king was in his counting-house
>   Counting out his money;
> The queen was in the parlour
>   Eating bread and honey;
> The maid was in the garden
>   Hanging out the clothes,
> There came a little blackbird,
>   And snapped off her nose.

The usual interpretation is that the 'blackbirds' refer to the monasteries which presented Henry VIII with a profitable 'pie' as a result of the Dissolution. The queen was Henry's wife CATHERINE OF ARAGON while the maid was ANNE BOLEYN, the blackbird her executioner.

> Here comes a candle to light you to bed,
> Here comes a chopper to chop off your head.

These last two lines of 'Oranges and Lemons' are also thought to refer to Henry VIII's fatal marriages.

> As I was going by Charing Cross,
> I saw a black man on a black horse;
> They told me it was King Charles the First –
> Oh dear, my heart was ready to burst!

The man on horseback was the statue of CHARLES I which was first erected in London's King Street and was later moved to the site of Old Charing Cross in 1675. The ditty mocked the sentiments of Royalists and was sung by those who were still loyal to the Parliamentarian ideal.

> Georgie Porgie, pudding and pie,
> Kissed the girls and made them cry;
> When the boys came out to play,
> Georgie Porgie ran away.

According to Andrew Lang, GEORGE I was the inspiration for 'Georgie Porgie', though other writers have claimed it was George Villiers, Duke of Buckingham; neither were noted for virtuous lifestyles.

O

OAK APPLE DAY The escape of PRINCE CHARLES, later Charles II, after the Battle of Worcester in 1651 is commemorated annually as Oak Apple Day on 29 May. The name comes from the incident in which the prince hid high in the foliage of an oak tree while his pursuers searched for him below. Each Oak Apple Day the Chelsea Pensioners march before a Reviewing Officer at the ROYAL HOSPITAL, and give three cheers for Charles while his statue is decorated with oak leaves. For a long time it was the custom across the kingdom to decorate trees in celebration of the royal escape and today it is still remembered at Castleton, Derbyshire, on Garland King Day on the same date. A procession with the 'merrie monarch' on horseback winds through the village, with appropriate pauses for refreshment, followed by maypole dancing.

OATLANDS When HENRY VIII acquired Oatlands in 1537 he used his familiar tactic of persuading the owner of a property he coveted to exchange it for another. In this case he traded some property, which had belonged to Tandridge Priory before it was suppressed, for the Oatlands estate which stretched between Walton and Weybridge, in order to enlarge the deerpark of HAMPTON COURT, which had been presented to him by CARDINAL WOLSEY eight years earlier. At first the king used the house at Oatlands as a hunting lodge but when he was planning to marry his fourth wife, Anne of Cleves, he set builders to work to transform it into the new queen's dower house. The marriage, which was celebrated in 1540, only lasted six months before it ended in divorce.

According to some accounts, when Henry secretly married CATHERINE HOWARD on

The Royal Hospital, Chelsea, where Oak Apple Day is celebrated annually on 29 May.

28 July of the same year the ceremony was held at Oatlands, which was still not fully completed. By the time Catherine Parr became the king's sixth wife in 1543 his interest in Oatlands had been overshadowed by his enthusiasm for NONSUCH PALACE.

In appearance Oatlands had a crenellated gate-tower set in the centre of a continuous line of gabled buildings behind which was the Middle Court containing the Great Hall, the chapel and the royal apartments. Beyond this was the Inner Court with its distinctive tower whose top storey overhung it and provided a panoramic view of the surrounding landscape including the nearby Thames. Like all Tudor palaces, Oatlands was splendidly furnished, the walls of its chambers being hung with tapestries and cloth of gold, a fabric that became associated with Henry after the Field of the Cloth of Gold.

After she ascended the throne ELIZABETH I visited Oatlands to hunt deer with a bow and arrow, as did JAMES I. His wife, ANNE OF DENMARK, had a special building constructed to house silkworms at a cost of £600, and though it was completed with her coat of arms on the stained-glass windows, it appears that the silkworms did not thrive.

It was at Oatlands that Henry, Duke of Gloucester was born to CHARLES I and QUEEN HENRIETTA MARIA in 1640. Two years later the king, at the head of his army, paid his last visit to the palace. After CHARLES II returned to his kingdom Oatlands became part of his mother's dower but she preferred to lease it out rather than reside there and it later passed out of royal ownership.

In 1791 it was bought back by Frederick, the second son of GEORGE III who became known as the 'Grand old Duke of York'. His wife Princess Frederica, daughter of Frederick William II of Prussia, resided there while he was in Flanders and had a narrow escape when the palace was destroyed by fire. It was rebuilt in 1794 under the supervision of Henry Holland, and the duke and duchess took up residence there again. The duke was often absent and the duchess spent many hours in the famous Oatlands' grotto which had been constructed by a previous owner. One of its rooms was designed for gambling while another was decorated with artificial stalactites. In other rooms the duchess enjoyed the company of her pets, which included parrots, monkeys and forty dogs. After the duchess died at Oatlands in 1820 the duke sold the house, after

The Cathedral of Notre-Dame in Bayeux, a splendid example of Norman Gothic architecture, was built by Bishop Odo.

which it was reconstructed and today is the Oatlands Park Hotel.

ODO The half-brother of Duke William II of Normandy, later WILLIAM I of England, Odo of Bayeux was born *c.* 1036 and had the bishopric of Bayeux bestowed upon him by William when he was in his early teens. In 1066 he was involved in the invasion of England and subsequently became the Earl of Kent, and on occasions acted as the king's viceroy. He amassed a vast fortune but, accused of extortion when William returned from Normandy in 1082, was imprisoned and had to forfeit his wealth. He was released in 1087, the year of the king's death, but the next year he took part in a rebellion against WILLIAM II and this time he was exiled to Normandy until his death in 1097.

OFFA One of the greatest Mercian kings, Offa came to be regarded as the King of the English, which caused Charlemagne to regard him as an equal. During his reign, which lasted from AD 757 to his death in AD 796, he expanded his kingdom, taking in Hwicce, Kent and the land of the southern Saxons. He is credited with introducing the first silver pennies on which his head was portrayed like that of a Roman emperor, and he initiated the first coronation at which anointing with holy oil was part of the ceremony.

His power as a ruler is testified by his great earthwork known as Offa's Dyke which ran as the boundary wall between Mercia and Wales. It consisted of a ditch 6ft deep and a bulwark that rose 20ft above ground level. Originally it stretched for 120 miles, and today 80 miles of its remains are to be seen. Its purpose would seem to have been as a deterrent to Welsh raiding parties, similar in function to Hadrian's Wall. Comparable earthen barriers were built in other parts of Europe but none came near the size of Offa's monumental work.

OLDCASTLE, SIR JOHN It has been written that it was the policy of HENRY IV in keeping his son out of state affairs that induced Prince Hal, the future HENRY V, 'to amuse his active mind by those youthful dissipations and escapades which have gained him a merry immortality from the pen of Shakespeare.' At this time one of his staunchest friends was Sir John Oldcastle, whom Shakespeare transformed into Falstaff. In reality, Oldcastle had a serious side to his nature, supporting the Lollard movement by paying for John Wycliffe's works to be transcribed and distributed.

When Prince Hal ascended the throne in 1413 a thought which must have dominated his mind was that the Crown had been usurped from its anointed owner by his father, and therefore his position was dependent upon the goodwill of the nobility and the Church. To keep the favour of the former he held out hopes of a profitable war; to the latter he promised to continue the late King's policy of repressing the Lollards. Thereupon the Archbishop of Canterbury applied for royal permission to indict Sir John Oldcastle, now Lord Cobham following his marriage to an heiress, for heresy.

Henry's reply to the Archbishop's request was that gentle persuasion was the best path to conversion. He announced that he would have a discussion with his old friend and, having studied divinity at Oxford, he was convinced he could argue him out of his heretical ideas. But when Sir John

obeyed the summons to Windsor, his extensive knowledge of the Bible made him more than a match for the King.

Henry's response was to tell the Archbishop to proceed against his old friend according to the law. At the same time magistrates were ordered to arrest all itinerant preachers. Sir John's response was to draw up his *Confession of Faith*, which he hoped would justify the Lollards' beliefs. Reading this credo today, one wonders what any true Roman Catholic could have found heretical about it. Beginning with the acceptance of the Apostles' Creed and the doctrine of the Trinity, it declared that no one could be saved unless he or she was a member of the Church. After acknowledging belief in the saints, purgatory and the Church militant, it stated that common folk should be obedient to their king, civil governors and priests. It concluded by emphasising the necessity of the sacraments. However, a significant clause in the *Confession* was that Lollards recognised the right of the state to compel priests to do their duty and to 'seclude' all false teachers. This doctrine of compulsion became embodied in the Reformation and resulted in the reformed church being as ready to persecute those who disagreed with it – especially Roman Catholics – as the Church of Rome had been to suppress the followers of John Wycliffe. This unfortunate legacy lasted until the Act of Toleration of 1689.

When Sir John returned to Windsor with his manifesto, the King refused to read it. After this rejection Sir John, in the spirit of the times, offered to purge himself of the charge of heresy by single combat with anyone who dared to challenge him. Henry ignored this dramatic gesture and Sir John was turned over to the Archbishop of Canterbury who, with the Bishops of London, Winchester and St David's, put him on trial. At the hearing the accused declared that 'the church had ceased to teach the doctrine of the Gospel from the moment that it became infected with the poison of worldly riches . . .'

For two days the accused lord argued his case and then was, in the words of the record, 'sweetly and modestly condemned to be burnt alive.' Henry, reluctant to see the companion of his youth chained to a stake with faggots piled round him, granted him a respite of fifty days. During this period Sir John managed to escape from the TOWER OF LONDON, some historians suggesting royal connivance. After four years of hiding in Wales, he was captured by retainers of the Earl of Powys in Montgomeryshire. In London he was tried before his peers for heresy and subsequently 'hanged and burnt hanging' as a heretic at St Giles's Fields in 1417.

OLD ROWLEY It was his reputation as a great lover which caused CHARLES II to be nicknamed after a famous stallion, Old Rowley, who was always in demand as a stud. One day in the palace the king heard a young woman singing a satirical ballad 'Old Rowley, the King'. When he knocked on her door she asked who was there, to which Charles replied with his usual humour, 'Old Rowley himself, madam.'

ORDERS OF CHIVALRY Grants of land were the original rewards for loyal service to the king and later titles were added as recognition of a subject's merit. Today British nationals who have distinguished themselves in service to the nation may have titles of honour conferred upon them by the sovereign, who can personally select recipients for the Order of the Garter, the Order of the Thistle, the Order of Merit, the Royal Victorian Order and long-service medals. The Prime Minister recommends all other honours while the Foreign Office advises on the granting of honorary decorations to foreign citizens in recognition of their contribution to rapport between their countries and Great Britain.
See also BATH, ORDER OF THE; BRITISH EMPIRE, ORDER OF THE; GARTER, MOST NOBLE ORDER OF THE; MERIT, ORDER OF; ST MICHAEL AND ST GEORGE, ORDER OF; ST PATRICK, MOST ILLUSTRIOUS ORDER OF; and ROYAL VICTORIAN ORDER.

OSBORNE HOUSE When QUEEN VICTORIA wrote to her dear Uncle Leopold, King of the Belgians, after she had bought Osborne House on the Isle of Wight, she stressed the pleasure it gave her 'to have a place of one's own'. With several royal residences, including BUCKINGHAM PALACE, at her disposal such a remark might have sounded odd to her subjects but it illustrated her desire for periods of quiet family life with PRINCE ALBERT and their children.

Married in February 1840, the royal couple had their first three children – Princess Victoria, Prince Edward and Princess Alice – by April 1843, and the need to have a refuge away from the capital became of increasing importance to the queen. Remembering

a pleasant visit to the Isle of Wight when she was a young girl, a fitting property was sought for her there. The property chosen was Osborne, an eighteenth-century house which afforded a panoramic view of the Solent and, a bonus for the royal children, had its own private beach.

The original plan was to take out a lease on the property but in May 1845 Victoria bought the house, with its accompanying land of around 1,000 acres, for £26,000 of her personal money. When it was found not to be large enough to accommodate the royal household it was decided to replace it by a new building designed by the versatile Albert. Inspired by Italian architecture he included two square towers suggestive of campaniles in his plans. The building work was planned in two phases, firstly a new block or 'pavilion' was to be built to house the royal family beside the original house. When this work was finished the old house would be replaced by the new block. The Italianate theme was continued in the gardens, laid out on two levels with fountains, classical balustrades and urns. Work on Osborne was completed in 1851.

Two years later a real Swiss chalet was dismantled for transportation and reassembled in Osborne's grounds, to the delight of the children. There they were introduced to such unroyal activities as woodwork and cookery – here one detects the prince's influence – and often their mother and father were invited to take tea and sample the results of their baking. It became the custom for the family to spend January and part of July and August at Osborne, the queen using her special horse-drawn bathing machine during the summer visit.

For the queen the Isle of Wight idyll ended abruptly in December 1861 when Albert died of typhoid at WINDSOR CASTLE. Within days she returned to grieve at Osborne House which, like their other retreat at BALMORAL, had brought them so much mutual happiness.

Although Victoria became known as 'the widow at Windsor' she had very little liking for the castle, the scene of Albert's death, and spent much of her time at Osborne House. After she became Empress of India in 1876 her interest in that huge piece of the empire blossomed and she had a wing added to Osborne House which housed the 'Durbar Room', designed by Rudyard Kipling's father who was the curator of the Lahore Museum. (It was ironical that Rudyard initiated the 'widow at Windsor' tag through his poem of the same name.) And it was at

Osborne that she took lessons in Hindi from her servant, Abdul Karim.

With her family about her, Queen Victoria died in the arms of her grandson – Kaiser Wilhelm, the son of Princess Victoria – at Osborne House on 22 January 1901. For EDWARD VII the house held no attraction, his favourite residence was SANDRINGHAM, and in the following reign GEORGE V gave it to the nation with public admission to the state apartments.

OUR LIFE IN THE HIGHLANDS When grief-stricken QUEEN VICTORIA gradually returned to the world of reality following the death of PRINCE ALBERT, one factor which helped her to assuage her grief was her editing of a five-volume biography of her husband by Theodore Martin. This work encouraged her to write *Leaves from a Journal of our Life in the Highlands*, which contained extracts from her remarkable diary. The book was printed privately in 1867 and then published commercially. It became the best-selling title of the following year. Never before had the public been allowed such glimpses into the domestic lives of royalty. It was a delightfully simple picture of the Queen's family freed from the pomp of court life, and described such homely incidents as Vicky (the Princess Royal) sitting on a wasps' nest and the pleasures and difficulties of picnicking.

OVERBURY SCANDAL There has been no shortage of court scandals down the centuries, but one that stands out because of its involvement with witchcraft and murder occurred during the reign of JAMES I. The king's favourite, Robert Carr, developed a passion for Frances Howard, the wayward wife of the 3rd Earl of Essex. In order to keep in close contact with her, Carr asked his friend the poet Thomas Overbury to act as intermediary. Carr had met him in 1601 at Edinburgh and a strong friendship developed between the two men, and

through Carr's influence with the doting king he had Overbury knighted in 1608.

It was therefore not surprising that Overbury fell in with Carr's wishes, but when Carr declared that he wanted to arrange for Frances to be divorced from the earl, he made the mistake of giving frank advice. Perhaps because he knew that she had secretly practised witchcraft, he did not hold her in high esteem and told Carr to have her for his mistress if he must but she was not suited to be his wife. Carr repeated this to Frances who was so infuriated that she decided Overbury should pay for the insult with his life, and to this end she offered £1,000 to Sir Davy Wood to murder him. Before this could take place Carr persuaded the king to imprison his erstwhile friend in the TOWER OF LONDON on 26 April 1613 on the trifling pretext of refusing to go on a diplomatic journey.

Although Overbury was temporarily out of circulation, the couple now feared that on his release he would make public Frances's involvement in witchcraft. Carr owed everything to being James's favourite and he knew what the reaction would be from the author of *Daemonologie* if there was any suggestion of witchcraft in the case. On 15 September Overbury was poisoned. Frances obtained a divorce on the grounds of non-consummation and three months after Overbury's murder she and Carr, now Earl of Somerset, were married.

Rumours of the crime persisted for the next two years and such was the popular feeling about the case that the king ordered an inquiry, and four of the minor characters who had been involved in the plot were hanged. In May 1616 Frances pleaded guilty and though Carr denied any knowledge of the affair, he was found equally guilty and the couple were sentenced to death by their peers. King James had no wish for Robert Carr to kneel at the block and he used the royal prerogative to get the sentence changed to one of imprisonment. In 1622 they were released; Frances lived for another ten years and Robert Carr survived until 1645.

P

PENDA The last great Anglo-Saxon pagan king, Penda was credited with slaying many Christian kings including St Oswald, King of Northumbria, who had restored Christianity to his kingdom after defeating Penda's ally Cadwallon of Gwynedd at the Battle of Heavenfield. Penda was first mentioned in history in AD 626 when he fought the West Saxons for the kingdom of Hwicce in the region that became known as Worcestershire. He is thought to have become King of Mercia in AD 633 and his reign was a succession of raids and campaigns, gaining Mercia areas corresponding to Cheshire, Shropshire and Hereford today. He frequently raided Northumbria, defeated Cenwalh of Wessex who had made the mistake of divorcing Penda's sister, killed the king of the East Angles in battle and in *c*. 654 led an invasion into Northumbria, ignoring King Oswio's offers to buy peace. When Oswio knew he had no alternative but to fight the pagan invader he met him on the banks of the river 'Winwaed' in Yorkshire and in the ensuing battle Penda was slain. Ironically it was his son Peada who introduced Christianity into the old pagan's kingdom.

PERCY, HENRY A border lord evocatively nicknamed 'Hotspur', Henry Percy was born in 1364, his father also being Henry Percy, 1st Earl of Northumberland. He became the Warden of the East March in 1385 but in 1388 he was pursuing a Scottish army when he was taken prisoner at the Battle of Otterburn, immortalised in 'Chevy Chase', which is one of the oldest English ballads. He was ransomed and continued his wardenship but ten years later the Percys were angered by RICHARD II's attempt to erode their domination of the Scottish border which had so well served the English Crown. In reply Hotspur and his father joined Henry of Bolingbroke who was laying claim to the Crown, and were instrumental in him becoming HENRY IV.

Hotspur was rewarded by being made Justiciar of North Wales with the brief of suppressing Owain Glyndwr's (*see* WALES, KINGS OF) rebellion. Soon, however, the Percys turned against the king who failed to repay large sums of money owed to them, and refused to let them keep the ransoms paid by Scottish prisoners captured when Hotspur was victorious at the Battle of Homildon Hill. As a result Hotspur conspired with the Welsh rebels to

The plain cross marking the site of the Battle of Heavenfield, south of Hexham in Northumberland.

replace King Henry with Edmund Mortimer, Earl of March and a nephew of his wife. Impulsively he launched what came to be known as the Percy Rebellion on 10 July 1403, but before his father or Glyndwr could join him he was intercepted at Shrewsbury on the 21st of the month by an army led by the king. He was slain in the battle whereupon Henry rode into the enemy lines shouting 'Henry Percy is dead! St George! Victory!' Hotspur's defeat brought about the surrender of Northumberland and the submission of Wales.

PHILIP, PRINCE Born on 10 June 1921 in Corfu, Philip was the son of Prince Andrew of Greece and Denmark and Victoria, daughter of Louis, Prince of Battenberg, Marquess of Milford Haven. He came to England in 1928 and subsequently entered the navy, beginning as a midshipman on HMS *Ramillies*. At the age of 21 he became a 1st lieutenant and when his seagoing career ended he was Lieutenant-Commander of HMS *Magpie*. In February 1947 Philip renounced his Greek nationality to become a British subject and adopted the surname of Mountbatten. In the same year he became a KNIGHT OF THE GARTER and was created Duke of Edinburgh. On 20 November 1947 he married Princess Elizabeth, who became ELIZABETH II in February 1952. In 1957 he was granted the title of HRH.

Apart from performing official engagements, Prince Philip has accompanied the Queen on overseas tours and given her discreet support on state occasions. In 1956 he established the Duke of Edinburgh's Award Scheme to help the development of young people. He also became patron or president of around eight hundred organisations. His interest in wildlife was reflected in the publication of his book *Seabirds in Southern Waters*.

PILGRIMAGE OF GRACE It was the suppression of the smaller monasteries that provoked the Pilgrimage of Grace in 1536. Following the Act of Supremacy, which asserted that HENRY VIII was the Supreme Head of the Church of England, a commission visited monasteries with annual incomes of less than £200 and its report, alleging widespread immorality and wrongdoing, was the justification for their dissolution. The revenues of these lesser monasteries were taken over by the Crown and the monks were either given pensions or sent to larger religious houses. The suppression of the larger monasteries began three years later.

The revolt against these closures, known as the Pilgrimage of Grace by its supporters, broke out in the north

The Duke of Edinburgh inspecting Canadian sailors at Pirbright, Surrey, 26 May 1953. *(Getty Images)*

and west of England. The Roman Catholic rebels of Yorkshire, where the Pilgrimage had the greatest support, were led by Robert Aske who until then had been an attorney at Gray's Inn in London. His demands were for the restoration of Roman Catholicism and the removal of Thomas Cromwell, the Vicar-General of the new Church of England.

When the Duke of Norfolk offered a general pardon to the insurgents if they disbanded they accepted, but new uprisings in Cumberland and Westmorland provided an excuse for them to be punished. Robert Aske was executed, as was the statesman Lord Thomas Darcy.

PIPER TO HER MAJESTY During QUEEN VICTORIA and PRINCE ALBERT's first visit to the Highlands of Scotland in 1842, they received a romantic welcome at Taymouth Castle by the Marquess of Breadalbane, with his kilted High-landers and personal piper. In her diary the queen wrote: 'We have heard nothing but bagpipes since we have been in the beautiful Highlands and I have become so fond of it that I mean to have a piper.' The marquess responded to her wish by finding a suitable piper named Angus Mackay who was solemnly sworn in as official 'Piper to Her Majesty'. His responsibility was to provide bagpipe music for the royal couple when they were staying at BALMORAL, which they had leased in 1847, and one of his routine duties was to play under the royal windows each morning.

When Mackay retired from royal service in 1854 the army arranged for his replacement, and for the last century and a half has continued to fill the post when necessary. As well as being a musician, the Queen's Piper is also a Page of the Presence. There are three such pages, and attending royal visitors and ambassadors on their arrival and departure at BUCKINGHAM PALACE is one of their most important functions.

PLANTAGENET KINGS When the disaster of the *White Ship* occurred in 1120, HENRY I lost both his sons who were heirs to his throne. When he died fifteen years later his legitimate successor was his daughter Matilda who was known as the Empress Maud when she returned to England after the death of her first husband the Emperor Henry V in 1125. Three years later she married Geoffrey Plantagenet, Count of Anjou and bore him a son who was to become HENRY II of England. The name Plantagenet came from the *planta genista*, or broom flower, which Geoffrey usually wore on his hat or helmet.

On the death of Henry I his nephew STEPHEN OF BLOIS seized the throne, which led to a civil war when Matilda fought against her cousin whom she hated as a usurper. When she gave up the struggle and retired to Normandy she promoted her son Henry as the rightful king. He took an army to England in 1153 and at Wallingford came to an agreement with Stephen that he would be his Justiciar and would inherit the Crown on his death, which came about the next year. Thus with Henry II

A manuscript portrait of Henry II, the first of the Plantagenet kings.

The Plantagenets

came the beginning of the Plantagenet dynasty which was to last for a record 331 years, though the first three sovereign kings are usually referred to as the Angevin kings, while as a result of the WARS OF THE ROSES the house split into the House of Lancaster and the House of York.

The Plantagenets were one of history's most dynamic royal families, which was strengthened by the fact that for much of the time the Crown passed peacefully from father to son. There was an enduring legend that the Plantagenets had Satanic blood, the story being that one of their female ancestors would always leave the Mass before the elevation of the host. Her odd behaviour concerned her husband and one day he prevented her walking out of the church, whereupon she rose into the air and flew out of the window, never to be seen again.

POET LAUREATE, OFFICE OF The custom of crowning exceptional poets with chaplets of laurel leaves originated in ancient Greece, the laurel (*laurea* in Latin) being sacred to Apollo, the god of poetry and music. The practice spread to Rome where generals and emperors received this honour as well as poets and orators. Although this ended with the fall of Rome, in the Middle Ages universities used the word 'laureate' as a verbal accolade for eminent poets of the day. In due course the word referred only to a poet retained by the sovereign as his or her personal versifier.

Ben Jonson is regarded as the first to take on the role of poet laureate. This was at the invitation of JAMES I and though the king did not formally bestow the title upon him, he was de facto the court poet.

The official laureateship did not commence until 1670 when John Dryden received letters patent granting him the title. CHARLES II found a valuable ally in his poet laureate, whose satire 'Absalom and Achitopel' was a devastating attack on the Whig party which championed the DUKE OF MONMOUTH. After Charles's death in 1685 Dryden served JAMES II equally well and followed the king's religious conviction by converting to Roman Catholicism. This was not for political advantage, as when Protestant WILLIAM OF ORANGE replaced James II Dryden remained staunchly Catholic and refused to take the oath of allegiance. As a result he was dismissed and the office he had held was bestowed upon his literary rival, Thomas Shadwell, in 1689. He was said to

have been the first of a number of poets whose work in flattering the monarch was more political than poetical.

As a court official the poet laureate was required to glorify the monarchy and produce suitable verses to celebrate such royal events as a coronation, the birth of an heir, or the death of a sovereign.

It was Thomas Shadwell who introduced the custom of composing annual birthday and new year odes, and Henry Pye, described by Sir Walter Scott as a man respectable in everything but his poetry, brought derision upon the office with his flattering tributes to unpopular Hanoverians. However, when William Wordsworth was offered the post he stipulated that he should not have to write to order matters that he regarded as trivial, such as birthday odes.

The poet laureate's remuneration varied from reign to reign. Ben Jonson had been paid an annual 100 marks and a butt of canary; Dryden received £300 and the canary. Rather than have the wine Henry Pye arranged to be paid an extra £27. Tennyson was paid £72 annually plus the extra money in lieu of the wine but when John Betjeman was appointed he asked that the old custom of providing the poet with wine should be revived.

Today the post of poet laureate is awarded mainly in recognition of a poet's talent and the odes and eulogies of the past are no longer required though poems written to commemorate certain royal events are still produced.

The following is the list of British court poets from Ben Jonson to the present office-holder: Ben Jonson (1617), Sir William Davenant (1638), John Dryden (1668), Thomas Shadwell (1689), Nahum Tate (1692), Nicholas Rowe (1715), Laurence Eusden (1718), Colley Cibber (1730), William Whitehead (1757), Thomas Warton (1785), Henry Pye (1790), Robert Southey (1813), William Wordsworth (1843), Alfred, Lord Tennyson (1850), Alfred Austin (1896), Robert Bridges (1913), John Masefield (1930), Cecil Day Lewis (1968), Sir John Betjeman (1972), Ted Hughes (1984), Andrew Motion (1999).

PRAEMUNIRE, STATUTES OF Passed in 1351, 1365 and 1393, the objective of these Acts of Parliament was to reduce the authority of the Pope in England. They decreed that outlawry and the confiscation of the accused's property should be the penalty for anyone procuring any papal processes, bulls or excommunications against the King of England or the supplanting of the jurisdiction of his courts. The statutes became of great importance during the Reformation when they were used to arraign those who continued to accept the Pope's authority after HENRY VIII's break with Rome which began in 1532.

PRINCE ARTHUR, DISAPPEARANCE OF

Born in 1187 shortly after his father, Geoffrey, Earl of Richmond and Duke of Brittany had been killed in a tournament, Arthur immediately became the Duke of Brittany and three years later his uncle RICHARD I named him as his heir presumptive to the English throne. However, as time passed the king's brother JOHN became increasingly regarded as the successor though technically the boy had a superior claim. In April 1199 John was staying in Brittany with his nephew Arthur and the boy's mother, the Duchess Constance, when news reached him that his brother King Richard had died as the result of an arrow wound received at the siege of the Castle of Chaluz. He hurried to safeguard his inheritance by hastening to Chinon to seize the royal treasury.

After attending Richard's funeral at Fontevrault Abbey, he continued to Le Mans only to find that a French army supporting Prince Arthur was about to capture the town. King Philip of France had taken over the guardianship of Arthur and sent him to Paris for safety. John retired to Normandy where there was no opposition to him taking the late king's title of duke. Soon afterwards he led a Norman army against Le Mans where he exacted his revenge by razing its castle and imprisoning its leading citizens.

In England there remained the question of whether Richard's brother John or the son of his brother Geoffrey should inherit the throne. It was largely through the support of two key figures, Hubert Walter, the Archbishop of Canterbury, and William Marshal, soon to become the Earl of Pembroke, that there was hardly any opposition when John was crowned at Westminster on 27 May.

Soon after the coronation the King divorced his childless wife Isabella and in August of the following year married the 12-year-old daughter of the Count of Angoulême, also named Isabella. Although she was a great heiress and was to bear the future HENRY III, it was an unfortunate match in that she was already betrothed to Hugh de

Lusignan, the son of the Count de la Marche. In revenge he attacked John's Poitou possessions.

Meanwhile, Philip of France had Prince Arthur betrothed to his own daughter and, declaring him to be the rightful heir to the English throne, demanded that John should compensate him by handing over his possessions in France. As John's suzerain – a paramount lord with nominal sovereignty over the ruler of an internally autonomous state – the French king commanded John to appear in Paris to surrender his French fiefs to Arthur. The summons was ignored.

On 30 July 1202 John received a message that his 80-year-old mother, ELEANOR OF AQUITAINE, was besieged at her castle at Mirebeau by Hugh de Lusignan and Prince Arthur. Mirebeau lay 100 miles away in Anjou but by hard riding John and his followers managed to reach the town and trap the besiegers between the walls of the castle and the donjon. In one stroke John had his principal opponents at his mercy. Prince Arthur was captured by William Braose who conveyed him to Falaise where he was kept in chains.

According to Roger of Wendover,

After a while, King John came to Falaise Castle and commanded that his nephew should be brought before him. When Arthur appeared, the King spoke to him with kindness, promising him many honours if he would break from the King of France and pledge his loyalty to his king and uncle. But Arthur unwisely replied with indignation and threats, demanding that the King should surrender to him the kingdom of England and all the territories that Richard had held at the time of his death. With an oath, Arthur asserted that all these possessions belonged to him by hereditary right, and that unless they were quickly restored to him, John would not enjoy much peace. The King was upset by these words, and ordered that Arthur should be removed to Rouen and kept under close guard there. Shortly afterwards, the said Arthur disappeared.

After rumours of Arthur's disappearance spread, King Philip vainly summoned John to appear in Paris to account for his prisoner and later claimed that the Supreme Court of France had found the English king in absentia guilty of murdering his nephew. Meanwhile, the Bretons, furious at the fate

Right: James VI and I, King of Scotland from 1567 and of England from 1603, the first of the Stuart kings. *(National Trust for Scotland)*

Below: Coronation procession of Charles II, 23 April 1661, by Dirck Stoop. *(Museum of London/ Bridgeman Art Library.*

Above: William III on a Grey Charger Observed by Neptune, Ceres and Flora, by Sir Godfrey Kneller. *(Christie's Images/Bridgeman Art Library)*

Right: Mary II, wife of William III and elder daughter of James II and Anne Hyde, by William Wissmig. *(Scottish National Portrait Gallery, Edinburgh/Bridgeman Art Library)*

Above: Kensington Palace.

Right: George II, by Charles Jervas. *(Guildhall Art Library, Corporation of London/Bridgeman Art Library)*

The Painted Hall at the Royal Naval College, Greenwich, by Sir James Thornhill. *(John Bethell/Bridgeman Art Library)*

The Distribution of the Premiums in the Society of Arts, by James Barry, painted *c*. 1778–1801. The Prince of Wales, a potential patron of the Society, is shown in his Garter robes. *(Royal Society of Arts/Bridgeman Art Libary)*

George III bathing at Weymouth, 1789, by John Nixon. *(Victoria Art Gallery, Bath/Bridgeman Art Library)*

Left: The Albert Memorial, Kensington Gardens.

Below: Westminster Abbey laid out in the traditional manner for Queen Victoria's coronation in 1838. *(Copyright: Dean and Chapter of Westminster)*

Interior of the Royal Mausoleum, Frogmore. *(Country Life/The Royal Collection © 2005, Her Majesty Queen Elizabeth II)*

The Regalia and Crown Jewels: St Edward's Crown, eagle-shaped Ampulla containing the anointing oil, the Sovereign's Orb, the Sceptre with Cross containing the 'Star of Africa' diamond, the Jewelled Sword of State, the Sceptre with Dove, the Armhills bracelets, the Spurs and Coronation Ring. *(Crown copyright: Historic Royal Palaces)*

Queen Elizabeth II in Westminster Abbey on the day of her coronation, 2 June 1953, photograph by Cecil Beaton. *(Bettmann/ Corbis)*

of their duke, joined with the French in invading Normandy, where many of the Norman barons preferred to open their castle gates to Philip's forces rather than defend them for John. In March 1204 Chateau Gaillard – the great bastion against the French which Richard I had dubbed his 'beautiful daughter' – fell and soon the French had control of all Normandy, and all that remained of England's Continental territories was a portion of Aquitaine.

There are several versions of Arthur's fate, none of which were ever verified. In the annals of Magram, written in a Cistercian abbey of that name whose patrons were the de Braose family, it was stated that 'after King John captured Arthur and kept him alive in prison for some time, at length in the castle of Rouen after dinner on the Thursday before Easter when he was drunk and possessed by the Devil, he slew him with his own hand, and tying a heavy stone to the body cast it into the Seine. It was discovered by a fisherman in his net, and being dragged to the bank and recognised, was taken for secret burial.'

Another version, recorded by Ralph of Coggeshall, set the scene in Falaise Castle where three executioners had been sent by John, infuriated by the success of the Bretons against him, to blind and castrate the royal prisoner. Hubert de Burgh, who had taken over command of the castle from William de Braose, refused to allow his prisoner to be harmed but reported his death to the king, hoping that the supposed loss of the duke would take the heart out of the Bretons. It had the opposite effect and when in hope of appeasing them de Burgh announced that Arthur still lived he was not believed.

This story was used by Shakespeare in his *The Life and Death of King John*. In Act IV, Scene I, Hubert and Arthur talk when Hubert shows him the order:

Hubert. Can you not read it? Is it not fair writ?
Arthur. Too fairly, Hubert, for so foul effect.
  Must you with hot irons burn out both
    mine eyes?
Hubert. Young boy, I must.
Arthur. And will you?
Hubert. I will
Arthur. Have you the heart? When your head did
    but ache
  I knit my handkercher about your brows –
  The best I had, a princess wrought it me
  And never did I ask it you again.

In the play Hubert relents and in Scene III Arthur attempts to escape, injures himself leaping from a wall and expires with this couplet:

O me! my uncle's spirit is in these stones:
  Heaven take my soul, and England keep my
    bones.

PRINCE OF WALES'S FEATHERS An almost legendary hero of the Battle of Crécy – the first major English land victory of the HUNDRED YEARS' WAR fought in 1346 – was Jean de Luxembourg, the blind King of Bohemia. When the battle turned against the French, whom the King supported with his troops, he is traditionally said to have cried out, 'I pray and beseech you to lead me into the fight that I might strike a good blow with this sword of mine.' Then, with a knight riding on either side of his destrier to guide him, and other knights linked to him by ropes, he charged into the battle where all met their chivalric deaths.

Jean de Luxembourg's emblem was a crest of three plumes attached to his helmet and Edward, Prince of Wales (the Black Prince), was so impressed by his act of valour that he adopted the blind King's insignia and his motto *Ich dien* – 'I serve'. This has remained the symbol of the Princes of Wales ever since. Today, a monument stands in the centre of the village of Crécy on which there is a medallion of the King, sword in hand on horseback, and a carving of a shield bearing his three plumes.

Jean de Luxembourg as portrayed on his monument in the village of Crécy complete with the plumes that were adopted by the Black Prince.

'PRINCESS OLIVIA' *See* HANNAH LIGHTFOOT

PROTECTOR, LORD When an under-age king ascended the throne or if a king became unfit to rule, as in the case of HENRY VI, and it was considered inappropriate to invest royal power in a regent, a Lord Protector of the Realm was appointed. Before EDWARD IV died in 1483 he named his brother RICHARD OF GLOUCESTER to be the Lord Protector and guardian of his son EDWARD V who disappeared in the TOWER OF LONDON when Richard claimed the throne, and later Edward Seymour, Duke of Somerset was appointed Lord Protector of his young nephew EDWARD VI. Richard was to die defending his crown at the Battle of Bosworth; Seymour was executed for treason. During the Interregnum the title of Lord Protector was chosen by OLIVER CROMWELL in 1653 and the period up to his death in 1658 was known as the Protectorate. His son succeeded him briefly as Lord Protector but resigned the following year.

PROVISIONS OF OXFORD *See* HENRY III

PSEUDONYM, PRINCE CHARLES'S In 1987, HRH the Prince of Wales submitted a watercolour for inclusion in the Royal Academy's annual summer exhibition. The painting was signed 'C/87'. It was entered and accepted under the pseudonym Arthur George Carrick. This pseudonym can be explained by examining the Prince's official title: His Royal Highness Prince Charles, Philip, Arthur, George, Prince of Wales, KG, KT, OM, GCB, AK, QSO, PC, ADC, Earl of Chester, Duke of Cornwall, Duke of Rothesay, Earl of Carrick, Baron of Renfrew, Lord of the Isles and Prince and Great Steward of Scotland.

Q

QUEEN REGNANT This is the designation of a queen who rules in her own right, as opposed to a 'Queen Consort' who holds her position because she is married to a king.

QUEEN'S BEASTS Armorial devices of aristocratic houses evolved from emblems – usually of the more aggressive animals – painted on the shields of knights to identify them in battle. Prior to the fifteenth century they could choose whatever they liked as their insignia, then HENRY V curtailed the custom and in 1483 EDWARD IV introduced the College of Heralds to regulate it. From such early heraldry developed the King's – now Queen's – Beasts. These statues of various animals, both natural and mythological, represent certain noble families and royal houses, and symbolise enduring majesty.

The lion has long been a symbol of English and British royalty, and it is understandable that an upright, crowned lion appears to dominate these regal creatures. A collection of the Queen's Beasts

Queen's Beasts, including the crowned lion of England, on display at Kew Gardens. (*Photograph by Simon Alexander*)

is to be seen in Kew Gardens where the insignia of the House of Windsor is inscribed on the shield of the royal griffin, originally the emblem of EDWARD III. At HAMPTON COURT PALACE a number of such beasts, or their replacements, have stood defiantly since the reign of HENRY VIII. These Hampton Court 'beasts' support shields with crests carved upon them which relate to the king and his queen Jane Seymour, both of whom delighted in such heraldic decoration.

QUEEN'S BODYGUARD OF YEOMEN OF THE GUARD Established at the beginning of HENRY VII's reign in 1485, the first duty of the Yeomen of the Guard was to attend the king at his coronation. Today the company is made up of eighty guards commanded by six officers, and remains the oldest royal bodyguard – and the oldest military corps – still functioning in the world. The Yeomen's Tudor-style uniform, with its black circular hats, white ruffs and knee-length coats, is similar to that of the Tower of London's Beefeaters, apart from the Yeomen's cross belts which were initially used to support arquebuses.

QUEEN'S CHAPEL When it was planned for CHARLES I to marry the Roman Catholic Infanta of Spain, Inigo Jones was commissioned to design a chapel where she could hear Mass in what had become a Protestant country. Standing at Marlborough Gate close to ST JAMES'S PALACE, it was to be England's first classical church, though when the wedding did not eventuate building work halted. It was revived with the arrival of QUEEN HENRIETTA MARIA who also needed a Catholic chapel in which to practise her faith, as later did CHARLES II's queen Catherine of Braganza. When WILLIAM AND MARY became joint sovereigns of Britain in 1689 the chapel saw the introduction of Dutch Reformed services which in turn gave way to German Lutheran observance for the Hanoverians.

QUEEN'S GUIDE OVER KENT SANDS One of the most naturally dangerous spots in Britain is the vast stretch of sand in Morecambe Bay. Not only are there areas of quicksand constantly on the move, but the River Kent which crosses the sands is erratic, and most threatening of all is the tide that sweeps in faster than a man can run. Logically it is a place to be avoided, yet it has been to the advantage of travellers to find their way across in order to shorten their journeys. ROBERT I ('The Bruce') of Scotland is credited with leading an army over the sands when invading England, and centuries earlier Agricola, the Roman Governor of Britain, also crossed safely with a legion.

Others were not so fortunate. In 1326 the abbot of Furness Abbey was so concerned by the loss of life on the sands that he appealed to EDWARD II for help, but in the same year the king was deposed. Later a succession of guides were employed who, by their intimate knowledge of the tides, the shifting sands and the wayward Kent, were able to lead travellers across the bay to safety.

It is known that in the sixteenth century the guide received a stipend from Furness Abbey until the Dissolution of the Monasteries. In 1540 the Duchy of Lancaster continued to pay a guide, one Richard Carter, an annual 10 marks in return for transporting travellers across the bay in his cart. The unique work of guiding remained the speciality of the Carter family, and in 1672 a William Carter requested a pay increase from the duchy on account of the cost of keeping the cart horses, coupled with the dangers of his calling. He pointed out that his father had died on the sands in an attempt to save two victims of the tide.

Today a guide continues to follow the tradition of his predecessors, escorting walkers across the bay and also taking parties out on the sands to lecture about his calling and the various types of sand that he has to contend with. His knowledge of safe routes is constantly revised as he tests them with a staff and every so often places a branch of laurel, known as a 'brob', on the otherwise invisible paths as markers.

Her Majesty the Queen continues to maintain the ancient appointment through the Duchy of Lancaster.

QUEEN'S MESSENGERS Even with today's sophisticated forms of electronic communication, the British government's most confidential messages to its embassies around the world are carried by the Corps of Queen's Messengers. This élite company began in the reign of HENRY VI when he gave the title of King's Messenger to his envoy Robert Ashewell. The service's legendary emblem of a silver greyhound goes back to HENRY VII when he chose one of the heraldic beasts supporting his coat of arms, the greyhound of Richmond, as the badge for his messengers. This was embroidered on their doublets. During the reign of Henry VIII the messengers became known as the Gentlemen of the Great Chamber in Ordinary or Extraordinary and had the status of being members of the king's household.

When CHARLES II was in exile as a result of the English Civil War, he is said to have removed the greyhounds decorating a silver dish and given them to his couriers as marks of identification. Later he ordained that the King's Messengers should wear the silver greyhound insignia suspended from their necks by blue ribands. These traditional badges of office are now worn only on special occasions.

As government ministers took over the affairs of the country from the monarchy, so control of the messengers shifted and in 1722 a number of King's Messengers were moved from the palace to the Foreign Office with the full title of the King's Foreign Service Messengers. Today it is estimated that a messenger travels an average of 250,000 miles annually, safeguarding diplomatic bags marked 'HBM Diplomatic Service', the initials standing for 'Her Britannic Majesty'.

QUEEN'S MUSIC, MASTER OF THE The lute-player Nicholas Lanier became the first official Master of the King's Musick* when he was assigned the post in 1625 by CHARLES II. Previously JAMES I had a group of musicians who performed at banquets and were known as 'the King's Music'. The musicians who have held the post since Nicholas Lanier are: Louis Grabu, appointed in 1666; Nicholas Staggins (1674); John Eccles (1700); Maurice Greene (1735); William Boyce (1757); John Stanley (1779); Sir William Parsons (1786); William Shield (1817); Christian Kramer (1829); Franz Cramer (1834); George Anderson (1848); Sir William Cusins (1870); Sir Walter Parratt (1893); Sir Edward Elgar (1924); Sir Henry Walford Davies (1934); Sir Arnold Bax (1941); Sir Arthur Bliss (1953); Malcolm Williamson (1975); Sir Peter Maxwell Davies (2004).

*This spelling was used until the appointment of Malcolm Williamson in 1975.

QUEEN'S REMEMBRANCER An ancient office that has survived since the twelfth century, and which still has practical as well as traditional roles, is that of the Queen's Remembrancer. The first man to be given the title was Richard of Ilchester during the reign of HENRY II and his remit was 'to put the Lord Treasurer and the Barons of the Court of Exchequer in remembrance of such things as were to be called upon and dealt with for the benefit of the Crown'. To put it briefly, the Remembrancer was responsible for overseeing money owed to the sovereign and later the Crown. He represented the Court of the Exchequer which later became known as the Treasury and the Inland Revenue.

Today, the office of Remembrancer is one of Britain's oldest legal institutions and though it is no longer as significant as it used to be, the Remembrancer still has a wide range of responsibilities. These range from his role as Senior Master of the Supreme Court to being in charge of the yearly scrutiny of the coinage. When a new Chancellor of the Exchequer is announced his position is not valid until he has been handed the seal of office from the Remembrancer, the custodian of the seal. When there is a change of government the Remembrancer must hasten to get the seal back from the departing Lord Chancellor so that he can bestow it upon his successor without delay, for until he does so the Treasury is unable to continue its business.

QUEEN'S WEATHER In Victorian times Queen's Weather meant a pleasant day for an outdoor occasion, as it was observed that when QUEEN VICTORIA appeared in public the weather would be fine. In Russia there was a similar notion that when the tsar appeared the sun would always shine upon him.

R

RAGNDVALSSON, ROBERT Usually known in history as 'Rollo', Robert Ragndvalsson was born in AD 860 in Norway. He was descended from the Jarls of Orkney and while he has been described as a pirate, it is true that he was an adventurer. With his Viking followers he rowed up the Seine to the walls of Paris in AD 912. Fear of the 'wrath of the Norsemen' – a fear that was widely felt in the tenth century – caused Charles III ('The Simple') to make terms with Rollo. By allowing themselves to be

Statue of Robert Ragndvalsson ('Rollo') in his home town of Alesund, a gift from Normandy. *(Photograph by Paul Abraham)*

baptised and technically becoming the king's vassals, they were given land on which to settle. Rollo was created Count of Rouen and held territory in that region, which continued to expand as the Northmen (Normans) were given more and more land in return for military aid. By the beginning of the eleventh century the Duchy of Normandy stretched from Brittany to Flanders and from the Channel to within 30 miles of Paris.

Rollo died *c.* AD 932 and was followed in succession by his descendants, the dukes of Normandy, whose names may have mirrored the history of the duchy – William Longsword, Richard the Fearless, Richard the Good, Robert the Magnificent and William the Bastard who became WILLIAM THE CONQUEROR.

REGENT'S PARK Land which included what is now Regent's Park was expropriated by HENRY VIII from the Abbess of Barking following the Dissolution of the Monasteries. Over 500 acres of it were designated as a royal hunting domain, which was enclosed by a ditch and an earthen wall to prevent the deer wandering away. Henry's son EDWARD VI used Marylebone Park – as the deer park was then called – to entertain important guests such as the French ambassador St André, and later, in 1582, ELIZABETH I hunted there in company with the Duke of Anjou. The royal connection with the park ended with the reign of CHARLES I when the king used it as collateral for the purchase of military supplies during the English Civil War.

At the close of the war the park, like all the Crown estates, was sold, the woods were felled and the land was let out to smallholders by the new owners. With the Restoration the land was returned to the Crown but it continued to be used for farming. At the beginning of the nineteenth century the expansion of the capital land resulted in a competition to be held for the development of Marylebone Park and a thoroughfare linking it to central London which was to become Regent Street.

The winning design was the work of John Nash, the Prince Regent's favourite architect, and his plan was to create a circle within a circle lined with villas and the famous 'Nash' terraces. The concept of graceful urban buildings overlooking spacious parkland was something completely new for London yet it was with great difficulty that the project was completed. Work could not be started until the end of the Napoleonic Wars and then there were difficulties both practical and economic, not least the bankruptcy of one of the main builders. For a number of years Nash was attacked harshly by his critics but during this difficult time he was defended and encouraged by the Prince Regent.

Two projected terraces at the north of the park were never built, and the area where they should have stood became the Regent's Park Zoo, while the gardens of the Inner Circle were the work of the Royal Botanic Society and later Queen Mary's Rose Garden became, and remains, one of the park's most delightful aspects. The park has been open to the public since the 1840s. Because of the encouragement the Prince Regent had given to Nash and the project, the park was named after him.

RICHARD I The life of Richard I, known down the centuries as 'Coeur de Lion', reads like a minstrel's tale. The son of HENRY II and ELEANOR OF AQUITAINE, he was born in Oxford in 1157 and at the age of 13 his mother took him to Bordeaux to be acknowledged as the future Count of Poitou. Richard's appearance matched his 'knight errant' image. He stood over 6ft tall, blue-eyed and with hair 'between yellow and red' and 'of beauty worthy of an empire'. He was admired for his physical strength and his long arms gave him an advantage when using the battleaxe, which was his favourite weapon.

His first taste of warfare came in 1173 when his mother and his elder brother Henry rebelled against his father in France. He soon proved his worth in the campaign, was knighted by the King of France and though at 16 he was no match for Henry II, he did manage to remain at large in Aquitaine, retreating from castle to castle until he was finally cornered. He then knelt at his father's feet in surrender and Henry took him back into favour.

Richard may have been a rebel but he had no mercy for those who rebelled against him, and when a revolt broke out in Aquitaine in 1176 he was in his element quelling it. The contemporary historian Girald de Barri wrote that 'fighting was the breath of his life; he was furious to rush to arms'. With his brother Henry he captured Limoges and Angoulême and then marched to the Pyrenees to crush the war lords who preyed on the pilgrims bound for Compostella.

On the death of his brother Henry in 1193 Richard became heir to the throne, but he was to fall out with his father again when the king wanted to divide his dominions in order to provide for his son JOHN. Four years later, as an ally of Philip Augustus, the new King of France, Richard was in open conflict with his father. At Chinon on 4 July 1189 they forced the old king to accept their terms. Two days later the ailing Henry II died and was interred in the abbey of Fontevrault.

As the new King, one of Richard's acts was to summon his father's advisers and in what appeared to be an act of gross ingratitude dismissed those who had supported him when he had been a rebel. Some saw it as a sign of repentance but it was more likely that Richard believed that men who had once sided with a rebel against his sovereign lord would be capable of doing so again.

In 1187 news swept Europe that Jerusalem had fallen to the Saracens under the inspired leadership of Salah-ed-din Yussuf ibn Ayub, the Sultan of Egypt and Syria and known to the West as Saladin. Christian anger was fuelled by rumours that the True Cross had been placed beneath Baghdad's

King Richard forgiving Bertrand de Gourdon, who fatally wounded him with an arrow.

main gateway so that every Muslim entering the city trod upon it. After his coronation at WEST-MINSTER ABBEY on 3 September 1189, Richard travelled to Tours where in the cathedral he was the first king 'to take the Cross', followed by his friend Philip of France. To raise money for the magnificent expedition he planned he was prepared to sell anything from castles to the Archbishopric of York, for which he received £3,000 (approximately £2,350,000 today), while the King of the Scots, who had done homage to Henry II, bought back Scotland's independence for only twice that amount. According to William of Newburgh, the king once declared he would sell London if he could find a buyer with enough money.

Prior to leaving England a match was negotiated between Richard and Berengaria, the daughter of Sancho of Navarre and a girl described as 'more learned than beautiful'. When the English and French armies reached Cyprus Richard and Berengaria were married in Limassol on 12 May 1191 and the Bishop of Evreux, who conducted the ceremony, anointed the bride as Queen of England. During the celebrations the king created a company of twenty-four knights as a guard for his new queen, in which each man wore a blue band at the knee, a forerunner of the Knights of the Garter. The crusaders then sailed to Acre where rivalry between the English and French, both wanting the honour of capturing the beleaguered Saracen garrison, resulted in the two armies mounting separate attacks. Although Richard was suffering from a local disease known as Arnoldia, which was most likely malaria, he had himself carried to the scene of the siege on a silvered litter. Then, reclining on cushions, he was able to fire crossbow bolts at the enemy.

Acre fell to the crusaders on 12 July 1191 and King Philip, piqued that in the eyes of the world the English king was outshining him, returned to France leaving the Duke of Burgundy in charge of the French army. At the same time Richard insulted Leopold, Duke of Austria by having his banner flung down when he ventured to raise it on the city's walls, declaring that only kings should raise their standards in victory.

On 22 August the crusaders began a march along the coast towards Jaffa. Tortured by thirst and heat made worse by their heavy armour, and always in danger from Saladin's whirlwind cavalry, the men struggled on, inspired by piety and Richard's leadership. Despite bad weather, disease and a shortage of food they reached Bethany 12 miles from Jerusalem, but they could go no further and fell back to Ascalon. Here the King toiled alongside his men repairing the city's fortifications. When the Duke of Austria refused to join him in this manual work an enraged Richard actually kicked him. This insult coupled with the tearing down of the ducal standard was never forgiven by Leopold.

By Easter 1192 letters from England warned Richard that his brother John was plotting to usurp the kingdom and urged his return. He was therefore eager to end the campaign quickly with the capture of Jerusalem but his plans were sabotaged by bickering between the various leaders. Disillusioned, he rode to the Fountains of Emmaus where it was possible to see the walls and domes of Jerusalem but, in despair at not being able to capture the Holy City for Christ, he held his shield before his eyes as being unworthy to look upon it.

Richard then went to Acre where he prepared to leave for England, but on 30 July word reached him that Jaffa was about to surrender Saladin. He immediately led a relief force to the city only to find that it had fallen. After a daring attack, led by the king swinging his famous battleaxe, the city was recaptured and a three-year truce was agreed with Saladin, both commanders having a chivalrous regard for each other. Thus ended the Third Crusade.

On the homeward journey Richard's ship was wrecked near Aquileia and, disguising himself as a cook, he began a long trek overland. He arrived at Vienna with his page William Marsh, who came under suspicion due to the large amount of money he was carrying when he went to buy food. He was taken before the Duke of Austria who soon learned the identity of his master, and eager to avenge the insults he had suffered on the crusade, seized Richard while he slept at an inn. At first he was imprisoned in the castle of Durrenstein on the Danube and then transferred to the castle of Trifels in the German Palatinate. The German Emperor Henry VI took charge of the prisoner from the duke with the argument that 'a duke has no right to imprison a king, that is the privilege of an emperor'.

For a time the King's whereabouts remained a mystery. One legend tells that he was found by Blondel de Nesle, a wandering troubadour, who recognised Richard's voice as he sang from his prison tower. Finally the King's ransom was set at £100,000, which Queen Eleanor raised with tremendous difficulty in England, Normandy, Anjou and Aquitaine. Then, despite being over 70 years of age, she travelled with the treasure convoy to Mainz, as she feared that John, her youngest son, might waylay it on the road. In fact a note had reached John which simply read 'The Devil is loose' which caused him to flee to France and put himself under the protection of King Philip.

On 20 March 1194 Richard arrived in England after an absence of four years and was received with joy despite the cost of his ransom, and to re-establish his authority he went through a second coronation ceremony at Winchester. He was dining in the Small Hall at Westminster when a message came that Philip of France had invaded Normandy. Richard made a vow that he would only go forward until he had defeated his erstwhile friend, and in order to keep to the letter of the oath a hole was made in the south wall of the palace through which he could set off. Then, having declared his mother regent of the realm, he left England for the last time. In France he suppressed a rebellion in Aquitaine and made a pact with Philip, which had little effect as he spent the remainder of his life at war with the French. John came to Richard to beg forgiveness, which the good-natured king readily gave, remarking that he wished he could forget his brother's crime and his brother could remember it.

In order to protect his territory he made himself a lasting monument by building the famous Chateau Gaillard overlooking the Seine at Eure. It was one of the most powerful medieval fortresses ever built and was constructed so rapidly that when it was completed in 1198 the king cried in delight, 'Behold what a beautiful daughter of one year!'

In 1199 a hoard of gold coins was found at the castle of Chaluz which was owned by the Viscount of Limoges who, as Richard's vassal, sent him half. Richard argued he was entitled to the whole amount

The ruins of Chateau Gaillard on the River Seine, built by Richard I a year before he died.
(Photograph by Mark Ronson)

and, when the viscount refused to part with another coin, he laid siege to the castle. During the operation he was struck in the shoulder by an arrow which some believed was poisoned, as the wound became infected and brought on a fever. By the time Chaluz fell Richard knew he was dying and ordered the archer who had wounded him, Bertrand de Gourdon, to be brought to him. 'What have I done to you that you would have taken my life?' the King asked from his bed. 'You have killed my father and my brother,' replied de Gourdon, 'and I hope I have killed you.' 'Youth I forgive you,' Richard said. 'Go unhurt.'

On 6 April 1199 Richard Coeur de Lion died of his wound. His last royal command was not obeyed as Bertrand de Gourdon was cruelly put to death by the King's grieving soldiers. Richard's body was interred close to his father in the abbey of Fontev-

Effigy of Richard I at Fontevrault Abbey.
(Photograph by Paul Abrahams)

rault where his effigy is still to be seen. During his ten-year reign Richard only visited his English kingdom twice, spending a total of ten months in it.

RICHARD II The son of Edward, the BLACK PRINCE and Lady Joan Plantagenet (the 'Fair Maid of Kent'), Richard II was born at Bordeaux on 6 January 1367. At the death of the Black Prince in June 1376 EDWARD III, Richard's grandfather, named him as his successor. The King died a year later and on 16 July 1377 the 10-year-old Richard was crowned at WESTMINSTER ABBEY.

The kingdom Richard inherited was in a state of unrest due to plague, heavy taxation and the disturbing ideas of the Lollards. The latter was originally a religious community established in Antwerp in 1300, but the name grew to have the same meaning as 'heretic. Not only were the powers of the Church questioned by the Lollards but the medieval social structure. Peasants began to ponder the equality of men expressed in the popular couplet: 'When Adam delved and Eve span, who was then the gentleman?'

Another anxiety was the powerful influence of JOHN OF GAUNT, Duke of Lancaster. The third son of Edward III, he was the most powerful noble in England and ambitious for the Crown. Against this background the boy king was put under the care of his mother while a council of eleven nobles was chosen to govern 'until he was of an age to know good and evil'.

Five years after his coronation Richard was to prove his regal qualities. Continuing the HUNDRED YEARS' WAR the French, in alliance with Spain and Scotland, attacked England, taking possession of the Isle of Wight and devastating areas of Kent and Sussex while the Scots invaded the northern counties.

To defend the realm taxation was increased on an already over-taxed population and in December 1380 a special shilling poll tax sparked the Peasants' Revolt when Wat Tyler led twenty

The son of the Black Prince, Richard II, in his robes of state.

RICHARD II

The crowning of Richard II at the age of ten in Westminster Abbey.

where Richard signed documents which freed them from villeinage and granted them amnesty.

In January 1382 Richard married ANNE OF BOHEMIA, a daughter of the Emperor Charles IV. The marriage brought him happiness, but his life was overshadowed by political difficulties and conspiracies. The king had to work to gain control of his kingdom from the barons and Parliament by removing members of his Council, who represented the old nobility, and replacing them with his supporters, heaping honours upon his favourites, especially his boyhood companion Robert de Vere whom he created Earl of Oxford. With no children he named his cousin Roger, Earl of March as the royal heir, which countered John of Gaunt's aspirations to the throne.

When his dreaded uncle went to claim the crown of Castile, Richard demonstrated his independence by increasing his household to ten thousand. In the royal kitchen there was a staff of three hundred and this extravagance alone outraged lords and commoners alike, while in October 1386 Parliament was further angered by the promotion of the royal favourite Robert to Duke of Ireland. The situation recalled that of EDWARD II and it was a reference to Edward's fate that checked the king, who agreed to a committee of nobles including his uncle Thomas, Duke of Gloucester to supervise the royal household. Gloucester now became the most powerful man in England while Richard was virtually deposed.

For a year the humbled king lived in retirement but before long people became dissatisfied with Gloucester's harsh rule. The 'problem' of the Lollards had grown and the faithful were anxious for action to be taken. Richard judged the time had come to strike and at midday on 13 May 1389 he strode into the Council hall at Westminster and demanded from the astonished members to be told his age. A chorus of voices answered that he was 22. 'Then I should be of no less account that any other heir in England,' he declared, 'since the law grants any man his full rights on his twenty-first year.' The king seized the Great Seal from the Chancellor and placed it in the hands of the old Bishop Wykeham, dismissed the Lords Appellant and announced he was assuming full control of the realm. The news was greeted joyously throughout England, and Richard responded by persecuting the Lollards.

In June 1394, Queen Anne died of the plague. The shock of her death unhinged the king who had

thousand rebels on London and burned down John of Gaunt's Savoy Palace overlooking the Thames. The court fled London, leaving the 16-year-old king to hold the mob. Richard sent a message direct to Wat Tyler, saying that if his followers would retire to Mile End he would go there and listen to their grievances. The meeting took place and Tyler presented the peasants' demands: the abolition of bondage, the reduction of land rent and a pardon for all past offences. Richard declared the complaints reasonable and promised to redress them by royal charter, but extremists refused to be placated.

On 15 June when Richard went to Smithfield to meet Wat Tyler for a second time, the rebel leader had new demands, including the repeal of the hated FOREST LAWS. While speaking he drew Richard aside and touched him. Perhaps it was merely a kindly gesture of reassurance but to Richard's attendants Tyler had committed the crime of laying a hand on the sovereign's person and the Mayor of London struck Tyler with a short sword. In the seconds that followed Tyler's death a flight of peasants' arrows could have altered the course of English history but Richard faced the crowd and cried, 'I am your king. I will be your captain and your leader. Follow me to the field and you shall have all you ask for!' The rebels hesitated, then were won over. A huge procession was formed and they marched behind the king to Clerkenwell Fields idolised her. He ordered her apartments at Shere to be demolished and for twelve months he was unable to enter a house they had visited together. Because the couple were childless the question of the succession was important and as he was without a direct heir Richard married Isabella, the 6-year-old daughter of Charles VI of France, in 1396. The political advantages of the marriage thwarted the Duke of Gloucester who wanted to renew the Hundred Years' War. And after meeting the French king it seemed that at last there would be a peaceful settlement between the two countries.

What Richard observed of Charles's exalted position in France stimulated his desire for absolute rule, free from meddling Parliament and bullying nobility. Inspired by these thoughts, on one occasion he signed himself 'Full Emperor of England'. He now surrounded himself with a new set of favourites who enjoyed immense power but their favours and honours added to serious popular discontent. This was fuelled by Gloucester and Arundel making political capital out of Richard's marriage settlement, by which England surrendered Cherbourg and Brest to France, and spreading the rumour that he was also about to hand over Calais.

The king had, however, achieved all his objectives when at the next Parliament at Shrewsbury, the country was virtually handed over to him with a series of articles including one which stated it was treason to renounce homage to the sovereign. New statutes retracted all the liberties that had been won over the years, and finally the members voted Richard a permanent income, making it unnecessary for any further parliaments to be called. In February 1399 John of Gaunt died and on the same day Richard deprived his absent son, Henry Bolingbroke, of his inheritance.

In July Richard was in Dublin when he received news that Henry Bolingbroke, now Duke of Lancaster, had landed in Yorkshire and was leading an army to Bristol. The King planned to take his army back to England until he learned that his uncle Edmund, Duke of York, was now supporting Henry Bolingbroke. At this point he realised his cause was lost and sent a message to Henry Bolingbroke at Chester asking his intentions. Henry answered he would meet Richard at Flint 'to implore his pardon' and escort him to London. Richard agreed and they met in the castle courtyard. 'Fair cousin of Lancaster, you are right welcome,' Richard said. Henry replied, 'The common report of the people is that for two-and-twenty years you have governed them badly and most harshly, and therefore they are not well contented with you but if it pleases our Lord I will help you govern them better than they have been governed in time past.' 'Fair cousin,' answered Richard, 'if it pleases you it pleases us well.'

A fortnight later the King was escorted to the TOWER OF LONDON and on 30 September 1399 representatives of the Lords and Commons visited the Tower for Richard's official abdication and his naming of Henry Bolingbroke as his successor. Perhaps if Richard had thus voluntarily abdicated there would have been no necessity for what immediately followed – a series of thirty-three articles of impeachment. The chief charges against the ex-king were violation of his coronation oath, the murder of Gloucester and his despotic conduct. On 13 October Henry Bolingbroke became HENRY IV and his Council ordered that Richard should be taken to a secret prison.

The death of the deposed King remains a mystery. In February his body was brought from Pontefract Castle and shown publicly in old St Paul's Cathedral where twenty thousand people filed past the coffin to see his emaciated face, the rest of the body being covered by a shroud. There is little doubt that Richard was murdered. According to tradition, the royal prisoner was at dinner in his cell when Sir Piers Exon entered with several men. Guessing their errand, Richard seized a stool to defend himself. It was said that he felled three of

The Great Seal of Richard II.

his attackers before Sir Piers knocked him down from behind and slew him. Richard was first buried in the Dominican abbey at King's Langley but later Henry V had his body removed to a tomb in Westminster Abbey.

RICHARD III A son of Richard, Duke of York, and Lady Cecily Neville, Richard III was born on 2 October 1452 at Fotheringhay Castle and was soon involved in the turmoil of the WARS OF THE ROSES. As children he and his brother George were made captive by the Lancastrians at Ludlow but were returned to their mother in London after the Yorkist victory at Northampton in 1460. Six months later their father was killed at Wakefield and the family fled across the Channel. Richard stayed at Utrecht until his elder brother, soon to be EDWARD IV, achieved a victory over the Lancastrians at Towton in May 1461.

At Edward's enthronement Richard and George were created dukes of Gloucester and Clarence respectively. Richard then joined the household of the EARL OF WARWICK, the redoubtable 'Kingmaker', at Middleham Castle in Wensleydale. The earl grew increasingly bitter over the favours Edward IV showered on the relatives of his queen Elizabeth Woodville and tried to subvert the boy dukes to his cause. In this he succeeded with George but Richard – who chose for his motto '*Layaulte me lie*' ('Loyalty binds me') – was to remain loyal to Edward despite the strains the king put upon him in later years.

Although Shakespeare depicted Richard as deformed, his feats of arms indicated he was an able soldier. At the age of 18 he led the van of the Yorkist army into battle at Barnet and soon after, clad in his white German armour, he took the leading part in routing the Lancastrians at the Battle of Tewkesbury.

After being made Great Chamberlain of England, Richard announced his intention of marrying his cousin Anne Neville, the second daughter of Warwick the Kingmaker, to whom he had been attracted since childhood. Richard's brother George, Duke of Clarence opposed the match as he was married to Warwick's eldest daughter and wanted to retain the inheritance of all of Warwick's vast possessions for himself. Richard and Anne married on 2 October 1472 and in the spring of 1476 their son Edward was born at their home of Middleham Castle, Yorkshire. Richard was given complete

The Great Seal of Richard III.

control of the north of England where he ruled almost like a king with his own Council in York, and such was his ability as an administrator that the region remained Yorkist in sympathy long after the House of York had fallen.

Before his death on 9 April 1483 King Edward named Richard in his will as Lord Protector until the royal heir Prince Edward should be of an age to rule in his own right. Richard had him lodged in the TOWER OF LONDON, then a royal palace as well as a fortress and prison, and arrangements were made for the boy's coronation on 22 June. On 13 June a meeting of the Council was held in the Tower where Bishop Morton of Ely, whose account of what happened is the only one we have, described Richard as being in a pleasant mood when the meeting opened but suddenly showed 'a wonderful sioure angrie countenance'. Richard accused both his late brother's widow and his former mistress JANE SHORE of using witchcraft to waste his body. He then struck the table with his fist and said to Lord Hastings, the Lord Chamberlain, 'I arrest thee traitor.' The bishop's account continues: '"For by Saint Paul (quoth he) I will not to dinner till I see thy head off." . . . So was he brought forth to the greene and his head laid down upon a log of timber and there stricken off.'

This was followed by the confinement of several persons Richard mistrusted – with good reason as time was to prove. Three days later, despite this drama Queen Elizabeth Woodville allowed her younger son Richard to leave the Westminster sanctuary and join Edward in the Tower. His arrival there was followed by an announcement that Edward's coronation would be postponed until November. From then on the fate of the two princes and the question of whether their uncle had them murdered remains one of the great mysteries of English history.

On 22 June a certain Friar Ralph Shaa, preaching at St Paul's on the text 'Bastard slips shall not take root', revealed a secret that had already been made known to the Council, namely that when Edward IV married Elizabeth Woodville he already had a pre-contract to Lady Eleanor Butler, the daughter of the 1st Earl of Shrewsbury, and consummation had taken place. According to the law of the time this meant that the children of Edward and Elizabeth Woodville were technically illegitimate. The Council had heard the story when Robert Stillington, the Bishop of Bath and Wells, announced that knowing of the contract between the late king and Lady Eleanor, his conscience would not permit him to see a bastard ascend the throne. Although proof that Stillington had actually married the couple has not survived, the story did seem to convince the Council and was later written into an Act of Parliament.

Bishop Stillington had been Chancellor of England and a favourite of Edward IV until the suspicious death of the King's brother Clarence, when he was suddenly imprisoned in the Tower of London and only released after taking an oath not to speak to the demerit of the king. This led to the theory that Stillington had been indiscreet enough to tell Clarence of the secret marriage. Clarence would know that the illegitimacy of his nephews would give his own son the right to inherit the throne, and it was the possession of this dangerous knowledge that was the real reason for King Edward having him killed.

If Edward IV's children were declared illegitimate the rightful heir should have been the son of the Duke of Clarence, but as he was barred by an attainder dating back to his father's death in the Tower, the next in line to inherit the throne was the late king's brother Richard of Gloucester. So, on 24 June, when peers and commons assembled for what had originally been planned as Edward V's first Parliament, a petition was presented to Richard requesting him to take his nephew's place on the throne.

Richard was crowned with his wife Anne on 6 July. He was so anxious that the ceremonial should be correct that he and Anne followed the old custom of walking barefoot from Westminster Hall to the abbey where, at the anointing, they 'put off their robes at the high altar and strode all naked from the medell upwards'. Meanwhile, the un-crowned Edward V and his brother remained in the Tower.

In September 1483 news reached Richard that the Duke of Buckingham was about to lead a rebellion. The duke, who was said to be affronted at not

A coin from the reign of Richard III.

receiving an earldom he had set his heart on, had listened to Bishop Morton's suggestion that the red and white rose feud could be solved for all time if the leading member of the House of Lancaster, Henry Tudor, won the throne and married Princess Elizabeth, the eldest daughter of the late Edward IV. Buckingham agreed to the plan and Henry Tudor, an exile in Brittany, was invited to invade England with the promised support of the Lancastrians, the Welsh and the Woodvilles. Richard acted swiftly and trapped the rebel force, which was unable to escape across the flooded Severn, while bad weather at sea prevented Henry Tudor from reaching England. Buckingham was beheaded for his part in the plot.

In January 1484 Richard held his only Parliament, which confirmed his position by an Act known as the Titulus Regis, endorsing the petition which had offered him the Crown six months earlier and gave his title authority of the Statute Book.

Soon afterwards Richard's son died at Middleham Castle. It was a heavy blow to the king both personally – he was said to have been a devoted father – and politically, as the delicate health of Queen Anne made it unlikely that he would father another child by her. This meant that yet again England could suffer from a disputed succession. Henry Tudor's supporters seized upon the opportunity to exploit Richard's problems by a propaganda campaign, and William Colyngbourne pinned to the door of St Paul's his famous couplet:

> The Cat, the Rat and Lovell our dog
> Rule all England under a Hog.

The first line referred to Richard's old friends and ministers Sir William Catesby, Sir Richard Ratcliffe and Lord Francis Lovell; the second line alluded to Richard whose emblem was a white boar. Colyngbourne was later executed for 'treasonable correspondence with Henry Tydder'.

As spring became summer Richard's spies informed him to expect a second Lancastrian rebellion. He was in Nottingham when word reached him that Henry Tudor, with two thousand mercenaries, had landed at Milford Haven on 7 August and the Welsh were flocking to his banner. In response he marched his army in the direction of Leicester and set up camp near Market Bosworth where next morning the last battle of the Wars of the Roses was fought. When the vanguards of the armies clashed, Richard ordered reinforcements from the rear but the Duke of Northumberland made no move and

Richmond Palace, which epitomised the authority of the new Tudor dynasty.

royal troops began to desert. Despite this the king rode into the fight, endeavouring to engage Henry Tudor in combat but as he neared him he was struck from the saddle with a mace blow and stabbed to death on the ground. His crown was placed on Henry's head and his mutilated body was stripped and slung over a pack horse to be carried to Leicester where it was left in a ditch for two days, an object of ridicule. It was then taken by charitable monks and interred in Greyfriars Church. Thus perished the last Plantagenet king, whose forebears had ruled over England for more than three centuries.

See also EDWARD IV and EDWARD V

RICHMOND PALACE When HENRY VII built Richmond Palace on the site of an earlier palace it was the largest and most splendid of England's royal residences, successfully underlining the power and grandeur of the new Tudor dynasty. It was situated to the west of London on the south bank of the Thames, a vital factor as it meant that the sovereign and members of the court could reach it from the capital in the comfort and comparative safety of royal barges. The original hall to stand on the site was known as Sheen and went back to the thirteenth century. It was first mentioned in history when EDWARD I met the Scottish Commissioners at Sheen where they had to acquiesce to his Ordinances for the Establishment of Government after WILLIAM WALLACE had been put to death at Smithfield in 1305.

In EDWARD II's troubled reign which followed, Sheen passed into the hands of his wife Queen Isabella. After her death her son EDWARD III made

it into one of the most outstanding royal houses in the kingdom, the work being continued enthusiastically after his death by his grandson RICHARD II. Two years after he married ANNE OF BOHEMIA in 1382 he built her a house on an island in the river opposite Sheen and provided a barge to take her to and from this retreat. Sheen was frequently used by the king and queen and their court until 1394 when Anne died of the plague at the palace. Richard was so heartbroken that he could no longer visit Sheen where they had been happy together, and he commanded that the palace and Anne's island house should be demolished.

When HENRY V came to the throne he resolved to re-create Sheen using building materials from two houses he owned but had no use for. This took the form of two manors, one being a royal residence and the other used for offices and lodging for court officials, but when he died in 1422 there was still work to be done. His son HENRY VI married Margaret of Anjou by proxy in 1444, and when she came to England the following year for a second ceremony she found that her apartments at Sheen were 'unfit for her reception'.

During the WARS OF THE ROSES the contestants for the throne had weightier matters on their minds than the refurbishment of palaces but when EDWARD IV had his turn upon the throne Sheen became part of Elizabeth Woodville's jointure. When the red rose of Lancashire was finally triumphant, Henry VII made Sheen his foremost residence, until 1497 when the palace was completely destroyed by fire. It was then that he decided to build a new palace that would symbolise the authority and majesty of the Tudor ascendancy. He also renamed it Richmond Palace as both he and his father had been the earls of 'Rychemonde' in Yorkshire.

No plans remain of Henry's magnificent palace but one aspect of it which excited admiration was the library, about which a French traveller wrote: '. . . the King of England testified his regard for literature by the establishment of a Royal Library which he formed at Richmond'. This was to establish the tradition of royal libraries, culminating in the KING'S LIBRARY which has become the priceless treasure of the British Library.

After the king died at Richmond Palace in 1509 his son HENRY VIII frequently stayed there and enjoyed taking part in tournaments on Richmond Green. CATHERINE OF ARAGON gave birth to a son at the palace on New Year's Day in 1511 and the arrival of a royal heir was greeted with jubilation by the king and his subjects. But their joy turned to bitter disappointment when the baby died on 22 February. When ELIZABETH I came to the throne she enjoyed Richmond Palace as much as her father and grandfather before her, and later in life referred to it as 'a warm winter box' which gave her shelter and comfort in her old age. When she died there in 1603 it seemed that the regal spirit of Richmond departed with her, the Stuarts seeming to have little interest in the palace loved by the Tudors. JAMES I rarely visited it and neither did CHARLES I.

During the Interregnum from 1649 to 1660, the palace fell into disrepair and although CHARLES II granted it to his brother JAMES after the Restoration, the latter's plans to have it rebuilt by Christopher Wren never materialised. His successor WILLIAM OF ORANGE took no interest in what was rapidly becoming a ruin. Today all that remains of old Richmond Palace is the gatehouse.

RICHMOND PARK Once known as Sheen Chase, the park of nearly 2,470 acres came into being in 1637 when the grounds of RICHMOND PALACE were extended by CHARLES I for hunting purposes. As a mark of appreciation for support in the English Civil War the new Commonwealth government presented it to the City of London in 1649. However, after the Restoration the City returned it to CHARLES II in 1660. Since then the closest connection between the park and royalty was when the Duke of Clarence, later WILLIAM IV, became ranger of the park and lived happily there with his mistress, the actress DOROTHEA JORDAN, and their ten children until political pressures forced him to marry Adelaide, daughter of George I, Duke of Saxe-Meiningen.

White Lodge in the park was the early home of QUEEN MARY and there in 1894 Edward, Prince of Wales and later EDWARD VIII, was born.

RIDOLFI PLOT In 1570 Roberto Ridolfi, a Florentine banker, set about organising the escape of MARY, QUEEN OF SCOTS with the encouragement of Thomas Howard, 4th Duke of Norfolk, Philip II of Spain and the pope. The plan was that Mary should be married to Norfolk and take ELIZABETH I's throne with the support of a Spanish invasion. The conspiracy was detected by

William Cecil, Lord Burghley, with the result that Norfolk was condemned to death for treason but Ridolfi managed to elude capture.

RIZZIO, DAVID Although it was love that decided MARY, QUEEN OF SCOTS, to marry her handsome cousin, Henry Stewart, LORD DARNLEY, in 1565, her affection soon turned to bitter disillusionment on account of his behaviour. His boorish animosity towards her was prompted by the fact that although he was proclaimed King after the wedding, Mary refused to grant him the crown matrimonial, which would have meant that if she died without issue the throne of Scotland should descend to his heirs. In her distress she found comfort in the company of her Italian secretary David Rizzio who, because of his Catholicism, had earned the enmity of the Protestant lords. Under the leadership of Lord Ruthven they devised a way to get rid of him and at the same time discredit the equally hated Darnley.

A document was prepared which, while it did not name Rizzio, stated that anyone who injured Darnley's honour should be dispatched. Darnley was induced to sign this and then, on the night of 9 March 1566, Darnley, with Lord Ruthven, Moray and a number of other Protestant conspirators, entered the cabinet of the Queen who was with several friends, her doctor and her doomed secretary. Realising their errand, Rizzio clung to the Queen's skirt and begged her to save him.

The author of *The Narrative of Lord Ruthven* wrote: '. . . Lord Ruthven took the Queen in his arms and put her into the King's arms, beseeching her majesty not to be afraid. And David (Rizzio) was thrown downstairs from the place where he was slain. The King's dagger was found sticking in his side.'

Rizzio's body had fifty stab wounds and during the bloody assassination Mary fainted. When she recovered consciousness James Hepburn, Earl of Bothwell, burst in and demanded an explanation. In reply Ruthven took the document with Darnley's signature from his pocket and said, 'What has been done was done in the King's name.'

ROBERT I ('THE BRUCE') OF SCOTLAND When WILLIAM WALLACE was defeated at Falkirk in 1298, EDWARD I of England could be pardoned for thinking that the question of Scottish independence was behind him, but his satisfaction

was to be of short duration. Among the nobles who had paid him homage in 1296 was Robert Bruce, born in 1274 the son of Robert de Bruce, Earl of Carrick who had accompanied Edward to Palestine in 1269. He was descended on his father's side from a Norman noble who had come to England with WILLIAM THE CONQUEROR while his mother Marjorie (or Margaret), the daughter of Walter, the Steward of Scotland, had the blood of the Celtic chiefs of Galloway. Robert's father was the Robert de Bruce who was one of the 'competitors' for the throne of Scotland following the death in 1290 of

Statue of Robert I, declared King of the Scots in 1306 at Bannockburn. (*Photograph by Paul Abrahams*)

little Queen Margaret, the Maid of Norway. Considering that it was John Balliol (*see* SCOTLAND, EARLY KINGS OF) who was finally chosen to be the Scottish king, it is understandable that both father and son took King Edward's part when Balliol fell from royal favour.

In 1295 Balliol renounced his allegiance to the English king and when Robert and his father, who had been made keeper of Carlisle Castle, continued to support Edward, Balliol retaliated by seizing the Bruces' lands at Annandale and conferring them on his adherent John Comyn, Earl of Buchan. Balliol's revolt against the English ended with him being captured and at Berwick on 7 July 1296 he formally surrendered 'crown and realm' to Edward. It was at this time that the Bruces, along with other Scottish nobles, took an oath of fealty to Edward, now King of Scotland as well as England, in the Ragman Rolls.

The following year the Scottish nobles, as vassals of Edward, were ordered to accompany him on his expedition to Flanders. This, they decided, was beyond the call of feudal obligation and along with a number of English barons ignored the summons for war service. The effect of this upon the Scots, coupled with the fact that Edward was out of England, gave William Wallace the opportunity to lead a rebellion in the cause of Scottish independence. Although Robert had sworn fealty to Edward on the host and Thomas à Becket's sword, he joined the insurrection.

Even after Wallace's defeat at Falkirk in July 1298 Robert continued his resistance until 1302 when he made his peace with Edward. His desertion from the Scottish cause greatly lessened the possibility of Balliol's return to the Scottish throne, which was no doubt part of Robert's long-term strategy to claim the Scottish throne through his descent from DAVID I (*see* SCOTLAND, EARLY KINGS OF) through David's granddaughter Isabella ('The Scot').

For the next two years he waited patiently for an opportunity to pursue his objective, possibly until he judged that Edward was close to the end of his life, and then on 10 February 1306 he met John Comyn of Badnoch at the church of the Friars Minor (Greyfriars) in Dumfries. Comyn, the nephew of Balliol and his ardent supporter, may have agreed to meet Robert to negotiate a truce between them in order to oppose Edward, but that is mere conjecture as mystery surrounds the whole incident. What is definitely known is that Robert stabbed him to death within the precincts of the church.

Robert now hurried to Scone where on Palm Sunday, 27 March 1306, the Bishop of St Andrews crowned him King of Scots.

Retribution overtook Robert for his sacrilegious act of spilling blood in a church when Pope Clement announced his excommunication. Meanwhile, King Edward learned of Comyn's death at Winchester and swore 'by God and the Swan' that he would destroy Robert and then devote the rest of his life to serving in the Crusades. He knighted his son, the future EDWARD II, and three hundred other young men in preparation for yet another campaign in Scotland. On 19 June Robert's rebel army was defeated by the king's newly appointed lieutenant, Aymer de Valence, Earl of Pembroke at Methven near Perth and he began his wanderings as a fugitive which became the stuff of legend.

Robert's family and supporters were ruthlessly hunted. His wife Elizabeth, his daughter Margaret and his sister Christina were captured when in the sanctuary of St Duthac at Tain and sent to England where they were to remain until after the Scots' victory at Bannockburn eight years later. Isabella, Countess of Buchan, and Robert's sister Mary were also captured and held ignominiously in cages. Neil, Robert's youngest brother, was executed in Berwick and the following year his brothers Thomas and Alexander, Dean of Glasgow, were

Robert the Bruce slaying John Comyn before the altar of Greyfriars Church, Dumfries.

captured, taken before King Edward in Carlisle and beheaded, their heads being mounted above the city gates. Yet, according to the *Chronicle of Lanercost*, 'the number of those who wished Bruce to be confirmed in the kingdom increased daily'.

Meanwhile, the fugitive Robert had been moving from one hiding place to another in various remote places including Arran, the Hebrides and the Orkneys. It was during this period that the story of how a spider inspired him to 'try, try and try again' originated and was destined to become an equal in royal legend to King Alfred burning the cakes.

In the spring of 1307 Robert landed at Carrick and in a surprise attack on his own castle of Turnberry defeated the English troops who were garrisoning it. This was followed by his victory over Pembroke's army at Loudon Hill.

Edward I, who had been wintering at Lanercost Priory near Carlisle, set out on his last invasion of Scotland but he never crossed the border, dying at Burgh by Sands on 7 July 1307. Despite his wish that his bones be carried at the head of the English army into Scotland, his son, the new Edward II, had other matters on his mind and did not continue the campaign.

No longer threatened by the dreaded 'Hammer of the Scots', Robert now had the opportunity to consolidate his position by attacking his Scottish rivals, defeating the Earl of Buchan, the Comyns, and the Lords of Lorne when he seized the strategic castle of Dunstaffnage. This meant that he had control of most of Scotland and in 1309 Philip of France arranged a truce between England and Scotland. A year later, despite the renewal of his excommunication by the Pope, the Church of Scotland accepted him as the rightful king. The final confirmation of his kingship was his victory over the English five years later at the BATTLE OF BANNOCKBURN, which is one of the beacons in the history of Scottish independence.

In 1312 he was in a position to complete the treaty that had been originally agreed between Alexander III and Magnus IV by which Norway ceded to Scotland the Isle of Man, the Sucheys and other islands with the exception of Orkney and Shetland.

Meanwhile, Robert's policy of taking strongholds garrisoned by the English continued until in 1314 only Berwick and Stirling Castle remained. When it was besieged its governor, Mowbray, agreed to surrender if he was not relieved by 24 June.

On 24 June, the day when the gates of Stirling Castle would have been opened to the Scots, the decisive battle was fought on the ground between the village of St Ninian and a stream known as the Bannock Burn. Although Robert was outnumbered by over three to one, he won his victory by his generalship and the fact that he knew the ground on which the battle would be joined.

One of the most important aspects of Robert's victory at Bannockburn was on 26 April 1315 when the Scottish Parliament at Ayr passed a unanimous resolution that following his demise the Crown should pass to 'the heirs male of his body, whom failing, his brother Edward, and the heirs male of his body, whom failing, on his daughter Marjorie and her heirs. . . .' As it turned out it was Marjorie, who married Walter, the High Steward of Scotland, who was to be the mother of Scotland's second king after her father, Robert II, the first of Scotland's kings to bear the surname of Stewart. Marjorie was the only issue of Robert and his first wife Isabel of Mar who died in 1302. The same year Robert married Elizabeth, the daughter of the Earl of Ulster, and by her had two sons and two daughters.

The success of the Scots in throwing off the English yoke encouraged the Celts of Ireland to follow their example and to this end Robert was offered the Irish Crown if he could lead his would-be subjects to independence. He declined the proposition but in May 1315 his brother Edward, an outstanding and ruthless soldier, arrived at Carrickfergus with an army of six thousand and began a campaign so brilliant that it has been said that at the time it seemed possible the line of Bruce might supplant that of the Plantagenets. On 2 May 1316 Edward was crowned King of Ireland though much of the country remained under the control of the English, and in 1317 Robert, who had subdued the Hebrides the previous year, crossed to Ireland with his army to help his brother. After defeating an Anglo-Irish army at Slane in Louth, the Scots marched remorselessly to the south to take Limerick and would have taken Dublin as well had not its inhabitants put it to the torch.

The appointment of Roger Mortimer to take control in Ireland stiffened the resolve of the English so that the Scots, whose success had been so fast that they had not had time to consolidate their gains, had to retreat to Ulster. On 14 October 1318 Edward was killed at the Battle of Dundalk.

Robert had returned to Scotland before this defeat of Irish hopes, to continue his reign of seemingly endless warfare. The English had taken advantage of his absence in Ireland to resume border fighting and added to this was the galling fact that Berwick was still an English stronghold and a symbol of the country's past subjugation.

In March 1318 the town, which had withstood Robert's siege during the winter, was captured, and a few days later the castle surrendered. Putting Walter the Steward in charge of it, Robert invaded and laid waste the north of England.

The feeling of King Robert's subjects towards him was made evident in 1320 when a Scottish Parliament wrote to the Pope offering to give him aid with a crusade in return for his recognition of Scotland's independence. Part of the letter read: 'He [Bruce] like another Joshua or Judas Maccabeus, gladly endured trials, distresses, the extremities of want, and every peril to rescue his people and inheritance out of the hands of the enemy. . . . To him in defence of our liberty we are bound to adhere . . . We fight not for glory, wealth or honour, but only for that liberty which no true man relinquishes but with his life.'

For the next few years hostilities between Scotland and England continued. Then, following Edward II's murder in 1326, Robert was approached by English commissioners proposing peace between the two countries and at a Parliament held at York in February 1328 it was agreed that Scotland 'according to its ancient bounds in the days of Alexander III, should remain to Robert king of Scots and his heirs and successors free and divided from the kingdom of England'. In April the Parliament of Northampton concluded the treaty by which there was finally peace between the two kingdoms. It was agreed that Joan, the 7-year-old daughter of the late Edward II and sister of Edward III, should marry Robert's 4-year-old son and heir David. The marriage of these children was performed at Berwick on 17 July 1328. Three years later, on 24 November 1331, Joan was crowned Queen Consort at Scone Abbey, Perthshire, and was the first Scottish queen consort to be thus honoured.

Eleven months after the marriage of his infant son to the little English princess, Robert I of Scotland died of leprosy at Cardross on 7 June 1329. At his dying request his heart was removed and entrusted to his old comrade, Sir James Douglas, with the injunction it should be embalmed and taken to the Holy Land and buried in Jerusalem. His body was buried beside his wife Elizabeth in Dunfermline Abbey. Sir James Douglas – the Black Douglas – set out for Palestine following the late king's wishes but while in Spain he was killed fighting the Moors. The royal relic was brought back to Scotland where it was finally interred in Melrose Abbey.

ROBERT II OF SCOTLAND When David II of Scotland died childless in 1371 the throne did not go to an English prince as the late king had suggested but to Robert, the son of James, the 6th High Steward of Scotland, and Marjorie, the only daughter of ROBERT I ('The Bruce'). He was born at Paisley in 1316, and after reaching manhood he twice acted as Regent of Scotland during the reign of his uncle David, the second time for the eleven years when King David was a 'captive' at the English court.

When Robert was crowned at Scone Abbey in 1371 he was the first king of the royal line of

Monument at the site of the Battle of Otterburn.

The Scottish House of Stewart

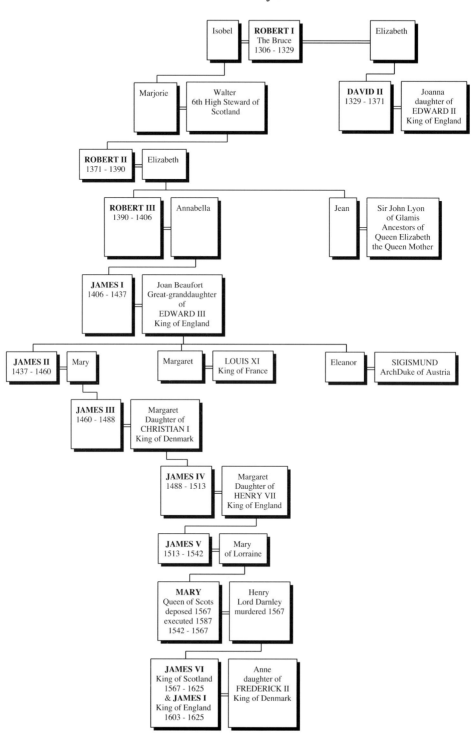

Stewart, the name coming from the word Steward which had been part of his father's title. It was his aspiration to bring peace and prosperity to his kingdom and in this he believed he would be free of outside influence as England was deeply involved in the HUNDRED YEARS' WAR. Unfortunately for the king there were barons who regarded themselves as noble as he and who brought about what was known as 'Scotland's bane', the conflict between the nobility and the sovereign which was to bedevil the country for many generations. Apart from their bloody quarrels among themselves when, according to one chronicler, 'justice was sent into banishment', their raiding of the 'debatable' land of the border created such misery and devastation it was inevitable that the country would suffer from reprisals.

Although Robert was now too old for battle, he used the younger members of the nobility to win back Scottish lands which had been occupied by the English. In 1377 he was confident enough to ignore payments due to England which had been incurred by agreeing to the huge ransom demanded for the late David II. Meanwhile, in England RICHARD II succeeded EDWARD III and before long was to prove a new threat to Scotland.

Due to the conflict on the border caused by re-prisal and counter-reprisal, open warfare became an inevitability and in 1384 a General Council, no doubt in consideration of the king's age, withdrew his control of justice and conferred it upon his son John.

The following year King Richard of England led an army into Scotland and razed Edinburgh. Inevitably the Scots sought revenge and in the summer of 1388 a two-pronged campaign was undertaken in which one army marched on Carlisle in the west and the other, under the command of James, Earl of Douglas, reached Durham, ravaging the countryside as it went, before being forced to retreat under the threat of HENRY PERCY, known in history as 'Hotspur'. He and his men overtook the Scots late on 15 August 1388 at Otterburn; fighting began immediately and continued after nightfall in a number of single combats. In reality Otterburn was little more than a border encounter but it gained fame through the ballads it inspired, the best known being 'Chevy Chase'. The Scottish commander Douglas was slain during the fighting and Henry Percy was captured.

Less than two years after Otterburn Robert died on 19 April 1390 at Dundonald Castle in Ayrshire and was buried in Scone Abbey. His son John

changed his name to Robert and succeeded him as ROBERT III.

Robert II had ten children by his first wife Elizabeth, whom he married in 1336, and four by his second wife Euphemia whom he wed in 1355. He also had eight illegitimate children by mostly unknown mothers.

ROBERT III OF SCOTLAND When ROBERT II died in 1390 the Scottish Crown went to his son John who, on becoming king, changed his name to become Robert III. He had been born *c.* 1337 and was created Earl of Carrick in 1368. His coronation was held at Scone Abbey on 14 August and the following day his wife Queen Annabella was crowned Queen Consort. Five years earlier he had received a crippling kick from a horse from which he never fully recovered, and referring to this he has been quoted as saying, 'I am the worst of kings and the most wretched of men.' Because of his poor health he allowed much of the government to pass into the hands of his ambitious brother Robert who in 1398 was created Duke of Albany.

The bickering between the Scottish nobles that had so darkened the previous reign continued and in 1399 it was obvious that the king's ill health made it difficult for him to restrain 'trespassers and rebellers' and he agreed to the kingdom being ruled by a regent, a state of affairs that in fact was to last for twenty-five years. The first regent appointed to take over the responsibility of the troubled kingdom for a three-year period was Robert's 20-year-old son David who was made Duke of Rothesay at the same time. Though he earned a reputation for licentious-ness, the young regent proved to be energetic in his duties until he was removed from office in a coup in which his uncle Robert, Duke of Albany, played a leading part. He was imprisoned at Falkland where he suffered an unknown fate. While some believed he had died as a result of dysentery, it was generally thought that Albany had starved him to death, though no proof of this was ever produced. The disappearance of the king's son meant that Albany was now the most powerful noble in Scotland and as such he took control of the kingdom as regent.

Following the Battle of Otterburn in 1388 there had been a truce along the border lands between Scotland and England. This ended when a small skirmish occurred at Nisbet Moor in which HENRY PERCY, the eldest son of the Earl of Northumber-land, and nicknamed 'Hotspur', got the best of the encounter. In retaliation an army of Scots entered Northumberland led by Archibald, 4th Earl of Douglas, who earned the sobriquet of 'the Tyneman' ('The Loser') due to the fact he was on the unsuccessful side of a number of battles. After ravaging the countryside the Scots were on their return march when their retreat was blocked by Hotspur near Wooler and a battle was fought at Homildon Hill on 14 September 1402, where English archers won the day with their deadly arrow fire.

The capture of Douglas by the English, along with a number of powerful nobles, strengthened the position of Albany as uncrowned King of Scotland as it removed potential opponents. Only too well aware of how ruthless his brother could be in eliminating political rivals, King Robert became anxious for the safety of his younger son and heir James. When a rumour reached him in 1406 that Albany was scheming to get him out of the way by giving him to the English, the king arranged for the 11-year-old boy to travel to France where he believed he would be safe from Albany's plotting. Off Flamborough Head the ship carrying James fell prey to English pirates who handed him over to HENRY IV of England, who held him as a hostage in the TOWER OF LONDON. News of this proved to be too much for the infirm and unhappy King Robert who died within a fortnight of it reaching him.

ROSES, WARS OF THE Known in their times as the 'Cousins' War', the Wars of the Roses were a dynastic struggle between the Houses of York and Lancaster from 1455 to 1487. The red rose was the symbol for the Lancastrians, the white rose for the Yorkists. The conflict began with a struggle for control of the royal government and escalated to a contest for the throne. In 1455 a Yorkist rebellion against HENRY VI was led by the Duke of York. Soon after claiming the throne for himself in 1460 the duke was killed at the Battle of Wakefield and his son EDWARD IV became king. In 1469 WARWICK THE KINGMAKER switched to the Lancastrian side, rebelled against Edward and restored Henry VI. Edward rallied, defeated the Lancastrians at the battles of Barnet and Tewkesbury, resumed the throne and lived out the rest of his reign in relative peace.

When he died in 1483 his young son Edward V was declared to be illegitimate and the late King's brother RICHARD was crowned in his place. HENRY TUDOR was now the head of the House of Lancaster and in August 1485 his forces defeated the Yorkists at the BATTLE OF BOSWORTH where Richard, the last Plantagenet king, was killed. Henry Tudor now became HENRY VII and married Elizabeth, the daughter of Edward IV in a gesture to unite the two Houses and symbolised by Elizabeth carrying a bouquet of red and white roses at her wedding.

The final act of the Wars of the Roses was in 1487 when King Henry defeated an invasion by Yorkist diehards led by the imposter LAMBERT SIMNEL at the Battle of Stoke.
See also EDWARD IV, HENRY VI, RICHARD III and WARWICK, RICHARD NEVILLE, EARL OF

ROUND TABLE Known as King Arthur's Round Table, a circular tabletop is mounted on a wall in Winchester Castle which Malory believed was once Camelot. The table is constructed of oak and measures 18ft across and has room for twenty-four seats. It is thought to go back to the thirteenth century, and during the reign of HENRY VIII it was decorated with the 'sieges' and names of Arthur's knights. In the centre was painted a Tudor rose to emphasise the claim by the Tudors that their house went back to the Pendragons.

ROYAL ARCHIVES The official and personal correspondence of the monarchy going back over the last two-and-a-half centuries is stored in the Round Tower at WINDSOR CASTLE. Under the supervision of the Keeper of the Royal Archives, it includes such items as the diaries of QUEEN VICTORIA and GEORGE V as well as the administration records of the departments of the Royal Household. Researchers are allowed access to the archives and there is an information service available for members of the general public.

ROYAL ASCOT The traditional appearance of the sovereign at the June Ascot race meeting goes back to 1711. However, the custom of the royal drive round the racecourse in an open carriage drawn by the famous Windsor greys and bays was originated by GEORGE IV. Today, after the drive, the sovereign watches the events from the royal box, while for the spectators the day is a time-honoured spectacle of high fashion.

ROYAL BURIAL GROUND *See* ROYAL MAUSOLEUM

ROYAL COMPOSERS Music was associated with most royal courts, ranging from the songs of troubadours particularly favoured by ELEANOR OF AQUITAINE, to music for masques and dances. The Chapel Royal – originally a body of clergy and musicians rather than a building – goes back to the twelfth century and is credited as being more influential in promoting English music down the centuries than any other institution. RICHARD III was so enthusiastic over the chapel's music that he empowered its members to visit cathedral choirs across the kingdom and take the most promising singers to join the élite group.

The pious HENRY VI is probably one of the earliest royal composers whose church music is still in existence. HENRY VIII, who played a number of instruments, was another king who composed Masses, though none of them are extant. Although there is some doubt over the authorship, the anthem 'O Lord, Maker of All Things' has been attributed to him. A more secular composition entitled 'Passtyme with Good Compayne' is his work, as are several other pieces for voices and viols. The well-known song 'Greensleeves' is said to be the work of the king and is referred to in Shakespeare's *Merry Wives of Windsor*. During the English Civil War the tune was popular with the Royalists who set their own political verses to it.

Music was part of the education of PRINCE ALBERT, consort of QUEEN VICTORIA, and as a result he was both an accomplished organist and composer. Some of his music was published and a Morning Service he composed is still to be found in cathedral choir libraries, while anthems he wrote were sung in WESTMINSTER ABBEY for the celebration of both Queen Victoria's jubilees.

ROYAL DUTIES Probably no monarch in the past undertakes as many official engagements as Her Majesty Queen Elizabeth. In the year up to April 2004 members of the royal family undertook 2,900 official engagements, 487 of these being carried out by the Queen. Apart from diplomatic functions, the Queen held twenty-seven investitures for 2,900 people and 9,000 guests, and hosted six garden parties with a total attendance of 37,000.

ROYAL EPIPHANY GIFTS As the name suggests this is a ceremony connected with the monarch and is enacted to commemorate the Gifts of the Magi on the Feast of the Epiphany (6 January) in the Chapel Royal at ST JAMES'S PALACE, London. Begun during the reign of GEORGE II, it used to be performed by the sovereign in person but since the days of the Prince Regent the role has usually been performed by the Lord Chamberlain. Today, two gentlemen ushers present three purses representing the gifts of gold, frankincense and myrrh during the offertory. These purses now contain money which is afterwards donated to the poor of the parish.

ROYAL EVENTS The royal family traditionally sees in the New Year at Sandringham.

6 January: The Royal Epiphany service is held at the Chapel Royal, St James's Palace.

February: During this month official overseas tours are arranged and investitures are held at Buckingham Palace.

March: Official overseas tours are undertaken.

March/April: The Royal Maundy service is held on Maundy Thursday.

21 April: The Queen's Birthday.

May: During this month state visits are made in the United Kingdom and there is a traditional visit to the Chelsea Flower Show.

June: Trooping the Colour is held at Horse Guards Parade, London, on the first or second Saturday of the month. Royal Ascot is held in the middle of the month, as is the Garter Ceremony at Windsor Castle.

10 June: Prince Philip's Birthday.

July: Early in the month the Thistle Ceremony is held at St Giles Cathedral, Edinburgh, followed by Buckingham Palace garden parties.

Summer: Traditionally the royal family spends a summer holiday at Balmoral.

September: A royal visit to the Braemar Highland Games.

October: Official overseas visits are undertaken.

November: During the month investitures are held at Buckingham Palace. Early in the month is the State Opening of Parliament and on the Saturday nearest to the 11th is the Festival of Remembrance at the Albert Hall with the Cenotaph ceremony the next day. Towards the end of the month the Royal Variety Performance is held.

14 November: The birthday of Charles, Prince of Wales.

December: Traditionally the royal family celebrates Christmas at Windsor Castle.

ROYAL FINANCES Official expenditure for Her Majesty the Queen as Head of State and Head of the Commonwealth is met by the Civil List. The up-keep of royal palaces and the cost of royal transport is provided by Grants-in-Aid from Parliament and, being official expenditure, is not taxed. The traditional income for the Queen's public use comes from the Privy Purse and is taxed, as is her personal income, which meets all her private expenditure. The Duchy of Lancaster, held in trust for the king or queen since 1399, provides part of Her Majesty's personal income. State money is not provided for the Prince of Wales. His income, which pays for public and private commitments, comes from the annual net surplus of the Duchy of Cornwall.

ROYAL FLAGS The royal standard is flown over a royal palace to indicate that the sovereign is in residence and it is also displayed on the sovereign's vehicle when on official journeys. It is a tradition that the royal standard is never flown at half-mast when a king or queen dies, the Union flag or the royal coat of arms of Scotland being used as a token of mourning. In 1960 the Queen's own flag was introduced which is displayed in the same manner as the royal standard, but cannot be used by other members of the royal family.

ROYAL GHOSTS The earliest English king said to have left a supernatural legacy is WILLIAM II, the unpopular Red King who met a mysterious death on 2 August 1100 in the New Forest. There his hunting party split up and the king found himself alone in a glade with Sir Walter Tirel. The next time he was seen he was lying dead, transfixed by an arrow. William's younger brother HENRY raced to Winchester to seize the royal treasury, knowing that his claim to the throne depended on being supported by cash. The dead king was left lying where he had fallen until a charcoal burner named Purkiss transported the body to Winchester on his cart, leaving a trail of blood through the forest.

Today the spot where the king met his mysterious fate is marked by a monument known as the Rufus Stone and it was here that, according to an old tradition, the Red King returned on the anniversary of his death before following the path that ten centuries ago was marked with his blood. Another anniversary manifestation was connected with the site of Castle Malwood which the king had used as a hunting lodge. Here a pond was credited with turning crimson on 2 August because Tirel paused here to wash blood off his hands – the legend ignoring the fact that an assassin's hands do not get stained if he shoots his victim with an arrow.

The next king to be associated with supernatural phenomena was EDWARD II though it is not his phantom that returns but that of his favourite, Piers Gaveston, who has haunted the ruins of Scarborough Castle where he was executed by the king's enemies in 1312.

The spectre of Queen Isabella ('The She Wolf of France') is said to appear running wildly on the ramparts of Castle Rising in Norfolk where EDWARD III banished her for her part in the downfall of his father EDWARD II. The other ghost connected with Edward II's unhappy reign is that of ROGER MORTIMER whose footsteps have been heard in the Trip to Jerusalem, which claims to be England's oldest inn, and which is partly hewn in the rock upon which Nottingham Castle was built. Mortimer, the paramour of Isabella, had ordered the ghastly murder of the abdicated Edward. When young Edward III reached manhood he arrested him and he was held in a natural chamber close to the inn's cellars before being taken to London where he became the first person to be hanged at Tyburn. His aural manifestation is restless pacing within a confined space, echoing from the rock dungeon still known as Mortimer's Hole.

Hall Place, near Bexley in Kent, was once used by the BLACK PRINCE, the eldest son of Edward III, as he prepared to campaign in France. The traditional explanation for rare appearances of his phantom at Hall Place is that it is a warning of some danger threatening either England or the owners of the manor. Wearing the black armour that gave him his name, his phantom has usually been glimpsed at twilight, accompanied by distant medieval music.

In 1483 the uncrowned boy king EDWARD V and his younger brother RICHARD were taken to the TOWER OF LONDON, after which their fate remains a mystery. Their uncle RICHARD III was crowned in Edward's place and it is widely assumed that he gave orders for the boys to be smothered. Over the past five centuries there have been glimpses of their pathetic wraiths in the Bloody Tower where they were supposed to have been murdered.

Queen ANNE BOLEYN's story has so caught the popular imagination down the centuries that it was not surprising she holds a prominent place in English ghostlore. On 15 May 1536 Anne was found guilty of high treason and four days later she was executed on Tower Green within the precincts of the Tower of London. Her body, said to have been placed in an ordinary arrow chest instead of a coffin, was interred in the Chapel Royal of ST PETER AD VINCULA where her spectre has been reported as walking down the aisle at the head of a phantom promenade. Her other appearances at the Tower were on the Green where she had been beheaded. Bollin Hall in Cheshire has been put forward as the birthplace of the queen and no doubt accounts of her ghost being sighted there supported the claim, but most authorities cite Blickling Hall in Norfolk as being her birthplace. The hall is the setting for her most dramatic reappearance which traditionally occurs on the anniversary of her execution. The manifestation takes the form of a spectral coach containing the queen, which drives up the avenue to the main door of the old red-brick house where it then vanishes. According to some accounts the queen, her coachman and the four horses are headless. The folklorist Christina Hole wrote: 'The occupants of the hall are so used to her annual appearance that they take little notice of her.'

In November 1541 HENRY VIII's fifth queen CATHERINE HOWARD was accused by ARCH-BISHOP CRANMER of having sexual relations with a relative before she married the king, and as a result she was beheaded the following February. When she was arrested at HAMPTON COURT she managed to break free from her captors and run along a gallery, to this day known as the Haunted Gallery, to the chapel where the King was at prayer. She hammered on the door and screamed for mercy but apparently Henry did not allow his wife's cries to interfere with his devotions and Catherine was dragged away by Yeomen of the Guard. In the past it is claimed the queen's ghost has been seen, and heard, re-enacting this pitiful scene on the anniversary of her arrest. Some who have seen the phenomenon described her as a figure running frantically with her hair streaming behind her before she 'dissolved'.

The ghost of JANE SEYMOUR, Henry's third queen is that seen at Marwell Hall in Hampshire for it was there in May 1536 that she married the king secretly in one of the upper rooms. Later at Hampton Court she bore a sickly son who lived to become EDWARD VI but she died seven days after the birth. According to tradition her phantom, dressed in white and carrying a candle, has been seen to glide from the old Queen's Apartments, through the Silver Stick Gallery and downstairs into the Clock Court.

Another of Henry's wives to find a posthumous place in English folklore was CATHERINE OF ARAGON. After Henry's history-making divorce from her, she spent the last two years of her life at Kimbolton Castle in Huntingdonshire. After her death in 1536 the castle was said to have been revisited by her spectre on numerous occasions. At the beginning of the eighteenth century part of the building collapsed but the Queen's Chamber remains intact and it was here Catherine would supervise the cooking of her food as she lived in fear of being poisoned.

The next in the line of royal Tudor ghosts is LADY JANE GREY whose ill-fated reign lasted nine days. After the death of EDWARD VI in 1553, she was presented to the Council by her husband Guildford Dudley who claimed that the late king had named her as his successor. The Council accepted his statement but thirteen thousand supporters of Henry VIII's daughter MARY marched with her from Framlingham Castle into London where she was proclaimed the rightful queen. The next year, fearing that Jane Grey, who was under house arrest, could be a focal point for rebellion Queen Mary ordered her execution, which was carried out on 9 February 1554. Like Anne Boleyn she was buried in St Peter ad Vincula which is the setting for her occasional reappearances, the last being reported in 1957.

The last of the House of Tudor ghosts was Queen Mary whose apparition has been seen at Sawston Hall which she rebuilt for her staunch supporter John Huddlestone after the original was razed by the Duke of Northumberland who supported Lady Jane Grey.

After Tudor times royalty became less likely to provide ghosts and the last Stuart phantom was that of the Young Pretender, PRINCE CHARLES EDWARD, whose phantom has been seen in the Country Hotel, Dumfries, where he stayed in 1745 in what is now known as Prince Charlie's room.

GEORGE II, who was Elector of Hanover as well as King of Great Britain and Ireland, was the final royal phantom. Like his father he preferred his Continental territory to that of Britain, and as he lay dying at KENSINGTON PALACE in October 1760 his main anxiety was caused by delay in the arrival of dispatches from Hanover. This was because the wind was in the wrong direction, making it impossible for the ship bringing the courier to cross the Channel. Through the window of his apartment the king watched a weather vane in the shape of a bird in the hope of seeing the wind change and complained, 'Vy don't dey come?' When the wind did change and the dispatches subsequently arrived it was too late, and since then the king's phantom is said to have been seen at Kensington Palace gazing upwards at the weather vane.

ROYAL GUN SALUTES A 41-gun salute is fired in Hyde Park at noon by the King's Troop, Royal Horse Artillery, on the following occasions: Accession Day (6 February), Her Majesty the Queen's Birthday (21 April), Coronation Day (2 June) and His Royal Highness the Duke of Edinburgh's Birthday (10 June). When an occasion falls on a Sunday it is normally held on the following day. Gun salutes also take place for TROOPING THE COLOUR and the STATE OPENING OF PARLIAMENT. The gunners use six quick-firing 13-pounders.

ROYAL HERB STREWER For much of its long history London suffered from malodorous air due to a large population living in close proximity, with only the most rudimentary system of sanitation. The tainted air was no respecter of rank and palaces were as likely to suffer from unpleasant odours as any other dwelling in the city. After the Restoration CHARLES II introduced the custom of herb strewing. This was performed by women employed to move through passages and apartments of the royal household, scattering herbs and sweet-smelling petals in the belief that if smells could not be eradicated, at least they could be disguised. Bridget Rummy was the first Royal Herb Strewer who began her fragrant work in 1660, for which she was paid £24 per year plus 6ft of red cloth for her official livery. It was a generous payment for the seventeenth century, which suggests how much her occupation was valued.

When GEORGE IV became king in 1820 improvements in the city's drainage system meant that herb strewers were no longer necessary, but as he planned to have the most lavish coronation in the history of the British monarchy, he included the

tradition of herb strewing in the ceremonial. Under the command of Anne Fellows, the Royal Herb Strewer of the day, six pretty young women scattered aromatic herbs and exotic blooms from silver gilt baskets along the carpet leading from the PALACE OF WESTMINSTER to WESTMINSTER ABBEY. A newspaper report stated later that 'a more interesting or lovely group was never exhibited on any occasion'.

ROYAL HOSPITAL In 1682 CHARLES II founded the Royal Hospital at Chelsea as a home for soldiers of the regular army who were no longer fit for military duty after twenty years of service, or were incapacitated as a result of wounds. The idea of providing such men with a place to live and be cared for rather than paying them pensions is thought to have been inspired by the Hôtel des Invalides which had been established in Paris by Louis XIV twelve years earlier. The king commissioned Sir Christopher Wren to design the building which, with additions, was completed in the reign of WILLIAM and MARY.

It was Charles's idea that the In-Pensioners should be organised on a military pattern with a governor and appropriate officers, and this system has continued to the present time. Today there are six companies of In-Pensioners whose scarlet coats and tricorn hats are based on the design of service dress in Marlborough's army.

ROYAL HOUSEHOLD Divided into six departments and employing a staff of more than six hundred, the Royal Household is under the direction of the Lord Chamberlain. He is appointed by the sovereign and it is his responsibility to ensure the smooth running of his or her duties. His insignia of office is a key and a white staff, which traditionally he breaks over the grave of a newly deceased sovereign to symbolise the end of that particular Household.

The departments of the Royal Household are:

THE MASTER OF THE HOUSEHOLD'S DEPARTMENT This office is responsible for the staff, catering arrangements and entertainment at Buckingham Palace and organises royal travel.

THE PRIVATE SECRETARY'S OFFICE The Private Secretary acts as the link between the sovereign and the Government.

THE PRIVY PURSE AND TREASURER'S OFFICE The Keeper of the Privy Purse is responsible for the management of the sovereign's finances. The name comes from the symbolic purse that the Keeper carries at the coronation service.

LORD CHAMBERLAIN'S OFFICE This office, which is separate from the Lord Chamberlain himself, has a number of duties which range from overseeing the royal swans on the River Thames to the organisation of state visits to Britain and other royal functions such as the State Opening of Parliament, investitures, and garden parties. The office is also responsible for royal warrants, matters of protocol and the overseeing of the CROWN JEWELS.

THE ROYAL COLLECTIONS DEPARTMENT Under the administration of the Director of the Royal Collection, the Surveyor of the Queen's Pictures, the Surveyor of the Queen's Works of Art and the Royal Librarian maintain the art treasures that have been collected by British royalty.

THE CROWN EQUERRY'S DEPARTMENT The function of this office is to organise royal transport and to maintain cars and carriages at the Royal Mews.

ROYAL HOUSEHOLD, COST OF In the year up to April 2004 the cost of maintaining the Royal Household was £36.8 million, which is the equivalent of 61p per head of the population of the United Kingdom. Included in the most expensive items of expenditure, the wages of household staff accounted for £7.1 million; travel, £4.7 million; garden parties, £514,000; housekeeping and furnishings, £488,000; ceremonial functions, £196,000.

ROYAL MARRIAGES ACT In 1772 GEORGE III had the Royal Marriages Act passed in Parliament, making it unlawful for any member of the royal family under the age of 25 to marry without the consent of the king. Any such marriages would be nullified. The King was no doubt prompted to do this by the marriage of his brother Henry, Duke of Cumberland, who was alleged to have privately married Olivia Wilmot and had a daughter who became known as Princess Olivia of Cumberland. In 1771 Henry did marry – perhaps bigamously – Anne, the daughter of the 1st Earl of Carhampton. King George must have also had in mind the rumours that when he was 21 in 1759 he had secretly married HANNAH LIGHTFOOT, which made him aware of the scandal that an unsanctioned marriage could generate. When his son GEORGE, PRINCE OF WALES, flouted the Act by marrying MARIA FITZHERBERT secretly in 1785 the marriage was invalid under British law, but as Mrs Fitzherbert was a Roman Catholic it was recognised by the Pope.
See also GEORGE IV, FITZHERBERT, MARIA, LIGHTFOOT, HANNAH, MARRIAGES ACT

ROYAL MAUSOLEUM Not long after their marriage QUEEN VICTORIA and Prince Albert decided that when they died they did not want to be buried in WESTMINSTER ABBEY or ST GEORGE'S CHAPEL but have their own special mausoleum. Soon after Prince Albert's death

The Royal Mausoleum at Frogmore, Windsor, which was built specially for Queen Victoria and Prince Albert.

in 1861 the grieving queen chose a site for the mausoleum in the grounds of Frogmore House, Windsor. The design was entrusted to Ludwig Gruner, though much reflected the interest that the queen and her eldest daughter Victoria took in the construction of the Romanesque-style building and the ornamentation of its interior. The result remains an amazing example of Victorian design and decoration. Construction work began in March 1862 and the fabric was completed quickly, though it was not until nine years later that the intricate decoration was completed. The entire cost of the mausoleum was paid for by Victoria from her private purse.

The building, in the form of a Greek cross, has a diameter of 70ft and is constructed of Portland stone and granite brought from different parts of the kingdom, while Australian copper sheaths the dome. Two bronze angels guard the entrance which has two sets of gates, the outer of bronze and the inner of brass.

In 1868 the body of the prince was translated from St George's Chapel to the tomb in what is known as the Central Octagon below a dome which rises to 70ft from the marble floor. Standing on a base of black marble, the sarcophagus is fashioned from the world's largest single block of unblemished worked granite. Resting on it are the recumbent effigies of the prince and his beloved Victoria which are magnificent examples of realistic sculpture. It is surrounded by what could be described as a 'time capsule' of nineteenth-century art – paintings, mosaics, stained glass and sculpture. The latter includes four statues of Biblical personages – Daniel, David, Isaiah and Solomon standing in niches – and the figures of the royal couple in Anglo-Saxon dress with Victoria holding Albert's hand and looking devotedly up at him.

The walls of the Octagon, from its inlaid floor to the dome, are lined with red Portuguese marble in which are set designs in coloured marbles brought from various European countries, North America and Africa. The vaulting ribs of the dome are decorated with angels while the inner surface has more angels holding wreaths against a backdrop of clouds and stars. Radiating from the ambulatory which encircles the Octagon are four chapels whose arched ceilings are decorated with paintings and bas-relief panels. Busts of some of Victoria's children and relatives are placed in the ambulatory, as is a memorial tablet to her Scottish retainer John Brown.

In 1928 a piece of land to the south-west of the mausoleum was consecrated as a private burial ground for members of the royal family. It is overlooked by a statue of Christ which was the gift of Queen Alexandra as a tribute to 'the best and greatest of Sovereigns and the kindest of mothers-in-law'. Among those who have been buried there are three of Victoria's children and EDWARD VIII and his wife the Duchess of Windsor. The burial ground is private but once a year in May the Royal Mausoleum is open to the public for a day.

ROYAL MEWS Situated close to BUCKINGHAM PALACE in Buckingham Palace Road, the Royal Mews began as the Riding House which was built in 1736 and ninety years later the Mews themselves were completed. Apart from stabling the Queen's coach horses, of which twenty are bays and ten are greys, the Mews houses twenty royal cars and seventy carriages which range from state coaches to phaetons, all of which are in perfect working order. The Mews is one of the sights of London and the main attraction is the Gold State Coach which was made for GEORGE III at the beginning of his reign and has been used for coronations ever since, and on past occasions for the STATE OPENING OF PARLIAMENT.

Weighing 4 tons and gilded all over, the coach is 24ft in length, 8ft in width and 12ft in height. Its panels were painted by Giovanni Cipriani, the famous Italian artist who came to London in the middle of the eighteenth century. Apart from these paintings the coach is adorned with carvings such as the two triton-like figures at the front holding conches, as though heralding the approach of the sovereign, or the cherubs on the raised centre of the roof symbolising England, Scotland and Ireland. When the coach was built in 1762 it cost £7,661 (approximately £780,000 today).

The next most important coach housed in the Mews is the Irish State Coach, or at least a reconstruction of the coach, whose woodwork was destroyed by fire in 1911. The meticulous work was begun in June 1988 and completed fifteen months later by the Royal Mews Carriage Restorers. It is this coach that is now used for the State Opening of Parliament. Other royal horse-drawn vehicles include the Scottish State Coach, Queen Alexandra's State Coach, and the Glass Coach which has been used for nearly all royal weddings since it was bought prior to GEORGE V's coronation.

ROYAL MINSTRELS Although minstrelsy was enjoyed before the Norman Conquest, it was only after 1066 that minstrels were known to have had regular employment at the royal court. At the BATTLE OF HASTINGS, WILLIAM I's minstrel Taillefer was killed while singing the song of 'Roland at Roncesvalles', the Domesday Book naming his successor as Berdic. After EDWARD I came to the throne in 1272 the number of court minstrels had greatly increased, and as they played a variety of musical instruments many were musicians as opposed to the traditional meaning of minstrels as 'a class of men in the Middle Ages who lived by singing and reciting'.

The minstrels at the court of King Edward, and those of the Plantagenet kings who followed him, had the status of squires, had regular remuneration, had allowances for their horses and were provided with livery. At the wedding of Edward's daughter Elizabeth to John I, Count of Holland and Zeeland in 1297 the king bestowed £40 (approximately £27,000 today) on his minstrels.

In the reign of ELIZABETH I itinerant minstrels were regarded as vagabonds and were classed as such in a statute of 1572, but this did not apply to liveried minstrels and minstrelsy continued to flourish at royal courts. During the reign of CHARLES I the King's Band was formed under the leadership of Nicholas Lanier which consisted of musicians playing a variety of instruments including recorders, flutes, oboes, sackbuts and violins. *See also* QUEEN'S MUSIC, MASTER OF THE

ROYAL MINT From Anglo-Saxon times onwards the coinage of the realm was under the control of the king, the early kings establishing their own mints which stamped their image on the coins together with the name of the place where they had been fashioned. It is believed that it was in the early ninth century that the London mint was established, though it was not until 1300 that it was housed within the precincts of the TOWER OF LONDON where it produced all the kingdom's coinage. Later, the mint was administered jointly by the king and the Master of the Mint, bound by a contract. From 1699 to 1727 the post of Master of the Mint was held very successfully by Isaac Newton.

Early in the nineteenth century the Royal Mint was moved from the Tower of London to a new site on Little Tower Hill where the production of coins began in 1810. The premises were not large enough to deal with the huge demand for new coins that came with decimalisation, and the Mint was moved to Llantrisant in South Wales where coins were first struck in 1968.

ROYAL MNEMONIC In the days when history lessons were more formal than today, children who had to learn the order of British reigns used the following mnemonic:

> Willy, Willy, Harry, Stee,
> Harry, Dick, John, Harry III,
> I, II, III Neds, Richard II,
> Harrys IV, V, VI . . . then who?
> Edwards IV, V, Dick the bad,
> Harrys twain, and Ned the Lad,
> Mary, Bessie, James the vain,
> Charlie, Charlie, James again . . .
> William and Mary, Anne Gloria,
> Four Georges, William and Victoria;
> Edward VII next and then
> George V in 1910;
> Edward VIII soon abdicated;
> George the VI was coronated;
> After which Elizabeth,
> and that's the end until her death.

ROYAL NEEDLEWORK During the twenty years that MARY, QUEEN OF SCOTS was a prisoner of ELIZABETH I, one of her favourite occupations was embroidery. Some of it, saved by the remarkable Bess of Hardwick, has lasted until the present day. The daughter of a country squire, Bess made a series of increasingly advantageous marriages until she finally wed one of Elizabeth's courtiers and became the Countess of Shrewsbury. The queen had entrusted the Earl of Shrewsbury with the care of her royal prisoner, whom he housed in a succession of his mansions and thus Bess came into contact with Mary. It was not a happy relationship as Bess mistrusted the Scottish queen's intentions in regard to her husband, but her suspicions did not prevent her collecting some of Mary's needlework.

When she was a widow of seventy years, Bess decided to build herself a magnificent new mansion. Named Hardwick Hall, its great array of windows, which became larger with each ascending storey, set an architectural fashion and inspired the saying, 'Hardwick Hall, more glass than wall'.

It was to enhance her new home with the embroidery worked by royal fingers that Bess collected what she could of the late Queen of Scots' work. Today embroidery attributed to Mary is to be seen at the hall.

At Hever Castle, the early home of ANNE BOLEYN, there is not only an example of her needlework but also that of her daughter Elizabeth I. Anne's exhibit consists of an elaborately embroidered coif and headpiece while Elizabeth's is an eighteen-piece layette which she sewed in her early twenties for her sister MARY, when she believed that she was carrying the child of her husband Philip of Spain. It turned out to be a phantom pregnancy and the baby clothes were never used. The tiny garments were made of linen and satin and included bootees, bibs and tiny shirts. Elizabeth had the reputation of being a fine needlewoman – she was credited with sewing a shirt for her little brother Edward when she was 5 years old – but once she became Queen of England she had little time for such a pastime.

As it was considered more than likely that VICTORIA would inherit the throne from her uncle WILLIAM IV who had no legitimate heir, the little princess suffered a rigid regime planned to prepare her for her expected role. Without full brothers or sisters, her childhood was lonely apart from her pets, and later her governess, Baroness Lehzen. When Victoria was 12, the baroness introduced the idea of her making costumes for wooden dolls, then known as Dutch dolls. This gave an outlet for the princess's artistic creativity as the elaborately costumed dolls were based on characters that she and the baroness had seen at operas and ballets, or on the dresses of ladies that she had met at court. With miniature stitches Victoria created the most elaborate ensembles from pieces of velvet, silk and linen, and these were adorned with tiny chains and other fragments of discarded jewellery, even to the making of diminutive earrings. For two years Victoria and her companionable baroness were absorbed in the hobby, which gave the princess an escape from her more taxing studies. During this period a hundred of these dolls were produced, many of which are now on display at the Museum of London.

ROYAL PETS The earliest royal pet to achieve fame was a white poodle that belonged to RUPERT OF THE RHINE. The dog was said to be so clever that superstitious Puritans, who may have renounced the Pope but not the devil, believed him to be an imp who slipped through their lines to spy for his master during the English Civil War. In reality his most popular trick was to raise his leg when Rupert said 'Pym' and leap into the air when he said 'Charles'.

QUEEN VICTORIA's childhood was a lonely one. Her father, Edward, Duke of Kent, had died when she was a baby and her domineering mother's main interest in her daughter was that she was likely to inherit the Crown. Deprived of the company of children of her own age, the young princess found a companion in Dash, a small King Charles spaniel. 'I dressed dear, sweet little Dash in a scarlet jacket and blue trousers', she wrote in her diary at the age of 13. When Victoria became queen in 1837 one of her concerns was how Dash would settle in BUCKINGHAM PALACE, but she was pleased to note in her journal that soon he 'was quite happy in the garden'. Her coronation was held on 28 June the following year and when she returned to the palace after five gruelling hours at WESTMINSTER ABBEY her first act was to give Dash a bath. As the new sovereign's love of Dash became public knowledge various dogs were presented to her, prompting the Prime Minister, Lord Melbourne, to declare, 'You'll be smothered with dogs.' But although other dogs, ranging from dachshunds to collies, took up residence at the palace, Dash was to remain the best loved, and it was a great sorrow for his mistress when he died in 1840. He was interred at Windsor where a memorial was inscribed:

Here lies DASH
The favourite spaniel of
Her Majesty Queen Victoria
In his tenth year.

The Queen enjoyed the company of dogs all her life and one of the most famous was a Pekinese named Looty. During the 1864 Taiping Rebellion British soldiers found Looty and four other Pekinese dogs in the room where the emperor's aunt had taken her life during the hostilities. The little dogs were cared for by the soldiers and when they were brought to England Looty was given to the Queen, which inspired the widespread popularity of the 'Lion Dogs of China'.

Victoria's last dog was a Pomeranian named Turi who became a second Dash to the old lady. When she lay dying at OSBORNE HOUSE in 1901 her last request was 'May I have little Turi?'

The words 'I am Caesar, the King's dog' were inscribed on the collar of EDWARD VII's favourite dog, a long-haired fox terrier. Caesar accompanied the king and his mistress, Alice Keppel, to Biarritz where he behaved in a way not entirely fitting for the 'King's dog'. He was ever eager to run away and dive into the sea to royal consternation, bite royal shoes and ignore royal commands. His saving grace was his love for his master who it would seem saw something of a fellow spirit in his disdain of conformity. The nearest the King ever came to punishing his canine companion for some misdemeanour was to wave his cane at him and repeat, 'You naughty dog. You naughty, naughty dog.' By evening any bad behaviour was forgotten as Caesar went to sleep in a chair next to the royal bed.

King Edward's Danish wife ALEXANDRA also shared the British royal family's fondness for animals. When she was still Princess of Wales she travelled to Egypt with her husband in the winter of 1868. While there she rescued a black ram that was about to be slaughtered and insisted that it should accompany them on a voyage along the Nile. The ram was so well behaved that it ate from its saviour's hand and tolerated the garlands of flowers which the sailors placed round its neck. Finally, Alexandra brought him to England, where he settled down to a peaceful existence at SANDRINGHAM HOUSE.

Because Edward was frequently away in pursuit of his social life, Alexandra spent much time on her own at Sandringham and found pleasure in the company of a wide variety of pets, which included a monkey, parakeets and an assortment of stray dogs whose good fortune had led them into the royal estate. Other dogs were gifts, such as the Russian wolfhounds presented to her by the tsar. In those days the kennels at Sandringham – still in use today – accommodated up to sixty dogs, ranging from a Samoyed who had been the mascot of an Arctic expedition, to a 180lb St Bernard.

At the onset of the First World War Alexandra refused advice to have her old dogs put down. 'It breaks my heart that this cruel war should be the cause of so many of my precious old friends and horses being slaughtered after all these years of faithful service,' she said and, while some horses did have to go, the aged dogs remained with their mistress.

Like his father and mother, GEORGE V had a fondness for dogs, his three favourites being a collie named Heather who lived for eleven years, followed by Happy, a terrier who lived for thirteen and then Jack, a Sealyham who reached fourteen. All lived at Sandringham where their memorials, each bearing the words 'the constant and faithful companion of His Majesty' are built into the wall of the stables. In the latter part of his reign the King's favourite was Bob, a cairn terrier, who missed his master so desperately the first time he left him to go to Balmoral that from then on he always accompanied him.

Another of the king's pets was Charlotte, his pink and grey parrot bought in Port Said when he was a naval officer. He would bring her to the breakfast table where she was allowed to wander among the crockery at will, the king placing the mustard pot over any droppings to hide them from Queen Mary. Charlotte, who was renowned for her command of 'nautical language', perched on the King's shoulder while he was at work at his desk, and when they were separated by his illness, she kept repeating stridently, 'Where's the captain?'

Following his family tradition, EDWARD VIII was fond of dogs, especially cairn terriers. He made a gift of cairn puppies to his mistress Freda Dudley Ward, and later gave a similar puppy to Wallis Simpson. In her autobiography *The Heart Has Its Reasons* the duchess wrote: 'Part of my affection for the Fort [FORT BELVEDERE, home of Edward when he was Prince of Wales] extended to the Prince's Cairns Cora and Jaggs. Unbeknown to me the Prince had observed the growth of our friendship. One afternoon he turned up at Bryanston Court [where she was then living] with a Cairn puppy under his arm. "This," he said, "is Slipper. He is yours."' Slipper was to become one of the links between them. He remained with the prince as a consolation when it was not possible for him to be with Wallis. Thus at the end of 1935 he took Slipper with him to Sandringham for the royal family's Christmas, which he found to be an ordeal, later writing that it was the worst Christmas he had ever spent with his relations. Much of the stress was due to the fact that while he wanted to raise the matter of marriage to Wallis Simpson, GEORGE V refused to discuss it.

After his father's death Edward and Wallis were free to stay at Balmoral, and QUEEN MARY was highly displeased when she heard that Wallis had allowed Slipper to sleep on the best beds. In his autobiography *A King's Story* Edward wrote that on the day of his abdication broadcast, 'The moment had come to leave the fort for good. . . . I discovered Slipper at my heels. In the commotion of packing he was obviously worried that he would be left behind. Patting the little dog to reassure him, I said, "Of course you are coming with me, Slipper." . . . And turning to Walter Monckton [the King's legal adviser], I said, "Be sure to bring Slipper with you in the car when you come to fetch me for the broadcast."'

Tragedy visited the ex-king and Wallis in April 1937, six weeks before their wedding. Wallis, separated from Edward while she waited for her divorce to become final, was staying at the Château de Candé near Tours, when she went for a stroll with Slipper on the local golf course. There the little dog suffered a fatal snakebite. She wrote to Edward: 'Now the principal guest at our wedding is no more. He was our dog – not yours or mine but ours and he loved us both.'

No other dog quite replaced Slipper, who had been with them through such a traumatic time, but later they had a number of pugs. The last of these was named Black Diamond and when Edward lay dying in 1972 he stretched out on the bed with his master's hand resting on him.

The Kennel Club awarded championship status to corgis in 1928 but they remained unfamiliar to the public until 1933 when a photograph appeared in the press showing PRINCESS ELIZABETH, then aged 7 years, with a strange-looking puppy on a lead. It was a Welsh Corgi named Dookie and since then Corgis have been synonymous with the royal family. Soon after the picture appeared, PRINCESS MARGARET was reported as having one, whose official name was Rozavel Lady Jane, to whom she read stories. When Princess Elizabeth married PRINCE PHILIP in 1947 her corgi Susan rode with them in the landau along the Mall after the ceremony, bringing added applause from the spectators.

Opposite: Princess Elizabeth holding a corgi dog, *c.* 1936. *(Getty Images)*

ROYAL PHILATELIC COLLECTION The world's finest collection of British and Commonwealth stamps is to be found in the Royal Philatelic Collection, which is housed in St James's Palace. It is a private collection belonging to Her Majesty the Queen and is maintained by a part-time staff of experts under the Keeper of the Royal Philatelic Collection who is responsible for the study, conservation of the stamps, the acquisition of new issues and the arranging of loans to philatelic exhibitions.

The collection dates back to 1865 when Edward, Prince of Wales and the future EDWARD VII, and his brother Alfred, Duke of Edinburgh, were presented with sets of current stamps. Alfred became a serious philatelist and prior to his death in 1900 he sold his collection to Edward who in turn gave it to his son George, Duke of York and the future GEORGE V, who was an enthusiastic stamp collector. In 1893 George became the Honorary Vice-President of what is now the Royal Philatelic Society London, a post he held for seventeen years.

In 1904 he bought two of the world's most prized stamps – a Mauritius one penny and a two-penny stamp, which in 1847 were the first stamps to be issued by a colonial post office. Afterwards a courtier remarked, 'Did you know that some damned fool has actually paid £1,400 for a stamp?'

'Yes,' George replied. 'You are talking to him.'

The King remained an avid philatelist all his life. It is said he spent three afternoons a week on his collection and when he died in 1936 it consisted of 328 albums each containing sixty pages of stamps. These were known as the Red Albums. His son GEORGE VI continued to expand the collection in the Blue Albums; today's acquisitions are mounted in the Green Albums. The first four of the Red Albums contain the results of a competition for the design of the first postage stamps to be issued in 1840 when Sir Roland Hill introduced the 'Penny Post'. Then the Penny Black, printed with black ink and showing QUEEN VICTORIA's profile, became the world's first adhesive postage stamp.

The actual number of stamps in St James's Palace has never been counted. The collection is constantly added to, as it receives mint blocks of four or six specimens of every stamp issued in the world. There is a backlog of unmounted specimens – enough, it is said, to fill several hundred albums.

The most poignant item in the collection is an album which once belonged to Alexis, the son of

Tsar Nicholas II, who with his family was murdered at Yekaterinburg in Russia by Red Guards in 1918. A soldier stole it and subsequently sold it to an Englishman working for a British company in Russia whose son later presented it to the Royal Collection.

ROYAL QUOTATIONS

ALBERT, PRINCE CONSORT On being incensed by a newspaper editorial in 1846: 'Soon there will not be room enough in the same country for the monarchy and *The Times*.'

ANNE Following an apoplectic fit, Queen Anne's dying injunction as she just managed to hand the white wand of office to her new Prime Minister, the Duke of Shrewsbury: 'For God's sake use it for the good of my people.'

ANNE, PRINCESS ROYAL As quoted in the *Observer*: 'When I appear in public people expect me to neigh, grind my teeth, paw the ground and swish my tail – none of which is easy.'

BOUDICCA According to Tacitus she encouraged her followers with these words before her final battle: 'It has been the custom of the Britons in the past to fight under the leadership of women, yet I am not fighting for a throne but as one of you, to avenge the loss of liberty, the lashes inflicted upon my body and the outrages done to my daughters. . . . We have the numbers and justice is on our side. We must conquer on this field or die. Such is my resolution as a woman. You men may live on and be slaves if you wish.'

CARACTACUS His words to the Emperor Claudius when taken before him as a captive in Rome: 'If you want to rule the world does it follow that everyone else welcomes enslavement?'

CHARLES I His protest after being silenced following the death sentence being passed on him: 'I am not suffered to speak, expect what justice other people will have.'

In a letter of advice to Lord Wentworth, 3 September 1636: 'Never make a defence of apology before you are accused.'

On the morning of his execution he told Sir Thomas Herbert after waking soon after five o'clock: 'I will get up, having a great work to do today.'

His last words, spoken to the headsman: 'Stay for the sign.'

CHARLES II His reply to his younger brother James when warning him against the possibility of assassination: 'I am sure no man in England will take away my life to make you King.'

His opinion of George of Denmark, who married his niece Anne: 'I've tried him drunk and I've tried him sober but there's nothing in him.'

His opinion of Presbyterianism: 'Not a religion for gentlemen.'

His last words reflecting his concern for his mistress Nell Gwynne: 'Let not poor Nelly starve.'

CHARLES, PRINCE OF WALES Referring to the intended extension to the National Gallery in an address to the Royal Institute of British Architects in 1984: 'A monstrous carbuncle on the face of a much-loved and elegant friend.'

His comment when it was suggested in a television broadcast that it was his wish that his mother the Queen should abdicate: 'I begin to tire of needing to issue denials of false stories about all manner of thoughts which I am alleged to be having.'

EDWARD I When the death of King Louis of France weakened the resolve of those who had undertaken the Seventh Crusade Edward vowed: 'Even if all my countrymen and comrades leave me, yet I with Fowen, the master of my horse, will enter Ptolomais, or Achan or Acre, and will keep my word until my body and soul are parted.'

On his journey home from the Crusade in 1272 Edward received news of the deaths of his young son, his uncle Richard of Cornwall and his father Henry III, and declared: 'I may get more children but never another father.'

EDWARD II The deposed king's reply when his captors humiliated him by giving him cold ditchwater with which to shave: 'Whether you will or no, I have warm tears for my beard.'

EDWARD III At the Battle of Crécy a courier took a message to the king that his son Edward, later known as the Black Prince, was hard pressed and in need of reinforcements to which, according to

Holinshed, the king replied: 'Return to him and them that sent you and say to them that they send me no more for any adventure that falleth, as long as my son is alive. Also say to them that they suffer him this day to win his spurs, for if God be pleased I will this journey be his and the honour thereof, and to them that be about him.' (Despite his words Edward sent a score of soldiers to aid his son, who did win his spurs upon the field of battle.)

His remark when retrieving the Countess of Salisbury's garter which fell to the floor during a dance: '*Honi soit qui mal y pense.*'

EDWARD VI Last words of the 15-year-old king: 'I am faint. Lord have mercy on me and take my spirit.'

EDWARD VII When asked if his mother Queen Victoria would be happy in heaven: 'She will have to walk behind the angels and she won't like that.'

A remark to the Archbishop of Canterbury during Victoria's Diamond Jubilee celebrations: 'I have no objection whatsoever to the Eternal Father but every objection to the concept of an Eternal Mother.'

EDWARD VIII Speaking in 1936 at steel works which had closed due to the Depression: 'These works brought all these people here. Something should be done to get them at work again.' (This became shortened to what many saw as a political credo: Something must be done!)

The opening of his famous radio broadcast following his abdication: 'At long last I am able to say a few words of my own. . . .'

ELIZABETH, THE QUEEN MOTHER Her remark to a policeman in September 1940: 'I'm glad we've been bombed. It makes me feel I can look the East End in the face.'

In reply to the proposal that the royal family should leave London during bombing by the German Luftwaffe: 'The Princesses would never leave without me and I couldn't leave the King, and the King will never leave.'

In a letter to Edith Sitwell following the death of her husband George VI: 'How small and selfish is sorrow. But it bangs one about until one is senseless.'

ELIZABETH I Her answer when, soon after her coronation, Parliament petitioned her to marry for fear that if she died without issue the succession

would go to Mary Stuart: 'This shall be for me sufficient, that a marble stone shall declare that a queen, having reigned such a time, has died a virgin.'

Her letter to the Bishop of Ely when he demurred over giving up his London residence to her favourite, Christopher Hatton: 'Proud Prelate, you know what you were before I made you what you are now. If you do not immediately comply with my request, I will unfrock you, by God.'

Her greeting to a deputation of eighteen tailors, playing on the adage – taken from a bell-ringing term – that Nine Tailors maketh a Man: 'Good morning, gentlemen both.'

From her speech at Tilbury when invasion by the Duke of Palma was feared: 'Let tyrants fear: I have placed my chiefest strength and safeguard in the loyal hearts and good will of my subjects. I know I have but the body of a weak and feeble woman, but I have the heart of a King, and a King of England too; and think foul scorn that Parma or Spain, or any other prince of Europe, should dare invade the borders of my realm. . . .'

While she was dying she was asked to name her heir and as she could not speak she was entreated to make a sign when the name of the person she favoured was spoken from a list. One name so incensed her that she forced herself to say out loud her last words: 'I will have no rascal's son in my seat. It is the throne of kings.'

ELIZABETH II Speaking at the Guildhall on the occasion of her 25th wedding anniversary: 'I think that everybody really will concede that on this, of all days, I should begin my speech with the words "My husband and I".'

GEORGE I His most quoted remark: 'I hate all Boets and Bainters.'

GEORGE II His retort when the Duke of Newcastle described General Wolfe as a madman: 'Mad, is he? Then I hope he will bite some of my other generals.'

When on her deathbed Queen Caroline enjoined him to marry again, he replied: 'No, I shall have mistresses.'

GEORGE III In his address to the House of Lords in 1760: 'Born and educated in this country, I glory in the name of Briton.'

Speaking to Edward Gibbon, author of *The Decline and Fall of the Roman Empire*: 'Another damned, thick square book! Always scribble, scribble, scribble! Eh! Mr Gibbon?' (Also attributed to the Duke of Gloucester.)

His response when his son Prince William told him he had settled £1,000 a year on his mistress Dorothea Jordan: 'A thousand, a thousand! Too much, too much! Five hundred a year quite enough! Quite enough!'

GEORGE IV His reaction on meeting Caroline of Brunswick whom he had agreed to marry in order to clear his debts: 'Harris, I am not well; pray fetch me a glass of brandy.'

GEORGE V His remark following H.G.Wells's description of the court as being 'alien and uninspiring': 'I may be uninspiring, but I'll be damned if I'm an alien.'

The king's reply from his deathbed when his doctor sought to cheer him up by saying he would soon be back in Bognor: 'Bugger Bognor!'

GEORGE VI His description of the British monarchy: 'The family firm.'

LADY JANE GREY Her words when, on being blindfolded for her execution, she was distressed at not being able to locate the headsman's block: 'What shall I do? Where is it?'

HAROLD II His reply, before the Battle of Stamford Bridge, when asked what Harold Hardrada, King of Norway would be given in return for a truce: 'Seven feet of ground or as much more as he needs as he is taller than most men.'

HENRY I A favourite expression according to William of Malmesbury: 'An illiterate king is a crowned ass.'

HENRY II Angered when Thomas à Becket excommunicated the bishops of Salisbury and Lincoln for supporting him, the king uttered the words that led to the archbishop's assassination: 'What a parcel of fools and dastards have I nourished in my house? Not one of them will avenge me of this one upstart clerk!'

His exclamation as he lay on his deathbed and learned that his favourite son John had been plotting against him: 'Let things take their course, I care no longer for myself or anything in this world.'

HENRY III When his royal barge was caught in a thunderstorm on the Thames, Henry, who had a dread of thunder, sought shelter at the Bishop of Durham's riverside palace only to be greeted by his political adversary Simon de Montfort who declared, 'What is there to be afraid of, sir? The storm is almost gone.' To which the king replied: 'I fear thunder and lightning excessively, but by God's head I fear you more.'

HENRY VI His response when shocked at a Christmas entertainment given by certain nobles in which young women with 'bared bosoms' took part: 'Fy, fy for shame, forsoothe ye be to blame.'

HENRY VIII A verse written during his wooing of Anne Boleyn:

> Now unto my lady
> Promise to her I make
> For all other only
> To her I me betake.

JAMES I On John Donne: 'Dr Donne's verses are like the peace of God, for they all pass understanding.'

His remark on being introduced to a girl who could converse in Hebrew, Greek and Latin: 'These are rare attainments for a damsel, but pray tell me, can she spin?'

JAMES II In his exile he turned to spiritual matters and deploring his earlier amatory adventures, wrote: 'I abhor and detest myself for having so often offended so gracious and merciful a God and having lived so many years in almost a perpetual course of sin, not only in the days of my youth when I was carried away with the heat of it and ill example, but even when I was come to years of more discretion.'

MARY I Due to pressure from Anne Boleyn, Henry VIII's Privy Council ordered her household to be disbanded and forbade her to use the title of princess. In reply the 17-year-old girl wrote: 'As touching upon my removal to Hatfield, I will obey his grace . . . but I protest before you and all others present that my conscience will in no wise suffer me to take any other than myself for princess, or for the king's daughter born in lawful matrimony, and that I will never wittingly or willingly say or do ought whereby any person might take occasion to think that I agree to the contrary.'

Ill and depressed at the end of her life, the queen was told by one of her ladies that her distress was due to the absence of her husband Philip of Spain, to which she replied: 'Not only that but when I am dead and opened, you shall find 'Calais' lying on my heart.'

MARY, QUEEN OF SCOTS Said to the commissioners trying her at Fotheringhay Castle on 13 October 1586: 'Look to your consciences and remember that the theatre of the world is wider than the realm of England.'

MARY, QUEEN CONSORT OF GEORGE V On returning to Marlborough House after the abdication of her son Edward VIII: 'All this thrown away for that.'

RICHARD II His comment to Adam of Usk who visited the deposed king when imprisoned in the Tower of London: 'My God, a wonderful land is this and a fickle: which has exiled, slain, destroyed and ruined so many kings, rulers and great men, and is ever tainted with strife and variance and envy.'

RICHARD III On 13 June 1483 Lord Hastings was arrested for treason and Richard, at that time Lord Protector, immediately declared: 'By Saint Paul, I will not to dinner till I see thy head off.'

STEPHEN During his troubled reign the king knew that Bishop Roger, the ex-Justiciar of England, was his secret enemy but he was forced to bide his time over the matter, explaining: 'By the birth of God, I would give him half of England if he asked for it – 'til the time be ripe he shall tire of asking ere I tire of giving.'

VICTORIA On seeing her name on the line of succession at the age of 11: 'I will be good.'

Describing her feelings on being introduced to Prince Albert: 'It was with some emotion that I beheld Albert – who is beautiful.'

Her complaint about Gladstone: 'He speaks to me as if I were a public meeting.'

Her comment on *King Lear*: 'A strange, horrible business, but I suppose good enough for Shakespeare's Day.'

Her annoyance with *The Times* in 1855: 'The Queen has been much disgusted with the late atrocious articles in *The Times* on the army in the Crimea. . . .'

WILLIAM THE CONQUEROR When he fell on all fours on landing at Pevensey beach his followers took it as an ill-omen until the quick-witted duke held up a handful of sand with the cry: 'By the Splendour of God, we have taken the seizin of England!'

Reflecting on his life after he had become King of England: 'Since I was a boy I have always worn my armour.'

WILLIAM II His order to a sea captain who argued that a violent storm was making the Channel too dangerous for a crossing to France: 'Cast off. Kings never drown.'

WILLIAM III In reply to the Duke of Buckingham who said, 'Do you not see your country is lost?': 'There can be one certain means by which I can be sure never to see my country's ruin: I will die in the last ditch.'

ROYAL STATUES OF LONDON Although there are statues of royalty to be found in towns and royal sites across Britain, the biggest collection is understandably in the capital. Below are London's major royal statues, apart from plaques and medallions:

PRINCE ALBERT A seated statue of the prince in the centre of his memorial by Joseph Durham. It is flanked by statuary originally designed to commemorate the Great Exhibition and was erected in 1899 opposite the Albert Hall.

An equestrian statue of the prince wearing the uniform of a field marshal by Charles Bacon. Erected in Holborn Circus in 1874.

QUEEN ALEXANDRA Sculpted in her coronation robes by George Edward Wade, the bronze statue commemorates the fact that she introduced a cure for leprosy into England. Erected at the London Hospital, Mile End Road.

KING ALFRED An ancient statue thought to be of Alfred was moved from Westminster Hall and erected in Trinity Church Square in 1824.

A 14th-century statue of King Alfred, removed from the site of Westminster Hall and set up in Trinity Church Square in 1842.

QUEEN ANNE A marble statue of the Queen sculpted by Richard Belt in 1886 and erected opposite St Paul's Cathedral.

QUEEN BOUDICCA With the Queen's daughters and chariot, complete with scythes attached to its wheel hubs, the bronze group by Thomas Thornycroft was erected on the Victoria Embankment at Westminster Bridge in 1902.

KING CHARLES I The bronze equestrian statue of the king standing in Trafalgar Square has an odd history. It was made by Hubert le Sueur in 1633, but no site was selected for it directly and sixteen years later a metal worker appropriately named Rivett was instructed to destroy it. Instead he secretly hid it away and made a good business out of souvenirs he falsely claimed were cast from 'the King's metal'. Some years later Charles II obtained it and in 1765 it was finally erected where it is to be seen today and where, on the anniversary of Charles's execution, a wreath is laid by the Royal Stuart Society.

KING CHARLES II This stone statue of the King, sculpted by Caius Gabriel Cibber, had once stood in Soho Square but was in the possession of W.S. Gilbert when he died in 1911. It was returned to the square by his widow and re-erected in 1938.

A bronze statue of the King in Roman attire by Grinling Gibbons was erected at the Chelsea Hospital in 1692. On the anniversary of Charles's birthday it is wreathed in oak leaves in remembrance of his escape by concealing himself in the Boscobel Oak after the Battle of Worcester.

QUEEN CHARLOTTE OF MECKLENBURG-STRELITZ A lead statue of the Queen stands in the garden which is the centre of Queen Square, opposite the National Hospital for Diseases of the Nervous System. On 1 April it became customary for the statue to appear expertly bandaged, doubtless the work of medical students.

KING EDWARD VI A bronze statue cast by Peter Scheemakers in 1737 and a stone figure sculpted by Thomas Cartwright half a century earlier stand at St Thomas's Hospital. They commemorate the fact that the young king reopened the hospital in 1551 after it had been closed by his father at the Dissolution of the Monasteries.

KING EDWARD VII A gift of East London's Jews, a memorial to King Edward was erected in Mile End Road the year after his death in 1910. Designed by W.S. Frith it consists of a pillar on which the figure of an angel holds a bronze medallion of the King.

With the figure of Queen Victoria beside him, a terracotta statue of Edward is to be seen on the frontage of Caxton Hall. Another statue of the King

in conjunction with his mother is the Temple Bar Memorial in Fleet Street, the marble statuary by Sir Joseph Edgar Boehm in 1918.

A bronze figure by L.F. Roselieb was erected in 1911 at Tooting Broadway, while an equestrian statue, also in bronze, by Sir Bertram Mackennal in 1922, stands in Waterloo Place.

QUEEN ELIZABETH I William Kerwin's statue of the Queen, completed in 1586, is to be seen at the church of St Dunstan in the West, Fleet Street, situated above the vestry porch.

KING GEORGE I Dressed in a toga and grasping a scroll, the figure of the King stands on the apex of the pyramid-shaped steeple of St George's Church in Bloomsbury.

KING GEORGE II Although its origin is obscure, this Portland stone statue, believed to be that of the King, has stood in Golden Square since 1753, the gift of an unidentified benefactor.

A statue of the King, sculpted by J.M. Rysbrack in marble taken from a captured French vessel, was erected at Greenwich Hospital in 1735.

Bronze equestrian statue of Edward VII in Waterloo Place, erected in 1922.

KING GEORGE III Financed by public subscription, the bronze equestrian statue of the King by Matthew Cotes Wyat was erected in Cockspur Street in 1820.

Statue of George III in Cockspur Street. The horse lost his tail at the unveiling in 1836 to the sculptor's dismay.

287

KING GEORGE IV Not noted for his modesty, George commissioned this bronze equestrian statue of himself in 1829. It was to be set above Marble Arch, then a gateway to Buckingham Palace, but as the work was not completed when the king died in 1830, it was later erected in Trafalgar Square.

KING GEORGE V Holding the Sword of State and wearing his Garter robes, the King's statue stands on a tall stone plinth at the Old Palace Yard, opposite the Palace of Westminster. The work of Sir William Reid Dick, it was erected in 1947.

KING GEORGE VI Sculpted by William Macmillan and erected at Carlton House Terrace in 1955, the stone statue shows the king dressed in the uniform of Admiral of the Fleet.

KING HENRY VIII The work of Francis Bird in 1702, a statue of the King stands above the gateway to St Bartholomew's Hospital which he allowed to be reopened in 1544 after it had been closed at the Dissolution of the Monasteries.

KING JAMES II Standing in front of the National Gallery, Trafalgar Square, the bronze statue of the King in a Roman costume is either by Grinling Gibbons or his pupils.

KING RICHARD I Originally cast to be displayed at the Great Exhibition, the bronze equestrian statue of the King holding his sword aloft stands at the Old Palace Yard, the Palace of Westminster.

QUEEN VICTORIA Sculpted by Victoria's daughter, Princess Louise, the marble statue – arguably the most attractive of London's royal statuary – shows the young Queen as she appeared soon after her coronation in 1838. It is situated in Kensington Gardens overlooking the Broad Walk.

A 13ft-high statue of the queen is the centrepiece of the Queen Victoria Memorial. Carved from a single block of marble, the seated figure looks along The Mall and is surrounded by groups of allegorical figures. Over 2,000 tons of marble went into the construction of the memorial, which was unveiled by George V in 1911.

A bronze statue of the Queen holding the sceptre by C.B. Birch, was erected at New Bridge Street in 1896, the year prior to the Diamond Jubilee.

KING WILLIAM III The hoof of the horse of this bronze equestrian statue is poised above the mole-hill responsible for the fall which brought death to William of Orange. The work was designed by John Bacon and completed by his son, also John Bacon, and erected in St James's Square in 1808.

Situated in front of Kensington Palace, a bronze statue of the King by Heinrich Baucke was given to Edward VII by his nephew Kaiser Wilhelm II as a token of goodwill towards Britain.

KING WILLIAM IV In 1844 a granite statue of the King by Samuel Nixon was appropriately erected in King William Street, but in 1938 it was relocated at William Walk in Greenwich.

'ROYAL TIME' EDWARD VII introduced the custom of setting all the clocks on the Sandringham Estate thirty minutes early to allow him more time to shoot. As a consequence, all business when the King was at Sandringham took place in this 'royal time'. GEORGE V maintained the tradition, but EDWARD VIII reset the clocks to 'ordinary time'.

ROYAL TITLES In the reign of HENRY IV it became customary to refer to the king as 'His Grace' and from then on there were several forms of title. HENRY VI was referred to as 'His Excellent Grace'; EDWARD IV, 'High and Mighty Prince', and with HENRY VII 'His Majesty' was introduced. After HENRY VIII 'His Sacred Majesty' was generally used. The present title is 'Her Most Gracious Majesty'.

ROYAL VICTORIAN ORDER The recipients of the Royal Victorian Order, usually members of the royal household, receive the honour in recognition for personal service to the sovereign and there is no limit to their number. The Order's chapel is the Queen's Chapel of the Savoy, though the special service for those who earn the award is held every four years at St George's Chapel in Windsor Castle.

ROYAL WARRANTS A company or person who has provided goods or services to Her Majesty,

Queen Elizabeth, the Duke of Edinburgh or Prince Charles for at least five years may apply for a Royal Warrant. A successful applicant may display the coat of arms of the member of the royal family they serve and use the words 'By Appointment'. The queen, duke and prince each only confer a single warrant on a particular company or individual, but a business serving more than one royal client may be granted a warrant from each royal patron. Warrants are issued by the Lord Chamberlain and are reviewed every five years. The Royal Warrant Holders Association ensures that the rules applying to the holding of a warrant are observed and that high standards are maintained.

ROYAL WATERMEN Until early Victorian times, when roads had improved enough to make coach travel comfortable, the Thames was in effect a royal highway. A number of palaces had been built along its banks from Greenwich to Richmond and when members of the court wished to travel between them they were carried by barges specially fitted out for the king's service. In Tudor times royal barges became particularly splendid as they had to reflect the majesty of the House of Tudor.

The creation of the company of Royal Watermen who rowed and maintained the sovereign's barge goes back to the fourteenth century and their duties continue to this day when members of royalty are rowed on the Thames for ceremonial occasions. The watermen are also members of the City of London Company of Watermen and Lightermen which a parliamentary Act sanctioned in 1514.

When river travel became outdated the Royal Watermen came ashore to continue their traditional duties, acting as royal coachmen and footmen on state occasions. Once the symbols of sovereignty were borne by barge to the PALACE OF WESTMINSTER for the STATE OPENING OF PARLIAMENT; today they arrive by carriage but Royal Watermen retain their traditional role by still accompanying it. As in the past it is the Queen's Bargemaster who has the honour of taking out the crown and presenting it with due solemnity to the official who carries it into the Houses of Parliament.

RUPERT OF THE RHINE The Royalists' hero and *beau sabreur* during the English Civil War, Prince Rupert was born in 1619, the third son of Frederick Henry of Wittelsbach, Elector Palatine of the Rhine, and Elizabeth, daughter of JAMES I of England. As a young man he spent eighteen months at the court of his uncle CHARLES I, after which he fought in the Thirty Years' War, was captured, and imprisoned for three years at Linz.

At the outbreak of the Civil War in 1642 he came to England to fight in his uncle's cause. He soon made a valiant reputation for himself as the 'Mad Cavalier' whose forte was to win battles by leading devastating cavalry charges – and sometimes to lose them by impetuous pursuits that took him and his horsemen away from the main action. Apart from skirmishes and cavalry raids on enemy positions, he fought in the major battles of Edgehill,

Prince Rupert of the Rhine, the epitome of the dashing cavalier, who became in inventor in later life.

289

Worcester, Brentford, Chalgrove, Newbury, Bolton, Marston, the Second Battle of Newbury and Naseby.

His brilliant if dashing military ability and his colourful bearing – the antithesis of Cromwell's psalm-singing soldiery – made him the mainstay of the royal army, the full control of which he was given at the end of 1644. In the following May the prince took Leicester, which caused the siege of Oxford to be lifted, but the next month he suffered defeat at Naseby. He was then ordered to hold Bristol but in September he was forced to surrender the city, to the anger of King Charles who dismissed him for 'so mean an action'. However, he was exonerated by a court martial and took up his duties again, only to surrender Oxford to General Fairfax in June 1646.

The next month he left England and in 1648 was given command of the naval ships that had remained Royalist, and though he was more cautious at sea than he had been on land, he still retained his old daring. After his little fleet was mauled by Admiral Blake when he took it to Ireland, he sailed to the West Indies where, with his brother Prince Maurice, he continued to be a threat to Commonwealth shipping.

After the Restoration he returned to England where he remained in the navy for the second and third wars with the Dutch, sharing command with the Duke of Albemarle under James, Duke of York. At sea his successes were less spectacular than they had been on land due to being up against seasoned Dutch admirals, but Pepys described his action off Lowestoft as 'a great victory, never known in the world'.

Rupert became one of the founders of the Hudson's Bay Company, a privy councillor and a Fellow of the Royal Society, his latter years being given over to his interest in mechanical and scientific matters. He invented an improved type of gunpowder and what became known as 'Prince's metal', and while he was not the originator of the mezzotint method of printing he improved the technique. He died in 1682.

S

ST DUNSTAN The son of a West Saxon noble, Dunstan was educated at Glastonbury Abbey and went to the court of King ATHELSTAN where he stayed until he was banished for practising 'unlawful arts'. One of the reasons for him being denounced as a magician was his construction of a harp that could play by itself. It is likely that the instrument was a form of aeolian harp whose strings were activated by the wind. After Athelstan's brother EDMUND inherited the throne he appointed Dunstan Abbot of Glastonbury where he worked to make it a centre of religious teaching. When an outlawed robber killed King Edmund he was followed by EDRED, who was so devout he allowed Dunstan to scourge him for the good of his soul. Edred died in AD 955 and was succeeded by the 15-year-old EDWY THE FAIR.

St Dunstan, who formulated the coronation ceremony.

At the coronation feast, Odo, the Archbishop of Canterbury, angered when he noticed the new king was missing from the high table, sent Dunstan to find him. Dunstan burst into the king's chamber to find him seated on a couch with Elgiva, his betrothed, and her mother. Dunstan had no compunction in physically dragging his successor back to the banquet. Edwy might have been young but he was not cowed and once the celebration was over he called upon Dunstan to account for the huge sums of money the previous king had entrusted him with. He refused, arguing that the money was given to him for religious purposes and he was answerable only to God. Thereupon Edwy banished him and Dunstan went to a monastery in Flanders where he mounted a whispering campaign against the king.

When Edgar, who was to become known as 'the Peaceable', assumed the throne in AD 959, one of his first acts was to appoint Dunstan as Archbishop of Canterbury, and as such was credited with contributing greatly to the peace and prosperity of the new reign. He worked to advance the clergy and make them mentors in secular subjects as well as religious. He also had it made law that landowners should pay church tithes.

Following Edgar's death in AD 975 he declared for EDWARD THE MARTYR, and when he was assassinated he crowned ETHELRED THE UNREADY, but he earned the king's antagonism which put an end to his political career. He died in AD 988 and his feast day is 19 May.

ST EDMUND Of the several murdered English kings whose enshrined remains have been credited with possessing beneficial powers, it was King Edmund of East Anglia who was the first to inspire a great centre of medieval pilgrimage. In AD 870 he was captured at Hoxne after a battle in which he had sought to repulse Danish invaders. His captors offered him his life and freedom if he would agree to renounce Christianity and accept a Danish overlord. When he refused he was shot to death with arrows, after which his head was severed from his body and flung into a thicket.

At this point the supernatural element enters the story. After the Danes had departed a search was made for the king's head and loyal servants were led to the thicket by a disembodied voice. Here they found that the head was being guarded by a wolf who followed the party to Hoxne for the interment of the mutilated remains. As a result the wolf became a symbol of the martyred king and was frequently portrayed in the churches dedicated to him after he had been elevated to sainthood.

In AD 903 Edmund's body, with the head miraculously reunited with the trunk, was exhumed and reinterred in a wooden church at the monastery of Beodriesworth that was to become the town of St Edmundsbury, later Bury St Edmunds. When the area was again under threat from marauding Norsemen the saint's bones were carried to London to be held in safety until 1013, when they were returned and placed in a magnificent reliquary in a specially built stone church which soon gained a miraculous reputation, attracting thousands of pilgrims annually.

There was something curious about some of Edmund's numerous miracles. Stories abounded in which those who offended the dead king came to untimely ends, the most famous relating to King Sweyn who died in 1040. In a dispute with the town, Sweyn threatened to enter it with his troops, thus posing a threat to its famous shrine. As he issued orders for the attack his retainers saw his mouth fall open and his eyes focus in horror on the far end of the room in which he was holding court. In a broken voice they heard him say that St Edmund had materialised and was advancing upon him with a spear. Seconds later he slumped to the floor in a fit and died three days later.

Such was the awesome reputation of St Edmund that when officials came to strip the shrine of its bejewelled ornamentation as an enforced contribution to RICHARD I's ransom, the abbot had the church doors opened and invited them to take the treasures – if they dared to risk Edmund's wrath. As a result, St Edmund's was the only shrine that was not plundered on behalf of the crusader. The protective magic had faded by 1538 when HENRY VIII's commissioners destroyed Edmund's gold and silver tomb as part of the Dissolution.

ST EDMUND THE KING, CHURCH OF One of England's oldest churches dedicated to a king is that of St Edmund the King, situated in London's Lombard Street. It goes back to the twelfth century when it was named after EDMUND (*c.* AD 841–70) who in AD 855 became King of the East Angles, succeeding King OFFA who had adopted him as his heir. He was defeated by invading Danes eleven years later, made prisoner and, when he refused to renounce Christianity, was shot to death with arrows in the manner of St Stephen at Hoxne. In 903 his remains were translated to Bury St Edmunds, which took its name from him. The church dedicated to him in London suffered in the Great Fire but was restored by Sir Christopher Wren.

ST GEORGE'S CHAPEL, WINDSOR CASTLE
Second only to WESTMINSTER ABBEY for its royal associations, St George's Chapel at WINDSOR CASTLE acts as a church for the castle, is a royal mausoleum and for over seven centuries has been the chapel of the MOST NOBLE ORDER OF THE GARTER, Britain's oldest and most prestigious order of chivalry. In 1240 when new lodgings were being erected for HENRY III at Windsor he resolved to build a chapel which, when it was completed nine years later, was dedicated to EDWARD THE CONFESSOR. Fire destroyed the royal apartments at the end of the century but the chapel escaped the conflagration and EDWARD III decided to make it the chapel for his newly established order of knighthood. He also instituted the College of St George, consisting of priests to serve the chapel and conduct daily services with prayers for Garter knights past and present.

After it seemed that the HOUSE OF YORK had emerged victorious from the WARS OF THE ROSES, EDWARD IV decided that the chapel was not magnificent enough to reflect the majesty of the new dynasty or to be a fitting place for his tomb and chantry, and decided to build a new St George's Chapel. Work commenced in 1473 with masons and artisans drafted in from all over the kingdom, but the work lapsed when the Yorkist regime ended on the FIELD OF BOSWORTH. It was only continued during the reign of HENRY VII through a munificent bequest willed by Sir Reginald Bray, a Knight of the Garter. It was finally completed in 1528. Apart from the choir and nave, described as 'the culmination of English late-Gothic style', St George's has nine chantry chapels where prayers could be said for the souls of their founders and their families. Garter knights have their own choir stalls with their heraldic plates, above which are suspended their banners. The fixing of a heraldic plate to a stall is the last act in the ritual of installing a knight, and around seven hundred of these plates on which coats of arms are depicted in enamel or paint are displayed in the chapel.

Apart from serving as a CHAPEL ROYAL and the spiritual centre of the Order of the Garter, St George's Chapel became the last resting place for several kings and queens. Edward IV had his wish to be interred there realised, his tomb being situated north of the high altar. Originally his effigy was placed above the vault but today all that remains to mark his grave is a slab of black marble bearing his name. As a result of paving work carried out at the spot in 1789 a vault was accidentally opened in which were the coffins of the king and Queen Elizabeth Woodville. Edward's coffin was opened and his remains measured, showing that his height had been 6ft 4in. Some strands of his hair were taken, a lock of which is preserved in the chapel's muniment room.

In 1484 RICHARD III had the body of HENRY VI translated from Chertsey Abbey to St George's where it was placed in a tomb south of the high altar, opposite that of Edward IV who brought about his downfall. Because of his saintly reputation Henry's tomb attracted pilgrims and soon reports circulated of miraculous cures taking place there. Today a stone marks the spot.

After CARDINAL WOLSEY's dramatic fall from favour, HENRY VIII not only took over HAMPTON COURT and WHITEHALL PALACE but also the cardinal's unfinished tomb. At the beginning of the sixteenth century construction of St George's Lady Chapel began on the site of Henry III's original chapel, which today is known as the Albert Memorial Chapel. At that time one of the canons was Thomas Wolsey, and remembering the chapel after he had embarked on his dazzling career he decided it would be the right setting for a tomb that would reflect his earthly glory. Work began in 1524 on his great black and white marble sarcophagus which was mounted on an 8ft-high base. Neither the chapel nor the tomb were ready when he died just before he was to be tried for treason. Henry decided that Wolsey's tomb which, like his palaces, was fit for a king, would be suitable for him, but when he died in 1547 the work was still not finished and he was buried in a vault in the chapel's choir. The unused tomb remained locked in

the incomplete Lady Chapel until 1808 when it was removed to St Paul's and set above the grave of Lord Nelson.

When CHARLES I was executed in 1649, the parliamentary government decided that he should not be interred in Westminster Abbey as his tomb could become an object of veneration by those who held Royalist sympathies, and so his body was taken to Windsor Castle, then garrisoned by Cromwell's troops. It was to be buried beneath the floor of St George's choir but as the grave was being dug workmen came to a vault which contained two coffins, those of Henry VIII and Queen Jane Seymour. There was a space reserved for Catherine Parr, but after she remarried she died in childbirth and was buried in the chapel of Sudely Castle. Charles's coffin was placed in the unoccupied section and the vault was resealed and covered over. It was not until 1837 that WILLIAM IV had a memorial slab placed above it.

GEORGE III, who took a great – and generous – interest in St George's Chapel, was responsible for the royal vault which is situated under the choir and the Albert Memorial Chapel. He was buried there, as was his son GEORGE IV, and WILLIAM IV. GEORGE V and Queen Mary were also placed there before being moved to their tomb in the nave. Finally a new memorial chapel was built for KING GEORGE VI where he was interred, as was later Queen Elizabeth, the Queen Mother and Princess Margaret. Of St George's 267 memorials the one most likely to capture attention is the marble monument to Princess Charlotte, the daughter of George IV, who if she had not died in childbirth would have inherited the throne instead of VICTORIA. The memorial, commissioned by her father in 1824 and executed by the sculptor Matthew Cotes Wyatt, consists of a marble tableau in which the princess's body lies draped by a sheet while above she appears to be rising towards heaven escorted by two angels, one of which holds her stillborn child.

ST JAMES'S PALACE For three centuries, from the reign of HENRY VIII onwards, St James's Palace was a foremost royal residence, and today it is still the Court of St James's to which ambassadors are accredited.

When the PALACE OF WESTMINSTER was partly destroyed by fire, King Henry decided that Whitehall was not adequate for his residential

ST JAMES'S PALACE

St James's Palace was begun by Henry VIII but it was not the principal royal palace until Whitehall Palace burned down in 1698.

requirements in London, and he acquired the Convent of St James the Less as the site for his new palace. All that is to be seen of the original building today is the gateway, on which the initials of Henry and ANNE BOLEYN remain, standing at the junction of Pall Mall and St James's Street. It is through this that the Colour Court, one of the palace's four courts, is reached, the other three being the Friary Court, the Engine Court and the Ambassadors' Court.

Although Henry's interest in the palace waned, it was where his Roman Catholic daughter MARY attended Mass, and found shelter within its walls when Sir Thomas Wyatt, outraged by her intention to marry Philip of Spain, led his rebels on London. After Mary died in the palace her half-sister ELIZABETH I held court in there. When JAMES I succeeded her he installed his son Henry, Duke of Cornwall in the palace but his residence was short as he died of fever in 1612.

CHARLES I took up residence in St James's after the death of his brother, and immediately after his marriage to HENRIETTA MARIA in 1625 he arranged that her French priests could say Mass daily for her – braving Protestant anger – in the Queen's Chapel which was designed by Inigo Jones. It was at St James's that the Queen gave birth to several of her children, including the future CHARLES II, and after the English Civil War it was where her husband spent his last night before being taken through St James's Park to Whitehall Palace for his execution on 30 January 1649. Several of his children were kept as prisoners in the palace by the victorious Parliamentarians though two, Henrietta and the future JAMES II, did manage to escape disguised as urchins.

During the Interregnum the palace was used as a military prison but with the Restoration Charles II renewed its royal status when he had Sir Christopher Wren improve the state apartments. He added 36 acres to St James's Park where he enjoyed walking by the lake and playing pall-mall in a special gallery. This game, after which Pall Mall was named, was similar to croquet and took its name from the Italian *pallo a maglio*.

Having owed its beginning to a fire in Whitehall Palace in 1698, St James's became the principal royal residence and was used extensively by the first three Hanoverian kings. GEORGE III was married to Queen Charlotte in the Chapel Royal, as was his son the future GEORGE IV when he wed CAROLINE OF BRUNSWICK-WOLFEN-BÜTTEL in 1795.

George III preferred to live in Buckingham House rather than St James's though it continued to be used by members of the royal family, including his son Ernest Augustus, Duke of Cumberland who later became the King of Hanover. On 31 May 1810 the duke was reported to have suffered a murderous attack in the palace by his Piedmontese valet, though the full facts of the sensational case are not known. Although the palace's state apartments fell into disuse, state functions continued to be held at St James's which included the marriages of QUEEN VICTORIA to PRINCE ALBERT in 1840, her eldest daughter Princess Victoria to Prince Frederick, later Frederick III, Emperor of Prussia in 1858, and her grandson the future GEORGE V to Princess Mary of Teck. And it was at St James's Palace on 8 February 1952 that, two days after her accession, ELIZABETH II made her first speech as Queen of England to the Accession Council which was made up of privy councillors.

Today the palace houses the Lord Chamberlain's department and other royal offices such as the Central Chancery of the Orders of Knighthood, as well as apartments for officers of the royal household.
See also CLARENCE HOUSE, LANCASTER HOUSE, MARLBOROUGH HOUSE

ST JAMES'S PARK London's oldest royal park was originally a miry field beside a leper hospital where the inmates were allowed to keep pigs, and its name of St James's goes back to the dreaded hospital. HENRY VIII, ever eager to extend his domains, had the pigs' field drained and established a tiltyard and bowling alley there. Later he extended it from the area which today lies between Birdcage Walk and The Mall, to Marylebone, Islington and Hampstead to make a royal hunting ground. His daughter ELIZABETH I hunted there but it was her successor JAMES I who began to create the park as we know it today. Gardens were laid out in the initial hospital grounds, as was a physic garden, and

The lake in St James's Park known as the Canal was created by Charles II, who enjoyed feeding the ducks there.

the king's private zoo which included a pair of crocodiles. The king's aviary gave its name to Birdcage Walk.

On 30 January 1649 CHARLES I was escorted across the park on his way to the scaffold, which had been erected outside the Banqueting House in Whitehall.

After a period of neglect during the Commonwealth, CHARLES II not only restored the park but increased its area by over 30 acres. Fruit trees were planted and a stretch of water which became known as the Canal was created by joining up several ponds. A tree-lined avenue was laid out and surfaced with powdered sea shells on which the king played pall-mall. Charles was particularly fond of the Canal where he enjoyed walking with his ladies and his dogs, feeding the ducks and sometimes swimming in its water. One of the aspects of the park was its variety of birds which included a couple of pelicans and a crane with an artificial leg.

When WILLIAM III came to the throne he had built a hide on an island, still known as Duck Island, from which he could watch the waterfowl. During the next reign, that of QUEEN ANNE, the park became a favourite venue for prostitutes to ply their ancient trade and the park lost much of its gentility. There was some improvement in the park's reputation in 1751 when Lord Pomfret became its ranger and made it against the law to draw a sword within its confines, so that fewer duels were fought there than in other London parks. Nevertheless 'ladies of the town', as James Boswell termed them, continued to use the park despite the fact that at nightfall the gates were locked.

In 1814 the Prince Regent, in collaboration with his architect John Nash, arranged a magnificent celebration in the park to mark the centenary of the foundation of the HOUSE OF HANOVER coupled with the anniversary of the Battle of the Nile. A Chinese-style pagoda was one of the attractions but during a display of fireworks it accidentally caught fire and was destroyed. When the Prince Regent became GEORGE IV in 1820 he set about improving the park and two years after his accession it was lighted by gas lamps and soon afterwards the Canal was altered to its present configuration.

During QUEEN VICTORIA's reign improvements to the park continued and these included the building of an iron suspension bridge spanning the water, which lasted until it was demolished in the 1950s. Today the park remains one of the most fashionable in London and its population of over thirty different varieties of wildfowl, including the traditional pelicans, is an enduring attraction for visitors to the capital.

ST MARGARET, QUEEN OF SCOTLAND

A granddaughter of EDMUND IRONSIDE, Princess Margaret was born c. 1045 in Hungary where her father EDWARD THE ATHELING lived in exile after CANUTE became King of England. In 1057 he returned to England with Margaret and her younger brother EDGAR THE ATHELING. Soon afterwards he died in mysterious circumstances, the *Anglo-Saxon Chronicle* stating enigmatically: 'We do not know for what reason it was brought about that he was not allowed to look on the face of his kinsman, King Edward [the Confessor].'

After 1066 Edgar the Atheling was the last hope of the supporters of the old English dynasty and thus became involved in futile revolts against the Normans with the result that he, Margaret and their mother sought sanctuary in Scotland in 1068. Here Margaret, who was renowned for her beauty as well as her intelligence, won the affections of Malcolm III (*see* SCOTLAND, EARLY KINGS OF). The king married her the following year at Dunfermline where Margaret later built an impressive church. During her marriage she bore three future kings of Scotland: EDGAR, ALEXANDER I and DAVID I.

Margaret's effect on her husband's kingdom was profound. With her experience of court life outside Scotland she introduced English fashions and customs to the royal household and greatly increased its prestige. But it was in religious matters that she had the greatest influence, bringing the Celtic Church into the orbit of Roman Catholicism and seeking to impose the concept of celibacy and Christian poverty upon its reluctant priests. She was also responsible for the rebuilding of the monastery on IONA.

On 13 November 1093, when invading Northumberland, King Malcolm was slain at the siege of Alnwick Castle. Three days later Queen Margaret died after giving thanks to God that her last hours were purified by the sorrow she felt over the death of her husband. She was canonised by Pope Innocent IV in 1250, her feast day being 16 November or 19 June.

ST MICHAEL AND ST GEORGE, ORDER OF

Instituted in 1818, the Order is bestowed on men

and women in recognition of exceptional service outside the military sphere or who have held or hold important office abroad. As with the Order of the Bath there are three classes of recipients: Knights and Dames Grant Cross with 125 members; Knights and Dames Commander, 375 members; and Companions, 1,750 members. The Order's chapel is St Paul's Cathedral and its motto is *Auspicium melioris aevi* – 'Token of a Better Age'.

ST PATRICK, MOST ILLUSTRIOUS ORDER OF Created in 1788 as the national order of Ireland, its membership consisted of the sovereign and twenty-two knights. No new knights were initiated after 1922.

ST PETER AD VINCULA Built for the use of prisoners in the TOWER OF LONDON, the appropriately named chapel ('St Peter in Chains') was established in the twelfth century. The present building on Tower Green goes back to the sixteenth century. Among those who were executed on the Green or on Tower Hill and interred in the chapel were SIR THOMAS MORE (1535), ANNE BOLEYN (1536), CATHERINE HOWARD (1542), LADY JANE GREY and her husband Lord Guildford Dudley (1554), ROBERT DEVEREUX, Earl of Essex (1601), the DUKE OF MONMOUTH (1685) and the Lords Lovat and Kilmarnock who were involved in the second Jacobite Rebellion in 1746.

ST THOMAS A BECKET *See* THOMAS A BECKET

SANDRINGHAM HOUSE Shortly before his death in 1861 PRINCE ALBERT arranged to buy Sandringham House in Norfolk for £220,000 from a nephew of Lord Palmerston, who had suggested it would make a suitable residence for the Prince of Wales, the future EDWARD VII, on his coming of age. It was Albert's hope that being in a remote rural area the prince would be distanced from the capital's temptations of which he so strongly disapproved. As it turned out, the prince was delighted with Sandringham because – so it was said – it was far from Windsor Castle where his disapproving mother QUEEN VICTORIA resided after being widowed, though the main attraction was the hunting and shooting that it offered. The prince turned the estate into a remarkable game reserve which, when it was fully stocked, provided the game bags of his shooting parties with up to thirty thousand partridges and pheasants a season.

After the prince married Princess Alexandra of Denmark in March 1863, the couple moved into Sandringham and the princess immediately fell in love with the place. This came as a surprise to some of her contemporaries as they considered the flat Norfolk landscape in which the house was set to be bleak and not improved by the cold wind that swept in from the North Sea, but to Alexandra it was a

The chapel of St Peter ad Vincula in the Tower of London.

reminder of the countryside she had known in her homeland. As for the prince, he once described Sandringham as 'the house that I like best'.

The disadvantage that they found with their new home was that it was not large enough to accommodate their household and the numerous guests that the gregarious prince took pleasure in entertaining. Thus it was decided to demolish it and build a more suitable residence in the Jacobean style. Work began in 1870 and Sandringham House, as it looks today, was completed three years later when an inscription over the entrance read 'This house was built by Albert Edward and Alexandra his wife in the year of Our Lord 1870.' The new mansion was constructed of red brick and dressings of yellowish stone, contained over 270 rooms and was noted for its ballroom, added some years after the building was completed.

In 1891 the prince planned a grand celebration at Sandringham to mark his 50th birthday but the night prior to the arrival of the guests a fire broke out on the third floor due to a faulty chimney, and as a result part of the building was destroyed. Despite this setback the prince was determined to continue with the festivity, which was held in part of the house that had escaped the flames beneath a temporary covering of tarpaulins.

As a young man Prince Edward's second son, the Duke of York and the future GEORGE V, was given the Bachelor's Cottage, once described as a modest villa with mock Tudor beams, which stood in the grounds of Sandringham and which was renamed York House. In 1893 the duke spent his honeymoon there with Mary of Teck and subsequently five of their six children were born there, the odd one out being the future EDWARD VIII who was born at White Lodge, Richmond. After he became king in 1910 George agreed to his mother continuing to live in Sandringham House, as had been his father's wish, so the dowager Queen Alexandra resided in the palatial house until her death in 1925 while the king and his family continued to live in the relatively humble York House.

King George died at his cherished Sandringham in January 1936 and after the brief reign of EDWARD VIII, his second son became GEORGE VI in December of that year. It was said that he was even more fond of Sandringham than his father, and it was there that he died peacefully in February 1952 after a day's shooting.

Today it is a tradition that after spending Christmas at WINDSOR CASTLE, the royal family moves to Sandringham for the New Year.

SCOTLAND, EARLY KINGS OF Today the Picts remain an enigmatic people but at the time the Romans left Britain in the fifth century they were the most powerful of the four races who inhabited Scotland, then known as Alban. Their territory extended from the Forth to where Caithness is today. The area south of the Forth was occupied by Angles who had crossed from northern Europe, while to the west the Britons of Strathclyde held the country stretching from the Clyde to Cumbria. The western land and isles were inhabited by Scots who, having crossed from Ireland in the previous century, established the kingdom of Dalriada and from then on were in fierce conflict with the Picts.

In the middle of the ninth century the unification of Scotland began when Kenneth MacAlpin, the King of Dalriada, conquered the Picts who, after centuries of being the most powerful folk north of Hadrian's Wall, faded from history. Next the king endeavoured to subject the Angles but when he died in 858 they were still undefeated. It was not until the beginning of the eleventh century that his descendant Malcolm II was successful in bringing them under Scottish domination. Malcolm's grandson and heir Duncan became King of the Strathclyde Britons when the previous king died without issue.

In 1034 Duncan became King of Scotland when he inherited Malcolm's throne but six years later he was slain in battle by Macbeth, the Mormaer of Moray, when he attempted to invade his kingdom. Macbeth seized Duncan's throne and, contrary to Shakespeare's portrayal of him, ruled Scotland so successfully for the next seventeen years that his reign was described by chroniclers as a time of plenty. He was the only Scottish king to make a pilgrimage to Rome where he 'scattered money like seed among the poor'. In 1054, four years after his visit to Rome, Macbeth lost a battle to Malcolm, the son of Duncan I, aided by Siward, Earl of Northumbria. Despite this setback Macbeth continued to rule Scotland. Known as 'Canmore', meaning 'great leader', Malcolm was eager to avenge his father and he accomplished this on 15 August 1057 when he slew Macbeth at the Battle of Lumphanan.

The Early Scots Kings - ALPIN - MALCOLM III

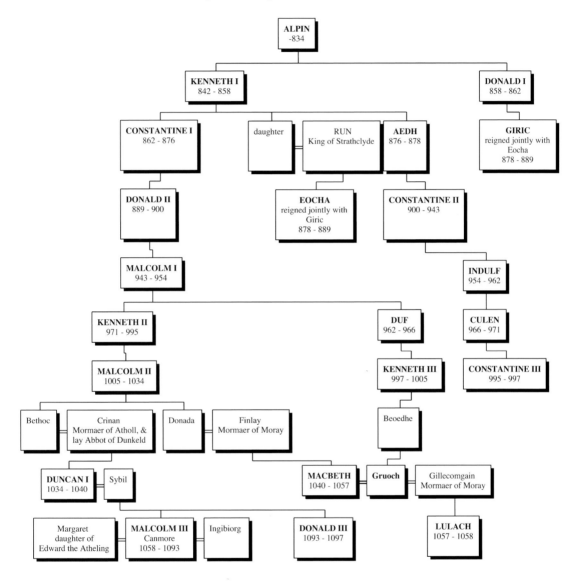

The following few weeks were chaotic, the throne of Scotland not going to Malcolm but to Lulach, the son of Gruoch, who had married Macbeth after he had killed her husband Gille Comgain, King of Moray, in 1032. However, eighteen weeks later Malcolm killed him 'by treachery' at Essie on March 17 and thus became Malcolm III of Scotland. He secured the throne by defeating Lulach's son Mael Snechta, King of Moray, in 1058. In 1070 the English royal family took refuge in Scotland following the Norman Conquest, and Malcolm married Margaret, the sister of EDGAR THE ATHELING. Two years later Malcolm submitted to WILLIAM I ('The Conqueror') at Abernethy but this did not prevent him raiding Northumbria. In August 1093 he laid the foundation stone of Durham Cathedral but soon afterwards was killed when he raided Alnwick.

The next three decades were chaotic as one ineffective king followed another. After the death of

Malcolm III the throne was seized by his pro-Celtic brother, Donald Bane, who reversed his predecessor's preference for English and Norman ways which had been encouraged by his wife Queen Margaret. His attitude found little favour with WILLIAM II who had ascended the throne of England in 1087. William had been holding hostage Duncan, Malcolm's son by his first marriage, but in 1094 he dispatched him to Scotland to supplant his uncle. Donald was deposed but Duncan had no chance to savour his success as almost immediately he was assassinated and once more Donald was king. Three years later William sent an army north of the border and this time Donald quit his throne for good, and Edgar, the son of Malcolm by his second wife Margaret, was installed in his place.

The new king understandably favoured those who had brought him to power, with the result that Norman influence increased in Scotland, especially in the south where a large number of Normans had settled. When Edgar died in 1107 he was succeeded by his brother Alexander who did not rule the whole of Scotland but the country between the Forth and the Spey, the country to the south of the Forth being governed by his brother David. During Alexander's reign the relationship with England deepened as his sister Maud married HENRY I of England and he married Henry's daughter Sibylla, so that he was not only the son-in-law of the English king but also his brother-in-law.

When Alexander died in 1124 his throne was inherited by his brother David, the most able of the sons born to Malcolm III by Queen Margaret. The Norman influence was strong in David who had not only received a Norman education but through his marriage to a Norman heiress he became Earl of Northampton and Huntingdon. This, added to the fact that he was Prince of Cumbria as well as King of Scotland, made him one of the most powerful men in Britain. Under David, Scotland was beginning to enjoy stability as he established a system of administration with a chancellor, chamberlain, marshal, and similar officials who, with bishops, formed a central council under his control to advise him and to attend to judicial and governmental matters.

The first Scottish king to have his own coinage, David established two royal mints and standardised weights and measures. He was also deeply concerned over Church matters, creating a number of bishoprics, increasing the number of monasteries and building new churches. Although he did not question the authority of Rome in ecclesiastical matters, he favoured the Church in Scotland preserving a certain independence. This was illustrated when Pope Innocent IV, who canonised the king's mother Queen Margaret in 1250, threatened excommunication when the bishops of Scotland, with David's support, refused to accept the primacy of the Archbishop of York.

During David's reign Scotland not only prospered but enjoyed a period of peace, apart from when the king became involved in the English dynastic struggle between Matilda, the daughter of the late Henry I, and her cousin STEPHEN. In this he was inspired by self-interest, supporting one side and then the other, and although he suffered defeat at the Battle of the Standard in 1138 he still managed to conclude a treaty that ceded him part of Northumbria, which had been his primary objective.

When David died in 1153 he was succeeded by his eldest grandson, 11-year-old Malcolm IV who was nicknamed 'The Maiden'. The security which Scotland had enjoyed under the late king eroded with the arrival of the boy king. On the east coast Aberdeen was pillaged by Norwegians; on the west Glasgow suffered similar treatment by the Lord of Argyll, while HENRY II of England compelled young Malcolm to give up Northumbria. Twelve years after he came to the throne Malcolm died and was followed by his brother William ('The Lion') who committed himself to the return of Northumbria. During 1165, the first year of his reign, he made a pact with France in order to have an ally against England which came to be known as the 'Auld Alliance'.

In 1173 the three sons of Henry II – Henry, RICHARD and Geoffrey – rebelled against their father and the troubles of the English king gave William the opportunity to invade Northumbria. While besieging Alnwick Castle he was surprised by an English force and taken as a prisoner to Normandy. Here he found that the price of his freedom was acceptance of the Treaty of Falaise. The document he was forced into signing placed the Scottish Church under the authority of the Archbishop of Canterbury, endorsed the English possession of Northumbria and stipulated that English soldiers should garrison the principal castles of southern Scotland. In effect the treaty transformed Scotland into a vassal state.

The Early Scots Kings - MALCOLM III - ROBERT I

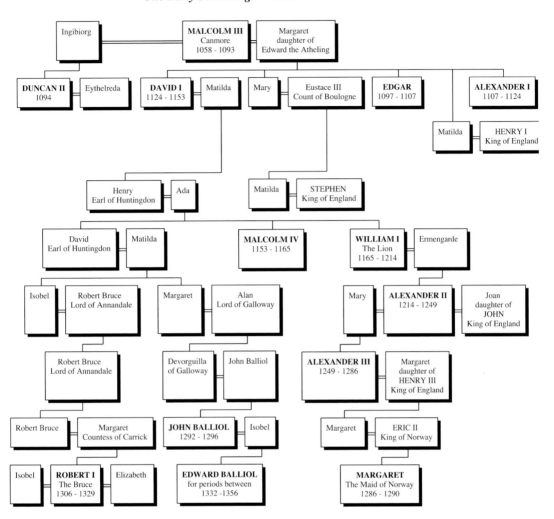

William the Lyon had to accept the situation until 1189 when he regained Scottish independence, not by force of arms but by the fact that RICHARD I, who had ascended the throne of England that year, was desperate for money to fund his participation in the Third Crusade. It was said he would sell London if he could find a buyer, and for 10,000 marks he restored Scotland's independence. This was further strengthened in 1192 when Pope Celestine III declared the Scottish Church should no longer be subject to the English archbishop but continue under the authority of Rome.

For the next century Scotland was to enjoy peace with England but William still had problems in the western quarter of the kingdom, where Celtic chieftains always resented the rule of a central monarchy and were ever ready to defy it. During the reign of Malcolm IV, the Prince of Galloway had raised the banner of insurrection, and after William the Lion came to the throne his sons followed his example by attacking the castles which, by the Treaty of Falaise, were held by English troops. In the region now known as Argyll-shire the Lords of Lorne and the Lords of the Isles had never willingly accepted the overlordship of a Scottish king and preferred to owe some allegiance to the royal house of Norway rather than that of Scotland.

More troublesome than rebellious lords were the claims to the throne made by members of the MacWilliam family, based on their descent from William, the son of Duncan II. In 1187 Donald MacWilliam sought to win the crown of William the Lion but this venture ended with his head being carried to the king. This did not deter his son Guthred from making a similar attempt in 1211 but he was taken prisoner and beheaded.

When William died in 1214 the throne was inherited by his son Alexander II who was soon faced with rebellion by Donald MacWilliam, the brother of Guthred, but he too lost his head. Like his forebears Alexander was eager for Scotland to have domination of Northumbria, and he hoped to regain it by supporting the barons who were opposed to KING JOHN of England, and eventually forced him to sign the MAGNA CARTA. In the event Alexander did not get Northumbria but accepted a number of estates in the north of England, while the peace between Scotland and England was further strengthened by his marriage to Joan, the sister of HENRY III, in 1221.

Finally Alexander formally renounced Scotland's long-standing claim to Northumbria in the Treaty of York in 1237, and the Anglo-Scottish borderline between the Tweed and the Solway was finally agreed. During his reign there were rebellions in Argyll, Caithness, Galloway and Moray but the peace between Scotland and England left him free to concentrate on these challenges. In 1221–2 he invaded Argyll and in 1234 he succeeded in subduing Galloway. In 1249 he was poised to seize the Western Isles, whose lords still owed fealty to Norway, when he died on the island of Kerrera in Oban Bay.

When Alexander III inherited his father's throne he was 8 years old, and two years later he was married to Princess Margaret, the daughter of Henry III, thereby continuing the kinship with the English royal family. At the age of 20 he assumed full control of the government and continued his father's plan to annex the Western Isles. His raids on the Hebrides, regarded by the Norwegians as their territory, provoked King Haakon into sending a war fleet to Scotland in the summer of 1263. Alexander entered into lengthy negotiations with the king in order to postpone hostilities until October when the Norwegian fleet would be struck by autumnal gales at its anchorage in the Firth of Clyde. On 2 October the Norwegians left their ships and fought the Battle of Largs which, although described in some history books as 'little more than a skirmish', was to have a far-reaching effect on Scotland. The Norwegians were forced from the battlefield in confusion and Haakon decided to return to Norway but died at Kirkwall on the journey.

As a direct result of the Battle of Largs, Haakon's successor King Magnus ('The Lawmaker') signed the Treaty of Perth on 2 July 1266 by which he sold the rights of Norway's kings to the Western Isles and Isle of Man to Alexander. Although Orkney and Shetland were to remain under Norwegian jurisdiction, the treaty ended the long period of Norway's hostile influence on Scottish history. The Lords of the Isles, however, still regarded themselves as independent of Scotland despite the end of their tenuous allegiance to Norway.

Scotland prospered greatly during the remainder of Alexander's reign. In 1283 his daughter Margaret was married to King Eric of Norway and this dynastic union underlined the new amicable relationship between the two countries which was to last down the centuries. The same year, Margaret died, it is thought in giving birth to her daughter who was named after her. This was yet another sorrow for Alexander who had also suffered the deaths of his wife and two sons. In 1284 he obtained the acceptance of his infant granddaughter Margaret, known as the Maid of Norway, as heir to the Crown of Scotland. Yet in the hope of still siring a son to follow him he married his second wife Yolande de Dreux in 1285. Only five months after the wedding he was killed by a fall from his horse as he was riding home after dark.

In England EDWARD I proposed that his son Edward should be betrothed to Alexander's granddaughter, the little Queen of Scotland who was still in Norway. In 1290 a marriage treaty was drawn up and signed by Scottish magnates at Birgham, guaranteeing that Scotland would remain an independent kingdom, and the following year a ship was sent to bring the 6-year-old Maid of Norway to Scotland. On the voyage Margaret died at Kirkwall in the Orkneys in September of that year. Her death was surrounded in mystery, some reports saying that she died at sea before reaching the Orkneys. A curious echo of the tragedy occurred in 1300 when a young woman from Leipzig declared that she was Queen Margaret, a claim that was ended when she was burned as a witch in Bergen.

Margaret's death brought about the dispute known as the Great Cause in which thirteen claimants to the throne, known as 'The Competitors', decided to accept the choice of Edward I. Of these contenders two with almost equally strong claims to the succession were John Balliol and ROBERT DE BRUCE (whose son was destined to become Robert I), both being descended from David I's youngest son on the distaff side. Each had estates in England as well as in Scotland, and each was on good terms with King Edward, having served in his army. After their claims had been considered by eighty Scottish and twenty-four English advisers to the king, Edward announced at Berwick Castle that Balliol was his choice. In making his decision he was influenced by the fact that of the two Balliol was likely to be the most amenable to his demands. These included that as the King of Scotland, Balliol should pay him homage and repudiate the Treaty of Birgham. This Balliol did, swearing fealty to the English king before and after his coronation at Scone in 1292.

In Scotland the new king was nicknamed 'Toom Tabard', meaning 'empty coat', on account of his weak acceptance of Edward's terms, which included demands for money towards England's approaching invasion of France. Finally the Scots became so disillusioned that in 1295 a council of twelve magnates was set up to supervise the king, with the result that he renounced his allegiance to Edward I; an alliance was concluded with France, then at war with England; and in 1296 Balliol planned to invade the north of England. As soon as he crossed the border Edward I replied by marching his army into Scotland where a number of Scottish nobles did him homage as, owning estates in England, they were technically his vassals and thus demonstrated the divisions that so often split the Scots. Among these was Robert de Bruce who had been Balliol's rival for the Crown. When news of this reached Balliol he confiscated all the lands that Bruce held in Scotland and bestowed them on his brother-in-law John Comyn, known as Red Comyn, the head of the most powerful Scottish baronial family.

Meanwhile, Edward I sacked Berwick, putting a large number of its inhabitants to the sword, after which he vanquished Balliol's army at Dunbar and took the Scottish king captive. As Edward's prisoner Balliol had to surrender his crown on 10 July 1296 and was then incarcerated in the TOWER OF LONDON for the next three years, after which he was released into papal custody and in 1306 was allowed to withdraw to his estates in Normandy where he remained until his death in 1315.

After his victory at Dunbar Edward I moved remorselessly through Scotland, capturing castles and stamping his mark on the country. Returning to Berwick in August 1296, two thousand prominent Scotsmen were coerced into doing him homage and placing their names on the 'Ragman's Roll', which was a document recognising him as the King of Scotland. Then, leaving castles garrisoned by English troops and an English council under the Earl of Surrey to administer the country, Edward returned to England. From Scone Abbey he took the 'Stone of Destiny', on which Scottish kings had been traditionally crowned since the days of Kenneth MacAlpin, and installed it under the Coronation Chair in WESTMINSTER ABBEY. It symbolised what appeared to be the end of Scotland's autonomy but in fact it was the beginning of the wars of Scottish independence.

Scotland's revolt against English rule began in the spring of 1297 when William Wallace, reputedly the second son of Sir Malcolm Wallace of Elderslie, became an outlaw. The traditional story is that Wallace, a protagonist of Scottish independence when so many accepted the rule of Edward I, became involved in a fracas with a number of English troops in Lanark's market place. He managed to elude his adversaries with the assistance

Terracotta statue of William Wallace.

of a young woman who, in some versions of the tale, was his wife. She was captured and, by the order of Hazelrig, the English Sheriff of Lanark, executed.

In reply Wallace led a band of like-minded men to Lanark, which they set afire, and put the sheriff to death. Wallace was outlawed but instead of fleeing he raised the standard of Scotland and in collaboration with a fellow esquire named Andrew Moray began a campaign to free the country from the English yoke. By September 1297 the two young men led an army which achieved a monumental victory against the English at Stirling Bridge, at which Andrew Moray was fatally wounded. As a result the English were expelled and for ten months after the battle Wallace was undisputed leader of the Scots and declared the Guardian of Scotland, his heroic reputation enhanced by a devastating incursion he led across the north of England. In 1298 Edward I, the dreaded 'Hammer of the Scots', retaliated by personally leading an avenging army across the border and at

Falkirk Wallace made the fatal error of engaging the royal army in a set-piece battle despite being outnumbered. He was deserted by his cavalry, which left the infantry at the mercy of Edward's bowmen with the consequence that the Scots were utterly defeated.

Wallace escaped the field and for a short while he continued to harass his enemies with guerrilla tactics before travelling to France where he endeavoured to persuade the French to support the Scots against their traditional enemy. In 1303 he returned to Scotland but in 1305 he was arrested in Glasgow by Sir John de Menteith, who later became the Earl of Lennox, and taken to London where he was found guilty of treason despite his argument that as he had never sworn fealty to the king he was innocent of the charge. He was condemned to a ghastly form of execution, sanctioned twenty years earlier, and was one of the first prisoners to be hanged, drawn and quartered at Smithfield. He was dismembered and parts of his body were displayed at Berwick, Newcastle, Perth and Stirling, and his head was placed on a spike on London Bridge.

Edward I may have rid himself of a troublesome rebel yet down the following centuries to the

Site of the Battle of Stirling Bridge where William Wallace defeated the army of Edward I.

present day William Wallace is regarded as a semi-legendary hero, personifying the Scots' love of liberty.

SCOTTISH CROWN JEWELS Known as the 'Honours of Scotland', the Scottish crown jewels comprise a crown, sceptre and sword. The crown was made for JAMES V of Scotland (1512–42) and consists of a circlet of Scottish gold decorated with twenty precious stones, twenty-two gemstones and a number of freshwater pearls found in Scottish rivers. The sceptre, which was remodelled in 1536, was presented to JAMES IV of Scotland (1473–1513) by Pope Alexander VI in 1494. Likewise, in 1507 the Sword of State was a gift to the king from Pope Julius II who had the 4ft 6in blade etched with a papal inscription and images of St Peter and St Paul. Until 1987, when the Order of the Thistle celebrated its 300th anniversary, the sword was used in the Order's ceremonial.

The jewels were first used together in 1543 for the coronation of MARY, QUEEN OF SCOTS, and at the coronation of her son JAMES VI of Scotland in 1567. They were used again at the enthronement of Mary's grandson CHARLES I in 1633 but during the Interregnum they were kept in a secret location after being smuggled out of Dunnottar Castle. They reappeared with the restoration of CHARLES II but were never again used in a coronation ceremony. In 1941 the jewels were again hidden in order to safeguard them against the possibility of a German invasion. They were formally presented to ELIZABETH II in 1953, the year of her coronation. Today they are displayed together with the STONE OF SCONE in Edinburgh Castle.

SEDLEY, CATHERINE In 1673 James, Duke of York and the future JAMES II replaced his long-term mistress ARABELLA CHURCHILL with Catherine Sedley. Her father was Charles Sedley, famous both as a poet and infamous as a debauched rake who set up house with his mistress after his wife went insane. Before she attracted James's attention it was said of Catherine that she was 'as mad as her mother and as vicious as her father'. On hearing of the new liaison CHARLES II declared that she must have been prescribed by his brother's confessor 'as a sort of penance'. She was described as 'clever but very pale and thin' and had a squint, but what was remarkable about Catherine Sedley was her outspokenness and wit which she used

unmercifully against the Roman Catholic priests who had come to England with Mary of Modena. Puzzled by James's passion for her, she once remarked, 'It cannot be my beauty for I have none, and it cannot be my wit for he has not enough to know I have any.'

A curious aspect of the relationship was that she was a strong Protestant while James was becoming more and more enthusiastic for the Roman Catholic faith, which was to lead to his downfall as the king of Protestant England. On coming to the throne in 1685, he had pangs of guilt about his way of life. Well aware that the Queen hated the royal favourite, he wanted to begin his reign as a moral monarch and to this end he dismissed Catherine from the court. She was given a house in St James's Square that had been previously occupied by Arabella Churchill, and an allowance of £4,000 a year.

This was a great relief to Queen Mary yet her triumph was diminished at the coronation when Catherine Sedley became the talk of London. One of her children, a baby of six months who had been fathered by the new sovereign, died on that very day. Disconsolate without his mistress, James met her by chance three months later and the relationship was resumed. It was widely believed that the meeting was not accidental but a plot engineered by Protestant nobles who wanted to counteract the influence of James's Roman Catholic wife by means of a Protestant mistress.

Things came to a head between Queen Mary and Catherine Sedley in January 1686 when the still-besotted James increased her allowance by £1,000 and created her Baroness of Darlington and Countess of Dorchester. These honours upset Catherine almost as much as they upset the queen. She was shrewd enough to realise that Mary could not overlook what appeared as an insult to her. The Queen assembled her priests and then summoned James to her apartment where she upbraided him bitterly and declared that unless he dismissed Catherine she would retire to a convent. The priests warned James that this 'blemish' in his life 'blasted' their plans to win the country back to the Roman Catholic fold. They even threatened to refuse him the Sacrament if he continued with his Protestant mistress, under whose gibes they had so often suffered.

James could not defend himself against this combined attack and answered that he was not intending to see Catherine any more and that he had given her the titles in order to break with her 'more decently'. Catherine was ordered back to her house in St James's Square, and James could not bear to watch her departure for fear of weakening his resolve. When she was gone from the court he scourged himself to dull his unfulfilled passion, and Mary of Modena later gave the whip to the convent of Chaillot as though it was a holy relic.

The banished mistress wrote to James: 'I know that your Majesty is surrounded and ensnared by many ravens hungering for their own purposes and for poor Catherine's downfall; but my good lord and master these men will wrought you evil, and perhaps bring sore trouble and distress upon you. The Queen, my lady, loves not her lord's true and faithful mistress, and perchance in that there can be nothing to surprise either of us, but if your loving Catherine must be sacrificed and driven from the presence of her good lord the King, let it be for the reason of my lady, the Queen, and not for the jealous hatred of cunning priests.'

Although she posed as a Protestant martyr and invoked the MAGNA CARTA to prove that she could not be banished without her agreement, Catherine Sedley, like Arabella Churchill before her, was sent to Ireland. She hated Dublin and after a few months managed to return to London, but now her power to influence the King was ended.

After James II lost his throne to WILLIAM AND MARY in 1689 the Protestant sovereigns granted Catherine a pension of £1,500 per annum. In 1696 she married David Colyer, who became the Earl of Portmore, and bore him two sons. She had had several children by James, but only one daughter, Lady Catherine Darnley, survived childhood.

Catherine was as bluntly spoken as NELL GWYNNE and became famous for a remark she made when the Hanoverian dynasty began in 1714. Invited to a court reception by GEORGE I she found that two other ex-royal favourites were present – the Duchess of Portsmouth, once the mistress to Charles II, and the Countess of Orkney, who had been the paramour of William III. 'By Jove,' she cried in ringing tones, 'who would have thought that we three whores should have met here!'

Catherine Sedley died in 1743 and was buried with great pomp in WESTMINSTER ABBEY.

SETTLEMENT, 1701, ACT OF The Act was passed to ensure that a Protestant would ascend the throne in the event of WILLIAM III or QUEEN ANNE dying without issue by declaring that JAMES I's granddaughter Sophia, Electress of Hanover and her heirs would inherit the Crown. The Act, which completely disregarded the superior claim of the Stuarts, ensured the establishment of the House of Hanover in 1714.

SHORE, JANE Of all the mistresses of English kings, Jane Shore is regarded as the most popular with the public of her day. She was born in London and at an early age married a goldsmith named William Shore. He abandoned her after she had begun an intrigue with EDWARD IV in about 1470, and from then on she was maintained in great luxury for the rest of his reign. After Edward's death in 1483 she lived under the protection of Lord Hastings until he was executed by order of RICHARD III. In order to discredit his late brother Richard fined Jane 2,000 marks and ensured that the Bishop of London forced her to do penance for her shameful life by walking with a lighted candle through the city streets wearing only her kirtle. According to a chronicler, Mistress Shore's popularity with the public was due to the fact that although she had great influence over the King while she was the royal paramour, she never exploited it 'to any man's hurt but to many a man's comfort and relief'. Eton School and King's College would not have continued to exist had not Jane persuaded the King to to support them. She died c. 1527.

SHREWSBURY, BATTLE OF Early in July 1403 HENRY PERCY, better known in history as 'Hotspur', led an army into Cheshire on the way to join up with Owain Glyndwr's Welsh rebels. Here he handed out White Hart badges to the locals, telling them that RICHARD II, who had been deposed by HENRY IV, had not been murdered in his prison, but was still alive.

In response, Henry hastened to Shrewsbury to occupy the town before the rebels arrived, and on the morning of 21 July he marched out to confront his enemies. At a spot known today as 'Battlefield' he placed his army in two divisions, the rear formation under the command of his son Prince Henry. The battle continued without respite for three hours and, according to the contemporary writer Thomas of Walsingham, 'the dead lay thick as leaves in autumn.'

Finally, Hotspur and the Earl of Douglas found that the ranks through which they had charged had closed behind them and they were assailed from all sides. Hotspur, nearly suffocating in his armour, raised his visor for air and at that instant an arrow struck him in the face and he fell dead from the saddle. Seeing this, Henry spurred towards the enemy shouting, 'Henry Percy is dead! St George! Victory!' Percy's lines broke and his men fled the field with their Welsh allies.

The body of Henry Percy was divided into four and spiked in Bristol, Chester, Newcastle and London as a warning to those who would challenge the King's authority.

SILVER STICK *See* GOLD STICK IN WAITING

SIMNEL, LAMBERT The son of either a baker or a joiner, Lambert Simnel was born *c.* 1477, and as a child was taken to Ireland where he was groomed to be a pretender to the throne of HENRY VII. Firstly it was claimed he was Prince Edward, the son of EDWARD IV, who had mysteriously vanished in the Tower of London. Later he avowed that he was Edward, the son of the Duke of Clarence. Supported by the Earl of Kildare and Margaret of Burgundy, his professed aunt, he was crowned in Dublin as 'Edward VI' in May 1487. The next month he sailed to England with two thousand German mercenaries. On 16 June Henry VII defeated this army at the Battle of Stoke Field, where John de la Pole, Earl of Lincoln, who had joined the rebels, was killed, with the result that the insurgency was quelled. As Simnel was no more than a pawn in the plot, the king put him to scullion's work and later he became a royal falconer. According to tradition, he originated Simnel cakes in the king's kitchen. Simnel was never the threat to the throne as PERKIN WARBECK was five years later.

SIMPSON, WALLIS Bessie Wallis was born in 1896 in Pennsylvania, the only child of Alice and Teackle Wallis Warfield. The Warfield family was one of America's oldest and most successful, having arrived in the New World in 1662. Alice was a member of the equally ancient Montague family, so from an American point of view Wallis's antecedents were impeccable, which gave a lie to the belief that she was devoid of 'breeding' or a social background.

In 1916 she married a U.S. Navy pilot, Earl Winfield Spencer, who she described in an ecstatic letter home as 'the world's most fascinating aviator'. They divorced in 1927 to the outrage of the Warfields and Montagues for whom divorce was the ultimate disgrace.

The following year Wallis married Ernest Aldrich Simpson of New York and in London they set up house close to Hyde Park. Ernest's sister, Mrs Kerr-Smiley, introduced them into London society, which finally led them to meeting Edward, Prince of Wales (the future EDWARD VIII), in 1930. It was not until 1932 that Edward invited them to his house, FORT BELVEDERE, then known as The Fort.

In the summer of 1934, the prince asked Wallis and Ernest Simpson to join his party at Biarritz in France. Ernest's business interests took him to the United States at that time, so Wallis went to Biarritz with her aunt Bessie Merryman as chaperone. From Biarritz the party took a cruise on the yacht *Rosaura* during which the Prince and Wallis (to quote her own words) 'crossed the line that marks the indefinable boundary between friendship and love'.

When Edward became King in January 1936 he was determined to marry Wallis despite the fact that as a divorced woman she would be unsuitable to become the Queen of England, because, apart from anything else, he was officially the head of the Church of England. The situation developed into what became known as the CONSTITUTIONAL CRISIS. This caused Wallis to write to Edward that while they had 'lovely beautiful times together' he must now attend to his role as sovereign. His reply, 'I do love you so entirely and in every way', touched her so deeply she abandoned any idea of parting.

Wallis and Ernest Simpson were divorced on 27 October. As a result of general opposition to his proposed marriage to Wallis, Edward, abdicated on 11 December in order to marry 'the woman I love'. He was given the title Duke of Windsor and Wallis became the Duchess of Windsor. GEORGE VI's Letters Patent of March 1937 prevented Wallis from being styled Her Royal Highness.

Wallis outlived her husband by fourteen years. She died at her home in Paris on 24 April 1986, and was buried beside Edward at Frogmore, Windsor. *See also* EDWARD VIII

SMITHFIELD A place of execution for four centuries, Smithfield was a large open space close to London. It was here in 1305 that WILLIAM WALLACE was hanged, drawn and quartered. It was also used as a market for horses, cattle and sheep, and for tournaments. One of the most famous of these was in 1357 when EDWARD III entertained the King of France. For refusing to accept HENRY VIII as supreme head of the Church, John Forest, prior of the Observant Convent at Greenwich, was burned alive in 1538. During the reign of Henry's daughter QUEEN MARY over two hundred Protestant 'martyrs' were led to the stake there.

SOMERSET HOUSE Described as the first Renaissance palace in England, Somerset House was built by Edward Seymour, 1st Duke of Somerset, when, as Lord Protector, he was the most powerful man in the kingdom. His rise to power began when his sister Jane Seymour became the third wife of HENRY VIII in 1536. Within a week of the marriage he was created Viscount Beauchamp and other honours followed. His royal brother-in-law made him the Earl of Hereford, a Knight of the Garter and Lord High Admiral. When his 9-year-old nephew EDWARD VI inherited the throne in 1547 he became Duke of Somerset and the Lord Protector of the realm.

Somerset House was a royal palace from the time of Elizabeth I until it was last used by the windowed Catherine of Braganza.

At this point he began to build a great palace, stretching from the Thames up to the Strand, which was to be an awe-inspiring symbol of his wealth and authority. Historians differ as to whether it was designed by Sir John Thynne, who was responsible for Longleat, or John of Padua, but there is no doubt about the grand scale of its plan. The Lord Protector had no qualms about demolishing existing buildings to make way for it. These included an inn of Chancery, the inns of the bishops of Chester, Worcester and Llandaff, the church of St Mary-le-Strand and the church of the Nativity of Our Lady and the Innocents. Building stone was obtained from the demolition of St Paul's charnel house and cloisters and the priory church of St John Clerkenwell, but when the duke looked to St Margaret's, Westminster, for more stone his men were put to flight by infuriated parishioners.

He was so eager to live in his new palace that he moved in before the building work was completed, and he must have been filled with pride when he entered through the entrance gate – carved by Nicholas Cave, the master mason who had worked on Nonsuch Palace – into the quadrangle, on three sides of which stood the principal buildings with their tall Tudor chimneys while to the south rose the Great Hall and gardens running down to the river.

If ever there was an example of how the mighty can fall – and how fast – it was provided by the duke. In the same year he started work on Somerset House

he underlined his ascendancy by defeating the Scots at the Battle of Pinkie Cleugh, yet after two and a half years of near absolute power he was supplanted by John Dudley, 1st Duke of Northumberland. He was divested of his protectorate in October 1549 and imprisoned in the TOWER OF LONDON. He regained his freedom briefly before being imprisoned once more and executed for treason in January 1552. Somerset House was claimed by the Crown.

When MARY I came to the throne the following year she bestowed the palace on her half-sister, ELIZABETH, in return for Durham House. When Elizabeth became queen she only stayed at the palace before commencing her famous progresses, and its main function was in providing accommodation for foreign ambassadors and as a venue for Council meetings.

In 1603 ANNE OF DENMARK, the wife of JAMES I, was given the palace, and here she indulged her love of the arts, patronising Ben Jonson and Inigo Jones, who in return produced lavish masques which delighted her but which the King found superficial. Soon after taking up residence, the Queen granted a lease of some land beside the palace to one John Gerard, a herbalist, on the understanding that he would keep her supplied with herbs and flowers. When the Queen's brother, Christian IV of Denmark, was a guest at the palace its name was changed to Denmark House as a token of esteem.

After the death of the Queen her son CHARLES I was given the house but, he much preferred ST JAMES'S PALACE. The next royal owner was HENRIETTA MARIA who was given it after her marriage to Charles in 1625. After the King became so exasperated with the behaviour of her French attendants and sent them packing, he built her a chapel designed by Inigo Jones at the palace. When the Queen left England after the outbreak of the English Civil War the palace was used by the army and Members of Parliament and the name Somerset House was resumed. The Queen returned to the palace after the Restoration and used it until 1665 when she left England for the last time.

It was now the turn of Catherine of Braganza, wife of CHARLES II, to use the palace as a place to retire to, and after the King's death in 1685 she took up residence there where she followed her love of music and introduced Italian opera to England. In 1693 she became Regent of Portugal, and from then on its days as a royal palace were over; instead it

was used to house grace and favour residents and gradually fell into neglect. In 1775 it was demolished and an imposing block of government offices was built on its site.

SOPHIA DOROTHEA OF CELLE In 1680 Ernest Augustus, Elector of Hanover, arranged for his eldest son George Louis, the future GEORGE I of England, to marry Sophia Dorothea, the only child of the Duke of Brunswick-Lüneburg-Celle, a union which would be politically advantageous to the astute elector. The wedding took place quietly in Sophia's apartment on 21 November 1682, and a few days later her new husband took her on a state journey of 30 miles to Hanover.

From the beginning of the marriage George Louis did not disguise the fact that he preferred the military camp to the company of his high-spirited wife. He was at the siege of Vienna and afterwards went on various campaigns, being at Buda when it was captured from the Turks, then soldiering in Greece, Germany and Flanders. In 1686 he returned to Hanover, not having seen his wife for two years, and openly took a mistress, encouraged by his father's mistress the Baroness von Platen, always referred to as 'La Platen'. It was said that she had encouraged the match between the Hanoverian heir and Sophia Dorothea as a favour to WILLIAM OF ORANGE, who feared the possibility of the elector's son marrying Princess Anne of England.

Having helped to bring Sophia to Hanover, La Platen found she made no secret of her disdain for her. When the elector showed a growing affection for his daughter-in-law, La Platen felt her position threatened and planned to isolate Sophia as much as possible. Her first move in this direction was to find a woman to control George Louis and the woman she chose was Ermengrada Melusina von der Schulenberg, who was to become the Duchess of Kendal when George became King of England. There was no pretence of discretion over George's relationship with La Platen's protégée, especially when she was given her own apartments in the palace.

In March 1688 a handsome Swedish soldier of fortune arrived at the Hanoverian court. His name was Count Philip Christopher von Königsmarck who, as a boy, had spent some time at the court of Celle where he was frequently in the company of little Sophia. Since those days he had built up an impressive military career and the elector gave him the highly prized post of Colonel of the Hanoverian Guards. In the following months it was natural that Sophia should enjoy the company of her old playmate and his sister Aurora. At court balls it was protocol that she should be paired with the count as he was the most distinguished nobleman present after the elector and his son.

The couple became lovers in 1692 when the count gave Sophia the choice of sharing his passion or seeing him volunteer to return to active service in Morea, but soon his friends were warning him of his danger. A court flirtation was acceptable provided it went no further than whispered words at a ball or reception, but to take Sophia as a lover, even though her husband had no use for her, was a deadly insult to the royal house. Instead of damping down the relationship, such warnings added to its intensity, and the couple began to consider elopement. One possible place of refuge was Brunswick-Wolfenbüttel whose duke, Anthony Ulrich, had a grudge against Hanover and would be delighted to shelter its royal runaway, or so he claimed years later when he said that he had expected the fugitives to seek sanctuary with him.

It appears that the elopement was finally decided upon in June 1694. That month the count made plans to sell his house, and on the night of 1 July he set out from his home at ten o'clock and was never seen again. Because of his irregular habits Königsmarck's servants did not feel anxiety on his failure to return the next morning, but after several days had passed rumours of his fate began to spread. From Celle, James Cresset, the English envoy wrote: 'Königsmarck's commerce with our electrol princess is all come out and the count is murdered . . . Königsmarck's papers have all been seized and the princess and her letters discovered. She is undone and her mother and father will hardly outlive the disgrace.'

Königsmarck's old friend, the Elector of Saxony, demanded an explanation for the count's disappearance. When no satisfactory reply was received his threats became so extreme that Hanover prepared for war. It took the intervention of the emperor and WILLIAM III of England to restore calm. Meanwhile, in Hanover the name of Sophia Dorothea was deleted from state prayers; in the palace every token of her presence was removed and she was confined in the castle of Ahlden where she was to remain until her death thirty-two years later. Her children were forbidden to see her but her son

George, the future GEORGE II of England, managed to secrete a portrait of his mother which he kept hidden during his father's lifetime.

The elector instituted proceedings on behalf of his son at an ecclesiastical court, which on 28 December 1694 granted a divorce and gave George permission to marry again if he so wished. This was granted on the grounds of desertion by Sophia, though throughout the case no mention was made of Königsmarck or adultery as this would have reflected on the honour of the House of Hanover.

There have been several accounts purporting to describe Königsmarck's fate, one of which was said to have been based on a confession by one of the guards involved in his assassination. Apart from minor details the main difference between these accounts is the amount of guilt apportioned to the elector, Ernest Augustus, his mistress La Platen and his son George. The foremost version of what happened on the fateful night was that the count was conducted by a lady-in-waiting to Sophia's chamber where the lovers discussed their proposed elopement.

Meanwhile, La Platen, learning of the clandestine meeting through one of her spies, took the story to the now ailing elector, saying that if he would leave the matter to her she would have Königsmarck discreetly arrested. On obtaining his agreement, La Platen hurried to the guardroom where she swore four halberdiers to secrecy and posted them in a corridor close to Sophia's apartment. When Königsmarck emerged they attacked him and though he put up a brave fight he was killed by a sword thrust.

Some authors laid the blame squarely on the elector and his son, claiming that the motive was not inspired by La Platen but because proof had come to light that the couple intended to elope and that the removal of a noble as celebrated as Königsmarck could only have been authorised by the elector.

Though nothing definite about the count's supposed assassination came to light during the lifetime of George I, his remains were said to have been discovered beneath the floor of Sophia's apartment when alterations were being made to the palace during the next century. George never saw his wife again but his son's anger over his mother's plight is said to have been the beginning of the Hanoverian tradition of animosity between the king and his eldest son.

STATE OPENING OF PARLIAMENT The State Opening of Parliament goes back to when the first representative assembly met to advise the king, and today it remains the most impressive ceremony in which the sovereign takes part. It is held after a general election and at the commencement of each parliamentary session, usually in November, and is still very much in the form it was when first chronicled in 1523. It begins with the sovereign travelling from Buckingham Palace to the PALACE OF WESTMINSTER, more widely known as the Houses of Parliament, in the Irish State Coach. (The reason that the coach used for this occasion is known as the Irish State Coach is that QUEEN VICTORIA purchased it at the Dublin Exhibition of 1852.) Meanwhile, the King's Troop of the Royal Horse Artillery fire a twenty-one gun salute in St James's Park.

On arrival at Westminster the sovereign is received by the Great Officers of State, made up of two hereditary members, the Earl Marshal and the Lord Great Chamberlain, and three non-hereditary Great Officers, the Lord High Chancellor, the Lord Privy Seal and the Lord President of the Council. The sovereign is accompanied by members of the royal family and such household officials as the Private Secretary, the KEEPER OF THE PRIVY PURSE and the MASTER OF HORSE.

In the Robing Room at the Palace of Westminster the traditional robes and crown are put on by the sovereign, while dignitaries including the Great Officers of State, Heralds and Pursuivants in traditional costume take their places in the Royal Gallery in the House of Lords. By tradition the sovereign cannot enter the House of Commons, as the result of an incident in January 1642 when CHARLES I burst into Parliament to demand the arrest of five Puritan members who, having been warned of what was afoot, had wisely disappeared.

A fanfare of trumpets sounds as the Garter King of Arms raises his sceptre to signal the approach of the royal procession. On entering the House of Lords the sovereign goes to the throne and when seated Black Rod, a member of the MOST NOBLE ORDER OF THE GARTER, summons the Speaker and members of the House of Commons. The Lord Chancellor then presents the 'Gracious Speech' to the sovereign, who reads it to the assembly which includes ambassadors, bishops, judges, peers and peeresses as well as the elected Members of Parliament. Because the British monarchy is constitutional the sovereign's speech does not reflect any personal views but is the traditional practice by which the government sets out its forthcoming policies.

STEPHEN Brave, generous, warm-hearted, affable to all classes . . . these are the words historians have used to describe Stephen, the last of England's Norman kings. Stephen was born *c.* 1096 at Chartres, the third son of Stephen Henry, Count of Blois and his wife Adela who was the fourth daughter of WILLIAM I. Soon afterwards Count Henry was killed in the First Crusade and his widow chose her son Theobald to succeed him with herself as regent.

In 1115 she sent Stephen to the English court where his uncle HENRY I promised to promote his career. True to his word he knighted him and gave him estates in England and lands in Normandy. Due to a sudden illness Stephen missed the disaster of the *White Ship* in 1120 in which perished his cousin William, the king's son and heir to the English throne. Henry kept Stephen at court and in 1124 arranged for him to be married to Matilda, the daughter of Eustace III, Count of Boulogne. Through her mother Mary she was a granddaughter of Malcolm III of Scotland and a niece of King Henry, and her dowry made Stephen one of the richest men in England.

An engraving of King Stephen from a manuscript portrait.

311

To many it appeared that Henry was grooming Stephen to be his heir, but the following year that possibility was ruled out. Henry's daughter Matilda had been married to the emperor Henry V of Germany for political reasons when she was 6 years old. When he died in 1125, Henry invited her to return to his court to proclaim her as his heir. His barons were required to swear fealty to her, Stephen being the first to pledge his loyalty. The king then arranged another political match for his daughter with Geoffrey of Anjou, which ensured the support of the Angevins, members of the House of Anjou, against the French.

When Henry was dying in 1135 he expected the barons to fulfil their vows to make his daughter 'the Lady of England', but when he died Stephen was a more popular contender for the throne.

Stephen had a lot in his favour – his mother was the last surviving child of William I; he was the nephew of the late king and his wife was niece of the queen, whereas Matilda had been out of the country for most of her life and was married to an Angevin. A council of prelates, officials and aldermen elected Stephen as the new king and he was crowned on 26 December 1135 at WESTMINSTER ABBEY.

For a while it seemed that Stephen's enthronement heralded a period of peace and prosperity but

Memorial to the Battle of the Standard at Northallerton in which a Scottish army was defeated by the Archbishop of York.

ambitious men realised that although the new king was cast in the mould of a knight errant, he lacked the ruthlessness by which his predecessors had maintained their royal authority, and they were not slow to take advantage of this. Two years after his coronation, when Stephen was taken ill at Oxford: it was the cue for revolt. There were risings in Devon and Norfolk, Normandy was threatened by Geoffrey of Anjou and in Scotland David I (*see* SCOTLAND, EARLY KINGS OF), Matilda's maternal uncle, prepared to invade England. Stephen left his sickbed and methodically crushed the insurrections in England and then crossed the Channel to secure Normandy.

In the summer of 1138 King David of Scotland began his greatest invasion of the North. As Stephen was fully occupied trying to keep the southern half of his kingdom intact, it fell to Thurston, the elderly Archbishop of York, to confront the invaders. On the morning of 22 August his army was victorious over the Scots at Northallerton in what became known as the Battle of the Standard. However, it did not deter King David who rallied his forces at Carlisle; Cumberland, Westmorland and Northumberland were to remain under Scottish influence for many years.

News of the victory gave encouragement to Stephen; for the rest of his reign his kingdom was rent by rebellion and anarchy. His difficulties increased dramatically when he heard that the Empress Matilda had arrived in England with

her followers to claim the Crown and established herself at Arundel Castle under the protection of Queen Adela, the widow of Henry I. Stephen captured the castle by surprise and took both royal ladies prisoner. Had he possessed the stern nature of previous Norman kings he could have ended the threat to his throne but he provided Matilda with an escort to conduct her safely to her half-brother, Robert of Gloucester, and Arundel Castle was returned to Adela. Stephen paid dearly for his gallantry when Matilda became mistress of the west of England and civil war again broke out.

At the beginning of 1141, while besieging a rebel army at Lincoln, Stephen was attacked by the whole of Robert of Gloucester's Norman and Welsh forces. Most of the royal troops fled, leaving the king with a small band of faithful followers to face his enemies. Finally, with only four companions he continued to fight until the handle of his battleaxe snapped and he was taken captive. Robert treated his royal prisoner well and conveyed him to Bristol where Matilda, forgetting how he acted when she was in his power, had him placed in chains.

On 10 April 1141 a Church Council ruled that Stephen had been deposed as the result of divine judgement and the Empress Matilda was the rightful sovereign of England. London welcomed her, its heavily taxed population hoping she would ease their burden, but when a delegation of leading citizens petitioned her help she imposed further taxes. Matilda's close supporters soon found her equally insensitive, contrasting her arrogance with Stephen's easy courtesy. One story tells how Stephen's wife, also called Matilda, was driven away in tears after she beseeched the 'Lady of England' to free her husband from Bristol Castle. If the story was true Matilda had her revenge when she led forces loyal to Stephen against London shortly before the empress's coronation and Londoners came out in support of the deposed king. As the empress was about to sit down to a grand entertainment she heard a tumult. She just had time to flee for the safety of Oxford before a mob broke into her apartments. Thus she missed her coronation. Stephen's supporters found new heart, especially when his queen held court in London and another Church Council decided that Stephen was the rightful king after all.

Still the civil war dragged on to become a stalemate and when Robert of Gloucester died in October 1147 the disheartened empress left England, never to return. In France she transferred her right to the English throne to her 16-year-old son HENRY PLANTAGENET. The ambitious youth landed with a small army in the south of England but soon ran out of silver to pay his troops and he turned to the king he hoped to depose for financial help. Stephen – 'being always compassionate' – sent money to relieve his young enemy of embarrassment. Henry returned to France where in 1152 he inherited his father's territories, giving him the power to mount a proper invasion of what he believed was his rightful kingdom. In England he was joined by his mother's old supporters and the war continued.

Meanwhile, Stephen, worried about the succession, was determined to have his son Eustace crowned as his heir, but Eustace died of fever in August 1153.

Towards the end of 1153 the armies of King Stephen and Henry Plantagenet faced each other across the Thames at Wallingford, but before the battle was joined a parley was arranged and the two leaders shouted terms at each other across the river. A reign of endless warfare and the recent deaths of his queen and his heir had sapped Stephen's spirit and on 6 November 1153 he made a contract with Henry that while he would remain King of England, Henry would be proclaimed

The Great Seal of King Stephen.

313

as his heir. Henry was also made Justiciar and he and Stephen travelled to London, Winchester and Oxford together to underline the agreement, which was received joyfully by a population demoralised by the long civil war.

Stephen's problems did not end there. The next year he discovered a plot to assassinate Henry by his own Flemish mercenaries, and saved his erstwhile enemy by sending him out of the country. He then set to work to make the country secure for his successor by bringing the barons into line. In the autumn he became ill and on 25 October 1154 he died of what was described as 'his old complaint the emrods with the iliac passion'. He was buried at Faversham Abbey, the last Norman King of England.

STONE OF DESTINY The ancient belief that certain stones have a beneficial power within them is demonstrated by the Stone of Destiny, also known as the Stone of Scone. Until the present time new sovereigns being crowned in WESTMINSTER ABBEY have been anointed by the Archbishop of Canterbury while seated on the legendary stone. Theories as to its origin include the possibility it was once part of a megalithic structure which later became the base of an early Christian cross.

A more intriguing tradition is that it came from the Holy Land where Jacob used it as a pillow at Bethel and was later taken to Ireland to be used as a coronation seat by the kings of Munster. What is definitely known is that when the Scots and Picts united in the eighth century, Scone became the principal town in the new kingdom of Pictavia and here Scottish kings were enthroned on the Stone of Destiny after it had been taken from Dunstaffnage by Kenneth Macalpine.

The stone was brought to Westminster Abbey by EDWARD I after his conquest of Scotland in 1296. Set under the Coronation Chair, it was first used at the enthronement of an English king in 1308 when EDWARD II was crowned. The stone remained in the abbey until Christmas Day 1950 when it was spirited away by Scottish Nationalists to a secret destination, where it was kept until it was returned in April of the following year. The next time the stone left the abbey was in 1996 when QUEEN ELIZABETH II authorised its return to Scotland where it remains in HOLYROODHOUSE PALACE, exactly seven centuries after it was seized by King Edward I.

STRAFFORD, THOMAS WENTWORTH, 1st EARL OF On 7 May 1641 CHARLES I was celebrating his daughter's wedding to the Prince of Orange when the festivities were interrupted by the arrival of a document from the Commons for the King's signature. It was a Bill of Attainder and its subject was the Roman Catholic statesman Thomas Wentworth, 1st Earl of Strafford, and nicknamed by those opposed to his policies 'Black Tom Tyrant'. Born into a Yorkshire family with royal connections in 1593, he became a Member of Parliament at the age of 21. At first he was opposed to Charles I, but later became an ardent royalist and in 1632 was appointed Lord Deputy of Ireland where his despotic policy was aimed at making Charles 'the most absolute prince in Christendom'. Five years later he became the King's chief adviser and was created Earl of Strafford.

When Charles's ill-judged policies provoked a rebellion in Scotland the Puritans saw Strafford as the only obstacle to their ascendancy, and his erstwhile friend John Pym, the leader of the Puritans in Parliament, had him impeached as the

The Earl of Strafford, whose ardent support of Charles I led to his execution.

'principal author and promoter of all those counsels which had exposed to so much ruin'. At his trial in Westminster Hall he defended himself with such ability against the twenty-eight charges brought against him that there were cries of 'Adjourn! Adjourn!' At this Strafford glanced at the king and winked, but when his accusers realised he would not be convicted they pressed for a Bill of Attainder. Provided it was passed by Parliament and the King gave his assent, the earl could be legally sent to the block by a simple declaration that it was necessary for the security of the state.

Thus when Charles received the Bill he knew if he signed it the man he had promised he would not let suffer in 'life, honour or fortune' would be put to death, and refused to put his signature to the paper. In the TOWER OF LONDON Strafford realised the consequences to the Crown if Charles refused the assent and wrote valiantly, 'I do most humbly beseech Your Majesty, for the prevention of evils which may happen by your refusal, to pass this bill.'

For two days the King held out against signing, despite the arguments of bishops and judges and the yells of the crowd that had assembled outside WHITEHALL PALACE. Finally it was the hysterical pleas of the queen, terrified of the mob and desperate to avert trouble by appeasing Parliament, that broke Charles's resistance and with tears running down his face he signed the fatal document and said, 'My Lord of Strafford's condition is happier than mine.'

On 12 May 1641 the earl, wearing his usual black, was taken to Tower Hill where he walked to the scaffold 'more like a general at the head of an army than like a condemned man to undergo death'.

What the King considered his betrayal of Strafford was to haunt him for the rest of his life and when it was his turn to stand on a scaffold he said, 'The unjust sentence that I suffered to take effect, is punished now by an unjust sentence on me.'

STRAFFORD'S GHOST CHARLES I's surrender to Parliament by giving his assent to the execution of his chief supporter the EARL OF STRAFFORD did little to stem the tide of hostility flowing against the monarchy. The next year it became clear that only warfare could settle the dispute between the Crown and Commons, and on 22 August 1642 the royal standard was raised at Nottingham and the English Civil War officially began. In June 1645 King Charles found himself with his army at Daventry in Northamptonshire where he made the Wheatsheaf Inn his headquarters. Here he planned the battle that he believed would be the turning point of the war.

On the night of 13 June the king had fallen into an uneasy sleep when he suddenly awoke to see a shadowy figure in his room, which he took to be the phantom of the executed Strafford. Next morning he described to his commanders how Strafford's ghost had not only appeared but had spoken to him, saying that the loyalty he still felt towards the king compelled him to return and warn him against the forthcoming battle. When Charles concluded his gloomy tale PRINCE RUPERT declared that it was probably nothing more than a nightmare and that military strategy should not be altered because of a bad dream. The others agreed, and persuaded Charles to continue with the proposed battle.

At Naseby the Royalists were defeated by Cromwell's Ironsides and the king, who showed exceptional gallantry, lost three thousand men, his 'park of artillery', his baggage and personal belongings. Many times afterwards, before and after the Scots had handed him over to the English Parliamentarians, Charles was heard to mutter, 'I wish to God I had paid heed to Strafford's warning.' After the Restoration the Wheatsheaf Inn became a place of pilgrimage as the location where Charles I spent his last few days as a real king.

STUART, THE HOUSE OF The Stuart dynasty began in England when James VI of Scotland was crowned JAMES I in WESTMINSTER ABBEY in 1603. The Scottish House of Stewart had originated with ROBERT II who took the name from his father's title of High Steward of Scotland. During the reign of MARY, QUEEN OF SCOTS the Stewarts began to spell their name in the French fashion.

After the powerful Tudor sovereigns there were unprecedented changes to the monarchy during the Stuart dynasty which began with the DIVINE RIGHT OF KINGS and ended with the beginnings of constitutional monarchy.

The Stuarts

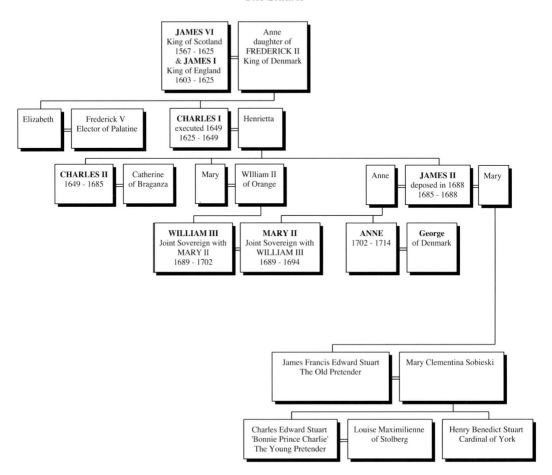

James I believed in the Divine Right of Kings and wrote two books, *The True Law of Free Monarchies* and the *Basilikon Doron*, expounding his conviction. CHARLES I inherited his father's doctrine, leading him to believe he was inherently above Parliament, which led to the English Civil War and his downfall. His execution sent a ripple of horror through the courts of Europe, for while kings may have been assassinated or killed in battle, Charles was the first to be officially condemned to death by his elected subjects.

His son CHARLES II regained the throne after the Interregnum and skilfully reconciled a country that had been divided, and re-established the place of the monarchy. JAMES II's Roman Catholicism led to a second revolution, this time the bloodless GLORIOUS REVOLUTION of 1688 when the king's flight to France was regarded as an act of abdication by Parliament. The king's daughter MARY and her husband WILLIAM OF ORANGE then accepted the invitation to take the throne of England as joint sovereigns, while accepting the Bill of Rights which lessened royal privilege and increased the authority of Parliament.

Like the Tudors before them the Stuarts were not of hardy stock and miscarriages were frequent. William and Mary produced three stillborn children but no heir. The Crown passed to ANNE, another of James II's daughters. In the hope of providing an heir with her husband George of Denmark she had eighteen pregnancies which resulted in offspring who were stillborn or died soon after birth, apart from Prince William who reached the age of 11 before dying of hydrocephalus.

STUART, JAMES EDWARD Pretender to the British throne, James Stuart was JAMES II's only surviving son. His mother was the king's second wife Mary of Modena, and when he was born on 10 June 1688 at ST JAMES'S PALACE rumours spread that the urgent need for a royal heir had resulted in the baby being smuggled into his mother's bed in a warming pan. With the impending GLORIOUS REVOLUTION his mother took him to the exiled court of St Germain in France where, on the death of his father in 1701, he was proclaimed James III and acknowledged as such by Louis XIV. Also known as the Chevalier de St George, he gained military experience serving with the French army, distinguishing himself at the Battle of Malplaquet.

In December 1715 he landed at Peterhead in Scotland to join the Jacobite rebellion launched by the Earl of Mar but after six weeks, under the threat of GEORGE I's army, he fled Scotland. Under the Treaty of Utrecht he was unable to return to France, so his court moved to Rome where in 1719 he married Princess Clementina Sobieski who bore him two sons, one of whom, Charles Stuart, was to become known in history as Bonnie Prince Charlie.

James's plans for further uprisings came to nothing and Jacobite hopes for a Stuart restoration turned to his son. When Charles left for Scotland for the second Jacobite Rebellion – 'The '45' – James was not informed until after he had set out.

James the 'Old Pretender' died in Rome in 1766 and was interred in St Peter's Basilica in the Vatican.

SUCCESSION, LINE OF The right to the throne is decreed by Parliament and is governed by descent following the ACT OF SETTLEMENT which was passed in 1701. The Act came about in order to provide for a Protestant heir following the death of QUEEN ANNE's son William, Duke of Gloucester, in 1700. In effect the Act debarred Roman Catholic Stuart claimants in favour of Sophie, a granddaughter of JAMES I and the Protestant Electress of Hanover. When she died in 1714 the succession passed to her son who became GEORGE I.

According to the formula for deciding the line of descent, male heirs have precedence over daughters and daughters have precedence over the brothers of the reigning king or queen. If a sovereign has no direct heir the succession passes to his or her eldest surviving brother and thence to his sons followed by his daughters.

The immediate successor to Her Majesty Queen Elizabeth is Prince Charles, then members of the royal family in the following order: Prince William of Wales; Prince Henry of Wales; Andrew, Duke of York; Princess Beatrice of York; Princess Eugenie of York; Edward, Earl of Wessex; Anne, Princess Royal; Peter Phillips and then Zara Phillips, both children of Princess Anne and Captain Mark Phillips.

SWEYN FORKBEARD The son of King Harold Bluetooth of Denmark, Sweyn Forkbeard was born *c.* AD 960 and succeeded his father in AD 986. For most of his reign he led raids upon England, and these intensified after the St Bride's Day Massacre of Danes in 1002 in which his sister Gunhilda perished. In 1013 his raiding turned to invasion when, with his son CANUTE, his ships entered England by sailing up the rivers Humber and Trent. He made his base at Gainsborough where he was acknowledged as master of Anglo-Danish England, after which he took Oxford and Winchester. At the end of the year London surrendered to the invader and ETHELRED II, who had been responsible for the massacre, fled to France. Sweyn was now King of England by right of conquest, but he was never crowned. He died at Gainsborough on 3 February 1014. Ethelred was restored, and following his death in 1016 was succeeded by his son EDMUND IRONSIDE. Edmund's reign only lasted from April to November, after which Sweyn's son Canute took the throne.

See also CANUTE *and* ETHELRED II

T

THEOBALDS PALACE It was the result of a visit by ELIZABETH I to Theobalds that upgraded it to the palace which later became the favourite residence of her successor JAMES I. In 1564 William Cecil had bought Theobalds, then a moated manor house near Cheshunt in Hertfordshire, and rebuilt it round two large courtyards. In September 1571 the queen honoured her minister with a visit, such an 'honour' invariably costing the host a great deal of money in entertaining the royal guest and her entourage. Theobalds was much to Elizabeth's liking and during her reign she made eleven more visits, with the result that Cecil spent far more lavishly on making it 'fit for a queen' than he had originally intended. But he understood Elizabeth probably better than anyone and saw the hospitality he provided – which cost him between £2,000 and £3,000 on each occasion – as a good investment. To flatter the queen he decorated the walls of the Great Gallery with genealogical tables depicting the royal line of England.

By the time Cecil had finished adding and refining, Theobalds was regarded as one of the finest houses in the kingdom, one of its principal features being its magnificent gardens complete with an ornamental lake large enough for the enjoyment of boating. There was also a maze, a summer house and a special arbour where the queen enjoyed al fresco meals.

In May 1607 Theobalds became a royal palace, albeit a short-lived one, when JAMES I coveted it and obtained possession by giving Cecil's son Robert, Lord Salisbury, HATFIELD HOUSE in exchange. Ben Jonson wrote a masque to celebrate the change of ownership and the King enlarged the park and enclosed it with a wall measuring 10 miles. When James was taken ill at Newmarket he demanded to be taken to Theobalds where he died on 27 March 1625. His son CHARLES I did not share his father's attachment for the palace and rarely visited it.

A year after the execution of the king in 1649, a report on Theobalds was prepared by parliamentary commissioners which described the various royal chambers, the towers decorated with statues of lions and the central tower with its corner pinnacles, chiming clock and a dozen bells. Although the report stated that the palace was in excellent repair, much of it was pulled down and sold for building materials, the proceeds going to the army. Following the Restoration Theobalds, or what remained of it, passed into the ownership of the Duke of Albemarle. In 1768 a new house, referred to as the Old Palace, was built on the site and included remnants of the former royal residence.

THISTLE, THE ORDER OF THE Also known as the Order of St Andrew, the Order of the Thistle goes back to 1687 when it was established by JAMES II – James VII of Scotland – as an order of Scottish knighthood. During the joint reign of WILLIAM AND MARY it fell into abeyance but was re-established by QUEEN ANNE in 1703. Scotland's highest honour, it is bestowed by the sovereign on eminent members of the Scottish nobility and is made up of the sovereign and knights, though extra numbers may be included by means of a special statute, and since 1987 women have been eligible for membership.

The principal article of the Order's insignia is a gold collar consisting of thistles entwined with sprigs of rue. The Order's chapel is at St Giles's Cathedral in Edinburgh and its motto is *Nemo me impune lacessit* – 'Let no one provoke me with impunity'.

TOWER OF LONDON WILLIAM THE CONQUEROR, who had brought prefabricated 'castles' from Normandy with his invasion fleet, saw castles as the key to controlling his new kingdom. The power of the castle was that it was not only a place of defence but was a base from which his forces were ready to emerge to deal with insurrection and, having dealt with it, retire to the safety of its walls.

The Bell Tower, built by the Bishop of Ely when, as custodian of the kingdom, he found it necessary to extend the Tower's fortifications.

Thus within weeks of his victory over HAROLD II he sent his castle builders into London, for, according to the contemporary chronicler, William of Poitiers, 'he [William] realised it was of the first importance to overawe the Londoners'.

The main fortification, a wooden keep partly defended by the city's ancient Roman wall overlooking the Thames, was to develop into the Tower of London, which for centuries cast its shadow across the political and court life of the country. By 1078 the king's Norman masons and Anglo-Saxon labourers were replacing the timber structure by a great three-storeyed keep of stone imported from Caen. Indeed, much of the Normans' success in colonising England was the dominating effect of their stone architecture, the like of which had not been seen since Roman times – castles, churches and cathedrals which not only 'overawed' the populace but, in modern parlance, 'created jobs'.

The foremost symbol of the new dynasty was the Tower of London, which was not only designed as a stronghold but a royal palace and a prison where the first inmate was Ranulf Flambard, Bishop of Durham, who was incarcerated in it in 1100. And no doubt remembering how his ancestor ROBERT RAGNDVALSSON ('Rollo') had sailed up the Seine to Paris and induced Charles the Simple, King of France, to cede Normandy to him, William saw the strategically placed Tower as London's bulwark against Norse invaders.

WILLIAM II carried on his father's work after his death in 1087, and while the interior did not have the comfort of later royal residences, its banqueting hall, the Chapel of St John the Evangelist and the Council Chamber kept it from being a mere fortress.

During the reign of HENRY III the Tower became more palatial as the king not only increased its defences with a surrounding wall reinforced by thirteen towers but extended the royal apartments, which were enhanced with wall paintings and marble columns. It was then that the keep became known as the White Tower following the king's decision to have it whitewashed.

Under Henry's direction – and that of his son EDWARD I – the Tower of London began to take on something of its present-day appearance, and this process was continued by William Longchamp, Chancellor and Bishop of Ely, who was put in charge of the kingdom while RICHARD I was crusading. With the king more interested in

The Tower of London which William the Conqueror began with stone imported from Caen.

Jerusalem than London, and with his brother JOHN casting a crafty eye on the throne, England was politically unstable and the bishop spent a vast amount of money making the Tower more secure as a bastion of the Crown. The Tower's area was doubled, deeper moat-type ditches were dug, sections of curtain wall were added and a tower – later named the Bell Tower – was built. These defences did not deter Prince John from laying siege to the Tower and though he was unable to breach them he still gained the fortress when the bishop was forced to surrender due to lack of supplies.

More work on the Tower was carried out during the reign of Henry III. In 1236 and 1238 the king was challenged by his barons and each time he sought refuge in the Tower. Here he saw that part of the defences had been neglected so, at a cost of £5,000 (£1.8 million today) he erected a massive curtain wall on three sides of the Tower which was protected by a moat and reinforced by nine towers, seven of which, including the Devereux, Martin and Salt corner towers, remain as they were first constructed. These new defences again doubled the area occupied by the Tower but found no favour with the citizens of London who saw them as visible signs of increasing royal power.

Henry's son EDWARD I extended his father's defences further at the enormous cost of £21,000 (£7.6 million today). He built a new wall and moat completely encircling the Tower and its existing wall, which meant that if attackers managed to breach the outer wall, they would still be facing another. This form of concentric defence made the Tower the most impregnable castle in the kingdom. The Beauchamp Tower was built at this time, and royal apartments were added to St Thomas's Tower. It was during this reign that the Tower began to be used for purposes other than a palace, fortress and prison. Within its precincts Edward set up the Royal Mint and the Treasury in which he deposited the CROWN JEWELS which until then had been kept at WESTMINSTER ABBEY.

The last royal building at the Tower was carried out by HENRY VII and HENRY VIII, the former by increasing the royal apartments, building a long gallery and library and laying out a garden. His son built a row of timber-framed houses to act as lodgings for the occasion of ANNE BOLEYN's coronation, but after she was beheaded on Tower Green the Tower ceased to be used as a royal

residence, though its reputation as a dreaded prison continued unabated and it is as such that it has since been regarded.

It is impossible to know the number of common folk who met their fate at the Tower during its long history, but its list of noble and ministerial victims proves that the menace of the Tower had no respect of blood or position. In Tudor times it was on ideological grounds as well as the posing of a threat to the Crown that caused the Tower's dungeons to be filled. The first celebrated victims of Henry VIII's break with the Roman Catholic Church were SIR THOMAS MORE and John Fisher, Bishop of Rochester, who refused to accept the king as head of the Church of England and paid for their presumption on Tower Hill in 1535. Exactly four centuries on they were canonised.

Almost a year later the Tower's most famous execution took place when Queen Anne Boleyn knelt at the block on Tower Green while her brother, Lord Rochford, and four commoners with whom she had been accused of having adulterous relationships were beheaded in front of the mob on Tower Hill. Partly because it was thought to be wrong for commoners to see the undignified executions of royal personages, and partly to provide privacy for the condemned, seven executions were carried out privately on Tower Green, the exact spot where the scaffolds were erected being marked by a plaque today.

In 1483 William, Lord Hastings was the first to die on the Green when RICHARD, Duke of Gloucester charged him with treason and had him executed out of hand. Anne Boleyn was the second to follow him, and after her came the 70-year-old Margaret Pole, Countess of Salisbury who was executed in 1541 because the king mistrusted her allegiance to the Roman Catholic faith coupled with her Yorkist blood. The next year Queen CATHERINE HOWARD, Henry's fifth wife, and her lady-in-waiting Jane, Viscountess Rochford were both beheaded. LADY JANE GREY paid the price for others' ambitions in 1554 and the last to die on the Green was ROBERT DEVEREUX, Elizabeth II's disgraced favourite, in 1601. Although he was not of royal blood he was granted a private execution because he was popular with the people and if he was taken to the usual execution site on Tower Hill the sight of his head falling might have caused the thousands of unruly spectators to riot. During the short reign of the under-

Tower Green in the Tower of London where aristocratic prisoners were executed away from public view.

age EDWARD VI his uncle and Protector Edward Seymour and his confederates were executed at Tower Hill in 1552 on the familiar charge of treason.

When pro-Catholic MARY succeeded to the throne many leading Protestants were taken to the Tower to be executed or imprisoned, including her half-sister ELIZABETH who famously entered the Tower through the riverside Traitor's Gate. Perhaps it was because she had feared the headsman herself that during her reign the axe became much less of a political expedient, the queen preferring imprisonment rather than execution for her enemies and recusants – those who refused to attend the Church of England when it was legally compulsory – with the result that the Tower had never had such an illustrious collection of prisoners, including bishops and some of England's principal nobility.

In 1747 the last prisoner to be executed on Tower Hill was Simon Fraser, Lord Lovat, for the part he had played in the second Jacobite Rebellion. He displayed great sangfroid as he walked through the jeering crowds to the scaffold. When a woman shouted, 'You'll get that nasty head of yours chopped off, you ugly old Scotch dog', he retorted, 'I believe I shall, you ugly old English bitch.'

While such executions were technically legal, there were several mysterious deaths and disappearances in the Tower that have become part of its folklore. Following the Battle of Tewkesbury the deposed HENRY VI was imprisoned in the Tower by the victor EDWARD IV and on the night of 21 May 1471 he died, it was said, 'of pure displeasure and melancholy' though tradition says that he was murdered while at prayer. In 1478 the king's brother Clarence was found guilty of treason and placed in the Tower where he was said to have drowned in a butt of Malmsey, his favourite wine. It was the fate of Edward's two sons, EDWARD V and his brother Richard, Duke of York that remains a riddle and still inspires heated argument. All that is known definitely is that in 1483 they were placed in the Tower by their uncle RICHARD III and never heard of again.

A less grim side to the Tower of London was its menagerie. In 1235 Henry III received a gift of three leopards from his brother-in-law Frederick II, Emperor of Germany. Thus began the Tower's royal menagerie which, housed in the Lion Tower, continued until 1835. Other exotic animals arrived including a white arctic bear from Norway. This private zoo remained popular with many succeeding kings and queens, though ELIZABETH I loathed it, her objection being that when she had been imprisoned in the Tower her sorry state had been made worse by the continuous roaring of the lions. Her successor JAMES I was fascinated by the collection and was constantly adding to it so that by the end of his reign his favourite beasts included eleven lions, a couple of leopards and – a great novelty – a tiger. When the King of Spain sent him an elephant it excited much curiosity as it was the first to be seen in Britain. It did not last long in the Tower, perhaps because its keeper tried to keep it warm during the winter months by giving it nothing to drink but wine.

In 1831 WILLIAM IV, who had ascended the throne the previous year, agreed with the Duke of Wellington, then Prime Minister, that the zoo – which was now open to the public – had become too popular and there was difficulty in controlling the crowds. Therefore he sanctioned the removal of the royal animals from the Tower and they became the nucleus of the Regent's Park zoo.

Although the Tower of London has not been a royal residence since the time of Henry VIII, it retains many royal aspects. It houses the Crown jewels, its Chapel of St John remains a royal chapel, and traditions continue such as the firing of royal salutes from the gun park at the riverside area known as the Wharf, and the CEREMONY OF THE KEYS.
See also ST PETER AD VINCULA

TRAINED BANDS The London Trained Bands, the forerunners of the militia, were formed during the reign of HENRY VIII and owed their unusual discipline to an alliance with the Honourable Artillery Company. During ELIZABETH I's reign the Trained Bands were said to number around four thousand musketeers and on one occasion paraded before the queen at Greenwich. Under her successor, JAMES I, the bands were reorganised into companies and four regiments under the command of the Lord Mayor. The Trained Bands were active during the English Civil War on the Parliamentary side, taking part in the relief of Gloucester and fighting in various actions including the Battle of Newbury. In 1794 the London Trained Bands were transformed into the City of London Militia.

TRANBY CROFT SCANDAL In 1890, Prince Edward (later EDWARD VII) became involved in a public scandal, which became known as the Tranby Croft Affair. In that autumn he accepted the invitation of shipowner Arthur Wilson to be a guest at his house, known as Tranby Croft, so that he could visit the nearby Doncaster races. At Edward's request his fellow guests played the then illegal game of baccarat, and it was at this game that Sir William Gordon-Cumming was accused of cheating.

The outcome was that in order to protect the prince from any unpleasantness public knowledge of his gambling might create, Sir William was merely asked to sign a confession of his guilt, which he admitted, and undertake never to play cards again. He believed this would remain a secret as promised, but when rumours of the affair spread he rashly brought an action for libel against the Tranby Croft witnesses in order to clear his name.

The case came to court on 1 June. As with the MORDAUNT CASE, Prince Edward sat through the proceedings while Sir William's counsel claimed his client had signed the confession in order to protect the Prince of Wales from public disclosure over his gambling and 'to save a tottering throne and prop a falling dynasty'.

On 9 June the jury took less than a quarter of an hour to decide against Sir William. While it was accepted that he was a cheat, it was the prince who was attacked from all quarters. The Kaiser wrote to Queen Victoria that anyone involved in a gaming scandal was not suitable to hold the honorary rank of colonel in the Prussian Hussars.

TROOPING THE COLOUR The object of the ceremony now known as Trooping the Colour was to familiarise troops with their regimental standards so that they would be able to recognise and rally to them in the press of battle. Originally it was known as 'Lodging the Colours', the word 'lodging' meaning the storing of a regiment's colours when not on active service, while 'trooping' came from the accompanying military music known as a 'Troop'. This parading of the colours used to be a daily exercise but in 1755 GEORGE II established it as an annual ceremony on Horse Guards Parade at Whitehall. It is held on the sovereign's official birthday, which is traditionally observed on the second Saturday in June.

The ceremony commences when the sovereign, accompanied by the mounted escort, travels in state along The Mall from BUCKINGHAM PALACE to the parade ground where the Brigade of Guards and the Household Cavalry are already drawn up. Only one colour, belonging to a regiment of which the sovereign is Colonel-in-Chief, is trooped each year. The appropriate regimental uniform is worn by the sovereign for the review.

On arriving at Horse Guards Parade the sovereign, escorted by an officer, inspects the ranks and then takes the salute at the march past to the accompaniment of regimental bands. At the conclusion of this display of precision marching the sovereign returns along The Mall at the head of the Guards regiments, which in turn mount guard at Buckingham Palace.

TUDOR, HOUSE OF When RICHARD III was killed at the Battle of Bosworth in 1465, the long Plantagenet dynasty was replaced by the House of Tudor whose name came from its first king, HENRY TUDOR. He won his place through right of conquest rather than having royal blood in his veins, his only connection with the Crown being that his mother Margaret Beaufort was descended from John Beaufort, the first of the illegitimate children born to JOHN OF GAUNT, Duke of Lancaster and his mistress Catherine Swynford. Henry's father Edmund was the illegitimate child of Catherine of France, widow of HENRY V, and Owen Tudor, a Welsh squire.

When Henry, who had led the Lancastrian party at the close of the WARS OF THE ROSES, became king he wisely married Elizabeth of York, the daughter of the Yorkist king, EDWARD IV, thereby endeavouring to unite a divided kingdom.

The dynasty that began with HENRY VII lasted for 138 years, during which royal courts reached an apex of magnificence while the kingdom underwent

The Tudors

Henry Tudor, the leader of the Lancastrian Party, became Henry VII when he defeated Yorkist Richard III and established the House of Tudor.

rapid transformations both good and bad due to the Renaissance and the Reformation. Although the personalities of the Tudor sovereigns retain an awesome sense of power and character to this day, they were of a sickly disposition and their lack of heirs brought about the premature end of their line. In desperation to get a male heir HENRY VIII married six times; his ailing son EDWARD VI died childless at the age of 16, the tragedy of his daughter MARY was that she was unable to bear children for her husband Philip of Spain and ELIZABETH I, who never married, once declared 'I am but a barren stock.'

One aspect of the Tudor reign was the ruthlessness with which political enemies were dealt with. The TOWER OF LONDON, the headsman, and the fires of Smithfield loomed large in the politics of the time, the same era of Caxton, Shakespeare, More, Tyndale, and Raleigh. While Salic Law was not recognised in England, there was a popular bias against a woman inheriting the throne, going back to the Empress Matilda and until the advent of ELIZABETH I, the last Tudor sovereign, who proved that a queen in her own right could be more effective at 'kingship' than many kings.

TUDOR EXECUTIONS On 19 May 1536 ANNE BOLEYN was led to the Green in the Tower of London where she declared to the assembled nobility and London aldermen that she blamed no one for her imminent death and, while not acknowledging the charges on which she had been found guilty of high treason, expressed her submission to the King's law. Sir William Kingston, Constable of the Tower, was so moved by the quiet courage with which she faced her executioner, that he wrote: 'This lady has much joy and pleasure in death.' The fact that the Queen was not beheaded by an axe but by a sword, which was the French custom until then unknown in England, was considered a sign of royal consideration.

Anne Boleyn's demeanour was typical of others who had offended HENRY VIII. They expressed a quiet acceptance of death on the scaffold and, considering they now had nothing to lose, refrained

Execution by beheading with a sword instead of an axe was introduced from France and first used for Anne Boleyn.

325

from cursing or denouncing the king. And while there may have been an occasional protestation of innocence, there was never a suggestion that a sentence was illegal or unfair. When Anne Boleyn's brother Lord Rochfort spoke his final words two days before her execution, he merely said that he had not come to preach but 'to serve as mirror and example'. When it was Thomas Cromwell's turn to put his head on the block he declared, 'I am by law condemned to die. I have offended my prince, for which I ask him heartily for forgiveness.'

These uncritical sentiments may have been the result of the king making everything conform to law, but it has been suggested that agreements were reached whereby the families of the victims might not be deprived of property if the condemned behaved correctly. A more sinister suggestion was that seemly behaviour on the scaffold was the price for an easy death. In 1530 William Tyndale, the English translator of the Bible, wrote in his *The Practyse of Prelates*: 'When any great man is put to death, how his confessor entreateth him, and what penance is enjoined him, concerning what he shall say when he cometh unto the place of execution, I would guess at a practice that might make men's ears glow.'

U

UNION FLAG, OFFICIAL FLYING OF The Union Flag is officially flown on the following occasions:

Queen's Accession	6 February
Prince Andrew's Birthday	19 February
St David's Day	1 March
Prince Edward's Birthday	10 March
Commonwealth Day	2nd Monday in March
Queen's Birthday	21 April
St George's Day	23 April
Europe Day	9 May
Coronation Day	2 June
Duke of Edinburgh's Birthday	10 June
Queen's Official Birthday	June
Princess Anne's Birthday	15 August
Remembrance Sunday	November
Prince of Wales's Birthday	14 November
Queen's Wedding Day	20 November
St Andrew's Day	30 November

(Getty Images)

V

VICTORIA Born Princess Alexandrina Victoria at Kensington Palace on 24 May 1819, Victoria was the only child of Edward, Duke of Kent, and Victoria, a daughter of the Duke of Saxe-Coburg. The duke died eight months after the baby's birth and his death was quickly followed by the death of his father GEORGE III. This meant that the infant princess was a successor to the Crown after her uncles the Duke of York and the Duke of Clarence, later William IV, and her highly ambitious mother saw the possibility of herself someday becoming the regent of Britain.

Conscious of not speaking English fluently herself, the duchess groomed Victoria for her possible role as sovereign by entrusting her education to Dr Davys, later Dean of Chester. The little princess was an apt pupil. She learned to sketch and paint, ride and dance, and in formal studies she learned to speak Italian, French and German.

Her governess, Baroness Lehzen, known as 'Fraulein', was to remain Victoria's lifelong friend. Having no relatives of her own to play with, the little princess's affection focused on her Uncle Leopold, later to become King of the Belgians, and with whom she remained on close terms for the rest of his life.

At the beginning of 1837 it became clear that Victoria's uncle, WILLIAM IV, did not have much longer to live. The Duchess of Kent, her chief adviser Sir John Conroy and Lady Flora Hastings, planned that if the old king lingered past Victoria's 18th birthday the girl should be pressured into acknowledging her mother as regent.

Engraving of the young Queen Victoria shortly after she came to the throne.

House of Saxe-Coburg & Gotha

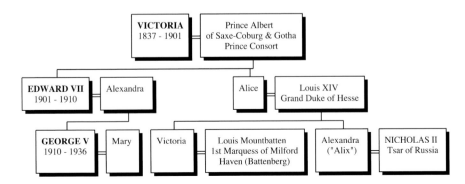

Victoria never wrote about this lonely and un-happy time in her life but three people rallied to the support of the princess – the Whig leader, Lord Melbourne; Baron Stockmar, who had been Uncle Leopold's physician; and the ever faithful Baroness Lehzen. Victoria never forgot her gratitude for their encouragement, the success of which was proved by the fact that when she became queen she had the courage to cut herself off from the tyranny of her mother.

Victoria became Queen of Great Britain on 20 June 1837 and was crowned at WESTMINSTER ABBEY a year later. There was much surprise at the aplomb with which she assumed her role as sovereign, presiding at her first Privy Council meeting with as much ease as if she had been doing it all her life. She showed also an extreme dignity and gracefulness of manner.

It was the wish of Victoria's Uncle Leopold to see his favourite niece married and his protégé was Albert, the younger son of the Duke of Saxe-Coburg-Gotha. He had a positive character, was highly intelligent and had an abiding interest in

culture. When he first visited Victoria's court, the young Queen had some reservations but a year later, she wrote ecstatically: 'My mind is quite made up and I told Albert this morning of it; the warm affection he showed me on learning this gave me great pleasure. He seems perfection. . . .'

The wedding took place on 10 February 1840 at ST JAMES'S PALACE. At the ceremony Albert wore the uniform of a field marshal and held a Bible bound in green. Of the two he was the most puritanical, but the lively Victoria did not allow this to influence her love of enjoyment.

When the Whigs lost power, Sir Robert Peel became Prime Minister, and, although the queen deeply regretted the absence of her old friend Lord Melbourne, she was determined to cooperate with his Tory successor. Her eldest son, ALBERT EDWARD, was born in November 1841, and although she was soon involved with a young family, she made it clear she was not going to become a mere figurehead. She had an acute know-ledge of foreign affairs and made a point of being shown drafts of all dispatches before they were sent abroad.

Albert toiled so hard for the advancement of his adopted country that he often appeared haggard. He was particularly interested in industrial develop-

A contemporary picture of the newly crowned Queen Victoria holding her first Privy Council meeting.

ment and the furtherance of science, and the Great Exhibition of Achievement in 1851 in Hyde Park was his inspiration. When it opened in May it was a personal triumph for the prince, who had seen it through against all manner of opposition.

The life of the royal couple was not wholly devoted to politics and advancement. Albert wanted to get away from London at times in order to enjoy a domestic period with Victoria and their family. To gain privacy a property named OSBORNE HOUSE was bought for the royal family on the Isle of Wight. While Osborne enchanted them, the wilder scenery of Scotland began to exercise a particular attraction for Victoria and Albert. In 1848 they leased BALMORAL CASTLE, which they bought four years later when it was rebuilt to the prince's plans. On the Balmoral estate, at some distance from the castle, a cottage was renovated so that they could have privacy and live like a private family. 'God knows how willingly I would have always lived with my beloved Albert and our children in the quiet and retirement of private life,' the queen told her uncle.

During these years of domestic happiness the queen had her share of political worries. The Crimean War began in 1854 and the British forces were so mismanaged that there was a public outcry and, after the resignation of Lord Aberdeen whose coalition government had seen the start of hostilities, she was forced to ask Lord Palmerston to form a government. She had never got on well with him due to his habit of sending off dispatches without her seeing them first, but now she treated him with politeness and tact and, with a firm Cabinet behind him, he concluded the war.

In 1857 she arranged for Albert to be given the title of Prince Consort, with a special precedence, an honour she believed he had earned by his promotion of social and industrial reforms. Over the years the prince had gained the trust both the public and parliament had felt towards him as a foreigner. Too intelligent to interfere openly in politics, his far-sighted and intelligent advice was passed on to the Cabinet through the queen. In November 1861, greatly troubled by what he and Victoria considered the bad behaviour of his eldest son, Albert suffered an attack of influenza. Then typhoid was diagnosed and he died just before midnight on 14 December.

'If I must live on (and I will do nothing to make me worse than I am), it is henceforth for our poor fatherless children – for my unhappy country, which has lost all in losing him . . .' Thus wrote the queen to her Uncle Leopold six days after the death of her beloved Albert. The tone of the letter was to be deeply reflected by the queen's attitude during her forty long years of bereavement, in which time she became known as the Widow of Windsor.

As a special royal train bore the heartbroken queen from Windsor to the Isle of Wight and Osborne House, she was heard to mutter, 'I will, I will do my duty.' And in her seclusion she forced herself to sign official documents and write to Cabinet ministers of affairs of state, though four years were to pass before she was able to make the effort to attend the opening of Parliament. Meanwhile, the Victorian Age, with its ever-accelerating ideas and technology, continued its momentum without her.

The splendid life she had shared with her husband was over and the public became impatient with a recluse who shut herself away in Balmoral in the Highlands of Scotland or Osborne House on the Isle of Wight. It has been estimated that for the remainder of her long reign the queen slept no more than twenty nights in Buckingham Palace.

Fifteen months after Albert's death, ALBERT EDWARD, Prince of Wales was married to Princess Alexandra, the daughter of King Christian IX of Denmark. The Queen would not allow the ceremony to be held in Westminster Abbey as it would have entailed her making a public appearance, and so it took place in St George's Chapel at Windsor where she merely observed it from a gallery.

In 1864 *The Times* published several articles urging the queen to return to public life. After a particularly harsh criticism of her she penned a reply to the newspaper in which she declared that she had 'other and higher duties' which she described as 'overwhelming her with work and anxiety' and which were more important than 'mere representation'.

In Scotland Victoria turned more and more to her Highland attendant, John Brown, for support. He had begun in the royal household as the Prince Consort's ghillie, which endeared him to the queen. She never resented his blunt manner – he got away with addressing her as 'Woman' and she overlooked his penchant for whisky. She explained in a letter to her Uncle Leopold that there was no question of his utter devotion to her and his understanding nature.

Gradually the Queen returned to the world of reality from her state of morbid grief, though for the

Queen Victoria in a small donkey-drawn carriage at Balmoral with her youngest daughter Princess Beatrice, *c.* 1895. *(Getty Images)*

rest of her life Albert's suit was laid out in his room at Windsor and his washbasin kept full of fresh water. One of the factor's which helped her was her editing of a five-volume biography of the Prince Consort by Theodore Martin, and this encouraged her to write *Leaves from a Journal of our Life in the Highlands* which contained extracts from her remarkable diary. The book was printed privately in 1867 and then published commercially to become the best-seller of the following year. Never before had the public been allowed such glimpses into the domestic lives of royalty, a delightfully simple picture of the queen's family freed from the pomp of court life, and describing such homely incidents as Vicky (the Princess Royal) sitting on a wasps' nest and the pleasures and difficulties of picnicking.

In 1868 William Ewart Gladstone became Prime Minister. He began his distinguished parliamentary career as a Tory and was responsible for far-reaching financial reforms, but in 1865 he became leader of the Liberal Party. The least successful aspect of his career was his inability to get along with Victoria. She said that 'he addressed her as though she was a public meeting'. While she sympathised with Conservative policies, she did give him correct support when he became premier, but the fact remained that her relations with him were the worst she had with the various statesmen who took principal office during her long reign.

In complete contrast to Gladstone was the Tory Benjamin Disraeli, who had briefly been Prime Minister in 1868. His flattering manner as well as his political policies were more sympathetic to the queen and he was further endeared to her by his continual tributes to the late Prince Consort.

Two years after Disraeli became Prime Minister in 1876 he mollified her by passing an Act that made her Empress of India, a title she thoroughly enjoyed.

The Queen remained closer to Disraeli than any other minister since Lord Melbourne and paid him the great honour of visiting his home in Bucking-

An early postage stamp showing Queen Victoria's head in profile. Such stamps came into use early in her reign.

hamshire. In 1880 when he lost an election and retired to resume novel writing he was created Earl of Beconsfield, and when he died a year later the Queen lost one of her greatest friends and supporters. She wrote to Lord Rowton, his private secretary, 'I cannot write in the third person at this terrible moment when I can scarcely see for my fast falling tears.'

Two years later Victoria came close to death when a would-be assassin named Roderick Maclean fired a revolver at her as she entered her carriage at Windsor Station. She showed the same courage as she had over the six previous attempts on her life, but she was angry when Maclean, who was charged with high treason, was pronounced not guilty but insane.

Victoria's personal life finally regained some of the happiness she had not known for twenty-four years with the marriage of her youngest daughter Princess Beatrice to Prince Henry of Battenberg in 1885. They shared the Queen's household, whether at Windsor, in Scotland or the Isle of Wight. Victoria became devoted to her son-in-law and they shared an interest in music. He arranged musical evenings for her, and London theatrical companies were booked to perform at Windsor. He also saw to it that interesting guests were invited to Windsor to dine

with the queen. It was almost a return to the days of Albert.

The following year one of the Queen's many concerns was cruelty to animals and she wrote an animal protection code which included this paragraph about dogs: 'No dogs should ever be killed by the police unless the veterinary surgeon declared they were mad. . . . Fits are no proof of this.'

The Queen was no doubt delighted that Lord Salisbury became Prime Minister after Gladstone was defeated over the Home Rule Bill, and she was able to look forward to her Golden Jubilee, to be held in 1887, with undiluted pleasure. For the celebration she spent a rare ten days in London, taking part in public ceremonies and going in procession to a service of thanksgiving at Westminster Abbey, followed by thirty members of her family – sons, sons-in-law and grandsons – all trotting behind her carriage. Although she was now close to 70 she gave audiences, made a 15-mile progress through London, attended a banquet, and visited Buffalo Bill's Wild West Show which she found 'very extraordinary and interesting'.

What some regarded as an eccentricity was her employment of Indians, who were housed in King John's Tower at Windsor where they were allowed to kill and cook chickens in their traditional way. For the rest of her life she was served by Indian attendants: her wheeled chair was pushed by an Indian servant; at meal times one always stood behind her chair no matter which of her three homes she was staying in, and one, Munshi Abdul Karim, took on something of the role of John Brown who had died in 1883. He gave her daily lessons in Hindustani and it delighted the queen to be able to greet visiting Indian dignitaries in their own tongue.

Queen Victoria's Diamond Jubilee, celebrated in 1897, was probably the greatest national celebration in British history. Representatives of British overseas dominions and foreign powers flocked to London for it, and the whole occasion, with huge processions, bonfires and reviews of naval and military strength, represented a peak of British achievement. The boom in commerce and the expansion of empire which had added so much pink to world maps, amazing advances in technology and social reform, culminated in one old lady's jubilee.

In 1899 the outbreak of the Boer War caused her much anxiety. She was in daily contact with her

Queen Victoria's Continental Legacy

```
┌──────────────┐  ┌──────────────┐
│ VICTORIA     │  │ Prince Albert│
│ 1837 - 1901  │  │ of Saxe-Coburg│
│              │  │ & Gotha,     │
│              │  │ Prince Consort│
└──────────────┘  └──────────────┘
```

Alice	Louis XIV Grand Duke of Hesse
	Victoria Adelaide	FRIEDRICH III Emperor of Germany

Victoria	Louis Mountbatten 1st Marquess of Milford Haven (Battenberg)

| WILHELM III
The Kaiser | Sophie | CONSTANTINE I
King of Greece |

| Louise | GUSTAV VI
King of Sweden |

| Alexandra
"Alix" | NICHOLAS II
Tsar of Russia | Alfred Ernest Albert
Duke of Edinburgh
and Saxe-Coburg &
Gotha | Maria
Grand Duchess of
Russia | Henry
of Battenberg | Beatrice M. Victoria |

| EDWARD VII
1901 - 1910 | Alexandra |

| Marie | FERDINAND I
King of Romania |

| Maud | HAAKON VII
King of Norway |

| Victoria E. Ena
Queen Ena of Spain | ALPHONSO XIII
King of Spain |

| OLAV
King of Norway | Martha
Princess of Sweden |

| HARALD
King of Norway |

ministers and, despite her age, constantly inspected troops before they left for Table Bay. She visited those invalided home and even travelled to Dublin to express her gratitude for the part played by Irish regiments.

In February 1900 she was cheered by the turn of the tide in favour of the British forces – apart from any other consideration, the queen disliked the Boers for their attitude to the black Africans – but the burden of age and the work she continued to do began to take their toll. Her physical condition deteriorated and she died in the arms of her oldest grandson, Kaiser Wilhelm II of Germany, on 22 January 1901, her final words being, 'Albert, Albert, Albert.' She was buried beside the Prince Consort in the ROYAL MAUSOLEUM at Frogmore in Windsor Park.

See also BALMORAL and OSBORNE HOUSE

VICTORIAN MOURNING After the death of PRINCE ALBERT in 1861, QUEEN VICTORIA set the standard for mourning. The period was decided not by personal sentiment but by a socially understood timetable:

Death of	Period of mourning
Husband	2 to 3 years
Wife	3 months
Parent or child	1 year
Siblings	6 months
Grandparents	6 months
Aunts and uncles	3 months
Nephews and nieces	2 months
Great uncles and aunts	6 weeks
First cousins	4 to 6 weeks

These individual periods of mourning were themselves subdivided into first mourning, second mourning, ordinary, and half-mourning. By tradition first mourning was the deepest and lasted a year and a day. Each of these periods had its own subtle code, down to the shade of black, the types of cloth worn, and the width of hat bands. Older children were expected to mourn alongside their parents, but often very young children were excused mourning dress. Servants' mourning was normally considered appropriate after the death of a senior member of the household and when imposed it usually lasted for at least six months. Victoria herself wore mourning dress for the rest of her reign after Albert's death.

VILLIERS, BARBARA The first of CHARLES II's celebrated mistresses was Barbara Villiers, whom he met just before the Restoration in 1660. Aged 19, she was already married to Roger Palmer, who was happy to trade her for the title of Earl of Castlemaine. Although a great beauty with a wistful expression, she was said to have such a temper that it was regarded a wonder that the king tolerated her hectoring ways and notorious amours for six years. But Charles was ever easy-going and the three sons he had by her were created respectively dukes of Cleveland, Grafton and Northumberland. Barbara's greatest mistake was to insult Queen Catherine, something that Charles, who was genuinely fond of his wife, would not tolerate. With his usual generosity he pensioned her off and created her Duchess of Cleveland. She found solace in the arms of an athletic rope-dancer.

VISCOUNT Originating in France when the *vicomte* was the deputy of a count, the title viscount ranks fourth in the British peerage between earl and baron. It was created in 1446 and latterly it became the custom to bestow this title upon Cabinet ministers raised to the peerage.

W

WALES, KINGS AND PRINCES OF Following the departure of the Romans in the fifth century Wales split into a number of small independent kingdoms. Four centuries later these had coalesced into two major ones: Gwynedd in the north of the country and Deheubarth in the south. Now there were only two kingdoms, the possibility of Wales having an overall king – as happened in Anglo-Saxon England on the other side of OFFA'S DYKE – became a reality in the form of Rhodri Mawr ('The Great'). Inheriting the throne of Gwynedd on the death of his father, Merfyn Frych ('The Freckled') in AD 844, Rhodri gradually inherited more territory from his relatives, so that by 872 he was also King of Deheubarth. Under his rule the people gained a sense of national identity, the benefits of which were demonstrated when Welsh armies under his leadership were victorious against Viking forces in a number of battles and fought off invaders from Wessex and Mercia. It was in battle against the latter that Rhodri was slain in AD 878.

It was Rhodri Mawr's grandson, Hywel ('The Good'), who extended the concept of kingship in Wales. His policy was to have good relations with England and, under threatened Viking incursions, he acknowledged the overlordship of EDWARD THE ELDER in AD 918 and that of ATHELSTAN in AD 927 and often visited their courts. In AD 928 he embarked upon a pilgrimage to Rome and like KING ALFRED became inspired to improve his kingdom by what he saw and learned by travelling. On his return to Wales he is credited with summoning a great assembly at Whitland which saw the codification of Welsh laws, the Cyfraith Hywel Dda, which further united the country, as did the minting of his own coinage. In this he was the only Welsh king to do so. After his death c. AD 949 his realm fell apart and regressed to a collection of independent kingdoms. One of the reasons for Wales's fragmentation was partible inheritance in which an estate did not go to the eldest son but was divided equally among all the deceased's male offspring; thus a kingdom might be divided among royal brothers.

It was only in the eleventh century that reunification came about with the advent of Gruffyd ap Llywelyn, a descendant of Hywel, who seized Gwynedd after its king was murdered, and with English and Scandinavian backing gained control of much of the country. Deheubarth held out against him despite a number of particularly fierce battles. He was more successful in winning land beyond Offa's Dyke, assisted by Mercia. In 1055 he finally won Deheubarth after killing two of its kings in battle and, establishing his court at Rhuddlan, he was recognised as the King of Wales. Although he acknowledged the overlordship of EDWARD THE CONFESSOR, the old warrior continued his border raiding, abetted by Mercia. This prompted HAROLD GODWINESON, Earl of Wessex to retaliate, attacking Rhuddlan in 1062. Gruffyd fled but when cornered by the English he was murdered by his own followers who sent his head to Harold as a token of submission.

As before, the country divided into a number of separate 'kingdoms' and more than a century was to pass before a leader was capable of restoring the concept of unity to Wales. Llywelyn ap Iorwert ('The Great'), taking profitable advantage out of family feuds, succeeded in taking control of Gwynedd in 1202, followed by the annexation of Powys and Deheubarth. He came to an understanding with KING JOHN whereby he accepted him as the ruler of Wales and in return acknowledged John as his overlord, rather as the independent dukes of Normandy and Aquitaine paid homage to the King of France. The agreement was strengthened by his marriage to Joan, John's illegitimate daughter, and in supporting him in his campaign against WILLIAM 'the Lyon' of Scotland (*see* SCOTLAND, EARLY KINGS OF).

In 1210 Llywelyn proclaimed himself Prince of Wales, and seeing this as an act of defiance King John invaded Gwynedd. Fortunately for Llywelyn the king's domestic problems prevented further conquest and in 1216 – the year of John's death – the Treaty of Worcester confirmed him as Prince of Wales. During his reign Llywelyn revised the laws of Wales, reorganised the administration and introduced the law of primogeniture – inheritance by the eldest son – which would ensure that the kingdom would continue to have a single ruler. Thus when Llywelyn died in 1240, his son Dafydd ap Llywelyn became Prince of Wales.

During the first year of Dafydd's reign relations with England deteriorated and HENRY III invaded Wales to force the return of lands which had been taken by the prince's father. Daffyd's illegitimate elder brother Gruffyd was taken hostage and an uneasy peace returned, Daffyd painfully aware that if he annoyed the English, Henry could endanger his position by supporting Gruffyd's long-held claim to their father's throne. This threat ended in 1244 when Gruffyd died in an attempt to escape from the TOWER OF LONDON.

Dafydd, supported by the Welsh nobles, felt he was now in a position to defy King Henry, with the result that there was an English expedition sent against him in 1245. Daffyd died unexpectedly at the beginning of the following year but Henry continued his campaign which gave him control of the land. In 1247 the Treaty of Woodstock was signed by Dafydd's nephew and successor Llywelyn ap Gruffydd ('Llywelyn the Last').

Llywelyn resented the terms of the treaty under which he and his two brothers were deprived of the territory east of the River Conway, and this fuelled his ambition to bring about a lasting and independent Welsh principality. His first step in this direction was to defeat his brothers at the Battle of Bryn Derwin in 1255 – thereby giving him sole control of Gwynedd – after which he regained the territory that had been annexed by the Treaty of Woodstock. With this success he won the loyalty of the various Welsh nobles who accepted him as their overlord. In 1258 the Peace of Montgomery was agreed between the Welsh and the English and in return for Llywelyn's homage King Henry acknowledged him as Prince of Wales.

After EDWARD I came to the throne of England in 1272, relations between the two countries changed. Llywelyn refused to pay the tribute to England that had been agreed under the Peace of Montgomery and refused to acknowledge the new king as his overlord. In 1276 King Edward's army

entered Wales, resulting in Llywelyn being bound to the humiliating Treaty of Aberconwy, which left him only with his original inheritance of west Gwynedd and the now empty title of Prince of Wales. The resultant period of peace ended in 1282 when Llywelyn's brother Dafydd besieged Hawarden Castle and Llywelyn had no option but to support him. Edward I's response was immediate and effective, and by the end of the year Llywelyn ap Gruffydd, the last Welsh Prince of Wales was dead.

In 1284 under the Statute of Rhuddlan, Wales lost its independence to English rule and King Edward gave his new-born son, the future EDWARD II, the title of Prince of Wales.

The idea of Welsh independence remained a remote, but not a forgotten, dream and in 1401 it seemed that it could become a reality when Wales's most popular hero began his rebellion. Born into a wealthy landowning family in Montgomeryshire, Owain Glyndwr – frequently spelt Owen Glendower – could claim descent from Llywelyn ap Gruffydd. He studied law at Westminster and became a squire to Richard Fitzalan, Earl of Arundel at Chirk. His rebellion began when he had a dispute with Lord Grey of Ruthin over some land, and when he could get no redress from HENRY IV he attacked Lord Grey's estates close to the Welsh border.

The country was ripe for rebellion. Would-be rebels rallied to Glyndwr, who was proclaimed Prince of Wales, and his border forays burgeoned into a war of independence. In 1401 he captured Lord Grey and Sir Edmund Mortimer, both of whom not only joined his cause giving it a great endorsement but also married his daughters. HENRY PERCY ('Hotspur') joined the rebellion and in 1403 met his death fighting for the coalition at the Battle of Shrewsbury, won by King Henry. Although this was a setback for Glyndwr, he continued the rebellion in south Wales where he captured a number of castles, and the next year he signed a treaty with Charles VI of France. He held several assemblies to plan the future of an independent Wales and the rebels were encouraged by the arrival of French troops at Milford Sound in 1405. Despite these reinforcements the rebels began to suffer defeats, with the result that their allies withdrew. Nevertheless, Glyndwr continued his campaign for the next five years. Then, after leading a raid into Shropshire, he vanished. There is no definite knowledge of his fate though it was said that when Henry V offered him a pardon in 1415 he refused it and died shortly afterwards.

See also HAROLD II, HENRY III, EDWARD I

WALLACE, WILLIAM See SCOTLAND, EARLY KINGS OF

WALSINGHAM, SIR FRANCIS Although ELIZABETH I did not always follow the advice of Francis Walsingham, she recognised his worth and made him her principal secretary in 1573. Coming from a Protestant family, he travelled abroad during the Roman Catholic reign of MARY I. In 1570 he was sent to France as a diplomat by William Cecil, Lord Burghley and proved himself to be so successful he was knighted, became a principal secretary of state and a member of the Privy Council. His most effective work was the establishment of a secret service using spies in England and abroad. His uncovering of the BABINGTON PLOT led to MARY, QUEEN OF SCOTS being tried for treason and executed in 1587, the same year that he was successful in obtaining advance information about the Spanish Armada. Despite his outstanding service to the Crown he earned little from Elizabeth, and when he died in 1590 he was poverty-stricken and in debt.

WARBECK, PERKIN After RICHARD III had been slain on Bosworth Field, Lancastrian HENRY TUDOR's right to rule England was questioned by

A coin struck by the supporters of the pretender Perkin Warbeck who claimed to be the son of Edward IV.

many of his subjects with Yorkist sympathies. This set the stage for false claimants to the Crown. In 1487 the imposter LAMBERT SIMNEL was crowned as Edward VI in Dublin, before being defeated by the king and set to work as a scullion in the royal kitchen. Four years later a more convincing imposter named Perkin Warbeck appeared on the scene. Born in 1472 at Tournai, he was the son of a prominent citizen and later came into contact with adherents of the House of York. At the age of 17 he entered the service of a Breton knight named Pregent Meno with whom he travelled to Ireland in 1491. Rumours spread that he was the son of the Duke of Clarence and nephew of EDWARD IV which at first he denied on oath. However, when the earls of Desmond and Kildare offered to support him he agreed to portray himself as RICHARD OF YORK, the younger of EDWARD IV's sons who had vanished mysteriously in the TOWER OF LONDON.

Warbeck was then taught to speak good English and behave in the courtly manner of a prince, and by March of the following year his mentors were so satisfied with his progress that they sent a letter to JAMES IV of Scotland in which Warbeck claimed to be 'King Edward's son'. His explanation was that when he was 9 years old his elder brother, Edward, was murdered in the Tower of London, but he was secretly sent out of England in the custody of two people after he had sworn an oath to remain silent about his name and rank for a certain number of years. Soon he was invited to the French court where, France being at war with England, he received royal honours until a treaty was signed between the two countries and it was not politic for him to remain as the French king's guest.

In Flanders King Henry's old enemy Margaret, Duchess of Burgundy and sister of Edward IV, acknowledged him as her nephew and called him 'The White Rose of England'. It was under her tutelage that his final coaching was completed. In response to the plot Henry suspended trade between England and Flanders, with the result that Londoners rioted at the loss of income caused by the ban. Meanwhile, Warbeck was confident enough to meet members of Europe's royal houses, including the Emperor Maximilian, while in England plans were laid for a rebellion on his behalf.

Henry's agents offered Sir Robert Clifford, a Yorkist living in exile, a pardon and £500 to name the conspirators. He accepted and a number of persons, said to be Warbeck's supporters, were put to death. Sir William Stanley, who had placed the crown on Henry's head on the battlefield of Bosworth, was among those sent to trial and then beheaded. These executions did not deter Warbeck, who travelled to Scotland where James IV greeted him royally at Stirling Castle, called him cousin and, as a sign of his favour, gave him his cousin Catherine Gordon, daughter of the Earl of Huntly, in marriage.

Plans now went ahead for Warbeck's invasion of England and in September 1496 the Scots, reinforced by Desmond's Irish troops, crossed the border into Northumberland, but when it became apparent that no Englishmen would follow the imposter's banner the Scots turned the campaign into an excuse to plunder. When Warbeck – shocked by the atrocities usual in such border strife – pleaded with King James to spare his 'subjects', he was ridiculed.

In 1498 Warbeck accepted an invitation from Cornish rebels to be their leader. Landing at Whitesand Bay he yet again proclaimed himself as Richard IV, and by the time he reached Bodmin he found himself at the head of three thousand men, a number which doubled as he marched towards Exeter. He laid siege to the town but when an army commanded by the Earl of Devonshire approached he withdrew to Taunton where he learned that another approaching force, under Lord Daubeney, had reached Glastonbury. At midnight on 21 September he abandoned his followers and fled to Beaulieu in Hampshire where he took sanctuary. Here he was persuaded to throw himself on the mercy of King Henry, who promised him his life if he would make a full confession of his imposture, which he did. In London he was led through the streets to the Tower but, having no wish to make him a martyr, the king allowed him to live at court under surveillance. He also treated Warbeck's pregnant wife with kindness, granting her a pension to cover the expenses of her estate.

When Warbeck attempted to escape in the summer of 1498, he was punished by being placed in the stocks at Westminster. His confession was now printed and distributed by royal command and once again he found himself in the Tower, where a fellow prisoner was the highly popular Edward, Earl of Warwick, the son of the Duke of Clarence and a genuine claimant of the Crown. They became great friends, and when they planned to seize the Tower news of the plot reached the authorities and Warbeck, Warwick and a number of other prisoners were indicted at the Guildhall. The result was that the earl was beheaded and Perkin Warbeck was hanged on 23 November 1499 after reading a confession.

Bacon wrote: 'The opinion of the King's great wisdom did surcharge him with a sinister frame, that Perkin was but his bait to entrap the Earl of Warwick.'

WARDE In 1400 RICHARD II resigned his crown to Henry of Lancaster, who then became HENRY IV, and was confined in Pontefract Castle where he died under mysterious circumstances. Many of his adherents ignored the rumours that he had been murdered and preferred to believe that he had escaped to Scotland. Four years later, a jester known as Warde was persuaded by a gentleman named Serle to impersonate Richard, to whom he bore a remarkable likeness. It was arranged for Richard's privy seal to be counterfeited and letters were sent to Richard's old supporters, including the elderly Countess of Oxford, proclaiming the imposter's intention to return to England to reclaim his rightful crown. Badges of gold and silver harts, such as Richard had given to his followers, were to be worn by those ready to rebel against Henry. He was appraised of the plot when one of Serle's messengers was seized and under interrogation revealed the identities of the plotters who were then arrested and imprisoned. Serle was drawn on a sledge through the principal towns between Pontefract and London where he was executed for treason.

WARWICK, RICHARD NEVILLE, EARL OF Known as 'The Kingmaker', he was born in 1428 the eldest son of Richard, Earl of Salisbury. Through his marriage to Anne Beauchamp, the daughter of the Earl of Warwick, he gained the earldom which provided him with so much land and wealth that when the WARS OF THE ROSES broke out in 1455 he was powerful enough to hold the balance between the Houses of York and Lancaster. His influence further increased in 1460 when he inherited his father's title. He backed the Yorkist cause with his enormous wealth and was instrumental in displacing HENRY VI in favour of EDWARD IV in 1461, thus earning his nickname. For the following four years he was the power behind the throne but then he and the king fell out, the latter resenting his influence and curtailing his authority, and finally exiling him to France. Warwick's attitude was that if he could make one king, he could make another. Back in England he briefly restored Henry VI to the throne after the Battle of Edgecote in July 1469. Edward escaped to Flanders but the next year, assisted by his brother-in-law, the Duke of Burgundy, returned and was victorious at the Battle of Barnet on 14 April 1471 where Warwick was slain.

See also HENRY VI

WESTMINSTER ABBEY Aptly called Britain's Pantheon, Westminster Abbey has been the ceremonial hub of royal events for the last thousand years. The site of the abbey is thought to go back to AD 785 when the Mercian king OFFA presented the land 'to St Peter and the needy people of God in Thorney [then an island in the Thames] in the terrible place which is called Westminster' where a religious community was established. Definite knowledge begins with the reign of EDWARD THE CONFESSOR who ascended the throne in 1043.

The king had sworn to travel to the tomb of St Peter, but his Council were against the idea of him leaving England so Pope Leo IX absolved him from the vow on condition that he established a monastery dedicated to the saint. Dutifully Edward began construction work on the monastery and the new abbey – to be pictured in the Bayeux Tapestry – which was designed in the shape of a cross beside an earlier building. The king was too ill to attend its consecration on 28 December 1065 and on 5 January he died and was interred before the high altar. In 1161 Pope Alexander III canonised the king for his spiritual virtues.

The first coronation in Westminster Abbey took place on Christmas Day 1066 when William, Duke of Normandy was crowned WILLIAM I. With the exceptions of EDWARD V and EDWARD VIII, all English and British sovereigns have been enthroned in the abbey since that date.

Westminster Abbey, which has been the centre of royal occasions since the coronation of William the Conqueror.

Born in 1207, HENRY III has been described as one of the most cultured monarchs ever to sit on the English throne, whose lavish spending on works of art and the decoration of royal palaces testified to his love of beauty. Doubtless the vicissitudes of his father's reign encouraged him to try and restore the monarchy to what he considered to be its former glory. This attitude was apparent with his fostering of the cult of the sainted Edward the Confessor and the transforming of Westminster Abbey into a magnificent royal necropolis. The rebuilding of the abbey commenced in 1245 under the master mason Henry de Reyns and, despite increasing economic problems in the kingdom, huge sums were spent on the project, most of which came from the king's own resources. By 1254 the work, now supervised by Master John of Gloucester, had reached a stage where the Chapter House, north front, rose windows, transepts and some of the cloisters had been completed. It is thought that much of the new abbey's design was inspired by ecclesiastical buildings the king had seen on the Continent, particularly those at Rheims and Amiens, and the rebuilt abbey has been described as the most French of English Gothic churches.

The body of Edward the Confessor had been translated to a shrine in the special chapel named after him, and when Henry died in 1272 he was interred where the saint had been originally buried before the high altar. His embalmed heart, however, was taken to France where it was placed close to the tombs of his grandparents, HENRY II and ELEANOR OF AQUITAINE, in Fontevrault Abbey.

During the reign of Henry's successor, EDWARD I, the crypt of the Chapter House became the Royal Treasury, but in spite of its seemingly impregnable location it was burgled and the Keeper of the Palace of Westminster was put to death for his role in the robbery, though it was thought likely that some of the abbey's clergy were involved.

In the latter part of the fourteenth century, building work, which had been largely discontinued after the reign of Henry, was recommenced on the nave by Abbot Nicholas Littlington after a previous abbot, Simon Langham, made funds available. RICHARD II also contributed generously to the continuation of the work, which followed the original plans of Henry de Reynes. Abbot Littlington also rebuilt the Abbot's House which contained an impressive room known as the Jerusalem Chamber. When praying before the shrine of Edward the Confessor, HENRY IV suffered a seizure due to a disease related to leprosy and was carried into the Jerusalem Chamber where he died on 20 March 1413. Thus a prediction that he would die in Jerusalem was considered to have been fulfilled.

During the reign of HENRY V the abbey's financial position was secured by an annual allocation of 1,000 marks, and when the king died in 1422 a chantry chapel was erected over his grave at the entrance to Edward the Confessor's shrine.

In 1471, when EDWARD IV regained the kingdom, Prior Thomas Millyng was rewarded with royal favour and made a bishop for providing sanctuary in the abbey for Queen Elizabeth Woodville during the dangers of the previous year when HENRY VI had briefly returned to the throne. The queen's gratitude was expressed by building the Chapel of St Erasmus next to the abbey's Lady Chapel.

After Henry VI was said to have 'died disconsolate and of pure melancholy' in the TOWER OF LONDON when Edward IV became king for a second time, he was interred at Windsor where miracles occurring at his tomb were reported. HENRY VII not only attempted to have him canonised, but decided to build a chapel in the abbey to which his body could be translated. When the petition for canonisation failed, the king decided to dedicate the new chapel to the Virgin Mary. When Henry died in 1509 he was interred in the chapel beside his queen, Elizabeth, the daughter of Edward IV.

At the Dissolution of the Monasteries the monastery of St Peter was closed but the abbey itself did not suffer as did other ecclesiastical establishments, its monuments and statuary remaining intact on account of its five centuries of royal patronage.

During the reign of EDWARD VI the abbey became the cathedral of the newly established diocese of Westminster and was administered by a dean and chapter in place of a bishop. When MARY I came to the throne she reinstated the monks but they were dismissed again when Protestant ELIZABETH I succeeded her Roman Catholic sister. Although Parliamentary troops were quartered in the abbey during the English Civil War the statuary escaped the iconoclasm that took place in other churches. Ironically the Lord Protector,

Oliver Cromwell, John Bradshaw, President of the Court that condemned CHARLES I to death, and Henry Ireton the king's implacable enemy, were all buried in the abbey beside the royal dead. On the Restoration their bodies were disinterred and buried beneath the Tyburn gallows.

Restoration work was carried out on the abbey under the direction of Sir Christopher Wren, who drew up plans for the West Towers which were modified by Nicholas Hawksmoor before the work was completed in 1745. By then the practice of erecting monuments to non-royal persons increased.

See also CORONATION CEREMONY

WESTMINSTER, PALACE OF The sainted EDWARD THE CONFESSOR was too ill to attend the consecration of the magnificent abbey he had built at Westminster, and eight days later, on 5 January 1066, he died in the Palace of Westminster, his other great building. For the site of WESTMINSTER ABBEY the king had chosen Thorney, meaning the Isle of Thorns, on land close to the Thames where there was already a small monastery dedicated to St Peter. Edward selected this spot because of his special veneration of the Apostle, and then chose a nearby site on the river bank for his palace. It was London's first royal palace, eventually being followed in succession by WHITEHALL PALACE, ST JAMES's and lastly BUCKINGHAM PALACE.

After WILLIAM I's coronation on Christmas Day 1066 he intended to rebuild the palace, but a fleet of ships bringing Caen stone from Normandy for the purpose was lost in a storm and it remained for his son WILLIAM II to build Westminster Hall beside Edward's palace, which gave its name to the 'Old Palace Yard'. The hall, a combination of royal residence and the king's seat of government, was completed in 1099 and was regarded as a marvel in its day. It was thought to be the largest in Europe and remains the oldest part of the palace. William planned to build even more grand additions but he was killed in the New Forest shortly after he had held his inaugural court in Westminster Hall.

London's first royal palace, the Palace of Westminster – better known as the Houses of Parliament – still belongs to the sovereign.

During the troubled reign of KING STEPHEN the palace suffered from neglect but his successor HENRY II refurbished it, building what became known as the White Hall for the royal household. His grandson HENRY III was the next king to leave his imprint on the palace by enlarging it to include his famous Painted Chamber, the walls of this 80ft-long hall being decorated with scenes from the life of Edward the Confessor and Biblical battle scenes. These murals were uncovered and reproduced when old layers of paper were stripped from the walls in the early nineteenth century.

In 1239 EDWARD I was born at Westminster Palace and has become known as 'Edward of Westminster', as in medieval times it was not unusual for the place of birth to become a surname. His contribution was to add St Stephen's Chapel, whose undercroft survived the great fire of 1834 and remains part of the palace.

Westminster Palace came to an end as a royal residence when HENRY VIII left it for York Place – soon to become Whitehall Palace – ten days after its owner CARDINAL WOLSEY was impeached under the STATUTE OF PRAEMUNIRE and fell from grace. Though royalty has preferred other palaces since then, the Palace of Westminster continued as the meeting place of the Lords and Commons and as such has remained at the core of British history.

In October 1834 a great stack of tally sticks – old forms of Exchequer accounts kept on notched sticks – was incinerated in a stove used for heating the House of Lords, but such was the heat they generated that panelling caught fire and most of the palace was razed. Six years later work began on the new Palace of Westminster, today also known as the Houses of Parliament, under the direction of Sir Charles Barry, with the Gothic ornamentation designed by Augustus Pugin. It was completed by 1860 with its long river frontage and its tower at each end, the western one being the Victoria Tower which rises 330ft, beneath which is the Sovereign's Entrance used by the sovereign for the STATE OPENING OF PARLIAMENT.

As the Eiffel Tower is to France and the Statue of Liberty is to the United States, so the square clock tower at the opposite end is probably the best known symbol of Britain abroad. It has four dials, each 23ft in diameter, and though it is erroneously referred to as 'Big Ben', it is actually the 13.5-ton bell which tolls the hours that is Big Ben, the name

coming from that of the First Commissioner of Works, Sir Benjamin Hall, who was in charge when it was placed in position in 1859.

During the Second World War its sonorous notes were broadcast around the world as a message of Britain's defiance despite the early military setbacks and the Blitz. It was during an air raid on 10 May 1941 that the palace's House of Commons was destroyed, but Westminster Hall, with RICHARD II's famed hammer-beam roof, was miraculously saved. With the firefighting equipment then available either the house or the hall could be saved and the agonising decision favoured the latter. The rebuilding of the House of Commons was completed by 1950. Westminster Hall did suffer some damage in 1974 from a device planted by Irish nationalists.

Today the Palace of Westminster is made up of eleven hundred apartments and offices, and covers an area of 8 acres, and while it has long been a symbol of a democratic Parliament it still belongs to the sovereign.

WHITE SHIP, THE *See* HENRY I

WILLIAM I Before he became 'The Conqueror', William I was referred to as 'The Bastard'. His father, Robert III, Duke of Normandy, became enamoured of a girl named Arlette when he saw her close to his castle in Falaise. Today a monument marks the spot where they met. A daughter of the tanner Fulbert, she gave birth to William in 1027.

Later, before setting out on a pilgrimage to the Holy Land, the duke made his barons swear fealty to his 7-year-old son, but they had no wish to see the illegitimate grandson of a tanner as their overlord, and in 1035, when the duke died, young William was in constant danger. His maternal uncle Walter now became his most devoted protector. His favourite companion was his cousin EDWARD, later known as 'The Confessor'. Exiled to Normandy during the reign of CANUTE, Edward was full of admiration for everything Norman.

The youthful duke was handsome but of stocky build. Describing him later in life, William of Malmesbury wrote that he was of 'moderate stature, extraordinary corpulence and fierce countenance, his forehead bare of hair. He was of such great strength of arm that no one was able to bend his bow. . . .'

When William was 24 years old he visited his childhood companion, Edward, now on the throne

The tower overlooking the town of Falaise in which William the Conqueror was born.

of England, and it was then, so William claimed, that the celibate king promised that he would be his successor.

In 1053 William wished to marry Matilda, the daughter of Baldwin V, Count of Flanders. Not only was he in love with the girl but their marriage would be a great alliance. Matilda's uncle was the King of France and she was descended both from Emperor Charlemagne and ALFRED THE GREAT, an important asset to her husband's aspirations to the English throne. When told of the proposal Matilda declared she would never marry a tanner's grandson. On hearing of this William rode out to find her, and seizing her by her long hair slapped her and immediately rode away. In response Matilda dropped her objection and after their marriage they were devoted to each other for the rest of their lives.

This sculpture marks the spot where William's father Robert III, Duke of Normandy first met Arlette, William's mother, when she was washing clothing in a spring.

In 1064 HAROLD GODWINESON was brought to William after being shipwrecked on the coast at Ponthieu. He was induced to be 'William's man' and support his claim to the English throne when the time came. Harold then found he had been tricked into swearing over holy relics, so giving the vow religious significance. Just before he died in January 1066 the childless King Edward named Harold as his heir and the WITAN, the council advising the King, offered him the Crown, which Harold accepted. Reminded of his oath, Harold replied that an oath made under duress was invalid. William then resolved to invade England. But

Harold's kingdom was larger and more powerful than Normandy, and he did not have enough troops for the campaign. He therefore wrote to Pope Alexander II claiming that Harold had usurped the throne promised to him by the sainted Edward and had broken a vow made before God on holy relics. He added that should he win his promised kingdom he would build a magnificent cathedral, as indeed he did.

Alexander endorsed his cause and sent him a ring containing a hair of St Peter and a holy banner depicting the saint. This changed the approaching invasion into a crusade with German, French, Flemish and Italian adventurers joining the Norman forces. By the middle of August, William had five thousand knights under his command. Adverse winds kept the ships at anchor until the night of 27 September when William led the fleet across the Channel to arrive off Pevensey beach by morning. After landing William erected prefabricated wooden forts brought over from France in sections and waited for Harold to march on him.

On Saturday 14 October 1066 William received Holy Communion, then led his army to the Field of Senlac where Harold had positioned his army on a ridge where Battle Abbey stands today. The conflict lasted all day and by nightfall King Harold and his two brothers had been killed and William, after giving thanks to God, held a victory feast on the battlefield.

Next, William took the Cinque Ports, then Canterbury, followed by the surrender of Winchester. He did not have enough men to take London, so he chose to intimidate its citizens rather than fight them. Crossing the Thames at Wallingford he approached the city, laying waste to the countryside. It was the smoke of Southwark which probably forced Londoners to capitulate.

On Christmas Day 1066 William was crowned in WESTMINSTER ABBEY. Because William was wary of London's 'fierce populace' he commanded Gundulf, Bishop of Rochester, to build a tower with Caen stone on the south-east corner of the city's Roman wall, which later evolved into the TOWER OF LONDON.

In 1067, having put his half-brother Odo temporarily in charge of England, William returned to Normandy with a quantity of treasure most of which he distributed to Norman churches. Returning to London, he found that under Odo's harsh rule there was rebellion in the kingdom and most

The dynamic statue of William the Conqueror rallying his men in battle stands in the centre of Falaise. *(Photograph by Paul Abrahams)*

dangerous of all were plots for the mass murder of Normans based on the St Brice's Day massacre of the Danes under ETHELRED II.

William realised he must rely on his barons to hold the country for him. Each baron would be responsible for his particular area, which he held technically as a tenant of the king in return for the military service of his knights. In turn these knights were tenants of the baron. The serf at the bottom of the new social order was granted his few acres in return for work done on his master's land. Thus every man was in the service of someone else, with the King at the apex of the pyramid. This system became known as feudalism from the word 'fee', meaning an estate.

Pockets of revolt were crushed and the last Saxon resistance ended in 1071 when HEREWARD THE

WAKE vanished after his fenland base was captured. When William felt secure in his kingdom he retained English law, under which Saxons and Normans were treated as equals. During his reign William's strong Norman government replaced the weak Saxon rule, relations with the Continent were established and Norman architecture was introduced. William's greatest achievement, though he might not have realised it, was to sow the seeds of the English nation.

The *Anglo-Saxon Chronicle* described him as 'very powerful and dignified, a true monarch and stronger than any of his ancestors, gentle to those good men who love God and beyond all measure stern to those who opposed his own will. He loved the tall deer as if he were their father.' The last sentence illustrates his passion for hunting and it was his creation of the New Forest in which thousands of acres were enclosed and villages demolished to make a vast royal hunting ground, coupled with the ruthless FOREST LAWS, that earned him the enmity of his peasant subjects. Indeed, the deaths of two of William's sons and two of his grandsons in the New Forest were regarded by many as divine retribution.

William's last act of importance was the compilation of the DOMESDAY BOOK, for which the

A stained glass representation of William the Conqueror's coat of arms in the Great Hall of Winchester Castle.

whole of England was surveyed. For seven months his commissioners travelled the realm so that, according to the *Anglo-Saxon Chronicle*, 'not a hide nor a yard of land, nor an ox, nor a cow, nor a swine was not set of his list'.

At 60 William showed his age, especially on account of his corpulence, and in the summer of 1087 he travelled to Rouen for treatment. A dispute had arisen between William and Philip of France over the right to the French Vexin, some French soldiers garrisoned at Mantes having plundered some of William's territory. Matters were not helped when it was reported that Philip had mocked William's appearance, saying that he was like a woman about to give birth. William swore 'by the Splendour of God', his favourite oath, that Philip would regret his joke and ordered his army to march on Mantes. He razed the town on 15 August and as he rode through the smoking ruins his horse trod on smouldering ash and reared, so that the pommel of the saddle struck William's heavy stomach causing an internal injury.

He was carried to Rouen and cared for in the priory of St Gervais. Aware that he was close to death he decreed that his eldest son Robert should succeed him in Normandy 'though he will rule it ill', and that his third son William Rufus (the future WILLIAM II), who was at his bedside, should have the Crown of England. To his remaining son Henry he bequeathed £5,000 in silver, remarking prophetically that in time he would get both his brothers' inheritance. He then gave instructions for all his prisoners to be released and his personal fortune to be divided between the poor and the Church.

William died on the morning of 9 September 1087. The moment he drew his last breath his nobles rushed from his bedside for, not knowing what dynastic struggle might occur, they wanted to get to their estates to protect their property. The royal servants seized all they could, to the extent of stripping their dead master of his linen. A faithful knight named Helwin took charge and had the King's body conveyed to Caen for burial in the cathedral he had built there. Even then there was little dignity for the king once feared as 'The Conqueror'. When the attendants tried to force the corpse into a stone sarcophagus that was too small it burst and filled the church with such a stench that the congregation rushed into the open air. *Sic transit gloria mundi*.

The Abbaye aux Dames in Caen, built by William in honour of his wife, who was subsequently interred there.

See also HAROLD II and HASTINGS, BATTLE OF

WILLIAM II Although he was only the third son of WILLIAM THE CONQUEROR, William Rufus, so named from his ruddy complexion and reddish hair, gained the English Crown on his father's death in 1087. His reign was one of the least popular in British history, and after his murder in the New Forest, a contemporary chronicler wrote: 'Though I hesitate to say it, all things that are loathsome to well nigh all his people and abominable to God and earnest men were customary in this land and this time.'

Born at some point between 1056 and 1060 in Normandy to William I and Queen Matilda, William Rufus was first mentioned in history eleven years after the Conquest. When his elder brother Robert intrigued against their father, he and his brother Richard remained loyal. In 1079 William was wounded during a siege of a castle loyal to Robert in Normandy and this shedding of blood on his behalf endeared the youth to his father. Two years later Richard, the most promising of the three brothers, was gored to death by a stag when hunting in the New Forest. Thus in 1087 the dying King William brooded on the disloyalty of his first-born son Robert and, with Richard dead, he decided to make the dutiful William his successor in England.

In appearance the new monarch had a broad forehead and eyes of 'varying colour flecked with white'. He was of middle height and, like his father, of stout build and immense strength. And, also like his father, his greatest love was for hunting. He spent so much time at the chase that he earned the nickname of 'the Wood-Keeper' as well as 'the Red King' from his colouring.

He had been reared as a typical Norman lord to hunt and fight and, like the knights of his time, he reconciled brutality with the precepts of chivalry. It was said his ambition was to become the most famous knight in Christendom yet he often treated the clergy with contempt and his subjects appeared

The tomb of William II – the Red King – in Winchester Cathedral, where he was interred without ceremony.

to have failed to inspire affection in him. Nor did he have any deep interest in women. He was the only adult English king never to marry, nor did he father illegitimate children.

One of the best opinions of William as a sovereign was recorded by William of Malmesbury who wrote: 'His greatness of soul was obscured by excessive severity and the world doubted for long to which side he would incline, but at last the desire after good grew cold – for he feared God but little and man not at all.'

Three months after his coronation, William learned that his father's half-brother ODO, the Bishop of Bayeux, was plotting to replace him with his more tractable brother Robert who had inherited the Duchy of Normandy. 'When the King understood these things and what treason they did towards him . . . he was greatly disturbed in his mood,' the *Anglo-Saxon Chronicle* recorded. 'Then he set after the Englishmen and set forth to them his need and prayed their help and promised the best laws everywhere in this land and that he would forbid unjust taxation and give them back their woods and hunting.' In London enthusiastic crowds flocked to the royal banner and marched to attack rebel strongholds in Kent. The campaign was successful, Odo was banished but the hated FOREST LAWS remained unrepealed and popular disillusion was fuelled by increased taxation. 'Who can fulfil all his promises?' William demanded – words that have an echo today.

The Great Seal of William II.

William became inspired by the example of fellow Normans who had seized the kingdom of Sicily for themselves. He wanted to be as renowned as his father 'The Conqueror', and if this was to be achieved he decided he must reunite Normandy with England. His first step was to bribe his brother's nobles, after which he took an army across the Channel to Europe, the threat of which gave him part of the duchy. An uneasy peace was agreed between the two brothers, who decided to unite in attacking their younger brother Count Henry.

On his father's death Henry's inheritance had been £5,000 in silver, £3,000 of which he gave to Robert, whose extravagance caused a perpetual shortage of money. In return he was given the rule of an area known as the Cotentin which covered nearly a third of Normandy. Robert now agreed to split this territory with William if it could be repossessed by force. To this end the brothers besieged Mont St Michel, a fortress on the coast remarkably similar to St Michael's Mount in Cornwall, where Henry had taken refuge.

At one stage of the siege Henry's water supply became dangerously low. Robert, the most good-natured of the Conqueror's sons, not only permitted Henry's soldiers to obtain more water but also sent him wine from his own table. William was furious at this chivalrous gesture but Robert argued, 'Shall we let our own brother die of thirst? Where shall we get another when he is gone?'

Unable to hold out indefinitely, Henry finally left Mont St Michel having been accorded the 'honours of war', and William returned to England.

In 1092 William carried out what has been described as the one good act of his reign. He went north to the ruins of Carlisle, which had been razed by his father, to restore the city. From the south he sent many 'churlish' folk to occupy it and recolonise the surrounding district which had turned into a wilderness.

Before long William and Robert were at war again. Bribes and payment of mercenaries had emptied the king's coffers so he introduced a novel method of replenishing his funds. An army of twenty thousand Englishmen was ordered to assemble at Hastings to embark for Normandy. Each shire had been obliged to send a required number of men and supply each with 10s to cover his expenses. When the force was assembled, William's favourite minister, Ranulf Flambard, collected this money and then sent the men home. The £10,000 thus raised was dispatched to the king who used it to bribe the King of France to withhold his support from Robert and pay his barons to continue the war. Despite this the war remained inconclusive and in 1096 Robert, eager to fulfil his ambition to 'take the Cross' and desperate for money to finance his part in the First Crusade, offered to pledge Normandy to William for 10,000 marks for the length of time he would be in the Holy Land. The need to raise this comparatively small sum gave William an excuse to levy more taxes, and when some members of the clergy protested that common folk were being driven to desperation they were told they could lessen the burden by selling Church treasures and contributing the proceeds to the King's fund. They dared not refuse this royal suggestion and even jewellery that adorned holy statues was no longer sacrosanct. William paid his brother and took temporary possession of Normandy but was never forgiven by the Church.

The news that Robert was returning from the holy wars to reclaim his dukedom reached William in the summer of 1100. As he had no intention of honouring the agreement, he ordered the construction of a fleet to carry an army to hold Normandy.

At the end of July William led a cavalcade of over a hundred members of his court from Winchester to Castle Malwood, a royal hunting lodge in the New Forest. With the king was his brother Henry – old enmities forgotten now that Robert was the enemy – his close friend Robert fitzHarmon, and Sir Walter Tirel of Poix who, according to the contemporary historian Geoffrey Gaimar, was a stranger at court. On 2 August the day's hunting was delayed because William had been taken ill during the night, probably due to a severe stomach upset. In the late afternoon he recovered enough to start out on the chase though Robert fitzHarmon tried to dissuade him. At that time of year it was still light enough for a couple of hours' hunting.

When the party was about to ride off a monk arrived with a message from Serlo, the Abbot of St Peter's Abbey at Gloucester. The abbot wrote that one of his monks had experienced a terrifying dream that was taken as a warning the King was in danger. William's reaction was to spur off, shouting,

The Rufus Stone – now encased in metal – marks the spot in the New Forest where William II met his mysterious death.

Coat of arms of William III.

'Does Serlo think I believe in the dreams of every monk?' The question remains as to whether it was a genuine dream that prompted the warning or whether Abbot Serlo was aware of a conspiracy and, wary of making dangerous accusations, invented it as a pretext for putting William on his guard.

Heedless of the warning, the King led his followers through the forest to take up positions to shoot deer as beaters drove them through the trees. When the party split up the King was alone in a glade with Sir Walter Tirel.

What happened next remains one of England's earliest royal mysteries. All that is known is that after a little while the King's body was found in the glade with an arrow protruding from it. Of Tirel there was no sign. He had fled from the spot to cross the Channel and claim the protection of the King of France. He declared that William had been struck by an arrow fired by an unseen archer and, knowing that he would be the obvious suspect, he had made his escape.

William's body was left abandoned by the hunting party, which made an undignified stampede away from the spot. A charcoal burner named Purkiss found the king's corpse and conveyed it in a cart to Winchester where it was interred in the cathedral without ceremony. No bell tolled, no prayers were said, and later when the roof of the cathedral collapsed the accident was blamed on the evil which clung to the king's remains.

WILLIAM III AND MARY II Mary, the eldest surviving child of James, Duke of York (later JAMES II) and his first wife Lady Anne Hyde, was born in London on 30 April 1662. She was a disappointment to her father, who, for dynastic reasons, had hoped for a male heir. With her sister ANNE she was entrusted to Lady Frances Villiers to be brought up a Protestant. In 1671 their mother died and in 1672 when, their father outraged Protestant England by becoming a Roman Catholic, public opinion forced CHARLES II to withdraw his

Mary, the daughter of the exiled James II, came to the throne with her husband William of Orange in the Glorious Revolution.

nieces from his brother's influence. The result of these changes in her young life was that Mary was deprived of normal family affection and in her loneliness she developed deep relationships with a few friends of the same sex. Her favourite of these was Frances Apsley, her playmate and companion.

As popular feeling against Roman Catholicism grew, Danby the Lord Treasurer advocated an alliance with William of Orange whom he regarded as the champion of European Protestants. Thus, in October 1677, William visited England and the match with Mary was agreed and despite her unhappy pleading the wedding took place on 4 November 1677.

A fortnight later Mary went to The Hague where for the next decade she lived unhappily. Despite the fact that she fell in love with her husband, marriage did not bring her the companionship she wanted so much. When, at the beginning of 1678, William left her to continue warring against the French, she wrote to Frances Apsley: 'What can be more cruel in the world than parting with what one loves, and not only common parting, but parting so as one may be never to meet again, to be perpetually in fear, for God knows when I may see him, or whether he is not now, at this instant in battle.'

William of Orange, who became William III of England after his father-in-law James II abdicated.

Throughout her relatively short life, Mary was to suffer constantly from these partings, even though William remained aloof, perhaps through jealousy that his wife was heir to a more powerful throne, perhaps because he was more at ease in male company, particularly that of his friend Hans William Bentinck. Preference for his favourite led to accusations of homosexuality but gossip did not prevent Prince William having a heterosexual relationship outside matrimony. Early in 1680 Mary was heartbroken to discover that one of her ladies-in-waiting, Elizabeth Villiers, was William's mistress.

William Henry Nassau, Prince of Orange, was born on 4 November 1650 at The Hague a week after his father had died. His mother was Mary Stuart, the eldest daughter of CHARLES I. In 1672 the Dutch elected William as Stadholder of the United Provinces and Captain-General following an unprovoked attack by the French, and for the next six years he was to devote all his energy to protecting the small Protestant states against the might of Catholic France. Despite William's personal valour, France retained the upper hand and William saw the political advantage of marriage with the heiress to the English throne.

Meanwhile, Princess Mary lived mainly outside The Hague at her home known as 'The House in the Wood' where she had the dining-room converted into a private chapel because 'her husband never dined with her'. To the delight of her subjects she learned to speak Dutch and wisely kept clear of politics, but Elizabeth Villiers continued to be a source of bitterness between Mary and William. Mary continued to love him and in the hope of winning his affection she agreed that he should not have to play the role of consort if she succeeded to the English throne, but even so the next couple of years were trying for Mary, torn between loyalty to her Roman Catholic father and love for her Calvinist husband. This came to a head when William grew more and more afraid that, with James II having appointed many Roman Catholic ministers, England would become an ally of France. However, the trial of the Seven Bishops so outraged Mary's Protestant ideals that she gave William her full support when he was invited to intervene in England by a letter signed by leading members of both the Tory and Whig parties.

On 1 November, the so-called 'Protestant wind' carried William's ships down the Channel, at the same time keeping King James's fleet locked in the Thames estuary. Four days later William and his army of fourteen thousand landed at Brixham. As a foreigner arriving with a foreign army William knew he had a delicate path to follow. Within a fortnight of his arrival, West Country gentry were joining his standard and in the Midlands and Yorkshire troops were raised on his behalf. The Duke of Grafton and John Churchill defected to the prince and were followed by James's other son-in-law, George of Denmark, the husband of Princess Anne, and then by Anne herself.

William's forces, swollen by desertions from the king's side, moved inexorably towards London and on 17 December James was informed that Dutch soldiers had reached Chelsea. The next day he was taken down the Thames to Rochester and 'allowed' to escape to France. William entered London and took up residence in ST JAMES'S PALACE.

The King's flight was a great relief to William as by quitting his kingdom voluntarily James had abdicated. This was the view taken by Parliament who offered the Crown jointly to William and Mary, but invested the power of administration in William.

When Mary arrived in England on 12 February 1688 William asked her for courage, and in order to please her husband she appeared indifferent to her father's downfall. William's court was very dull after those of his predecessors. His cold manner did not endear him to his new courtiers and the Dutch favourites, especially Bentinck, were deeply resented. He found it difficult to rule with a

Parliament where the Whigs and the Tories were always in conflict, and in addition many Roman Catholics still supported the exiled James. These Jacobites, as they were called, were even to be found among William's ministers. Knowing that France, William's arch-enemy, planned to restore King James to his throne, many influential men, including Marlborough, were anxious to protect their interests no matter which king prevailed.

On 11 April 1689 William and Mary were crowned at WESTMINSTER ABBEY. King James, supported by France, had landed unopposed in Ireland and summoned a parliament in Dublin which declared in his favour. William crossed to Ireland in June 1690 and Queen Mary found herself governing England with the advice of the Council, a role she was destined to play often, with the king so frequently abroad campaigning against the French.

In Ulster on 30 June William with a multinational force reached the River Boyne, on the south side of which James was encamped. The next day he put himself at the head of his cavalry and, sword in hand, led them to the victory which Ulster Protestants celebrate to this day.

After his successful campaign in Ireland, William briefly visited London and found the London fog affected his asthma so the royal couple lived at first at HAMPTON COURT and then at KENSINGTON HOUSE, later enlarged by Sir Christopher Wren.

William's relations with his English subjects reached their lowest ebb after the death of Queen Mary of smallpox on 28 November 1694. She accepted the news of her fatal illness with great dignity and, burning papers and some of her diaries, she set her affairs in order. She also wrote a letter to be given to William after her death imploring him to give up Elizabeth Villiers.

The prospect of Mary's death sent William into a frenzy of despair and when she died on 28 December 1694 he became so ill that there were fears for his life and two months passed before he recovered. When he read Mary's last letter he respected her posthumous plea by marrying Elizabeth Villiers off to one of his military commanders. For the remainder of his life he carried Mary's wedding ring and a lock of her hair in a black ribbon above his left elbow.

Queen Mary was interred in Westminster Abbey. Her lasting memorial was the Royal Hospital for Seamen, designed by Sir Christopher Wren, which she and the king built at Greenwich and which

A coin from the reign of William III.

became the Royal Naval College in 1873. In her memory William had the building enlarged from a plan she had improved. Mary had achieved a genuine popularity with the people and with the Stuart Queen dead the King was more deeply resented as a foreigner; Jacobites plotted against him and Parliament opposed his plans. Abroad he suffered a series of military failures until 1697 when the Treaty of Ryswick brought peace with France.

After his wife's death William did not seek feminine consolation. Since boyhood his greatest friend had been Hans William Bentinck, but in 1691 he had found a new favourite in a Dutch youth named Arnold Jost van Keppel, a royal page.

When the deposed King James died at St Germain in September 1701, Louis XIV recognised his son JAMES FRANCIS EDWARD as James III of England. This brought English opinion into line with William's anti-French feeling. Encouraged by this support he declared war yet again on his old enemy. But the king did not go into battle again. On 20 February 1702 he was thrown from his horse near Hampton Court, breaking his collar bone. He was carried to Kensington Palace where he stubbornly continued working until his condition worsened. On 18 March 1702 he died from pleurisy and was interred with Mary in Westminster Abbey.

WILLIAM IV The third son of GEORGE III and Queen Charlotte, William was born on 21 August 1765 at BUCKINGHAM PALACE. While the King's eldest son George was brought up as heir to the Crown, it was planned that the second son Frederick would have an army career, and that William should go into the navy. Thus at the age of 14 the prince joined the *Prince George* of ninety-eight guns. He was anxious to be regarded as one of the crew, saying to his shipmates, 'I am nothing more than a sailor like yourselves.' He also insisted on being known only as William Guelph, which made him popular with the ship's company.

It was this side of his character that later revived the monarchy after the intense unpopularity of GEORGE IV for, despite his highly eccentric nature, when he became bluff King William, the Sailor King, he had something that few previous sovereigns had possessed – the common touch. In 1780 he was present at Admiral Rodney's relief of Gibraltar, after which he was promoted to midshipman. On his return to England William presented

his father with an enemy flag and then, in the tradition of sailors home from the wars, celebrated in the company of his two brothers with such enthusiasm that he was taken to the watch-house for brawling in the Vauxhall pleasure gardens. He was sent back to his ship, which sailed for New York – then surrounded by rebel colonists – as it was considered that his royal presence would encourage pro-British elements.

Returning to London he fell deeply in love with a certain Miss Fortesque and had it not been for the ROYAL MARRIAGES ACT they would have married. The youthful romance ended when he went off to sea for a second time, followed by the customary 'grand tour' in France and Italy.

In 1785 he was back at sea again as a lieutenant on HMS *Pegasus* in the West Indies. Here he became a close friend of Horatio Nelson, giving away the bride when the then obscure captain married in Nevis. The friendship was to last until Nelson was shot close to the *Victory*'s foremast at the Battle of Trafalgar. Afterwards William had a piece of the mast removed and kept it in his dining-room as a memento mori.

In 1789 William was created Duke of Clarence, a title which had not been used since Plantagenet

William IV, the unexpected king, who according to Queen Victoria, 'meant well'.

times when George, Duke of Clarence and brother of EDWARD IV, was reputedly drowned in a butt of Malmsey. When George III was struck by his illness, which was taken for insanity, William aligned himself with his brother George, Prince of Wales in pressing for an immediate regency. This estranged him from his parents and when the King's sanity returned he took his revenge by ending William's naval career. He was appointed ranger of Bushey Park and remained without work or purpose for the next forty years.

Soon after this he fell in love with DOROTHEA JORDAN, who became one of the most remarkable of Britain's royal mistresses. Born in Waterford in 1762, she started her acting career in Dublin and when William became enamoured with her she was a highly successful comedy actress at the Drury Lane Theatre. In the autumn of 1791 she moved into the Ranger's Lodge, and became a loyal companion to the prince for the next twenty-one years. They had ten children whom he loved dearly and on whom he bestowed the name of Fitz-Clarence. One of Dorothea's advantages was that when she was not bearing FitzClarences she would return to the stage, the money she earned being a very welcome contribution to the housekeeping, as William was forever short of money. In October 1797 he wrote to his banker: 'Mrs Jordan is getting both fame and money; to her I owe very much, and lately she has insisted on my accepting four and twenty hundred pounds which I am to repay as I think proper.'

The liaison between William and Dorothea ended in 1811 when she was on tour. The reason for the break had a great deal to do with finance. In that year George III went permanently insane and the impecunious prince was informed that if he made a suitable marriage Parliament would increase his income. If it had not been for these pressures there was little doubt that William would have been happy to continue living with Dorothea in their lively home at Bushey.

Desperate efforts were made to find a bride for William, but no suitable applicants were to be found in England, Germany or even Russia. No lady of royal blood wanted to marry a notoriously needy prince who already had ten illegitimate children and a reputation for eccentricity. Indeed, this quest for a bride became a national joke.

In 1818, to the sorrow of the nation, Princess Charlotte, the daughter of the Prince Regent, died in childbirth. As she had been the prince's only child and as his brother Frederick, Duke of York was without legitimate issue, the need for William to make a suitable marriage and produce an heir became more urgent. It was finally arranged for him to wed Princess Adelaide, the eldest daughter of George I, Duke of Saxe-Meiningen. On 13 July the 53-year-old William married the 25-year-old princess at KEW PALACE. The marriage was surprisingly happy. The couple spent their first year in Hanover and then for the next decade lived in placid obscurity in the Ranger's Lodge at Bushey. The princess gave birth to two baby daughters but both died in infancy.

The death of the Duke of York in 1827 made William the heir presumptive and he was given the sinecure post of Lord High Admiral; by the time George IV died in 1830 William was living a life of retirement and his subjects hardly knew him when he became William IV. William wished to forgo a coronation ceremony, arguing that it was a 'useless and ill-timed expense'. He was finally persuaded to go through with it though he stipulated that the cost of the whole event was to be kept under £30,000, a sum less than his brother had spent on his coronation robes and regalia alone. William was also the innovator of the 'royal walkabout', often strolling down a public street unattended. Once in St James's Street a cheering crowd surrounded him and a 'woman of the town' kissed him, to the delight of everybody. His only comment was, 'When I have walked about a few times they will get used to it.'

After the coronation the Whig party, led by Lord Grey, came into power on the strength of the Reform Bill, known as the Great Charter of 1832, which was intended to do away with 'rotten boroughs'. Unlike the previous king, William was sympathetic to the Bill until Lord Grey informed him that unless new peers were created the Opposition would be able to block it in the House of Lords, and he declared that he would resign unless he was allowed to create them. The King could not agree to this and accepted Lord Grey's resignation with tears in his eyes. He gave the Tories the opportunity to form a government, but this move was so unpopular that when he drove from Windsor to London cavalry protection was needed. When the Tories were unable to form an alternative government, William was forced to accept Lord Grey's proposals and he signed the Bill on 7 June 1832.

After Grey had retired, the King's political activity lessened, and when he arbitrarily dismissed the Prime Minister, Viscount Melbourne, in 1834 it was the last time this royal prerogative was exercised. Peel's Tory government was short-lived.

Meanwhile, the King's home life was a model of domestic stability, and he frequently remarked, 'The Queen and I are quiet folk, she does nothing but her knitting after dinner.' But he was still capable of his impetuous outbursts. On one occasion when walking round the Royal Academy the president pointed out a portrait of Admiral Napier, who at that time was in political trouble over his intervention in a Spanish civil war. 'Captain Napier may be damned, sir,' the King shouted, 'and may you be damned, sir, and if the Queen was not here, sir, I would kick you downstairs.'

In May 1837 William became dangerously ill and for ten days Queen Adelaide was in such constant attendance at his bedside that she did not have time to change her clothes. His last words to her were, 'Bear! Oh come – bear up, bear up!' He died on 20 June and was interred in ST GEORGE'S CHAPEL.

'Poor man, he was always very kind to me and he *meant* well I know,' wrote QUEEN VICTORIA before her coronation. 'He was odd, very odd and singular, but his intentions were often ill-interpreted.'

WINDSOR CASTLE The castle has been a royal residence since the time of the Norman Conquest. Today, Her Majesty Queen Elizabeth leaves London to spend private weekends there, and traditionally is in official residence during Easter and Ascot Week. Thus for a thousand years, while other palaces have been built, had their span of royal patronage and been abandoned or given over to other roles, Windsor Castle has remained an enduring symbol of Britain's royal heritage. Four years after he had taken the throne of England, WILLIAM I founded the castle as one of the ring of fortresses he built to protect – and hold – London. The site he chose was conveniently close to the Thames, 25 miles west of the city, and, though the Conqueror was more concerned with fortresses than palaces, the castle took on the role of a royal palace. After the King's death in 1087 his son WILLIAM II is chronicled as having entertained the nobility of England and Normandy at Windsor during Eastertide in the year 1097. In 1110 his younger brother and successor HENRY I held his first court in the castle, and eleven years later the first royal wedding was celebrated there when he married his second wife, Adeliza of Louvain. Nine centuries later, the most

Built by William the Conqueror, Windsor Castle has remained a royal residence for over nine centuries.

recent royal wedding in the castle was when Prince Edward and Sophie Rhys-Jones were married at Windsor's St George's Chapel in 1999.

In the beginning the castle was a rugged affair, centred in the usual style on a high earthen mound and defended by walls of timber which allowed the new masters of the kingdom to build their strongholds in as short a time as possible.

When Plantagenet HENRY II came to the throne in 1154, he built the Round Tower on the original mound and began constructing an encircling wall of stone. Inside he added the Domus Regis in the Upper Ward and the Great Hall in the lower. The wall was completed by HENRY III – the two intervening kings being more concerned with plotting or crusading – but it was under the direction of EDWARD III, assisted by William of Wykeham, that the castle was improved to a degree that, according to one chronicler, 'there was not another more splendid within the bounds of Europe'. In HOLINSHED we read that, because Edward had been born in the castle and had great affection for it, he did not count the cost of adding beautiful new buildings. It was in the magnificent new surroundings of his favourite residence that he founded the ORDER OF THE GARTER in 1348.

Although minor improvements were continued during the next four reigns, it was EDWARD IV who gave the castle its glorious St George's Chapel, dedicated to the patron saint of the Order of the Garter and in which are the tombs of ten British sovereigns.

Although ELIZABETH I complained that she found the castle cold, it did not discourage her from reconstructing the North Terrace and having a long gallery built where she could take walks regardless of the weather. This gallery was later transformed into the castle's library. It is believed that the Queen prevailed upon Shakespeare to write *The Merry Wives of Windsor* for her, which had its first performance at the castle.

Following the indecisive Battle of Edgehill the Parliamentarians used Windsor Castle as the headquarters for OLIVER CROMWELL's army and as a prison, CHARLES I being held there prior to his execution. During Cromwell's rule the castle suffered from neglect – HAMPTON COURT and the PALACE OF WHITEHALL being more to the Lord Protector's taste as residences – and John Evelyn, writing later in his diary, described it as 'exceedingly ragged and ruinous'. Returned to England as king in 1660, CHARLES II set about the repair and refurbishment of Windsor Castle. The royal apartments were restored and enhanced, Grinling Gibbons providing the wood carvings, while Antonio Verrio was commissioned to paint a number of ceilings. Outdoors the construction began of an avenue that was to run through the Great Park from the castle to Snow Hill 3 miles away.

QUEEN ANNE preferred to stay in a small house in the castle's grounds, perhaps delighting in its unostentatious atmosphere in the same way that QUEEN VICTORIA and PRINCE ALBERT did at BALMORAL. But she did enjoy the Great Park, through which a road was laid – known as Queen Anne's Ride – and which runs between what later were called Queen Anne's Gate and the Prince Consort's Gate. The Queen's indifference to the castle was shared by GEORGE I and GEORGE II, but royal interest was renewed when GEORGE III, with James Wyatt, the Surveyor-General, began alterations reflecting the Gothic revival. These ended with the onset of the King's illness, the seriousness of which was realised when he stopped his carriage in the Great Park and addressed an oak tree under the delusion it was the King of Prussia.

Windsor Castle as it is seen today owes much to GEORGE IV's passion for building and design. Jeffry (*sic*) Wyatville, the nephew of George III's James Wyatt, was appointed to oversee the work, which included the building of the Grand Corridor, linking the private apartments, while the exterior work included the addition of battlemented towers which became a great feature of the castle. Charles II's Long Walk was completed to Snow Hill, on the summit of which was set a huge equestrian statue of George III. Known locally as 'The Copper Horse' – the horse presumably being more impressive than the king – the bronze monument was said to have been inspired by an equestrian statue of Peter the Great in St Petersburg. As the relationship between George IV and his father could never have been described as cordial, it was perhaps a sense of regret that promoted the king to have the statue erected. He ordered that the statue's right hand should be outstretched in the direction of the castle that had meant so much to his father and where he spent his latter days sadly playing a harp, and where he died on 29 January 1820.

In 1992 Windsor Castle suffered severe damage when a fire started in ELIZABETH II's private chapel, but by the end of 1997 a remarkable feat of restoration had been accomplished in time for a ball to be held celebrating the golden wedding of the Queen and the DUKE OF EDINBURGH.

WINDSOR, HOUSE OF The death of QUEEN VICTORIA in 1901 signalled the official end of the HOUSE OF HANOVER, which was replaced by the House of Saxe-Coburg-Gotha. This was because Saxe-Coburg-Gotha was the family name of EDWARD VII's father PRINCE ALBERT. Sixteen years later there was another name change when GEORGE V decided that the House of Windsor was more appropriate in view of popular feeling during the First World War. Similarly, the name Battenberg, which had royal connections in Europe, became Mountbatten. Although present members of the royal family belong to the House of Windsor, the children of QUEEN ELIZABETH and PRINCE PHILIP MOUNTBATTEN are officially named Mountbatten-Windsor.

WITAN Also known as Witenagemot, the Witan was a council convened by an Anglo-Saxon king when he decided he needed advice on certain matters concerning the kingdom, or required endorsement for his laws or the granting of lands. For example, KING ALFRED sought the Witan's counsel on the terms and bequests of his will. Although a king would listen to 'the Witan of my people', he was the one who selected its participants from members of the royal family, the nobility, bishops, and officials of the royal household. Thegns might also be included. These were substantial men who were required to provide military service to the king on request and owned at least 5 hides of land, a hide being as much land as could be tilled with a single plough in a year.

In the later Anglo-Saxon period the Witan became involved in court ceremonial such as attending the king when he received foreign ambassadors. In the eleventh century the royal

House of Windsor

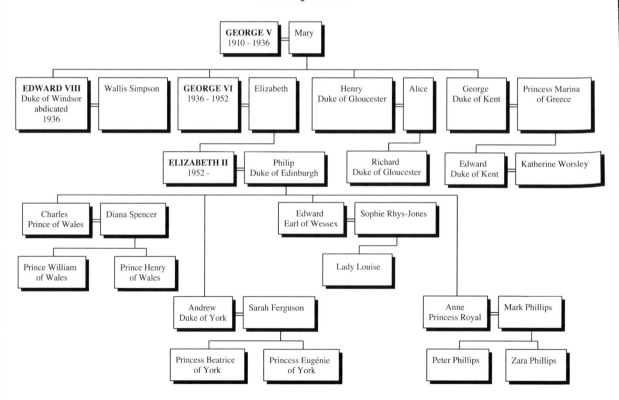

The Anglo-Saxon Witan, a council that met when summoned by the king for advice on the government of the kingdom.

family and the Witan would assemble for a traditional public feast at Christmas, Easter and Whitsuntide, and on other occasions when summoned by the king. It would seem that at the end of the Anglo-Saxon period the Witan had become a very influential body, as it is believed that it coerced EDWARD THE CONFESSOR to name HAROLD GODWINESON as his successor and then declared him king on Edward's death.

It was because he did not listen to the advice of his Witan that ETHELRED II earned the sobriquet of 'The Unready' or more accurately 'Unraed' meaning 'Without Counsel'.

After WILLIAM I ('The Conqueror') took the Crown of England the Witan was replaced by the feudal Great Council.

WITCHCRAFT ACT It was a series of royal scandals in the fifteenth and sixteenth centuries that gave witchcraft a sinister reputation in England. In 1419 HENRY V prosecuted his stepmother, Joan of Navarre, for attempting to bring about his death 'in the most horrible manner that one could devise'

through witchcraft. Forty-two years later Eleanor Cobham, Duchess of Gloucester was accused of conspiring with Roger Bolingbroke, 'a most notorious evoker of demons', to kill young HENRY VI by magical means so that her husband, the Duke of Gloucester and the king's uncle, could replace him on the throne.

In 1476 the Woodville faction at the court of EDWARD IV was involved in a plot to discredit the king's brother, the Duke of Clarence, by suggesting involvement in the black arts. It was arranged that an Oxford clerk, reputed to be a wizard, should be arrested. Under torture he denounced one Thomas Burdet, a member of Clarence's household, for practising witchcraft and 'having composed the death of the King'. Both men were hanged at Tyburn, and soon afterwards Clarence met with a mysterious death in the TOWER OF LONDON.

When Edward's other brother RICHARD III became king in 1483 he astonished a Council meeting by declaring the dowager queen Elizabeth Woodville had used 'sorcery and witchcraft' to trap his late brother into their clandestine marriage. He also accused her of using witchcraft to waste his own body, with the assistance of Edward's former mistress Jane Shore. No action was taken against the Queen, but Jane Shore was forced to walk barefoot through London streets wearing only her shift as a penance.

After HENRY VIII had married ANNE BOLEYN in 1533, enemies of the new queen circulated rumours that she had used witchcraft to ensnare the king and bring about the downfall of CATHERINE OF ARAGON. These slanders were endorsed by the fact that Anne had a sixth finger on her left hand, a minor deformity that she attempted to conceal by having the ends of her sleeves widened so much that most of the hand was hidden, a style that became known as 'Anne Boleyn sleeves'. Her detractors claimed that this extra finger was a mark of the devil. According to Eustace Champuys, the imperial ambassador, the King once declared, after Anne had been delivered of a stillborn male child in 1536, 'I was seduced into this marriage. I was wrought upon by witchcraft. Yea, that is why God will not suffer me to have male children.'

Matters came to a head as regards magic being a threat to the monarchy in 1562 when the Pole brothers were imprisoned in the Tower of London for attempting to bring about the death of ELIZABETH I by means of witchcraft. At the same time the Countess of Lennox was found guilty of treason for having consulted witches on how long the Queen would live – a treasonable act in Tudor times. Thus the climate was right for the introduction of the Witchcraft Act of 1563, which, while not authorising the death penalty for practising witchcraft, did so for using witchcraft 'with intent to kill or destroy'. When a death penalty was delivered for witchcraft crime in England, the method of execution was by hanging – the stake, though accepted in Scotland, was reserved for wives who poisoned their husbands and women found guilty of treason.

A second Witchcraft Act was passed in 1604 during the reign of JAMES I in which a wider range of witchcraft activities were made punishable by death. Following the decline of the 'witchcraft mania' that had swept England and the Continent, the Act was repealed in 1736 and replaced with a relatively mild law stating that for the practice 'of witchcraft, sorcery, enchantment or conjuration' the penalty would be a year in prison with a period in the stocks each quarter.

See also OVERBURY SCANDAL

WOLSEY, CARDINAL THOMAS Few, if any, commoners have risen to such power, riches and royal favour only to lose everything in a matter of months as Cardinal Wolsey. The son of a well-to-do butcher, he was born *c.* 1475 at Ipswich, and after making his mark as a scholar at Magdalen College, Oxford, he became a master at a seminary. In 1502 the chaplaincy of Calais was bestowed upon him and such was his proficiency in this role that he came to the notice of HENRY VII who appointed him as his chaplain in 1507. When HENRY VIII came to the throne in 1509, Wolsey succeeded in his aim of making himself indispensable to the new sovereign. For his part in organising the king's campaign in France in 1513 he was rewarded with the bishoprics of Lincoln and Tournai, shortly after which he became the Archbishop of York. In 1513 he became both a cardinal and the Lord Chancellor of England, and Pope Leo X honoured him with appointment as papal legate. As his state responsibilities increased so did his wealth, and in 1514 he had work begun on HAMPTON COURT, which was to become his private palace.

While thus enjoying the confidence of the king, as his chief adviser on the management of the realm, Wolsey gained more power than any other minister since the days of THOMAS À BECKET, and his continuing aim was to make England an

Cardinal Wolsey being forced to give up the Great Seal following his fall from Henry VIII's favour.

absolute monarchy with himself as the power behind the throne. It was believed that he had his eye on eventually achieving the office of Pope. Meanwhile, the core of his policy was to achieve both military and diplomatic success for his royal master. After Henry's first campaign in France Wolsey endeavoured to heighten the King's prestige in Europe through peace negotiations, famous for their lavish display such as those at the FIELD OF THE CLOTH OF GOLD in 1520.

In domestic matters Wolsey, as Lord Chancellor, was resolute in retaining and reinforcing traditional policies such as the reintroduction of Henry VII's campaign against those nobles who sought to challenge royal justice by having inordinate numbers of supporters. In Church matters his achievement was the establishment of educational foundations, the most notable being Cardinal College at Oxford, which was not completed until after his death and was later known as Christ Church.

Wolsey's rapid fall from royal favour to disaster began with the King's wish to be divorced from QUEEN CATHERINE OF ARAGON. Wolsey was well aware of Henry's obsession with ANNE BOLEYN and he knew that a dangerous time lay ahead. He endeavoured to insure himself against royal disfavour by giving the King his Thames-side palace of Hampton Court, but this gesture did nothing to halt his approaching nemesis. Henry commanded him to petition the Pope for the royal divorce, but aware of the difficulties, Wolsey tried to have the matter put before a commission which included himself and the reluctant Cardinal Campeggio. His plan failed when Queen Catherine presented her case directly to the Vatican.

The delay infuriated Henry who, impatient to make Anne Boleyn his wife, took note of her endless complaints against the cardinal. Understandably the Boleyn faction joined the growing intrigue against Wolsey, as did many influential men who had resented his haughty demeanour, his influence over the King and his vast wealth. The result was that, in October 1529, he lost all his official posts and had to give up the Great Seal when he was prosecuted under the STATUTE OF PRAEMUNIRE, which imposed penalties for seeking papal authority to override the jurisdiction of the king's courts. He pleaded guilty to this dubious charge and retired to Winchester, but impeachment by the House of Lords was followed by the forfeiture of all his property. The final blow came when he was arrested on a charge of treason, and in November 1530 he set out from his York diocese to stand trial in London. Halting at Leicester, he was taken ill and died after saying, 'Had I but served God as diligently as I have served the King, he would not have given me over in my grey hairs.'

WOODSTOCK PALACE The first recorded royal connection with Woodstock goes back to when ETHELRED THE UNREADY – who was born exactly a hundred years before the victory of the Normans at Hastings – held a council there. In the Domesday Book it was described as a royal forest, and soon afterwards HENRY I, who surrounded the parkland with a wall 7 miles in length, followed his interest in exotic animals by having a menagerie there, which included camels and lions and even a porcupine. In 1163 HENRY II held a council at Woodstock, and it was there that he took ROSAMOND CLIFFORD to be his mistress, popular tradition claiming erroneously that she was murdered in Woodstock by QUEEN

Woodstock Palace was a royal residence from the reign of Ethelred the Unready until the Civil War.

ELEANOR. The earliest surviving written English law, the assize of Woodstock, was passed at Woodstock in 1184 to safeguard 'the peace of the king's venison'.

So often did Henry stay at Woodstock, then one of the most impressive of medieval palaces, that the nearby borough of New Woodstock was created in order to accommodate the court which came with him. It was at Woodstock that he knighted his son Geoffrey, and later the palace was the scene of the wedding of William the Lyon of Scotland to Henry's relative Ermengarde, daughter of Richard, Viscount of Beaumont-le-Maine.

When staying at Woodstock in 1238 HENRY III narrowly escaped assassination by a madman who claimed that the king had usurped the throne from him. He was found in Henry's bedchamber armed with a dagger, but luckily for the king he had decided to spend the night with his queen, Eleanor of Provence.

EDWARD, THE BLACK PRINCE, was also known as Edward of Woodstock, as he was born at the palace in 1330, and it continued to be a favourite residence with the monarchy until MARY TUDOR came to the throne. In 1554 the Queen had her sister ELIZABETH I placed under house arrest there for six months, and as a result Elizabeth disliked the scene of captivity, where she declared she had been worse off than if she had been in Newgate Prison.

The end of the palace came when it was besieged during the English Civil War, after which the parliamentary commissioners found it in a decrepit state. Following the Restoration the manor and park of Woodstock was returned to the Crown.

After the Battle of Blenheim QUEEN ANNE bestowed the manor on John, Duke of Marlborough and Blenheim Palace was built on its land. The remains of the old Woodstock Palace were demolished, as it was considered they marred the view.

APPENDIX I

REIGNS OF ENGLISH AND BRITISH SOVEREIGNS

	Birthdate	Reign	Line of succession
SAXON KINGS			
Egbert	?	802–39	King of Wessex, hailed in 829 as Bretwalda – Overlord of England – by other English kings
Ethelwulf	?	839–58	Egbert's son
Ethelbald	*c.* 834	858–60	Ethelwulf's son
Ethelbert	*c.* 836	860–5	Ethelwulf's second son
Ethelred I	*c.* 840	865–71	Ethelwulf's third son
Alfred the Great	849	871–99	Ethelwulf's fourth son
Edward the Elder	*c.* 870	899–924	Alfred's son
Athelstan the Glorious	*c.* 895	924–39	Edward the Elder's first son
Edmund I	*c.* 921	939–46	Edward the Elder's second son
Edred	*c.* 923	946–55	Edward the Elder's third son
Edwy the Fair	*c.* 941	955–9	Edmund's son
Edgar the Peaceable	944	959–75	Edmund's younger son
Edward the Martyr	*c.* 963	975–8	Edgar the Peaceable's son
Ethelred II	968	978–1016	Edgar the Peaceable's son by his second wife Elfryth
Sweyn of Denmark	*c.* 960	1013–14	Known as Forkbeard, he usurped Ethelred in 1013, claiming to be King of England by right of conquest. He died in 1014, after which Ethelred resumed as king
Edmund II Ironside	*c.* 981	1016	Ethelred II's son
DANISH KINGS			
Canute	*c.* 995	1016–35	Son of Sweyn Forkbeard of Denmark; also King of Denmark (1018) and Norway (1030)
Hardicanute	*c.* 1018	1035–42	Canute's son by Emma; also King of Norway
Harold I Harefoot	*c.* 1016	1037–40	Canute's illegitimate son who usurped the English throne in 1037 after which Hardicanute resumed as king
SAXON KINGS			
Edward the Confessor	*c.* 1003	1042–66	Ethelred II's younger son
Harold II	*c.* 987	1066	Edward the Confessor's brother-in-law
HOUSE OF NORMANDY			
William I	1027	1066–87	Duke of Normandy, won English Crown at Battle of Hastings

William II Rufus	*c.* 1056	1087–1100	William I's third son
Henry I	1068	1100–35	William I's youngest son

HOUSE OF BLOIS

Stephen	*c.* 1097	1135–54	William I's grandson through his daughter Adela and Stephen, Count of Blois

HOUSE OF PLANTAGENET

Henry II	1133	1154–89	Henry I's grandson through his daughter Matilda and her second husband, Geoffrey Plantagenet
Richard I	1157	1189–99	Henry II's third son
John	1167	1199–1216	Henry II's youngest son
Henry III	1207	1216–72	John's son
Edward I	1239	1272–1307	Henry III's son
Edward II	1284	1307–27	Edward I's son by Eleanor of Castile
Edward III	1312	1327–77	Edward II's son
Richard II	1367	1377–99	Edward III's grandson and son of the Black Prince

HOUSE OF LANCASTER

Henry IV	1367	1399–1413	Edward III's grandson through John of Gaunt
Henry V	1387	1413–22	Henry IV's son by Mary de Bohun
Henry VI	1421	1422–61	Henry V's son by Catherine of Valois

HOUSE OF YORK

Edward IV	1442	1461–70	Son of Richard, Duke of York and Edward III's great-grandson
Edward V	1470	1483	Edward IV's son, the elder of the 'Princes in the Tower'
Richard III	1452	1483–5	Edward IV's brother

HOUSE OF TUDOR

Henry VII	1457	1485–1509	The grandson of Owen Tudor who married Catherine of Valois, widow of Henry V
Henry VIII	1491	1509–47	Henry VII's son
Edward VI	1537	1547–53	Henry VIII's son by Jane Seymour
Mary I	1516	1553–8	Henry VIII's daughter by Catherine of Aragon
Elizabeth I	1533	1558–1603	Henry VIII's daughter by Anne Boleyn

HOUSE OF STUART

James I	1566	1603–25	Son of Mary, Queen of Scots
Charles I	1600	1625–49	James I's son by Anne of Denmark

THE INTERREGNUM 1649–60

Charles II	1630	1660–85	Charles I's son by Henrietta Maria
James II	1633	1685–8	Charles II's younger brother; deposed in the 'Glorious Revolution' and died in 1701
William III	1650	1689–1702	Son of William II of Orange and Mary Henrietta, the eldest daughter of Charles I; ruled in conjunction with his wife Mary II
Mary II	1662	1689–94	James II's daughter
Anne	1665	1702–14	James II's younger daughter

REIGNS OF ENGLISH AND BRITISH SOVEREIGNS

HOUSE OF HANOVER

George I	1660	1714–27	James I's great-grandson
George II	1683	1727–60	George I's son
George III	1738	1760–1820	George II's grandson through Frederick Louis, Prince of Wales
George IV	1762	1820–30	George III's son
William IV	1765	1830–7	George III's third son
Victoria	1819	1837–1901	George III's granddaughter through Edward, Duke of Kent

HOUSE OF SAXE-COBURG

Edward VII	1841	1901–10	Victoria's son

HOUSE OF WINDSOR

George V	1865	1910–36	Edward VII's son
Edward VIII	1894	1936	George V's son, abdicated, died in 1972
George VI	1895	1936–52	George V's second son
Elizabeth II	1926	1952–	George VI's daughter

Appendix II

ROYAL RESTING PLACES

ENGLISH AND BRITISH KINGS AND QUEENS

EGBERT Died AD 839 and was buried in Winchester Cathedral where his bones remain in a mortuary chest.

ETHELWULF Died in AD 858 and was buried in Winchester Cathedral.

ETHELBALD Died in AD 860 and was buried in Sherborne Abbey.

ETHELBERT Died in AD 865 and was buried in Sherborne Abbey.

ETHELRED I Killed in AD 871 at the Battle of Merton and was buried in Wimborne Abbey.

ALFRED Died in AD 899 and was originally buried in Newminster Abbey then translated to Hyde Abbey, later demolished at the Reformation. It is possible the king's bones were placed in a mortuary chest in Winchester Cathedral. The king's wife Ethelswitha died c. AD 905 at St Mary's Abbey in Winchester, where she had spent her last years as a nun, and was interred there before being translated to Winchester Cathedral. She gained a posthumous reputation for sainthood.

EDWARD THE ELDER Died in AD 924 at Farndon-on-Dee and was interred in Winchester Cathedral. His first wife Egwina died c. AD 901 but her burial place is not known. His second wife Elfleda died in 920 and was interred in Winchester Cathedral.

ATHELSTAN Died in AD 939 at Gloucester and was buried in Malmesbury Abbey.

EDMUND I Murdered in AD 946 at Pucklechurch in Dorset and was buried in Glastonbury Abbey. The King's first wife Elgiva (posthumously St Elgiva) died c. AD 944 and was said to have been interred at Shaftesbury Abbey in Dorset. His second wife Ethelfleda became a nun later in life at Shaftesbury Abbey where she was interred. The date of her death is unknown.

EDRED Died in AD 955 at Frome in Somerset and was buried in Winchester Cathedral where his bones are now in a mortuary chest.

EDWY THE FAIR Died in AD 959 at Gloucester and was buried in Winchester Cathedral.

EDGAR Died in AD 975 at Winchester and was buried in Glastonbury Abbey. His first wife Ethelfleda ('The Fair') died c. AD 962 and was interred in Wilton Abbey in Wiltshire. His second wife, Queen Elfrida, was crowned with the King in 973, making it the first coronation of an English Queen. She died in c. 1002 and was most likely interred in Wherewell Abbey.

EDWARD THE MARTYR Murdered in AD 978 at Corfe Castle and was buried in Wareham Abbey, later translated to Shaftesbury Abbey.

ETHELRED II ('The Redeless') Died in 1016 in London and was interred in old St Paul's Cathedral which was destroyed in the Great Fire of London. The king's first wife, Queen Elgiva, died in 1002 at Winchester but her grave is not known. His second wife Emma of Normandy, who later married King Canute, died in 1052 and a mortuary chest at Winchester Cathedral now contains her bones.

SWEYN Died in 1014 at Gainsborough and was buried in England at a now unidentified site, and later was translated to Roeskild Cathedral in Denmark.

EDMUND II ('Ironside') Died in 1016 either in London or Oxford and was buried in Glastonbury Abbey.

CANUTE Died in 1035 at Shaftesbury and was buried in Winchester Cathedral where his bones are now in a mortuary chest. His wife, Queen Emma, died in 1052 and her bones are also in a Winchester mortuary chest.

HARDICANUTE Died in 1042 at London and was buried in Winchester Cathedral.

HAROLD I ('Harefoot') Died in 1040 at Oxford and his original burial place is uncertain. His remains may have been reinterred at St Clement Danes Church, London.

EDWARD THE CONFESSOR Died 1066 at Westminster and was interred in Westminster Abbey which he had built and was just completed. His wife, Queen Edith, died in 1075 and was also interred in the abbey.

HAROLD II Slain in 1066 at the Battle of Hastings, after which his remains were finally interred at Waltham Abbey where today a stone marks the site of the grave.

WILLIAM I ('The Conqueror' and 'The Bastard') Died of wounds in 1087 following the siege of Mantes and was interred in St Stephen's Abbey at Caen. His wife, Queen Matilda, died in 1083 and was interred at the abbey of the Holy Trinity at Caen.

WILLIAM II ('Rufus') Killed by an arrow when hunting in the New Forest in 1100 and was interred in Winchester Cathedral.

HENRY I ('Beauclerk') Died of food poisoning in 1135 at St Denis le Fremont in Normandy and was buried in Reading Abbey, his tomb being destroyed at the Reformation. His first wife Matilda, daughter of Malcolm III of Scotland, died in 1118 and was interred in Westminster Abbey. His second wife, Queen Adela, who later married William d'Albini,

Earl of Cornwall, died in 1151 at Affligem Abbey, in South Braban, where she was buried.

STEPHEN Died at Dover in 1154 and was interred in Faversham Abbey. His wife Matilda, Countess of Boulogne, died in 1152 and was also interred in the abbey. During the Reformation both tombs were demolished.

HENRY II ('Curtmantle') Died in 1189 at Chinon Castle in France and was interred at Fontevrault Abbey where his tomb with effigy is still to be seen. His wife, Eleanor of Aquitaine, died in 1204 and was interred in a similar tomb at the abbey.

RICHARD I ('The Lionheart') Died of an arrow wound at the siege of Chalus, France, in 1199 and was interred in Fontevrault Abbey where his tomb and effigy is still to be seen. His wife, Queen Berengaria, died at the abbey of L'Espan in Anjou, which she founded, and was interred in the abbey. The date of her death is not known.

JOHN ('Lackland' and 'Softsword') Died in 1216 at Newark and was interred in Worcester Cathedral. The king's first wife Isabella, daughter of William, Earl of Gloucester, whom he divorced in 1199, died 1217 and was interred in Canterbury Cathedral. His second wife, Isabella of Angoulême, whom he married in 1200, died in 1246 at Fontevrault Abbey where she was interred.

HENRY III Died in 1272 at Westminster Palace and was interred in Westminster Abbey. His wife, Eleanor of Provence, died in 1291 and was interred in Amesbury Abbey.

EDWARD I ('Longshanks') Died in 1307 at Burgh by Sands, Cumbria and was interred in Westminster Abbey. His first wife, Eleanor of Castile, died in 1290 and was also interred in the abbey. His second wife, Margaret of France, died *c.* 1317 and was interred in Greyfriars Church, London.

EDWARD II Murdered in 1327 at Berkeley Castle and was interred in Gloucester Cathedral. His wife Isabella ('The She-wolf of France') died in 1358 and was interred in Greyfriars Church in London.

EDWARD III Died in 1377 at Sheen Palace and was interred in Westminster Abbey. His wife,

Phillipa of Hainault, died in 1369 and was also interred in the abbey.

RICHARD II ('Richard of Bordeaux') Most likely put to death at Pontefract Castle in 1400, King Richard was first buried in King's Langley Church but soon after was translated to Westminster Abbey. His wife Anne, daughter of the Holy Roman Emperor Charles IV, died in 1394 and was also interred in the abbey. His second wife, Isabella of France, died in 1409 and was interred in St Laumer's Abbey, Blois.

HENRY IV Died, possibly of leprosy, in 1413 at Westminster and interred in Canterbury Cathedral. His first wife Queen Mary, daughter of Humphrey de Bohun, Earl of Hereford, died in 1394 and was interred in St Mary's Church in Leicester. His second wife, Joan of Navarre, died in 1437 and was interred in Canterbury Cathedral.

HENRY V Died in 1422 at the castle of Bois-de-Vincennes in France and was interred in Westminster Abbey. His wife Catherine of Valois, who later married Owen Tudor, died in 1437 at Bermondsey Abbey and was interred in Westminster Abbey.

HENRY VI Murdered in 1471 and buried in Chertsey before being translated to St George's Chapel, Windsor Castle. His wife, Margaret of Anjou, died in 1482 and was interred in St Maurice's Cathedral in Anjou.

EDWARD IV Died in 1483 at the Palace of Westminster and was interred in St George's Chapel, Windsor Castle. His wife, Elizabeth Woodville, died in 1492 and was also interred in the chapel.

EDWARD V (Eldest of 'The Princes in the Tower') Presumed murdered in 1483 in the Tower of London. In 1674 bones thought to be those of Edward and his brother Richard were found beneath a staircase in the Tower and interred in Westminster Abbey.

RICHARD III Killed at the Battle of Bosworth in 1485, King Richard's mutilated remains were interred in the church of St Mary in Leicester, but during the Reformation the tomb was destroyed. His wife Anne, daughter of Richard Neville, Earl of Warwick, died also in 1485 and was interred in Westminster Abbey.

HENRY VII Died in 1509 at Richmond Palace and was interred in Westminster Abbey. His wife Elizabeth, daughter of Edward IV, died in 1503 and was also interred in the abbey.

HENRY VIII Died at Whitehall Palace in 1547 and was interred in St George's Chapel in Windsor Castle. His queens:

1. Catherine of Aragon, died in 1536 and was interred in Peterborough Cathedral.
2. Anne Boleyn, executed in 1536 and was interred in the chapel of St Peter ad Vincula in the Tower of London.
3. Jane Seymour, died in 1537 and was interred in St George's Chapel in Windsor Castle.
4. Anne of Cleves, died in 1557 and was interred in Westminster Abbey.
5. Catherine Howard, executed in 1542 and was interred in the chapel of St Peter ad Vincula in the Tower of London.
6. Catherine Parr, died in 1548 and was interred in Sudely Castle Chapel in Gloucestershire.

EDWARD VI Died at Greenwich Palace in 1553 and was interred in Westminster Abbey.

JANE (Lady Jane Grey) Executed in 1554 at the Tower of London and was interred in the Tower's chapel of St Peter ad Vincula.

MARY I ('Bloody Mary') Died in 1558 at St James's Palace and was interred in Westminster Abbey. Her husband Philip of Spain died in 1598 and was interred in the Escorial in Madrid.

ELIZABETH I Died in 1603 at Richmond Palace and was interred in Westminster Abbey.

JAMES VI (of Scotland) and **JAMES I** (of England) Died in 1625 at Theobalds Park and was interred in Westminster Abbey. His wife, Anne of Denmark, died in 1619 and was also interred in the abbey.

CHARLES I Executed in 1649 and was interred in St George's Chapel, Windsor Castle. His wife,

Queen Henrietta Maria, died in 1669 in France and was interred in the cathedral of St Denis in Paris.

CHARLES II Died in 1685 at Whitehall Palace and was interred in Westminster Abbey. His wife, Catherine of Braganza, died in 1705 and was interred at the monastery of Belém in Lisbon.

JAMES II Died in exile in 1688 at the Chateau of St Germain-en-Laye and was interred in the church of the English Benedictines, Paris, where his tomb was desecrated during the French Revolution. Later a story circulated that due to intervention by George IV his bones were given burial at St Germain-en-Laye. His first wife, Anne Hyde, died in 1671. His second wife, Mary of Modena, died in 1718 at Germain-en-Laye and was interred in the abbey of the Visitation of St Mary, Chaillot.

WILLIAM III and **MARY II** (joint sovereigns of Great Britain) Queen Mary died in 1694 at Kensington Palace and King William died there in 1702. Both were interred in Westminster Abbey.

ANNE Died in 1714 and was interred at Westminster Abbey. Her husband, Prince George of Denmark, died in 1708 and was also interred at the abbey.

GEORGE I Died in 1712 while travelling near Osnabrück in Hanover and was interred in the Leine Schloss Chapel, his remains being translated to the Schloss Herrenhausen Chapel following the Second World War. His divorced wife, Sophia Dorothea of Brunswick-Lüneberg-Celle, died in 1726 and was interred in Celle Church.

GEORGE II Died in 1760 at Kensington Palace and was interred in Westminster Abbey. His wife, Caroline of Brandenburg-Ansbach, died in 1737 and was also interred in the abbey.

GEORGE III Died in 1820 at Windsor Castle and was interred in St George's Chapel at Windsor Castle. His wife, Charlotte of Mecklenburg-Strelitz, died in 1818 and was also interred in the chapel.

GEORGE IV Died in 1830 at Windsor Castle and was interred in St George's Chapel. His first wife, Maria Anne Fitzherbert (privately married), died in 1837 and was interred at the church of St John the Baptist in Brighton. His second wife, Caroline of Brunswick-Wolfenbüttel, died in 1821 in London and was interred in Brunswick.

WILLIAM IV Died in 1837 at Windsor Castle and was interred there in St George's Chapel. His wife, Adelaide of Saxe-Meiningen, died in 1849 and was also interred in the chapel.

VICTORIA Died in 1901 and was interred in the Royal Mausoleum at Frogmore. Her consort, Prince Albert, who had died in 1861, was first buried in St George's Chapel, Windsor Castle, and then interred in the Mausoleum when it was completed.

EDWARD VII Died in 1910 at Buckingham Palace and was interred in St George's Chapel, Windsor Castle. His wife, Alexandra of Denmark, died in 1925 and was also interred in the chapel.

GEORGE V Died in 1936 at Sandringham House in Norfolk and was interred in St George's Chapel, Windsor Castle. His wife, Mary of Teck, died in 1953 and was also interred in the chapel.

EDWARD VIII Died in 1972 in Paris and was buried at Frogmore, Windsor. His wife, Wallis, died in 1986 and was also buried at Frogmore.

GEORGE VI Died in 1952 at Sandringham House in Norfolk and was buried in the King George VI Memorial Chapel in St George's Chapel, Windsor Castle. His wife, Elizabeth Bowes-Lyon, died in 2002 and was interred in the chapel.

KINGS AND QUEENS OF SCOTLAND

The names of kings whose burial places are unknown are omitted

KENNETH I Died in AD 859 and was interred on Iona.

CONSTANTINE I Killed AD 877 in battle against the Danes and was interred on Iona.

DONALD II Slain in AD 900 and was interred on Iona.

CONSTANTINE II Died in AD 952 at St Andrews in Fife and is thought to have been interred there.

MALCOLM I Killed in AD 954 and was interred on Iona.

KENNETH II Died, possibly murdered, in AD 995 and was interred on Iona.

MALCOLM II Died of wounds in 1034 at Glamis Castle and was buried on Iona.

DUNCAN I Murdered by Macbeth, or slain fighting him in battle in 1040, and was interred on Iona.

MACBETH Killed in 1057 at the Battle of Lumphanan and was interred on Iona.

LULACH Killed in 1058 at Essie in Strathbogie and was interred on Iona.

MALCOLM III ('Canmore') Killed in battle at Alnwick in 1093 and was interred in Dunfermline Abbey. Later his remains were translated to the Escorial in Madrid. Details of his first wife Ingibiorg's death and grave are not known. His second wife Margaret – afterwards St Margaret – died in 1093 and was interred in Dunfermline Abbey. Later her remains were also translated to the Escorial in Madrid, though her head was taken to the Jesuit College at Douai.

DONALD III Died a prisoner at Rescobie in Forfarshire in 1097 and was interred in Dunkeld Abbey. Later his remains were translated to Iona.

DUNCAN II Killed at the Battle of Monthechin in 1094 and was interred in Dunfermline Abbey in Fife. The date of his wife Ethelreda's death is uncertain but she was also interred in Dunfermline Abbey.

EDGAR Died in 1107 either at Dundee or Edinburgh and was interred in Dunfermline Abbey in Fife.

ALEXANDER I ('The Fierce') Died in 1124 at Stirling Castle and was interred in Dunfermline Abbey in Fife. His wife, Sybilla, died in 1122 and was interred in a church on the Island of the Woman on Loch Tay.

DAVID I ('The Saint') Died at Carlisle in 1153 and was interred in Dunfermline Abbey in Fife. His wife, Matilda, died c. 1130 and was interred at Scone Abbey.

MALCOLM IV ('The Maiden') Died at Jedburgh Castle in 1165 and was interred in Dunfermline Abbey.

WILLIAM ('The Lion') Died at Stirling in 1214 and was interred in Arbroath Abbey. His wife, Ermengarde, died c. 1233 and was interred at Balmerino Abbey, Fife.

ALEXANDER II Died on the Isle of Kerrara in 1249 and was interred in Melrose Abbey in Roxburghshire. His wife, Joan, died in 1238 and was interred at Tarrant Crawford Abbey, Dorset.

ALEXANDER III ('The Glorious') Died as a result of a riding accident near Kinghorn in 1286 and was interred in Dunfermline Abbey. His wife, Margaret, died in 1275 and was also interred in the abbey.

MARGARET ('The Maid of Norway') Died on her voyage to Scotland from Norway in 1290 and was buried in Bergen.

JOHN BALLIOL ('Toom Tabard') Died in France, probably at Chateau Gaillard, in 1314 and may have been interred in the church of St Waast in Normandy.

ROBERT I ('The Bruce') Died at Cardross Castle in Dumbartonshire in 1329 and was interred in Dunfermline Abbey. The burial place of his first wife Isabella, said to have been a granddaughter of Lywelyn the Great, Prince of Wales, is unknown. His second wife, Elizabeth, died in 1327 and was also interred at Dunfermline Abbey.

DAVID II Died at Edinburgh Castle in 1371 and was interred in Holyrood Abbey. His first wife Joan, the daughter of Edward II of England and the first Scottish queen consort to be crowned, died in 1362 and was interred at Greyfriars Church, London.

Appendix II

ROBERT II Died at Dundonald Castle in Ayrshire in 1390 and was interred in Scone Abbey.

ROBERT III Died at Dundonald Castle in 1406 and was buried in Paisley Abbey. His wife, Queen Annabella, died in 1401 and was interred at Dunfermline Abbey.

JAMES I Assassinated in 1437 and buried in a monastery at Perth, possibly the monastery of the Carthusians. His wife Joan, daughter of John Beaufort, Earl of Somerset, died in 1445 and was interred in the monastery of Charterhouse, Perth.

JAMES II Killed when a gun exploded at the siege of Roxburgh in 1460 and was interred in Holyrood Abbey in Edinburgh. His wife, Mary of Gueldres, died in 1463 and was interred in Holy Trinity Church, Edinburgh.

JAMES III Murdered in 1488 and was interred at Cambuskenneth Abbey. His wife, Margaret of Denmark, died in 1486 and was also interred at Cambuskenneth Abbey.

JAMES IV Slain at the Battle of Flodden in 1513 and possibly interred in Sheen Abbey, Surrey. His wife Margaret, daughter of Henry VII of England, died in 1541 and was interred in the Carthusian abbey in Perth.

JAMES V Died at Falkland Palace in 1542 and was buried in Holyrood Abbey in Edinburgh. His first wife Madeleine, daughter of Francis I of France, died in 1537 and was also interred at the abbey. His second wife, Mary of Guise-Lorraine, died in 1560 and was interred at Rheims Cathedral in France.

MARY ('Queen of Scots') Executed at Fotheringhay Castle in 1587 and was first interred in Peterborough Cathedral and later translated to Westminster Abbey. Her first husband, Francis II of France, died in 1560 and was interred at the cathedral of St Denis in Paris. Her second husband Henry, Lord Darnley, was murdered in 1567 and interred in the Chapel Royal, Holyrood Palace. Her third husband Patrick Hepburn, 3rd Earl of Bothwell, died in prison in Denmark in 1578 and was interred in the Faarevejle Church in Dragsholm.

JAMES VI Became James I of England in 1603. He died at Theobalds Park in 1625 and was interred in Westminster Abbey. His wife, Anne of Denmark, died in 1619 and was also interred in the abbey.